Emeritus Professor Robert Ely FRSA, FIoD, Ed.D, B.Ed(Hons)

© 2012 TPG

All rights reserved.
No part of this publication may be reproduced, stored in a retriever system, or transmitted in any form or by any means, electronic, mechanical, photocopying, recording, or otherwise, without prior permission of the author.
All enquiries to: info@tpgroup.net.au

ISBN-13: 978-0-9871351-6-2

BISAC: LIT015000

Shakespeare
The Natural World
A Reference Guide

Professor
Robert S. Ely

Jean-Norman Benedetti 1930-2012
Clarence Bahs
And our common heritage,
Rose Bruford College.

Foreword

In setting out to examine the Bard's ecological credentials, a number of operational questions and issues emerged. For example, what to include? And, how to present the findings? The intention was to involve the Complete Works of Shakespeare. But, even that descriptor is open to interpretation and opinion. Do I include works written collaboratively, with no clear indications of the level or extent of the collaboration?
Sir Thomas More
The Lamentable Tragedy of Locrine
The Life and Death of The Lord Cromwell
King Edward the Third
The Puritaine Widdow
The Life of Sir John Oldcastle
A Yorkshire Tragedy
The Two Noble Kinsmen c. 1613; pub. 1634
The Merry Devill of Edmonton
Faire Em
A Most Pleasant Comedy of Mucedorus.
I decided, not.
And what of recently attributed work, excluded from the First Folio, for, allegedly, political reasons: *Edward III*?
I decided not.
Why so?
Well, whilst the intent of this work is not to enter or contribute to the authorship debate, I asserted, that the inclusion of such works added little, if anything, to the tapestry of nature woven by Shakespeare. They were unlikely to produce any surprising insights or new knowledge; nor were they likely to create any sense of completeness, when so many questions remain about their authorship. It seemed to me, that Shakespeare must have written some, if not the majority of scenes in *Edward III*, but, interesting though that is, how does it help this survey?
As to the second question, of how to present the findings, simple, yet important issues emerged. List works by genre? By date? Alphabetically? Or, even by the weight of their natural credentials? Should I include line numbers? Line numbers by scene or by work?
And, in any case...what *is* the Natural World?
Well, for the purposes of this exercise, it includes anything that grows, lives and is not manufactured. It encompasses, plants and trees, rocks and stones, gases and liquids, as we find them. The stars and planets as they were understood at the time, the insects and animals and the subatomic world; and, it includes body parts and products thereof.
Organised alphabetically, I have tried to include everything I have observed in the complete works of Shakespeare. If I have missed something, I apologise to the reader.
Is there a reader?
Not really; this is largely, a reference book.
Each word is given the definition at the time it was written, as far as we understand it; and each is given an origin, if we know what it is. Some words, of course, have no history, as Shakespeare invented them. Many have infused the English language as we speak it; some have evolved, others have reached an evolutionary cul-de-sac; and a few were strangled at birth.
I am indebted to the Oxford English Dictionary for some definitions and to T.F. Thistleton-Dyer for his 1883 book, *Folk-lore of Shakespeare*. This is a

comprehensive study of the folklore aspects of Shakespeare, providing a full-spectrum exposure to the cultural background of Elizabethan society. The Reverend Dyer, who also wrote *Folk-lore of Women*, delves into the source of innumerable passages in Shakespeare which were *mysterious* in Victorian times. Although, usually he manages to clear up the mystery, in a few instances he has to admit defeat. He is not alone in that. Sometimes, I have no idea what Shakespeare was talking about, or why he spells things so variously. But, hey, we are talking about a man here, who couldn't seem to sign his own name, consistently.

But then, nobody is perfect.

Not least, whilst every effort has been made to include all natural references, and to do so accurately, there will be mistakes and omissions. Wherever they are, and I hope they will be few, some sympathy would be much appreciated. This was a huge undertaking, complex, and painfully tedious at times; and yet, I was rewarded with some new insights, new layers, and the occasional nugget of knowledge.

Should it be obvious, for example, that *Hamlet* is littered with more references to 'ear' than any other play? At first, you might think so, given that Hamlet's father is poisoned through the ear. But, these references are not concerned with the action on the ear. They are general references. Or are they? Is Shakespeare subtly playing with our senses? Is he creating a resonance to remind us of the dreadful deed that is the trigger of the play?

Some things surprised, whilst others, seemingly obvious, provided reassurances that I was dealing with the greatest writer in the English Language. For example, it seems that, in hindsight, it should obvious that the two most frequently used natural references in the Sonnets are: *eyes* and *heart*. To *see* and to *feel*. But, until I mapped the references I had no idea that these tools of the poet, or indeed any artist, we're so prevalent. And who's to say why the word *breath* is so common in *King John*?

Note on References

The referencing system used in this guide utilises a continuous line numbering system. That is, all works are line numbered from the first line (1) until the last line without breaking for Act and Scene partitions. These partitions, are in any case rather false, in that, they make no appearance in the performance of a play. In this case, however, the line numbering assists in locating the line, word or expression using on-line databases such as:
www. opensourceshakespeare.org

As such, line referencing can also be approximate depending on the exact layout of the page. In the vast majority of instances they will be exact. However, on occasion, they may not. If using for research purposes, quotations should be checked from more than one source.

Introduction: How Green is my Shakespeare?

It's a reasonable question. Just as there is no one history, so too, there is no one Shakespeare. Perspectives change with time, distance, fashions and fads; or, they simply morph according to the cultural and social milieu of the time. The multifarious approaches to literary criticism keep literature alive. After all, who's interested in a dead poet espousing dead ideas. Whether it be a Marxist perspective of a Feminist review, each age has its Shakespeare.

Samuel Johnson, in his *Preface to Shakespeare* (1755) set the tone for much that is misunderstood about the relationship between Shakespeare and the Natural World:

Shakespeare is above all writers, at least above all modern writers, the poet of nature; the poet that holds up to his readers a faithful mirror of manners and of life.

By focussing on human nature, as if it is somehow above the rest of nature.

So, how should I proceed? Do I consider animal studies, early modern zoology, bio-politics, climate theory, geohumoralism, food, medicine, botany, demonology, and more?

Ecological literary criticism is not new. The Victorians, obsessed with the natural sciences, we're also obsessed with Shakespeare; the Pre-Raphaelite Brotherhood, were obsessed with both. But, this work is not intended to tease out whether Shakespeare's ink was green, blue or black. Rather, it is a survey of the extent to which the natural world pervades his work; and what then does it contribute to his ideas about the world of which he writes. Some, take a bold view:

The concept of Nature in Shakespeare's King Lear is not simply one of many themes to be uncovered and analysed, but rather it can be considered to be the foundation of the whole play. From Kingship through to personal human relations, from representations of the physical world to notions of the heavenly realm, from the portrayal of human nature to the use of animal imagery; Nature permeates every line of King Lear[1].

Well, maybe not *every* line.

A play is a play; it's not a novel; and a poem is what it is, and is written to be read. The thing that is the play, is for playing. It is meant to be heard and seen. And, so, the language, although dense and layered to the modern ear, is rich with references to nature that bombard our senses. What we see and feel and imagine, plays on the mind, creating the landscape of emotions as the backdrop to character and action. These references to the natural world are no accident; they are there to shape our response to the play. The two most common natural words in the Sonnets are, by far: *eyes* and *heart*. To see and to feel. Is that not what the poetry is all about?

Do I need to consider what constitutes early modern environmental studies? How did early modern writers define *nature*, as opposed to *supernature*, or *preternature*, or culture? In what ways did travel, global exchanges, or economic shifts affect the construction of early modern *nature*? What role does gender play in conceptions of nature? What was natural knowledge? Who had access to it? How do these questions, and others, inform the created worlds[2] represented in Shakespeare's plays?

---

[1] Doncaster, Sarah. *Representations of Nature in King Lear*. Shakespeare Online. 20 Aug. 2000. (accessed: February 5th 2013) < http://www.shakespeare-online.com/essays/learandnature.html >.

[2] Ely, Robert S., *Created Worlds: The Chaos of Film.* (2006) ICA Publications, Singapore. ISBN-981-05-3774-3

Shakespeare, as far as we know, came from the country; a place of nature. His audiences, as far as we know, came from the city, a place largely devoid of nature.

Works included:

- All's Well That Ends Well
- Antony and Cleopatra
- As You Like It
- Comedy of Errors
- Coriolanus
- Cymbeline
- Hamlet
- Henry IV, Part I
- Henry IV, Part II
- Henry V
- Henry VI, Part I
- Henry VI, Part II
- Henry VI, Part III
- Henry VIII
- Julius Caesar
- King John
- King Lear
- Lover's Complaint
- Love's Labour's Lost
- Macbeth
- Measure for Measure
- Merchant of Venice
- Merry Wives of Windsor
- Midsummer Night's Dream
- Much Ado About Nothing
- Othello
- Passionate Pilgrim
- Pericles
- Phoenix and the Turtle
- Rape of Lucrece
- Richard II
- Richard III
- Romeo and Juliet
- Sonnets
- Taming of the Shrew
- Tempest
- Timon of Athens
- Titus Andronicus
- Troilus and Cressida
- Twelfth Night
- Two Gentlemen of Verona
- Venus and Adonis
- Winter's Tale

Reference A-Z

* Denotes first use.
**Denotes first use, but not absorbed into common English.
Old English: 400-1100 C.E.
Middle English: 1100-1500 C.E.
Old French: 900-1400 C.E.
Old Norse: 700-1100 C.E.
r Denotes a repeat on the same line.
Multiple lines denote repeat in the same speech.

Abysm: Abyss: bottomless gulf, greatest depths, now chiefly poetic, c.1300, from Old French *abisme*.
   Antony and Cleopatra, III 13 line 2430.
   Sonnet CXII line 9.
   Tempest, I 2 line 144.

Acre: Old English *æcer* tilled field, open land, from Proto-Germanic *akraz*: field, pasture (cf. Old Norse *akr*, Old Saxon akkar, Old Frisian *ekker*, Middle Dutch *acker*, Dutch *akker*, Old High German *achar*, German *acker*, Gothic *akrs*). Originally in English without reference to dimension; in late Old English the amount of land a yoke of oxen could plough in a day, afterward defined by statute as a piece 40 poles by 4, or an equivalent shape. Original sense retained in *God's acre: churchyard*.
   As You Like It, V 3 line 2382.
   Hamlet, V 1 line 3625.
   Henry IV, Part I, I 1 line 26.
   King Lear, IV 4 line 2522.
   Tempest, I 1 line 80; Tempest, IV 1 line 1792.
   Winter's Tale, I 2 line 178.

Aconite: This plant from the deadly virulence of its juice. Also known as monkshood and wolf's bane, 1570s, from French: *aconit*, from Latin: *aconitum*. It is probably derived from the Greek: ἀκόνιτον: *without a struggle*, in allusion to the intensity of its poisonous qualities. Virgil speaks of it, and tells us how the aconite deceives the wretched gatherers, because often mistaken for some harmless plant. The ancients fabled it as the invention of Hecate, who caused the plant to spring from the foam of Cerberus, when Hercules dragged him from the gloomy regions of Pluto.
   Henry IV, Part II, IV 4 line 2794.

Acorn: Old English: *æcern: nut*, originally the mast of any forest tree, and ultimately related (through notion of *fruit of the open or unenclosed land*) to Old English: *æcer: open land*. The sense gradually restricted in English to the most important of the forest produce for feeding swine, the mast of the oak tree. Spelling changed 15c.-16c. by folk etymology. Acorns hold significance as a Celtic symbol for life, fertility, and immortality. For this reason it is often sacred to the god *Thor*, who is ruler of fire and fertility. When it is carried on

the person, it can often preserve youthfulness. Commonly believed to be androgynous. Also acts as the symbol for strength.
> **As You Like It**, III 2 line 1335.
> **Cymbeline**, III 5 line 1388.
> **Midsummer Night's Dream**, II 1 line 397; Midsummer Night's Dream, III 2 line 1381.
> **Tempest**, I 2 line 646.

Adder: Old English: *næddre* a snake, serpent, viper. *Nedder* is still a northern English dialect form. Folklore connection with deafness is via *Psalm lviii:1-5*. The adder is said to stop up its ears to avoid hearing the snake charmer called in to drive it away. *Adderbolt* (late 15c.) was a former name for a dragonfly.
> **Cymbeline**, IV 2 line 2439.
> **Hamlet**, III 4 line 2608.
> **Henry VI, Part II**, III 2 line 1757.
> **Henry VI, Part III**, I 4 line 552.
> **Julius Caesar**, II 1 lines 615, 623, 625.
> **King Lear,** V 1 line 3094.
> **Macbeth**, IV 1 line 1563.
> **Midsummer Night's Dream**, III 2 lines 1104, 1105, 1106.
> **Rape of Lucrece**, line 922.
> **Richard II**, III 2 line 1428; Richard II, V 1 line 2390.
> **Richard III**, I 2 line 192.
> **Sonnet** CXII line 10.
> **Taming of the Shrew**, IV 3 line 2136.
> **The Tempest**, II 2 line 1094.
> **The Winter's Tale**, IV 4 line 2149.
> **Timon of Athens**, IV 3 line 1867.
> **Titus Andronicus**, III 2 line 768.
> **Troilus and Cressida**, II 2 line 1170.
> **Venus and Adonis**, line 900.

Ague: malarial fever involving shivering, c.1300, from Old French: *ague: an acute fever.*
> **Henry VIII**, I 1 line 40.
> **Julius Caesar**, II 2 line 1097.
> **Macbeth**, V 5 line 2356.
> **Merchant of Venice**, I 1 line 25.
> **Richard II**, III 2 line 1600.
> **Tempest**, II 2 line 1157; Tempest, II 2 line 1182; Tempest, II 2 line 1223.
> **Troilus and Cressida**, III 3 line 2115.

Aierie: or aerie, or aery, or aiery, or eyie: nest, or brood of a bird of prey, and particularly of hawks.
> **Hamlet**, II 2 line 1427.

Air: c.1300, *invisible gases that make up the atmosphere*, from Old French: air *atmosphere, breeze, weather* (12c.), from Latin: *aerem: air, lower atmosphere, sky*, from Greek: *aer: air* (related to *aenai: to blow, breathe*), of unknown origin, possibly from a base *awer-* and thus related to *aeirein: to raise*. Air is traditionally seen as one of the four elements and along with fire is considered active and male. In this respect it is represented by the arc or the circle, and the colours blue or gold. It is light, mobile, and has the quality of dryness. Being that which we breathe, it is essential to life and can be thought of as the primary element. The Greek *spiro* means *breath*, from this we get inspiration, as if the gods were filling us with the divine breath. Also connected with stormy wind (creation) and a medium for movement.

All's Well That Ends Well, III 2 line 1521; All's Well That Ends Well, III 2 line 1535.

Antony and Cleopatra, II 2 line 940; Antony and Cleopatra, IV 3 line 2597; Antony and Cleopatra, IV 10 line 2884; Antony and Cleopatra, IV 14 line 2984; Antony and Cleopatra, V 2 line 3747; Antony and Cleopatra, V 2 line 3776.

As You Like It, II 6 line 890.

Comedy of Errors, I 2 line 227; Comedy of Errors, III 2 line 834.

Coriolanus, I 6 line 688; Coriolanus, II 3 line 1496; Coriolanus, III 3 line 2495; Coriolanus, IV 6 line 3179; Coriolanus, V 3 line 3664; Coriolanus, V 6 line 3879.

Cymbeline, I 1 line 50; Cymbeline, I 1 line 135; Cymbeline, I 2 line 237r; Cymbeline, I 3 line 297; Cymbeline, II 3 line 994; Cymbeline, II 4 line 1294; Cymbeline, V 2 line 2995; Cymbeline, V 4 line 3293; Cymbeline, V 5 line 3907; Cymbeline, V 5 line 3916.

Hamlet, I 1 line 168; Hamlet, I 1 line 176; Hamlet, I 4 line 626; Hamlet, I 4 line 627; Hamlet, I 5 line 796; Hamlet, II 2 line 1308; Hamlet, II 2 line 1310; Hamlet, II 2 line 1395; Hamlet, II 2 line 1563; Hamlet, III 2 line 1886; Hamlet, III 2 line 1976; Hamlet, III 4 line 2517; Hamlet, IV 1 line 2673.

Henry IV, Part I, I 3 line 465; Henry IV, Part I, III 1 line 1776; Henry IV, Part I, V 1 line 2760.

Henry IV, Part II, I 3 line 633; Henry IV, Part II, IV 4 line 2869; Henry IV, Part II, V 3 line 3402.

Henry V, Prologue, line 15; Henry V, I 1 line 87; Henry V, II Chorus line 471; Henry V, II 4 line 957; Henry V, III 6 line 1618; Henry V, III 7 line 1656; Henry V, III 7 line 1661; HenryV, IV 2 line 2207.

Henry VI, Part I, IV 7 line 2347.

Henry VI, Part II, I 1 line 266; Henry VI, Part II, III 2 line 1978; Henry VI, Part II, III 2 line 2066; Henry VI, Part II, III 2 line 2087; Henry VI, Part II, IV 1 line 2158; Henry VI, Part II, IV 10 line 2938; Henry VI, Part II, V 2 line 3212.

Henry VI, Part III, II 6 line 1271; Henry VI, Part III, III 1 line 1453; Henry VI, Part III, III 2 line 1667.

Henry VIII, I 2 line 430; Henry VIII, I 4 line 805.

Julie Caesar, I 2 line 343; Julie Caesar, II 1 line 648; Julie Caesar, II 1 line 894; Julie Caesar, II 2 line 998.

King John, II 1 line 698; King John, V 1 line 2268; King John, V 7 line 2635.
King Lear, II 4 line 1504; King Lear, III 4 line 1886; King Lear, III 6 line 2007; King Lear, IV 1 line 2253; King Lear, IV 3 line 2363; King Lear, IV 6 line 2613; King Lear, IV 6 line 2656; King Lear, IV 6 line 2784.
Love's Labour's Lost, I 1 line 234; Love's Labour's Lost, III 1 line 768; Love's Labour's Lost, IV 3 lines 1433, 1438, 1439; Love's Labour's Lost, V 2 line 2207.
Macbeth, I 1 line 14; Macbeth, I 3 line 183; Macbeth, I 5 line 348; Macbeth, I 6 line 433; Macbeth, I 7 line 496; Macbeth, II 3 line 825; Macbeth, III 4 line 1299; Macbeth, III 5 line 1470; Macbeth, IV 1 line 1703; Macbeth, IV 1 line 1717; Macbeth, IV 3 line 2035; Macbeth, IV 3 line 2068; Macbeth, V 8 line 2486.
Measure for Measure, II 4 line 1028; Measure for Measure, II 4 line 1035.
Merchant of Venice III 2 line 1475; Merchant of Venice V 1 line 2506; Merchant of Venice V 1line 2531.
Midsummer's Night's Dream, I 1 line 191; Midsummer's Night's Dream, II 1 line 473; Midsummer's Night's Dream, II 1 line 494.
Much Ado About Nothing, II 3 line 876; Much Ado About Nothing, II 3 line 877; Much Ado About Nothing, III 1 line 1153; Much Ado About Nothing, V 1 line 2095.
Othello, III 1 line 1557; Othello, III 3 line 1995; Othello, III 4 line 2328; Othello, V 1 line 3267.
Passionate Pilgrim, lines 231, 237.
Pericles, I 1 line 149; Pericles I 2 line 332; Pericles, I 4 line 430; Pericles, I 4 line 450; Pericles, III 1 line 1228; Pericles, III 2 line 1394; Pericles, IV 1 line 1575; Pericles, IV 6 line 2042.
Rape of Lucrece, lines 829, 1093, 1056.
Richard II, I 3 line 454; Richard II, I 3 line 492; Richard II, I 3 line 585; Richard II, III 2 line 1410; Richard II, IV 1 line 2174.
Richard III, I 1 line 131; Richard III, I 3 line 753; Richard III, I 4 line 872; Richard III, III 4 line 2056; Richard III, IV 4 line 2803; Richard III, V 3 line 3507.
Romeo and Juliet, I 1 line 172; Romeo and Juliet, I 4 line 601; Romeo and Juliet, II 2 line 879; Romeo and Juliet, II 6 line 1478; Romeo and Juliet, III 5 line 2233; Romeo and Juliet, IV 3 line 2586.
Sonnet XXI line 8; Sonnet XXI line 12; Sonnet XLV line 1; Sonnet LXX line 4.
Taming of the Shrew, I 1 line 466.
Tempest, I 2 line 346; Tempest, I 2 lines 550, 556; Tempest, II 1 line 750; Tempest, IV 1 line 1780; Tempest, IV 1 line 1881r; Tempest, IV 1 line 1907; Tempest, IV 1 line 2012; Tempest, V 1 line 2040; Tempest, V 1 line 2087; Tempest, V 1 line 2132.
Timon of Athens, I 1 line 102; Timon of Athens, IV 2 line 1621; Timon of Athens, IV 2 line 1631; Timon of Athens, IV 3 line 1667; Timon of Athens, IV 3 line 1790; Timon of Athens, IV 3 line 1910; Timon of Athens, V 1 line 2281; Timon of Athens, V 2 line 2540.

Titus Andronicus, III 2 line 1508; Titus Andronicus, IV 2 line 1862.
Troilus and Cressida, I 3 line 519; Troilus and Cressida, II 3 line 1390; Troilus and Cressida, III 2 line 1706; Troilus and Cressida, III 2 line 1843; Troilus and Cressida, III 3 line 106; Troilus and Cressida, IV 5 line 2598; Troilus and Cressida, IV 5 line 2812.
Twelfth Night, I 1 line 22; Twelfth Night, I 5 lines 564, 566; Twelfth Night, III 4 line 1674; Twelfth Night, IV 3 line 2152.
Two Gentlemen of Verona, II 1 line 561; Two Gentlemen of Verona, II 4 line 680; Two Gentlemen of Verona, IV 4 line 1994.
Venus and Adonis, lines 84, 293, 675, 1107.
Winter's Tale, III 1 line 1182; Winter's Tale, III 2 line 1322; Winter's Tale, III 3 line 1529; Winter's Tale, IV 4 line 2708; Winter's Tale, IV 4 line 2741; Winter's Tale, V 1 line 2980;Winter's Tale, V 1 line 3026; Winter's Tale, V 3 line 3381.

Alabaster: translucent form of gypsum or calcite, known for its whiteness; late Middle English: via Old French from Latin: *alabaster, alabastrum*, from Greek: *alabastos, alabastros*.
    Merchant of Venice, I 1 line 91.
    Othello, V 2 line 3307.
    Rape of Lucrece, line 470.
    Richard III, IV 3 line 2744.
    Venus and Adonis, line 383.

Allicholy: melancholy
    Merry Wives of Windsor, I 4 line 552.

Alligator*: 1560s, *lagarto*, a corruption of Spelling: *el lagarto* (de Indias): *the lizard* (of the Indies). *Alligarter* was an early variant.
    Romeo and Juliet, V 1 line 2852.

Almond: c.1300, from Old French *almande, amande,* from Vulgar Latin *amendla, amandula*, from Latin *amygdala* (plural), from Greek *amygdalos* an almond tree, of unknown origin, perhaps a Semitic word. Virginity; the self-productive; conjugal happiness. As the first flower of the year the blossom is the Awakener, hence it depicts watchfulness; it also represents sweetness, charm, delicacy. In the Christian tradition, the almond signifies divine favour and approval, and the purity of the Virgin. The nut is concealed within an outer skin, bringing the idea of the essence hidden within things of little apparent importance: for example, the divinity of Christ hidden within the mortal human form. It is often connected with sex, across cultures and eras; in India, the almond is the vulva, and eating the almond signifies the sexual act. In mythology, it is attributed to *Atys*, who was conceived by a virgin from an almond. A Jewish myth places the entrance to the underworld at the base of an almond tree.
    Troilus and Cressida, V 2 line 3271.

Anchovies: 1590s, from Portuguese: *anchova*, from Genoese or Corsican dialect, perhaps ultimately from Basque: *anchu: dried fish*, from *anchuva: dry*.
    Henry IV, Part I, II 4 line 1528.

Animal: early 14c. (but rare before c.1600), any living creature (including humans), from Latin: *animale:* living being, being which breathes, from *anima:* breath, soul; a current of air. Drove out the older *beast* in common usage. Used of brutish humans from 1580s. Often, the use of animal imagery seeks to depict generally negative qualities and instincts relevant to human nature. Almost all symbols of animals can be related to three main ideas: the animal as a mount or mode of transportation, as an object of sacrifice, and as an inferior form of life.
    As You Like It, I 1 line 13; As You Like It, II 1 line 589; As You Like It, II 1 line 617.
    Hamlet, II 2 line 1401.
    King Lear, III 4 line 1902.
    Love's Labour's Lost, IV 2 line 1169.
    Merchant of Venice, IV 1 line 2067.
    Much Ado About Nothing, IV 1 line 1701.

Ant: c.1500, from Middle English *ampte* (late 14c.), from Old English *æmette*. The ant is consistently a symbol of diligence and industriousness. In Indian myth, however, they show the fragility of all living creatures. Often the ant is also associated with prudence and forethought, as even though they are not strong they gather food for winter. The multiplicity surrounding ants gives it unfavourable symbolism, sometimes compared with swarming humanity, and a sudden great increase in ants can spell war.
    Henry IV, Part I, III 1 line 1694.
    King Lear, II 4 line 1345.

Anthropophaginian: cannibal.
    Merry Wives of Windsor, IV 5 line 2302.

Antre: a cave.
    Othello, I 3 line 484.

Ape: Old English: *apa*: ape, monkey. Apes were noted in medieval times for mimicry of human action, hence, perhaps, the other figurative use of the word, to mean *a fool*. In Christian symbology, however, they have long been considered a symbol of malice and physical ugliness, as a pejorative epithet dating back to the ancient world.
    As You Like It, IV 1 line 1925.
    Comedy of Errors, II 1 line 588.
    Coriolanus, I 4 line 529.
    Cymbeline, I 6 line 646; Cymbeline, II 2 line 953; Cymbeline, IV 2 line 2570.
    Hamlet, III 4 line 2598; Hamlet, IV 2 line 2695.
    Henry IV, Part I, II 3 line 940.

Henry IV, Part II, II 2 line 1032; Henry IV, Part II, II 4 line 1491; Henry IV, Part II, IV 5 line 3014.
Love's Labour's Lost, III 1 line 851; Love's Labour's Lost, III 1 line 857; Love's Labour's Lost, IV 2 line 1275; Love's Labour's Lost, V 2 line 2253.
Julius Caesar, V 1 line 2392.
Measure for Measure, II 2 line 885.
Merry Wives of Windsor, III 1 line 1271.
Midsummer Night's Dream, II 1 line 555.
Much Ado About Nothing, II 1 line 433; Much Ado About Nothing, II 1 line 439; Much Ado About Nothing, V 1 line 2166; Much Ado About Nothing, V 1 line 2276r.
Richard III, III 1 line 1703.
Romeo and Juliet, II 1 line 815.
Taming of the Shrew, II 1 line 874.
Tempest, II 2 line 1090; Tempest, IV 1 line 1989.
Winter's Tale, V 2 line 3208.

Apish: primitive or foolish.
As You Like It, III 2 line 1485.
King John, V 2 line 2413.
King Lear, I 4 line 693.
Richard II, II 1 line 704.
Richard III, I 3 line 509.

Apple: In Middle English and as late as 17c., it was a generic term for all fruit other than berries but including nuts (e.g. Old English: *fingeræppla* meaning *dates*, lit. finger-apples; Middle English: *appel of paradis* meaning *banana*, c. 1400). The *Crab* roasted before the fire and put into ale was a very favourite indulgence, especially at Christmas. It is a complex symbol, with a variety of meanings and incorporated in a variety of contexts. It can mean love, knowledge, wisdom, joy, death, and/or luxury. The apple could be an erotic association with a woman's breasts, with the core sliced in half representing the vulva. In Greek mythology, the apple appears repeatedly; Hera received an apple as a symbol of fertility upon her engagement to Zeus. The apple of the Garden of Eden, is the symbol of temptation and of original sin. In secular terms, the apple functions as a symbol for the cosmos or totality, due to its nearly perfect spherical shape.
Henry V, III 7 line 1773.
Henry VIII, V 4 line 3332.
King Lear, I 5 line 892.
Love's Labour's Lost, V 2 line 2404.
Merchant of Venice, I 3 line 428.
Midsummer Night's Dream, III 2 line 1140.
Sonnet XCIII line 13.
Taming of the Shrew, I 1 line 427; Taming of the Shrew, IV 2 line 1935.
Tempest, II 1 line 791.
Twelfth Night, I 5 line 450; Twelfth Night, V 1 line

2423.

Apple-john: called in France *deux-années* or *deux-ans*, because it will keep two years, and considered to be in perfection when shrivelled.
    Henry IV, Part I, III 3 line 2011.
    Henry IV, Part II, II 4 lines 1227, 1229.

Apricock: 1550s, *abrecock*, from Catalan: *abercoc*. It was called *the precocious tree* because it flowered and fruited earlier than the peach.
    Midsummer Night's Dream, III 1 line 991.
    Richard II, III 4 line 1893.

April: c.1300, *aueril*, from Old French: *avril* (11c.), from Latin (mensis) *Aprilis: (month) of Venus,* second month of the ancient Roman calendar, dedicated to the goddess Venus and perhaps based on *Apru*, an Etruscan borrowing of Greek: Aphrodite. In English in Latin form from mid-12c. Replaced Old English: *Eastermonað*, which was similarly named for a fertility goddess. Respelled in Middle English on Latin model (*apprile* first attested late 14c.).
    Antony and Cleopatra, III 2 line 1644.
    As You Like It, IV 1 line 1920.
    King John, IV 2 line 1852.
    Lover's Complaint, line 102.
    Merchant of Venice, II 9 line 1228.
    Merry Wives of Windsor, II 2 line 1377.
    Rape of Lucrece, line 446.
    Romeo and Juliet, I 2 line 297.
    Sonnet III line 11; Sonnet XXI line 6; Sonnet XCVIII line 2; Sonnet CIV line 7.
    Tempest, IV 1 line 1775.
    Timon of Athens, IV 3 line 1706.
    Titus Andronicus, III 1 line 1144.
    Troilus and Cressida, I 2 line 319.
    Two Gentlemen of Verona, I 3 line 390.
    Winter's Tale, IV 4 line 1858; Winter's Tale, IV 4 line 2161.

Arbour: c.1300, *herber: herb garden*, from Old French: *erbier: field, meadow; kitchen garden*, from Latin: *herba: grass, herb*. Later, a grassy plot (early 14c., a sense also in Old French), a shaded nook (mid-14c.). Probably not from Latin: *arbor: tree*, though perhaps influenced by its spelling.
    Henry IV, Part II, V 3 line 3395.
    Julius Caesar, III 2 line 1793.
    Much Ado About Nothing, II 3 line 848.

Arm: upper limb, Old English: *earm*.
    All's Well That Ends Well, II 3 line 1151; All's Well That Ends Well, II 3 line 1184.
    Antony and Cleopatra, II 5 line 1054; Antony and Cleopatra, IV 14 line 3068.
    As You Like It, II 6 line 886; As You Like It, II 7 line 1042.

Coriolanus, I 6 line 706; Coriolanus, IV 3 line 2583; Coriolanus, IV 5 line 2872; Coriolanus, IV 5 line 2888.
Cymbeline, IV 2 lines 2573, 2576; Cymbeline, IV 2 line 2599; Cymbeline, V 5 line 3368; Cymbeline, V 5 line 3743.
Hamlet, I 1 line 136; Hamlet, I 5 line 927; Hamlet, II 2 line 1528; Hamlet, IV 5 line 3020; Hamlet, V 1 line 3377; Hamlet, V 1 line 3581.
Henry IV, Part I, I 3 line 636; Henry IV, Part I, II 3 line 884; Henry IV, Part I, III 2 line 1929.
Henry IV, Part II, I 1 line 201.
Henry V, IV 1 line 1982.
Henry VI, Part I, I 1 line 15; Henry VI, Part I, I 1 line 85; Henry VI, Part I, I 5 line 592; Henry VI, Part I, II 3 line 868; Henry VI, Part I, II 3 line 896; Henry VI, Part I, II 5 line 1086; Henry VI, Part I, II 5 line 1114; Henry VI, Part I, III 3 line 681; Henry VI, Part I, III 3 line 1687; Henry VI, Part I, IV 7 lines 2281, 2284;Henry VI, Part I, IV 7 line 2300.
Henry VI, Part III, I 4 line 507; Henry VI, Part III, II 3 line 1073; Henry VI, Part III, II 5 line 1220.
Henry VIII, II 2 line 1142; Henry VIII, III 2 line 2193.
Julius Caesar, I 1 line 41; Julius Caesar, II 1 line 867.
King John, I 1 line 167; King John, IV 3 line 2169; King John, V 2 line 2313.
King Lear, II 3 line 1256; King Lear, III 6 line 2089; King Lear, III 7 line 2151; King Lear, V 3 line 3372; King Lear, V 3 line 3473.
Love's Labour's Lost, III 1 line 780; Love's Labour's Lost, III 1 line 944; Love's Labour's Lost, IV 3 line 1463; Love's Labour's Lost, V 2 line 2493.
Lover's Complaint, line 272.
Measure for Measure, III 1 line 1315; Measure for Measure, V 1 line 2602.
Merry Wives of Windsor, III 1 line 1227; Merry Wives of Windsor, V 5 line 2619.
Midsummer Night's Dream, IV 1 line 1584.
Othello, I 3 line 423; Othello, II 1 line 857.
Passionate Pilgrim, line 149.
Pericles, III 1 line 1209; Pericles, III 3 line 1422; Pericles, V 2 line 2573.
Rape of Lucrece, lines 78, 161, 568, 844, 1885.
Richard II, I 3 line 349; Richard II, II 3 line 1261; Richard II, II 3 line 1279.
Richard III, I 4 line 1074; Richard III, II 2 line 1329; Richard III, III 1 line 1604; Richard III, IV 3 line 2737.
Romeo and Juliet, III 2 line 1725; Romeo and Juliet, V 3 line 3059.
Taming of the Shrew, III 1 line 1071.
Tempest, I 2 line 348; Tempest, II 1 line 820; Tempest, II 2 line 1120.
Titus Andronicus, II 3 line 757; Titus Andronicus, III 1 line 1422; Titus Andronicus, III 2 line 1451; Titus Andronicus, IV 1 line 1575; Titus Andronicus, IV 2 line 1738; Titus Andronicus, IV 2 line 1746; Titus Andronicus, V 1 line 2151; Titus Andronicus, V 2 line 2374; Titus Andronicus, V 3 line 2647; Titus Andronicus, V 3 line 2659.

Troilus and Cressida, I 3 lines 733, 737; Troilus and Cressida, II 3 line 1466; Troilus and Cressida, III 3 line 2046; Troilus and Cressida, III 3 line 2153; Troilus and Cressida, IV 5 line 2756; Troilus and Cressida, III 3 line 2153; Troilus and Cressida, V 6 line 3533.
Two Gentlemen of Verona, II 1 line 417.
Venus and Adonis, lines 88, 245, 246, 276, 560, 613, 834,
Winter's Tale, I 2 lines 271, 284; Winter's Tale, IV 4 line 2012; Winter's Tale, IV 4 line 2495; Winter's Tale, V 1 line 2920.

Ashes: powdery remains of fire. Symbol of grief or repentance; hence *Ash Wednesday* (c.1300), from custom introduced by *Pope Gregory the Great* of sprinkling ashes on the heads of penitents on the first day of Lent. Ashes meaning *mortal remains of a person* is late 13c., in reference to the ancient custom of cremation.
    Antony and Cleopatra, V 2 line 3600.
    Coriolanus, IV 5 line 2875.
    Henry IV, Part II, I 2 line 524.
    Henry V, III 3 line 1281.
    Henry VI, Part I, I 6 line 652; Henry VI, Part I, III 1 line 1425; Henry VI, Part I, IV 7 line 2349; Henry VI, Part I, V 4 line 2764.
    Henry VI, Part II, II 3 line 1050.
    Henry VI, Part III, I 4 line 473.
    Henry VIII, IV 2 line 2638; Henry VIII, V 5 line 3424.
    King John, III 1 line 1274; King John, IV 1 line 1700.
    Pericles, I line 3.
    Rape of Lucrece, line 1239.
    Richard II, V 1 line 2383.
    Richard III, I 2 lie 179.
    Romeo and Juliet, III 2 line 1777; Romeo and Juliet, IV 1 line 2466.
    Sonnet LXXIII line 10.

Aspen: According to a medieval legend, the perpetual motion of this tree dates from its having supplied the wood of the Cross, and that its leaves have trembled ever since at the recollection of their guilt. Late 14c., from adjective or genitive form of Old English: *æspe: aspen tree, white poplar.*
    Henry IV, Part II, II 4 line 1367.

Ass: beast of burden, Old English: *assa* (Old Northumbrian *assal, assald*) *he-ass* probably from Old Celtic: as(s): *donkey*. Since ancient Greek times, in fables and parables, the animal typified clumsiness and stupidity (hence *asshead*, late 15c., etc.). To make an ass of oneself is from 1580s. In Middle English, someone uncomprehending or unappreciative would be *lik an asse that listeth on a harpe*. In 15c., an *ass man* was a donkey driver. This beast of burden is the epitome of humility, patience, and stupidity. It is stubborn yet persistent, and often represents the poor. In Christian tradition, the ass had many meanings, among them are: the nativity and Satan. In dreams, the ass is usually a messenger of death or as the destroyer of a life-span.

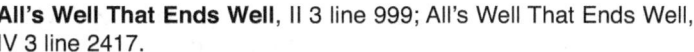

All's Well That Ends Well, II 3 line 999; All's Well That Ends Well, IV 3 line 2417.
Antony and Cleopatra, IV 2 line 2563; Antony and Cleopatra, V 2 line 3769.
As You Like It, II 5 line 865.
Comedy of Errors, II 1 line 286; Comedy of Errors, II 2 line 589; Comedy of Errors, II 2 line 591; Comedy of Errors, II 2 line 569; Comedy of Errors, III 1 line 626; Comedy of Errors, III 1 line 630; Comedy of Errors, III 1 line 668; Comedy of Errors, III 2 line 842; Comedy of Errors, IV 4 line 1276; Comedy of Errors, IV 4 line 1277.
Coriolanus, II 1 line 967; Coriolanus Ii 1 line 1004; Coriolanus, IV 5 line 2800.
Cymbeline, I 2 line 264; Cymbeline, II 1 line 904.
Hamlet, II 2 line 1657; Hamlet, V 1 line 3396; Hamlet, V 1 line 3421.
Henry IV, Part II, II 1 line 751; Henry IV, Part II, II 2 line 1036.
Henry V, III 2 line 1200; Henry V, IV 1 lines 1924, 1926.
Julius Caesar, IV 1 lines 1883, 1888.
King John, II 1 lines 440, 441.
King Lear, I 4 line 686; King Lear, I 4 line 746; King Lear, I 5 line 909.
Love's Labour's Lost, III 1 line 811; Love's Labour's Lost, III 1 line 813; Love's Labour's Lost, V 2 line 2566; Love's Labour's Lost, V 2 line 2569.
Measure for Measure, III 1 line 1248; Measure for Measure, V 1 line 2947.
Merchant of Venice, IV 1 line 2023.
Merry Wives of Windsor, I 1 line 155; Merry Wives of Windsor, II 2 line 1085r; Merry Wives of Windsor, V 5 line 2694.
Midsummer Night's Dream, III 1 line 917; Midsummer Night's Dream, III 1 line 940; Midsummer Night's Dream, III 2 line 1046; Midsummer Night's Dream, III 2 line 1077; Midsummer Night's Dream, IV 1 line 1569; Midsummer Night's Dream, IV 1 line 1625; Midsummer Night's Dream, IV 1 line 1768; Midsummer Night's Dream, V 1 line 1997; Midsummer Night's Dream, V 1 line 2156.
Much Ado About Nothing, IV 2 line 2051r; Much Ado About Nothing, IV 2 line 2053, 2054, 2055, 2064; Much Ado About Nothing, V 1 line 2327; Much Ado About Nothing, V 1 line 2382.
Othello, I 1 line 48; Othello I 3 line 759; Othello, II 1 line 1110.
Richard II, V 5 line 2844.
Taming of the Shrew, I 2 line 708; Taming of the Shrew II 1 line 1047; Taming of the Shrew, III 1 line 1276; Taming of the Shrew, III 2 line 1598; Taming of the Shrew, V 1 line 2422.
Tempest, V 1 line 2371.
Timon of Athens, I 1 line 317; Timon of Athens, II 2 line 746; Timon of Athens, III 5 line 1358; Timon of Athens, IV 3 line 2033r; Timon of Athens, IV 3 line 2052.
Titus Andronicus, IV 2 line 1710.
Troilus and Cressida, I 2 line 391; Troilus and Cressida, II 1 line 901; Troilus and Cressida, III 3 line 2193; Troilus and Cressida, V 1 lines 2990r, 2991; Troilus and Cressida, V 4 line 3414.

Twelfth Night, I 3 line 183; Twelfth Night, II 3 line 719; Twelfth Night, II 3 line 846; Twelfth Night, II 3 line 867; Twelfth Night, II 3 line 868; Twelfth Night, III 2 line 1415; Twelfth Night, IV 2 line 2010; Twelfth Night, V 1 lines 2205, 2206.
Two Gentlemen of Verona, II 3 line 629; Two Gentlemen of Verona, II 5 line 900; Two Gentlemen of Verona, II 5 line 918; Two Gentlemen of Verona, V 2 line 2094.

Assinego: see Ass.
    Troilus and Cressida, II 1 line 900.

Atomies: atomy, 1590s, *atoms*, also *diminutive beings,* from atomy, from Latin: *atomi*, plural of *atomus*, but taken as a singular in English and re-pluralized in the native way. Perhaps also in some cases a plural of *atomy* (from division of *anatomy*).
    As You Like It, III 2 line 1332; As You Like It, III 4 line 1664.
    Romeo and Juliet, I 4 line 557.
    Henry IV, Part II, V 4 line 3584.

Autumn: late 14c., *autumpne* from Old French: *autumpne, automne* (13c.), from Latin: *autumnus* (also: *auctumnus*, perhaps influenced by *auctus* meaning *increase*), of unknown origin, but referring to the season of harvest.
    Antony and Cleopatra, V 2 line 3495.
    Henry VI, Part III, V 7 line 3097.
    King Lear, IV 6 line 2804.
    Merchant of Venice, I 3 line 407.
    Midsummer Night's Dream, III 1 line 481.
    Sonnet XCVII line 6; Sonnet CIV line 5.
    Taming of the Shrew, I 2 line 644.
    Troilus and Cressida, I 2 line 276.

Azure: Middle English (denoting a blue dye): from Old French: *asur, azur*, from medieval Latin: *azzurum, azolum*, from Arabic: *al lazaward* (from Persian *lazward: lapis lazuli*).
    Cymbeline, II 2 line 944; Cymbeline, IV 2 line 2610.
    Rape of Lucrece, line 470.
    Tempest, V 1 line 2064.

Baboons: type of ape, c.1400, *babewyn*, earlier *a grotesque figure used in architecture or decoration* (early 14c.), also *gaping figure (such as a gargoyle)*, so perhaps from Old French: *baboue: grimacing*; or perhaps it is imitative of the ape's babbling speech-like cries.
    Henry IV, Part II, II 4 line 1521.
    Macbeth, IV 1 line 1584.
    Merry Wives of Windsor, II 2 line 803.
    Othello, I 3 line 674.
    Pericles, IV 1 line 2119.
    Timon of Athens, I 1 line 274.

Back: Middle English, from *back*. Old English: *bæc*, of Germanic origin; related to Middle Dutch and Old Norse: *bak*. The adverb use dates from late Middle English and is a shortening of *aback*.

Antony and Cleopatra, IV 7 line 2772; Antony and Cleopatra, IV 14 line 3051; Antony and Cleopatra V 2 line 3097.
As You Like It, IV 3 line 2110; As You Like It, IV 3 line 2131.
Coriolanus, I 4 line 530; Coriolanus, III 3 line 2506.
Cymbeline, III 5 line 2115; Cymbeline, V 3 line 3029.
Hamlet, V 1 line 3517.
Henry IV, Part I, II 4 line 1138; Henry IV, Part I, II 4 line 1207; Henry IV, Part I, III 3 line 2077; Henry IV, Part I, V 4 line 3098; Henry IV, Part I, V 4 line 3128.
Henry IV, Part II, I 1 line 189; Henry IV, Part II, I 3 line 685; Henry IV, Part II, II 4 line 1602; Henry IV, Part II, II 2 line 1996.
Henry V, III 7 line 1688; Henry V, V 2 lines 3120, 3143.
Henry VI, Part I, I 1 line 145; Henry VI, Part I, II 5 line 1121; Henry VI, Part I, III 2 line 1439.
Henry VI, Part II, II 1 line 949; Henry VI, Part II, II 4 line 1191; Henry VI, Part II, IV 8 line 2786.
Henry VI, Part III, I 4 line 515; Henry VI, Part III, II 2 line 858; Henry VI, Part III, II 5 line 1242; Henry VI, Part III, III 2 line 1646; Henry VI, Part III, V 1 line 2659; Henry VI, Part III, V 7 line 3119.
Henry VIII, I 1 line 131; Henry VIII, I 2 line 376; Henry VIII, II 3 line 1251; Henry VIII, II 3 line 1321.
Julius Caesar, II 1 line 626; Julius Caesar, II 2 line 986; Julius Caesar, IV 3 line 2222.
King John, II 1 line 361; King John, II 1 lines 439, 441.
King Lear, I 1 line 187; King Lear, I 4 line 570; King Lear, I 4 line 687; King Lear, III 4 line 1929; King Lear, IV 6 line 2766.
Love's Labour's Lost, I 2 line 374; Love's Labour's Lost, V 2 lines 2050, 2051; Love's Labour's Lost, V 2 line 2404.
Macbeth, III 1 line 1045; Macbeth, III 6 line 1535; Macbeth, V 5 line 2413.
Measure for Measure, III 1 line 1248; Measure for Measure, III 2 line 1533.
Merchant of Venice, IV 1 line 1960; Merchant of Venice, IV 1 line 2238.
Merry Wives of Windsor, V 5 line 2071; Merry Wives of Windsor, V 5 line 2619.
Midsummer Night's Dream, II 1 line 521; Midsummer Night's Dream, III 2 line 1278.
Othello, I 1 line 127.
Passionate Pilgrim, line 55.
Richard II, I 2 line 264; Richard II, III 2 line 1453; Richard II V 5 lines 2835, 2840.
Richard III, III 7 line 2441.
Romeo and Juliet, I 1 line 48; Romeo and Juliet, I 4 line 592; Romeo and Juliet, II 5 line 1427rr; Romeo and Juliet, III 2 line 1727; Romeo

and Juliet, III 3 line 2023; Romeo and Juliet, IV 1 line 2393; Romeo and Juliet, V 1 line 2882; Romeo and Juliet, V 3 line 3177.
Taming of the Shrew, line 155; Taming of the Shrew, III 2 line 1436.
Tempest, II 1 line 816; Tempest, III 1 line 1308; Tempest, V 1 line 2121.
Timon of Athens, II 1 line 653; Timon of Athens, IV 2 line 1616.
Titus Andronicus, IV 1 line 1643; Titus Andronicus, IV 3 line 1928.
Troilus and Cressida, I 2 line 409; Troilus and Cressida, III 3 line 2021.
Twelfth Night, I 2 line 62.
Venus and Adonis, lines 320, 416, 615, 684, 836.
Winter's Tale, IV 4 line 2748.

Bacon: early 14c., *meat from the back and sides of a pig* (originally either fresh or cured, but especially cured), from Old French: *bacon*.
    Henry IV, Part I, II 1 line 665.
    Merry Wives of Windsor, IV 1 line 1932.

Balm: early 13c., *basme*, aromatic substance made from resins and oils, from Old French: *basme* from Latin: *balsamum*. Arabic *basham: balsam, spice, perfume*. Spelling refashioned 15c.-16c. on Latin model. Sense of *healing or soothing influence* (1540s) is from aromatic preparations from balsam.
    Antony and Cleopatra, V 2 line 3376.
    Coriolanus, I 6 line 692.
    Henry IV, Part II, IV 5 line 3010.
    Henry V, IV 1 line 2107.
    Henry VI, Part III, III 1 line 1384; Henry VI, Part III, IV 8 line 2563.
    King Lear, I 1 line 234.
    Macbeth, II 2 line 698.
    Merry Wives of Windsor, V 5 line 2627.
    Rape of Lucrece, line 1517.
    Richard II, I 1 line 176; Richard II, III 2 line 1463; Richard II, IV 1 line 2195.
    Richard III, I 2 line 186.
    Taming of the Shrew, line 49.
    Timon of Athens, V 4 line 2574.
    Troilus and Cressida, I 1 line 91.
    Venus and Adonis, line 47.

Balmy: c.1500, delicately fragrant. Figurative use for *soothing* dates from c. 1600.
    Othello, II 3 line 1411; Othello, V 2 line 3318.
    Sonnet CVII, line 9.

Balsamum: 1570s, Latin: *balsamum:* gum of the balsam tree. There is an isolated Old English reference from c.1000, and Middle English used: *basme, baume*, from the French form of the word.
    Comedy of Errors, IV 1 line 1043.

Ban-dog: fierce dogs, which are kept tied up.
    Henry VI, Part II, I 4 line 645.

Bank: earthen incline, edge of a river, c.1200, probably in Old English: but not attested in surviving documents.
    Cymbeline, II 4 line 1260; Cymbeline, V 4 line 3248.
    Hamlet, III 2 line 2019.
    Henry IV, Part I, I 3 lines 423, 432. Henry IV, Part I, III 1 line 1588; Henry IV, Part I, III 1 line 1608.
    Henry IV, Part II, III 1 line 1512; Henry IV, Part II, III 2 line 1754; Henry IV, Part II, IV 1 line 2382.
    Julius Caesar, I 1 line 46; Julius Caesar, I 1 line 58.
    King John, II 1 line 753.
    Macbeth, I 7 line 479.
    Merchant of Venice, V 1 line 2456. Merchant of Venice, V 1 line 2508.
    Midsummer Night's Dream, II 1 line 628; Midsummer Night's Dream, II 2 line 694.
    Pericles, II 4 line 976.
    Rape of Lucrece, lines 1170, 1489.
    Richard II, III 4 line 1974.
    Richard III, IV 4 line 3356.
    Sonnet, LVI line 11.
    Tempest, I 2 line 552; Tempest IV 1 line 1774.
    Troilus and Cressida, I 3 line 791; Troilus and Cressida, III 2 line 1658.
    Twelfth Night, I 1 line 7.
    Venus and Adonis, lines 92, 171.
    Winter's Tale, IV 4 line 2010.

Barefoot: Old English: *bærfot*.
    All's Well That Ends Well, III 4 line 1565.
    Hamlet, II 2 line 1579.
    Othello, IV 3 line 3060.
    Tempest, II 2 line 1092.
    Troilus and Cressida, I 2 line 226.

Bark: tree skin, c.1300, from a Scandinavian source akin to Old Norse: *borkr*. Also, any small ship, early 15c. More precise sense of three-masted ship (17c.) often is spelled *barque* to distinguish it. Unrelated in reference to a dog sound, Old English: *beorcan: to bark*.
    Antony and Cleopatra, I 4 line 496.
    As You Like It, III 2 line 1127; As You Like It, III 2 line 1360; As You Like It, III 2 line 1446.
    Comedy of Errors, I 1 line 118; Comedy of Errors, III 2 line 909; Comedy of Errors, IV 1 line 1039; Comedy of Errors, IV 1 line 1053; Comedy of Errors, IV 3 line 1186.
    Coriolanus, II 3 line 1666.
    Hamlet, IV 3 line 2755.
    Henry IV, Part II, III 1 line 1332; Henry IV, Part II, III 2 line 2108.

Henry IV, Part III, II 1 line 643; Henry IV, Part III, V 4 line 2832.
Henry VI, Part I, III 4 line 1741.
Henry VIII, I 2 line 427; Henry VIII, II 4 line 1531.
Julius Caesar, V 1 line 2420.
King Lear, III 6 line 2036; King Lear, IV 6 line 2618; King Lear, IV 6 line 2761.
Love's Labour's Lost, V 2 line 2198.
Macbeth, I 3 line 122.
Measure for Measure, III 1 line 1300.
Merchant of Venice, I 1 line 100; Merchant of Venice, II 6 line 924.
Merry Wives of Windsor, I 1 line 276.
Midsummer Night's Dream, III 1 line 927.
Much Ado About Nothing, I 1 line 118.
Othello, II 1 line 817; Othello, II 1 line 978.
Pericles, V 0 line 2165.
Rape of Lucrece, lines 1218, 1220.
Richard II, III 4 line 1924.
Richard III, I 1 line 24; Richard III, III 7 line 2373; Richard III, IV 4 line 3037.
Romeo and Juliet, III 5 lines 2238, 2240; Romeo and Juliet, III V line 3075.
Sonnet LXXX line 7; Sonnet, CVI line 7.
Tempest, I 2 line 253; Tempest, I 2 line 545; Tempest, II 2 line 1211.
Timon of Athens, IV 2 line 1628; Timon of Athens, V 1 line 2308.
Titus Andronicus, I 1 line 87; Titus Andronicus, V 1 line 2273.
Troilus and Cressida, I 0 line 12; Troilus and Cressida, I 1 line 135; Troilus and Cressida, I 3 line 490.
Venus and Adonis, line 260.
Winter's Tale, III 3 line 1495; Winter's Tale, IV 4 line 1969; Winter's Tale, V 2 line 3176.

Barley: Old English: *bærlic*, originally an adjective, *of barley*, from *bere: barley*. Also refers to beer: *barley juice*.
   Henry V, III 5 line 1409.
   Tempest, IV 1 line 1771.

Barm: Old English *beorma*: yeast, leaven, also, head of a beer.
   Coriolanus, II 1 line 978.
   Midsummer Night's Dream, II 1 line 405.

Barnacle: early 13c., *species of wild goose*; as a type of shellfish, first recorded 1580s. Often derived from a Celtic source, but the application to the goose predates that of the shellfish in English. The goose nests in the Arctic in summer and returns to Europe in the winter, hence the mystery surrounding its reproduction. It was believed in ancient superstition to hatch from barnacle's shell, possibly because the crustacean's feathery stalks resemble goose down.

Tempest, IV 1 line 1989.

Bat: It has generally been an object of superstitious dread, and proved to the poet and painter a fertile source of images of gloom and terror. In Scotland it was connected with witchcraft, and if, while flying, it rise and then descend again earthwards, it is a sign that the witches' hour is come; the hour in which they are supposed to have power over every human being who is not specially shielded from their influence. A flying mammal, 1570s, a dialectal alteration of Middle English: *bakke* (early 14c.), which is probably related to Old Swedish: *natbakka*, Old Danish: *nathbakkæ night bat*, and Old Norse: *leðrblaka*: *leather flapper*, so original sense is likely *flapper*. Old English word for the animal was *hreremus*, from *hreran*: *to shake*. It has qualities of both the bird and the mouse, rendering this animal a symbol of Androgyne; it also has strong associations with darkness and obscurity, as a creature of the night. As a contemptuous term for an old woman, perhaps a suggestion of witchcraft, or from *bat* as a prostitute who plies her trade by night.
    Macbeth, III 2 line 1214; Macbeth, IV 1 line 1562.
    Tempest, I 2 line 491; Tempest, V 1 line 2129.

Bate: the flutter of a hawk.
    Taming of the Shrew, IV 1 line 1807.
    Venus and Adonis, line 676.

Bavin: used as an a piece of waste wood, applied contemptuously to anything worthless.
    Henry IV, Part I, III 2 line 1884.

Bay: The withering and death of this tree were considered to be a prognostic of evil.
    Henry VIII, IV 2 lines 2649, 2650.
    Pericles, IV 6 line 2093.
    Richard II, II 4 line 1338.

Beach: 1530s, loose, water-worn pebbles of the seashore, probably from Old English: *bæce, bece: stream*. Extended to loose, pebbly shores (1590s), and in dialect around Sussex and Kent beach still has the meaning "pebbles worn by the waves.
    Coriolanus, V 3 line 3558.
    Cymbeline, I 6 line 643.
    Henry IV, Part II, III 1 line 1755.
    Henry V, V 0 line 2847.
    King Lear, IV 6 line 2616.
    Merchant of Venice, IV 1 line 2003.
    Midsummer Night's Dream, II 1 line 454.
    Timon of Athens, V I line 2005.

Beagle: Middle English: *begle*; late 15c., of unknown origin, possibly from French *becguele*: *noisy person*, literally *gaping throat*, from *bayer:open wide*.

Refers to a breed of hunting dog, known for its baying, energy and gaping mouth.
>**Timon of Athens**, IV 3 line 1858.

Beak: horny jaw of bird. Middle English: from Old French: *bec*, from Latin: *beccus*, of Celtic origin.
>**Cymbeline**, V 4 line 3269.
>**Henry VI, Part II**, III 2 line 1878.
>**King Lear**, II 2 line 1145.
>**Rape of Lucrece**, line 559.
>**Tempest**, I 2 line 315.
>**Venus and Adonis**, line 76.

Bean: Old English: *bean: bean, pea, legume*. As a metaphor for *something of small value* it is from c.1300. The notion of lucky or magic beans in English folklore is from the exotic beans or large seeds that wash up occasionally in Cornwall and western Scotland, carried from the Caribbean or South America by the Gulf Stream. They were cherished, believed to ward off the evil eye and aid in childbirth. Beans are also phallic, especially when they are green and can symbolise male sex organs, and can connote immortality. Can be thought of also as an elementary food or way of counting. The flowers that can grow from beans emit a smell that produces accidents, lunacy, bad dreams and terrifying visions.
>**Henry IV, Part I**, II 1 line 651.
>**Midsummer Night's Dream**, II 1 line 413.

Bear: Old English: *bera*. Irish equivalent: *the good calf*, Welsh: *honey-pig*. According to an old idea, the bear brings forth unformed lumps of animated flesh, and then licks them into shape. In the time of Queen Elizabeth, bear-baiting was still a favourite pastime, being considered a fashionable entertainment for the ladies of the highest rank. The bear is a creature of contrasts, as it possesses enormous strength and yet generally thrives on fruit and honey. Because of their habit of hibernation during winter months, bears can stand for resurrection. It was the emblem for the kingdoms of Persia and Russia. For the Celts, it is a symbol of the warrior, and in Christian symbolism we encounter the fable of the she-bear who gives birth to shapeless offspring and must lick them to give them form. Similarly, we are ignorant creatures who find our way only through spiritual knowledge. The word *berserk* most likely means 'bear-coat' and refers to a Norse warrior who morphs into a furious bear.
>**Antony and Cleopatra**, IV 14 line 2980.
>**Comedy of Errors**, III 2 line 913.
>**Coriolanus**, II 1 line 927; Coriolanus, II 1 line 928.
>**Henry V**, III 7 line 1772.
>**Henry VI, Part II**, V 1 line 3193; Henry VI, Part II, V 1 lines 3198, 3200r; Henry VI, Part II, V 2 line 3210.
>**Henry VI, Part III**, II 2 line 855.
>**Julius Caesar**, IV 3 line 2196.
>**King John**, II 1 line 550.

King Lear, III 1 line 1629; King Lear, III 4 lines 1808, 1810; King Lear IV 2 line 2386.
Macbeth, III 4 line 1396.
Midsummer Night's Dream, II 1 line 555; Midsummer Night's Dream, II 2 line 683; Midsummer Night's Dream, II 2 line 753; Midsummer Night's Dream, III 1 lines 925, 927; Midsummer Night's Dream, IV 1 line 1668; Midsummer Night's Dream, V 1 line 1852.
Othello, II 1 line 777; Othello, IV 1 line 2620.
Troilus and Cressida, I 2 line 176.
Venus and Adonis, line 906.
Winter's Tale, III 3 line 1551; Winter's Tale, IV 4 line 2781; Winter's Tale, V 2 line 3172; Winter's Tale, V 3 line 3364.

Beard: Old English: *beard: beard*. Pubic hair sense is from 1600s (but also: *neþir berd: pubic hair*, late 14c. As a verb: c.1300, *to grow or have a beard*. The sense of *confront boldly and directly* is from Middle English, phrases such as *rennen in berd: oppose openly* (c.1200), *reproven in the berd: to rebuke directly and personally* (c.1400). The beard is a symbol of manhood, virility, and sovereignty. It is wisdom, a mark of the knowledge of the elders, and is often the mark of male dignity. Hence, a bearded woman is often a witch. In the Old Testament, the beard can only be cut as a form of penance, mourning, punishment or putting someone to shame. It is also a sign of living, as Christ has a beard on earth and is clean-shaven after his death.

All's Well That Ends Well, II 3 line 957; All's Well That Ends Well, IV 1 line 1951; All's Well That Ends Well, V 3 line 2750.
Antony and Cleopatra, II 2 line 688.
As You Like It, I 2 line 205; As You Like It, I 2 line 206; As You Like It, II 7 line 1048; As You Like It, II 7 line 1053; As You Like It, III 2 line 1310; As You Like It, III 2 line 1311; As You Like It, III 2 line 1312; As You Like It, III 2 lines 1459, 1460; As You Like It, V 4 line 2470r; As You Like It, V 4 line 2480; As You Like It, V 4 lines 2610, 2612.
Comedy of Errors, V 1 line 1606.
Coriolanus, I 10 line 889r; Coriolanus, II 1 lines 1002r; Coriolanus, IV 3 line 2671.
Cymbeline, V 3 line 3041.
Hamlet, I 2 line 457; Hamlet, II 2 line 1301; Hamlet II 2 line 1503; Hamlet, II 2 line 1573; Hamlet, II 2 line 1647; Hamlet, IV 5 line 3070; Hamlet, IV 7 line 3164.
Henry IV, Part I, II 4 line 1343; Henry IV, Part I, IV 1 line 2241.
Henry IV, Part II, I 2 line 293; Henry IV, Part II, IV 1 line 2248; Henry IV, Part II, V 1 line 3208; Henry IV, Part II, V 1 line 3434.
Henry V, III 2 line 1201; Henry V, III 3 line 1308; Henry V, III 6 line 1539; Henry V, IV 6 line 2489; Henry V, V 2 line 3144; Henry V, V 2 line 3191.
Henry VI, Part I, I 3 line 399; Henry VI, Part I, I 3 line 400; Henry VI, Part I, I 3 line 403.
Henry VI, Part II, III 2 line 1860; Henry VI, Part I, IV 10 line 2925.

King John, II 1 line 434.
King Lear, II 2 line 1133; King Lear, II 4 line 1486; King Lear, III 7 line 2159; King Lear, III 7 line 2160; King Lear, III 7 line 2207; King Lear, IV 6 lines 2706, 2707.
Love's Labour's Lost, II 1 line 696; Love's Labour's Lost, V 2 line 2766.
Macbeth, I 3 line 146; Macbeth, V 5 line 2360r.
Measure for Measure, IV 2 line 2080; Measure for Measure, IV 3 line 2191.
Merchant of Venice, I 3 line 444; Merchant of Venice, II 2 line 658; Merchant of Venice, III 2 line 1452.
Merry Wives of Windsor, I 4 line 423; Merry Wives of Windsor, I 4 line 426r.
Midsummer Night's Dream, I 2 line 307; Midsummer Night's Dream, I 2 line 345; Midsummer Night's Dream, I 2 lines 349r, 350r; Midsummer Night's Dream, II 1 line 464; Midsummer Night's Dream, IV 2 line 1817.
Much Ado About Nothing, II 1 line 424; Much Ado About Nothing, II 1 line 425; Much Ado About Nothing, II 1 lines 428, 429; Much Ado About Nothing, II 1 line 650; Much Ado About Nothing, III 2 line 1243; Much Ado About Nothing, V 1 line 2083.
Othello, I 3 line 700; Othello, III 3 line 2123; Othello, IV 1 line 2490.
Rape of Lucrece, line 1456.
Romeo and Juliet, III 1 line 1516.
Sonnet, XII line 8.
Taming of the Shrew, III 2 line 1537.
Tempest, V 1 line 2033.
Timon of Athens, IV 3 line 1791; Timon of Athens, V 1 line 2456.
Troilus and Cressida, I 3 line 618; Troilus and Cressida, I 3 line 757; Troilus and Cressida, IV 5 line 2833.
Twelfth Night, II 3 line 855; Twelfth Night, III 1 line 1277; Twelfth Night, III 2 line 1430; Twelfth Night, IV 2 line 2021; Twelfth Night, IV 2 line 2080.
Two Gentlemen of Verona, IV 2 line 1563.
Winter's Tale, II 3 line 1125; Winter's Tale, IV 4 line 2318; Winter's Tale, IV 4 line 2685; Winter's Tale, IV 4 line 2691.

Beast: c.1200, from Old French: *beste* animal, wild beast, figuratively: fool, idiot. Replaced Old English: *deor* as the generic word for wild creature. Of persons felt to be animal-like in various senses from early 13c. Of the figure in the Christian apocalypse story from late 14c.
> **Antony and Cleopatra**, I 1 line 44; Antony and Cleopatra, I 4 line 494.
> **As You Like It**, II 7 line 894; As You Like It, IV 3 line 2051; As You Like It, IV 3 line 2119; As You Like It, V 4 line 2440.
> **Comedy of Errors**, II 1 line 290; Comedy of Errors, II 2 line 471; Comedy of Errors, III 2 lines 848, 849; Comedy of Errors, V 1 line 1515.
> **Coriolanus**, III 1 line 922; Coriolanus, IV 3 line 2522; Coriolanus, IV 6 line 3167.
> **Cymbeline**, V 3 line 3051.

Hamlet, I 2 line 354; Hamlet, I 5 line 781; Hamlet, IV 4 line 2824; Hamlet, IV 5 line 2947; Hamlet, IV 7 line 3228; Hamlet, V 2 lines 3742, 3743.
Henry IV, Part I, III 3 line 2133; Henry IV, Part I, III 3 line 2135; Henry IV, Part I, III 3 line 2136.
Henry IV, Part II, II 1 line 752.
Henry V, III 7 lines 1660, 1666; Henry V, IV 3 line 2332.
Henry VI, Part II, V 2 line 3221.
Henry VI, Part III, II 2 line 854.
Julius Caesar, I 3 line 490; Julius Caesar, II 2 line 1018; Julius Caesar, II 2 line 1020; Julius Caesar, III 2 line 1648.
King John, IV 3 line 2183.
King Lear, II 3 line 1260; King Lear, III 4 line 1898.
Love's Labour's Lost, I 1 line 236; Love's Labour's Lost, II 1 line 721.
Macbeth, I 7 line 526.
Measure for Measure, III 1 line 1373; Measure for Measure, III 2 line 1515; Measure for Measure, III 2 line 1544.
Merchant of Venice, I 2 line 279.
Merry Wives of Windsor, I 1 line 18; Merry Wives of Windsor, III 4 line 1742; Merry Wives of Windsor, V 5 lines 2564, 2565, 2568.
Midsummer Night's Dream, II 1 line 603; Midsummer Night's Dream, II 2 line 754; Midsummer Night's Dream V 1 line 1984; Midsummer Night's Dream, V 1 line 2061; Midsummer Night's Dream, V 1 line 2071; Midsummer Night's Dream, V 1 line 2072.
Much Ado About Nothing, I 1 line 126; Much Ado About Nothing, V 4 line 2595.
Othello, I 1 line 127; Othello, II 3 line 1446; Othello, II 3 line 1460; Othello, IV 1 line 2485; Othello, IV 1 line 2486.
Passionate Pilgrim, lines 379, 396.
Rape of Lucrece, lines 596, 1199r.
Richard II, V 1 line 2368; Richard II, V 1 line 2369r.
Richard III, I 2 line 246; Richard III, I 2 line 247.
Romeo and Juliet, I 1 line 103; Romeo and Juliet, III 2 line 1819; Romeo and Juliet, III 3 lines 1992, 1994.
Sonnet L line 5; Sonnet LI line 5; Sonnet CXIII line 6.
Taming of the Shrew, Prologue 1 line 35; Taming of the Shrew, IV 1 line 1640; Taming of the Shrew, IV 1 line 1642.
Tempest, I 2 line 526; Tempest, II 1 line 1074; Tempest, II 2 line 1116; Tempest, IV 1 line 1868.
Timon of Athens, III 2 lines 1055, 1061; Timon of Athens, III 6 line 1538; Timon of Athens, IV 1 line 1600; Timon of Athens, IV 3 line 1718; Timon of Athens, IV 3 line 2024; Timon of Athens, IV 3 line 2026r; Timon of Athens, IV 3 lines 2045, 2046r; Timon of Athens, IV 3 lines 2051; Timon of Athens, IV 3 line 2075; Timon of Athens, IV 3 lines 2097; Timon of Athens, IV 3 lines 2136; Timon of Athens, IV 3 lines 2137; Timon of Athens, V 3 line 2547.
Titus Andronicus, II 4 line 1098; Titus Andronicus, V 3 line 2743.
Troilus and Cressida, I 2 line 174; Troilus and Cressida, V 6 line 3553.

Two Gentlemen of Verona, V 4 line 2183.
Venus and Adonis, lines 346, 1021.
Winter's Tale, IV 4 line 1886.

Bee: stinging insect, Old English: *beo*. Used metaphorically for *busy worker* since 1530s.
Cymbeline, III 2 line 1545.
Henry IV, Part II, IV 4 line 2847; Henry IV, Part II, IV 5 line 2967; Henry IV, Part II, IV 5 line 2970.
Henry VI, Part I, I 5 line 607.
Henry VI, Part II, III 2 line 1807; Henry VI, Part II, IV 2 line 2383; Henry VI, Part II, IV 2 line 2384.
Julius Caesar, V 1 line 2384.
Pericles, II 1 line 628.
Rape of Lucrece, lines 887, 1820.
Tempest, I 2 line 480; Tempest, V 1 line 2118.
Titus Andronicus, V 1 line 2145.
Two Gentlemen of Verona, I 2 line 266.

Beef: 13c. from Old French: *buef: ox; beef; ox hide*, from Latin: *bovem: ox, cow*. Original plural was beeves.
Henry IV, Part I, III 3 line 2187.
Henry V, III 7 line 1778; Henry V, III 7 line 1780.
Henry VI, Part II, IV 10 line 2944.
Measure for Measure, III 2 line 1568.
Taming of the Shrew, Prologue 2 line 154; Taming of the Shrew, IV 3 line 1979; Taming of the Shrew, IV 3 line 1982; Taming of the Shrew, IV 3 line 1984; Taming of the Shrew, IV 3 line 1986.
Twelfth Night, I 3 line 195.

Beetle: type of insect, Old English: *bitela: beetle, little biter*, from *bitel: biting*, related to *bitan: to bite*.
Antony and Cleopatra, III 2 line 1615.
Cymbeline, III 3 line 1623.
Hamlet, I 4 line 704.
Henry IV, Part II, I 2 line 575.
King Lear, IV 6 line 2614.
Macbeth, III 2 line 1216.
Measure for Measure, III 1 line 1308.
Midsummer Night's Dream, II 2 line 672.
Romeo and Juliet, I 4 line 528.
Tempest, I 2 line 491.

Beeves: flesh of a cow, ox or bull, used as food. Middle English: from Old French *boef*, from Latin: *bos, bov: ox*.
Henry IV, Part II, III 2 line 2195.

Belly: *to swell out*. Old English: *belig: bag*, of Germanic origin, from a base meaning: *swell, be inflated*.

As You Like It, II 7 line 1052; As You Like It, III 2 line 1308.
Coriolanus, I 1 line 88; Coriolanus, I 1 line 98; Coriolanus, I 1 line 101; Coriolanus, I 1 line 115; Coriolanus, I 1 line 119; Coriolanus, I 1 line 125; Coriolanus, I 1 line 146.
Henry IV, Part I, II 4 line 1436; Henry IV, Part I, III 3 line 2058; Henry IV, Part I, IV 2 line 2388.
Henry IV, Part II, I 2 line 462; Henry IV, Part II, I 2 line 508; Henry IV, Part II, I 2 line 517; Henry IV, Part II, I 2 line 799; Henry IV, Part II, II 4 line 1483; Henry IV, Part II, IV 3 lines 2599, 2601.
Henry V, IV 8 line 2771.
Henry VI, Part III, II 3 line 1048.
King Lear, III 6 line 2035.
Love's Labour's Lost, V 2 line 2617; Love's Labour's Lost, V 2 line 2631.
Measure for Measure, IV 3 line 2283.
Merchant of Venice, III 5 line 1876.
Merry Wives of Windsor, I 3 line 360; Merry Wives of Windsor, II 1 line 628; Merry Wives of Windsor, III 5 line 1781; Merry Wives of Windsor, V 5 line 2715.
Pericles, II 1 line 621.
Taming of the Shrew, IV 1 line 1626.
Timon of Athens, I 1 line 246.
Troilus and Cressida, I 2 line 409; Troilus and Cressida, II 1 line 930.
Venus and Adonis, line 615.
Winter's Tale, I 2 line 295.

Berry: Old English: *berie*. This, and *Apple*, are the only native fruit names.
Antony and Cleopatra, I 4 line 493.
Henry V, I 1 line 100.
Midsummer Night's Dream, III 2 line 1251.
Pericles, V 0 line 2149.
Tempest, I 2 line 485; Tempest, II 2 line 1246.
Timon of Athens, IV 3 line 2135.
Titus Andronicus, IV 2 line 1873.
Venus and Adonis, lines 481, 625, 1126.

Bilberry: late 16c., probably of Scandinavian origin; compare with Danish: *bøllebær*. It is known in English by a very wide range of local names. These include: *blaeberry, whortleberry, (ground) hurts, whinberry, winberry, windberry, wimberry, myrtle blueberry* and *fraughan*.
Merry Wives of Windsor, V 5 line 2609.

Bill: Old English: *bill, bird's beak*, related to *bill*, a poetic word for a kind of sword (especially one with a hooked blade). Used also in Middle English of beak-like projections of land.
As You Like It, III 3 line 1570.
Cymbeline, IV 2 line 2612r.
Midsummer Night's Dream, III 1 line 947.
Winter's Tale, I 2 line 270.

Venus and Adonis, line 1124.

Billing: stroking beaks as in courtship. Old English: *bile*, of unknown origin.
Troilus and Cressida, III 2 line 1710.

Bird: rare form of *bridd*, originally *young bird, nestling*. Middle English, in which bird referred to various young animals and even human beings, may be used in a figurative sense of *secret source of information* from 1540s. Also, confused with *burd*, meaning a maiden or young girl c.1300.
Antony and Cleopatra, III 2 line 1605.
As You Like It, II 5 line 824; As You Like It, IV 1 line 1967; As You Like It, V 3 line 2380.
Cymbeline, I 6 line 623; Cymbeline, III 3 line 1647; Cymbeline, IV 2 line 2577; Cymbeline, V 4 line 3268.
Hamlet, I 1 line 184; Hamlet, I 5 line 857; Hamlet, III 4 line 2598.
Henry IV, Part I, V 1 line 2694.
Henry IV, Part II, IV 4 line 2841; Henry IV, Part II, V 5 line 3707.
Henry V, III 2 line 1145.
Henry VI, Part II, I 3 line 480; Henry VI, Part II, II 1 line 734; Henry VI, Part II, III 2 line 1867.
Henry VI, Part III, I 4 line 474; Henry VI, Part III, II 1 line 718; Henry VI, Part III, II 1 line 798; Henry VI, Part III, III 3 line 1858; Henry VI, Part III, IV 3 line 2326; Henry VI, Part III, V 6 lines 3008, 3010.
Henry VIII, IV 1 line 2518; Henry VIII, V 5 line 3424.
Julius Caesar, I 3 line 447; Julius Caesar, I 3 line 490.
King Lear, IV 6 line 2701; King Lear, V 3 line 3132.
Love's Labour's Lost, I 1 line 107; Love's Labour's Lost, I 1 line 236; Love's Labour's Lost, IV 3 line 1343; Love's Labour's Lost, V 2 line 2890.
Macbeth, I 6 line 439; Macbeth, II 3 line 828; Macbeth, IV 2 line 1750; Macbeth, IV 2 line 1776; Macbeth, IV 2 line 1779; Macbeth, IV 2 line 1781.
Measure for Measure, II 1 line 454.
Merchant of Venice, III 1 line 1265.
Merry Wives of Windsor, II 1 line 684; Merry Wives of Windsor, III 1 lines 1208, 1214; Merry Wives of Windsor, III 3 line 1618; Merry Wives of Windsor, III 5 line 1787; Merry Wives of Windsor, III 5 line 1865; Merry Wives of Windsor, IV 2 line 1974; Merry Wives of Windsor, IV 2 line 2018.
Midsummer Night's Dream, III 1 line 957r; Midsummer Night's Dream, IV 1 line 1697; Midsummer Night's Dream, V 1 line 2244.
Much Ado About Nothing, I 1 line 38; Much Ado About Nothing, I 1 line 126; Much Ado About Nothing, II 1 line 605; Much Ado About Nothing, II 1 line 612.
Othello, II 1 line 905.
Passionate Pilgrim, lines 284, 361, 379, 383, 399, 401.
Pericles, IV 0 line 1518; Pericles, IV 6 line 2041; Pericles, V 0 line 2149.
Phoenix and the Turtle, lines 1, 68.

Rape of Lucrece, lines 139, 384, 508, 922, 1158, 1172, 1193.
Richard II, I 3 line 357; Richard II, I 3 line 588.
Romeo and Juliet, II 2 line 867; Romeo and Juliet, II 2 line 1041; Romeo and Juliet, II 5 line 1452.
Sonnet LXXIII line 4; Sonnet XCVII line 12; Sonnet XCVIII line 5; Sonnet CXIII line 6.
Taming of the Shrew, V 2 line 2537; Taming of the Shrew, V 2 line 2542.
Tempest, IV 1 line 1941.
Timon of Athens, III 6 line 1467; Timon of Athens, IV 3 line 2136; Timon of Athens, IV 3 line 2137.
Titus Andronicus, II 3 line 745; Titus Andronicus, II 3 line 893; Titus Andronicus, III 1 line 1215; Titus Andronicus, IV 4 line 2097; Titus Andronicus, V 3 line 2743.
Twelfth Night, I 4 line 384; Twelfth Night, IV 2 line 2070.
Venus and Adonis, lines 87, 476, 553, 581, 622, 625, 1123.
Winter's Tale, IV 3 line 1729.

Bladder: inflated or hollow bag or chamber. Old English: *blædre*, of Germanic origin; related to Dutch: *blaar* and German: *Blatter*.
   Henry IV, Part I, II 4 line 1319.
   Henry VIII, III 2 line 2263.
   Romeo and Juliet, V 1 line 2856.
   Troilus and Cressida, V 1 line 2951.

Blind-worms: also known as *slow worms* Old English: *slawyrm*, are burrowing lizards spending much of the time hiding underneath objects. The skin of the varieties of slow worm is smooth with scales that do not overlap one another. Like many other lizards, slow worms autotomise, meaning that they have the ability to shed their tail. Copper in *oloyr*, they give birth to live young.
   Midsummer Night's Dream, II 2 line 671.

Blister: c.1300, perhaps via Old French: *blestre: blister, lump, bump*. To *become covered in blisters*, late 15c.; *to raise blisters on*, 1540s.
   Hamlet, III 4 line 2435.
   Henry VIII, I 3 line 607.
   Love's Labour's Lost, V 2 line 2253.
   Macbeth, IV 3 line 1855.
   Measure for Measure, II 3 line 977.
   Romeo and Juliet, I 4 line 577; Romeo and Juliet, III 2 line 1814.
   Tempest, I 4 line 474.
   Timon of Athens, V 1 line 2410.
   Winter's Tale, II 2 line 885.

Blood: from the Old English: *blod*, that which spurts out. Popularly used for describing disposition or temperament. Red blood was considered a traditionary sign of courage. The absence of blood in the liver was the supposed property of a coward. Blood globally represents life itself, as the element of divine life that functions within the human body. It is repeatedly referred to as having magic powers and as the only food for the supernatural beings, and it is also associated with popular notions, including blood brotherhood, blood vengeance, blood baptism. Since it corresponds so readily with the colour red, it represents the end of a series which begins with sunlight (yellow) and follows intermediately with vegetable life (green). Closely tied with passion, but also with death, war, sacrifice (specifically sheep, hog, bull and man) and the warding off of malicious powers. Close ties to guilt, especially as bloodstains.

All's Well That Ends Well, I 1 line 59; All's Well That Ends Well, I 3 line 356; All's Well That Ends Well, I 3 lines 367, 368r, 369; All's Well That Ends Well, I 3 line 348r; All's Well That Ends Well, II 1 line 808; All's Well That Ends Well, II 3 line 996; All's Well That Ends Well, II 3 line 1019; All's Well That Ends Well, II 3 line 1095; All's Well That Ends Well, III 1 line 1371; All's Well That Ends Well, III 2 line 1469; All's Well That Ends Well, III 4 line 1566; All's Well That Ends Well, III 7 line 1870.

Antony and Cleopatra, I 1 line 37; Antony and Cleopatra, I 2 line 285; Antony and Cleopatra, I 3 line 391; Antony and Cleopatra, I 4 line 481; Antony and Cleopatra, I 5 line 602; Antony and Cleopatra, I 5 line 608; Antony and Cleopatra, III 1 line 1554; Antony and Cleopatra, III 13 line 2462; Antony and Cleopatra, IV 2 line 2524; Antony and Cleopatra, IV 8 line 2784; Antony and Cleopatra, IV 14 line 3091; Antony and Cleopatra, V 1 line 3308; Antony and Cleopatra, V 1 line 3328; Antony and Cleopatra, V 2 line 3831.

As You Like It, I 1 lines 39, 42; As You Like It, II 3 lines 681r; As You Like It, II 3 lines 693; As You Like It, III 5 lines 1657; As You Like It, IV 3 lines 2095; As You Like It, IV 3 lines 2161; As You Like It, IV 3 lines 2165; As You Like It, V 4 lines 2458.

Comedy of Errors, I 1 line 11; Comedy of Errors, II 2 line 530; Comedy of Errors, IV 3 line 1221; Comedy of Errors, V 1 line 1630; Comedy of Errors, V 1 line 1752.

Coriolanus, I 1 line 132; Coriolanus, I 1 line 157; Coriolanus, I 3 line 397; Coriolanus, I 3 line 401r; Coriolanus, I 3 line 405; Coriolanus, I 5 line 592; Coriolanus, I 6 line 647; Coriolanus, I 6 line 684; Coriolanus, I 8 line 748; Coriolanus, I 9 line 781; Coriolanus, I 9 line 874; Coriolanus, I 10 line 878; Coriolanus, II 1 line 990; Coriolanus, II 2 line 1356; Coriolanus, III 1 line 1824; Coriolanus, III 1 line 2112; Coriolanus, III 1 line 2147; Coriolanus, III 2 line 2240; Coriolanus, IV 5 line 2834; Coriolanus, IV 5 line 2980; Coriolanus, V 1 lines 3338, 3341; Coriolanus, V 2 line 3428; Coriolanus, V 3 line 3518; Coriolanus, V 3 line 3525; Coriolanus, V 6 line 3872; Coriolanus, V 6 line 3912.

Cymbeline, I 1 line 2; Cymbeline, I 1 line 160; Cymbeline, I 1 line 202; Cymbeline, I 2 line 239; Cymbeline, I 4 line 376; Cymbeline, III 2 line 1519; Cymbeline, III 3 line 1702; Cymbeline, III 4 line 1861; Cymbeline, IV 2 line 2537; Cymbeline, IV 2 line 2547; Cymbeline, IV 2 line 2700; Cymbeline, IV 2 line 2775; Cymbeline, IV 4 line 2926; Cymbeline, IV 4 line 2947; Cymbeline, V 1 line 2952; Cymbeline, V 5 line 3460; Cymbeline, V 5 line 3552; Cymbeline, V 5 line 3779; Cymbeline, V 5 line 3959.

Hamlet, I 1 line 133; Hamlet, I 3 line 488; Hamlet, I 3 line 603; Hamlet, I 5 lines 352, 358; Hamlet, I 5 lines 703, 708; Hamlet, II 1 line 983; Hamlet, II 2 line 1449; Hamlet, II 2 line 1534; Hamlet, II 2 line 1654; Hamlet, III 2 line 1948; Hamlet, III 2 line 2247; Hamlet, III 2 line 2266; Hamlet, III 3 line 2326; Hamlet, III 4 line 2414; Hamlet, III 4 line 2416; Hamlet, III 4 line 2461; Hamlet, III 4 line 2529; Hamlet, IV 1 line 2643; Hamlet, IV 3 line 2781; Hamlet, IV 4 lines 2847, 2845; Hamlet, IV 5 line 2986; Hamlet, IV 5 line 3022; Hamlet, IV 7 line 3289; Hamlet, V 2 line 4032; Hamlet, V 2 lines 4042, 4048.

Henry IV, Part I, I 1 line 7; Henry IV, Part I, I 1 line 57; Henry IV, Part I, I 1 line 70; Henry IV, Part I, I 2 line 179; Henry IV, Part I, I 2 line 245; Henry IV, Part I, I 3 line 323; Henry IV, Part I, I 3 lines 430, 433; Henry IV, Part I, I 3 line 463; Henry IV, Part I, I 3 line 475; Henry IV, Part I, I 3 line 516; Henry IV, Part I, I 3 line 528; Henry IV, Part I, I 3 line 582; Henry IV, Part I, II 3 line 776; Henry IV, Part I, II 2 line 903; Henry IV, Part I, II 3 line 956; Henry IV, Part I, II 4 line 1229; Henry IV, Part I, II 4 line 1296; Henry IV, Part I, II 4 line 1354; Henry IV, Part I, II 4 line 1426; Henry IV, Part I, III 1 line 1726; Henry IV, Part I, III 1 line 1767; Henry IV, Part I, III 2 lines 1829, 1839. Henry IV, Part I, III 2 line 1858; Henry IV, Part I, III 2 line 1929; Henry IV, Part I, III 2 lines 1959, 1960; Henry IV, Part I, III 3 line 2058; Henry IV, Part I, III 3 line 2094; Henry IV, Part I, IV 1 line 2250; Henry IV, Part I, IV 1 line 2343; Henry IV, Part I, IV 3 line 2535; Henry IV, Part I, V 1 line 2621; Henry IV, Part I, V 1 line 2722; Henry IV, Part I, V 2 line 2787; Henry IV, Part I, V 2 line 2852; Henry IV, Part I, V 2 line 2870; Henry IV, Part I, V 4 lines 3073, 3075; Henry IV, Part I, V 4 line 3079.

Henry IV, Part II, Prologue 1 lines 24, 27; Henry IV, Part II, I 1 line 90; Henry IV, Part II, I 1 lines 165, 185; Henry IV, Part II, I 1 line 218; Henry IV, Part II, I 1 line 262; Henry IV, Part II, I 2 line 419; Henry IV, Part II, I 3 line 627; Henry IV, Part II, II 2 line 947; Henry IV, Part II, II 2 line 1076; Henry IV, Part II, II 3 line 1184; Henry IV, Part II, II 4 line 1261; Henry IV, Part II, II 4 line 1587; Henry IV, Part II, IV 1 lines 1939, 1945, 1955; Henry IV, Part II, IV 1 line 2287; Henry IV, Part II, IV 1 line 2296; Henry IV, Part II, IV 2 line 2498; Henry IV, Part II, IV 3 lines 2684, 2687, 2697, 2709; Henry IV, Part II, IV 4 lines 2786, 2792; Henry IV, Part II, IV 4 lines 2806, 2811; Henry IV, Part II, IV 5 lines 2926, 2930; Henry IV, Part II, IV 5 line 2979; Henry IV, Part II, IV 5 line 3065; Henry IV, Part II, IV 5 line 3090; Henry IV, Part II, V 2 line 3377; Henry IV, Part II, V 4 line 3569; Henry IV, Part II, IV 5 line 3065.

Henry V, I 2 lines 164, 170; Henry V, I 2 lines 246, 255; Henry V, I 2 line 263; Henry V, I 2 line 269; Henry V, I 2 line 276; Henry V, II 2 line 710; Henry V, II 2 line 769; Henry V, II 3 line 886; Henry V, II 4 line 950; Henry V, II 4 lines 1000, 1010; Henry V, III 1 lines 1098, 1108, 1114; Henry V, III 2 line 1136; Henry V, III 3 lines 1284, 1306, 1313; Henry V, III 5 lines 1410, 1411; Henry V, III 5 line 1439; Henry V, III 6 line 1597; Henry V, III 6 line 1628; Henry V, IV 1 line 1989; Henry V, IV 1 lines 2147, 2150; Henry V, IV 2 line 2173; Henry V, IV 2 line 2175; Henry V,

IV 2 line 2184; Henry V, IV 3 line 2296; Henry V, IV 4 line 2388; Henry V, IV 4 line 2433; Henry V, IV 6 line 2482; Henry V, IV 6 lines 2484, 2490, 2502; Henry V, IV 7 lines 2592, 2596, 2598; Henry V, IV 8 line 2716; Henry V, IV 8 line 2798; Henry V, V 2 line 3041; Henry V, V 2 line 3205; Henry V, V 2 line 3329.

Henry VI, Part I, I 1 line 21; Henry VI, Part I, I 1 line 163; Henry VI, Part I, I 3 line 442; Henry VI, Part I, I 5 line 586; Henry VI, Part I, II 2 lines 768, 778; Henry VI, Part I, II 3 line 864; Henry VI, Part I, II 4 line 986; Henry VI, Part I, II 4 line 1026; Henry VI, Part I, II 4 line 1042; Henry VI, Part I, II 4 line 1073; Henry VI, Part I, II 5 line 1181; Henry VI, Part I, II 5 line 1213; Henry VI, Part I, III 1 line 1313; Henry VI, Part I, III 1 line 1348; Henry VI, Part I, III 1 line 1391; Henry VI, Part I, III 1 line 1392; Henry VI, Part I, III 3 line 1664; Henry VI, Part I, III 4 line 1749; Henry VI, Part I, IV 1 line 1804; Henry VI, Part I, IV 1 line 1915; Henry VI, Part I, IV 2 line 1974; Henry VI, Part I, IV 2 lines 1982, 2004; Henry VI, Part I, IV 2 lines 2016, 2019; Henry VI, Part I, IV 4 line 2103; Henry VI, Part I, IV 5 line 2150; Henry VI, Part I, IV 6 lines 2208, 2212, 2214, 2215; Henry VI, Part I, IV 6 line 2235; Henry VI, Part I, IV 7 lines 2257, 2266; Henry VI, Part I, IV 7 line 2289; Henry VI, Part I, IV 7 line 2291; Henry VI, Part I, IV 7 line 2301; Henry VI, Part I, IV 7 line 2353; Henry VI, Part I, V 1 line 2364; Henry VI, Part I, V 1 line 2368; Henry VI, Part I, V 3 lines 2463, 2471; Henry VI, Part I, V 3 line 2497; Henry VI, Part I, V 4 line 2678; Henry VI, Part I, V 4 lines 2715, 2723; Henry VI, Part I, V 4 line 2733.

Henry VI, Part II, I 1 line 125; Henry VI, Part II, I 1 line 159; Henry VI, Part II, I 1 line 245; Henry VI, Part II, I 2 line 338; Henry VI, Part II, II 1 line 856; Henry VI, Part II, II 2 line 1022; Henry VI, Part II, III 1 lines 1410, 1413; Henry VI, Part II, III 1 line 1494; Henry VI, Part II, III 1 line 1542; Henry VI, Part II, III 1 line 1596; Henry VI, Part II, III 1 line 1654; Henry VI, Part II, III 2 lines 1742, 1744; Henry VI, Part II, III 2 line 1845, 1847, 1853; Henry VI, Part II, III 2 line 1878; Henry VI, Part II, III 2 line 1912; Henry VI, Part II, III 2 line 1913; Henry VI, Part II, IV 1 line 2162; Henry VI, Part II, IV 1 line 2189; Henry VI, Part II, IV 1 lines 2203, 2204; Henry VI, Part II, IV 1 line 2265; Henry VI, Part II, IV 1 line 2283; Henry VI, Part II, IV 1 line 2304; Henry VI, Part II, IV 2 line 2432; Henry VI, Part II, IV 4 line 2533; Henry VI, Part II, IV 7 line 2717; Henry VI, Part II, IV 10 line 2924; Henry VI, Part II, IV 1 line 2957; Henry VI, Part II, V 1 lines 3102, 3103; Henry VI, Part II, V 1 line 3160.

Henry VI, Part III, I 1 line 15; Henry VI, Part III, I 1 line 16; Henry VI, Part III, I 1 line 43; Henry VI, Part III, I 1 line 104; Henry VI, Part III, I 1 line 176; Henry VI, Part III, I 1 line 193; Henry VI, Part III, I 1 lines 240, 241; Henry VI, Part III, I 2 line 328; Henry VI, Part III, I 3 line 377; Henry VI, Part III, I 3 line 398; Henry VI, Part III, I 3 line 400; Henry VI, Part III, I 3 lines 431, 432; Henry VI, Part III, I 4 lines 448, 465; Henry VI, Part III, I 4 line 518; Henry VI, Part III, I 4 line 578; Henry VI, Part III, I 4 lines 594, 598, 599, 609; Henry VI, Part III, II 1 line 689; Henry VI, Part III, II 1 lines 735, 754; Henry VI, Part III, II 2 line 974; Henry VI, Part III, II 2 line 1014; Henry VI, Part III, II 2 line 1018; Henry VI, Part III, II 3 lines 1043, 1049; Henry VI, Part III, II 3

line 1051; Henry VI, Part III, II 5 line 1175; Henry VI, Part III, II 5 line 1177; Henry VI, Part III, II 5 line 1204; Henry VI, Part III, II 5 line 1241; Henry VI, Part III, II 6 line 1278; Henry VI, Part III, II 6 line 1286; Henry VI, Part III, II 6 line 1336; Henry VI, Part III, III 2 line 1671; Henry VI, Part III, IV 1 line 2115; Henry VI, Part III, IV 4 line 2264; Henry VI, Part III, V 1 line 2652; Henry VI, Part III, V 1 line 2688; Henry VI, Part III, V 2 lines 2730, 2741, 2745; Henry VI, Part III, V 2 line 2760; Henry VI, Part III, V 5 lines 2953, 2961; Henry VI,
Part III, V 5 line 2980; Henry VI, Part III, V 5 line 2986; Henry VI, Part III, V 6 line 3058; Henry VI, Part III, V 7 line 3097.
Henry VIII, I 1 line 185; Henry VIII, II 1 line 902; Henry VIII, II 1 line 943; Henry VIII, II 2 line 1133; Henry VIII, II 3 line 1326; Henry VIII, III 2 line 2170; Henry VIII, V 3 line 3207; Henry VIII, V 5 line 3422.
Julius Caesar, I 1 line 52; Julius Caesar, I 2 line 242; Julius Caesar, I 3 line 559; Julius Caesar, II 1 line 757; Julius Caesar, II 1 lines 722, 788; Julius Caesar, II 2 line 996; Julius Caesar, II 2 line 1059; Julius Caesar, II 2 lines 1066, 1069; Julius Caesar, III 1 lines 1241, 1244; Julius Caesar, III 1 line 1272; Julius Caesar, III 1 line 1320; Julius Caesar, III 1 lines 1373, 1377; Julius Caesar, III 1 line 1386; Julius Caesar, III 1 lines 1406, 1420, 1423; Julius Caesar, III 1 lines 1487, 1494; Julius Caesar, III 1 line 1525; Julius Caesar, III 2 line 1678; Julius Caesar, III 2 lines 1723, 1734, 1737; Julius Caesar, III 2 line 1747; Julius Caesar, IV 2 line 1944; Julius Caesar, IV 3 line 2058; Julius Caesar, IV 3 line 2104; Julius Caesar, IV 3 line 2289; Julius Caesar, IV 3 line 2309; Julius Caesar, V 1 line 2360; Julius Caesar, V 3 line 2572.
King John, I 1 line 19; King John, I 1 line 21r; King John, I 1 line 41; King John, II 1 line 292; King John, II 1 line 332; King John, II 1 lines 335, 338; King John, II 1 line 402; King John, II 1 lines 514, 522; King John, II 1 lines 556, 567; King John, II 1 line 579; King John, II 1 line 624; King John, II 1 line 637r; King John, II 1 line 644; King John, II 1 line 651; King John, II 1 lines 661, 670; King John, II 1 line 700; King John, II 1 line 742; King John, II 1 line 773; King John, II 1 line 805; King John, III 1 line 917r; King John, III 1 line 1022; King John, III 1 lines 1036, 1044; King John, III 1 line 1164, 1171; King John, III 1 line 1228; King John, III 1 line 1254; King John, III 1 lines 1271, 1272r; King John, III 1 line 1274; King John, III 3 line 1343; King John, III 4 line 1391; King John, III 4 line 1513;
King John, III 4 lines 1535, 1536; King John, III 4 line 1556; King John, IV 1 line 1659; King John, IV 2 line 1798; King John, IV 2 line 1828; King John, IV 2 lines 1834, 1837; King John, IV 2 line 1954; King John, IV 2 line 1969; King John, IV 2 line 1990; King John, IV 2 line 1997; King John, IV 2 line 2009; King John, IV 3 line 2045; King John, IV 3 line 2067; King John, IV 3 line 2075; King John, IV 3 line 2077; King John, V 1 line 2204; King John, V 2 line 2316; King John, V 2 line 2337; King John, V 2 lines 2409, 2434, 2440; King John, V 5 line 2557; King John, V 7 line 2628; King John, V 7 line 2682.
King Lear, I 1 line 118; King Lear, II 1 line 961; King Lear, II 4 line 1380; King Lear, II 4 line 1507; King Lear, II 4 lines 1517, 1521; King

Lear, III 1 line 1659; King Lear, III 2 line 1730; King Lear, III 4 line 1887; King Lear, III 4 line 1937; King Lear, III 4 line 1960; King Lear, III 4 line 1981; King Lear, III 5 line 2002; King Lear, IV 2 line 2411; King Lear, IV 6 line 2765; King Lear, IV 7 line 3017; King Lear, V 3 line 3217; King Lear, V 3 line 3324; King Lear, V 3 line 3342; King Lear, V 3 line 3324; King Lear, V 3 line 3384; King Lear, V 3 line 3388.
Love's Labour's Lost, I 1 line 183; Love's Labour's Lost, I 2 line 336; Love's Labour's Lost, II 1 line 677; Love's Labour's Lost, IV 1 line 1007; Love's Labour's Lost, IV 2 line 1144; Love's Labour's Lost, IV 3 line 1424; Love's Labour's Lost, IV 3 line 1425; Love's Labour's Lost, IV 3 lines 1559, 1561; Love's Labour's Lost, IV 3 line 1607; Love's Labour's Lost, V 2 line 1955; Love's Labour's Lost, V 2 line 2631; Love's Labour's Lost, V 2 line 2646; Love's Labour's Lost, V 2 line 2742; Love's Labour's Lost, V 2 line 2864.
Lover's Complaint, lines 47, 53, 163, 185, 199, 202.
Macbeth, I 2 line 18; Macbeth I 2 line 37; Macbeth I 5 line 93; Macbeth I 7 line 482; Macbeth I 7 line 557; Macbeth II 1 lines 625, 627; Macbeth II 2 line 711; Macbeth II 2 line 724; Macbeth II 3 line 883; Macbeth II 3 line 888; Macbeth II 3 line 900; Macbeth II 3 line 922; Macbeth II 3 lines 938, 939; Macbeth II 4 line 954; Macbeth II 4 line 974; Macbeth III 1 line 1036; Macbeth III 1 line 1135; Macbeth III 2 line 1223; Macbeth III 4 line 1287; Macbeth III 4 line 1366; Macbeth III 4 line 1389; Macbeth III 4 lines 1425rr, 1429; Macbeth III 4 line 1440; Macbeth III 6 line 1528; Macbeth IV 1 line 1584; Macbeth IV 1 line 1620; Macbeth IV 1 line 1638; Macbeth IV 1 line 1641; Macbeth IV 1 line 1695; Macbeth IV 3 line 1910; Macbeth IV 3 line 1962; Macbeth V 1 line 2064; Macbeth V 1 line 2173; Macbeth V 6 line 2427; Macbeth V 8 line 2480; Macbeth V 8 line 2482.
Measure for Measure, I 3 line 345; Measure for Measure, I 4 line 411; Measure for Measure, II 1 line 464; Measure for Measure, II 4 line 1031r; Measure for Measure, II 4 line 1041; Measure for Measure, II 4 lines 1210, 1213; Measure for Measure, III 1 line 1380; Measure for Measure, V 1 line 2913.
Merchant of Venice, I 1 line 89; Merchant of Venice, I 2 line 212; Merchant of Venice, II 1 line 521; Merchant of Venice, II 2 line 657; Merchant of Venice, II 3 line 794; Merchant of Venice, III 1 line 1270; Merchant of Venice, III 1 line 1272; Merchant of Venice, III 1 line 1274; Merchant of Venice, III 2 line 1546; Merchant of Venice, III 2 line 1641; Merchant of Venice, III 3 line 1745; Merchant of Venice, IV 1 lines 2045, 2046; Merchant of Venice, IV 1 line 2073; Merchant of Venice, IV 1 lines 2252, 2256; Merchant of Venice, IV 1 line 2273; Merchant of Venice, V 1 line 2530.
Merry Wives of Windsor, IV 4 line 2227; Merry Wives of Windsor, V 5 line 2561; Merry Wives of Windsor, V 5 line 2662.
Midsummer Night's Dream, I 1 lines 73, 79; Midsummer Night's Dream, I 1 line 141; Midsummer Night's Dream, II 2 line 760; Midsummer Night's Dream, III 2 line 1081; Midsummer Night's Dream, III 2 line 1108; Midsummer Night's Dream, III 2 line 1132; Midsummer

Night's Dream, V 1 lines 1986, 1989, 1990; Midsummer Night's Dream, V 1 line 2125.
Much Ado About Nothing, I 1 line 117; Much Ado About Nothing, I 1 line 224; Much Ado About Nothing, I 3 line 354; Much Ado About Nothing, II 1 line 565; Much Ado About Nothing, II 3 lines 976, 977; Much Ado About Nothing, III 2 line 1216; Much Ado About Nothing, III 3 line 1446; Much Ado About Nothing, IV 1 line 1677; Much Ado About Nothing, IV 1 line 1700; Much Ado About Nothing, IV 1 line 1771; Much Ado About Nothing, IV 1 line 1844; Much Ado About Nothing, V 1 line 2102; Much Ado About Nothing, V 1 line 2316.
Othello, I 1 line 5; Othello, I 1 line 185; Othello, I 3 line 405; Othello, I 3 line 445; Othello, I 3 line 468; Othello, I 3 line 487; Othello, I 3 line 493; Othello, II 1 line 1025; Othello, II 3 line 1330; Othello, II 3 line 1353; Othello, III 3 line 2000; Othello, III 3 line 2137rrr; Othello, III 3 line 2143; Othello, III 3 line 2158; Othello, IV 1 line 2517; Othello, IV 1 line 2717; Othello, V 1 line 3180; Othello, V 1 line 3216; Othello, V 1 line 3250; Othello, V 2 line 3304; Othello, V 2 line 3352; Othello, V 2 line 3725.
Passionate Pilgrim, line 281.
Pericles, I 2 line 333; Pericles, I 2 line 342; Pericles, I 2 line 359; Pericles, I 4 line 513; Pericles, II 3 line 903; Pericles, II 5 line 1102; Pericles, II 5 line 1112; Pericles, IV 1 line 1571; Pericles, IV 1 line 1599; Pericles, IV 3 line 1822; Pericles, IV 6 line 1977; Pericles, V 1 line 2361.
Rape of Lucrece, lines 481, 706, 1050, 1080, 1232; 1258; 1368; 1409; 1429; 1488, 1505, 1538; 1648; 1699; 1706; 1787; 1789; 1796; 1799, 1800, 1887, 1891.
Richard II, I 1 lines 54, 61; Richard II, I 1 line 74; Richard II, I 1 lines 106, 107; Richard II, I 1 line 116; Richard II, I 1 line 122; Richard II, I 1 line 152; Richard II, I 1 line 156; Richard II, I 1 line 176; Richard II, I 2 line 214; Richard II, I 2 lines 223, 225, 230, 234, 235; Richard II, I 3 line 352; Richard II, I 3 line 364; Richard II, I 3 line 378; Richard II, I 3 lines 423, 435; Richard II, II 1 line 802; Richard II, II 1 lines 810, 815; Richard II, II 1 lines 869, 870; Richard II, II 1 line 931; Richard II, II 3 line 1213; Richard II, II 4 line 1340; Richard II, III 1 lines 1364, 1368, 1375, 1384; Richard II, III 2 lines 1485, 1487; Richard II, III 2 line 1541; Richard II, III 2 line 1581; Richard II, III 3 line 1680; Richard II, III 3 lines 1720, 1737, 1741; Richard II, III 3 line 1748; Richard II, III 4 line 1925; Richard II, IV 1 line 1985; Richard II, IV 1 line 2010; Richard II, IV 1 line 2121; Richard II, V 5 line 2867; Richard II, V 5 line 2871; Richard II, V 6 lines 2929, 2933.
Richard III, I 2 lines 180r; 189r; Richard III, I 2 lines 232, 233, 236, 237; Richard III, I 2 line 271; Richard III, I 2 line 276; Richard III, I 3 line 588; Richard III, I 3 line 589; Richard III, I 3 lines 642, 645; Richard III, I 3 line 676; Richard III, I 3 line 738; Richard III, I 3 line 780; Richard III, I 4 line 887; Richard III, I 4 line 1017; Richard III, I 4 line 1047; Richard III, I 4 line 1103; Richard III, II 1 line 1217r; Richard III, II 4 line 1550r; Richard III, III 1 line 1758; Richard III, III 3 line 1924; Richard III, III 3 lines 1927, 1932; Richard III, III 3 line 1939; Richard

III, III 4 line 2048; Richard III, III 4 line 2061; Richard III, III 7 line 2346r; Richard III, IV 1 line 2538; Richard III, IV 2 line 2656; Richard III, IV 3 lines 2727, 2732, 2748; Richard III, IV 4 line 2823; Richard III, IV 4 line 2845; Richard III, IV 4 line 2970; Richard III, IV 4 line 2997r; Richard III, IV 4 line 3003; Richard III, IV 4 line 3015; Richard III, IV 4 line 3040; Richard III, IV 4 line 3081; Richard III, IV 4 line 3097; Richard III, IV 4 lines 3105, 3109; Richard III, IV 5 line 3376; Richard III, V 2 lines 3435, 3437, 3444; Richard III, V 2 line 3445; Richard III, V 3 line 3562; Richard III, V 3 lines 3636, 3637; Richard III, V 3 line 3669; Richard III, V 3 lines 3753, 3754r; Richard III, V 3 line 3858; Richard III, V 5 line 3894; Richard III, V 5 line 3897; Richard III, V 5 lines 3916, 3928, 3929.

Romeo and Juliet, Prologue 1 line 4; Romeo and Juliet, I 1 line 106; Romeo and Juliet, II 5 line 1386; Romeo and Juliet, II 5 line 1448; Romeo and Juliet, III 1 line 1502; Romeo and Juliet, III 1 lines 1664, 1666r; Romeo and Juliet, III 1 line 1668; Romeo and Juliet, III 1 line 1701; Romeo and Juliet, III 1 line 1707; Romeo and Juliet, III 2 line 1732; Romeo and Juliet, III 2 lines 1776, 1777, 1778; Romeo and Juliet, III 2 line 1793; Romeo and Juliet, III 3 line 1974; Romeo and Juliet, III 5 line 2159; Romeo and Juliet, IV 1 line 2428; Romeo and Juliet, IV 3 line 2594; Romeo and Juliet, IV 5 line 2683; Romeo and Juliet, V 3 line 3043; Romeo and Juliet, V 3 lines 3097, 3103; Romeo and Juliet, V 3 line 3141.

Sonnet II line 14; Sonnet XI line 3; Sonnet XVI line 2; Sonnet XIX line 4; Sonnet L line 9; Sonnet LXIII line 3; Sonnet LXVII line 10; Sonnet LXXXII line 14; Sonnet CIX line 10; Sonnet CXXI line 6; Sonnet CXXIX line 3.

Taming of the Shrew, Prologue 2 line 205; Taming of the Shrew, Prologue 2 line 274; Taming of the Shrew, Prologue 2 line 279.

Timon of Athens, I 2 line 382; Timon of Athens, II 2 line 913; Timon of Athens, III 4 line 1273; Timon of Athens, III 5 line 1308; Timon of Athens, III 5 line 1318; Timon of Athens, III 5 line 1362; Timon of Athens, III 5 line 1399; Timon of Athens, IV 2 line 1649; Timon of Athens, IV 3 line 1729; Timon of Athens, IV 3 lines 2142, 2143; Timon of Athens, IV 3 line 2250.

Titus Andronicus, I 1 line 133; Titus Andronicus, I 1 lines 159, 161; Titus Andronicus, II 3 lines 772, 778; Titus Andronicus, II 3 line 946; Titus Andronicus, II 3 line 957; Titus Andronicus, II 3 line 963; Titus Andronicus, II 3 lines 973, 979; Titus Andronicus, II 3 line 1034; Titus Andronicus, II 4 lines 1086, 1093; Titus Andronicus, III 1 lines 1129, 1141, 1148; Titus Andronicus, III 1 line 1296; Titus Andronicus, III 1 line 1299; Titus Andronicus, III 1 line 1398; Titus Andronicus, IV 1 line 1624; Titus Andronicus, IV 1 line 1638; Titus Andronicus, IV 2 line 1699; Titus Andronicus, IV 2 line 1773; Titus Andronicus, IV 2 line 1813; Titus Andronicus, IV 4 line 2048;

Titus Andronicus, V 1 line 2182; Titus Andronicus, V 1 line 2236; Titus Andronicus, V 2 line 2320; Titus Andronicus, V 2 line 2343; Titus Andronicus, V 2 lines 2500, 2504, 2515, 2521; Titus Andronicus, V 3 line 2649; Titus Andronicus, V 3 line 2698.

Troilus and Cressida, I 0 line 2; Troilus and Cressida, I 1 line 121; Troilus and Cressida, I 2 line 168; Troilus and Cressida, I 2 line 381; Troilus and Cressida, I 3 line 587; Troilus and Cressida, I 3 line 762; Troilus and Cressida, II 2 line 1111; Troilus and Cressida, II 2 line 1167; Troilus and Cressida, II 2 line 1195; Troilus and Cressida, II 3 line 1244; Troilus and Cressida, II 3 line 1395; Troilus and Cressida, II 3 line 1435; Troilus and Cressida, III 1 line 1523; Troilus and Cressida, III 1 line 1615r; Troilus and Cressida, III 2 line 1812; Troilus and Cressida, III 3 line 1891; Troilus and Cressida, IV 1 line 2215; Troilus and Cressida, IV 2 line 2396; Troilus and Cressida, IV 5 line 2605; Troilus and Cressida, IV 5 line 2696; Troilus and Cressida, IV 5 lines 2742, 2747; Troilus and Cressida, IV 5 line 2849; Troilus and Cressida, V 1 line 2930; Troilus and Cressida, V 1 lines 2979, 2981; Troilus and Cressida, V 3 lines 3285, 3288; Troilus and Cressida, V 4 line 3440; Troilus and Cressida, V 5 line 3489; Troilus and Cressida, V 7 line 3560; Troilus and Cressida, V 8 line 3591.
Twelfth Night, II 3 line 777; Twelfth Night, II 5 line 1131; Twelfth Night, II 5 line 1169; Twelfth Night, III 2 line 1463; Twelfth Night, III 3 lines 1520, 1522; Twelfth Night, III 4 line 1567; Twelfth Night, III 4 line 1767; Twelfth Night, III 4 line 1811; Twelfth Night, III 4 line 1910; Twelfth Night, IV 1 line 1993; Twelfth Night, V 1 line 2220; Twelfth Night, V 1 line 2259; Twelfth Night, V 1 line 2376; Twelfth Night, V 1 lines 2388, 2389; Twelfth Night, V 1 line 2409; Twelfth Night, V 1 line 2465.
Two Gentlemen of Verona, II 4 line 679; Two Gentlemen of Verona, III 1 line 1191.
Venus and Adonis, lines 576, 686, 764, 913, 924, 1021, 1059, 1078, 1144, 1189, 1191, 1204, 1206.
Winter's Tale, I 2 line 138; Winter's Tale, I 2 line 184; Winter's Tale, I 2 line 254; Winter's Tale, I 2 line 438; Winter's Tale, I 2 line 543; Winter's Tale, II 1 line 670; Winter's Tale, II 3 line 1115; Winter's Tale, II 3 line 1131; Winter's Tale, III 2 line 1391; Winter's Tale, IV 3 line 1727; Winter's Tale, IV 4 line 2029; Winter's Tale, IV 4 line 2045; Winter's Tale, IV 4 line 2352; Winter's Tale, IV 4 line 2666; Winter's Tale, IV 4 lines 2670, 2671, 2672; Winter's Tale, IV 4 line 2681; Winter's Tale, V 2 line 3198; Winter's Tale, V 3 line 3364.

Bloodhound: type of large dog used in hunting, c.1300, from *blood + hound*.
    Henry IV, Part II, V 4 line 3582.

Blossom: late 14c., from Old English: *blostmian*, from *blostma: blossom, flower*.
    Antony and Cleopatra, IV 12 line 2929.
    As You Like It, II 3 line 708.
    Hamlet, I 5 line 814.
    Henry IV, Part II, II 2 line 1055.
    Henry VI, Part I, II 4 line 970; Henry VI, Part I, II 4 line 1005; Henry VI, Part I, IV 7 line 2267.
    Henry VI, Part II, III 1 line 1368.

Henry VIII, III 2 line 2257.
Love's Labour's Lost, IV 3 line 1432; Love's Labour's Lost, V 2 line 2744.
Lover's Complaint, line 236.
Measure for Measure, I 4 line 393.
Othello, II 3 line 1530.
Passionate Pilgrim, line 230.
Tempest, V 1 line 2124.
Titus Andronicus, IV 2 line 1761.
Winter's Tale, III 3 line 1538; Winter's Tale, V 2 line 3235.

Bluebottle: common blow fly with a metallic blue body, often used as a term of reproach.
Henry IV, Part II, V 4 line 3575.

Blush: a reddening of the skin due to embarrassment,
shyness or shame. Old English *blyscan*; related to modern
Dutch *blozen*.
All's Well That Ends Well, II 3 lines 965, 966; All's Well That Ends Well, IV 3 line 2417; All's Well That Ends Well, V 3 line 2836; All's Well That Ends Well, V 3 line 2899.
Antony and Cleopatra, I 1 line 37; Antony and Cleopatra, III 11 line 2123; Antony and Cleopatra, V 2 line 3571.
As You Like It, I 1 line 131; As You Like It, I 2 line 169; As You Like It, II 7 line 1015.
Coriolanus, I 9 line 845; Coriolanus, II 2 line 1403; Coriolanus, IV 6 line 3010; Coriolanus, IV 6 line 3938.
Hamlet, III 4 line 2432; Hamlet, III 4 line 2474.
Henry IV, Part I, II 4 line 1297; Henry IV, Part I, II 4 line 1301; Henry IV, Part I, V 2 line 2835.
Henry IV, Part II, II 2 line 1037r.
Henry V, I 2 line 480; Henry V, V 2 line 3095; Henry V, V 2 line 3218.
Henry VI, Part I, II 4 line 993; Henry VI, Part I, IV 1 line 1858.
Henry VI, Part II, II 4 line 1208; Henry VI, Part II, III 1 line 1378; Henry VI, Part II, III 2 line 1852.
Henry VI, Part III, I 4 line 484; Henry VI, Part III, I 4 line 662; Henry VI, Part III, III 3 line 1791; Henry VI, Part III, V 1 line 2703.
Henry VIII, II 3 line 1251; Henry VIII, III 2 line 1287; Henry VIII, III 2 line 2207; Henry VIII, III 2 line 2258.
King John, IV 1 line 1702; King John, IV 3 line 2097; King John, V 2 line 2435; King John, V 5 line 2553.
King Lear, I 1 line 10.
Love's Labour's Lost, I 2 line 400; Love's Labour's Lost, I 2 line 429; Love's Labour's Lost, IV 3 line 1457; Love's Labour's Lost, IV 3 lines 1459, 1466.
Lover's Complaint, lines 201, 306.
Measure for Measure, II 4 line 1193.
Merchant of Venice, II 6 line 948.

Much Ado About Nothing, IV 1 lines 1674, 1682; Much Ado About Nothing, IV 1 lines 1809, 1811.
Othello, I 3 line 437.
Passionate Pilgrim, lines 132, 352.
Pericles, I 1 line 187; Pericles, I 2 line 258; Pericles, IV 2 line 1789.
Rape of Lucrece, lines 105, 106, 530, 843, 1133, 1391, 1406, 1407, 1562, 1801.
Richard II, III 2 line 1459; Richard II, III 3 line 1703.
Richard III, I 2 line 231r; Richard III, I 4 line 966.
Romeo and Juliet, I 4 line 528; Romeo and Juliet, I 5 line 721; Romeo and Juliet, II 2 line 935; Romeo and Juliet, III 3 line 1910.
Sonnet LXVII line 10; Sonnet XCIX line 9; Sonnet CXXVIII line 8.
Timon of Athens, IV 3 line 2090.
Titus Andronicus, II 4 line 1096; Titus Andronicus, III 1 line 1141; Titus Andronicus, IV 2 line 1805; Titus Andronicus, IV 2 line 1807; Titus Andronicus, V 1 line 2256.
Troilus and Cressida, I 2 line 313; Troilus and Cressida, I 3 line 684; Troilus and Cressida, III 2 line 1681; Troilus and Cressida, III 2 line 1693; Troilus and Cressida, III 2 line 1752.
Two Gentlemen of Verona, V 4 line 2259; Two Gentlemen of Verona, V 4 line 2323.
Venus and Adonis, lines 53, 579, 611.
Winter's Tale, III 2 line 1243; Winter's Tale, IV 4 line 1868; Winter's Tale, IV 4 line 1933; Winter's Tale, IV 4 line 2541.

Boar: a tusked wild pig, from Old English: *bar*. It appears that in former times boar-hunting was a favourite recreation; many allusions to which we find in old writers. Indeed, in the middle ages, the destruction of a wild boar ranked among the deeds of chivalry.
Antony and Cleopatra, IV 13 line 2963.
As You Like It, I 3 line 527.
Cymbeline, II 5 line 1387.
Henry IV, Part II, II 2 line 1118.
Midsummer Night's Dream, II 2 line 683.
Passionate Pilgrim, line 127.
Richard III, III 2 line 1790; Richard III, III 2 lines 1807r, 1808, 1812; Richard III, III 2 lines 1857, 1858; Richard III, III 4 line 2040; Richard III, IV 5 line 3376; Richard III, V 2 line 3435; Richard III, V 3 line 3650.
Taming of the Shrew, I 2 line 752.
Timon of Athens, V 1 line 2447.
Titus Andronicus, IV 2 line 1829.
Venus and Adonis, lines 430, 609, 610, 635, 662, 683, 733, 906, 922, 928, 1021, 1025, 1052, 1074, 1127, 1134.

Bog: a wetland of acidic soil, dominated by peaty moss, c.1500, from Gaelic and Irish: *bogach: bog*.
Comedy of Errors, III 2 line 878.
Henry V, III 7 line 1696.
King Lear, III 4 line 1854.

Midsummer Night's Dream, III 1 line 933.
Tempest, II 2 line 1083.

Bones: plural of bone. As a colloquial way to say *dice*, it is attested from late 14c. To make bones about something (mid-15c.) refers to bones found in soup, etc., as an obstacle to being swallowed. They are the last earthly traces of the dead, and seem to last forever: bones symbolise the indestructible life, yet also may represent mortality and the transitory.
    Antony and Cleopatra, I 4 line 452.
    Comedy of Errors, IV 4 line 1328.
    Coriolanus, III 1 line 1949.
    Hamlet, I 4 line 676; Hamlet, III 4 line 2475; Hamlet, IV 5 line 3091; Hamlet, V 1 line 3431.
    Henry IV, Part II, IV 5 line 2962; Henry IV, Part II, V 4 line 3583.
    Henry V, I 2 line 375; Henry V, IV 2 line 2204; Henry V, IV 3 lines 2329, 2336; Henry V, IV 7 line 2588.
    Henry VI, Part I, I 2 line 228; Henry VI, Part I, III 1 line 1428; Henry VI, Part I, IV 7 line 2302.
    Henry VI, Part II, I 3 line 591; Henry VI, Part II, IV 10 line 2944.
    Henry VI, Part III, III 2 line 1614; Henry VI, Part III, V 2 line 2725.
    Henry VIII, III 2 line 2309; Henry VIII, IV 2 line 2582.
    Julius Caesar, III 2 line 1620; Julius Caesar, V 5 line 2719; Julius Caesar, V 5 line 2764.
    King John, I 1 line 84; King John, II 1 line 331; King John, III 4 line 1413; King John, IV 3 line 2026; King John, IV 3 line 2178.
    King Lear, II 4 line 1447; King Lear, IV 2 line 2413.
    Love's Labour's Lost, V 2 line 2250; Love's Labour's Lost, V 2 line 2257; Love's Labour's Lost, V 2 line 2603.
    Lover's Complaint, line 45.
    Macbeth, I 7 line 536; Macbeth, II 4 line 991; Macbeth, III 4 line 1389; Macbeth, V 3 line 2284.
    Measure for Measure, I 2 line 148; Measure for Measure, IV 2 line 1952.
    Merchant of Venice, I 2 line 244; Merchant of Venice, IV 1 line 2045.
    Midsummer Night's Dream, IV 1 line 1574.
    Much Ado About Nothing, V 1 line 2359; Much Ado About Nothing, V 3 line 2530.
    Othello, IV 2 line 2903.
    Pericles, III 1 line 1258.
    Rape of Lucrece, lines 260, 1812.
    Richard II, II 1 line 767; Richard II, III 2 line 1564; Richard II, III 3 line 1720; Richard II, III 3 line 1747.
    Richard III, I 4 line 866; Richard III, IV 4 line 2826.
    Romeo and Juliet, I 4 line 563; Romeo and Juliet, II 4 line 1195r; Romeo and Juliet, II 5 line 1403; Romeo and Juliet, II 5 line 1404; Romeo and Juliet, II 5 line 1441; Romeo and Juliet, IV 1 line 2448; Romeo and Juliet, IV 3 lines 2593, 2606; Romeo and Juliet, V 1 line 2850.
    Sonnet XXXII line 2.

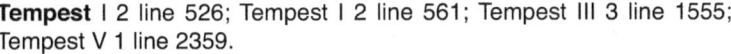

Tempest I 2 line 526; Tempest I 2 line 561; Tempest III 3 line 1555; Tempest V 1 line 2359.
Timon of Athens, III 5 line 1421; Timon of Athens, III 6 line 1561; Timon of Athens, IV 3 line 1833; Timon of Athens, IV 3 line 2245.
Titus Andronicus, I 1 line 116; Titus Andronicus, I 1 line 412; Titus Andronicus, I 1 line 433; Titus Andronicus, IV 3 line 1927; Titus Andronicus, V 2 lines 2503, 2516.
Troilus and Cressida, I 3 line 506; Troilus and Cressida, I 3 line 506; Troilus and Cressida, II 1 line 927; Troilus and Cressida, II 3 line 1233; Troilus and Cressida, III 3 line 2050; Troilus and Cressida, V 1 line 2952; Troilus and Cressida, V 3 line 3399; Troilus and Cressida, V 8 line 3603; Troilus and Cressida, V 10 lines 3672, 3687.
Twelfth Night, II 4 line 939; Twelfth Night, II 4 line 958.
Venus and Adonis, lines 76, 314.
Winter's Tale, III 3 line 1592; Winter's Tale, IV 2 line 1673; Winter's Tale, IV 4 line 2382.

Bosky: covered by trees or bushes, 16c., from Middle English: *bosk* meaning *bush*.

Tempest, IV 1 line 1792.

Bosom: Old English: *bosm:* breast; womb; surface; ship's hold. Sometimes an enclosure formed by the breast and the arms.
All's Well That Ends Well, I 3 line 441; All's Well That Ends Well, III 1 line 1377; All's Well That Ends Well, IV 1 line 1977; All's Well That Ends Well, IV 4 line 2429.
Antony and Cleopatra, II 3 line 980; Antony and Cleopatra, II 6 line 1280; Antony and Cleopatra, IV 12 line 2933.
As You Like It, V 4 line 2508.
Coriolanus, III 2 line 2236; Coriolanus, IV 4 line 2734.
Cymbeline, V 2 line 2993; Cymbeline, V 5 line 3898.
Hamlet, I 5 line 825; Hamlet, II 2 line 1209; Hamlet, III 2 line 2270; Hamlet, III 3 line 2339.
Henry IV, Part I, I 3 line 604; Henry IV, Part I, III 3 line 2163; Henry IV, Part I, IV 1 line 2347; Henry IV, Part I, V 5 line 3174.
Henry IV, Part II, I 1 line 217; Henry IV, Part II, I 3 line 618; Henry IV, Part II, I 3 line 704; Henry IV, Part II, IV 1 line 2390.
Henry V, II 0 line 485; Henry V, II 2 line 637; Henry V, II 2 line 718; Henry V, II 3 line 841r; Henry V, IV 1 line 1875; Henry V, IV 1 line 2013; Henry V, V 2 line 3335.
Henry VI, Part I, II 5 line 1115; Henry VI, Part I, III 3 line 1664; Henry VI, Part I, IV 3 line 2077.
Henry VI, Part II, IV 1 line 2153; Henry VI, Part II, V 2 line 3250.
Henry VI, Part II, I 4 line 520; Henry VI, Part II, II 6 line 1280.
Henry VIII, I 1 line 165; Henry VIII, II 4 line 1252; Henry VIII, III 2 line 1962.
Julius Caesar, I 3 line 475; Julius Caesar, II 1 line 935; Julius Caesar, V 1 line 2351; Julius Caesar, V 3 line 2545.

King John, II 1 line 720; King John, III 3 line 1325; King John, IV 1 line 1576; King John, IV 1 line 1609; King John, IV 2 line 1998; King John, IV 2 line 2306; King John, IV 2 line2319; King John, IV 7 line 2262; King John, IV 7 line 2672.
King Lear, I 1 line 122; King Lear, I 1 line 296; King Lear, II 1 line 1068; King Lear, IV 5 line 2580; King Lear, V 1 line 3028; King Lear, V 3 line 3177.
Love's Labour's Lost, IV 3 line 1351; Love's Labour's Lost, IV 3 line 1464.
Lover's Complaint, lines 128, 255.
Macbeth, I 2 line 92; Macbeth, II 1 line 604; Macbeth, III 1 line 1119; Macbeth, IV 3 line 1843; Macbeth, V 1 line 2177; Macbeth, V 3 line 2299.
Measure for Measure, I 3 line 293; Measure for Measure, II 2 line 903; Measure for Measure, IV 3 line 2261; Measure for Measure, V 1 line 2397.
Merchant of Venice, III 4 line 1766; Merchant of Venice, IV 1 line 1963; Merchant of Venice, IV 1 line 2188; Merchant of Venice, IV 1 line 2195.
Midsummer Night's Dream, I 1 line 31; Midsummer Night's Dream, I 1 line 224; Midsummer Night's Dream, II 2 line 696; Midsummer Night's Dream, II 2 lines 703, 704; Midsummer Night's Dream, II 2 line 764.
Much Ado About Nothing, I 1 line 295.
Othello, I 2 line 290; Othello, III 1 line 1613; Othello, III 3 line 2133; Othello, IV 2 line 2753; Othello, IV 3 line 3064.
Pericles, IV 1 line 1551; Pericles, V 3 line 2574.
Rape of Lucrece, lines 839, 1394.
Richard II, I 1 line 152; Richard II, I 2 line 262; Richard II, II 3 lines 1250, 1255; Richard II, III 2 line 1426; Richard II, III 2 line 1557; Richard II, IV 1 line 2086; Richard II, V 1 line 2336; Richard II, V 2 line 2499; Richard II, V 2 line 2517; Richard II, V 3 line 2633.
Richard III, I 1 line 5; Richard III, I 2 line 304; Richard III, I 2 line 362; Richard III, I 4 line 967; Richard III, IV 3 line 2770; Richard III, IV 4 line 3038; Richard III, V 1 line 3420; Richard III, V 2 line 3429; Richard III, V 3 line 3632; Richard III, V 3 line 3645; Richard III, V 3 line 3866.
Romeo and Juliet, I 4 line 603; Romeo and Juliet, II 2 line 879; Romeo and Juliet, II 3 line 1070; Romeo and Juliet, II 4 line 1181; Romeo and Juliet, III 5 line 2359; Romeo and Juliet, V 1 line 2807; Romeo and Juliet, V 3 line 3115; Romeo and Juliet, V 3 line 3178.
Sonnet IX line 13; Sonnet XXIV line 7; Sonnet XXXI line 1; Sonnet CXX line 12; Sonnet CXXXIII line 9.
Taming of the Shrew, Prologue 1 line 127.
Tempest, II 1 line1016.
Timon of Athens, I 1 line 84; Timon of Athens, I 2 line 467; Timon of Athens, IV 1 line 1593; Timon of Athens, IV 3 line 1873; Timon of Athens, V 1 line 2365.
Titus Andronicus, II 1 line 606; Titus Andronicus, III 1 line 1352; Titus Andronicus, IV 1 line 1662; Titus Andronicus, V 3 line 2650.

Troilus and Cressida, I 3 line 565; Troilus and Cressida, II 2 line 1152; Troilus and Cressida, III 2 line 1687.
Twelfth Night, I 5 line 514; Twelfth Night, I 5 line 515r; Twelfth Night, II 1 line 646; Twelfth Night, III 1 line 1358; Twelfth Night, III 1 line 1397.
Two Gentlemen of Verona, I 2 line 273; Two Gentlemen of Verona, III 1 line 1216; Two Gentlemen of Verona, III 1 line 1323; Two Gentlemen of Verona, V 4 line 2223.
Venus and. Adonis, lines 101, 667, 980, 1195.
Winter's Tale, I 2 lines 188, 194; Winter's Tale, I 2 line 235; Winter's Tale, I 2 line 337; Winter's Tale, II 2 line 907; Winter's Tale, IV 4 line 2512.

Bots: parasitical worm or maggot which infests horses (1520s), of unknown origin; some imagined that poverty or improper food engendered these worms, or that they were the offspring of putrefaction.
Henry IV, Part I, II 1 line 652.
Pericles, II 1 line 687.
Taming of the Shrew, III 2 line 1414.

Bough: from Old English: *bog*: shoulder, arm. The sense in which this becomes the limb of a tree is unique to English.
As You Like It, II 7 line 1007; As You Like It, III 2 line 1247; As You Like It, IV 3 line 2107.
Cymbeline, III 3 line 1667.
Hamlet, IV 7 line 3321.
Henry V, III 2 line 1145.
Macbeth, V 4 line 2349; Macbeth, V 6 line 2416.
Richard II, III 4 line 1930.
Sonnet LXXIII line 3; Sonnet CII line 11.
Tempest, V 1 line 2125.
Timon of Athens, IV 3 line 1960.
Titus Andronicus, I 1 line 90.
Venus and Adonis, line 57.
Winter's Tale, V 3 line 3450.

Bourn*: a boundary or a brook or a destination, 1520s, from French borne, apparently a variant of *bodne*. Used by Shakespeare in Hamlet's soliloquy, from which it entered into English poetic speech. He meant it probably in the correct sense of boundary. Also *bourne*, small stream, especially of the winter torrents of the chalk downs, Old English *brunna, burna* brook, stream.
Antony and Cleopatra, I 1 line 20.
Hamlet, III 1 line 1772.
King Lear, III 6 line 2030; King Lear, IV 6 line 2664.
Pericles, IV 4 line 1878r.
Tempest, II 1 line 861.
Troilus and Cressida, II 3 line 1470.
Winter's Tale, I 2 line 213.

Bowels: c.1300, from Old French: *boele: intestines, bowels, innards.* Also from Latin *botellus: small intestine*, originally *sausage*. Greek *splankhnon* was a word for the principal internal organs, which also were felt in ancient times to be the seat of various emotions. Greek poets, from Aeschylus down, regarded the bowels as the seat of the more violent passions such as anger and love, but by the Hebrews they were seen as the seat of tender affections, especially kindness, benevolence, and compassion.

    Coriolanus, IV 5 line 2897; Coriolanus, V 3 line 3610.
    Henry IV, Part I, I 3 line 386; Henry IV, Part I, V 3 line 2919.
    Henry V, II 1 line 556; Henry V, II 4 line 1005.
    Henry VI, Part I, I 1 line 136; Henry IV, Part I, IV 7 line 2297.
    Julius Caesar, V 3 line 2545.
    King John, II 1 line 511; King John, V 6 line 2611; King John, V 7 line 2663.
    Measure for Measure, III 1 line 1251.
    Richard III, I 4 line 1034; Richard III, III 4 line 2059; Richard III, V 2 line 3431.
    Titus Andronicus, III 1 line 1227; Titus Andronicus, III 1 line 1369; Titus Andronicus, IV 2 line 1776.
    Troilus and Cressida, II 1 line 906; Troilus and Cressida, II 2 line 1000.

Bower: Old English: *bur: room, hut, dwelling, chamber*. Sense of *leafy arbor* (place closed in by trees) is first attested 1520s.

    Coriolanus, III 2 line 2275.
    Henry IV, Part I, III 1 line 1758.
    Midsummer Night's Dream, III 1 line 1022; Midsummer Night's Dream, III 2 line 1037; Midsummer Night's Dream, IV 1 line 1609.
    Much Ado About Nothing, III 1 line 1079; Much Ado About Nothing, III 1 line 1109.
    Romeo and Juliet, III 2 line 1803.
    Sonnet CXXVII line 7.
    Twelfth Night, I 1 line 45.

Box: Old English, from the Greek: *puxos*, type of shrub. Slang meaning *vulva* is attested 17c.

    Twelfth Night, II 5 line 1042.

Brach: bitch hound (archaic), mid-14c., *brache*, originally: hound that hunts by scent, from Old French *braches* hound, hunting dog.

    Henry IV, Part I, III 1 line 1788.
    King Lear, I 4 line 641; King Lear, III 6 line 2070.
    Taming of the Shrew, Prologue 1 lines 17, 18.
    Troilus and Cressida, II 1 line 971.

Brain: Old English: *brægen: brain*. The custom of using the plural to refer to the substance (literal or figurative), as opposed to the organ, dates from 16c. Figurative sense of *intellectual power* is from late 14c.

All's Well That Ends Well, III 2 line 1412; All's Well That Ends Well, IV 3 line 2277.
Antony and Cleopatra, II 1 line 644; Antony and Cleopatra, II 7 line 1493; Antony and Cleopatra, III 7 line 1949; Antony and Cleopatra, III 13 line 2487; Antony and Cleopatra, IV 8 line 2810.
As You Like It, II 7 line 932; As You Like It, IV 1 line 1879; As You Like It, IV 3 line 2003; As You Like It, IV 3 line 2035.
Coriolanus, I 1 line 133; Coriolanus, II 1 line 1010; Coriolanus, III 2 line 2203.
Cymbeline, I 2 line 256; Cymbeline, II 1 line 904; Cymbeline, IV 2 line 2473; Cymbeline, IV 2 line 2704; Cymbeline, V 4 line 3212; Cymbeline, V 4 line 3300; Cymbeline, V 4 lines 3318, 3319; Cymbeline, V 5 line 3383; Cymbeline, V 5 line 3604.
Hamlet, I 4 line 708; Hamlet, I 5 line 842; Hamlet, II 2 line 1134; Hamlet, II 2 line 1143; Hamlet, II 2 line 1666; Hamlet, III 1 line 1865; Hamlet, III 2 line 2120; Hamlet, III 4 line 2539; Hamlet, IV 1 line 2637; Hamlet, IV 5 line 3032; Hamlet, V 1 line 3396; Hamlet, V 2 line 3681.
Henry IV, Part I, II 3 lines 874, 881; Henry IV, Part I, II 4 line 1212; Henry IV, Part I, V 2 line 2789.
Henry IV, Part II, I 2 line 425; Henry IV, Part II, III 1 line 1722; Henry IV, Part II, IV 3 line 2693; Henry IV, Part II, IV 4 line 2862; Henry IV, Part II, IV 5 line 2962.
Henry V, III 7 line 1763; Henry V, IV 1 line 2128.
Henry VI, Part I, I 2 line 205; Henry VI, Part I, I 2 line 230; Henry VI, Part I, I 4 line 572; Henry VI, Part I, III 1 line 1310; Henry VI, Part I, IV 1 line 1876.
Henry VI, Part II, I 2 line 376; Henry VI, Part II, III 1 line 1328; Henry VI, Part II, III 1 line 1626; Henry VI, Part II, IV 10 line 2898; Henry VI, Part II, V 1 line 3153.
Henry VIII, I 0 line 20; Henry VIII, III 2 line 1979; Henry VIII, III 2 line 2066; Henry VIII, III 2 line 2102.
Julius Caesar, II 1 line 857.
King John, V 7 line 2629.
King Lear, I 2 line 392; King Lear, I 5 line 886; King Lear, IV 6 line 2623; King Lear, IV 6 line 2800.
Love's Labour's Lost, I 1 line 170; Love's Labour's Lost, IV 3 lines 1670, 1674; Love's Labour's Lost, V 2 line 2791.
Lover's Complaint, line 210.
Macbeth, I 3 line 265; Macbeth, I 7 line 537; Macbeth, I 7 line 546; Macbeth, II 1 line 618; Macbeth, II 2 line 706; Macbeth, III 4 line 1370; Macbeth, V 3 line 2297.
Measure for Measure, IV 3 line 2170; Measure for Measure, V 1 line 2820.
Merchant of Venice, I 2 line 211.
Merry Wives of Windsor, III 2 line 1338; Merry Wives of Windsor, III 5 line 1753; Merry Wives of Windsor, IV 2 line 2115; Merry Wives of Windsor, IV 2 line 2171; Merry Wives of Windsor, V 5 line 2710.
Midsummer Night's Dream, V 1 line 1834.

Much Ado About Nothing, II 3 line 1047; Much Ado About Nothing, V 4 line 2640; Much Ado About Nothing, V 4 line 2657.
Othello, II 1 line 916; Othello, II 3 line 1165; Othello, III 3 line 1758; Othello, IV 1 line 2718; Othello, IV 2 line 3001.
Rape of Lucrece, lines 226, 511.
Richard II, V 5 line 2754.
Richard III, IV 1 line 2531; Richard III, IV 4 line 3140.
Romeo and Juliet, I 3 line 414; Romeo and Juliet, I 4 line 570; Romeo and Juliet, I 4 line 599; Romeo and Juliet, II 3 line 1097; Romeo and Juliet, IV 3 line 2606.
Sonnet LIX line 2; Sonnet LXXVII line 11; Sonnet LXXXVI line 3; Sonnet CVIII line 1; Sonnet CXXII lines 1, 5.
Taming of the Shrew, III 2 line 1373; Taming of the Shrew, III 2 line 1525.
Tempest, III 2 line 1401; Tempest, III 2 line 1483; Tempest, IV 1 line 1890; Tempest, V 1 line 2098.
Timon of Athens, I 1 line 233; Timon of Athens, IV 1 line 1579; Timon of Athens, V 1 line 2458; Timon of Athens, V 4 line 2649.
Titus Andronicus, V 2 line 2378; Titus Andronicus, V 3 line 2678.
Troilus and Cressida, I 3 line 775; Troilus and Cressida, I 3 line 790; Troilus and Cressida, I 3 line 844; Troilus and Cressida, II 1 line 900; Troilus and Cressida, II 1 line 927; Troilus and Cressida, II 1 line 959; Troilus and Cressida, II 3 line 1476; Troilus and Cressida, III 3 line 2137; Troilus and Cressida, III 3 line 2183; Troilus and Cressida, V 1 lines 2979, 2980, 2983.
Twelfth Night, I 1 line 41; Twelfth Night, I 3 line 153; Twelfth Night, I 5 line 349; Twelfth Night, I 5 line 374; Twelfth Night, I 5 line 406; Twelfth Night, IV 2 line 2134.
Venus and Adonis, lines 932, 1062, 1090.
Winter's Tale, I 2 line 224; Winter's Tale, II 3 line 931; Winter's Tale, II 3 line 1101; Winter's Tale, III 3 line 1558; Winter's Tale, IV 4 line 2661.

Brake: a thicket. Old English: *bracu* (first recorded in the plural in *fearnbraca: thickets of fern*), related to Middle Low German brake: *branch, stump*.
Henry VI, Part III, III 1 line 1376.
Henry VIII, I 2 line 405.
Midsummer Night's Dream, II 1 line 602; Midsummer Night's Dream, III 1 line 823; Midsummer Night's Dream, III 1 line 886; Midsummer Night's Dream, III 1 line 923; Midsummer Night's Dream, III 2 line 1045.
Passionate Pilgrim, line 127.
Venus and Adonis, lines 257, 898, 935.

Brambles: Old English *bræmbel, bræmel*, of Germanic origin; related to *broom*.
As You Like It, III 2 line 1447.
Venus and Adonis, line 650.

Bran: c.1300, *the husk of wheat, barley, etc., separated from the flour after grinding*, from Old French: *bren: bran, scurf, scales, faeces*. The word also was used 16c. in English for *dandruff flakes*.
    Coriolanus, I 1 line 145; Coriolanus, III 1 line 2140.
    Cymbeline, IV 2 line 2347.
    Love's Labour's Lost, I 1 line 293.
    Measure for Measure, IV 3 line 2282.
    Troilus and Cressida, I 2 line 391r.

Brat: mid 16c perhaps an abbreviation of synonymous Scottish: *bratchet*, from Old French *brachet: hound, bitch*.
    Comedy of Errors, IV 4 line 1286.
    Henry VI, Part I, V 4 line 2755.
    Henry VI, Part III, I 3 line 380; Henry VI, Part III, V 5 line 2922.
    Richard III, I 3 line 658.
    Titus Andronicus, V 1 line 2160.
    Winter's Tale, II 3 line 1044; Winter's Tale, III 2 line 1303.

Breast: Old English: *breost: breast, bosom; mind, thought, disposition*. The spelling conforms to the Scottish and northern England dialectal pronunciation. Figurative sense of *seat of the emotions* was in Old English. In Christian iconography, the female breast does not have erotic implications; in classical antiquity it represents the universal mother nursing all of humanity and mature motherhood. It is closely linked to fertility and milk, evoking protection, love, and tenderness.
    All's Well That Ends Well, III 2 line 1523.
    Antony and Cleopatra, I 1 line 9; Antony and Cleopatra, V 2 line 3765; Antony and Cleopatra, V 2 line 3773; Antony and Cleopatra, V 2 line 3830.
    Comedy of Errors, III 2 line 902.
    Coriolanus, I 3 line 403; Coriolanus, II 2 line 1369; Coriolanus, III 1 line 2058; Coriolanus, IV 5 line 2865; Coriolanus, V 2 line 3459.
    Cymbeline, II 2 line 960; Cymbeline, II 4 line 1343; Cymbeline, V 4 line 3259; Cymbeline, V 5 line 3368.
    Hamlet, III 2 line 2070.
    Henry IV, Part I, III 1 line 1812; Henry IV, Part I, IV 3 line 2502.
    Henry IV, Part II, IV 1 line 2330.
    Henry V, II 0 line 467; Henry V, III 0 line 1065; Henry V, IV 6 line 2493.
    Henry VI, Part I, I 5 line 591; Henry VI, Part I, II 5 line 1202; Henry VI, Part I, III 1 line 1259; Henry VI, Part I, III 2 line 1554; Henry VI, Part I, III 3 line 1661; Henry VI, Part I, III 3 line 1697; Henry VI, Part I, V 4 line 2698; Henry VI, Part I, V 5 line 2937.
    Henry VI, Part II, III 1 line 1631; Henry VI, Part II, III 2 line 1724; Henry VI, Part II, III 2 line 1919; Henry VI, Part II, IV 4 line 2527; Henry VI, Part II, IV 7 line 2719.
    Henry VI, Part III, I 1 line 9; Henry VI, Part III, II 1 line 710; Henry VI, Part III, II 3 line 1082; Henry VI, Part III, II 5 line 1113r; Henry VI, Part III, II 5 line 1223; Henry VI, Part III, II 6 line 1280; Henry VI, Part III, III

1 line 1404; Henry VI, Part III, V 4 line 2844; Henry VI, Part III, V 6 line 3022.
Henry VIII, I 2 line 557; Henry VIII, II 4 line 1545; Henry VIII, III 2 line 1983; Henry VIII, III 2 line 2081.
Julius Caesar, I 2 line 137; Julius Caesar, I 3 line 477; Julius Caesar, IV 3 line 2088.
King John, II 1 line 407; King John, III 1 line 936; King John, IV 2 line 1802.
Love's Labour's Lost, II 1 line 641; Love's Labour's Lost, IV 3 line 1504; Love's Labour's Lost, IV 3 line 1517; Love's Labour's Lost, IV 3 line 1569; Love's Labour's Lost, V 2 line 2758.
Lover's Complaint, lines 260, 294.
Macbeth, I 5 line 397; Macbeth, IV 3 line 1971; Macbeth, IV 3 line 2072.
Merchant of Venice, IV 1 line 2196; Merchant of Venice, IV 1 line 2248.
Midsummer Night's Dream, II 2 line 807; Midsummer Night's Dream, V 1 line 1990; Midsummer Night's Dream, V 1 line 2189.
Othello, II 3 line 1329; Othello, III 3 line 1786; Othello, V 2 line 3627.
Passionate Pilgrim, line 384.
Pericles, I 1 line 66; Pericles, I 2 line 271; Pericles, III 0 line 1121.
Phoenix and the Turtle, line 58.
Rape of Lucrece, lines 458, 490, 514, 810, 902, 1172, 1614, 1774, 1788, 1893.
Richard II, I 1 line 186; Richard II, I 2 line 237; Richard II, I 2 line 261; Richard II, I 3 line 391; Richard II, III 4 line 1963; Richard II, IV 1 line 2040; Richard II, V 3 line 2684.
Richard III, I 2 line 214; Richard III, I 2 line 272; Richard III, I 2 line 364; Richard III, I 2 line 393; Richard III, II 1 line 1273.
Romeo and Juliet, I 1 line 213; Romeo and Juliet, I 4 line 612; Romeo and Juliet, II 2 line 975; Romeo and Juliet, II 2 line 1053; Romeo and Juliet, III 1 line 1676; Romeo and Juliet, III 2 line 1775.
Sonnet XXII line 7; Sonnet XXIII line 10; Sonnet XXIV line 11;
Sonnet XLVIII line 11; Sonnet CIX line 4; Sonnet CX line 14; Sonnet CXXX line 3; Sonnet CLIII line 10.
Tempest, I 2 line 425; Tempest, II 1 line 817; Tempest, III 3 line 1619.
Timon of Athens, IV 3 line 1865; Timon of Athens, IV 3 line 2228.
Titus Andronicus, III 2 line 1452; Titus Andronicus, V 3 line 2707; Titus Andronicus, V 3 line 2724.
Troilus and Cressida, I 3 line 486; Troilus and Cressida, III 3 line 2016; Troilus and Cressida, III 3 line 2031.
Twelfth Night, II 3 line 720; Twelfth Night, V 1 line 2316.
Two Gentlemen of Verona, V 4 line 2155.
Venus and Adonis, lines 316, 416, 603, 669, 804, 834, 977, 1204, 1205.
Winter's Tale, III 2 line 1316.

Breath: Old English: *bræd, odour, scent, stink, exhalation, vapour* (Old English word for *air exhaled from the lungs* was: *ædm*).

All's Well That Ends Well, I 2 line 255; All's Well That Ends Well, II 1 line 757; All's Well That Ends Well, IV 3 line 2141.
Antony and Cleopatra, I 3 line 313; Antony and Cleopatra, II 2 line 958; Antony and Cleopatra, III 10 line 2093; Antony and Cleopatra, III 13 line 2341; Antony and Cleopatra, III 13 line 2467; Antony and Cleopatra, IV 1 line 2543; Antony and Cleopatra, V 2 line 3653.
As You Like It, II 7 line 1080; As You Like It, V 4 lines 2611, 2613.
Comedy of Errors, II 2 line 561; Comedy of Errors, III 2 line 789; Comedy of Errors, III 2 line 889; Comedy of Errors, III 2 line 893; Comedy of Errors, IV 1 line 1010; Comedy of Errors, IV 2 line 1104; V 1 line 1616.
Coriolanus, I 1 line 52; Coriolanus, I 2 line 968; Coriolanus, II 1 line 1179; Coriolanus, II 2 line 1409; Coriolanus, III 1 line 1963; Coriolanus, III 3 line 2492; Coriolanus, IV 5 line 2882; Coriolanus, IV 6 line 3136; Coriolanus, V 2 line 3419.
Cymbeline, I 3 line 312; Cymbeline, III 2 line 940; Cymbeline, II 4 line 1278; Cymbeline, III 4 line 1756; Cymbeline, IV 2 line 2612; Cymbeline, V 1 line 2977; Cymbeline, V 3 line 3112; Cymbeline, V 4 line 3265.
Hamlet, I 2 line 282; Hamlet, I 3 line 617; Hamlet, III 1 line 1793; Hamlet, III 2 line 2238; Hamlet, III 4 lines 2601, 2602; Hamlet, V 2 line 3772; Hamlet, V 2 line 3813; Hamlet, V 2 line 3914; Hamlet, V 2 line 3938; Hamlet, V 2 line 4008.
Henry IV, Part I, I 3 line 427; Henry IV, Part I, II 3 line 920; Henry IV, Part I, II 4 line 1231; Henry IV, Part I, II 4 line 1520; Henry IV, Part I, V 2 line 2822; Henry IV, Part I, V 4 line 3118.
Henry IV, Part II, II 2 line 1094; Henry IV, Part II, III 2 line 2039; Henry IV, Part II, IV 2 line 2577; Henry IV, Part II, IV 5 line 2919; Henry IV, Part II, IV 5 line 3046.
Henry V, I 1 line 63; Henry V, II 4 line 1049; Henry V, III 1 line 1107; Henry V, IV 1 line 2080.
Henry VI, Part I, II 5 line 1140; Henry VI, Part I, IV 2 line 1997; Henry VI, Part I, IV 3 line 2069; Henry VI, Part I, IV 6 line 2196; Henry VI, Part I, IV 7 line 2276; Henry VI, Part I, V 5 line 2860.
Henry VI, Part II, I 1 line 222; Henry VI, Part II, I 2 line 294; Henry VI, Part II, V 7 line 2637.
Henry VI, Part III, II 1 line 736; Henry VI, Part III, V 2 line 2763.
Henry VIII, I 4 line 694; Henry VIII, II 2 line 1076.
Julius Caesar, I 2 line 339; Julius Caesar, V 3 line 2523.
King John, II 1 line 444; King John, II 1 line 730; King John, II 1 line 789; King John, III 1 line 923; King John, III 1 line 1070; King John, III 1 line 1155; King John, III 4 line 1403; King John, III 4 line 1416; King John, III 4 line 1422; King John, III 4 lines 1515, 1522; King John, IV 1 line 1699; King John, IV 1 line 1701; King John, IV 2 line 1763; King John, IV 2 line 1990; King John, IV 3 line 2086; King John, IV 3 line 2165; King John, V 1 line 2210; King John, V 2 line 2347; King John, V 2 line 2363; King John, V 2 line 2409; King John, V 4 line 2522; King John, V 4 line 2524.

King Lear, I 1 line 60; King Lear, I 4 line 657; King Lear, II 2 line 1122; King Lear, II 4 line 1380; King Lear, IV 6 line 2831; King Lear, V 3 line 3439; King Lear, V 3 line 3496.
Love's Labour's Lost, I 1 line 7; Love's Labour's Lost, IV 3 line 1391r; Love's Labour's Lost, IV 3 line 1437; Love's Labour's Lost, V 2 line 1972; Love's Labour's Lost, V 2 line 2178; Love's Labour's Lost, V 2 line 2456; Love's Labour's Lost, V 2 line 2594; Love's Labour's Lost, V 2 line 2603; Love's Labour's Lost, V 2 line 2663; Love's Labour's Lost, V 2 line 2676.
Lover's Complaint, line 328.
Macbeth, I 3 line 184; Macbeth, I 5 line 383; Macbeth, I 6 line 438; Macbeth, II 1 line 640; Macbeth, IV 1 line 1667; Macbeth, V 3 line 2278; Macbeth, V 6 line 2426.
Measure for Measure, III 1 line 1230; Measure for Measure, V 1 line 2526; Measure for Measure, V 1 line 2634.
Merchant of Venice, I 3 line 451; Merchant of Venice, II 9 line 1225; Merchant of Venice, III 1 line 1331; Merchant of Venice, III 2 line 1488; Merchant of Venice, III 2 line 1673; Merchant of Venice, III 4 1766. merchant of Venice, V 1 line 2606.
Midsummer Night's Dream, II 1 line 522; Midsummer Night's Dream, II 2 line 747; Midsummer Night's Dream, III 1 line 897; Midsummer Night's Dream, III 2 line 1027; Midsummer Night's Dream, III 2 line 1206; Midsummer Night's Dream, IV 2 line 1824.
Much Ado About Nothing, II 1 line 733; Much Ado About Nothing, II 2 line 629; Much Ado About Nothing, II 3 line 988; Much Ado About Nothing, V 1 line 2335; Much Ado About Nothing, V 2 line 2457r.
Othello, II 1 line 855; Othello, II 1 line 1059; Othello, III 3 line 1764; Othello, IV 2 line 2741; Othello, V 2 line 3318; Othello, V 2 line 3543.
Passionate Pilgrim, lines 37r, 154, 162, 235.
Pericles, I 1 line 92; Pericles, I 1 line 148; Pericles, I 1 line 219; Pericles, I 4 lines 431, 435; Pericles, II 1 line 585; Pericles, II 4 line 929; Pericles, II 4 line 980.
Phoenix and the Turtle, line 19.
Rape of Lucrece, lines 263, 451, 830, 1091, 1231, 1458, 1717, 1771, 1777, 1828.
Richard II, I 1 line 177; Richard II, I 3 line 361; Richard II, I 3 line 430; Richard II, I 3 line 470r; Richard II, I 3 line 515; Richard II, I 3 line 532; Richard II, II 1 line 685; Richard II, II 1 line 712r; Richard II, III 1 line 1379; Richard II, III 2 line 1464; Richard II, III 2 line 1574; Richard II, III 2 line 1595; Richard II, III 3 line 1670; Richard II, IV 1 line 2030; Richard II, IV 1 2112; Richard II, IV 1 line 2198; Richard II, V 3 line 2625; Richard II, V 3 line 2650.
Richard III, I 1 line 22; Richard III, I 3 line 707; Richard III, III 5 line 2070; Richard III, III 5 line 2096; Richard III, III 7 line 2226; Richard III, IV 2 line 2607; Richard III, IV 2 line 2632; Richard III, IV 4 line 2883; Richard III, IV 4 line 2929; Richard III, IV 4 line 2929; Richard III, IV 4 line 3196; Richard III, V 3 line 3671.
Romeo and Juliet, I 1 line 131; Romeo and Juliet, I 4 line 576; Romeo and Juliet, II 2 line 972; Romeo and Juliet, II 5 line 1407; Romeo and

Juliet, II 5 lines 1408r, 1409; Romeo and Juliet, II 6 line 1485; Romeo and Juliet, III 1 line 1674; Romeo and Juliet, III 3 line 1944; Romeo and Juliet, IV 1 line 2464; Romeo and Juliet, V 1 line 2813; Romeo and Juliet, V 1 line 2874; Romeo and Juliet, V 3 lines 3038, 3060; Romeo and Juliet, V 3 line 3185; Romeo and Juliet, V 3 line 3204.
Sonnet LIV line 8; Sonnet LXV line 5; Sonnet LXXXI line 14; Sonnet LXXXV line 13; Sonnet XCVIX line 3; Sonnet XCVIX line 11; Sonnet CXXX line 7; Sonnet CXLV line 2.
Taming of the Shrew, Prologue 2 lines 192, 197; Taming of the Shrew, I 1 line 466.
Tempest, I 2 line 476; Tempest, IV 1 line 1908; Tempest, V 1 line 2201; Tempest, V 1 2413.
Timon of Athens, I 1 line 15; Timon of Athens, I 2 line 388; Timon of Athens, II 2 line 710; Timon of Athens, II 2 line 842; Timon of Athens, II 2 line 862; Timon of Athens, III 4 line 1288; Timon of Athens, IV 1 line 1594r; Timon of Athens, IV 3 line 1822; Timon of Athens, IV 3 line 1901; Timon of Athens, IV 3 line 1944; Timon of Athens, V 4 line 2564.
Titus Andronicus, II 1 line 608; Titus Andronicus, II 4 line 1089.
Troilus and Cressida, I 3 line 701; Troilus and Cressida, II 2 line 1067; Troilus and Cressida, II 3 line 1329; Troilus and Cressida, III 2 line 1684; Troilus and Cressida, III 3 line 2084; Troilus and Cressida, IV 1 line 2277; Troilus and Cressida, IV 4 line 2468; Troilus and Cressida, IV 5 line 2706; Troilus and Cressida, IV 5 line 2718; Troilus and Cressida, IV 5 line 2816; Troilus and Cressida, V 7 line 3559; Troilus and Cressida, V 8 line 3590; Troilus and Cressida, V 8 line 3596.
Twelfth Night, II 3 line 722; Twelfth Night, II 3 line 755; Twelfth Night, II 4 line 949; Twelfth Night, III 4 line 1680; Twelfth Night, V 1 line 2306.
Two Gentlemen of Verona, II 3 line 622; Two Gentlemen of Verona, III 1 line 1394; Two Gentlemen of Verona, III 1 line 1397.
Venus and Adonis, lines 209, 434, 464, 495, 531, 951, 956, 957, 1194.
Winter's Tale, III 2 line 1443; Winter's Tale, IV 4 line 2001; Winter's Tale, V 1 line 2924; Winter's Tale, V 2 line 3206; Winter's Tale, V 3 line 3363; Winter's Tale, V 3 line 3382.

Breathe: c.1300, not in Old English, but it retains the original Old English vowel of its source word, *breath*.
All's Well That Ends Well, II 1 line 673; All's Well That Ends Well, II 3 line 1157.
Antony and Cleopatra, II 2 line 960; Antony and Cleopatra, III 12 line 2214.
Coriolanus, I 6 line 609.
Cymbeline, V 5 line 3653.
Hamlet, II 1 line 980; Hamlet, II 1 line 996; Hamlet, III 2 line 2265; Hamlet, III 2 line 2602; Hamlet, IV 7 line 3203.
Henry IV, Part I, I 1 line 4; Henry IV, Part I, II 4 line 1000; Henry IV, Part I, II 4 line 1234; Henry IV, Part 1, IV 1 line 2230; Henry IV, Part 1,

V 3 line 2930; Henry IV, Part I, V 4 line 2964; Henry IV, Part I, V 4 1 line 3002.
Henry IV, Part II, I 1 line 90; Henry IV, Part II, IV 5 line 3079.
Henry VI, Part I, V 4 line 2802.
Henry VI Part II, III 2 line 1979; Henry VI Part II, III 2 lines 2087, 2094; Henry VI Part II, IV 1 line 2158.
Henry VI Part III, I 2 line 307; Henry VI Part III, I 4 line 481; Henry VI Part III, I 4 line 549; Henry VI Part III, II 3 line 1027; Henry VI Part III, II 6 line 1284; Henry VI Part III, III 1 line 1449; Henry VI Part III, IV 1 line 2088; Henry VI Part III, V 3 line 2793.
King John, III 1 line 1181; King John, III 2 line 1283; King John, IV 2 line 1873; King John, V 7 line 2701.
King Lear, IV 6 line 2658; King Lear, V 3 line 3292.
Love's Labour's Lost, V 2 line 2663.
Lover's Complaint, line 103.
Measure for Measure, II 2 line 839.
Merry Wives of Windsor, IV 5 line 2296.
Othello, IV 1 line 2719.
Pericles, III 2 line 1396.
Rape of Lucrece, lines 813, 1717.
Richard II, I 3 line 450; Richard II, I 3 line 558; Richard II, II 1 line 683; Richard II, II 1 line 690r; Richard II, II 1 line 776; Richard II, III 4 line 1949; Richard II, IV 1 line 2056.
Richard III, I 1 line 169; Richard III, I 2 line 320; Richard III, I 3 line 753; Richard III, III 7 line 2327.
Romeo and Juliet, IV 3 line 2586.
Sonnet XVIII line 13; Sonnet XXXVIII line 2.
Taming of the Shrew, Prologue 0 line 32; Taming of the Shrew, Prologue 1 line 33; Taming of the Shrew, I 1 line 301.
Tempest, II 1 line 750; Tempest, II 2 line 1154; Tempest, IV 1 line 1749.
Timon of Athens, III 5 line 1339; Timon of Athens, III 5 line 1368.
Titus Andronicus, III 1 line 1350; Titus Andronicus, III 1 line 1389.
Twelfth Night, I 1 line 7; Twelfth Night, II 2 line 696.
Two Gentlemen of Verona, III 1 line 1313; Two Gentlemen of Verona, V 4 line 2289.
Winter's Tale, IV 4 line 2259.

Bred: *race, lineage, stock* (originally of animals), 1550s, from *breed*. Of persons, from 1590s. Meaning *kind, species* is from 1580s.
Antony and Cleopatra, II 7 line 1402; Antony and Cleopatra, V 2 line 3595.
As You Like It, I 1 line 10; As You Like It, I 1 line 95; As You Like It, II 7 line 993.
Comedy of Errors, V 1 line 1506.
Coriolanus, III 1 line 2138; Coriolanus, III 2 line 2262.
Cymbeline, I 1 Line 185; Cymbeline, II 3 line 1114.
Henry IV, Part I, I 1 line 12.
Henry IV, Part II, I 1 line 76; Henry IV, Part II, V 3 line 3470.

Henry V, II 4 line 950; Henry V, III 5 line 1419.
Henry VI, Part I, I 2 line 223.
Henry VI, Part III, II 2 line 966; Henry VI, Part III, II 2 line 1009; Henry VI, Part III, III 3 line 171.
King John, I 1 line 130.
King Lear, I 1 line 99; King Lear, IV 2 line 2422.
Love's Labour's Lost, I 2 line 400; Love's Labour's Lost, IV 2 line 1165.
Measure for Measure, IV 2 line 2036.
Merchant of Venice, II 1 line 517; Merchant of Venice, III 2 line 1430; Merchant of Venice, III 2 line 1463; Merchant of Venice, III 2 line 1532.
Midsummer Night's Dream, IV 1 line 1674.
Much Ado About Nothing, III 1 line 1083.
Pericles, I 1 line 157; Pericles, V 1 line 2312; Pericles, V 1 line 2376; Pericles, V 1 line 2382.
Rape of Lucrece, lines 462, 541, 988, 1239.
Richard III, I 4 line 940.
Romeo and Juliet, I 1 line 109.
Sonnet CVIII line 13; Sonnet CXII line 13.
Timon of Athens, I 1 line 155; Timon of Athens, I 1 line 293; Timon of Athens, IV 3 line 1946.
Titus Andronicus, V 3 line 2596.
Twelfth Night, I 2 line 69; Twelfth Night, III 1 line 1283.
Venus and Adonis, lines 90, 234.
Winter's Tale, V 1 line 2832.

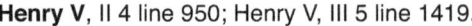

Breese: also called the *gadfly* or *brize*. It is said that the terror this insect causes in cattle proceeds solely from the alarm occasioned by the peculiar sound it emits while hovering.
    Antony and Cleopatra, III 10 line 2079.

Brier: thorny shrub, heath, 1540s, variant of Middle English: *brere*, from Old English: *brer* (Anglian), *brær* (W.Saxon) *brier, bramble, prickly bush*, of unknown origin. Briar is the most recent variant (c.1600). Originally used of prickly, thorny bushes in general, now mostly restricted to wild rose bushes. Used figuratively (in plural) for *troubles* from c.1500.
    All's Well That Ends Well, IV 4 line 2458.
    As You Like It, I 3 line 417.
    Comedy of Errors, II 2 line 567.
    Coriolanus, III 3 line 2410.
    Henry VI, Part I, II 4 line 952.
    Midsummer Night's Dream, II 1 line 370; Midsummer Night's Dream, III 1 line 907; Midsummer Night's Dream, III 1 line 923; Midsummer Night's Dream, III 2 line 1060; Midsummer Night's Dream, III 2 line 1518; Midsummer Night's Dream, V 1 line 2244.
    Tempest, IV 1 line 1916.
    Timon of Athens, IV 3 line 2132.
    Titus Andronicus, II 3 line 945.
    Venus and Adonis, line 727.

Winter's Tale, IV 4 line 2347.

Brim: c.1200, *brymme: edge of the sea*, of obscure origin (Old English: *brim: sea, surf*). Extended by 1520s to cups, basins, hats.
    All's Well That Ends Well, II 4 line 1249.
    Antony and Cleopatra, III 13 line 2266.
    Henry IV, Part II, III 1 line 1772.
    Henry V, I 2 line 295.
    King Lear, IV 1 line 2330.
    Passionate Pilgrim, line 81.
    Pericles, II 3 line 873.
    Tempest, IV 1 line 1774.
    Venus and Adonis, line 1110.

Brimstone: Old English: *brynstan*, from *brin-* stem of *brinnen: to burn*. In Middle English the first element also recorded as *brem-, brom-, brum-, bren-, brin-, bron-, brun-, bern-, born-, burn-, burned-*, and *burnt-*. Formerly the mineral: *sulphur*.
    Othello, IV 1 line 2669.
    Twelfth Night, II 5 line 1078; Twelfth Night, III 2 line 1422.

Brine: salty water. Old English: *brine*, of unknown origin.
    All's Well That Ends Well, I 1 line 45.
    Antony and Cleopatra, II 5 line 1134.
    Lover's Complaint, line 17.
    Pericles, III 1 line 1242.
    Rape of Lucrece, line 847.
    Romeo and Juliet, II 3 line 1129.
    Tempest, I 2 line 332; Tempest, III 2 line 1459.
    Twelfth Night, I 1 line 34.

Brock: Old English *brocc* badger, a borrowing from Celtic (cf. Old Irish *brocc*, Welsh *broch*). After c.1400, often with the adjective stinking, and meaning: a low, dirty fellow.
    Twelfth Night, II 5 line 1127.

Brook: *small stream*, Old English: *broc: flowing stream, torrent*, of obscure origin. In Sussex and Kent, it means *water-meadow*, and in plural, *low, marshy ground*.
    As You Like It, II 1 line 563; As You Like It, II 1 lines 581, 591; As You Like It, III 2 line 1383.
    Hamlet, IV 7 lines 3315, 3324.
    Henry VI, Part II, III 1 line 1330.
    Henry VI, Part III, IV 8 line 2578.
    Merchant of Venice, II 7 line 1033; Merchant of Venice, V 1 line 2553.
    Midsummer Night's Dream, II 1 line 453.
    Othello, V 2 line 3608.
    Passionate Pilgrim, lines 43, 76, 77, 81.
    Taming of the Shrew, Prologue 2 line 195.

Tempest, I 2 line 645; Tempest, IV 1 line 1849; Tempest, V 1 line 2054.
Timon of Athens, IV 3 line 114.
Venus and Adonis, lines 182, 1121.

Broom: Old English: *brom: broom, brushwood*, the common flowering shrub whose twigs were tied together to make a tool for sweeping. Both the flowers and sweeping with broom twigs were traditionally considered unlucky in May (Suffolk, Sussex, Wiltshire, etc.). The witch's flying broomstick was originally one among many such objects (pitchfork, trough, bowl), but the broomstick became fixed as the popular tool of supernatural flight via engravings from the Lancashire witch trial of 1612.
Tempest, IV 1 line 1777.

Brow: words for *eyelid, eyelash*, and *eyebrow* changed about in Old and Middle English. Lacking a distinctive word for it, the Anglo-Saxons called an eyebrow *ofer-bru*, and in early MiddleEnglish they were known as *uvere breyhes* or *briges aboue þe eiges*. By c.1200, everything had changed again: *Bru/brouw* (from *bræw*) became *eyelid*; and *brew/breow* (from Old English: *bru*) became *eyebrow*. It remained the word for *eyebrow* in Scottish and northern English, where it naturally evolved into colloquial *bree*. In southern English, however, Middle English: *bru/brouw* took over the sense of *eyebrows*, in the form: *brues*, and yielded the usual modern form of the word. To make matters worse, if possible, some southern writers 15c.-17c. used *bree* for *eyelashes*. By 1530s, *brow* had been given an extended sense of *forehead*, especially with reference to movements and expressions that showed emotion or attitude.
All's Well That Ends Well, I 1 line 95.
Antony and Cleopatra, I 3 line 340; Antony and Cleopatra, I 5 line 557; Antony and Cleopatra, I 3 line 340.
As You Like It, III 2 line 1317; As You Like It, III 3 line 1555; As You Like It, III 5 line 1700; As You Like It, IV 3 line 2010.
Comedy of Errors, II 2 line 525.
Coriolanus, I 3 line 376; Coriolanus, I 3 line 397; Coriolanus, I 3 line 401; Coriolanus, II 1 line 1042; Coriolanus, IV 5 line 2827.
Cymbeline, III 1 line 1475.
Hamlet, I 2 line 204; Hamlet, II 1 line 1048; Hamlet, III 4 line 2448; Hamlet, IV 5 line 2988; Hamlet, V 2 line 3939.
Henry IV, Part I, I 1 line 86; Henry IV, Part I, I 3 line 341; Henry IV, Part I, II 3 line 917; Henry IV, Part I, IV 3 line 2542.
Henry IV, Part II, I 1 line 116; Henry IV, Part II, I 1 line 209; Henry IV, Part II, II 1 line 848; Henry IV, Part II, IV 5 line 2915; Henry IV, Part II, V 1 line 3224.
Henry V, III 1 line 1102.
Henry VI, Part I, III 1 line 1355; Henry IV, Part II, V 3 line 2490.
Henry VI, Part II, I 2 line 276; Henry VI, Part II, III 1 line 1292; Henry VI, Part II, III 1 line 1436; Henry VI, Part II, V 1 line 3082; Henry VI, Part II, V 3 line 3322.

Henry VI, Part III, II 2 line 862; Henry VI, Part III, III 2 line 1565; Henry VI, Part III, V 2 lines 2741, 2744.
Henry VIII, I 0 line 2.
Julius Caesar, I 2 line 275; Julius Caesar, II 1 line 691; Julius Caesar, II 1 line 938; Julius Caesar, V 3 lines 2594, 2597.
King John, II 1 line 328; King John, II 1 line 394; King John, II 1 line 818; King John, III 1 line 1172; King John, III 4 line 1414; King John, IV 1 line 1624; King John, IV 2 line 1819; King John, IV 2 line 1936; King John, V 1 line 2244; King John, V 2 line 2334; King John, V 6 line 2597.
King Lear, I 4 line 811; King Lear, IV 2 line 2397.
Love's Labour's Lost, III 1 line 959; Love's Labour's Lost, IV 1 line 999; Love's Labour's Lost, IV 1 line 1101; Love's Labour's Lost, IV 3 line 1517; Love's Labour's Lost, IV 3 line 1571; Love's Labour's Lost, IV 3 lines 1603, 1609; Love's Labour's Lost, V 2 line 2314; Love's Labour's Lost, V 2 line 2685.
Macbeth, IV 1 line 1654; Macbeth, IV 1 line 1686; Macbeth, IV 3 line 1870; Macbeth, IV 3 line 2087.
Measure for Measure, IV 2 line 2059.
Merchant of Venice, III 2 line 1445; Merchant of Venice, IV 1 line 2215.
Merry Wives of Windsor, III 2 line 1455; Merry Wives of Windsor, III 3 line 1458.
Midsummer Night's Dream, III 2 line 1421; Midsummer Night's Dream, III 2 line 1443; Midsummer Night's Dream, V 1 line 1841.
Much Ado About Nothing, I 1 line 164; Much Ado About Nothing, III 5 line 1591.
Othello, II 1 line 824; Othello, III 3 line 1757.
Passionate Pilgrim, line 312.
Pericles, I 2 line 291; Pericles, V 1 line 2304.
Rape of Lucrece, lines 760, 800, 845, 858, 1560.
Richard II, I 1 line 18r; Richard II, IV 1 line 2328.
Richard III, I 1 line 6; Richard III, I 3 line 639; Richard III, IV 1 line 2530; Richard III, IV 4 line 3194; Richard III, V 5 line 3898.
Romeo and Juliet, I 1 line 260; Romeo and Juliet, I 3 line 423; Romeo and Juliet, I 3 line 437; Romeo and Juliet, I 4 line 528; Romeo and Juliet, III 2 line 1729; Romeo and Juliet, III 2 line 1816; Romeo and Juliet, III 5 line 2117; Romeo and Juliet, V 1 line 2848.
Sonnet II line 1; Sonnet XIX line 9; Sonnet XXXIII line 10; Sonnet LX line 10; Sonnet LXIII line 3; Sonnet LXVIII line 4; Sonnet CVI line 6; Sonnet CXII line 2; Sonnet CXXVII line 9.
Taming of the Shrew, V 2 line 2644.
Twelfth Night, V 1 line 2443.
Two Gentlemen of Verona, I 2 line 214.
Venus and Adonis, lines 79, 159, 203, 360, 511.
Winter's Tale, I 2 line 194; Winter's Tale, I 2 line 225; Winter's Tale, I 2 line 230; Winter's Tale, II 1 line 607r; Winter's Tale, IV 4 line 2619.

Bubble: early 14c. As a noun and mid-15c. Of financial schemes originally in South Sea Bubble (1590s), on notion of *fragile and insubstantial*.
    All's Well That Ends Well, III 6 line 1733.
    As You Like It, II 7 line 1050.
    Hamlet, V 2 line 3829.
    Henry IV, Part I, II 3 line 918.
    Macbeth, I 3 line 181; Macbeth, IV 1 line 1558; Macbeth, IV 1 line 1566; Macbeth, IV 1 line 1568; Macbeth, IV 1 line 1583.
    Measure for Measure, V 1 line 2735.
    Richard III, IV 4 line 2883.

Bubbles:** facetiously compounded from the French word *bube*, a blotch or sore, and from the word *buccal* (pertaining to the cheek; Latin, *bucca*, the cheek), to signify a cheek-blotch.
    Henry V, III 6 line 1568.

Buck: *male deer*, c.1300, earlier *male goat*; from Old English: *bucca: male goat*.
    Comedy of Errors, III 1 line 704.
    Henry VI, Part II, IV 2 line 2352.
    Love's Labour's Lost, IV 2 line 1151.
    Merry Wives of Windsor, III 3 lines 1548r, 1549rrrr; Merry Wives of Windsor, V 5 line 2583; Merry Wives of Windsor, V 5 line 2675.
    Troilus and Cressida, III 1 line 1602.

Bud: late 14c., *budde*, origin unknown.
    Antony and Cleopatra, III 13 line 2292.
    Cymbeline, I 3 line 313; Cymbeline II 3 line 1001.
    Henry IV, Part II, I 3 line 644.
    Henry V, I 2 line 330.
    Henry VI, Part II, III 1 line 1368.
    Henry VIII, I 1 line 144.
    King John, III 4 line 1468.
    Love's Labour's Lost, V 2 line 2209; Love's Labour's Lost, V 2 line 2850.
    Merry Wives of Windsor, III 3 line 1470.
    Midsummer Night's Dream, I 1 line 193; Midsummer Night's Dream, II 1 line 479; Midsummer Night's Dream, II 2 line 653; Midsummer Night's Dream, IV 1 lines 1601, 1621.
    Much Ado About Nothing, IV 1 line 1699.
    Passionate Pilgrim, lines 133, 172, 366.
    Pericles, V 0 line 2149.
    Rape of Lucrece, lines 655, 899.
    Romeo and Juliet, I 1 line 171; Romeo and Juliet, I 2 line 299; Romeo and Juliet, II 2 line 972.
    Sonnet I line 11; Sonnet XVIII line 3; Sonnet XXXV line 4; Sonnet LIV line 8; Sonnet LXX line 7; Sonnet XCVIX line 7.
    Taming of the Shrew, V 2 line 2648.
    Twelfth Night, II 4 line 1012.

Two Gentlemen of Verona, I 1 line 44; Two Gentlemen of Verona, I 1 lines 47, 50.
Venus and Adonis, lines 436, 1164.
Winter's Tale, IV 4 line 1970.

Budding: late 14c., *budde*, origin unknown.
Henry IV, Part I, V 4 line 3030.
Sonnet XCV line 3.
Taming of the Shrew, IV 5 line 2304.

Bug: insect, 1620s (earliest reference is to bedbugs), probably from Middle English: *bugge* something frightening, scarecrow (late 14c.), a meaning obsolete except in *bugbear* (1570s) probably connected with Scottish: *bogill: goblin, bugbear*, or obsolete Welsh *bwg: ghost, goblin*. See also *bogey* and German: *bögge, böggel-mann: goblin*.
Cymbeline, V 3 line 3077.
Hamlet, V 2 line 3672.
Henry VI, Part III, V 2 line 2723.
Taming of the Shrew, I 2 line 760.
Winter's Tale, III 2 1309.

Bull: Old English: *bula: a bull, a steer*. An uncastrated male, reared for breeding, as opposed to a bullock or steer. Extended after 1610s to males of other large animals (elephant, alligator, whale, etc.). Once upon a time there was scarcely a town or village of any magnitude which had not its bull-ring.
Henry IV, Part I, II 4 line 1230; Henry IV, Part I, II 4 line 1246; Henry IV, Part I, IV 1 line 2329.
Henry IV, Part II, II 2 line 1148.
Henry VI, Part III, II 5 line 1235.
Merry Wives of Windsor, V 5 line 2562.
Midsummer Night's Dream, II 1 line 554.
Much Ado About Nothing, I 1 line 234; Much Ado About Nothing, I 1 lines 236, 237; Much Ado About Nothing, V 1 line 2255; Much Ado About Nothing, V 4 line 2591; Much Ado About Nothing, V 4 lines 2596, 2597.
Tempest, II 1 line 1059; Tempest, III 3 line 1617.
Titus Andronicus, IV 3 line 1955; Titus Andronicus, V 1 line 2163.
Troilus and Cressida, II 3 line 1469; Troilus and Cressida, V 1 line 2985; Troilus and Cressida, V 7 lines 3569, 3570.
Winter's Tale, IV 4 line 1887.

Burning: Old English *birnan: be on fire* and *bærnan:consume by fire*, both from the same Germanic base; related to German: *brennen*.
Coriolanus, II 1 line 1156; Coriolanus, V 1 line 3294.
Cymbeline, II 2 line 925.
Hamlet, II 2 line 1591; Hamlet, V 1 line 3626.
Henry IV, Part I, III 1 line 1557; Henry IV, Part I, III 3 line 2034; Henry IV, Part I, III 3 line 2040r; Henry IV, Part I, III 3 line 2213; Henry IV, Part I, IV 1 line 2261.

Henry V, II 1 line 623; Henry V, II 3 line 872; Henry V, V 2 line 3130.
Henry VI, Part I, III 2 line 1470; Henry VI, Part I, III line 1473; Henry VI, Part I, III 2 line 1476.
Henry VI, Part II, I 4 line 672; Henry VI, Part II, II 4 line 1175; Henry VI, Part II, III 2 line 1799.
Henry VI, Part III, II 1 line 707; Henry VI, Part III, II 6 line 1263.
King John, IV 1 line 1698; King John, V 2 line 2331; King John, V 4 line 2522; King John, V 7 line 2636.
King Lear, III 6 line 2020; King Lear, IV 3 line 2504; King Lear, IV 6 line 2739.
Love's Labour's Lost, I 1 line 273.
Lover's Complaint, lines 229, 306.
Measure for Measure, I 3 line 295; Measure for Measure, V 1 line 2709.
Merchant of Venice, V 1 line 2546.
Merry Wives of Windsor, I 3 line 365; Merry Wives of Windsor, II 1 line 678.
Othello, II 1 line 777; Othello, III 3 line 2153; Othello, V 2 line 3300; Othello, V 2 line 3459.
Pericles, II 2 line 787; Pericles, III 0 line 1123.
Rape of Lucrece, lines 298, 486, 1525, 1608.
Romeo and Juliet, I 2 line 319; Romeo and Juliet, II 3 line 1063.
Sonnet VII line 2.
Titus Andronicus, III 1 line 1199; Titus Andronicus, III 1 line 1382; Titus Andronicus, IV 2 line 1779; Titus Andronicus, IV 3 line 1924; Titus Andronicus, V 1 line 2176; Titus Andronicus, V 3 line 2622.
Troilus and Cressida, V 2 line 3273.
Two Gentlemen of Verona, I 3 line 383.
Venus and Adonis, lines 70, 163, 198, 761.

Burs: prickly seed case. Middle English: probably of Scandinavian origin and related to Danish *burre: burr, burdock*, Swedish: *kard-borre: burdock*.
    As You Like It, I 3 line 418; As You Like It, I 3 line 421.
    Henry V, V 2 line 3035.
    Troilus and Cressida, III 2 line 1761.

Bush: *many-stemmed woody plant*, Old English: *bysc*. To *beat the bushes* (mid-15c.) is a way to rouse birds so that they fly into the net which others are holding, which originally was the same thing as *beating around the bush*.
    As You Like It, III 3 line 1572; As You Like It, IV 3 line 2116r; As You Like It, V 4 lines 2598, 2599.
    Cymbeline, IV 2 line 2694.
    Henry VI, Part II, I 3 line 479; Henry VI, Part II, II 4 line 1214.
    Henry VI, Part III, II 5 line 1144; Henry VI, Part III, V 6 line 3007; Henry VI, Part III, V 6 lines 3008, 3009.
    King Lear, II 4 line 1608.
    Love's Labour's Lost, IV 1 line 978; Love's Labour's Lost, IV 3 line 1465.
    Merry Wives of Windsor, III 3 line 1619.

Midsummer Night's Dream, II 1 line 370; Midsummer Night's Dream, III 1 line 871; Midsummer Night's Dream, III 1 line 923; Midsummer Night's Dream, III 2 line 1469; Midsummer Night's Dream, III 2 line 1471; Midsummer Night's Dream, V 1 line 1852; Midsummer Night's Dream, V 1 line 1978; Midsummer Night's Dream, V 1 line 2098r.
Rape of Lucrece, lines 139, 1024.
Taming of the Shrew, V 2 line 2537.
Tempest, II 2 line 1101; Tempest, II 2 line 1228.
Timon of Athens, IV 3 line 2133.
Titus Andronicus, II 3 line 745.
Venus and Adonis, lines 650, 893.

Butter: Old English: *butere*.
Henry IV, Part I, I 2 line 132; Henry IV, Part I, II 1 line 701; Henry IV, Part I, II 4 line 1111; Henry IV, Part I, II 4 line 1500; Henry IV, Part I, IV 2 line 2430.
King Lear, II 4 line 1402.
Merry Wives of Windsor, II 2 line 1088; Merry Wives of Windsor, III 5 line 1753; Merry Wives of Windsor, III 5 line 1853.

Butterfly: Old English *buttorfleoge*, but of obscure signification. Perhaps based on the old notion that the insects (or witches disguised as butterflies) consume butter or milk that is left uncovered. Or, less creatively, simply because the pale yellow colour of many species' wings suggests the colour of butter. Applied to persons from c.1600, originally in reference to vain and gaudy attire. n its metamorphosis from the common, colorless caterpillar to the exquisite winged creature of delicate beauty, the butterfly has become a metaphor for transformation and hope; across cultures, it has become a symbol for rebirth and resurrection, for the triumph of the spirit and the soul over the physical prison, the material world. Among the ancients, is an emblem of the soul and of unconscious attraction towards light. It is the soul as the opposite of the worm. In Western culture, the butterfly represents lightness and fickleness. Wantonness, especially in Shakespeare.

Coriolanus, I 3 line 426; Coriolanus, IV 6 line 3131; Coriolanus, V 4 lines 3740, 3741.
King Lear, V 3 line 3136.
Midsummer Night's Dream, III 1 line 997.
Troilus and Cressida, III 3 line 1950.

Buttock: late 13c.,
All's Well That Ends Well, II 2 lines 840, 841r, 842r.
Comedy of Errors, III 2 line 878.
Coriolanus, II 1 line 966.
Venus and Adonis, lines 318, 335.

Button: or *Bachelor's Buttons*. This was a name given to several flowers, and perhaps in Shakespeare's time was more loosely applied to any flower in bud. It is now usually understood to be a double variety of ranunculus. It was formerly supposed by country people to have some magical effect upon the

fortunes of lovers. Hence, it was customary for young people to carry its flowers in their pockets, judging of their good or bad success, in proportion as these retained or lost their freshness.
    Comedy of Errors, IV 2 line 1109.
    Hamlet, I 3 line 525; Hamlet, II 2 line 1331.
    King Lear, V 3 line 3498.
    Merry Wives of Windsor, III 2 line 1378.
    Romeo and Juliet, II 4 line 1181.

Buzzard: c.1300, from Old French: *buisart: buzzard, harrier, inferior hawk*, from *buson, buison*, from Latin: *buteonem: a kind of hawk*. May also mean, a beetle or flying insect: imitative.
    Richard III, I 1 line 140.
    Taming of the Shrew, II 1 line 1055; Taming of the Shrew, II 1 line 1056; Taming of the Shrew, II 1 line 1057.

Caddis: larva of the May-fly, 1650s, of unknown origin.
    Henry IV, Part I, II 4 line 1055.
    Winter's Tale, IV 4 line 2099.

Caelo: Latin, literally, sky or heaven.
    Love's Labour's Lost, IV 2 line 1146.

Calf: young cow, Old English: *cealf*. Also, fleshy part of the lower leg, early 14c.
    Comedy of Errors, IV 3 line 1167.
    Hamlet, III 2 line 1986.
    Henry VI, Part II, III 1 line 1492; Henry VI, Part II, IV 2 line 2332.
    King John, I 1 line 132; King John, III 1 line 1050; King John, III 1 line 1052; King John, III 1 line 1054; King John, III 1 line 1122; King John, III 1 line 1145; King John, III 1 line 1225.
    Love's Labour's Lost, V 1 line 1756; Love's Labour's Lost, V 2 line 2154; Love's Labour's Lost, V 2 line 2155; Love's Labour's Lost, V 2 line 2156; Love's Labour's Lost, V 2 line 2162; Love's Labour's Lost, V 2 line 2581.
    Much Ado About Nothing, III 3 line 1387; Much Ado About Nothing, V 1 line 2229; Much Ado About Nothing, V 4 line 2598.
    Tempest, II 2 line 1194; Tempest, II 2 line 1196; Tempest, II 2 line 1221; Tempest, III 2 lines 1416, 1417; Tempest, IV 1 line 1915.
    Titus Andronicus, V 1 line 2165.
    Troilus and Cressida, III 2 line 1834.
    Winter's Tale, I 2 lines 202, 204, 205.

Camel: Old English, from Latin: *camelus*, from Greek: *kamelos*, of Semitic origin.
    Coriolanus, II 1 line 1198.
    Hamlet, III 2 line 2253; Hamlet, III 2 line 2254.
    Richard II, V 5 line 2764.
    Troilus and Cressida, I 2 line 398; Troilus and Cressida, II 1 line 910.

Camomile: an aromatic plant of the daisy family. Middle English: from Old French: *camomille*, from late Latin *chamomilla*, from Greek *khamaimelon*: *earth-apple* (because of the apple-like smell of its flowers). It was formerly imagined that this plant grew the more luxuriantly for being frequently trodden or pressed down.
    Henry IV, Part I, II 4 line 1383.

Canary: type of small songbird, 1650s (short for *Canary-bird*, 1570s), from French: *canarie*, from Spanish: *canario: canary bird*, literally: of the Canary Islands, from Latin: *Insula Canaria: Canary Island*, largest of the Fortunate Isles, literally: *island of dogs*, (canis) so called because large dogs lived there. The name was extended to the whole island group (Canariæ Insulæ) by the time of Arnobius (c.300). As a type of wine (from the Canary Islands) from 1580s.
    All's Well That Ends Well, II 1 line 674.
    Henry IV, Part II, II 4 line 1260.
    Love's Labour's Lost, III 1 line 774.
    Merry Wives of Windsor, II 2 line 854; Merry Wives of Windsor, II 2 line 857; Merry Wives of Windsor, III 2 line 1397.
    Twelfth Night, I 3 line 190; Twelfth Night, I 3 line 192.

Canker: Old English: *cancer*, from Latin: *cancer*; influenced in Middle English by Old Norman: *cancre*. The word was the common one for *cancer* until c. 1700. Also, a caterpillar; the dog rose.
    Coriolanus, IV 5 line 2857.
    Hamlet, I 3 line 523; Hamlet, V 2 line 3723.
    Henry IV, Part I, I 3 line 466; Henry IV, Part I, I 3 line 506; Henry IV, Part I, IV 2 line 2397.
    Henry VI, Part I, II 4 line 996; Henry VI, Part I, II 4 line 1000.
    Henry VI, Part II, I 2 line 291; Henry IV, Part II, II 2 line 1055.
    King John, II 1 line 493; King John, III 4 line 1468; King John, V 2 line 2292.
    King Lear, V 3 line 3268.
    Midsummer Night's Dream, II 2 line 652.
    Much Ado About Nothing, I 3 line 353.
    Romeo and Juliet, I 1 line 115r; Romeo and Juliet, II 3 line 1078.
    Sonnet XXXV line 4; Sonnet LXX line 7; Sonnet XCV line 2; Sonnet XCVIX line 12.
    Tempest, I 2 line 560; Tempest, IV 1 line 1931.
    Timon of Athens, IV 3 line 1718.
    Two Gentlemen of Verona, I 1 line 45; Two Gentlemen of Verona, I 1 line 48.
    Venus and Adonis, line 677, 789.

Canker-bloom: dog rose, as above, *canker blossom* is recorded from 1580s.
    Midsummer Night's Dream, III 2 line 1329.
    Sonnet LIV line 5.

Capon: Old English: a *castrated cock*, from Latin: *caponem*.
    As You Like It, II 7 line 1052.
    Comedy of Errors, I 2 line 209; Comedy of Errors, III 1 line 645.
    Cymbeline, II 1 line 874.
    Hamlet,III 2 line 1977.
    Henry IV, Part I, I 2 line 119; Henry IV, Part I, I 2 line 223; Henry IV, Part I, II 4 line 1440; Henry IV, Part I, II 4 line 1525.
    Love's Labour's Lost, IV 1 line 1027.
    Much Ado About Nothing, V 1 line 2230.
    Two Gentlemen of Verona, IV 4 line 1842.

Cantle: the arch of a horse at the neck or back. Middle English: (in the sense a *corner*): from Anglo-Norman French: *cantel*, variant of Old French: *chantel*, from medieval Latin: *cantellus*, from *cantus: corner, side*.
    Antony and Cleopatra, III 10 line 2070.
    Henry IV, Part I, III 1 line 1643.

Carbuncle: early 13c., *fiery jewel*, from Old French: *carbuncle-stone*, also *carbuncle, boil*, from Latin: *carbunculus: red gem*, also *red, inflamed spot*, literally, *a little coal*, from *carbo: coal*. Originally of rubies, garnets, and other red jewels; in English the word was applied to tumours from late 14c.
    Antony and Cleopatra, IV 8 line 2818.
    Comedy of Errors, III 2 line 892.
    Coriolanus, I 4 line 558.
    Cymbeline, V 5 line 3597.
    Hamlet, II 2 line 1539.
    King Lear, II 4 line 1520.

Carcass: dead body, originally of an animal. Middle English: from Anglo-Norman French: *carcois*, variant of Old French: *charcois*; of unknown ultimate origin.
    Coriolanus, III 3 line 2494.
    Cymbeline, I 2 line 241; Cymbeline, V 3 line 3098.
    Julius Caesar, II 1 line 793.
    King John, II 1 line 768.
    Lover's Complaint, line 11.
    Merchant of Venice, III 1 line 1243.
    Midsummer's Night's Dream, III 2 line 1097.
    Tempest, I 2 line 253.

Carp: This fish was proverbially the most cunning of fishes. This notion is founded on fact, the brain of the carp being six times as large as the average brain of other fishes. Type of freshwater fish, late 14c., from Old French: *carpe* (13c).
    All's Well That Ends Well, V 2 line 2637.

Carrion: decaying flesh on dead animal, Middle English, early 13c., *carione*, from Anglo-French: *carogne*. Originally from Latin: *caro: flesh*.
    Hamlet, II 2 line 1287.

Henry IV, Part II, IV 4 line 2828.
Henry V, IV 2 line 2204.
Henry VI, Part II, V 2 line 3220.
Julius Caesar, II 1 line 749; Julius Caesar, III 1 line 1504.
King John, III 4 line 1417.
Measure for Measure, II 2 line 941.
Merchant of Venice, II 1 line 1051; Merchant of Venice, III 1 line 1271; Merchant of Venice, IV 1 line 1973.
Romeo and Juliet, III 3 line 1906; Romeo and Juliet, III 5 line 2263.
Troilus and Cressida, IV 1 line 2275.

Caraway: seeds of a plant from the parsley family, late 13c., from Old Spanish: *alcarahuaya*, from Arabic: *al-karawiya*, of unknown origin.
Henry IV, Part II, V 3 line 3397.

Cat: Old English: *catt* (c.700), from West Germanic (c.400-450). Cats were domestic in Egypt from c.2000 B.C.E., but not a familiar household animal to classical Greeks and Romans. The nine lives have been proverbial since at least 1560s. Extended to lions, tigers, etc. c.1600. As a term of contempt for a woman, from early 13c. Slang sense of prostitute is from at least c.1400. (Cat's foot 1590s) refers to old folk tale in which the monkey tricks the cat into pawing chestnuts from a fire; the monkey gets the nuts, the cat gets a burnt paw.

All's Well That Ends Well, IV 3 lines 2320, 2321; All's Well That Ends Well, IV 3 line 2346; All's Well That Ends Well, IV 3 line 2357; All's Well That Ends Well, V 2 line 2634r.
As You Like It, III 2 line 1181; As You Like It, III 2 line 1214.
Coriolanus, I 6 line 667; Coriolanus, IV 2 line 2636.
Cymbeline, I 5 line 539; Cymbeline, V 5 lie 3671.
Hamlet, V 1 line 3638.
Henry IV, Part I, I 2 line 180; Henry IV, Part I, III 1 line 1561; Henry IV, Part I, III 1 line 1698; Henry IV, Part I, IV 2 line 2427.
Henry V, I 2 line 317; Henry V, I 2 line 319.
King Lear, III 4 line 1899; King Lear, III 6 line 2049.
Macbeth, I 7 line 522; Macbeth, IV 1 line 1548.
Merchant of Venice, IV 1 lines 1980, 1987.
Midsummer's Night's Dream, I 2 line 290; Midsummer's Night's Dream, II 2 line 682; Midsummer's Night's Dream, III 2 line 1303.
Much Ado About Nothing, I 1 line 231; Much Ado About Nothing, V 1 line 2210.
Othello, I 3 line 695.
Pericles, III 0 line 1123.
Rape of Lucrece, line 605.
Romeo and Juliet, II 4 line 1177; Romeo and Juliet, III 1 line 1576; Romeo and Juliet, III 1 line 1606; Romeo and Juliet, III 3 line1901.
Taming of the Shrew, I 2 line 662.
Tempest, II 1 line 1026; Tempest, II 2 line 1172; Tempest, IV 1 line 2007.
Troilus and Cressida, V 1 line 2992.

Two Gentlemen of Verona, II 3 line 599.

Caterpillar: mid-15c., *catyrpel*, probably altered from Old French: *caterpilose*, literally, *hairy cat;* a reference to the variety with spiny bristles.
  Pericles, V 1 line 2244.

Cattle: mid-13c., from Anglo-French: *catel: property* (Old French: *chatel*). Original sense was of moveable property, especially livestock; not limited to *cows* until 1550s.
  As You Like It, III 2 line 1192; As You Like It, III 2 line 1488.
  Lover's Complaint, line 57.
  Merry Wives of Windsor, IV 4 line 2227.
  Titus Andronicus, V 1 line 2267.

Carnation: cultivated variety of the clove pink, 1530s, either a corruption of *coronation*, from the flower's being used in chaplets or from the toothed crown-like look of the petals.
  Henry V, II 3 line 865.
  Love's Labour's Lost, III 1 line 908.
  Winter's Tale, IV 4 line 1954.

Cave: early 13c., from Old French *cave*: a cave, vault, cellar (12c.)
  Antony and Cleopatra, V 2 line 3835.
  As You Like It, II 7 line 1098; As You Like It, IV 3 line 2150; As You Like It, V 4 line 2592.
  Cymbeline, III 3 line 1600; Cymbeline, III 3 line 1643; Cymbeline, III 3 line 1692; Cymbeline, III 6 line 2172; Cymbeline, III 6 line 2185; Cymbeline, III 6 line 2187; Cymbeline, III 6 line 2247; Cymbeline, IV 2 line 2314; Cymbeline, IV 2 line 2316; Cymbeline, IV 2 line 2376; Cymbeline, IV 2 line 2499; Cymbeline, IV 2 line 2701.
  Henry V, II 4 line 1028.
  Henry VI, Part II, III 2 line 1770; Henry VI, Part II, III 2 line 2009.
  Julius Caesar, II 1 line 693.
  King Lear, III 2 line 1721.
  Measure for Measure, I 3 line 312.
  Rape of Lucrece, lines 820, 1301.
  Richard II, I 1 line 108.
  Richard III, V 3 line 3529.
  Romeo and Juliet, II 2 line 1022; Romeo and Juliet, III 2 line 1796.
  Timon of Athens, IV 3 line 1663; Timon of Athens, IV 3 line 2257; Timon of Athens, V 1 line 2259; Timon of Athens, V 1 line 2289; Timon of Athens, V 1 line 2387; Timon of Athens, V 1 line 2393; Timon of Athens, V 1 line 2402; Timon of Athens, V 1 line 2407; Timon of Athens, V 1 line 2513; Timon of Athens, V 2 line 2532.
  Titus Andronicus, II 3 line 758; Titus Andronicus, III 1 line 1411; Titus Andronicus, IV 2 line 1875; Titus Andronicus, V 2 line 2341; Titus Andronicus, V 2 line 2358.
  Twelfth Night, IV 1 line 1998.
  Two Gentlemen of Verona, V 3 line 2143.

Venus and Adonis, lines 267, 852, 1056.

Caviare: 1550s, from French *caviar* (16c.), from Italian *caviaro* (modern *caviale*) or Turkish *khaviar*, from Persian *khaviyar*, from *khaya* egg.
    Hamlet, II 2 line 1514.

Cedar: Old English: *ceder*, blended in Middle English: with Old French: *cedre*, from Latin: *cedrus*, from Greek: *kedros cedar, juniper*, origin uncertain. Cedar oil was used by the Egyptians in embalming as a preservative against decay and the word for it was used figuratively for immortality by the Romans.
    Coriolanus, V 3 line 3560.
    Cymbeline, V 4 line 3293; Cymbeline, V 5 line 3907; Cymbeline, V 5 lines 3225, 3929.
    Henry VI, Part II, V 1 line 3195.
    Henry VI, Part III, V 2 line 2730.
    Henry VIII, V 5 line 3437.
    Love's Labour's Lost, IV 3 line 1414.
    Rape of Lucrece, lines 715, 716.
    Richard III, I 3 line 731.
    Tempest, V 1 line 2069.
    Titus Andronicus, IV 3 line 1925.
    Venus and Adonis, line 890.

Celestial: late 14c., from Old French: *celestial: celestial, heavenly, sky-blue*, from Latin: *caelestis: heavenly, pertaining to the sky*, from *caelum: heaven, sky; abode of the gods*; of uncertain origin.
    Cymbeline, V 4 line 3265.
    Hamlet, I 5 line 794; Hamlet, II 2 line 1205.
    Henry V, I 1 line 69.
    Henry VI, Part I, V 4 line 2711; Henry VI, Part I, V 5 line 2918.
    Henry VIII, IV 2 line 2643.
    Love's Labour's Lost, IV 2 line 1266; Love's Labour's Lost, V 2 line 2739.
    Merry Wives of Windsor, III 1 line 1293.
    Midsummer's Night's Dream, III 2 line 1267.
    Passionate Pilgrim, line 70.
    Pericles, I 1 line 67; Pericles, V 1 line 2473.
    Sonnet XXXIII line 6.
    Tempest, II 2 line 1205.
    Two Gentlemen of Verona, II 6 lines 940, 964.
    Venus and Adonis, line 209.
    Winter's Tale, III 1 line 1186.

Chaff: husks. From Old English: *ceaf*.
    Coriolanus, V 1 line 3307; Coriolanus, V 1 line 3313.
    Cymbeline, I 6 line 808.
    Henry IV, Part II, IV 1 line 2402.
    Henry VIII, V 1 line 2913.
    Merchant of Venice, I 1 line 123; Merchant of Venice, II 9 line 1177.

Troilus and Cressida, I 2 line 391r.
Winter's Tale, IV 4 line 2578.

Chameleon: slow moving lizard with independently rotating eyes and a prehensile tail; has the ability to change colour to match the environment. Mid-14c., from Old French: *chaméléon*, from Latin: *chamaeleon*, from Greek: *khamaileon: the chameleon*. Figurative sense of variable person is 1580s. It was formerly supposed to live on air.
Henry VI, Part III, III 2 line 1680.
Two Gentlemen of Verona, II 1 line 560; Two Gentlemen of Verona, II 4 line 678.

Chanticleer: c.1300, from Old French: *chante-cler: sing-loud.*
As You Like It, II 7 line 924.
Tempest, I 2 line 549.

Charles' Wain: the constellation called also Ursa Major, or the Great Bear.
Henry VI, Part I, II 1 line 644.

Chaudron: entrails
Macbeth, IV 1 line 1580.

Cheek: Old English: *ceace, cece: jaw, jawbone,* also: *the fleshy wall of the mouth.* Aristotle considered the chin as the front of the jaws and the cheeks as the back of them. The other Old English word for cheek was *ceafl*.
All's Well That Ends Well, I 1 line 48; All's Well That Ends Well, I 1 line 162; All's Well That Ends Well, I 3 line 499; All's Well That Ends Well, II 1 line 640; All's Well That Ends Well, II 3 lines 965, 967; All's Well That Ends Well, IV 5 lines 2553r, 2554.
Antony and Cleopatra, I 1 line 38; Antony and Cleopatra, I41 line 500; Antony and Cleopatra, II 2 line 928; Antony and Cleopatra, II 7 line 1388; Antony and Cleopatra, II 7 line 1524; Antony and Cleopatra, IV 14 line 3062.
As You Like It, III 2 line 1258; As You Like It, III 2 line 1457; As You Like It, III 5 line 1681; As You Like It, III 5 line 1701; As You Like It, III 2 line 1777.
Comedy of Errors, I 2 line 211; Comedy of Errors, II 1 line 364.
Coriolanus, II 1 line 1155; Coriolanus, III 2 line 2304; Coriolanus, V 3 line 3662.
Cymbeline, I 6 line 722; Cymbeline, III 3 line 1702; Cymbeline, III 4 line 1903; Cymbeline, IV 2 line 2596; Cymbeline, IV 2 line 2735; Cymbeline, V 5 line 3409.
Hamlet, III 1 line 1742; Hamlet, III 4 line 2587.
Henry IV, Part I, I 3 line 471; Henry IV, Part I, II 3 line 903; Henry IV, Part I, III 1 line 1552; Henry IV, Part I, III 3 line 2087.
Henry IV, Part II, I 1 line 125; Henry IV, Part II, I 2 line 294; Henry IV, Part II, I 2 line 507; Henry IV, Part II, IV 5 line 2977.
Henry V, II 2 line 709; Henry V, IV 0 line 1814.

Henry VI, Part I, I 2 line 274; Henry VI, Part I, I 3 line 406; Henry VI, Part I, I 4 line 535; Henry VI, Part I, II 4 line 988; Henry VI, Part I, II 4 line 992; Henry VI, Part I, II 5 line 1116; Henry VI, Part I, IV 1 line 1858.
Henry VI, Part II, III 2 line 1852; Henry VI, Part II, IV 7 line 2703.
Henry VI, Part III, I 4 line 522; Henry VI, Part III, II 1 line 688; Henry VI, Part III, II 5 line 1205; Henry VI, Part III, III 2 line 1673; Henry VI, Part III, V 1 line 2703.
Henry VIII, I 4 line 716.
Julius Caesar, I 2 line 277.
King John, II 1 line 309; King John, II 1 line 526; King John, III 3 line 1347; King John, III 4 line 1469; King John, IV 2 line 1838; King John, V 2 line 2324.
King Lear, I 4 line 812; King Lear, II 4 line 1580; King Lear, III 2 line 1678; King Lear, IV 2 line 2396; King Lear, IV 3 line 2466; King Lear, II 4 line 1580.
Love's Labour's Lost, I 2 lines 400, 405; Love's Labour's Lost, IV 3 line 1349; Love's Labour's Lost, IV 3 line 1579; Love's Labour's Lost, V 2 line 2392; Love's Labour's Lost, V 2 line 2558.
Lover's Complaint, lines 32, 286, 326.
Macbeth, III 4 line 1414; Macbeth, V 3 line 2265.
Measure for Measure, I 4 line 367.
Merchant of Venice, I 3 line 427; Merchant of Venice, III 2 line 1619.
Midsummer Night's Dream, I 1 line 134; Midsummer Night's Dream, III 2 line 1391; Midsummer Night's Dream, IV 1 line 1547; Midsummer Night's Dream, V 1 line 2177.
Much Ado About Nothing, III 2 line 1241.
Othello, IV 2 line 2823.
Passionate Pilgrim, line 236.
Pericles, I 1 line 85; Pericles, I 2 line 342; Pericles, I 4 line 467; Pericles, V 1 line 2290.
Rape of Lucerne, lines 112, 437, 759, 807, 1268, 1276, 1322, 1409, 1503, 1561.
Richard II, II 1 line 802; Richard II, II 1 line 856; Richard II, III 1 line 1373; Richard II, III 3 line 1694.
Richard III, I 2 line 306; Richards III, I 2 line 347; Richard III, II 1 line 1210; Richard III, II 2 line 1294.
Romeo and Juliet, I 5 line 667; Romeo and Juliet, II 2 lines 864, 868, 870; Romeo and Juliet, II 2 line 935; Romeo and Juliet, II 3 lines 1130, 1135; Romeo and Juliet, II 5 line 1448; Romeo and Juliet, III 2 line 1732; Romeo and Juliet, IV 1 line 2465; Romeo and Juliet, V 1 line 2880; Romeo and Juliet, V 3 line 3041.
Sonnet LIII line 7; Sonnet LXVII line 5; Sonnet LXVIII line 1; Sonnet LXXIX line 11; Sonnet LXXXII line 14; Sonnet XCVIX line 4; Sonnet CXVI line 9; Sonnet CXXX line 6; Sonnet CXXXII line 6.
Taming of the Shrew, III 2 line 1416; Taming of the Shrew, IV 5 line 2298.
Tempest, I 2 line 88; Tempest, II 1 line 956.
Timon of Athens, IV 3 line 1761; Timon of Athens IV 3 line 1794.

Titus Andronicus, II 3 line 796; Titus Andronicus, II 4 line 1095; Titus Andronicus, III 1 line 1132; Titus Andronicus, III 1 line 1242; Titus Andronicus, III 1 line 1254; Titus Andronicus, III 1 line 1272; Titus Andronicus, III 1 line 1277; Titus Andronicus, III 2 line 1483.
Troilus and Cressida, I 1 line 84; Troilus and Cressida, I 3 lines 452, 468; Troilus and Cressida, I 3 line 684; Troilus and Cressida, IV 2 line 2405; Troilus and Cressida, IV 4 line 2557; Troilus and Cressida, IV 5 line 2603; Troilus and Cressida, IV 5 line 2661; Troilus and Cressida, IV 5 line 2748; Troilus and Cressida, V 2 line 3109.
Twelfth Night, II 4 line 1013; Twelfth Night, V 1 line 2441.
Two Gentlemen of Verona, IV 4 line 1994.
Venus and Adonis, lines 23, 65, 70, 79, 85, 103, 205, 239, 262, 272, 368, 372, 373, 489, 496, 612, 979, 988, 1004, 1191.
Winter's Tale, I 2 line 388r; Winter's Tale, II 3 line 1053; Winter's Tale, IV 4 line 2528.

Cheese: Old English: *cyse*. Earliest references would be to compressed curds of milk used as food; pressed or moulded cheeses with rinds are 14c.
All's Well That Ends Well, I 1 line 144.
Henry IV, Part I, III 1 line 1707.
Henry IV, Part II, III 2 line 2180.
Henry V, II 1 line 515.
Henry VI, Part II, IV 7 line 2632.
King Lear, IV 6 line 2700.
Merry Wives of Windsor, I 1 line 118; Merry Wives of Windsor, I 2 line 302; Merry Wives of Windsor, II 1 line 696; Merry Wives of Windsor, II 2 line 1089; Merry Wives of Windsor, V 5 line 2646; Merry Wives of Windsor, V 5 line 2714.
Troilus and Cressida, II 3 line 1254; Troilus and Cressida, V 4 line 3420.

Cherries: see *Cherry*.
Midsummer Night's Dream, III 2 line 1178.
Venus and Adonis, line 1125.

Cherry: small, soft, round, stoned fruit, typically red or black; mid 13c from Anglo-French: *cherise*.
Henry VIII, V 1 line 2987r.
King John, II 1 line 459.
Midsummer Night's Dream, III 2 line 1249; Midsummer Night's Dream, V 1 line 2034; Midsummer Night's Dream, V 1 line 2176.
Pericles, V 0 line 2151.
Richard III, I 1 line 100.
Twelfth Night, III 4 line 1661.

Cherry-stone: the pip or seed of the cherry, sometimes associated with the fleeting quality of life's pleasures.
Comedy of Errors, IV 3 line 1222.

Chestnut: 1560s, from *chesten nut* (1510s), from Middle English: *chasteine*, from Old French: *chastain*. Of the dark reddish-brown colour, 1650s.
    As You Like It, III 4 line 1604.
    Macbeth, I 3 line 101.
    Taming of the Shrew, I 2 line 759.

Cheveril: kid leather.
    Henry VIII, II 3 line 1239.
    Romeo and Juliet, II 4 line 1239.
    Twelfth Night, III 1 line 1247.

Child: Old English: *cild: child, infant*. Also meaning: *a youth of gentle birth* (archaic, usually written *childe*). In 16c., especially: *girl child*. The difficulty with the plural began where the nominative plural was at first *cild*, identical with the singular, then c.975 a plural form *cildru* arose, only to be pluralized in the late 12c. as *children*, which is thus a double plural. Middle English plural *cildre* survives in Lancashire dialect *childer* and in *Childermas* (c.1000, *cildramæsse*) festival of the Holy Innocents (Dec. 28th).
    All's Well That Ends Well, I 1 line 36: All's Well That Ends Well, III 2 line 1440; All's Well That Ends Well, III 2 line 1459; All's Well That Ends Well, III 2 line 1470; All's Well That Ends Well, IV 3 line 2274; All's Well That Ends Well, V 3 line 3018; All's Well That Ends Well, V 3 line 3034.
    Antony and Cleopatra, I 2 line 107; Antony and Cleopatra, I 2 line 114; Antony and Cleopatra, I 3 line 364; Antony and Cleopatra, III 7 line 1495; Antony and Cleopatra, III 13 line 2273; Antony and Cleopatra, V 2 line 3553; Antony and Cleopatra, V 2 line 3640.
    As You Like It, I 2 line 159; As You Like It, I 3 line 416; As You Like It, II 7 lines 1060, 1063; As You Like It, III 3 line 1515; As You Like It, III 4 line 1602; As You Like It, III 5 line 1707; As You Like It, IV 1 line 1943.
    Comedy of Errors, I 1 line 85; Comedy of Errors, V 1 line 1802; Comedy of Errors, V 1 line 1848.
    Coriolanus, I 3 line 378; Coriolanus, I 3 line 394; Coriolanus, I 3 line 433; Coriolanus, II 3 line 1621; Coriolanus, III 1 line 1763; Coriolanus, III 1 line 2105; Coriolanus, IV 5 line 2995; Coriolanus, IV 6 line 3034; Coriolanus, V 1 line 3311; Coriolanus, V 2 line 3456; Coriolanus, V 3 line 3518; Coriolanus, V 3 line 3555; Coriolanus, V 3 lines 3608, 3625; Coriolanus, V 3 line 3639; Coriolanus, V 3 lines 3668, 3690; Coriolanus, V 6 line 3881; Coriolanus, V 6 line 4005.
    Cymbeline, I 1 line 57; Cymbeline, I 1 line 64; Cymbeline, I 1 line 65; Cymbeline, I 1 line 73; Cymbeline, V 4 line 3149; Cymbeline, V 5 line 3688; Cymbeline, V 5 line 3789; Cymbeline, V 5 line 3804.
    Hamlet, II 2 line 1329; Hamlet, II 2 line 1427; Hamlet, II 2 line 1432; Hamlet, II 2 line 1468; Hamlet, IV 5 line 3024.
    Henry IV Part I, I 1 line 7; Henry IV Part I, I 1 line 89; Henry IV Part I, III 2 line 1871; Henry IV Part I, III 2 line 1963.
    Henry IV Part II, Prologue 1 line 15; Henry IV Part II, II 1 line 734; Henry IV Part II, II 2 line 969; Henry IV Part II, V 4 line 3565.

Henry V, II 0 line 482; Henry V, II 3 line 843; Henry V, IV 1 line 1987; Henry V, IV 1 line 2078.
Henry VI, Part I, I 3 line 397; Henry VI, Part I, I 4 line 501; Henry VI, Part I, II 3 line 851; Henry VI, Part I, III 1 line 1329; Henry VI, Part I, III 1 line 1364; Henry VI, Part I, IV 1 line 1961; Henry VI, Part I, V 3 line 2616; Henry VI, Part I, V 4 line 2734; Henry VI, Part I, V 4 line 2736; Henry VI, Part I, V 4 line 2743.
Henry VI, Part II, I 1 line 257; Henry VI, Part II, II 3 line 1073; Henry VI, Part II, III 1 line1513; Henry VI, Part II, IV 2 line 2445; Henry VI, Part II, IV 2 line 2485.
Henry VI, Part III, I 3 line 384; Henry VI, Part III, I 4 line 590; Henry VI, Part III, II 2 line 878; Henry VI, Part III, II 2 line 957; Henry VI, Part III, II 2 line 958; Henry VI, Part III, III 2 line 1500; Henry VI, Part III, III 2 line 1502; Henry VI, Part III, III 2 line 1515; Henry VI, Part III, III 2 line 1556; Henry VI, Part III, III 2 line 1586; Henry VI, Part III, V 4 line 2843; Henry VI, Part III, V 4 line 2854; Henry VI, Part III, V 5 lines 2956, 2957, 2963, 2965.
Henry VIII, II 4 line 1393; Henry VIII, II 4 line 1560; Henry VIII, IV 2 line 2564; Henry VIII, V 3 line 3083; Henry VIII, V 5 line 3373; Henry VIII, V 5 line 3391; Henry VIII, V 5 line 3446r; Henry VIII, V 5 lines 3450, 3453.
Julius Caesar, I 3 line 492; Julius Caesar, III 1 line 1243; Julius Caesar, III 1 line 1310; Julius Caesar, V 3 line 2577.
King John, I 1 line 70; King John, I 1 line 137; King John, II 1 line 456; King John, II 1 line 457r; King John, II 1 line 476; King John, II 1 line 488; King John, II 1 lines 546, 558; King John, III 1 line 1110; King John, II 1 line 1168; King John, III 4 lines 1461, 1465; King John, III 4 line 1478; King John, III 4 line 1479; King John, IV 1 line 1720; King John, IV 2 line 1810; King John, IV 2 line 1817; King John, IV 2 line 1826; King John, IV 2 line 2003; King John, IV 3 line 2152; King John, IV 3 line 2186; King John, V 2 line 2303.
King Lear, I 1 line 59; King Lear, I 2 line 436; King Lear, I 2 line 466; King Lear, I 4 line 785; King Lear, I 4 lines 809, 816; King Lear, II 1 line 1044; King Lear, II 4 lines 1326, 1328; King Lear, II 4 line 1464; King Lear, II 4 line 1515; King Lear, III 2 line 1693; King Lear, III 4 line 1978; King Lear, III 6 line 2114; King Lear, III 7 line 2195; King Lear, III 7 line 2203; King Lear, IV 7 line 2928; King Lear, IV 7 line 2989.
Love's Labour's Lost, I 1 line 175; Love's Labour's Lost, I 1 line 260; Love's Labour's Lost, I 2 line 371; Love's Labour's Lost, I 2 line 396; Love's Labour's Lost, III 1 line 765; Love's Labour's Lost, IV 2 line 1306; Love's Labour's Lost, IV 3 line 1416; Love's Labour's Lost, V 1 line 1793; Love's Labour's Lost, V 2 line 2561; Love's Labour's Lost, V 2 line 2616; Love's Labour's Lost, V 2 line 2701.
Macbeth, I 3 line 188; Macbeth I 3 line 229; Macbeth, I 4 line 304; Macbeth, I 7 line 554; Macbeth, II 2 line 716; Macbeth, IV 1 line 1638; Macbeth, IV 1 line1650; Macbeth, IV 3 line 1873; Macbeth, IV 3 line 1974; Macbeth, IV 3 line 2048; Macbeth, IV 3 line 2090; Macbeth, IV 3 line 2091; Macbeth, IV 3 line 2099; Macbeth, V 7 line 2453.

Measure for Measure, I 2 line 163; Measure for Measure, I 2 line 182; Measure for Measure, I 2 line 247; Measure for Measure, I 3 line 315; Measure for Measure, I 4 line 380; Measure for Measure, I 4 line 397; Measure for Measure, II 1 line 540; Measure for Measure, II 1 line 550; Measure for Measure, II 1 line 616; Measure for Measure, II 3 line 977; Measure for Measure, III 2 lines 1708, 1709; Measure for Measure, IV 3 line 2298; Measure for Measure, V 1 line 2957.
Merchant of Venice, I 1 line 151; Merchant of Venice, II 2 line 642; Merchant of Venice, II 2 line 650; Merchant of Venice, II 3 line 793; Merchant of Venice, III 5 line 1842; Merchant of Venice, III 5 line 1877.
Merry Wives of Windsor, II 2 line 919; Merry Wives of Windsor, III 4 line 1702; Merry Wives of Windsor, III 4 line 1729; Merry Wives of Windsor, IV 1 line 1930; Merry Wives of Windsor, IV 1 line 1945; Merry Wives of Windsor, IV 1 line 1947; Merry Wives of Windsor, IV 4 line 2263; Merry Wives of Windsor, IV 4 line 2265; Merry Wives of Windsor, IIV 5 line 2587.
Midsummer Night's Dream, I 1 lines 27, 31, 33; Midsummer Night's Dream, I 1 line 164; Midsummer Night's Dream, I 1 line 249; Midsummer Night's Dream, II 1 line 390; Midsummer Night's Dream, II 1 line 481; Midsummer Night's Dream, II 1 line 492; Midsummer Night's Dream, III 2 line 1242; Midsummer Night's Dream, III 2 line 1472; Midsummer Night's Dream, IV 1 line 1607; Midsummer Night's Dream, IV 1 line 1726; Midsummer Night's Dream, V 1 line 1965; Midsummer Night's Dream, V 1 line 2265.
Much Ado About Nothing, I 1 line 96; Much Ado About Nothing, I 1 line 266; Much Ado About Nothing, III 2 line 1204; Much Ado About Nothing, III 3 line 1382; Much Ado About Nothing, III 2 line 1385; Much Ado About Nothing, IV 1 line 1719; Much Ado About Nothing, V 1 line 2076; Much Ado About Nothing, V 1 line 2101; Much Ado About Nothing, V 1 lines 2136, 2140; Much Ado About Nothing, V 1 line 2153; Much Ado About Nothing, V 1 line 2336; Much Ado About Nothing, V 1 line 2363.
Othello, I 3 line 540; Othello, IV 2 line 2877.
Pericles, I 0 line 28; Pericles, I 1 line 117; Pericles, I 1 line 180; Pericles, I 4 line 523; Pericles, II 4 line 532; Pericles, II 2 line 754; Pericles, III 0 lines 1138, 1168; Pericles, III 1 line 1227; Pericles, III 1 line 1253; Pericles, III 3 line 1454; Pericles, III 3 line 1458; Pericles, IV 3 line 1819; Pericles, IV 3 line 1828; Pericles, IV 3 line 1850; Pericles, IV 4 line 1922; Pericles, V 1 line 2430; Pericles, V 3 lines 2525, 2526.
Rape of Lucerne, lines 325, 482, 576, 584, 836, 864, 1005r, 1145, 1804, 1807, 1876.
Richard II, I 3 line 539; Richard II, II 1 line 764; Richard II, II 1 line 936; Richard II, III 2 line 1416; Richard II, III 3 line 1729; Richard II, III 4 line 1894; Richard II, IV 1 line 2133rr.
Richard III, I 2 line 194; Richard III, I 2 lines 339,344; Richard III, I 3 line 605; Richard III, I 3 line 668; Richard III, I 4 line 905; Richard III, II 2 line 1270; Richard III, II 2 line 1287; Richard III, II 2 line 1296; Richard III, II 2 line 1328; Richard III, II 2 line 1427; Richard III, II 3 line 1444; Richard III, II 4 line 1520; Richard III, III 1 line 1624; Richard III,

III 5 line 2146; Richard III, III 7 line 2205; Richard III, III 7 line 2395; Richard III, III 7 line 2420; Richard III, IV 1 line 2511; Richard III, IV 3 line 2734; Richard III, IV 4 line 2888; Richard III, IV 4 line 2941; Richard III, IV 4 line 2994; Richard III, IV 4 line 3045; Richard III, IV 4 line 3051; Richard III, IV 4 line 3053; Richard III, IV 4 lines 3108, 3112; Richard III, IV 4 line 3195; Richard III, IV 4 lines 3204, 3207; Richard III, IV 4 line 3236; Richard III, V 1 line 3399; Richard III, V 1 line 3411; Richard III, V 3 lines 3768, 3769r.
Romeo and Juliet, Prologue 1 line 11; Romeo and Juliet, I 1 line 240; Romeo and Juliet, I 2 line 278; Romeo and Juliet, I 3 line 425; Romeo and Juliet, I 4 line 599; Romeo and Juliet, II 3 line 1069; Romeo and Juliet, III 1 line 1663; Romeo and Juliet, III 2 line 1748; Romeo and Juliet, III 3 line 1973; Romeo and Juliet, III 4 line 2071; Romeo and Juliet, III 5 line 2213; Romeo and Juliet, IV 5 line 2675; Romeo and Juliet, IV 5 lines 2721rr, 2722, 2723.
Sonnet II line 10; Sonnet VIII line 11; Sonnet IX line 8; Sonnet XVII line 13; Sonnet XXI line 11; Sonnet XXXVII line 2; Sonnet LIX line 4; Sonnet LXXVII line 11; Sonnet CXXIV line 1; Sonnet CXLIII line 5.
Taming of the Shrew, I 1 line 396; Taming of the Shrew, II 1 lines 1264, 1265; Taming of the Shrew, IV 3 line 2038; Taming of the Shrew, IV 5 line 2306; Taming of the Shrew, V 2 line 2690.
Tempest, I 1 line 74; Tempest, I 2 line 405; Tempest, I 2 line 500; Tempest, III 3 line 1650; Tempest, V 1 2253.
Timon of Athens, IV 1 line 1568; Timon of Athens, IV 3 line1867.
Titus Andronicus, II 3 line 851; Titus Andronicus, II 3 line 892; Titus Andronicus, II 3 line 968; Titus Andronicus, IV 2 line 1738; Titus Andronicus, IV 2 line 1777; Titus Andronicus, IV 2 line 1821; Titus Andronicus, IV 2 lines 1846, 1849; Titus Andronicus, V 1 line 2151; Titus Andronicus, V 1 line 2156; Titus Andronicus, V 1 line 2184; Titus Andronicus, V 1 line 2188; Titus Andronicus, V 1 line 2203; Titus Andronicus, V 3 lines 2658, 2659; Titus Andronicus, V 3 line 2710.
Troilus and Cressida, III 2 line 1772.
Two Gentlemen of Verona, III 1 lines 1140, 1145; Two Gentlemen of Verona, III 1 line 1194.
Venus and Adonis, lines 920, 1174.
Winter's Tale, I 1 line 21; Winter's Tale I 1 line 38; Winter's Tale I 2 line 253; Winter's Tale II 2 line 916; Winter's Tale II 3 line 956; Winter's Tale II 3 line 1009; Winter's Tale II 3 line 1061; Winter's Tale II 3 line 1093; Winter's Tale II 3 line 1159; Winter's Tale III 2 line 1319; Winter's Tale III 2 line 1469; Winter's Tale III 3 line 1486; Winter's Tale III 3 lines 1556, 1564; Winter's Tale III 3 line 1610; Winter's Tale IV 2 line 1682; Winter's Tale IV 4 line 2314; Winter's Tale V 1 line 2866; Winter's Tale IV 1 line 2967; Winter's Tale V 2 line 3113; Winter's Tale V 2 line 3169; Winter's Tale V 2 line 3179; Winter's Tale V 2 line 3236.

Chin: Old English: *cin, cinn*. Protruding part of the face, below the mouth.
As You Like It, I 2 line 204; As You Like It, III 2 line 1310; As You Like It, III 2 line 1314.

Comedy of Errors, III 2 line 886.
Coriolanus, II 2 line 1338.
Henry IV, Part I, i 3 line 359.
Henry IV, Part II, I 2 line 292; Henry IV, Part II, I 2 line 509; Henry IV, Part II, I 2 line 590.
Henry V, III 0 line 1075; Henry V, III 4 line 1363.
King Lear, III 7 line 2164; King Lear, III 7 line 2207.
Lover's Complaint, line 92.
Merchant of Venice, II 2 line 659; Merchant of Venice, III 2 line 1451.
Rape of Lucerne, lines 471, 523.
Tempest, II 1 line 982; Tempest, IV 1 line 1919.
Troilus and Cressida, I 2 line 263; Troilus and Cressida, I 2 line 286; Troilus and Cressida, I 2 line 289; Troilus and Cressida, I 2 line 290; Troilus and Cressida, I 2 line 299; Troilus and Cressida, I 2 line 305.
Twelfth Night, I 5 line 537; Twelfth Night, III 1 line 1281.
Venus and Adonis, lines 79, 105.
Winter's Tale, II 3 line 1054.

Choleric: mid-14c., *colrik: bilious of temperament or complexion*, from Old French: *colerique*. Meaning *easily angered, hot-tempered* is from 1580s (from the supposed effect of excess choler).
Comedy of Errors, II 2 line 455; Comedy of Errors, II 2 line 459.
Henry VI, Part II, I 2 line 324.
Julius Caesar, IV 3 line 2025.
King Lear, I 1 322.
Measure for Measure, II 2 897.
Pericles, IV 6 line 2108.
Taming of the Shrew, IV 1 line 1783; Taming of the Shrew, IV 3 line 1975; Taming of the Shrew, IV 3 1978.

Chough: Middle English, denoting a member of the crow family. The chough or jackdaw was one of the birds considered ominous.
All's Well That Ends Well, IV 1 line1920.
Hamlet, V 2 line 3744.
King Lear, IV 6 line2613.
Macbeth, III 4 1428.
Midsummer Night's Dream, III 2 line 1051.
Tempest, II 1 line 101.
Winter's Tale, IV 4 line 2571.

Chuck: a chicken, also a term of endearment.
Antony and Cleopatra, IV 4 line 2621.
Henry V, III 2 line 1152.
Love's Labour's Lost, V 1 line 1838; Love's Labour's Lost, V 2 line 2602.
Macbeth, III 2 1220.
Othello, III 4 line 2227; Othello, IV 2 line 2765.
Twelfth Night, III 4 line 1658.

Civet: a slender, nocturnal mammal with a spotted coat and powerful scent glands. 1530s, from French: *civette*.
> **As You Like it**, III 2 line 1178; As You Like It, III 2 line 1180.
> **King Lear**, IV 6 line 2739.
> **Much Ado About Nothing**, III 2 line 1244.

Claws: Old English:*clawu*. Also, *clapper-claw*: to claw with the nail (1590).
> **As you Like It**, V 2 line 2269.
> **Hamlet**, V 1 line 3414.
> **Henry Iv, Part II**, II 4 line 1547.
> **Love's Labour's Lost**, IV 2 line 1211r.
> **Merry Wives of Windsor**, II 3 line 1157; Merry Wives of Windsor, II 3 line 1158; Merry Wives of Windsor, II 3 line 1160.
> **Midsummer Night's Dream**, IV 2 line 1823.
> **Much Ado About Nothing**, I 3 line 445.
> **Rape of Lucerne**, line 594.
> **Troilus and Cressida**, V 4 line 3410.

Clay: stiff, sticky earth that can be moulded when wet. Old English:*clæg*, of West Germanic origin; related to Dutch: *klei*.
> **Antony and Cleopatra**, I 1 line 43.
> **Cymbeline**, IV 2 line 2320r.
> **Hamlet**, V 1 line 3437; Hamlet, V 1 line 3459; Hamlet, V 1 line 3541.
> **Henry IV, Part I**, II 4 line 1212.
> **Henry IV, Part II**, I 2 line 282.
> **Henry V**, IV 8 line 2834.
> **Henry VI, Part I**, II 5 1089.
> **Henry VI, Part II**, III 1 line 1596.
> **King John**, IV 3 line 2166; King John, V 7 line 2705.
> **King Lear**, I 4 line 833.
> **Rape of Lucerne**, line 660.
> **Richard II**, I 1 line184.
> **Sonnet** LXXI line 10.

Climate: late 14c., Scottish, from Old French: *climat*, from L. *clima: region, slope of the Earth*. The angle of sun on the slope of the Earth's surface defined the zones assigned by early geographers. Meaning moved from *region* to *weather associated with a region* by c.1600.
> **Henry V**, III 5 line 1406.
> **Julius Caesar**, I 3 line 453.
> **King John**, II 1 line 654.
> **Othello**, I 1 line 74.
> **Richard II**, IV 1 line 2114.
> **Tempest**, II 1 line 917.
> **Winter's Tale**, II 3 line 1145; Winter's Tale, III 1 line 1162; Winter's Tale, V 1 line 3027.

Clod: lump of earth or clay, Old English: *clod-* (in *clod-hamer: field-goer*). Meaning, person (mere lump of earth) is from 1590s; that of *blockhead* is from

c.1600. It also was a verb in Middle English: meaning both, to coagulate, form into clods and to break up clods after ploughing.
    King John, III 1 line 999; King John, V 7 line 2692.
    Measure for Measure, III 1 line 1356.
    Much Ado About Nothing, II 1 line 454.

Cloud: Old English: *clud: mass of rock*, related to *clod*. Metaphoric extension 13c. based on similarity of cumulus clouds and rock masses. Old English word for cloud was *weolcan*. In Middle English: *skie* also originally meant *cloud*. Also, the spot between the eyes of a horse.
    All's Well That End's Well, V 3 line 2714.
    Antony and Cleopatra, III 2 line 1655; Antony and Cleopatra, IV 14 line 2979; Antony and Cleopatra, V 2 line 3654; Antony and Cleopatra, V 2 line 3758.
    Coriolanus, III 1 line 1791; Coriolanus, IV 5 line 2871.
    Hamlet, I 2 line 268; Hamlet, I 2 line 329; Hamlet, III 2 line 2253; Hamlet, IV 5 2950; Hamlet, IV 5 line 2971.
    Henry IV, Part I, I 2 line 301; Henry Iv, Part I, III 2 line 1906; Henry IV, Part I, IV 1 line 2334.
    Henry IV, Part II, I 3 line 666; Henry IV, Part II, II 2 line 1113; Henry IV, Part II, III 1 line 1728; Henry IV, Part II, IV 5 line 2994.
    Henry V, III 3 lines 1303, 1312; Henry V, III 5 line 1398.
    Henry VI, Part II, II 1 line 741: Henry VI, Part II, II 4 line 1157; Henry VI, Part II, III 1 line 1436; Henry VI, Part II, III 2 line2079.
    Henry VI, Part III, II 1 line 653; Henry VI, Part III, II 3 line 1033; Henry VI, Part III, II 5 line 1104; Henry VI, Part III, II 6 line 1315; Henry VI, Part III, IV 1 line 2049; Henry VI, Part III, V 3 line 2781; Henry VI, Part III, V 3 lines 2787, 2790.
    Henry VIII, I 1 line 309; Henry VIII, V 5 line 3428.
    Julius Caesar, I 3 line 429; Julius Caesar, II 1 line 627; Julius Caesar, II 1 line 722; Julius Caesar, II 2 line 1004; Julius Caesar, V 3 line 2574.
    King John, II 1 line 553.
    Love's Labour's Lost, V 2 line 2095; Love's Labour's Lost, V 2 lines 2096r; 2098; Love's Labour's Lost, V 2 line 2211; Love's Labour's Lost, V 2 line 2662; Love's Labour's Lost, V 2 line 2689.
    Macbeth, III 4 line 1410; Macbeth, III 5 line 1506; Macbeth, III 6 line 1535.
    Midsummer Night's Dream, III 2 line 1436.
    Much Ado About Nothing, V 4 line 2590.
    Othello, II 1 line 775.
    Passionate Pilgrim, line 313.
    Pericles, I 1 line 122; Pericles, I 4 line 440; Pericles, II 2 line 792; Pericles, III 1 line 1242.
    Rape of Lucerne, lines 166, 422, 424, 598, 827, 1058, 1135, 1275, 1422, 1778.
    Richard II, I 1 line 45; Richard II, III 1 line 1380; Richard II, III 2 line 1477; Richard II, III 3 lines1685, 1695; Richard III, 3 line 1727.

Richard III, I 1 line 3; Richard III, I 3 lines 659, 660; Richard IIII, I 3 line 735; Richard III, II 2 line 1385; Richard III, II 3 line 1465; Richard III, V 4 line 3404.
Romeo and Juliet, I 1 line 153r; Romeo and Juliet, II 2 line 878; Romeo and Juliet, II 3 line 1060; Romeo and Juliet, III 1 line 1625; Romeo and Juliet, III 2 line 1722; Romeo and Juliet, III 5 line 2105; Romeo and Juliet, III 5 line 2311; Romeo and Juliet, IV 5 line 2733.
Sonnet XXVIII line 10; Sonnet XXXIII line 5; Sonnet XXXIV line 3; Sonnet XXXIV line 5; Sonnet XXXV line 3.
Taming of the Shrew, I 2 line 644; Taming of the Shrew, IV 3 line 2132.
Tempest, I 2 line 310; Tempest, II 1 line 848; Tempest, II 2 lines 1104, 1107; Tempest, III 2 line 1539; Tempest, IV 1 line 1806; Tempest, IV 1 line 1883.
Timon of Athens, II 2 line 863; Timon of Athens, III 4 line 1212.
Titus Andronicus, I 1 line 290; Titus Andronicus, II 3 line 766; Titus Andronicus, II 4 line 1096; Titus Andronicus, III 1 line 1351.
Troilus and Cressida, I 2 line 276; Troilus and Cressida, IV 5 line 2844.
Two Gentlemen of Verona, I 3 line 392.
Venus and Adonis, lines 511, 554, 747, 842, 994.
Winter's Tale, I 2 line 382.

Cloven: split in two, usually referring to the hoof; such as the goat. Old English: *cleofan*, of Germanic origin; related to Dutch: *klieven* and German: *klieben*.
    Coriolanus, I 4 line 509.
    Love's Labour's Lost, V 2 line 2590.
    Tempest, I 2 line 413; Tempest, II 2 line 1093.
    Troilus and Cressida, I 2 line 270; Troilus and Cressida, I 2 line 271.

Clover: or honey-stalks. It was not uncommon for cattle to overcharge themselves with clover and die. Old English: *clafre*. First reference in English to the supposed luck of a four-leaf clover is from c.1500.
    Henry V, V 2 line 330.

Cloy: weary by too much, fill to loathing, surfeit, 1520s, from Middle English *cloyen* hinder movement, encumber (late 14c.), a shortening of *accloyen* (early 14c.), from Old French *encloer*: to fasten with a nail, grip, grasp, figuratively, to hinder, check, stop, curb, from Late Latin *inclavare*: drive a nail into a horse's foot when shoeing, from Latin *clavus* a nail. The meaning fill to a satiety, overfill is attested for accloy from late 14c.
    Antony and Cleopatra, II 2 line 964.
    Richard II, I 3 line 597.
    Richard III, IV 4 line 2857.
    Venus and Adonis, line 39.

Coal: Old English: *col: charcoal, live coal*. Meaning *mineral consisting of fossilized carbon* is from mid-13c. Traditionally good luck, coal was given as a

New Year's gift in England, said to guarantee a warm hearth for the coming year. The phrase drag (or rake) over the coals was a reference to the treatment meted out to heretics by Christians. To carry coals *do dirty work*, also *submit to insult* is from 1520s. To carry coals to Newcastle (c.1600).
    Coriolanus, I 1 line 174; Coriolanus, IV 6 line 3186; Coriolanus, V 1 line 3297.
    Henry IV, Part II, II 1 814.
    Henry V, III 2 line 1175; Henry V, III 6 line 1570.
    Henry VI, Part II, II 1 line 858; Henry VI, Part II, V 2 line 3251.
    Henry VI, Part III, II 1 line 710; Henry VI, Part III, V 1 line 2650.
    Henry VIII, II 4 line 1441; Henry VIII, II 4 line 1457.
    King John, IV 1 line 1698; King John, V 2 line 2363.
    Merchant of Venice, III 5 line 1864.
    Merry Wives of Windsor, I 4 line 412.
    Pericles, III 0 line 1123.
    Rape of Lucerne, lines 98, 1060, 1431.
    Richard II, V 1 line 2383.
    Romeo and Juliet, I 1 line 16.
    Titus Andronicus, III 2 line 1525; Titus Andronicus, IV 2 line 1789; Titus Andronicus, V 1 line 2165.
    Troilus and Cressida, II 3 line 1418.
    Venus and Adonis, lines 55, 358, 407, 554.
    Winter's Tale, V 1 line 2903.

Cobweb: old, dusty spider's web. Middle English: *coppeweb, copweb*, from obsolete *coppe* meaning, *spider*.
    Merchant of Venice, III 2 line 1492.
    Midsummer Night's Dream, III 1 line 982; Midsummer Night's Dream, III 1 line 983; Midsummer Night's Dream, III 1 line 1006; Midsummer Night's Dream, III 1 line 1008; Midsummer Night's Dream, IV 1 line 1543; Midsummer Night's Dream, IV 1 line 1544; Midsummer Night's Dream, IV 1 line 1554; Midsummer Night's Dream, IV 1 line 1566.
    Taming of the Shrew, IV 1 line 1657.

Cock: notion which represents the cock as crowing all night long on Christmas Eve, and by its vigilance dispelling every kind of malignant spirit and evil influence. For the time being, mankind is said to be released from the influence of all those evil forces which otherwise exert such sway. The notion that spirits fly at cock-crow is very ancient. In Shakespeare, the word cock was used as a vulgar corruption or purposed disguise of the name of God.
    Antony and Cleopatra, II 3 line 1022.
    As You Like It, II 7 line 987.
    Cymbeline, II 1 line 872; Cymbeline, II 1 lines 874, 875.
    Hamlet, I 1 line 158; Hamlet, I 1 line 170; Hamlet, I 1 line 173; Hamlet, I 1 line 180; Hamlet, I 2 line 429; Hamlet, IV 5 line 2923.
    Henry IV, Part I, II 1 line 660.
    Henry IV, Part II, V 1 line 3140.

Henry V, II 1 line 557; Henry V, IV 0 line 1802; Henry V, V 1 line 2901; Henry V, V 1 line 2903.
King Lear, III 2 line 1680; King Lear,III 4 line 1911; King Lear, IV 6 line 2619r.
Macbeth, II 3 line 785.
Merry Wives of Windsor, I 1 line 282.
Midsummer Night's Dream, II 1 line 646; Midsummer Night's Dream, III 1 line 946.
Passionate Pilgrim, line 339.
Richard III, V 3 line 3712.
Romeo and Juliet, IV 4 line 2616.
Taming of the Shrew, II 1 line 1076; Taming of the Shrew, II 1 line 1077; Taming of the Shrew, IV 1 line 1717.
Tempest, II 1 line 735.
Two Gentlemen of Verona, II 1 line 425.
Winter's Tale, IV 3 line 1760; Winter's Tale, IV 4 line 2722.

Cockerel: see Cock.
Tempest, II 1 line 736.

Cockscomb: c.1400, comb or crest of a cock. Meaning *cap worn by a professional fool* is from 1560s; hence *conceited fool* (1560s), a sense passing into the derivative coxcomb. As a plant name, from 1570s.
Merry Wives of Windsor, III 1 line 1276

Cock-pigeon: the male of the species. Old English: *cocc*, from medieval Latin: *coccus*; reinforced in Middle English by Old French: *coq*.
As You Like It, IV 1 line 1923.

Cockle: flowering weed that grows in wheat fields, Old English *coccel*: darnel, used in Middle English to translate the Bible word now usually given as *tares*. Also, burrowing bivalve mollusc. Middle English, from Old French: *coquille: shell*, based on Greek: *konkhulion*, from *konkhē: conch*. The badge of a pilgrim was formerly a cockleshell, which was worn usually in the front of the hat. The scallop was sometimes used, and either of them was considered as an emblem of the pilgrim's intention to go beyond the sea.
Coriolanus, III 1 line 1815.
Hamlet, IV 5 line 2885.
Love's Labour's Lost, IV 3 line 1682; Love's Labour's Lost, IV 3 line 1728.
Pericles, IV 4 line 1876.
Taming of the Shrew, IV 3 line 2029.

Codling: an apple, which was the popular term for an immature apple, such as would require cooking to be eaten, being derived from *coddle*, to stew or boil lightly, hence it denoted a boiling apple, an apple for coddling or boiling. An involucrum or kell, and was used for that early state of vegetation, when the fruit, after shaking off the blossom, began to assume a globular and

determinate form. Late Middle English: from Anglo-Norman French *quer de lion*: *lionheart*.
    Twelfth Night, I 5 line 450.

Colt: young, uncastrated, male horse. Old English; perhaps related to Swedish: *kult*, applied to boys or half-grown animals. From its wild tricks, the colt was formerly used to designate, youthful energy.
    Cymbeline, II 4 line 1341.
    Henry IV, Part I, II 2 line 778; Henry IV, Part I, II 2 line 779r.
    Henry VIII, I 3 line 627.
    Love's Labour's Lost, III 1 line 793.
    Merchant of Venice, I 2 line 233; Merchant of Venice, V 1 line 2528.
    Midsummer Night's Dream, V 1 line 1962.
    Richard II, II 1 line 754.
    Tempest, IV 1 line 1911.
    Venus and Adonis, line 439.

Columbine: This was anciently termed a *thankless flower*, and was also emblematical of forsaken lovers, c.1300, from Old French: *columbine*; of Latin: *columbinus*, literally, dove-like, from *columba*: *dove*. The inverted flower supposedly resembles a cluster of five doves.
    Hamlet, IV 5 line 3056.
    Love's Labour's Lost, V 2 line 2598.

Comet: c.1200, from Old French: *comete* (12c), from Latin: *cometa*, from Greek: *kometes: long-haired* (star). So called from resemblance of a comet's tail to streaming hair. From the earliest times comets have been superstitiously regarded, and ranked among omens. Thus Thucydides tells us, that the Peloponnesian war was heralded by an abundance of earthquakes and comets; and Virgil, in speaking of the death of Caesar, declares that at no other time did comets and other supernatural prodigies appear in greater numbers.
    Henry IV, Part I, III 2 line 1870.
    Henry VI, Part I, I 1 line 6; Henry VI, Part I, I 4 line 560; Henry VI, Part I, II 1 line 719; Henry VI, Part I, III 2 line 1477.
    Julius Caesar, II 2 line 1006.
    Pericles, V 1 line 2279.
    Taming of the Shrew, III 2 line 1455.

Coney: c.1200, from Anglo-French: *conis*, long-eared rabbit (*Lepus cunicula*) from Latin: *cuniculus*. Rabbit arose 14c. to mean the young of the species, but gradually pushed out the older word after British slang picked up coney as a punning synonym for *cunny: cunt* (*connyfogle:* to deceive in order to win a woman's sexual favors). The word was in the King James Bible [Prov. xxx:26, etc.], however, so it couldn't be entirely dropped, and the solution was to change the pronunciation of the original short vowel (rhyming with honey, money) to rhyme with boney. In the Old Testament the word translates from: *shaphan: rock-badger*. Rabbits not being native to northern Europe, there was no Germanic or Celtic word for them.

As You Like It, III 2 line 1429.

Conger: 1300c. From Latin: *conger: sea eel.*
   Henry IV, Part II, II 4 line 1298; Henry IV, Part II, II 4 line 1527.

Constellation: early 14c., from Old French *constellacion:* constellation, conjuncture (of planets), from Late Latin *constellationem* from *constellatus.* Originally in astrology, of position of planets (stars) in regard to one another on a given day, usually one's birth day, as a determination of one's character. Modern astronomical sense is from 1550s.
   Twelfth Night, II 4 line 283.

Coppice: woodland of trees and shrubs of managed growth and regrowth. late Middle English: from Old French: *copeiz,* based on medieval Latin: *colpus: a blow.*
   Love's Labour's Lost, IV 1 line 980.

Coral: c.1300, from Old French: *coral* (12c) from Latin: *corallium,* from Greek: *korallion;* originally just the red variety found in the Mediterranean, hence use of the word as a symbol of red.
   Passionate Pilgrim, line 367.
   Rape of Lucerne, lines 471, 1285.
   Sonnet CXXX line 2.
   Taming of the Shrew, I 1 line 465.
   Tempest, I 2 line 561.
   Venus and Adonis, line 563.

Corn: a cereal crop seed; also, a painful growth of hardened skin, usually on the foot. Old English, of Germanic origin; related to Dutch: *koren* and German: *korn.*
   Coriolanus, I 1 line 9; Coriolanus, I 1 line 191; Coriolanus, I 1 line 214; Coriolanus, I 1 line 270; Coriolanus, II 3 line 1438; Coriolanus, III 1 line 1781; Coriolanus, III 1 line 1805; Coriolanus, III 1 line 1870; Coriolanus, III 1 lines 1879, 1884.
   Henry IV, Part II, IV 1 line 2402.
   Henry VI, Part I, III 2 line 1444; Henry VI, Part I, III 2 line 1455; Henry VI, Part I, III 2 line 1494; Henry VI, Part I, III 2 line 1500.
   Henry VI, Part II, I 2 line 274; Henry VI, Part II, III 2 line 1860.
   Henry VI, Part III, V 7 line 3098.
   Henry VIII, V 1 line 2916; Henry VIII, V 5 line 3415.
   King Lear, III 2 1708; King Lear, III 6 line 2046; King Lear, IV 4 line
   Love's Labour's Lost, I 1 line 98; Love's Labour's Lost, IV 3 line 1728.
   Macbeth, IV 1 line 1607.
   Midsummer Night's Dream, II 1 line 436; Midsummer Night's Dream, II 1 line 463.
   Pericles, I 4 line 515; Pericles, III 3 line 1443.
   Rape of Lucerne, line 332.
   Richard II, II 1 line 847; Richard II, III 3 line 1804.

Tempest, II 1 line 862.
Titus Andronicus, II 3 line 861; Titus Andronicus, V 3 line 2609.

Corpse: a corpse. Middle English: from Old French *cors: body*, from Latin: *corpus*.
Henry IV, Part I, I 1 line 44.
Henry IV, Part II, I1 line 250.
Henry VI, Part I, II 2 line 773.
Henry VI, Part II, III 2 line 1814.
Julius Caesar, III 2 line 1596; Julius Caesar, III 2 line 1702.
Pericles, III 1 line 1259.
Richard III, I 2 line 172; Richard III, V 3 line 3773.
Titus Andronicus, V 1 line 2240.
Twelfth Night, II 4 line 958.
Winter's Tale, V 1 line 2889.

Cormorant: sea bird: early 14c., from Old French: *cormarenc*.
The proverbial voracity of this bird gave rise to a man of large appetite being likened to it, a sense in which Shakespeare employs the word.
Coriolanus, I 1 line 115.
Love's Labour's Lost, I 1 line 6.
Richard II, II 1 line 720.
Troilus and Cressida, II 2 line 995.

Costard: late 13c., coster, perhaps from Anglo-French: *coste: rib* (from Latin: *costa*). A kind of large apple with prominent ribs, i.e. one having a shape more like a green pepper than a plain, round apple. Also applied derisively to the head. Common 14c.-17c. but limited to fruit-growers afterward.
King Lear, IV 6 line 2861.
Love's Labour's Lost, I 1 line 184; Love's Labour's Lost, I 1 line 186; Love's Labour's Lost, I 1 line 223; Love's Labour's Lost, I 1 line 253; Love's Labour's Lost, I 2 line 416; Love's Labour's Lost, I 2 line 423; Love's Labour's Lost, I 2 line 424; Love's Labour's Lost, I 2 line 462; Love's Labour's Lost, III 1 line 832; Love's Labour's Lost, III 1 line 833; Love's Labour's Lost, III 1 line 868; Love's Labour's Lost, III 1 line 874; Love's Labour's Lost, III 1 line 877; Love's Labour's Lost, III 1 line 881; Love's Labour's Lost, III 1 line 896; Love's Labour's Lost, III 1 line 907; Love's Labour's Lost, IV 1 line 1014; Love's Labour's Lost, IV 1 line 1140; Love's Labour's Lost, IV 2 line 1229; Love's Labour's Lost, IV 2 line 1238; Love's Labour's Lost, IV 2 line 1293; Love's Labour's Lost, IV 2 line 1295; Love's Labour's Lost, IV 3 line 1522; Love's Labour's Lost, IV 3 line 1535; Love's Labour's Lost, IV 3 line 1544; Love's Labour's Lost, IV 3 line 1557; Love's Labour's Lost, V 1 line 1766; Love's Labour's Lost, V 1 line 1772; Love's Labour's Lost, V 2 line 2413; Love's Labour's Lost, V 2 line 2480; Love's Labour's Lost, V 2 line 2523; Love's Labour's Lost, V 2 line 2836.
Merry Wives of Windsor, III 1 line 1204.
Richard III, I 4 line 982.

Country: mid-13c., district, native land, from Old French: *contree*. Sense narrowed 1520s to rural areas, as opposed to cities. Replaced Old English: *land*. As an adjective from late 14c.

All's Well That Ends Well, III 2 line 1410; All's Well That Ends Well, III 2 line 1513; All's Well That Ends Well, III 5 line 1658; All's Well That Ends Well, IV 3 line 2350; All's Well That Ends Well, IV 3 line 2405; All's Well That Ends Well, V 3 line 2840.

Antony and Cleopatra, IV 14 line 3076; Antony and Cleopatra, IV 15 line 3233; Antony and Cleopatra, V 2 line 3457; Antony and Cleopatra, V 2 line 3817.

As You Like It, II 1 line 609; As You Like It, III 2 lines 1163, 1164; As You Like It, III 2 line 1229; As You Like It, IV 1 1827; As You Like It, V 3 line 2384; As You Like It, V 4 line 2457.

Comedy of Errors, I 1 lines 9, 14.

Coriolanus, I 1 line 25; Coriolanus, I 1 line 31; Coriolanus, I 1 line 47; Coriolanus, I 3 line 387; Coriolanus, I 6 line 701; Coriolanus, I 9 line 784; Coriolanus, II 2 line 1248; Coriolanus, II 2 line 1270; Coriolanus, II 3 line 1478; Coriolanus, II 3 line 1521; Coriolanus, II 3 line 1607; Coriolanus, II 3 line 1689; Coriolanus, III 1 line 1824; Coriolanus, III 1 line 2001; Coriolanus, III 1 lines 2014, 2015; Coriolanus, III 1 line 2119; Coriolanus, III 3 line 2482; Coriolanus, III 3 line 2489; Coriolanus, IV 2 line 2631; Coriolanus, IV 3 line 2697; Coriolanus, IV 4 line 2747; Coriolanus, IV 5 lines 2835, 2852, 2857, 2865; Coriolanus, IV 5 line 2908; Coriolanus, V 1 lines 3318, 3320; Coriolanus, V 1 line 3364; Coriolanus, V 2 line 3450; Coriolanus, V 3 lines 3611, 3615, 3618, 3619, 3624, 3631; Coriolanus, V 3 line 3658; Coriolanus, V 6 line 3908.

Cymbeline, I 4 line 358; Cymbeline, I 4 line 375; Cymbeline, I 6 line 790; Cymbeline, II 4 line 1192; Cymbeline IV 3 line 2877; Cymbeline, IV 4 line 2940; Cymbeline, V 2 line 2995; Cymbeline, V 3 line 3042: Cymbeline, V 4 line 3218.

Hamlet, I 1 lines 142, 151; Hamlet, II 1 line 1000; Hamlet, III 1 line 1772; Hamlet, III 2 line 1997.

Henry IV, Part I, IV 3 line 2541.

Henry IV, Part II, IV 1 line 2342.

Henry V, II 2 line 826; Henry V, III 6 line 1574; Henry V, IV 0 lines 1803, 1822; Henry V, IV 1 line 2128; Henry V, IV 3 line 2256; Henry V, IV 6 line 2477; Henry V, IV 7 line 2627; Henry V, IV 7 line 2633; Henry V, V 2 line 3039; Henry V, V 2 lines 3254, 3258.

Henry VI, Part I, I 2 line 222; Henry VI, Part I, I 2 line 278; Henry VI, Part I, I 5 line 612; Henry VI, Part I, II 3 line 871; Henry VI, Part I, III 1 line 1368; Henry VI, Part I, III 2 line 1472; Henry VI, Part I, III 3 line 1648; Henry VI, Part I, III 3 lines 1654, 1664, 1667; Henry VI, Part I, III 3 line 1685; Henry VI, Part I, III 3 line 1691r; Henry VI, Part I, IV 1 line 1805; Henry VI, Part I, IV 1 line 1819; Henry VI, Part I, V 1 line 2382; Henry VI, Part I, V 1 line 2419; Henry VI, Part I, V 3 line 2622; Henry VI, Part I, V 4 line 2673; Henry VI, Part I, V 4 line 2779; Henry VI, Part I, V 4 line 2801.

Henry VI, Part II, I 1 line 217; Henry VI, Part II, I 3 line 557; Henry VI, Part II, II 3 line 1055; Henry VI, Part II, IV 5 line 2598; Henry VI, Part II, IV 7 line 2683; Henry VI, Part II, IV 7 line 2730; Henry VI, Part II, IV 8 line 2768; Henry VI, Part II, IV 9 line 2850; Henry VI, Part II, IV 9 line 2878; Henry VI, Part II, IV 10 line 2890.
Henry VI, Part III, II 5 line 1212; Henry VI, Part III, III 1 line 1442; Henry VI, Part III, III 3 line 1913; Henry VI, Part III, IV 6 line 2386; Henry VI, Part III, V 7 line 3131.
Henry VIII, I line 622; Henry VIII, III 1 line 1723; Henry VIII, III 2 2361.
Julius Caesar, I 1 line 56; Julius Caesar, II 1 line 741; Julius Caesar, III 1 line 1333; Julius Caesar, III 2 lines 1546, 1566; Julius Caesar, III 2 line 1591; Julius Caesar, III 2 line 1617; Julius Caesar, III 2 line 1736; Julius Caesar, III 2 line 1751; Julius Caesar, III 2 line 1778; Julius Caesar, V 1 line 2376; Julius Caesar, V 3 line 2355; Julius Caesar, V 4 line 2632; Julius Caesar, V 4 line 2636; Julius Caesar, V 4 line 2639; Julius Caesar, V 5 line 2711.
King John, I 1 line 49; King John, I 1 line 162.
King Lear, I 1 line 201; King Lear, II 3 line 1264.
Love's Labour's Lost, I 2 line 415; Love's Labour's Lost, III 1 line 892.
Macbeth, I 3 line 221; Macbeth, III 4 line 1323; Macbeth, III 6 line 1543; Macbeth, IV 3 line 1879; Macbeth, IV 3 line 1889; Macbeth, IV 3 line 1991; Macbeth, IV 3 line2025; Macbeth, IV 3 line 2031; Macbeth, V 2 line 2239; Macbeth, V 3 line 2288.
Measure for Measure, III 2 line 1726.
Merchant of Venice, II 8 line 1102; Merchant of Venice, III 2 line 1594; Merchant of Venice, III 2 line 1662.
Merry Wives of Windsor, I 1 line 203; Merry Wives of Windsor, V 5 line 2809.
Midsummer Night's Dream, III 2 line 1535.
Othello, I 3 line 438; Othello, II 3 line 1227; Othello, II 3 line 1453; Othello, III 3 line 1853; Othello, III 3 line 1895; Othello, IV 2 line 2891; Othello, V 1 line 3244.
Pericles, II 1 line 645; Pericles, II 3 line 856; Pericles, III 3 line 1443; Pericles, IV 6 line 1996; Pericles, IV 6 line 2067; Pericles, V 1 line 2297; Pericles, V 3 line 2523.
Rape of Lucerne, line 1889.
Richard II, I 3 line 429; Richard II, I 3 line 473; Richard II, I 4 line 647; Richard II, II 1 line 983; Richard II, II 3 line 1326; Richard II, II 4 line 1338; Richard II, IV 1 line 2081; Richard II, V 2 line 2462.
Richard III, I 3 line 569; Richard III, I 3 line 615; Richard III, III 7 line 2222; Richard III, III 7 line 2345; Richard III, V 3 lines 3744, 3764, 3765; Richard III, V 3 line 3834.
Romeo and Juliet, IV 1 line 2475.
Taming of the Shrew, I 1 line 491; Taming of the Shrew, I 2 line 738; Taming of the Shrew, IV 2 line 1860; Taming of the Shrew, IV 2 line 1910.
Tempest, IV 1 line 1860; Tempest, IV 1 line 1984; Tempest, V 1 line 2137.

Timon of Athens, IV 3 line 1786; Timon of Athens, V 1 line 2448; Timon of Athens, V 1 line 2453; Timon of Athens, V 1 line 2477; Timon of Athens, V 1 line 2481; Timon of Athens, V 4 line 2601.
Titus Andronicus, I 1 line 7; Titus Andronicus, I 1 line 64; Titus Andronicus, I 1 lines 91, 108; Titus Andronicus, I 1 line 129; Titus Andronicus, I 1 line 199; Titus Andronicus, I 1 lines 218, 221; Titus Andronicus, IV 1 line 1655; Titus Andronicus, IV 2 line 1844.
Troilus and Cressida, II 2 line 1088; Troilus and Cressida, IV 1 line 2271; Troilus and Cressida, IV 1 line 2272.
Twelfth Night, I 2 line 48; Twelfth Night, I 2 line 68; Twelfth Night, V 1 line 2431.
Two Gentlemen of Verona, II 4 line 704; Two Gentlemen of Verona, III 2 line 1463.
Winter's Tale, IV 2 line 1671; Winter's Tale, IV 2 line 1687; Winter's Tale, V 1 line 3052.

Cow: Old English: *cu* perhaps ultimately imitative of lowing. In Germanic and Celtic, of females only; in most other languages, of either gender.
  Antony and Cleopatra, III 10 line 2079.
  As You Like It, II 4 line 766.
  Henry VIII, V 4 line 3296.
  King John, I 1 line 130.
  Macbeth, V 8 line 2496.
  Much Ado About Nothing, II 1 line 419r; Much Ado About Nothing, V 4 line 2597.

Cowslips: primula with clusters of yellow, fragrant flowers, growing on grassy river banks. Old English: *cūslyppe*, from *cū*. From combination with slipa, slyppe, slime, i.e. cow slobber or dung.
  Cymbeline, I 5 line 590; Cymbeline, II 2 962.
  Henry V, V 2 line 3029.
  Midsummer Night's Dream, II 1 lines 378, 383; Midsummer Night's Dream, V 1 line 2177.
  Tempest, V 1 line 2118.

Crab: crustacean, Old English: *crabba*. The constellation name is attested in English from c.1000; French: *crabe* (13c.) is from Dutch. Also a fruit, see Apple.
  Coriolanus, II 1 line 1119.
  Hamlet, II 2 line 1306.
  Henry VI, Part II, III 2 line 1900.
  Henry VIII, V 4 line 3275.
  King Lear, I 5 line 892; King Lear, I 5 line 895r.
  Love's Labour's Lost, IV 2 line 1147; Love's Labour's Lost, V 2 line 2922.
  Measure for Measure, III 2 line 1609.
  Midsummer Night's Dream, II 1 line 416.
  Passionate Pilgrim, line 158.

Taming of the Shrew, II 1 line 1079; Taming of the Shrew, II 1 line 1080.
Tempest, II 2 line 1253; Tempest, III 1 line 1285.
Two Gentlemen of Verona, II 3 line 597; Two Gentlemen of Verona, II 3 line 634; Two Gentlemen of Verona, IV 4 line 1857.
Winter's Tale, I 2 line 175.

Craven: a dunghill cock.
Hamlet, IV 4 line 2829.
Henry V, IV 7 line 2654.
Henry VI, Part I, II 4 line 1019.
Taming of the Shrew, II 1 line 1077.

Cream: white or yellowish fatty liquid derived from milk. Middle English: from Old French: *cresme*, from a blend of late Latin: *cramum* (probably of Gaulish origin) and ecclesiastical Latin: *chrisma*.
As You Like It, III 5 line 1701.
Henry IV, Part I, IV 2 line 2428; Henry IV, Part I, IV 2 line 2429.
Macbeth, V 3 line 2258.
Merchant of Venice, I 1 line 95.
Winter's Tale, IV 4 line 2046.

Creature: an animal as distinct from a human. Middle English (in the sense *something created*): via Old French from late Latin: *creatura*, from the verb: *creare*.
All's Well That Ends Well, I 2 line 283; All's Well That Ends Well, I 3 line 355; All's Well That Ends Well, II 3 line 1042; All's Well That Ends Well, III 5 line 1682; All's Well That Ends Well, III 6 line 1842; All's Well That Ends Well, IV 1 line 1932; All's Well That Ends Well, V 3 line 2762; All's Well That Ends Well, V 3 line 2879.
Antony and Cleopatra, II 5 line 1152; Antony and Cleopatra, III 3 line 1741; Antony and Cleopatra, V 2 line 3489.
As You Like It, I 2 line 183.
Comedy of Errors, II 2 line 600; Comedy of Errors, III 2 line 795; Comedy of Errors, III 2 line 850; Comedy of Errors, V 1 line 1523.
Cymbeline, I 1 line 23; Cymbeline, I 5 line 513; Cymbeline, I 6 line 701; Cymbeline, III 2 line 1552; Cymbeline, IV 2 line 2354; Cymbeline, IV 2 line 2702; Cymbeline, V 5 line 3519; Cymbeline, V 5 line 3671.
Hamlet, II 2 line 1664; Hamlet, III 1 line 1837; Hamlet, III 2 line 2148; Hamlet, IV 3 line 2733; Hamlet, IV 7 line 3328.
Henry IV, Part I, II 4 line 1176; Henry IV, Part I, II 4 line 1313; Henry IV, Part I, V 5 line 3148.
Henry IV, Part II, II 2 line 957.
Henry V, I 2 line 334; Henry V, II 2 line 731; Henry V, III 7 line 1770.
Henry VI, Part I, I 6 line 632.
Henry VI, Part II, II 1 line 733.
Henry VI, Part III, II 2 line 868.

Henry VIII, I 2 line 509; Henry VIII, II 3 line 1272; Henry VIII, II 4 line 1603; Henry VIII, III 2 line 1872; Henry VIII, III 2 line 1891; Henry VIII, V 1 line 2807.
Julius Caesar, I 1 line 2; Julius Caesar, I 2 line 207; Julius Caesar, II 1 line 750; Julius Caesar, IV 1 line 1894.
King John, III 4 line 1567; King John, IV 1 line 1709.
King Lear, I 4 line 804; King Lear, II 4 line 1555; King Lear, III 4 line 1914; King Lear, IV 6 line 2763.
Measure for Measure, IV 3 line 2185.
Merchant of Venice, II 1 line 518; Merchant of Venice, III 2 1652.
Merry Wives of Windsor, II 2 line 849; Merry Wives of Windsor, III 4 line 1689; Merry Wives of Windsor, IV 1 line 1952; Merry Wives of Windsor, IV 2 line 2089.
Midsummer Night's Dream, II 1 line 544.
Much Ado About Nothing, I 1 line 63; Much Ado About Nothing, IV 1 line 1834.
Othello, II 3 line 1154; Othello, II 3 line 1462; Othello, III 3 line 1901; Othello, III 3 line 1930; Othello, III 3 line 2104; Othello, III 4 line 2198; Othello, IV 1 line 2522; Othello, IV 1 line 2615.
Passionate Pilgrim, line 136.
Pericles, I 4 line 432; Pericles, I 4 line 452; Pericles, III 2 line 1336; Pericles, III 2 line 1408; Pericles, IV 1 line 1555; Pericles, IV 1 line 1632; Pericles, IV 2 line 1673; Pericles, IV 6 line 1987; Pericles, IV 6 line 2018.
Rape of Lucerne, lines 1198, 1284, 1399, 1678.
Richard II, V 3 line 2591; Richard II, V 5 line 2751.
Richard III, I 2 line 312; Richard III, III 5 line 2091; Richard III, V 2 line 3452; Richard III, V 3 line 3702.
Romeo and Juliet, IV 5 line 2775; Romeo and Juliet, IV 5 line 2776; Romeo and Juliet, V 3 line 2990.
Sonnet I line 1; Sonnet CXIII line 10; Sonnet CXLIII line 2.
Taming of the Shrew, Prologue 2 line 211.
Tempest, I 2 line 91; Tempest, I 2 line 121; Tempest, I 2 line 182; Tempest, III 1 line 1307; Tempest, III 1 line 1335; Tempest, III 3 line 1653; Tempest, V 1 line 2234.
Timon of Athens, I 1 line 69; Timon of Athens, I 1 line 146; Timon of Athens, I 2 line 435; Timon of Athens, IV 3 line 1916.
Titus Andronicus, II 3 line 922; Titus Andronicus, III 2 line 1449.
Troilus and Cressida, III 3 line 1288.
Twelfth Night, II 4 line 908; Twelfth Night, V 1 line 2424.
Two Gentlemen of Verona, II 4 line 811.
Venus and Adonis, lines 698, 1027, 1103.
Winter's Tale, I 2 line 581; Winter's Tale II 1 line 700; Winter's Tale, III 2 line 1436; Winter's Tale, III 3 1500; Winter's Tale, III 3 line 1511; Winter's Tale, V 1 line 2953; Winter's Tale, V 2 line 3145.

Creek: 1550c., *creke: narrow inlet in a coastline*, altered from *kryk* (early 13c.; in place names from 12c.) perhaps influenced by Anglo-French: *crique*, itself from a Scandinavian source via Norman. Perhaps ultimately related to *crook*

and with an original notion of *full of bends and turns*. Extended to *inlet or short arm of a river* by 1570s.
    Comedy of Errors, IV 2 line 1114.
    Cymbeline, IV 2 line 2515.

Cricket: the insect, early 14c., from Old French: *criquet* (12c.) a cricket, from *criquer: to creak, rattle, crackle*, of echoic origin. he presence of crickets in a house has generally been regarded as a good omen, and said to prognosticate cheerfulness and plenty.
    Cymbeline, II 2 line 933.
    Henry IV, Part I, II 4 line 1079.
    Macbeth, II 2 line 666.
    Merry Wives of Windsor, V 5 line 2607.
    Pericles, III 0 line 1125.
    Romeo and Juliet, I 4 line 563.
    Taming of the Shrew, IV 3 line 2073.
    Winter's Tale, II 1 line 637.

Crocodile: According to fabulous accounts, the crocodile was the most deceitful of animals; its tears being proverbially fallacious. 1560s, restored spelling of Middle English: *cokedrille*, kokedrille (c.1300).
    Antony and Cleopatra, II 7 line 1403; Antony and Cleopatra, II 7 line 1419.
    Hamlet, V 1 line 3620.
    Henry VI, Part II, III 1 line 1510.
    Othello, IV 1 line 2688.

Crow: large perching bird with black, glossy plumage and a loud cry. Associated with death ad the aftermath of war, due to its attraction to carrion. Old English: *craw*, of West Germanic origin; related to Dutch: *kraai* and German: *Krähe*. This has from the earliest times been reckoned a bird of bad omen.
    All's Well That Ends Well, IV 3 line 2367.
    As You Like It, II 7 line 924.
    Comedy of Errors, III 1 line 715; Comedy of Errors, III 1 lines 716, 718r; Comedy of Errors, III 1 line 719.
    Coriolanus, III 1 line 1898; Coriolanus, IV 5 line 2799; Coriolanus, IV 5 line 2800.
    Cymbeline, I 3 line 289; Cymbeline, II 1 line 874; Cymbeline, III 1 line 1500; Cymbeline III 3 line 1615; Cymbeline, V 3 line 3127.
    Hamlet, I 1 line 158.
    Henry V, II 1 line 591; Henry V, IV 0 line 1803; Henry V, IV 2 line 2216.
    Henry VI, Part II, IV 10 line 2973; Henry VI, Part II, V 2 line 3220.
    Julius Caesar, V 1 2461.
    King John, V 2 line 2426.
    King Lear, IV 6 line 2613.
    Macbeth, III 2 line 1225.
    Merchant of Venice, V 1 line 2559.

Midsummer Night's Dream, II 1 466; Midsummer Night's Dream II 1 line 647; Midsummer Night's Dream, III 2 line 1180.
Much Ado About Nothing, I 1 line 118.
Pericles, IV 0 line 1525.
Phoenix and the Turtle, line 17.
Rape of Lucerne, line 1060.
Romeo and Juliet, I 2 line 364; Romeo and Juliet, I 5 line 670; Romeo and Juliet, IV 4 line 2616; Romeo and Juliet, V 2 line 2921; Romeo and Juliet, V 3 line 3071.
Sonnet LXX line 4; Sonnet CXIII line 12.
Taming of the Shrew, II 1 line 1077.
Tempest, II 1 line 734.
Troilus and Cressida, I 2 line 394r; Troilus and Cressida, IV 2 line 2297.
Venus and Adonis, line 344.
Two Gentlemen of Verona, II 1 line 425.
Winter's Tale, III 2 line 1426; Winter's Tale, IV 4 line 2110.

Crow-flower: This name, which in Shakespeare's time was applied to the *ragged robin*, is now used for the buttercup.
Hamlet, IV 7 line 3318.

Crystal: Old English: *cristal: clear ice, clear mineral,* from Old French: *cristal* (12c), from Latin: *crystallus*: crystal, ice, from Greek: *krystallos*, from *kryos*: frost. Spelling adopted the Latin form 15c.-17c. The mineral has been so-called since Old English; it was regarded by the ancients as a sort of fossilised ice. As a shortened form of crystal-glass it dates from 1590s. As an adjective, from late 14c.
Cymbeline, V 4 line 3228; Cymbeline, V 4 line 3252.
Henry IV, Part I, II 4 line 1054.
Henry V, II 3 line 884.
Henry VI, Part I, I 1 line 7.
King John, II 1 469.
Love's Labour's Lost, II 1 843; Love's Labour's Lost, IV 3 line 1470.
Lover's Complaint, lines 37, 288.
Midsummer Night's Dream, III 2 line 1177.
Rape of Lucerne, line 1302.
Richard II, I 1 line 44.
Romeo and Juliet, I 2 line 373.
Sonnet XLVI line 6.
Two Gentlemen of Verona, II 4 line 740.
Venus and Adonis, lines 511, 654, 979, 985.

Cuckoo: mid-13c., from Old French: *cocu: cuckoo*, also *cuckold*, echoic of the male bird's mating cry. Noun meaning *stupid person* is first recorded 1580s, perhaps from the bird's unvarying, oft-repeated call. The Old English name was *geac*. Many superstitions have clustered round the cuckoo, and is looked upon as a mysterious bird, being supposed to possess the gift of second sight. The notion which couples the name of the cuckoo with the character of the man whose wife is unfaithful to him, appears to have been derived from the Romans, and is first found in the middle ages in France, and in the countries of which the modern language is derived from the Latin. But the ancients more correctly gave the name of the bird, not to the husband of the faithless wife, but to her paramour, who might justly be supposed to be acting the part of the cuckoo. They applied the name of the bird in whose nest the cuckoo's eggs were usually deposited, *carruca*, to the husband. It is not quite clear how, in the passage from classic to medieval, the application of the term was transferred to the husband.

All's Well That Ends Well, I 3 line 382.
Antony and Cleopatra, II 6 line 1243.
Henry IV, Part I, II 4 line 1338; Henry IV, Part I, III 2 line 1898; Henry IV, Part I, V 1 line 2683.
King Lear, I 4 line 737.
Love's Labour's Lost, V 2 line 2832; Love's Labour's Lost, V 2 lines 2840, 2847, 2848, 2849r.
Merchant of Venice, V 1 line 2571.
Merry Wives of Windsor, II 1 line 684.
Midsummer Night's Dream, III 1 line 953.
Rape of Lucerne, line 900.

Cuckoo-buds: or pile-wort, this flower appears earlier in spring.
Love's Labour's Lost, V 2 line 2845.

Cuckoo-flowers (see Cuckoo-bud): By this flower, the *ragged robin* is also (see Crow-flower) meant, a well-known meadow and marsh plant, with rose-coloured flowers and deeply-cut narrow segments. It blossoms at the time the cuckoo comes, hence one of its names.
King Lear, IV 4 line 2519.

Curds: white creamy fat that forms when milk coagulates. Late Middle English: of unknown origin. c.1500, metathesis of crud (late 14c.), originally *any coagulated substance*, probably from Old English: *crudan: to press, drive*.
All's Well That End's Well, I 3 line 468.
Cymbeline, V 3 line 3567.
Hamlet, I 5 line 807.
Henry VI, Part III, II 5 line 1159.
Titus Andronicus, IV 2 line 1874.
Winter's Tale, IV 4 line 2046.

Current: c.1300, *running, flowing*, from Old French: *corant: running, lively, eager, swift*. Meaning *prevalent, generally accepted* is from 1560s.
Coriolanus, III 1 line 1850.
Hamlet, III 1 line 1781; Hamlet, III 3 line 2339; Hamlet, V 2 line 4019.
Henry IV, Part I, I 3 line 394; Henry IV, Part I, I 3 line 523; Henry IV, Part I, II 1 line 695; Henry IV, Part I, II 3 line 914; Henry IV, Part I, III 1 line 1644; Henry IV, Part I, IV 1 line 2024.
Henry IV, Part II, II 1 line 860.
Henry VIII, I 3 line 626.
Julius Caesar, IV 3 2234.

King John, II 1 line 645; King John, II 1 line 752.
Lover's Complaint, line 286.
Measure for Measure, III 1 line 1483.
Merchant of Venice, IV 1 line 1996.
Othello, III 3 line 2140; Othello, IV 2 line 2808.
Rape of Lucerne, line 1620.
Richard II, I 3 line 531; Richard II, III 3 line 1749; Richard II, V 3 line 2641; Richard II, V 3 line 2707.
Richard III, I 2 line 259; Richard III, i 3 line 723; Richard III, II 1 line 1219; Richard III, II 2 line 1340; Richard III, IV 2 line 2591.
Timon of Athens, I 1 line 34.
Two Gentlemen of Verona, II 7 line 1000.

Cuttle: reference to the squid or cuttlefish. Due to the practice of squirting ink, the word is used to describe a person who is foul mouthed. Old English: *cudele*.
Henry IV, Part II, II 4 line 1388.

Cygnet: c.1400, also signet before 17c., from Old French: *cigne, cisne*: swan.
Henry IV, Part I, V 3 line 2515.
King John, V 7 line 2652.
Troilus and Cressida, I 1 line 88.

Cypress: type of evergreen tree (sacred to Pluto), late 12c., from Old French: *cipres* (12c.), from Latin: *cupressus*, from Greek: *kyparissos*, probably from an unknown pre-Greek Mediterranean language. From the earliest times the cypress has had a mournful history, being associated with funerals and churchyards. Formerly coffins were frequently made of cypress wood.
Coriolanus, I 10 line 910.
Henry VI, Part II, III 2 line 2017.
Taming of the Shrew, II 1 line 1204.
Twelfth Night, II 4 line 948; Twelfth Night, III 1 line 1358.

Daffodils: 1540s, variant of Middle English: *affodill: asphodel* (c.1400), from Latin: *asphodelus*, from Greek: *asphodelos*, of unknown origin. The initial d- is perhaps from merging of the article in Dutch: *de affodil*, the Netherlands being a source for bulbs. First reference to the flower we know by this name (Narcissus pseudo-Narcissus) is from 1590s. The daffodil of Shakespeare is the wild daffodil which grew abundantly in many parts of England.
Winter's Tale, IV 3 line 1724: Winter's Tale, IV 4 line 1997.

Daisied: covered in daisies. Old English: *dægesege*, from *dæges eage: day's eye*, because the petals open at dawn and close at dusk. In Medieval Latin it was *solis oculus: sun's eye*.
Cymbeline, IV 2 line 2817.

Dale: Old English: *dæl: dale, valley, gorge*. Preserved from extinction by Norse influence in north of England

Henry IV, Part II, IV 3 lines 2585, 2587; Henry IV, Part II, IV 3 line 2622.
Midsummer Night's Dream, II 1 line 369; Midsummer Night's Dream, II 1 line 452.
Passionate Pilgrim, line 356.
Rape of Lucerne, 1128.
Venus and Adonis, line 252.
Winter's Tale, IV 3 line 1725.

Darnel: a rye grass. Middle English: of unknown origin; apparently related to French (Walloon dialect) *darnelle*. This plant, like the cockle, was used in Shakespeare's day to denote any hurtful weed.
Henry V, V 2 line 3026.
Henry Vi, Part I, III 2 line 1497.
King Lear, IV 4 line 2520.

Dates: the fruit, late 13c., from Old French: *date*, from Greek: *daktylos*, originally *finger, toe*; so called because of fancied resemblance between oblong fruit of the date palm and human digits. This fruit of the palm-tree was once a common ingredient in all kinds of pastry, and some other dishes, and often supplied a pun for comedy.
All's Well That Ends Well, I 1 line 160.
Romeo and Juliet, IV 4 line 2614.
Sonnet CXXIII line 5.
Troilus and Cressida, I 2 line 405.
Winter's Tale, IV 3 line 1771.

Dawn: c.1200, *dauen*, to dawn, grow light, shortened or back-formed from *dauinge, dauing* period between darkness and sunrise, (c.1200), from Old English *dagung*, from *dagian* to become day, from root of *dæg*: day. Dawn suggests the notions of illumination and hope, the beginning of a new day and thus a chance for happiness and improvement. Sunrise is a symbol of birth and rebirth, of awakening. The coming of light, resurrection.
Henry V, IV 1 line 2119.
Measure for Measure, IV 2 line 2114.

Daws: early 15c., perhaps imitative of bird's cry.
Coriolanus, IV 5 line 2801.
Love's Labour's Lost, V 2 line 2853.
Othello, I 1 line 67.
Troilus and Cressida, I 2 line 394r.
Twelfth Night, III 4 line 1580.

Dead Men's Fingers: see Long Purples.
Hamlet, IV 7 line 3320.

Decay: late 15c., *to decrease*. Meaning *decline, deteriorate* is c.1500; that of *to decompose, rot* is from 1570s.
All's Well That Ends Well, V 2 line 2637.

Antony and Cleopatra, II 1 line 620.
Comedy of Errors, II 1 line 370; Comedy of Errors, IV 3 line 1175.
Coriolanus, III 1 line 1826; Coriolanus, V 2 line 3416.
Cymbeline, I 5 line 560.
Hamlet, V 1 line 3504.
Henry IV, Part II, I 1 line 223; Henry IV, Part II, IV 4 line 2814.
Henry VI, Part I, I 1 line 38; Henry VI, PartI, II 5 line 1076.
Henry VI, Part II, III 1 line 1475; Henry VI, Part II, IV 4 line 2258.
Julius Caesar, IV 2 line 1939.
King John, I 1 line 30; King John, IV 3 line 2184.
King Lear, V 3 line 3471; King Lear, V 3 line 3485.
Merchant of Venice, V 1 line 2518.
Merry Wives of Windsor, V 5 line 2718.
Passionate Pilgrim, line 182.
Pericles, III 2 line 1338.
Rape of Lucerne, lines 74, 567, 784, 998, 1219.
Richard II, III 2 line 1512.
Richard III, IV 4 line 3223.
Sonnet XI line 6; Sonnet XIII line 9; Sonnet XV line 11; Sonnet XVI line 3; Sonnet XVII line 3; Sonnet XXIII line 7; Sonnet LXIV line 10; Sonnet LXV line 8; Sonnet LXXI line 12; Sonnet LXXIX line 3; Sonnet LXXX line 14; Sonnet C line 11.
Timon of Athens, IV 3 line 2174.
Troilus and Cressida, III 2 line 1812.
Twelfth Night, I 5 line 365.

Deep: The noun is Old English: *deop: deep water*, especially the sea.
Henry IV, Part I, I 3 line 534; Henry IV, Part I, III 1 line 1596.
Henry IV, Part II, II 4 line 1418.
King Lear, IV 1 line 2329; King Lear, IV 2 line 2394.
Love's Labour's Lost, IV 3 line 1351.
Midsummer Night's Dream, III 1 line 978; Midsummer night's Dream, III 2 line 1081.
Pericles, III 1 line 1194.
Richard III, I 4 line 868; Richard III, III 4 line 2059.
Sonnet LXXX line 10.
Taming of the Shrew, I 1 line 316.
Tempest, I 2 line 386.

Deer: Old English: *deor: animal, beast*. Sense specialization to a specific animal began in Old English (usual for what we now call a deer was *heorot*), common by 15c., now complete. Probably via hunting, deer being the favourite animal of the chase. Shakespeare frequently refers to the popular sport of hunting the deer; and by his apt allusions shows how thoroughly familiar he was with the various amusements of his day. Shooting with the cross-bow at deer was an amusement of great ladies. Buildings with flat roofs, called *stands*, partly concealed by bushes, were erected in the parks for the purpose. Shakespeare has several pretty allusions to the tears of the deer, this animal being said to possess a very large secretion of tears.

All's Well That Ends Well, I 3 line 375.
As You Like It, II 1 line 597; As You Like It, II 1 line 616; As You Like It, III 3 line 1550; As You Like It, IV 2 line 1981; As You Like It, IV 2 line 1984; As You Like It, IV 2 line 1989.
Comedy of Errors, II 1 line 374.
Cymbeline, II 3 line 1057; Cymbeline, III 4 line 1839.
Hamlet, III 2 line 2159.
Henry IV, Part I, V 4 line 3071.
Henry VI, Part I, IV 2 lines 2014, 2016, 2022.
Henry VI, Part II, V 2 line 3225.
Henry VI, Part III, III 1 lines 1368, 1370; Henry VI, Part III, III 1 line 1389; Henry VI, Part III, IV 5 line 2297.
Julius Caesar, III 1 line 1431.
King Lear, III 4 line 1931.
Love's Labour's Lost, IV 1 line 1007; Love's Labour's Lost, IV 1 line 1097; Love's Labour's Lost, IV 2 line 1144; Love's Labour's Lost, IV 2 line 1154; Love's Labour's Lost, IV 2 line 1161; Love's Labour's Lost, IV 2 line 1162; Love's Labour's Lost, IV 2 lines 1195, 1196; Love's Labour's Lost, IV 3 line 1319.
Macbeth, IV 3 line 2084.
Merry Wives of Windsor, I 1 line 103; Merry Wives of Windsor, V 5 line 2577r; Merry Wives of Windsor, V 5 line 2693; Merry Wives of Windsor, V 5 line 2805.
Passionate Pilgrim, line 301.
Rape of Lucerne, line 1200.
Taming of the Shrew, V 2 line 2548.
Titus Andronicus, III 1 line 1219; Titus Andronicus, III 1 line 1221.
Venus and Adonis, lines 251, 259, 711.
Winter's Tale, I 2 line 193.

Desert: wasteland, early 13c., from Old French: *desert* (12c.) *desert, wilderness, wasteland; destruction, ruin*. Sense of *waterless, treeless region* was in Middle English and gradually became the main meaning
    As You Like It, II 1 line 571; As You Like It, II 4 line 789; As You Like It, II 6 line 892; As You Like It, II 7 line 1006; As You Like It, III 2 line 1237; As You Like It, IV 3 line 2147.
Macbeth, III 4 line 1400; Macbeth, IV 3 line 2068.
Merchant of Venice, II 7 line 1027.
Midsummer Night's Dream, II 1 line 593.
Othello, I 3 line 485.
Rape of Lucerne, line 1195.
Tempest, II 1 line 740.
Timon of Athens, I 1 line 82.
Titus Andronicus, I 1 line 29.
Two Gentlemen of Verona, V 4 line 2150.
Winter's Tale, II 3 line 1142; Winter's Tale, III 3 line 1488.

Dew: Old English: *deaw* of Germanic origin; related to Dutch: *dauw*. Amongst the many virtues ascribed to dew was its supposed power over the

complexion, a source of superstition which still finds many believers, especially on May morning. All dew, however, does not appear to have possessed this quality, some being of a deadly or malignant quality.
    Antony and Cleopatra, III 12 line 2208.
    Coriolanus, II 3 line 1454; Coriolanus, V 6 line 3845.
    Cymbeline, I 5 line 491; Cymbeline, IV 2 line 2684; Cymbeline, V 5 line 3800.
    Hamlet, I 1 line 134; Hamlet, I 2 line 334; Hamlet, I 3 line 525.
    Henry IV, Part II, IV 5 line 3009.
    Henry V, IV 4 lines 2380, 2381, 2382.
    Henry VI, Part II, III 2 line 2034; Henry VI, Part II, V 2 line 3270.
    Henry VIII, I 3 line 640; Henry VIII, II 4 line 1442; Henry VIII, IV 2 line 2732.
    Julius Caesar, II 1 line 855; Julius Caesar, V 3 line 2574.
    King John, II 1 line 586; King John, V 2 line 2323.
    Love's Labour's Lost, IV 3 line 1349.
    Macbeth, V 2 line 2242.
    Merchant of Venice, V 1 line 2451.
    Midsummer Night's Dream, II 1 line 376; Midsummer Night's Dream, III 2 line 1518; Midsummer Night's Dream, VI 1 line 1601; Midsummer Night's Dream, IV 1 line 1676; Midsummer Night's Dream, V 1 line 2266.
    Othello, I 2 line 279.
    Passionate Pilgrim, line 72.
    Rape of Lucerne, lines 75, 447, 1283, 1880.
    Richard II, III 3 line 1742; Richard II, V 1 line 2343.
    Richard III, IV 1 line 2554; Richard III, V 3 line 3796.
    Romeo and Juliet, I 1 line 152; Romeo and Juliet, I 4 line 605; Romeo and Juliet, III 5 line 2233; Romeo and Juliet, V 3 line 2948.
    Taming of the Shrew, II 1 line 1018.
    Tempest, I 2 line 354; Tempest, I 2 line 471.
    Titus Andronicus, II 3 line 977; Titus Andronicus, III 1 line 1242.
    Venus and Adonis, lines 86, 725.
    Winter's Tale, II 1 line 729.

Dewberry: bramble resembling blackberry, first used in 1578. Probably a descriptive of *dew* settling on berries.
    Midsummer Night's Dream, III 1 line 991.

Dewdrops: literally, drops of dew. See above.
    Midsummer Night's Dream, II 1 line 381.
    Troilus and Cressida, III 3 line 2105.

Dewlap: mid-14c., dewe lappe, from lappe: *loose piece* (Old English læppa), first element of unknown origin or meaning. Originally of cattle.
    Midsummer Night's Dream, II 1 line 418; Midsummer Night's Dream, IV 1 line 1677.
    Tempest, III 3 line 1617.

Diamond: a precious stone from carbon, known for hardness. Middle English: from Old French: *diamant*, from medieval Latin: *diamas, diamant*, variant of Latin: *adamans*.
>**Comedy of Errors**, IV 3 line 1218; Comedy of Errors, V 1 line 1836.
>**Cymbeline**, I 1 line 137; Cymbeline, I 4 lines 390, 393; Cymbeline, I 4 line 457; Cymbeline, I 4 line 465; Cymbeline II 4 line 1296; Cymbeline, V 5 line 3538.
>**Henry VI, Part I**, V 3 line 2638.
>**Henry VI, Part II**, III 2 line 1788.
>**Henry VI, Part III**, III 1 line 1430.
>**King Lear**, IV 3 line 2476.
>**Love's Labour's Lost**, V 2 line 1883.
>**Lover's Complaint**, line 212.
>**Macbeth**, II 1 line 586.
>**Merchant of Venice**, III 1 line 1319.
>**Merry Wives of Windsor**, III 3 line 1454.
>**Pericles**, II 3 line 859; Pericles, II 4 line 1005; Pericles, III 2 line 1406.
>**Timon of Athens**, III 6 line 1562.

Die: to cease to live, mid-12c., possibly from Old Danish: *døja* or Old Norse: *deyja*: *to die, pass away*. It has been speculated that Old English had *diegan*, from the same source, but it is not in any of the surviving texts. Languages usually don't borrow words from other languages for central life experiences, but *die* words are an exception, since they are often hidden or changed euphemistically out of superstitious dread. Regularly spelled *dege* through 15c., and still pronounced *dee* by some in Lancashire and Scotland. Used figuratively, for example: *to die away* (referring to sounds)from 1580s.
>**All's Well That Ends Well**, I 1 line 93; All's Well That Ends Well, I 1 line 136; All's Well That Ends Well, I 1 line 145; All's Well That Ends Well, I 2 line 313; All's Well That Ends Well, I 3 line 480; 543; All's Well that Ends Well, I 3 line All's Well That Ends Well, II 1 line 604; All's Well That Ends Well, II 1 line 797; All's Well That Ends Well, II 1 line 799; All's Well That Ends Well, IV 2 line 2088; All's Well That Ends Well, IV 3 line 2325; All's Well That Ends Well, IV 5 line 2541.
>**Antony and Cleopatra**, I 2 line 140; Antony and Cleopatra, I 2 line 208; Antony and Cleopatra, I 2 lines 231, 235; Antony and Cleopatra, I 3 line 365; Antony and Cleopatra, I 4 line 498; Antony and Cleopatra, I 5 line 558; Antony and Cleopatra, I 5 line 595; Antony and Cleopatra, III 13 line 2245; Antony and Cleopatra, IV 1 line 2500; Antony and Cleopatra, IV 6 line 2750; Antony and Cleopatra, IV 9 line 2861; Antony and Cleopatra, IV 12 line 2957; Antony and Cleopatra, IV 14 line 3010; Antony and Cleopatra, IV 14 line 3048; Antony and Cleopatra, IV 14 line 3105; Antony and Cleopatra, IV 15 line 3211; Antony and Cleopatra, IV 15 line 3231; Antony and Cleopatra, IV 15 line 3236; Antony and Cleopatra, V 2 line 3472; Antony and Cleopatra, V 2 line 3702; Antony and Cleopatra, V 2 line 3704; Antony and Cleopatra, V 2 line 3708; Antony and Cleopatra, V 2 line 3750; Antony and Cleopatra, V 2 line 3780; Antony and Cleopatra, V 2 line 3800; Antony and Cleopatra, V 2 line 3837.

As You Like It, I 1 line 96; As You Like It, I 2 line 160; As You Like It, I 3 line 493; As You Like It, II 3 line 720; As You Like It, II 6 line 879; As You Like It, II 6 lines 887, 891; As You Like It, II 7 line 995; As You Like It, II 7 line 997; As You Like It, II 7 line 1000; As You Like It, III 2 line 1266; As You Like It, III 5 1657; As You Like It, IV 1 lines 1876, 1878, 1880; As You Like It, IV 3 line 2065; As You Like It, V 2 line 2260; As You Like It, V 4 line 2414.
Comedy of Errors, I 1 line 27; Comedy of Errors, I 1 line 156; Comedy of Errors, I 2 line 169; Comedy of Errors, II 1 line 389; Comedy of Errors, III 2 line 813; Comedy of Errors, V 1 line 1566.
Coriolanus, I 1 line 5; Coriolanus, I 3 line 381; Coriolanus, I 3 line 386; Coriolanus, I 8 line 742; Coriolanus, II 1 line 1079; Coriolanus, II 3 line 1546; Coriolanus, III 1 2102; Coriolanus, III 1 line 2008; Coriolanus, III 3 line 1656; Coriolanus, V 2 line 3479; Coriolanus, V 3 line 3685; Coriolanus, V 6 line 3870; Coriolanus, V 6 line 3963.
Cymbeline, I 1 line 42; Cymbeline, I 1 line 203; Cymbeline, I 4 line 436; Cymbeline, II 4 line 1179; Cymbeline, III 3 line 1656; Cymbeline, III 4 line 1799; Cymbeline, III 6 line 2177; Cymbeline, III 6 line 2211; Cymbeline, IV 2 line 2326; Cymbeline, IV 2 line 2342; Cymbeline, IV 2 line 2449; Cymbeline, IV 4 line 2926; Cymbeline, IV 4 line 2943; Cymbeline, V 1 line 2977; Cymbeline, V 3 line 3036; Cymbeline, V 3 lines 3048, 3076; Cymbeline, V 3 line 3099; Cymbeline, V 4 line 3175; Cymbeline, V 4 line 3184; Cymbeline, V 4 line 3327; Cymbeline, V 4 line 3357; Cymbeline, V 5 line 3438; Cymbeline, V 5 line 3494; Cymbeline, V 5 line 3494; Cymbeline, V 5 line 3516; Cymbeline, V 5 line 3556; Cymbeline, V 5 line 3687; Cymbeline, V 5 line 3750; Cymbeline, V 5 line 3751; Cymbeline, V 5 line 3836.
Hamlet, I 2 line 274; Hamlet, I 2 line 307; Hamlet, III 2 line 2006; Hamlet, III 2 line 2010; Hamlet, III 2 line 2107; Hamlet, III 3 line 2293; Hamlet, IV 4 line 2816; Hamlet, IV 5 line 3061; Hamlet, IV 7 line 3262; Hamlet V 1 line 3498; Hamlet, V 1 line 3537; Hamlet, V 2 line 3966; Hamlet, V 2 line 3984; Hamlet, V 2 line 4014; Hamlet, V 2 line 4019.
Henry IV, Part I, I 3 line 399; Henry IV, Part I, II 1 line 653; Henry IV, Part I, II 2 line 754; Henry IV, Part I, II 4 line 1118; Henry IV, Part I, III 2 line 1983; Henry IV, Part I, III 2 line 1984; Henry IV, Part I, IV 1 line 2362r; Henry IV, Part I, V 1 line 2763; Henry IV, Part I, V 2 line 2861r; Henry IV, Part I, V 4 line 3050; Henry IV, Part I, V 4 line 3081.
Henry IV, Part II, I 1 line 211; Henry IV, Part II, I 3 line 718; Henry IV, Part II, II 2 line 1068; Henry IV, Part II, II 4 line 1437; Henry IV, Part II, III 1 line 1761; Henry IV, Part II, III 2 line 1863; Henry IV, Part II, III 2 line 2093; Henry IV, Part II, III 2 line 2096; Henry IV, Part II, IV 1 line 2260; Henry IV, Part II, IV 4 line 2881; Henry IV, Part II, IV 5 line 3001; Henry IV, Part II, IV 5 line 3048; Henry IV, Part II, IV 5 line 3135; Henry IV, Part II, V 3 line 3462; Henry IV, Part II, V 3 line 3523; Henry IV, Part II, V 4 line 3558; Henry IV, Part II, V 5 line 3685; Henry IV, Part II, V 5 line 3733; Henry IV, Part II, V 5 line 3737.
Henry V, I 1 line 65; Henry V, I 2 line 204; Henry V, I 2 line 245; Henry V, II 0 line 495; Henry V, III 2 line 1134; Henry V, III 6 line 1518; Henry V, IV 1 line 1972; Henry V, IV 1 line 1984; Henry V, IV 1 lines 1987,

1988, 1990; Henry V, IV 1 lines 1999, 2022; Henry V, IV 1 line 2035; Henry V, IV 3 lines 2255, 2273, 2274; Henry V, IV 5 line 2462; Henry V, IV 6 line 2487; Henry V, V 1 line 2918; Henry V, V 2 line 3023; Henry V, V 2 line 3134.

Henry VI, Part I, I 4 line 552; Henry VI, Part I, I 5 line 624; Henry VI, Part I, II 2 line 769; Henry VI, Part I, II 4 line 1030; Henry VI, Part I, II 5 line 1197; Henry VI, Part I, II 5 line 1207; Henry VI, Part I, III 2 line 1534; Henry VI, Part I, III 2 line 1578; Henry VI, Part I, III 2 line 1601; Henry VI, Part I, IV 3 line 2057; Henry VI, Part I, IV 4 line 2093; Henry VI, Part I, IV 5 line 2154; Henry VI, Part I, IV 5 line 2179; Henry VI, Part I, IV 5 line 2185; Henry VI, Part I, IV 5 line 2185; Henry VI, Part I, IV 5 line 2186; Henry VI, Part I, IV 5 line 2188; Henry VI, Part I, IV 6 line 2230; Henry VI, Part I, IV 6 lines 2226, 2227; Henry VI, Part I, IV 6 lines 2239, 2244; Henry VI, Part I, IV 6 line 2249; Henry VI, Part I, IV 7 line 2265; Henry VI, Part I, IV 7 line 2280; Henry VI, Part I, IV 7 line 2285; Henry VI, Part I, V 4 line 2676; Henry VI, Part I, V 4 line 2746.

Henry VI, Part II, I 1 lines 102, 104; Henry VI, Part II, I 1 line 120; Henry VI, Part II, I 4 line 663; Henry VI, Part II, I 4 line 666; Henry VI, Part II, I 4 lines 699, 704; Henry VI, Part II, II 2 line 973; Henry VI, Part II, II 2 line 988; Henry VI, Part II, II 2 line 997; Henry VI, Part II, II 3 line 1091; Henry VI, Part II, II 3 line 1122; Henry VI, Part II, II 3 line 1143; Henry VI, Part II, III 1 line 1519; Henry VI, Part II, III 1 line 1527; Henry VI, Part II, III 1 line 1541; Henry VI, Part II, III 2 line 1801; Henry VI< Part II, III 2 line 1813; Henry VI, Part II, III 2 line 1938; Henry VI, Part II, III 2 line 2048; Henry VI, Part II, III 2 lines 2085, 2096r, 2097; Henry VI, Part II, III 3 line 2123; Henry VI, Part II, III 3 line 2144; Henry VI, Part II, III 3 line 2123; Henry VI, Part II, IV 1 line 2171; Henry VI, Part II, IV 1 line 2177; Henry VI, Part II, IV 1 line 2188; Henry VI, Part II, IV 1 line 2290; Henry VI, Part II, IV 1 line 2294; Henry VI, Part II, IV 2 line 2397; Henry VI, Part II, IV 2 line 2433; Henry VI, Part II, IV 4 line 2547; Henry VI, Part II, IV 10 line 2964; Henry VI, Part II, IV 17 line 2722; Henry VI, Part II, IV 10 line 2966; Henry VI, Part II, V 1 line 3030; Henry VI, Part II, V 2 line 3241; Henry VI, Part II, V 2 line 3266.

Henry VI, Part III, I 1 line 33; Henry VI, Part III, I 1 line 195; Henry VI, Part III, I 1 line 234; Henry VI, Part III, I 2 line 329; Henry VI, Part III, I 3 line 381; Henry VI, Part III, I 3 line 395; Henry VI, Part III, I 3 line 426; Henry VI, Part III, I 3 line 429; Henry VI, Part III, I 4 line 622; Henry VI, Part III, II 1 line 676; Henry VI, Part III, II 1 line 715; Henry VI, Part III, II 6 line 1251; Henry VI, Part III, II 6 line 1295; Henry VI, Part III, IV 4 line 2277; Henry VI, Part III, V 2 line 2722r; Henry VI, Part III, V 2 line 2740; Henry VI, Part III, V 2 line 2773; Henry VI, Part III, V 6 line 3052; Henry VI, Part III, V 6 line 3057.

Henry VIII, I 2 line 471; Henry VIII, II 1 line 893; Henry VIII, II 2 line 1182; Henry VIII, II 4 line 1560; Henry VIII, III 1 line 1635; Henry VIII, IV 2 line 2567; Henry VIII, IV 2 line 2630; Henry VIII, V 5 line 3423; Henry VIII, V 5 line 3444.

Julius Caesar, II 1 line 808; Julius Caesar, II 1 line 811; Julius Caesar, II 2 line 1006; Julius Caesar, II 2 line 1008; Julius Caesar, III 1 line 1287; Julius Caesar, III 1 line 1313; Julius Caesar, III 1 line 1380;

Julius Caesar, III 2 line 1557; Julius Caesar, III 2 line 1753; Julius Caesar, IV 1 line 1860; Julius Caesar, IV 1 line 1861; Julius Caesar, IV 1 line 1878; Julius Caesar, IV 3 line 2156; Julius Caesar, IV 3 line 2183; Julius Caesar, IV 3 lines 2198, 2199; Julius Caesar, V 1 line 2409; Julius Caesar, V 1 line 2411; Julius Caesar, V 3 line 2552; Julius Caesar, V 4 line 2645; Julius Caesar, V 5 line 2735; Julius Caesar, V 5 line 2750.
King John, II 1 line 396; King John, II 1 line 730; King John, III 1 lines 945, 948; King John, III 1 line 1223; King John, III 1 line 1266; King John, III 3 line 1303; King John, III 4 line 1472; King John, III 4 line 1552; King John, IV 2 lines 1852, 1854; King John, IV 3 line 2023r; King John, IV 3 line 2027; King John, V 4 line 2517; King John, V 7 line 2700.
King Lear, II 2 line 1119; King Lear, III 3 line 1792; King Lear, III 7 line 2215; King Lear, IV 6 line 2655; King Lear, IV 6 line 2686; King lear, IV 6 line 2720r; King Lear, IV 6 line 2806; King Lear, IV 6 line 2833; King Lear, IV 6 line 2872; King Lear, IV 7 line 2966; King Lear, IV 7 line 2970; King Lear, V 3 lines 3345, 3346; King Lear, V 3 line 3500.
Love's Labour's Lost, I 1 line 34; Love's Labour's Lost, IV 3 line 1550; LOve's Labour's Lost, V 2 lines 1895, 1897; Love's Labour's Lost, V 2 line 1924; Love's Labour's Lost, V 2 line 2162; Love's Labour's Lost, V 2 line 2163; Love's Labour's Lost, V 2 line 2252; Love's Labour's Lost, V 2 line 2374; Love's Labour's Lost, V 2 line 2407; Love's Labour's Lost, V 2 line 2450; Love's Labour's Lost, V 2 line 2619.
Macbeth, I 4 lines 280, 285; Macbeth, II 2 line 655; Macbeth, II 3 line 874; Macbeth, III 2 line 1181; Macbeth, III 3 line 1262; Macbeth, III 4 line 1370; Macbeth, IV 3 line 1969; Macbeth, IV 2 line 1838; Macbeth, V 1 line 2182; Macbeth, V 5 line 2374; Macbeth, V 5 line 2413; Macbeth, V 8 line 2525; Macbeth, V 8 line 2473.
Measure for Measure, I 2 line 221; Measure for Measure, II 1 line 484; Measure for Measure, II 1 line 575; Measure for Measure, II 2 line 741; Measure for Measure, II 2 line 744; Measure for Measure, II 2 line 785; Measure for Measure, II 2 line 802; Measure for Measure, II 2 line 844; Measure for Measure, II 2 line 850; Measure for Measure, II 2 line 869; Measure for Measure, II 3 line 979; Measure for Measure, II 3 line 981; Measure for Measure, II 3 line 1007; Measure for Measure, II 3 line 1011; Measure for Measure, II 4 line 1058; Measure for Measure, II 4 line 1108; Measure for Measure, II 4 line 1131; Measure for Measure, II 4 line 1133; Measure for Measure, II 4 line 1135; Measure for Measure, II 4 line 1149; Measure for Measure, II 4 line 1172; Measure for Measure, II 4 line 1196; Measure for Measure, II 4 line 1215; Measure for Measure, III 1 line 1226; Measure for Measure, III 1 line 1265; Measure for Measure, III 1 lines 1306, 1310; Measure for Measure, III 1 line 1313; Measure for Measure, III 1 line 1317; Measure for Measure, III 1 line 1353; Measure for Measure, III 1 line 1381; Measure for Measure, III 1 line 1409; Measure for Measure, III 1 line 1433; Measure for Measure, III 2 line 1677; Measure for Measure, III 2 line 1678; Measure for Measure, III 2 line 1717; Measure for

Measure, III 2 line 1757; Measure for Measure, IV 2 line 1891; Measure for Measure, IV 2 line 1993; Measure for Measure, IV 3 line 2171; Measure for Measure, IV 3 line 2174; Measure for Measure, IV 3 line 2180; Measure for Measure, IV 3 line 2189; Measure for Measure, IV 3 line 2200; Measure for Measure, IV 3 line 2202; Measure for Measure, V 1 line 2876; Measure for Measure, V 1 lines 2883, 2884; Measure for Measure, V 1 line 2904; Measure for Measure, V 1 line 2932.
Merchant of Venice, I 2 line 296; Merchant of Venice, II 1 line 553; Merchant of Venice, III 1 line 1300; Merchant of Venice, III 2 line 1435; Merchant of Venice, III 4 line 1823; Merchant of Venice, IV 1 line 2338; Merchant of Venice, V 1 line 2676; Merchant of Venice, V 1 line 2765.
Merry Wives of Windsor, II 3 line 1176; Merry Wives of Windsor, III 3 line 1445; Merry Wives of Windsor, IV 2 line 2025; Merry Wives of Windsor, IV 2 line 2108; Merry Wives of Windsor, V 5 line 2611.
Midsummer Night's Dream, I 1 line 70; Midsummer Night's Dream, I 1 lines 83, 84; Midsummer Night's Dream, I 1 line 88; Midsummer Night's Dream, II 1 line 504; Midsummer Night's Dream, II 1 line 620; Midsummer Night's Dream, V 1 line 1992; Midsummer Night's Dream, V 1 lines 2144, 2151rrrr; Midsummer Night's Dream, V 1 lines 2152, 2153; Midsummer Night's Dream, V 1 line 2194.
Much Ado About Nothing, I 1 line 107; Much Ado About Nothing, I 1 line 209; Much Ado About Nothing, I 1 line 222; Much Ado About Nothing, II 3 lines 985, 986r, 987; Much Ado About Nothing, II 3 lines 1033, 1049; Much Ado About Nothing, III 1 lines 1157, 1158; Much Ado About Nothing, III 2 line 1258; Much Ado About Nothing, IV 1 line 1773; Much Ado About Nothing, IV 1 line 1804; Much Ado About Nothing, IV 1 line 1875; Much Ado About Nothing, IV 1 line 1906; Much Ado About Nothing, IV 1 line 1971; Much Ado About Nothing, IV 2 line 2040; Much Ado About Nothing, V 1 line 2356; Much Ado About Nothing, V 1 line 2366; Much Ado About Nothing, V 2 line 2479; Much Ado About Nothing, V 2 line 2502; Much Ado About Nothing, V 3 line 2514; Much Ado About Nothing, V 3 line 2513; Much Ado About Nothing, V 4 line 2614; Much Ado About Nothing, V 4 line 2617.
Othello, I 3 line 668; Othello, II 1 line 980; Othello, II 3 line 1320; Othello, III 3 line 1654; Othello, IV 3 line 3044; Othello, IV 3 line 3051; Othello, V 1 line 3146; Othello, V 1 line 3159; Othello, V 2 line 3307; Othello, V 2 line 3363; Othello, V 2 line 3368; Othello, V 2 line 3450; Othello, V 2 line 3454; Othello, V 2 lines 3600, 3605r, 3606; Othello, V 2 line 3651; Othello, V 2 line 3728; Othello, V 2 line 3729.
Passionate Pilgrim, line 173.
Pericles, I 0 lines 23, 40; Pericles, I 1 line 68; Pericles, I 1 line 78; Pericles, I 1 line 151; Pericles, I 1 line 202; Pericles, I 4 line 462; Pericles, II 1 line 658; Pericles, III 1 line 1208; Pericles, IV 1 line 1566; Pericles, IV 2 line 1740; Pericles, IV 3 lines 1831, 1834; Pericles, IV 6 line 2056; Pericles, V 1 line 2195; Pericles, V 1 line 2369; Pericles, V 3 line 2525; Pericles, V 3 line 2537.

Rape of Lucrece, lines 243, 255, 282, 325, 430, 559, 955, 1083, 1103, 1190, 1205, 1228, 1262, 1528, 1536, 1703, 1737, 1820, 1822, 1827.

Richard II, I 1 line 189; Richard II, I 2 line 240; Richard II, I 2 line 286; Richard II, I 3 line 381; Richard II, II 1 line 741; Richard II, II 1 line 773; Richard II, II 1 line 818; Richard II, II 1 line 824; Richard II, II 2 line 1095; Richard II, II 3 line 1284; Richard II, III 2 line 1594; Richard II, III 3 line 1772; Richard II, III 3 line 1817; Richard II, V 3 line 2648; Richard II, V 5 line 2770; Richard II, V 5 line 2869; Richard II, V 5 line 2870;Richard II, V 6 line 2909.

Richard III, I 1 line 153; Richard III, I 2 line 336; Richard III, I 3 lines 661, 665, 671, 673; Richard III, I 4 line 955; Richard III, I 4 line 1007; Richard III, I 4 line 1078; Richard III, II 1 line 1212; Richard III, II 2 line 1315; Richard III, II 2 line 1382; Richard III, II 4 line 1553; Richard III, III 1 line 1664; Richard III, III 1 line 1671; Richard III, III 2 line 1831; Richard III, III 2 line 1845; Richard III, III 3 line 1921; Richard III, III 5 line 2122; Richard III, IV 1 line 2516; Richard III, IV 1 line 2533; Richard III, IV 2 line 2606; Richard III, IV 2 lines 2642, 2648; Richard III, Iv 4 line 2817; Richard III, IV 4 line 2986; Richard III, IV 4 line 3009; Richard III, IV 4 line 3018; Richard III, V 3 line 3596; Richard III, V 3 lines 3605, 3606; Richard III, V 3 line 3617; Richard III, V 3 line 3625r; Richard III, V 3 line 3630; Richard III, V 3 line 3638; Richard III, V 3 line 3647; Richard III, V 3 line 3659; Richard III, V 3 lines 3669, 3673; Richard III, V 3 line 3703; Richard III, V 3 line 3065; Richard III, V 4 line 3884.

Romeo and Juliet, I 1 lines 245r; Romeo and Juliet, I 1 line 268, Romeo and Juliet, I 2 line 324; Romeo and Juliet, I 2 line 367; Romeo and Juliet, II 0 line 782; Romeo and Juliet, II 6 line 1468; Romeo and Juliet, III 1 line 1693; Romeo and Juliet, III 2 line 1739; Romeo and Juliet, III 2 line 1859; Romeo and Juliet, III 3 line 2026; Romeo and Juliet, III 4 line 2062; Romeo and Juliet, III 5 line 2305; Romeo and Juliet, III 5 line 2361; Romeo and Juliet, IV 1 line 2431; Romeo and Juliet, IV 3 line 2587; Romeo and Juliet, IV 5 line 2676; Romeo and Juliet, IV 5 line 2698; Romeo and Juliet, IV 5 line 2737; Romeo and Juliet, V 1 line 2880; Romeo and Juliet, V 3 lines 2990, 2997; Romeo and Juliet, V 3 line 3018; Romeo and Juliet, V 3 line 3067; Romeo and Juliet, V 3 line 3018; Romeo and Juliet, V 3 line 3049; Romeo and Juliet, V 3 line 3137; Romeo and Juliet, V 3 line 3138; Romeo and Juliet, V 3 line 3265.

Sonnet I line 2; Sonnet III line 14; Sonnet IX line 3; Sonnet XI line 14; Sonnet XII line 12; Sonnet XXV line 6; Sonnet XXXII line 13; Sonnet LIV line 11; Sonnet LXVI line 14; Sonnet LXVIII line 2; Sonnet LXXXI line 6; Sonnet XCII line 12; Sonnet XCIV line 10; Sonnet CXXIV line 14.

Taming of the Shrew, II 1 line 1214; Taming of the Shrew, II 1 line 1242; Taming of the Shrew, II 1 line 1244; Taming of the Shrew, III 1 line 1345; Taming of the Shrew, III 2 line 1608; Taming of the Shrew, IV line 1685.

Tempest, I 1 line 82; Tempest I 2 line 415; Tempest, II 2 line 1132; Tempest, III 1 lines 1373, 1378; Tempest, III 2 line 1530.
Timon of Athens, I 1 line 234; Timon of Athens, I 2 line 486; Timon of Athens, II 2 lines 765, 768; Timon of Athens, II 3 line 855; Timon of Athens, III 5 line 1308; Timon of Athens, III 5 line 1385; Timon of Athens, III 5 line 1386; Timon of Athens, III 5 line 1397; Timon of Athens, IV 3 line 1943; Timon of Athens, V 4 lines 2596, 2597.
Titus Andronicus, I 1 line 142; Titus Andronicus, I 1 line 238; Titus Andronicus, I 1 line 421; Titus Andronicus, I 1 line 435; Titus Andronicus, I 1 line 509; Titus Andronicus, I 1 line 516; Titus Andronicus, II 3 line 840; Titus Andronicus, II 3 line 911; Titus Andronicus, III 1 line 1136; Titus Andronicus, III 1 line 1306; Titus Andronicus, III 1 line 1394; Titus Andronicus, IV 1 line 1638; Titus Andronicus, IV 2 line 1770; Titus Andronicus, IV 2 line 1781; Titus Andronicus, IV 4 line 2067; Titus Andronicus, V 1 line 2275; Titus Andronicus, V 1 line 2280; Titus Andronicus, V 3 lines 2578r, 2580; Titus Andronicus, V 3 line 2599, Titus Andronicus, V 3 line 2727.
Troilus and Cressida, I 2 line 392; Troilus and Cressida, I 3 629; Troilus and Cressida, III 1 line 1606; Troilus and Cressida, III 3 line 1959; Troilus and Cressida, IV 1 line 2228; Troilus and Cressida, IV 4 line 2481; Troilus and Cressida, IV 4 line 2517; Troilus and Cressida, V 5 line 3478; Troilus and Cressida, V 7 line 3564.
Twelfth Night, I 1 line 4; Twelfth Night, I 2 lines 84, 86; Twelfth Night, II 3 line 807; Twelfth Night, II 4 line 934; Twelfth Night, II 4 line 1020; Twelfth Night, IV 2 line 2034; Twelfth Night, V 1 line 2325; Twelfth Night, V 1 line 2445.
Two Gentlemen of Verona, II 4 line 767; Two Gentlemen of Verona, III 1 line 1244; Two Gentlemen of Verona, III 1 line 1305; Two Gentlemen of Verona, IV 3 line 1802.
Venus and Adonis, lines 182, 224, 266, 517, 519, 748, 825, 1039; 1082, 1096, 1102.
Winter's Tale, I 1 line 42; Winter's Tale III 2 line 1325; Winter's Tale, IV 3 line 1749; Winter's Tale, IV 4 line 2002; Winter's Tale IV 4 lines 2381r, 2388, 2389; Winter's Tale, V 1 line 2971; Winter's Tale, V 1 line 3095; Winter's Tale, V 3 line 3418.

Dimples: c.1400, perhaps existing in Old English as a word meaning *pothole*. As a verb, from 1570s (implied in dimpled).
    Antony and Cleopatra, II 2 line 926.
    Rape of Lucrece, line 471.
    Timon of Athens, IV 3 line 1789.
    Troilus and Cressida, I 2 line 272.
    Venus and Adonis, line 262.
    Winter's Tale, II 3 line 1054.

Disclose: the coming forth of a chicken from a shell.
    Hamlet, III 1 line 1858.

Docks: Old English: *docce*, of Germanic origin; related to Dutch dialect *dokke*. These plants have many uses. Broad-leaved docks used to be called *butter dock* because its large leaves were used to wrap and conserve butter.
Henry V, V 2 line 3033.
Tempest, II 1 line 853.

Dog: Old English: *docga*, a late, rare word used of a powerful breed of canine. It forced out Old English: *hund* by 16c. and subsequently was picked up in many continental languages, but the origin remains one of the great mysteries of English etymology. Many expressions: *a dog's life* (c.1600), *go to the dogs* (1610s), etc. reflect earlier hard use of the animals as hunting accessories, not pampered pets. The dog not unnaturally possesses an extensive history, besides entering largely into those superstitions which, more or less, are associated with every stage of human life. It is not surprising, therefore, that Shakespeare frequently speaks of the dog, making it the subject of many of his illustrations. Thus he has not omitted to mention the fatal significance of its howl; which is supposed either to foretell death or misfortune. Also a scavenger, envy, flattery, fury, war, greed, pitiless, bragging and folly. Shakespeare often linked them negatively with kites.
All's Well That Ends Well, II 3 line 1176; All's Well That Ends Well, III 4 line 1574.
Antony and Cleopatra, IV 15 line 3262; Antony and Cleopatra, V 2 line 3435; Antony and Cleopatra, V 2 line 3580.
As You Like It, I 1 line 68; As You Like It, I 1 line 69; As You Like It, I 3 line 410.
Comedy of Errors, III 2 line 904; Comedy of Errors, V 1 line 1501.
Coriolanus, I 1 line 24; Coriolanus, I 1 line 212; Coriolanus, II 1 line 1205; Coriolanus, II 3 line 1666; Coriolanus, IV 5 line 2810.
Cymbeline, I 5 line 538; Cymbeline, II 1 line 865; Cymbeline, V 3 line 3125; Cymbeline, V 5 line 3632; Cymbeline, V 5 line 3671.
Hamlet, II 2 line 1286; Hamlet, IV 5 line 2975; Hamlet, V 1 line 3634.
Henry IV, Part I, line 651; Henry IV, Part I, III 3 line 2095; Henry IV, Part I, IV 2 line 2393.
Henry IV, Part II, I 2 line 462; Henry IV, Part II, I 3 line 704; Henry IV, Part II, II 4 line 1419; Henry IV, Part II, II 4 line 1437; Henry IV, Part II, IV 5 line 3027.
Henry V, I 2 line 362; Henry V, II 1 line 548; Henry V, II 1 line 551; Henry V, II 2 line 720; Henry V, II 3 line 882; Henry V, II 4 line 970; Henry V, III 2 line 1147; Henry V, III 2 line 1204; Henry V, II 6 line 1505; Henry V, IV 5 line 2466.
Henry VI, Part I, I 2 line 216; Henry VI, Part I, I 5 line 609; Henry VI, Part I, II 4 line 932.
Henry VI, Part II, I 4 line 645; Henry VI, Part II, III 1 line 1452; Henry VI, Part II, IV 2 line 2329.
Henry VI, Part III, II 1 line 641; Henry VI, Part III, V 6 line 3041; Henry VI, Part III, V 6 line 3075.
Henry VIII, V 4 line 3312.
Julius Caesar, III 1 line 1502; Julius Caesar, IV 3 line 2006.
King John, II 2 line 772; King John, IV 1 line 1705.

King Lear, I 4 line 609; King Lear, I 4 line 640; King Lear, II 2 line 1207; King Lear, II 4 line 1284; King Lear, III 4 line 1888; King Lear, III 4 line 1926; King Lear, III 6 line 2064; King Lear, III 6 line 2074; King Lear, III 7 line 2206; King Lear, IV 3 line 2503; King Lear, IV 6 line 2706; King Lear, IV 6 line 2761; King Lear, IV 6 line 2764; King Lear, IV 7 line 2952; King Lear, V 3 line 3347; King Lear, V 3 line 3495.
Love's Labour's Lost, IV 2 line 1203.
Macbeth, III 1 line 1110; Macbeth, IV 1 line 1562; Macbeth, V 3 line 2303.
Merchant of Venice, I 1 line 100; Merchant of Venice, I 3 lines 438, 448 454; Merchant of Venice, II 8 line 1085; Merchant of Venice, III 3 lines 1714, 1715; Merchant of Venice, IV 1 line 2023; Merchant of Venice, IV 1 line 2063.
Merry Wives of Windsor, I 1 line 86; Merry Wives of Windsor, I 1 line 88r; Merry Wives of Windsor, I 1 line 267; Merry Wives of Windsor, I 4 line 515; Merry Wives of Windsor, II 1 line 671; Merry Wives of Windsor, II 3 line 1155; Merry Wives of Windsor, III 1 line 1271; Merry Wives of Windsor, III 5 line 1754; Merry Wives of Windsor, IV 2 line 2084; Merry Wives of Windsor, V 5 line 2805.
Midsummer Night's Dream, II 1 line 585; Midsummer Night's Dream, III 2 line 1098; Midsummer Night's Dream, V 1 line 1978; Midsummer Night's Dream, V 1 line 2098r.
Much Ado About Nothing, I 1 line 119; Much Ado About Nothing, II 3 line 898; Much Ado About Nothing, III 3 line 1380.
Othello, II 3 line 1184; Othello, II 3 line 1429; Othello, III 3 line 2040; Othello, IV 1 line 2572; Othello, V 1 line 3215; Othello, V 2 line 3722; Othello, V 2 line 3732.
Passionate Pilgrim, line 272.
Rape of Lucrece, line 787.
Richard II, III 2 line 1540; Richard II, V 3 line 2725; Richard II, V 5 line 2821.
Richard III, I 1 line 23; Richard III, I 2 line 213; Richard III, I 3 line 680; Richard III, I 3 line 757; Richard III, IV 1 line 2060; Richard III, IV 3 line 2732; Riched III, IV 4 line 2844; Richard III, IV 4 line 2873; Richard III, V 5 line 3894.
Romeo and Juliet, I 1 line 23; Romeo and Juliet, I 1 line 26; Romeo and Juliet, II 4 line 1362; Romeo and Juliet, III 1 line 1524; Romeo and Juliet, III 1 line 1605; Romeo and Juliet, III 3 line 1901.
Taming of the Shrew, Prologue 1 line 21; Taming of the Shrew, Prologue 1 line 25; Taming of the Shrew IV 1 line 1769; Taming of the Shrew, IV 2 line 1889.
Tempest, I 1 line 51; Tempest, I 2 line 546; Tempest, II 2 line 1228; Tempest, III 2 line 1414; Tempest, IV 1 line 1997.
Timon of Athens, I 1 line 223; Timon of Athens, I 1 line 241; Timon of Athens, I 1 line 242; Timon of Athens, I 1 line 316; Timon of Athens, I 1 line 317; Timon of Athens, I 2 line 395; Timon of Athens, II 1 lines 631, 632; Timon of Athens, II 2 lines 769, 770; Timon of Athens, III 6 line 1521; Timon of Athens, IV 3 line 1723; Timon of Athens, IV 3 line 1888; Timon of Athens, IV 3 line 1946; Timon of Athens, IV 3 line 2018;

Timon of Athens, IV 3 line 2058; Timon of Athens, IV 3 line 2067; Timon of Athens, IV 3 line 2245; Timon of Athens, V 1 line 2386.
Titus Andronicus, II 2 line 723; Titus Andronicus, IV 2 line 1766; Titus Andronicus, V 1 line 2237; Titus Andronicus, V 1 line 2257; Titus Andronicus, V 3 line 2539.
Troilus and Cressida, II 1 line 864; Troilus and Cressida, II 1 line 907; Troilus and Cressida, II 3 line 1455; Troilus and Cressida, V 1 line 2992; Troilus and Cressida, V 1 line 3041; Troilus and Cressida, V 4 lines 3420, 3422; Troilus and Cressida, V 7 line 3569.
Twelfth Night, II 3 line 761; Twelfth Night, II 3 line 762; Twelfth Night, II 3 line 840; Twelfth Night, V 1 lines 2194, 2195.
Two Gentlemen of Verona, II 3 line 592; Two Gentlemen of Verona, II 3 lines 597, 598, 603, 614r, 615r, 624; Two Gentlemen of Verona, II 3 line 634; Two Gentlemen of Verona, II 5 line 909; Two Gentlemen of Verona, IV 2 line 1708; Two Gentlemen of Verona, IV 4 line 1833; Two Gentlemen of Verona, IV 4 lines 1840, 1846, 1847, 1852, 1854, 1859, 1860; Two Gentlemen of Verona, IV 4 line 1881; Two Gentlemen of Verona, IV 4 line 1883; Two Gentlemen of Verona, IV 4 line 1885; Two Gentlemen of Verona, IV 4 line 1891; Two Gentlemen of Verona, IV 4 line 1893.
Venus and Adonis, lines, 260, 908.

Dog-ape: meaning a *dog faced baboon*: a common insult.
    As You Like It, II 5 line 840.

Dogfish: bottom dwelling shark with long tail.
    Henry VI, Part I, I 4 line 570.

Dolphin: mid-14c., from Old French: *daulphin*.
    All's Well That Ends Well, II 3 line 917.
    Antony and Cleopatra, V 2 line 3497.
    Henry IV, Part II, II 1 line 814.
    Henry V, IV 8 line 2803.
    Henry VI, Part I, I 4 line 569.
    King Lear, III 4 line 1893.
    Midsummer Night's Dream, II 1 line 521.
    Twelfth Night, I 2 line 62.

Dormouse: early 15c., possibly from Anglo-French: *dormouse: tending to be dormant* (from stem of *dormir*: to sleep), with the second element mistaken for mouse; or perhaps it is from a Middle English dialectal compound of *mouse* (Old English: *mus*) and *dormir*. The rodent is inactive in winter.
    Twelfth Night, III 2 line 1421.

Dove: probably from Old English: *dufe*; perhaps related to words for *dive*, in reference to its flight. Originally applied to all pigeons, now mostly restricted to the turtle dove. A symbol of gentleness from early Christian times, also of the Holy Spirit (cf. Gen. viii.8-12), and of peace and deliverance from anxiety.

The young nestlings, when first disclosed, are only covered with a yellow down, and the mother rarely leaves the nest, in consequence of the tenderness of her young; hence the dove has been made an emblem of patience.
>   **Antony and Cleopatra**, III 13 line 2488.
>   **Coriolanus**, V 3 line 3521; Coriolanus, V 6 line 3956.
>   **Hamlet**, IV 5 line 3046; Hamlet, V 1 line 3631.
>   **Henry IV, Part II**, III 2 2012; Henry IV, Part II, IV 1 line 2251.
>   **Henry VI, Part I**, I 2 line 339; Henry VI, Part I, I 5 line 607; Henry VI, Part I, II 2 line 790.
>   **Henry VI, Part II**, III 1 line 1349; Henry VI, Part II, III 1 line 1353.
>   **Henry VI, Part III**, I 4 line 479; Henry VI, Part III, II 2 line 860.
>   **Henry VIII**, IV 1 line 2433.
>   **Merchant of Venice**, II 2 line 698.
>   **Merry Wives of Windsor**, I 3 line 396.
>   **Midsummer Night's Dream**, I 1 line 178; Midsummer Night's Dream, I 2 line 339; Midsummer Night's Dream, II 1 line 607; Midsummer Night's Dream, II 2 line 775; Midsummer Night's Dream, V 1 line 2170.
>   **Passionate Pilgrim**, Lines 87, 119.
>   **Pericles**, IV 0 line 1524.
>   **Phoenix and the Turtle**, line 50.
>   **Rape of Lucrece**, lines 109, 411.
>   **Romeo and Juliet**, I 3 lines 412, 418; Romeo and Juliet, I 5 line 670; Romeo and Juliet, II 1 line 809; Romeo and Juliet, II 5 line 1381; Romeo and Juliet, III 2 line 1798.
>   **Sonnet** CXIII line 12.
>   **Taming of the Shrew**, II 1 line 1144; Taming of the Shrew, III 2 line 1519.
>   **Tempest**, IV 1 line 1807.
>   **Troilus and Cressida**, III 1 line 1614.
>   **Twelfth Night**, V 1 line 2323.
>   **Venus and Adonis**, lines, 30, 173, 386, 1212.
>   **Winter's Tale**, IV 4 line 2262.

Dowle: feathery or wool-like down, or filament of a feather.
>   **Tempest**, III 3 line 1643.

Down: Fine, soft, fluffy feathers forming the first plumage of a young bird and underlying the contour feathers in certain adult birds. Middle English *doun*, from Old Norse *dnn*.
>   **All's Well That Ends Well**, I 1 line 66.
>   **Antony and Cleopatra**, III 2 line 1651.
>   **Henry VI, Part I**, V 3 line 2515.
>   **Henry VIII**, I 4 line 680.
>   **Macbeth**, II 3 line 851.
>   **Troilus and Cressida**, I 1 line 88.
>   **Winter's Tale**, IV 4 line 2255.

Drone: Old English: *dran, dræn: male honeybee*, probably imitative; given a figurative sense of idler, lazy worker (male bees make no honey) 1520s.
    Comedy of Errors, II 2 line 583.
    Henry IV, Part I, I 2 line 182.
    Henry V, I 2 line 350.
    Henry VI, Part II, IV 1 line 2265.
    Merchant of Venice, II 5 line 896.
    Pericles, II 4 line 555; Pericles, II 1 line 627.
    Rape of Lucrece, line 887.

Duck: Old English: *duce*. Waterfowl, name denoting the female of the species, as well as the species generally, due to the preponderance of females in the population. A pastime in Shakespeare's time was hunting a tame duck in the water with spaniels. For the performance of this amusement it was necessary to have recourse to a pond of water sufficiently extensive to give the duck plenty of room for making its escape from the dogs when closely pursued.
    Henry IV, Part I, II 2 line 842; Henry IV, Part I, IV 2 line 2387.
    Henry V, II 3 line 882.
    Midsummer Night's Dream, V 1 line 2122.
    Othello, II 1 line 979.
    Pericles, III 0 line 1178.
    Richard III, I 3 line 510.
    Tempest, II 2 lines 1216, 1217; Tempest, II 2 line 1219.
    Timon of Athens, IV 3 line 1681.
    Troilus and Cressida, III 2 line 1706; Troilus and Cressida, IV 4 line 2439.
    Venus and Adonis, line 107.
    Winter's Tale, IV 4 line 2209.

Dugs: animal nipple, or, contemptuously, the human female breast, 1520s, origin obscure, related to Swedish: *dagga*, Danish: *dægge* to suckle.
    Antony and Cleopatra, V 2 line 3380.
    As You Like It, II 4 line 766.
    Hamlet, V 2 line 3824.
    Henry VI, Part II, III 2 line 2089.
    Richard II, V 3 line 2670.
    Richard III, II 2 line 1300.
    Romeo and Juliet, I 3 lines 411, 416, 417.
    Venus and Adonis, line 897.

Dunghill: early14c.
    As You Like It, I 1 line 13.
    Henry IV, Part II, V 3 line 3513.
    Henry V, IV 3 line 2337.
    Henry VI, Part I, I 3 line 365.
    Henry VI, Part II, I 3 line 594; Henry VI, Part II, IV 10 line 2970.
    King John, IV 3 line 2110.
    King Lear, III 7 line 2232; King Lear, IV 6 line 2863.

Love's Labour's Lost, V 1 line 1805; Love's Labour's Lost, V 1 line 1807.
Merry Wives of Windsor, I 3 line 361.

Dungy: spread with animal excrement. Old English, of Germanic origin; related to German: *Dung*, Swedish: *dynga*, Icelandic: *dyngja: dung, dunghill, heap*, and Danish: *dynge*: *heap*.
Antony and Cleopatra, I 1 line 43.
Winter's Tale, II 1 line 785.

Eagle: mid-14c., from Old French: *egle*. It signifies inspiration, release from bondage, victory, longevity, speed, pride, father and royalty; it is often an emblem for powerful nations. The Roman, French, Austrian, German, and American peoples have all adopted this image as their symbol. Hence, a two-headed eagle has come to often mean the union of two nations, but it also means creative power.
Antony and Cleopatra, II 2 line 906.
Coriolanus, III 1 line 1898; Coriolanus, V 6 line 3956.
Cymbeline, I 1 line 176; Cymbeline, III 3 line 1624; Cymbeline, IV 2 line 2758; Cymbeline, V 3 line 3068; Cymbeline, V 4 line 3241; Cymbeline, V 4 line 3263; Cymbeline, V 4 line 3266; Cymbeline, V 5 line 3895; Cymbeline, V 5 lines 3943, 3946.
Henry IV, Part I, II 4 line 1316; Henry IV, Part I, IV 1 line 2325.
Henry V, I 2 line 314.
Henry VI, Part I, I 2 line 340.
Henry VI, Part II, III 1 line 1532; Henry VI, Part II, IV 1 line 2265.
Henry VI, Part III, I 1 line 286; Henry VI, Part III, II 1 line 718; Henry VI, Part III, V 2 line 2734.
Julius Caesar, V 1 line 2437.
King John, V 2 line 2431.
Love's Labour's Lost, IV 3 line 1565; Love's Labour's Lost, IV 3 line1667.
Macbeth, I 2 line 56.
Pericles, IV 3 line 1869.
Phoenix and the Turtle, line 9.
Rape of Lucrece, line 1066.
Richard II, I 3 line 426; Richard II, III 3 line 1709.
Richard III, I 1 line 139; Richard III, I 3 line 532.
Romeo and Juliet, III 5 line 2336.
Timon of Athens, I 1 line 63; Timon of Athens, IV 3 line 1912.
Titus Andronicus, IV 4 line 2097.
Troilus and Cressida, I 2 line 393.
Twelfth Night, II 3 line 878.
Venus and Adonis, line 75.

Ear: organ of hearing, Old English: *eare*: *ear*. The belief that itching or burning ears means someone is talking about you is mentioned in Pliny's *Natural History* (77 C.E.). According to a well-known superstition, much credited in days gone by, and still extensively believed, a tingling of the right ear is considered lucky, being supposed to denote that a friend is speaking well of one, whereas a tingling of the left is said to imply the opposite. This notion, however, varies in different localities, as in some places it is the tingling of the left ear which denotes the friend, and the tingling of the right ear the enemy. In Shakespeare's day it was customary for young gallants to wear a long lock of hair dangling by the ear, known as a *love-lock*. The ear is associated with the spiral, the whorled shell, and the shell, in turn, is a symbol of the vulva. Thus, there is a close connection between the ear and birth itself. It has long been considered the seat of memory, receptivity, inquisitiveness and awakening. Small ears represent shyness and low self-esteem, while large ears reflect an extroverted personality and adaptive ease. Seen as the portal for temptation or flattery

All's Well That Ends Well, I 2 line 235; All's Well That Ends Well, I 2 line 296; All's Well That Ends Well, I 3 line 364; All's Well That Ends Well, I 3 line 422; All's Well That Ends Well, III 2 line 1538; All's Well That Ends Well, III 5 line 1662; All's Well That Ends Well, IV 3 line 2315; All's Well That Ends Well, V 1 line 2573; All's Well That Ends Well, V 3 line 2692; All's Well That Ends Well, V 3 line 3010.

Antony and Cleopatra, I 2 line 128; Antony and Cleopatra, I 4 line 478; Antony and Cleopatra, I 5 line 569; Antony and Cleopatra, II 1 line 655; Antony and Cleopatra, II 5 line 1079; Antony and Cleopatra, II 5 line 1116; Antony and Cleopatra, II 7 line 1412; Antony and Cleopatra, II 7 line 1508; Antony and Cleopatra, III 2 line 1648; Antony and Cleopatra, III 4 line 1756; Antony and Cleopatra, III 6 line 1887; Antony and Cleopatra, III 12 line 2221; Antony and Cleopatra, III 13 line 2634; Antony and Cleopatra, IV 8 line 2825.

As You Like It, III 5 line 1712; As You Like It, III 5 line 1757.

Comedy of Errors, II 1 line 318; Comedy of Errors, II 1 line 321; Comedy of Errors, II 2 line 503; Comedy of Errors, II 2 line 573; Comedy of Errors, III 2 line 924; Comedy of Errors, IV 1 line 1055; Comedy of Errors, IV 4 line 1255; Comedy of Errors, IV 4 line 1278; Comedy of Errors, IV 4 line 1303; Comedy of Errors, V 1 line 1450; Comedy of Errors, V 1 line 1697; Comedy of Errors, V 1 line 1755.

Coriolanus, I 1 line 247; Coriolanus, II 1 line 1220; Coriolanus, II 2 line 1258; Coriolanus, II 2 line 1285; Coriolanus, II 2 line 1328; Coriolanus, III 2 line 2163; Coriolanus, IV 3 line 2581; Coriolanus, IV 5 line 2821; Coriolanus, IV 5 line 2971; Coriolanus, IV 6 line 3138; Coriolanus, V 2 line 3383; Coriolanus, V 2 line 3462; Coriolanus, V 3 line 3495; Coriolanus, V 3 line 3510; Coriolanus, V 6 line 3820; Coriolanus, V 6 line 3962.

Cymbeline, I 3 line 282; Cymbeline, I 6 line 757; Cymbeline , I 6 line 770; Cymbeline, II 1 line 863; Cymbeline, II 3 line 1008; Cymbeline, III 1 line 1413; Cymbeline, III 2 line 1510; Cymbeline, III 4 line 1845; Cymbeline, III 4 line 1891; Cymbeline, III 4 line 1920; Cymbeline, IV 4 line 2906; Cymbeline, V 5 line 3443.

Hamlet, I 1 line 41; Hamlet, I 2 line 377; Hamlet, I 2 line 401; Hamlet, I 3 line 514; Hamlet, I 3 line 553; Hamlet, I 5 line 758; Hamlet, I 5 line 773; Hamlet, I 5 line 801; Hamlet, II 2 line 1225; Hamlet, II 2 line 1464; Hamlet, II 2 line 1550; Hamlet, II 2 line 1636; Hamlet, II 2 line 1639;

Hamlet, III 2 line 2019; Hamlet, III 2 line 2148; Hamlet, III 4 line 2455; Hamlet, III 4 line 2470; Hamlet, III 4 line 2490; Hamlet, IV 2 line 2699; Hamlet, IV 5 lines 2950, 2954r; Hamlet, IV 6 line 3122; Hamlet, IV 7 line, 3133; Hamlet, V 2 line 4035.
Henry IV, Part I, I 2 line 256; Henry IV, Part I, I 3 line 551; Henry IV, Part I, I 3 line 557; Henry IV, Part I, I 3 line 573; Henry IV, Part I, II 2 line 772; Henry IV, Part I, III 2 line 1847; Henry IV, Part I, IV 1 line 2343; Henry IV, Part I, V 4 line 3108.
Henry IV, Part II, Prologue 1 lines 2, 9; Henry IV, Part II, I 1 lines 136, 137; Henry IV, Part II, I 2 line 436; Henry IV, Part II, I 2 line 522; Henry IV, Part II, II 2 line 1022; Henry IV, Part II, II 4 line 1545; Henry IV, Part II, II 4 line 1583; Henry IV, Part II, IV 5 line 3008; Henry IV, Part II, V 2 line 3367.
Henry V, I 1 line 87; Henry V, II 2 line 771; Henry V, III 1 line 1096; Henry V, III 7 line 1720; Henry V, IV 0 line 1798; Henry V, IV 1 line 2062; Henry V, IV 7 line 2649; Henry V, IV 7 line 2694; Henry V, V 2 line 3084; Henry V, V 2 line 3222.
Henry VI, Part I, II 3 line 835.
Henry VI, Part II, I 3 line 534; Henry VI, Part II, IV 7 line 2662; Henry VI, Part II, IV 7 line 2704.
Henry VI, Part III, I 1 line 7; Henry VI, Part III, II 6 line 1349; Henry VI, PartIII, III 3 line 1756; Henry VI, Part III, III 3 line 1830; Henry VI, Part III, IV 8 line 2561; Henry VI, Part III, V 1 line 2712; Henry VI, Part III, V 6 line 3023.
Henry VIII, II 4 line 1516; Henry VIII, III 2 line 1890; Henry VIII, IV 2 line 2566; Henry VIII, V 1 line 2797; Henry VIII, V 1 line 2830.
Julius Caesar, I 2 line 305; Julius Caesar, I 3 line 468; Julius Caesar, II 1 line 684; Julius Caesar, II 1 line 952; Julius Caesar, III 1 line 1254; Julius Caesar, III 2 line 1617; Julius Caesar, IV 1 line 1888; Julius Caesar, V 3 lines 2585, 2587.
King John, I 1 line 45; King John, I 1 line 148; King John, II 1 line 443; King John, II 1 line 507; King John, II 1 line 776; King John, II 1 line 891; King John, III 3 lines 1350, 1352; King John, III 4 line 1497; King John, IV 2 line 1851; King John, IV 2 line 1933; King John, V 2 line 2456; King John, V 6 line 2595; King John, V 7 line 2701.
King Lear, II 4 line 1530; King Lear, II 4 line 1614; King Lear, III 4 line 1887; KIng Lear, IV 6 lines 2759, 2760; King Lear, V 3 line 3366.
Love's Labour's Lost, II 1 line 560; Love's Labour's Lost, IV 1 line 1032; Love's Labour's Lost, IV 2 line 1146; Love's Labour's Lost, IV 3 line 1364; Love's Labour's Lost, IV 3 lines 1679, 1962; Love's Labour's Lost, V 2 line 2110; Love's Labour's Lost, V 2 line 2199; Love's Labour's Lost, V 2 line 2362; Love's Labour's Lost, V 2 line 2370; Love's Labour's Lost, V 2 line 2693; Love's Labour's Lost, V 2 lines 2804, 2806; Love's Labour's Lost, V 2 lines 2850, 2858.
Macbeth, I 5 line 370; Macbeth, II 3 line 863; Macbeth, III 4 line 1369; Macbeth, IV 1 line 1640; Macbeth, IV 3 line 2078; Macbeth, V 7 line 2441; Macbeth, V 8 2499.
Measure for Measure, I 3 line 305; Measure for Measure, II 1 line 626; Measure for Measure, III 1 line 1440; Measure for Measure, IV 1

line 1857; Measure for Measure, IV 2 line 2001; Measure for Measure, IV 3 line 2227; Measure for Measure, V 1 line 2543; Measure for Measure, V 1 line 2725; Measure for Measure, V 1 line 2982.
Merchant of Venice, I 1 line 104; Merchant of Venice, I 2 line 271; Merchant of Venice, II 5 line 882; Merchant of Venice, III 1 line 1324; Merchant of Venice, III 2 line 1457; Merchant of Venice, V 1 lines 2510, 2522.
Merry Wives of Windsor, I 1 line 134; Merry Wives of Windsor, I 1 line 199; Merry Wives of Windsor, I 4 line 505; Merry Wives of Windsor, II 2 line 890; Merry Wives of Windsor, II 3 line 1156; Merry Wives of Windsor, III 1 line 1267; Merry Wives of Windsor, IV 5 line 2388.
Midsummer Night's Dream, I 1 lines 192, 196; Midsummer Night's Dream, II 1 line 382; Midsummer Night's Dream, III 1 line 960; Midsummer Night's Dream, III 2 lines 1218, 1222; Midsummer Night's Dream, IV 1 line 1549; Midsummer Night's Dream, IV 1 line 1573; Midsummer Night's Dream, IV 1 line 1676; Midsummer Night's Dream, IV 1 line 1773.
Much Ado About Nothing, II 1 line 557; Much Ado About Nothing, II 1 line 693; Much Ado About Nothing, III 1 line 1076; Much Ado About Nothing, III 1 line 1107; Much Ado About Nothing, III 1 line 1187; Much Ado About Nothing, IV 2 line 2008; Much Ado About Nothing, V 1 lines 2071, 2074; Much Ado About Nothing, V 1 line 2219; Much Ado About Nothing, V 1 line 2384.
Othello, I 3 line 469; Othello, I 3 line 494; Othello, I 3 line 568; Othello, I 3 line 596; Othello, I 3 line 751; Othello, II 3 line 1508; Othello, III 3 line 1791; Othello, IV 1 line 2459; Othello, IV 2 line 2923.
Passionate Pilgrim, lines 47, 327, 350.
Pericles, I 0 line 5; Pericles, I 2 line 304; Pericles, II 5 line 1042; Pericles, III 1 line 1199; Pericles, IV 1 line 1624; Pericles, IV 2 line 1745; Pericles, IV 4 line 1896; Pericles, IV 6 line 2109; Pericles, V 1 line 2275; Pericles, V 1 line 2290; Pericles, V 1 line 2308; Pericles, V 3 line 2355.
Rape of Lucrece, lines 86, 90, 157, 334, 609, 1177, 1377, 1459, 1467.
Richard II, I 1 line 115; Richard II, I 1 line 118; Richard II, II 1 line 686; Richard II, II 1 line 698; Richard II, II 1 lines 702, 709; Richard II, II 1 line 925; Richard II, III 2 line 1503; Richard II, III 2 line 1624; Richard II, III 3 line 1671; Richard II, IV 1 line 2036; Richard II, V 3 line 2708; Richard II, V 5 lines 2792, 2795.
Richard III, I 3 line 507; Richard III, I 4 line 855; Richard III, I 4 line 892; Richard III, II 2 line 1305; Richard III, II 4 line 1521; Richard III, III 2 line 1902; Richard III, III 7 line 2312; Richard III, IV 2 line 2673; Richard III, IV 4 line 3034; Richard III, IV 4 line 3133.
Romeo and Juliet, Prologue 1 line 13; Romeo and Juliet, I 1 line 131; Romeo and Juliet, I 4 line 539; Romeo and Juliet, I 4 line 585; Romeo and Juliet, I 5 line 640; Romeo and Juliet, I 5 line 668; Romeo and Juliet, II 2 line 907; Romeo and Juliet, II 2 line 1027; Romeo and Juliet, II 3 line 1134; Romeo and Juliet, II 4 line 1172; Romeo and

Juliet, II 4 line 1234; Romeo and Juliet, III 1 lines 1580, 1581; Romeo and Juliet, III 3 line 1932; Romeo and Juliet, III 5 line 2100; Romeo and Juliet, V 3 line 2937; Romeo and Juliet, V 3 line 3167.
Sonnet VIII line 6; Sonnet C line 7; Sonnet CXXVIII line 4; Sonnet CXL line 12; Sonnet CXLI line 5.
Taming of the Shrew, I 1 line 464; Taming of the Shrew, I 2 line 569; Taming of the Shrew, I 2 line 749; Taming of the Shrew, IV 1 line 1668; Taming of the Shrew, IV 3 line 2040; Taming of the Shrew, IV 4 line 2211.
Tempest, I 2 line 129; Tempest, I 2 line 185; Tempest, I 2 line 465; Tempest, II 1 line 806; Tempest, II 1 line 1060; Tempest, II 1 line 1062; Tempest, III 1 line 1329; Tempest, III 2 line 1536; Tempest, IV 1 lines 1911, 1913; Tempest, IV 1 line 1956; Tempest, V 1 line 2392.
Timon of Athens, I 1 line 100; Timon of Athens, I 2 line 467; Timon of Athens, I 2 line 624; Timon of Athens, III 6 line 1468; Timon of Athens, IV 3 line 1803; Timon of Athens, IV 3 line 1903; Timon of Athens, V 1 line 2484.
Titus Andronicus, II 1 line 684; Titus Andronicus, II 3 line 848; Titus Andronicus, II 3 line 899; Titus Andronicus, III 1 line 1216; Titus Andronicus, IV 4 line 2015; Titus Andronicus, IV 4 lines 2110, 2112, 2113; Titus Andronicus, V 2 line 2345; Titus Andronicus, V 3 line 2536; Titus Andronicus, V 3 lines 2621, 2623.
Troilus and Cressida, I 3 line 520; Troilus and Cressida, I 3 line 597; Troilus and Cressida, I 3 line 674; Troilus and Cressida, I 3 line 706; Troilus and Cressida, I 3 line 709; Troilus and Cressida, II 1 line 926; Troilus and Cressida, II 2 line 1057; Troilus and Cressida, II 2 line 1170; Troilus and Cressida, V 2 line 3084; Troilus and Cressida, V 2 line 3194; Troilus and Cressida, V 2 line 3248; Troilus and Cressida, V 2 line 3256; Troilus and Cressida, V 3 line 3277.
Twelfth Night, I 1 line 6; Twelfth Night, I 5 line 500; Twelfth Night, I 5 line 504; Twelfth Night, II 3 line 825; Twelfth Night, III 1 line 1324; Twelfth Night, V 1 line 2300; Twelfth Night, V 1 line 2503.
Two Gentlemen of Verona, III 1 line 1279; Two Gentlemen of Verona, III 1 line 1313; Two Gentlemen of Verona, IV 2 line 1646; Two Gentlemen of Verona, IV 2 line 1695.
Venus and Adonis, lines 13, 94, 165, 291, 317, 453r, 457, 680, 720, 800, 801, 830, 911, 946, 1045, 1147.
Winter's Tale, I 2 line 276; Winter's Tale, I 2 line 377; Winter's Tale, II 1 line 639; Winter's Tale, IV 4 line 2077; Winter's Tale, IV 4 line 2571; Winter's Tale, IV 4 line 2647; Winter's Tale, V 1 line 2899; Winter's Tale, V 1 line 3064; Winter's Tale, V 2 line 3171.

Eanling: a yeanling or lamb.
Merchant of Venice, I 3 line 405.

Earth: Old English: *eorthe*, of Germanic origin; related to Dutch *aarde* and German *Erde*. Also, *eorþe: ground, soil, dry land*, also used (along with *middangeard*) for the (material) world (as opposed to the heavens or the underworld). The earth considered as a planet was so called from c.1400. The earth was also one of the elements in ancient and medieval philosophy.

All's Well That Ends Well, II 3 line 915; All's Well That Ends Well, II 4 line 1215; All's Well That Ends Well, IV 2 line 2079.

Antony and Cleopatra, I 1 line 21; Antony and Cleopatra, I 1 line 43; Antony and Cleopatra, I 2 line 258; Antony and Cleopatra, I 5 line 548; Antony and Cleopatra, II 7 line 1455; Antony and Cleopatra, III 6 line 1899; Antony and Cleopatra, III 7 line 2018; Antony and Cleopatra, III 12 line 2214; Antony and Cleopatra, IV 3 line 2598; Antony and Cleopatra, IV 6 line 2742; Antony and Cleopatra, IV 8 line 2828; Antony and Cleopatra, IV 15 line 3241; Antony and Cleopatra, V 2 line 3487; Antony and Cleopatra, V 2 line 3842.

As You Like It, 1 2 line 312; As You Like It, V 4 line 2503.

Comedy of Errors, I 1 line 100; Comedy of Errors, II 1 line 289; Comedy of Errors, II 2 line 602; Comedy of Errors, III 2 lines 794r, 796; Comedy of Errors, III 2 line 828.

Coriolanus, II 1 line 1015; Coriolanus, III 1 line 1743; Coriolanus, IV 2 line 2638; Coriolanus, V 3 line 3523; Coriolanus, V 3 line 3546; Coriolanus, V 6 line 3969.

Cymbeline, I 1 line 24; Cymbeline, II 1 line 868; Cymbeline, III 6 line 2193; Cymbeline, V 4 line 3189; Cymbeline, V 5 line 3624.

Hamlet, I 1 lines 140, 155; Hamlet, I 1 line 176; Hamlet, I 2 line 309; Hamlet, I 2 line 331; Hamlet, I 2 line 345; Hamlet, I 2 line 479; Hamlet, I 5 line 830; Hamlet, I 5 line 915; Hamlet, I 5 line 919; Hamlet, II 2 line 1329; Hamlet, II 2 line 1393; Hamlet, III 1 line 1820; Hamlet, III 2 line 2108; Hamlet, IV 4 line 2835; Hamlet, IV 5 line 3093; Hamlet, V 1 line 3497; Hamlet, V 1 line 3505; Hamlet, V 1 lines 3539r, 3543; Hamlet, V 1 line 3572; Hamlet, V 1 line 3586; Hamlet, V 2 line 3768; Hamlet, V 2 line 3920.

Henry IV, Part I, I 3 lines 381, 385; Henry IV, Part I, II 2 line 853; Henry IV, Part I, II 3 line 901; Henry IV, Part I, II 4 line 1119; Henry IV, Part I, III 1 line 1558; Henry IV, Part I, III 1 line 1563; Henry IV, Part I, III 1 line 1564; Henry IV, Part I, III 1 line 1566; Henry IV, Part I, III 1 lines 1567, 1570, 1574, 1576; Henry IV, Part I, V 2 line 2875; Henry IV, Part I, V 4 line 3047; Henry IV, Part I, V 4 lines 3055, 3056.

Henry IV, Part II, Prologue 1 line 6; Henry IV, Part II, I 1 line 168; Henry IV, Part II, I 1 line 211; Henry IV, Part II, I 3 line 723; Henry IV, Part II, IV 1 line 2286; Henry IV, Part II, IV 5 line 3086.

Henry V, Prologue 1 line 28; Henry V, I 2 line 267; Henry V, III 7 lines 1653, 1657; Henry V, III 7 line 1663; Henry V, IV 3 line 2340; Henry V, IV 7 line 2663.

Henry VI, Part I, I 2 line 192; Henry VI, Part I, I 2 line 343; Henry VI, Part I, II 2 line 761; Henry VI, Part I, IV 2 line 1978; Henry VI, PartI, IV 3 line 2046; Henry VI, Part I, V 3 line 2459; Henry VI, Part I, V 4 line 2712.

Henry VI, Part II, I 1 line 26; Henry VI, Part II, I 2 line 278; Henry VI, Part II, I 4 line 637; Henry VI, Part II, II 1 line 745; Henry VI, Part II, II 1 line 762; Henry VI, Part II, II 1 line 810; Henry VI, Part II, III 2 line 1830; Henry VI, Part II, III 2 line 2067; Henry VI, Part II, III 2 line 2081;

Henry VI, Part II, IV 9 line 2832; Henry VI, Part II, IV 10 line 2939; Henry VI, Part II, V 1 line 3158; Henry VI, Part II, V 2 line 3258.
Henry VI, Part III, I 4 line 452; Henry VI, Part III, II 1 line 664; Henry VI, Part III, II 3 line 1043; Henry VI, Part III, II 3 line 1051; Henry VI, Part III, II 3 lines 1063, 1071; Henry VI, Part III, II 6 line 1263; Henry VI, Part III, III 2 line 1654; Henry VI, Part III, V 2 lines 2731, 2750.
Henry VIII, I 1 line 53; Henry VIII, I 1 line 99; Henry VIII, II 4 line 1510; Henry VIII, III 1 line 1783; Henry VIII, III 2 line 2000; Henry VIII, III 2 line 2014; Henry VIII, III 2 line 2288; Henry VIII, IV 2 line 2560; Henry VIII, IV 2 line 2583; Henry VIII, IV 2 line 2684; Henry VIII, V 1 line 2946.
Julius Caesar, I 3 line 424; Julius Caesar, I 3 line 471; Julius Caesar, II 2 line 973; Julius Caesar, II 1 line 1483.
King John, I 1 line 271; King John, II 1 line 472; King John, II 1 line 613; King John, II 1 line 654; King John, III 1 line 988; King John, III 1 line 999; King John, III 1 line 1069; King John, IV 2 line 1960; King John, IV 3 line 2056; King John, V 7 line 2709.
King Lear, I 2 line 424; King Lear, II 4 line 1584; King Lear, III 1 line 1622; King Lear, III 4 line 1914; King Lear, IV 4 line 2534; King Lear, V 3 line 3438.
Love's Labour's Lost, I 1 line 90; Love's Labour's Lost, I 1 line 221; Love's Labour's Lost, IV 2 line 1148; Love's Labour's Lost, IV 2 line 1235; Love's Labour's Lost, IV 2 line 1266; Love's Labour's Lost, IV 3 lines 1389, 1392; Love's Labour's Lost, IV 3 line 1411; Love's Labour's Lost, V 2 line 2047.
Lover's Complaint, line 25.
Macbeth, I 3 line 141; Macbeth, I 3 line 181; Macbeth, II 1 line 635; Macbeth, II 3 line 829; Macbeth, II 4 line 957; Macbeth, III 4 line 1388; Macbeth, IV 1 line 1664; Macbeth, IV 2 line 1821; Macbeth, IV 3 line 1956.
Measure for Measure, II 4 line 1072; Measure for Measure, II 4 line 1121; Measure for Measure, V 1 line 2927.
Merchant of Venice, II 1 line 543; Merchant of Venice, II 7 line 1023; Merchant of Venice, II 8 line 1107; Merchant of Venice, III 5 lines 1912, 1913, 1916; Merchant of Venice, IV 1 line 2137.
Merry Wives of Windsor, III 2 line 1357; Merry Wives of Windsor, III 4 line 1718; Merry Wives of Windsor, V 5 line2644.
Midsummer Night's Dream, I 1 line 81; Midsummer Night's Dream, I 1 line 152; Midsummer Night's Dream, II 1 line 528; Midsummer Night's Dream, II 1 line 547; Midsummer Night's Dream, III 2 line 1086; Midsummer Night's Dream, V 1 line 1843r.
Much Ado About Nothing, II 1 line 451; Much Ado About Nothing, IV 1 line 1769.
Othello, III 3 line 2049; Othello, IV 1 line 2687; Othello, IV 2 line 2828; Othello, V 2 line 3435.
Passionate Pilgrim, lines, 35, 38, 71.
Pericles, I 1 lines 95, 98; Pericles, I 1 lines 150, 152; Pericles, I 2 line 359; Pericles, I 4 line 450; Pericles, II 1 line 581; Pericles, III 1 line

1229; Pericles, III 2 line 1303; Pericles, IV 3 line 1823; Pericles, IV 4 lines 1920, 1921.
Rape of Lucrece, lines 136, 538, 600, 623, 847, 1181, 1277,1888.
Richard II, I 1 line 26; Richard II, I 1 line 40; Richard II, I 1 line 108; Richard II, I 2 line 220; Richard II, I 3 line 364; Richard II, I 3 line 422; Richard II, II 1 lines 723, 732; Richard II, II 2 line 1075; Richard II, II 4 line 1340; Richard II, II 4 line 1351; Richard II, III 2 lines 1414, 1418, 1420, 1432; Richard II, III 2 line 1477; Richard II, III 2 lines 1557, 1562; Richard II, III 3 lines 1695, 1696; Richard II, III 3 line 1810; Richard II, III 3 line 1839; Richard II, III 4 line 1944; Richard II, IV 1 line 2034; Richard II, IV 1 line 2052; Richard II, IV 1 line 2081; Richard II, IV 1 line 2131; Richard II, IV 1 line 2208; Richard II, V 1 line 2338; Richard II, V 1 line 2364; Richard II, V 3 line 2606; Richard II, V 3 line 2722.
Richard III, I 2 lines 225, 237, 239; Richard III, I 2 line 286; Richard III, I 2 line 320; Richard III, II 1 line 1126; Richard III, III 5 line 2096; Richard III, IV 4 line 2821; Richard III, IV 4 2847; Richard III, IV 4 line 2870; Richard III, IV 4 line 2665r; Richard III, IV 4 line 3048; Richard III, V 3 line 3782.
Romeo and Juliet, I 2 lines 284, 285, 295; Romeo and Juliet, I 5 line 669; Romeo and Juliet, II 1 line 797; Romeo and Juliet, II 3 lines 1067, 1075, 1076; Romeo and Juliet, III 1 line 1626; Romeo and Juliet, III 2 line 1781r; Romeo and Juliet, III 2 line 1818; Romeo and Juliet, III 3 lines 2000, 2001; Romeo and Juliet, III 5 lines 2321, 2322, 2325; Romeo and Juliet, IV 3 lines 2694, 2699; Romeo and Juliet, V 1 line 2856; Romeo and Juliet, V 3 line 2984.
Sonnet XIV line 4; Sonnet XVII line 8; Sonnet XIX line 2; Sonnet XIX line 2; Sonnet XXI line 6; Sonnet XXIX line 12; Sonnet XLIV lines 6, 11; Sonnet LXV line 1; Sonnet LXXIV line 7r; Sonnet LXXXI line 2; Sonnet LXXXI line 7.
Taming of the Shrew, Prologue 2 line 190.
Tempest, I 2 line 94; Tempest, I 2 line 388; Tempest, I 2 line 409; Tempest, I 2 line 459; Tempest, I 2 line 550; Tempest, I 2 line 571; Tempest, Tempest, I 2 line 683; Tempest, II 1 line 962; Tempest, II 1 line 1019; Tempest, II 2 line 1214; Tempest, III 1 line 1358; Tempest, IV 1 line 1793; Tempest, IV 1 line 1826; Tempest, V 1 line 2076.
Timon of Athens, II 2 line 915; Timon of Athens, IV 1 line 1566; Timon of Athens, IV 3 lins 1664, 1685; Timon of Athens, IV 3 line 2130; Timon of Athens, IV 3 line 2153; Timon of Athens, IV 3 line 2177.
Titus Andronicus, I 1 lines 116, 118; Titus Andronicus, I 1 line 251; Titus Andronicus, II 1 line 557; Titus Andronicus, II 3 line 976; Titus Andronicus, II 3 line 998; Titus Andronicus, III 1 lines 1139, 1141; Titus Andronicus, III 1 line 1344; Titus Andronicus, III 1 lines 1360, 1365, 1367; Titus Andronicus, IV 1 line 1628; Titus Andronicus, IV 3 line 1892; Titus Andronicus, IV 3 line 1930; Titus Andronicus, V 2 line 2510; Titus Andronicus, V 3 line 2724.
Troilus and Cressida, I 3 line 454; Troilus and Cressida, I 3 line 550; Troilus and Cressida, III 2 line 1828; Troilus and Cressida, III 2 line 1843; Troilus and Cressida, IV 2 line 2381; Troilus and Cressida, IV 2 line 2402; Troilus and Cressida, IV 5 line 2613; Troilus and Cressida, V

2 line 3223; Troilus and Cressida, V 8 line 3609; Troilus and Cressida, V 10 line 3660.
Twelfth Night, I 5 line 566; Twelfth Night, V 1 line 2288.
Two Gentlemen of Verona, II 4 line 796; Two Gentlemen of Verona, II 4 line 803; Two Gentlemen of Verona, II 4 line 811; Two Gentlemen of Verona, II 4 line 818; Two Gentlemen of Verona, II 7 line 1053; Two Gentlemen of Verona, IV 2 line 1685; Two Gentlemen of Verona, V 4 2234.
Venus and Adonis, lines 48, 189, 190, 218, 287, 360, 505, 514, 567, 709, 744, 775, 816, 885, 955, 1069.
Winter's Tale, I 2 line 422r; Winter's Tale II 1 785; Winter's Tale, III 1 line 1189; Winter's Tale III 3 line 1536; Winter's Tale, IV 4 line 1977; Winter's Tale, IV 4 line 2274; Winter's Tale, IV 4 line 2411; Winter's Tale, IV 4 line 2425; Winter's Tale, V 1 line 2939; Winter's Tale, V 1 line 2984; Winter's Tale, V 1 line 3006; Winter's Tale, V 1 line 3062; Winter's Tale, V 2 line 3184.

Earthquake: late 13c., *eorthequakynge*, from earth + quake. In this sense Old English had *eorddyn, eordhrernes, eordbeofung, eordstyren*.
All's Well That Ends Well, I 3 line 404.
As You Like It, III 2 line 1293.
Henry V, II 4 line 1004.
King John, V 2 line 2320.
Much Ado About Nothing, I 1 line 245.
Romeo and Juliet, I 3 line 408.
Tempest, II 1 line 1063.

Ebb: Old English: *ebba: ebb, low tide*. The verb is Old English: *ebbian*. Figurative sense of decline, decay is c.1400
Antony and Cleopatra, I 4 line 471; Antony and Cleopatra, II 7 line 1397.
As You Like It, II 7 line 968.
Henry IV, Part I, I 2 lines 142, 1148.
Henry IV, Part II, II 2 line 964; Henry IV, Part II, IV 4 line 2878; Henry IV, Part II, V 2 line 3379.
Henry VI, Part III, IV 8 line 2580.
King Lear, V 3 line 3142.
Love's Labour's Lost, IV 3 line 1560.
Othello, III 3 lines 2141, 2144.
Rape of Lucrece, lines 1382, 1620.
Romeo and Juliet, III 5 line 2240.
Tempest, I 2 line 606; Tempest, II 1 line 947; Tempest, II 1 line 952; Tempest, V 1 line 2056; Tempest, V 1 line 2344.
Timon of Athens, II 2 line 828.
Troilus and Cressida, II 3 line 1349.
Winter's Tale, V 1 line 2948.

Ebony: 1590s, from *hebenyf* (late 14c.), perhaps a Middle English misreading of Latin: *hebeninus: of ebony*, from Greek: *ebeninos*, from *ebenos* probably

from Egyptian *hbnj* or another Semitic source. Figurative use to suggest intense blackness is from 1620s. As an adjective, from 1590s. The wood of this tree was regarded as the typical emblem of darkness, the tree itself, however, was largely unknown in Shakespeare's time.
>   **Love's Labour's Lost**, IV 3 line 1591; Love's Labour's Lost, IV 3 line 1592.
>   **Twelfth Night**, IV 2 line 2059.

Eclipse: late 13c., from Old French: *eclipse: eclipse, darkness* (12c.), figurative use is from 1580s.
>   **Antony and Cleopatra**, III 13 line 2439.
>   **Hamlet**, I 1 line 137.
>   **Henry VI, Part I**, IV 5 line 2187.
>   **Henry VI, Part III**, IV 6 line 2377.
>   **King Lear**, I 2 line 429; King Lear, I 2 line 459; King Lear, I 2 line 463.
>   **Macbeth**, IV 1 line 1575.
>   **Othello**, V 2 line 3420.
>   **Rape of Lucrece**, line 1275.
>   **Sonnet** XXXV line 3; Sonnet CVII line 5.

Eel: Old English: *æl*. Used figuratively for slipperiness from at least 1520s.
>   **King Lear**, II 4 line 1399.
>   **Love's Labour's Lost**, I 2 line 333; Love's Labour's Lost, I 2 line 334; Love's Labour's Lost, I 2 line 335.
>   **Pericles**, IV 2 line 1806.
>   **Taming of the Shrew**, IV 3 line 2136.

Eglantine: sweet briar, c.1400, from Old French: *aiglent* : *dog rose*.
>   **Cymbeline**, IV 2 line 2611.
>   **Midsummer Night's Dream**, II 1 line 631.

Egg: mid-14c., from northern England dialect, from Old Norse: *egg*, which vied with Middle English: *eye, eai* (from Old English: *æg*) until finally displacing it after 1500. Its physical characteristics are unique and well-defined; the egg is fragile, a repository of new life, with a shape resembling that of the testicles. The new life that lies dormant in the egg came to be associated with life-energy. In general the egg symbolises a primeval embryonic form from which the world later emerged.
>   **All's Well That Ends Well**, IV 3 line 2332.
>   **As You Like It**, II 5 line 831; As You Like It, III 2 line 1155.
>   **Coriolanus**, IV 4 line 2742.
>   **Henry IV, Part I**, I 2 line 132; Henry IV, Part I, II 1 line 701.
>   Henry V, I 2 line 316.
>   **Julius Caesar**, II 1 line 633.
>   **King Lear**, I 4 line 681; King Lear, I 4 lines 684, 685; King Lear, III 7 line 2243; King Lear, IV 6 line 2658.
>   **Love's Labour's Lost**, V 1 line 1802.
>   **Macbeth**, IV 2 line 1833.
>   **Merry Wives of Windsor**, III 5 line 1775.

Romeo and Juliet, III 1 lines 1520, 1522.
Troilus and Cressida, I 2 line 282; Troilus and Cressida, I 2 line 283; Troilus and Cressida, V 1 line 2966.
Winter's Tale, I 2 line 209; Winter's Tale, I 2 line 242.

Eggshell: early 15c., from egg + shell. Earlier *ay-schelle* (c.1300).
Cymbeline, III 1 line 1440.
Hamlet, IV 4 line 2841.

Eglantine: sweet briar, c.1400, from Old French: *aiglent: dog rose.*
Cymbeline, IV 2 line 2611.
Midsummer Night's Dream, II 1 line 631.

Eisel: vinegar.
Sonnet CXI line 10.

Elbow: c.1200, *elbowe*, from Old English: *elnboga*, from *ell* (length of the forearm) + *boga* (bow, arch). According to a popular belief the itching of the elbow denoted an approaching change of some kind or other.
Henry IV, Part I, V 1 line 2700.
Henry IV, Part II, I 2 line 365; Henry IV, Part II, II 1 line 738.
Henry V, III 4 line 1352; Henry V, III 4 line 1353; Henry V, III 4 line 1358; Henry V, III 4 line 1359; Henry V, III 4 line 1374; Henry V, III 4 line 1375; Henry V, III 4 line 1378.
Julius Caesar, III 1 line 1321.
King John, I 1 line 200; King John, V 7 line 2660.
King Lear, IV 3 line 2500.
Love's Labour's Lost, V 2 line 1993.
Measure for Measure, II 1 line 515.
Merchant of Venice, II 2 line 567.
Much Ado About Nothing, III 3 line 1414; Much Ado About Nothing, III 3 line 1415.
Othello, V 1 line 3138.
Richard III, I 4 line 974.
Troilus and Cressida, II 1 line 900.
Venus and Adonis, line 64.

Elder: This plant whilst surrounded by an extensive folklore, has from time immemorial possessed an evil reputation, and been regarded as one of bad omen. Type of berry tree, c.1400, from earlier ellen, from Old English: *ellæn, ellærn: elderberry tree.*
Cymbeline, IV 2 line 2394.
Merry Wives of Windsor, II 3 line 1127.
Titus Andronicus, II 3 lines 1024, 1029.

Elements: Middle English (denoting fundamental constituents of the world or celestial objects): via Old French from Latin: *elementum* : *principle, rudiment*, translating Greek *stoikheion: step, component part.*

Antony and Cleopatra, II 7 line 1423; Antony and Cleopatra, III 2 line 1641; Antony and Cleopatra, V 2 line 3747.
Coriolanus, I 10 line 888.
Henry V, III 7 line 1663.
Julius Caesar, V 5 line 2759.
King Lear, III 1 line 1621; King Lear, III 2 line 1692.
Love's Labour's Lost, IV 3 line 1675.
Othello, II 1 line 813; Othello, II 3 line 1189; Othello, II 3 line 1494; Othello, III 3 line 2153.
Pericles, III 1 line 1254.
Richard II, III 3 line 1691.
Sonnet XLIV line 13; Sonnet XLV line 5.
Tempest, I 1 line 26; Tempest, III 3 line 1639; Tempest, V 1 line 2399.
Timon of Athens, IV 3 line 1918.
Troilus and Cressida, I 3 line 491.
Twelfth Night, I 5 line 566; Twelfth Night, II 3 line 710.

Elephant: c.1300, *olyfaunt*, from Old French: *oliphant* (12c.), from Latin: *elephantus*, from Greek: *elephas*. Re-spelled after 1550 on Latin model. According to a vulgar error current in bygone times, the elephant was supposed to have no joints.
Julius Caesar, II 1 line 829.
Troilus and Cressida, I 2 line 176; Troilus and Cressida, II 3 line 1216; Troilus and Cressida, II 3 line 1322.
Twelfth Night, III 3 line 1530; Twelfth Night, III 3 line 1540; Twelfth Night, IV 3 line 2156.

Embers: Old English: *æmerge*, merged with or influenced by Old Norse: *eimyrja*.
Antony and Cleopatra, II 2 line 697.
Rape of Lucrece, line 56.

Emerald: Middle English: from Old French e(s)*meraud*, ultimately via Latin from Greek (s)*maragdos*, via Prakrit from Semitic (compare with Hebrew *bāreqet*, from *bāraq* 'flash, sparkle').
Lover's Complaint, line 214.
Merry Wives of Windsor, V 5 line 2635.

Eryngoes: could be some kind of artichoke. Or, could be a reference to *erygium*, a kind of parsley, late 16c, from Latin *eryngion*, from a diminutive of Greek *erungos*: sea holly. It is said to have aphrodisiac qualities, and a legend has it that the ancient Greek poetess, Sappho, wore it to attract the love of a particularly handsome Greek boatman, *Phaon*.
Merry Wives of Windsor, V 5 line 2580.

Estridge: flightless bird.
Antony and Cleopatra, III 13 line 2488.
Henry IV, Part I, IV 1 line 2324.

Ewes: Old English: *eowu*, feminine of *eow: sheep*,(Welsh: *ewig: hind*).
> **As You Like It**, III 2 line 1168; As You Like It, III 2 line 1189; As You Like It, III 2 line 1190.
> **Henry IV, Part II**, III 2 line 1876; Henry IV, Part II, III 2 line 1880.
> **Henry VI, Part III**, II 5 line 1137.
> **Merchant of Venice**, I 3 lines 406, 412; Merchant of Venice, I 3 line 421.
> **Passionate Pilgrim**, line 247.
> **Winter's Tale**, IV 4 line 2374.

Excrement: 1530s, waste discharged from the body, from Latin: *excrementum.* Originally any bodily secretion, especially from the bowels.
> **Comedy of Errors**, II 2 line 470.
> **Hamlet**, III 4 line 2520.
> **Love's Labour's Lost**, V 1 line 1831.
> **Merchant of Venice**, III 2 line 1454.
> **Timon of Athens**, IV 3 line 2155.
> **Winter's Tale**, IV 4 line 2690.

Eyas: a hawk.
> **Hamlet**, II 2 line 1427.

Eyas-musket: a nestling of the musket or merlin, the smallest species of British hawk.
> **Merry Wives of Windsor**, III 3 line 1424.

Eye: c.1200, from Old English: *ege* (Mercian), *eage* (W. Saxon). Eyes are probably the most important symbolic sensory organ. They can represent clairvoyance, omniscience, and/or a gateway into the soul. Other qualities that eyes are commonly associated with are: intelligence, light, vigilance, moral conscience, and truth. Looking someone in the eye is a western custom of honesty. In this way covering of the eyes, by wearing a helmet, sunglasses, etc. can mean mystery, not seeing the complete truth, or deceit.
> **All's Well That Ends Well**, I 1 line 95; All's Well That Ends Well, I 1 line 223; All's Well That Ends Well, I 3 line 453; All's Well That Ends Well, I 3 line 471; All's Well That Ends Well, I 3 line 499; All's Well That Ends Well, II 1 line 716; All's Well That Ends Well, II 3 line 947; All's Well That Ends Well, II 3 line 978; All's Well That Ends Well, II 3 line 1007; All's Well That Ends Well, II 3 line 1069; All's Well That Ends Well, III 2 line 1517; All's Well That Ends Well, IV 1 line 1967; All's Well That Ends Well, V 3 line 2692; All's Well That Ends Well, V 3 line 2728; All's Well That Ends Well, V 3 line 2766; All's Well That Ends Well, V 3 line 2810; All's Well That Ends Well, V 3 line 3024; All's Well That Ends Well, V 3 line 3041.
> **Antony and Cleopatra**, I 1 line 3; Antony and Cleopatra, I 3 line 320; Antony and Cleopatra, I 3 line 339; Antony and Cleopatra, I 3 line 412; Antony and Cleopatra, I 5 line 556; Antony and Cleopatra, II 1 line 760; Antony and Cleopatra, II 2 line 932; Antony and Cleopatra, II 2 line 952; Antony and Cleopatra, II 5 line 1131; Antony and Cleopatra, II 6

line 1333; Antony and Cleopatra, II 7 line 1387; Antony and Cleopatra, III 2 line 1644; Antony and Cleopatra, III 6 line 1833; Antony and Cleopatra, III 6 line 1892; Antony and Cleopatra, III 9 line 2053; Antony and Cleopatra, III 10 line 2065; Antony and Cleopatra, III 10 line 2082; Antony and Cleopatra, III 11 line 2167; Antony and Cleopatra, III 13 line 2390; Antony and Cleopatra, III 13 line 2442; Antony and Cleopatra, IV 2 line 2563; Antony and Cleopatra, IV 12 line 2930; Antony and Cleopatra, IV 14 line 2984; Antony and Cleopatra, IV 15 line 3198; Antony and Cleopatra, V 1 line 3312; Antony and Cleopatra, V 2 line 3450; Antony and Cleopatra, V 2 line 3581; Antony and Cleopatra, V 2 line 3668; Antony and Cleopatra, V 2 line 3785.

As You Like It, I 2 line 290; As You Like It, I 2 line 299; As You Like It, I 2 line 323; As You Like It, I 3 line 440; As You Like It, II 7 line 915; As You Like It, II 7 line 1018; As You Like It, II 7 line 1052; As You Like It, II 7 line 1094; As You Like It, III 2 lines 1124, 1128; As You Like It, III 2 line 1263; As You Like It, III 2 line 1457; As You Like It, III 5 lines 1661, 1663, 1667, 1670, 1671, 1675, 1677; As You Like It, III 5 line 1697; As You Like It, III 5 lines 1772, 1785; As You Like It, IV 1 line 1817; As You Like It, IV 1 line 1975; As You Like It, IV 3 line 2049; As You Like It, IV 3 line 2085; As You Like It, IV 3 line 2105; As You Like It, V 2 line 2271; As You Like It, V 2 line 2287; As You Like It, V 2 line 2306.

Comedy of Errors, I 1 line 96; Comedy of Errors, I 2 line 264; Comedy of Errors, II 1 line 288; Comedy of Errors, II 1 line 378; Comedy of Errors, II 2 line 504; Comedy of Errors, II 2 line 573; Comedy of Errors, II 2 line 594; Comedy of Errors, III 2 line 781; Comedy of Errors, III 2 line 817; Comedy of Errors, III 2 lines 827r; Comedy of Errors, IV 2 line 1073; Comedy of Errors, IV 2 line 1099; Comedy of Errors, IV 4 line 1355; Comedy of Errors, V 1 lines 1479, 1482; Comedy of Errors, V 1 lines 1677, 1680; Comedy of Errors, V 1 line 1773.

Coriolanus, I 1 line 108; Coriolanus, I 1 line 278; Coriolanus, II 1 line 953; Coriolanus, II 1 line 1016; Coriolanus, II 1 line 1106; Coriolanus, II 1 line 1148; Coriolanus, II 1 line 1220; Coriolanus, II 2 line 1253; Coriolanus, III 2 line 2257; Coriolanus, III 3 line 2433; Coriolanus, IV 3 line 2546; Coriolanus, IV 5 line 2767; Coriolanus, IV 5 line 2966; Coriolanus, IV 6 line 3088; Coriolanus, IV 7 line 3239; Coriolanus, V 1 line 3354; Coriolanus, V 3 line 3521; Coriolanus, V 3 line 3533; Coriolanus, V 3 line 3577; Coriolanus, V 3 line 3605; Coriolanus, V 3 line 3710; Coriolanus, V 4 line 3750; Coriolanus, V 6 line 3962.

Cymbeline, I 1 line 86; Cymbeline, I 1 line 108; Cymbeline, I 1 line 119; Cymbeline, I 3 line 282; Cymbeline, I 3 line 290; Cymbeline, I 3 lines 292, 297; Cymbeline, I 4 line 332; Cymbeline, I 6 line 638; Cymbeline, I 6 line 646; Cymbeline, I 6 line 690; Cymbeline, I 6 lines 726, 731; Cymbeline, II 2 line 923; Cymbeline, II 2 line 982; Cymbeline, II 3 line 1002; Cymbeline, II 4 line 1310; Cymbeline, III 1 line 1413; Cymbeline, III 2 line 1553; Cymbeline, III 5 line 2115; Cymbeline, IV 2 line 2492; Cymbeline, IV 2 lines 2703, 2707; Cymbeline, IV 2 line 2821; Cymbeline, IV 4 line 2905; Cymbeline, V 4 line 3203; Cymbeline, V 4 line 3334; Cymbeline, V 4 line 3341;

Cymbeline, V 4 line 3345; Cymbeline, V 5 line 3441; Cymbeline, V 5 line 3504; Cymbeline, V 5 line 3518; Cymbeline, V 5 line 3572; Cymbeline, V 5 line 3853.

Hamlet, I 1 line 38; Hamlet, I 1 line 73; Hamlet, I 1 line 129; Hamlet, I 2 line 211; Hamlet, I 2 line 271; Hamlet, I 2 line 283; Hamlet, I 2 line 319; Hamlet, I 2 line 360; Hamlet, I 2 line 392; Hamlet, I 2 line 412; Hamlet, I 2 line 449; Hamlet, I 2 line 479; Hamlet, I 5 line 753; Hamlet, II 1 line 1057; Hamlet, II 2 line 1301; Hamlet, II 2 line 1386; Hamlet, II 2 line 1538; Hamlet, II 2 line 1591; Hamlet, II 2 line 1594; Hamlet, II 2 lines 1628, 1639; Hamlet, III 1 line 1842; Hamlet, III 2 line 1964; Hamlet, III 4 lines 2449, 2457, 2459, 2470, 2471; Hamlet, III 4 line 2482; Hamlet, III 4 lines 2516, 2518; Hamlet, IV 3 line 2712; Hamlet, IV 4 line 2790; Hamlet, IV 5 line 3028; Hamlet, IV 5 line 3033; Hamlet, IV 7 line 3180; Hamlet, IV 7 line 3243; Hamlet, V 2 line 3922.

Henry IV, Part I, I 1 line 10; Henry IV, Part I, I 2 line 317; Henry IV, Part I, I 3 line 338; Henry IV, Part I, I 3 line 472; Henry IV, Part I, II 3 lines 901, 905; Henry IV, Part I, II 4 line 1368; Henry IV, Part I, II 4 line 1377; Henry IV, Part I, II 4 line 1387; Henry IV, Part I, II 4 line 1405; Henry IV, Part I, III 2 lines 1863, 1893, 1899, 1906; Henry IV, Part I, IV 1 line 2293; Henry IV, Part I, IV 1 line 2340; Henry IV, Part I, IV 2 line 2405; Henry IV, Part I, V 1 line 2698; Henry IV, Part I, V 2 line 2778; Henry IV, Part I, V 4 line 3094; Henry IV, Part I, V 4 lines 3106, 3107.

Henry IV, Part II, I 1 line 144; Henry IV, Part II, I 1 line 152; Henry IV, Part II, I 1 line 165; Henry IV, Part II, I 2 line 507; Henry IV, Part II, II 2 line 1043; Henry IV, Part II, II 3 line 1215; Henry IV, Part II, III 1 line 1722; Henry IV, Part II, III 1 lines 1769, 1772; Henry IV, Part II, IV 1 line 2327; Henry IV, Part II, IV 2 line 2481; Henry IV, Part II, IV 2 line 2507; Henry IV, Part II, IV 5 line 2892; Henry IV, Part II, IV 5 line 2981.

Henry V, I 2 line 348; Henry V, I 2 line 429; Henry V, II 2 line 690; Henry V, II 2 line 740; Henry V, III 1 lines 1100, 1120; Henry V, III 2 line 1243; Henry V, III 6 line 1492; Henry V, IV 0 line 1831; Henry V, IV 1 line 2119; Henry V, IV 2 line 2173; Henry V, IV 2 line 2212; Henry V, IV 6 line 2506; Henry V, IV 6 line 2511; Henry V, IV 7 line 2586; Henry V, V 0 line 2882; Henry V, V 2 lines 2995, 2996; Henry V, V 2 line 3011r; Henry V, V 2 line 3059; Henry V, V 2 lines 3132, 3146; Henry V, V 2 line 3295.

Henry VI, Part I, I 1 line 16; Henry VI, Part I, I 1 line 53; Henry VI, Part I, I 1 line 92; Henry VI, Part I, I 4 lines 535, 543, 544; Henry VI, Part I, II 3 line 835; Henry VI, Part I, II 4 line 935; Henry VI, Part I, II 4 line 942; Henry VI, Part I, II 4 line 945; Henry VI, Part I, II 5 line 1083; Henry VI, Part I, III 3 line 1658; Henry VI, Part I, IV 2 line 2003; Henry VI, Part I, V 3 line 2494; Henry VI, Part I, V 3 line 2524.

Henry VI, Part II, I 1 line 63; Henry VI, Part II, I 1 line 125; Henry VI, Part II, I 2 line 278; Henry VI, Part II, II 1 line 745; Henry VI, Part II, II 1 line 851; Henry VI, Part II, II 3 line 1061; Henry VI, Part II, II 4 line 1173; Henry VI, Part II, II 4 line 1182; Henry VI, Part II, III 1 line 1292; Henry VI, Part II, III 1 line 1435; Henry VI, Part II, III 1 lines 1500, 1481; Henry VI, Part II, III 2 line 1715; Henry VI, Part II, III 2 line 1732; Henry VI, Part II, III 2 line 1791; Henry VI, Part II, III 2 line 2011; Henry

VI, Part II, III 2 line 2091; Henry VI, Part II, III 3 line 2128; Henry VI, Part II, III 3 line 2134; Henry VI, Part II, III 3 line 2146; Henry VI, Part II, IV 1 line 2176; Henry VI, Part II, IV 4 line 2569; Henry VI, Part II, IV 10 line 2932.

Henry VI, Part III, I 1 line 27; Henry VI, Part III, I 3 line 388; Henry VI, Part III, I 4 line 475; Henry VI, Part III, I 4 line 521; Henry VI, Part III, I 4 line 579; Henry VI, Part III, I 4 line 592; Henry VI, Part III, II 1 line 651; Henry VI, Part III, II 2 line 869; Henry VI, Part III, II 3 line 1059; Henry VI, Part III, II 3 line 1064; Henry VI, Part III, II 5 line 1181; Henry VI, Part III, II 5 lines 1190, 1192; Henry VI, Part III, II 5 line 1240; Henry VI, Part III, III 2 lines 1626, 1633; Henry VI, Part III, III 3 line 1702; Henry VI, Part III, III 3 line 1812; Henry VI, Part III, V 2 line 2738; Henry VI, Part III, V 4 line 2812; Henry VI, Part III, V 4 line 2882; Henry VI, Part III, V 6 line 3011; Henry VI, Part III, V 6 line 3035.

Henry VIII, I 0 line 4; Henry VIII, I 1 line 69; Henry VIII, I 1 line 111; Henry VIII, I 1 line 172; Henry VIII, I 1 line 190; Henry VIII, I 2 line 557; Henry VIII, II 2 line 1063; Henry VIII, III 1 line 1663; Henry VIII, III 2 line 1867; Henry VIII, III 2 line 1984; Henry VIII, III 2 line 1998; Henry VIII, III 2 line 2091; Henry VIII, III 2 line 2345; Henry VIII, IV 1 line 2513; Henry VIII, IV 2 line 2684; Henry VIII, IV 2 line 2764; Henry VIII, V 2 line 3017.

Julius Caesar, I 2 line 120; Julius Caesar, I 2 line 140; Julius Caesar, I 2 line 145; Julius Caesar, I 2 line 213; Julius Caesar, I 2 line 278; Julius Caesar, II 1 line 716; Julius Caesar, II 1 line 799; Julius Caesar, II 3 line 1122; Julius Caesar, III 1 line 1422; Julius Caesar, III 1 line 1514; Julius Caesar, III 2 line 1660; Julius Caesar, IV 2 line 1966; Julius Caesar, IV 3 line 2077; Julius Caesar, IV 3 line 2087; Julius Caesar, IV 3 line 2282; Julius Caesar, IV 3 line 2305; Julius Caesar, V 5 line 2688; Julius Caesar, V 5 line 2719.

King John, I 1 line 26; King John, I 1 line 95; King John, II 1 line 394; King John, II 1 line 467; King John, II 1 lines 509, 516; King John, II 1 line 636; King John, II 1 lines 808, 810, 815; King John, II 1 line 817; King John, II 1 line 897; King John, III 1 line 937; King John, III 1 line 962; King John, III 1 line 998; King John, III 3 lines 1346, 1349, 1352; King John, III 3 line 1360; King John, III 4 line 1508; King John, IV 1 line 1619; King John, IV 1 lines 1638, 1639; King John, IV 1 lines 1645, 1649, 1652; King John, IV 1 line 1658; king John, IV 1 line 1679; King John, IV 1 line 1704; King John, IV 1 line 1711; King John, IV 2 line 1729; King John, IV 2 line 1742; King John, IV 2 line 1801; King John, IV 2 line 1837; King John, IV 2 line 1900; King John, IV 2 line 1935; King John, IV 2 line 1977; King John, IV 2 line 2009; King John, IV 3 line 2069; King John, IV 3 line 2133; King John, IV 3 line 2179; King John, V 1 lines 2242, 2245; King John, V 2 lines 2329, 2334; King John, V 4 line 2499; King John, V 4 line 2519; King John, V 4 line 2548; King John, V 6 line 2592; King John, V 7 line 2686.

King Lear, I 1 line 56; King Lear, I 1 line 167; King Lear, I 1 line 251; King Lear, I 1 line 292; King Lear, I 4 line 749; King Lear, I 4 line 830; King Lear, I 4 line 877; King Lear, I 5 line 898; King Lear, II 2 line 1247; King Lear, II 4 line 1347; King Lear, II 4 line 1451; King Lear, II 4 line

1458; King Lear, III 1 line 1625; King Lear, III 4 line 1912; King Lear, III 6 line 2028; King Lear, III 7 line 2126; King Lear, III 7 line 2197; King Lear, III 7 line 2214; King Lear, III 7 line 2231; King Lear, IV 1 lines 2268, 2274; King Lear, IV 2 line 2397; King Lear, IV 2 line 2420; King Lear, IV 2 line 2421; King Lear, IV 2 line 2431; King Lear, IV 2 line 2440; King Lear, IV 2 line 2450; King Lear, IV 3 line 2475; King Lear, IV 3 line 2485; King Lear, IV 4 line 2523; King Lear, IV 4 line 2531; King Lear, IV 5 line 2561; King Lear, IV 6 line 2604; King Lear, IV 6 line 2612; King Lear, IV 6 line 2667; King Lear, IV 6 line 2679; King Lear, IV 6 line 2745; King Lear, IV 6 line 2752; King Lear, IV 6 lines 2753, 2754; King Lear, IV 6 line 2757; King Lear, IV 6 line 2775; King Lear, IV 6 line 2781; King Lear, IV 6 line 2803; King Lear, IV 6 line 2845; King Lear, V 3 line 3147; King Lear, V 3 line 3178; King Lear, V 3 line 3205; King Lear, V 3 line 3330; King Lear, V 3 line 3435; King Lear, V 3 line 3461.

Love's Labour's Lost, I 1 lines 78, 81, 82, 83, 84; Love's Labour's Lost, II 1 line 499; Love's Labour's Lost, II 1 line 555; Love's Labour's Lost, II 1 line 680; Love's Labour's Lost, II 1 lines 735, 737, 739, 742, 747r; Love's Labour's Lost, III 1 line 780; Love's Labour's Lost, III 1 line 958; Love's Labour's Lost, IV 1 lines 1040, 1060; Love's Labour's Lost, IV 2 lines 1255, 1261; Love's Labour's Lost, IV 3 lines 1328r, 1329; Love's Labour's Lost, IV 3 line 1348; Love's Labour's Lost, IV 3 line 1383; Love's Labour's Lost, IV 3 line 1410; Love's Labour's Lost, IV 3 line 1470; Love's Labour's Lost, IV 3 line 1486; Love's Labour's Lost, IV 3 line 1515; Love's Labour's Lost, IV 3 line 1570; Love's Labour's Lost, IV 3 lines 1576r, 1587; Love's Labour's Lost, IV 3 line 1596; Love's Labour's Lost, IV 3 line 1622; Love's Labour's Lost, IV 3 lines 1647, 1655, 1658, 1661, 1668, 1674, 1679, 1685, 1686, 1702; Love's Labour's Lost, V 1 line 1743; Love's Labour's Lost, V 2 line 1974; Love's Labour's Lost, V 2 line 2052r; Love's Labour's Lost, V 2 line 2053; Love's Labour's Lost, V 2 lines 2058, 2059; Love's Labour's Lost, V 2 line 2061; Love's Labour's Lost, V 2 line 2068; Love's Labour's Lost, V 2 line 2296r; Love's Labour's Lost, V 2 line 2300; Love's Labour's Lost, V 2 line 2344; Love's Labour's Lost, V 2 line 2372; Love's Labour's Lost, V 2 lines 2403, 2408; Love's Labour's Lost, V 2 lines 2702r, 2705, 2708, 2710; Love's Labour's Lost, V 2 line 2757; Love's Labour's Lost, V 2 line 2781.

Lover's Complaint, lines 22, 50, 81, 89, 136, 191, 248, 251, 263, 283, 292, 325.

Macbeth, I 2 line 70; Macbeth, I 4 lines 335, 336; Macbeth, I 7 line 497; Macbeth, II 1 lines 623, 628; Macbeth, II 2 line 716; Macbeth, II 2 line 723; Macbeth, II 4 line 969; Macbeth, III 1 line 1144; Macbeth, III 2 line 1204; Macbeth, III 2 line 1222; Macbeth, III 4 line 1390; Macbeth, IV 1 line 1561; Macbeth, IV 1 line 1688; Macbeth, IV 3 line 2014; Macbeth, IV 3 line 2058; Macbeth, IV 3 line 2114; Macbeth, V 1 line 2150; Macbeth, V 1 line 2200.

Measure for Measure, I 1 line 78; Measure for Measure, I 2 line 199; Measure for Measure, II 2 line 952; Measure for Measure, IV 1 line 1797; Measure for Measure, IV 1 line 1862; Measure for Measure, IV 3 line 2246; Measure for Measure, IV 3 line 2254; Measure for Measure, IV 3 line 2274; Measure for Measure, IV 3 line 2281; Measure for Measure, V 1 line 2410; Measure for Measure, V 1 line 2566; Measure for Measure, V 1 line 2940.

Merchant of Venice, I 1 line 55; Merchant of Venice, I 1 line 144; Merchant of Venice, I 1 line 170; Merchant of Venice, I 2 line 307; Merchant of Venice, II 1 line 528; Merchant of Venice, II 1 line 542; Merchant of Venice, II 2 line 640; Merchant of Venice, II 2 line 728; Merchant of Venice, II 2 line 748; Merchant of Venice, II 2 line 759; Merchant of Venice, II 5 line 847; Merchant of Venice, II 5 line 890; Merchant of Venice, II 6 line 967; Merchant of Venice, II 7 line 1051; Merchant of Venice, II 8 line 1119; Merchant of Venice, II 9 line 1156; Merchant of Venice, III 1 line 1293; Merchant of Venice, III 2 line 1377; Merchant of Venice, III 2 lines 1411, 1434; Merchant of Venice, III 2 line 1477; Merchant of Venice, III 2 lines 1485, 1492, 1512; Merchant of Venice, III 2 line 1567; Merchant of Venice, III 3 line 1722; Merchant of Venice, IV 1 line 1959; Merchant of Venice, IV 1 line 2215; Merchant of Venice, V 1 line 2516; Merchant of Venice, V 1 line 2534; Merchant of Venice, V 1 line 2710; Merchant of Venice, V 1 lines 2713, 2714.

Merry Wives of Windsor, I 3 line 358; Merry Wives of Windsor, I 3 line 364; Merry Wives of Windsor, I 4 line 546; Merry Wives of Windsor, II 1 line 619; Merry Wives of Windsor, II 1 line 683; Merry Wives of Windsor, II 2 line 865; Merry Wives of Windsor, II 2 line 977; Merry Wives of Windsor, III 2 line 1314r; Merry Wives of Windsor, III 2 line 1338; Merry Wives of Windsor, III 2 line 1376; Merry Wives of Windsor, III 3 line 1454; Merry Wives of Windsor, V 5 line 2612.

Midsummer Night's Dream, I 1 line 61; Midsummer Night's Dream, I 1 line 63; Midsummer Night's Dream, I 1 line 137; Midsummer Night's Dream, I 1 lines 191, 196r; Midsummer Night's Dream, I 1 line 226; Midsummer Night's Dream, I 1 lines 241, 245, 248; Midsummer Night's Dream, I 2 line 287; Midsummer Night's Dream, II 1 line 552; Midsummer Night's Dream, II 1 lines 636, 640; Midsummer Night's Dream, II 2 line 684; Midsummer Night's Dream, II 2 line 719; Midsummer Night's Dream, II 2 lines 724, 734; Midsummer Night's Dream, II 2 lines 750, 751, 752; Midsummer Night's Dream, II 2 line 779; Midsummer Night's Dream, II 2 line 786; Midsummer Night's Dream, III 1 line 961; Midsummer Night's Dream, III 1 lines 990, 995, 998; Midsummer Night's Dream, III 1 line 1019; Midsummer Night's Dream, III 1 line 1023; Midsummer Night's Dream, III 2 line 1030; Midsummer Night's Dream, III 2 line 1050; Midsummer Night's Dream, III 2 line 1068; Midsummer Night's Dream, III 2 line 1072; Midsummer Night's Dream, III 2 line 1140; Midsummer Night's Dream, III 2 line 1194; Midsummer Night's Dream, III 2 lines 1217, 1221; Midsummer Night's Dream, III 2 line 1228; Midsummer Night's Dream, III 2 line 1263; Midsummer Night's Dream, III 2 line 1345; Midsummer Night's Dream, III 2 line 1408; Midsummer Night's Dream, III 2 lines 1423, 1433; Midsummer Night's Dream, III 2 line 1508; Midsummer Night's Dream, III 2 lines 1527, 1529, 1534; Midsummer Night's Dream, IV 1 lines 1603, 1611; Midsummer Night's Dream, IV 1 line 1628;

Midsummer Night's Dream, IV 1 line 1635; Midsummer Night's Dream, IV 1 line 1727; Midsummer Night's Dream, IV 1 line 1747; Midsummer Night's Dream, IV 1 line 1772; Midsummer Night's Dream, V 1 line 1906; Midsummer Night's Dream, V 1 line 2121; Midsummer Night's Dream, V 1 line 2167; Midsummer Night's Dream, V 1 lines 2174, 2180.

Much Ado About Nothing, I 1 line 168; Much Ado About Nothing, I 1 line 226; Much Ado About Nothing, I 1 line 270; Much Ado About Nothing, II 1 line 470; Much Ado About Nothing, II 1 line 561; Much Ado About Nothing, II 3 line 836; Much Ado About Nothing, III 1 line 1128; Much Ado About Nothing, III 1 line 1128; Much Ado About Nothing, III 4 line 1571; Much Ado About Nothing, IV 1 line 1714; Much Ado About Nothing, IV 1 line 1714; Much Ado About Nothing, IV 1 lines 1772, 1779; Much Ado About Nothing, IV 1 line 1812; Much Ado About Nothing, IV 1 lines 1881, 1895; Much Ado About Nothing, V 1 line 2304; Much Ado About Nothing, V 1 line 2331; Much Ado About Nothing, V 2 line 2503; Much Ado About Nothing, V 4 line 2567; Much Ado About Nothing, V 4 line 2568; Much Ado About Nothing, V 4 line 2569.

Othello, I 1 line 28; Othello, I 3 line 595; Othello, I 3 line 649; Othello, II 1 lines 1023, 1041; Othello, II 3 line 1134; Othello, II 3 line 1155; Othello, II 3 line 1157; Othello, III 3 line 1817; Othello, III 3 line 1840; Othello, III 3 line 1850; Othello, III 3 line 1864; Othello, III 3 line 2081; Othello, III 4 lines 2242, 2247; Othello, IV 2 line 2767; Othello, IV 2 line 2922; Othello, IV 3 line 3080; Othello, V 1 line 3179; Othello, V 1 line 3269; Othello, V 2 line 3345; Othello, V 2 line 3540; Othello, V 2 line 3715.

Passionate Pilgrim, lines 29, 47, 61, 67, 81, 194, 197, 203, 214, 300.

Pericles, I 0 lines 5, 38; Pericles, I 1 line 78; Pericles, I 1 line 120; Pericles, I 1 lines, 146, 148; Pericles, I 1 line 225; Pericles, I 2 lines 238, 242r; Pericles, I 2 line 319; Pericles, I 2 line 342; Pericles, I 4 line 424; Pericles, I 4 line 430; Pericles, I 4 line 467; Pericles, I 4 line 506; Pericles, II 4 line 546; Pericles, II 3 line 847; Pericles, II 4 line 961; Pericles, II 5 line 1024; Pericles, III 1 line 1233; Pericles, III 3 line 1432; Pericles, IV 1 line 1590; Pericles, IV 4 line 1894; Pericles, V 1 line 2278; Pericles, V 1 line 2296; Pericles, V 1 line 2306; Pericles, V 1 line 2454.

Rape of Lucrece, lines 81, 124, 135, 146, 150, 156, 214, 230, 256, 280, 306, 327, 341, 342, 407, 425, 443, 448, 468, 477, 486, 487, 497, 510, 512, 534, 547, 571, 591, 612, 666, 689, 734, 760, 799, 801, 809, 881, 908, 1022, 1066, 1127, 1134, 1139, 1141, 1189, 1194, 1264, 1290, 1377, 1391, 1395, 1408, 1430, 1435, 1438, 1449, 1477, 1499, 1508, 1520, 1526, 1527, 1550, 1559, 1599, 1603, 1637, 1643, 1702, 1713, 1719, 1731, 1868.

Richard II, I 1 line 97; Richard II, I 1 line 118; Richard II, I 2 line 296; Richard II, I 3 line 354; Richard II, I 3 line 393; Richard II, I 3 line 424; Richard II, I 3 line 506; Richard II, I 3 line 576; Richard II, II 1 line 788; Richard II, II 1 line 961; Richard II, II 2 lines 1009, 1012, 1019; Richard II, II 3 line 1274; Richard II, II 4 line 1349; Richard II, III 1 line 1372;

Richard II, III 2 line 1445; Richard II, III 2 line 1557; Richard II, III 2 line 1606; Richard II, III 3 line 1708; Richard II, III 3 line 1811; Richard II, III 3 line 1841; Richard II, III 3 line 1850; Richard II, IV 1 lines 2233, 2236; Richard II, IV 1 line 2329; Richard II, V 2 line 2455; Richard II, V 2 lines 2464, 2468; Richard II, V 3 line 2683; Richard II, V 3 line 2708; Richard II, V 5 lines 2765, 2800.
Richard III, I 1 line 99; Richard III, I 2 line 185; Richard III, I 2 line 220; Richard III, I 2 line 307; Richard III, I 2 line 333; Richard III, I 2 line 334; Richard III, I 2 lines 338, 340, 349; Richard III, I 2 lines 425, 438; Richard III I 3 line 640; Richard III, I 3 line 689; Richard III, I 3 line 828r; Richard III, I 4 lines 856, 863, 864; Richard III, I 4 line 997; Richard III, I 4 line 1094; Richard III, II 2 line 1340; Richard III, II 4 line 1544; Richard III, III 4 line 2024; Richard III, III 5 line 2152; Richard III, III 7 line 2323; Richard III, III 7 line 2397; Richard III, IV 1 line 2526; Richard III, IV 2 line 2615; Richard III, IV 2 line 2657; Richard III, IV 4 lines 2844, 2848; Richard III, IV 4 line 3035; Richard III, IV 4 line 3084; Richard III, V 3 lines 3582, 3589.
Romeo and Juliet, I 1 line 196; Romeo and Juliet, I 1 line 218; Romeo and Juliet, I 1 line 242; Romeo and Juliet, I 1 line 256; Romeo and Juliet, I 1 line 263; Romeo and Juliet, I 2 line 323; Romeo and Juliet, I 2 line 365; Romeo and Juliet, I 2 line 372; Romeo and Juliet, I 3 lines 471, 476; Romeo and Juliet, I 3 line 483; Romeo and Juliet, I 4 line 527; Romeo and Juliet, II 1 line 816; Romeo and Juliet, II 2 lines 858, 861, 863, 865; Romeo and Juliet, II 2 line 876; Romeo and Juliet, II 2 line 920; Romeo and Juliet, II 2 line 930; Romeo and Juliet, II 2 line 1053; Romeo and Juliet, II 3 lines 1059, 1063; Romeo and Juliet, II 3 line 1095; Romeo and Juliet, II 3 line 1128; Romeo and Juliet, II 4 line 1172; Romeo and Juliet, II 4 line 1204; Romeo and Juliet, III 1 lines 1518, 1519r; Romeo and Juliet, III 1 line 1550; Romeo and Juliet, III 1 line 1551; Romeo and Juliet, III 1 line 1632; Romeo and Juliet, III 2 line 1724; Romeo and Juliet, III 2 lines 1769, 1771; Romeo and Juliet, III 2 line 1774; Romeo and Juliet, III 2 line 1780; Romeo and Juliet, III 3 line 1933; Romeo and Juliet, III 3 line 1945; Romeo and Juliet, III 5 line 2116; Romeo and Juliet, III 5 line 2128; Romeo and Juliet, III 5 line 2157; Romeo and Juliet, III 5 line 2239; Romeo and Juliet, III 5 line 2336; Romeo and Juliet, IV 1 line 2466; Romeo and Juliet, V 1 line 2881; Romeo and Juliet, V 3 line 3058; Romeo and Juliet, V 3 line 3077.
Sonnet XIV line 9; Sonnet XVII line 12; Sonnet XVIII line 6; Sonnet XVIII line 13; Sonnet XX line 5; Sonnet XX line 8; Sonnet XXIII line 14; Sonnet XXIV line 1; Sonnet XXIV line 8; Sonnet XXIV line 9r; Sonnet XXIV line 10; Sonnet XXIV line 13; Sonnet XXV line 6; Sonnet XXIX line 1; Sonnet XXX line 5; Sonnet XXXI line 6; Sonnet XXXIII line 2; Sonnet XLIII line 1; Sonnet XLIII line 8; Sonnet XLIII line 9; Sonnet XLIII line 12; Sonnet XLVI line 1; Sonnet XLVI line 3; Sonnet XLVI line 4; Sonnet XLVI line 6; Sonnet XLVI line 12; Sonnet XLVI line 13; Sonnet XLVII line 1; Sonnet XLVII line 3; Sonnet XLVII line 5; Sonnet XLVII line 14; Sonnet XLIX line 6; Sonnet LV line 9; Sonnet LVI line 6; Sonnet LXI line 10; Sonnet LXII line 1; Sonnet LXIX line 1; Sonnet

LXIX line 8; Sonnet LXIX line 11; Sonnet LXXVIII line 5; Sonnet LXXXI line 8; Sonnet LXXXI line 10; Sonnet LXXXIII line 13; Sonnet LXXXVIII line 2; Sonnet XCIII line 5; Sonnet XCV line 12; Sonnet CIV line 2r; Sonnet CIV line 12; Sonnet CVI line 6; Sonnet CVI line 11; Sonnet CVI line 14; Sonnet CXIII line 1; Sonnet CXIII line 14; Sonnet CXIV line 13; Sonnet CXIV line 12; Sonnet CXIV line 14; Sonnet CXIX line 7; Sonnet CXXI line 5; Sonnet CXXVII line 10; Sonnet CXXX line 1; Sonnet CXXXII line 1; Sonnet CXXXII line 9; Sonnet CXXXIII line 5; Sonnet CXXXVII line 1; Sonnet CXXXVII line 5; Sonnet CXXXVII line 11; Sonnet CXXXVII line 13; Sonnet CXXXIX line 6; Sonnet CXL line 14; Sonnet CXLI line 1; Sonnet CXLII line 10; Sonnet CXLVIII line 1; Sonnet CXLVIII line 5; Sonnet CXLVIII line 8; Sonnet CXLVIII line 9; Sonnet CXLVIII line 14; Sonnet CXLIX line 12; Sonnet CLII line 11; Sonnet CLIII line 9; Sonnet CLIII line 14.

Taming of the Shrew, Prologue, 1 line 136; Taming of the Shrew, I 1 line 375; Taming of the Shrew, I 1 line 514; Taming of the Shrew, I 2 line 661; Taming of the Shrew, II 1 line 893; Taming of the Shrew, II 1 line 1193; Taming of the Shrew, III 1 line 1360; Taming of the Shrew, III 2 line 1460; Taming of the Shrew, IV 2 line 1850; Taming of the Shrew, IV 3 line 2137; Taming of the Shrew, IV 5 line 2300; Taming of the Shrew, IV5 line 2312; Taming of the Shrew, V 2 line 2645.

Tempest, I 2 line 115; Tempest, I 2 line 241; Tempest, I 2 line 562; Tempest, I 2 line 572; Tempest, I 2 line 606; Tempest, I 2 line 614; Tempest, II 1 line 758; Tempest, II 1 line 828; Tempest, II 1 line 904; Tempest, II 1 line 956; Tempest, II 1 line 1068; Tempest, III 1 line 1328; Tempest, III 2 line 1403; Tempest, IV 1 line 1720; Tempest, IV 1 line 1743; Tempest, IV 1 line 1766; Tempest, V 1 line 2092; Tempest, V 1 line 2200; Tempest, V 1 line 2303.

Timon of Athens, I 1 line 44; Timon of Athens, I 1 line 85; Timon of Athens, I 1 line 113; Timon of Athens, I 2 line 445; Timon of Athens, I 2 line 448; Timon of Athens, I 2 line 469; Timon of Athens, I 2 line 516; Timon of Athens, II 2 line 852; Timon of Athens, IV 1 line 1572; Timon of Athens, IV 3 line 1719; Timon of Athens, IV 3 lines 1796, 1803; Timon of Athens, IV 3 line 1869; Timon of Athens, IV 3 line 1956; Timon of Athens, IV 3 line 2184; Timon of Athens, IV 3 line 2197; Timon of Athens, IV 3 line 2200; Timon of Athens, V 1 line 2282; Timon of Athens, V 1 line 2439.

Titus Andronicus, I 1 line 15; Titus Andronicus, I 1 line 194; Titus Andronicus, I 1 line 478; Titus Andronicus, II 1 line 563; Titus Andronicus, II 1 lines 684, 687; Titus Andronicus, II 3 line 765; Titus Andronicus, II 3 line 917; Titus Andronicus, II 3 line 951; Titus Andronicus, II 3 line 960; Titus Andronicus, II 3 line 965; Titus Andronicus, II 4 lines 1117, 1119; Titus Andronicus, III 1 line 1188; Titus Andronicus, III 1 line 1268; Titus Andronicus, III 1 line 1404; Titus Andronicus, III 2 line 1463; Titus Andronicus, III 2 line 1501; Titus Andronicus, IV 2 line 1747; Titus Andronicus, V 1 line 2153; Titus Andronicus, V 1 lines 2175, 2177; Titus Andronicus, V 2 line 2372; Titus Andronicus, V 3 line 2601.

Troilus and Cressida, I 1 line 84; Troilus and Cressida, I 2 line 185; Troilus and Cressida, I 2 line 292; Troilus and Cressida, I 2 line 295r; Troilus and Cressida, I 2 line 388; Troilus and Cressida, I 2 line 393; Troilus and Cressida, I 2 line 401; Troilus and Cressida, I 2 line 446; Troilus and Cressida, I 3 line 544; Troilus and Cressida, I 3 line 680; Troilus and Cressida, I 3 line 685; Troilus and Cressida, I 3 line 829; Troilus and Cressida, I 3 line 834; Troilus and Cressida, II 1 line 939; Troilus and Cressida, II 2 line 1056; Troilus and Cressida, II 2 line 1096; Troilus and Cressida, II 2 line 1103; Troilus and Cressida, II 3 line 1337; Troilus and Cressida, III 2 line 1691; Troilus and Cressida, III 2 line 1720; Troilus and Cressida, III 3 line 1911; Troilus and Cressida, III 3 line 1949; Troilus and Cressida, III 3 lines 1980r, 1982r; Troilus and Cressida, III 3 line 2011; Troilus and Cressida, III 3 lines 2056, 2059; Troilus and Cressida, IV 2 line 2290; Troilus and Cressida, IV 4 line 2557; Troilus and Cressida, IV 5 line 2605; Troilus and Cressida, IV 5 line 2661; Troilus and Cressida, IV 5 line 2783; Troilus and Cressida, IV 5 line 2857; Troilus and Cressida, IV 5 line 2869; Troilus and Cressida, V 1 line 2950; Troilus and Cressida, V 1 line 2963; Troilus and Cressida, V 2 lines 3176, 3177, 3179, 3181; Troilus and Cressida, V 2 line 3194; Troilus and Cressida, V 2 line 3210; Troilus and Cressida, V 3 line 3339; Troilus and Cressida, V 3 line 3372; Troilus and Cressida, V 3 line 3399; Troilus and Cressida, V 7 line 3563; Troilus and Cressida, V 10 line 3684.
Twelfth Night, I 1 line 21; Twelfth Night, I 1 line 34; Twelfth Night, I 2 line 112; Twelfth Night, I 5 line 592; Twelfth Night, I 5 line 607; Twelfth Night, II 1 line 648; Twelfth Night, II 2 line 671; Twelfth Night, II 2 line 677; Twelfth Night, II 3 line 805; Twelfth Night, II 3 line 857; Twelfth Night, II 4 line 913; Twelfth Night, II 5 line 1074; Twelfth Night, II 5 line 1157; Twelfth Night, III 1 line 1299; Twelfth Night, III 3 line 1535; Twelfth Night, III 4 line 1568; Twelfth Night, IV 3 line 2163; Twelfth Night, V 1 line 2219; Twelfth Night, V 1 line 2328; Twelfth Night, V 1 line 2397.
Two Gentlemen of Verona, I 3 line 335; Two Gentlemen of Verona, II 1 line 437; Two Gentlemen of Verona, II 1 lines 465, 466; Two Gentlemen of Verona, II 3 line 605; Two Gentlemen of Verona, II 4 line 740; Two Gentlemen of Verona, II 4 line 746; Two Gentlemen of Verona, II 4 line 747; Two Gentlemen of Verona, II 4 line 791; Two Gentlemen of Verona, II 4 line 800; Two Gentlemen of Verona, III 1 line 1158; Two Gentlemen of Verona, IV 2 line 1679; Two Gentlemen of Verona, IV 4 lines 2033, 2045; Two Gentlemen of Verona, V 2 line 2077; Two Gentlemen of Verona, V 2 line 2079; Two Gentlemen of Verona, V 4 line 2217; Two Gentlemen of Verona, V 4 line 2271.
Venus and Adonis, lines 90, 140r, 160, 198, 202, 216, 233, 239, 295, 301, 316, 362, 376r, 377r, 378r, 380, 419, 453, 457, 507, 521, 524, 605, 623, 642, 653, 665, 682, 838, 949, 961, 974r, 983, 984r, 1002, 1045, 1052, 1059, 1072, 1084, 1087, 1094, 1095, 1128, 1149, 1201.
Winter's Tale, I 2 line 146; Winter's Tale, I 2 line 215; Winter's Tale, I 2 lines 370, 377; Winter's Tale, I 2 line 393; Winter's Tale, I 2 line 409; Winter's Tale, I 2 line 416; Winter's Tale, I 2 line 490; Winter's Tale, II 1

line 643; Winter's Tale, II 1 line 652; Winter's Tale, II 1 line 755; Winter's Tale, II 3 line 1004; Winter's Tale, II 3 line 1052; Winter's Tale, III 2 line 1341; Winter's Tale, III 2 line 1442; Winter's Tale, III 3 line 1517; Winter's Tale, IV 2 line 1703; Winter's Tale, IV 4 line 2000; Winter's Tale, IV 4 line 2063; Winter's Tale, IV 4 line 2277; Winter's Tale, IV 4 line 2622; Winter's Tale, IV 4 line 2647; Winter's Tale, IV 4 line 2768; Winter's Tale, V 1 line 2882; Winter's Tale, V 1 line 2898; Winter's Tale, V 1 line 2903; Winter's Tale, V 1 line 2912; Winter's Tale, V 1 line 2952; Winter's Tale, V 1 line 3094; Winter's Tale, V 2 line 3119; Winter's Tale, V 2 line 3155; Winter's Tale, V 2 line 3182; Winter's Tale, V 2 line 3191; Winter's Tale, V 2 line 3218; Winter's Tale, V 3 line 3367.

Eyeball*: also eye-ball, 1580s, from eye + ball.
    As You Like It, III 5 line 1670.
    Cymbeline, III 4 line 1830.
    Henry VI, Part I, IV 7 line 2336.
    Henry VI, Part II, III 2 line 1730; Henry VI, Part II, III 2 line 1854.
    King John, III 4 line 1414.
    Macbeth, IV 1 line 1685.
    Midsummer Night's Dream, III 2 line 1426.
    Rape of Lucrece, line 419.
    Tempest, I 2 line 444.
    Venus and Adonis, line 139.

Eyebrow: also eye-brow, early 15c., from eye + brow(Old English *eagbræw* meant *eyelid*).
    As You Like It, II 7 line 1046.
    Winter's Tale, II 1 line 613; Winter's Tale, II 1 line 616.

Eyelids: Mid 13c., from eye + lid.
    As You Like It, II 7 line 1011.
    Hamlet, V 1 line 3611.
    Henry IV, Part I, III 1 line 1766; Henry IV, Part I, III 2 line 1900.
    Henry IV, Part II, III 1 line 1711.
    King Lear, IV 5 line 2579.
    Love's Labour's Lost, III 1 line 775.
    Midsummer Night's Dream, II 1 line 542; Midsummer Night's Dream, II 2 line 678; Midsummer Night's Dream, II 2 line 737.
    Much Ado About Nothing, IV 1 line 1751.
    Pericles, III 2 line 1403.
    Sonnet XXVI line 7; Sonnet LXI line 2.
    Tempest, II 1 line 919; Tempest, IV 1 line 1912.
    Venus and Adonis, line 978.

Eyne: archaic plural of eye.
    Antony and Cleopatra, II 7 line 1516.
    As You Like It, IV 3 line 2052.
    Love's Labour's Lost, V 2 line 2097.

Lover's Complaint, line 15.
Midsummer Night's Dream, I 1 line 253; Midsummer Night's Dream, II 2 line758; Midsummer night's Dream, III 2 line 1176; Midsummer Night's Dream, V 1 line 2020.
Pericles, III 0 line 1123.
Rape of Lucrece, lines 694, 1280.
Taming of the Shrew, V 1 line 2455.
Venus and Adonis, line 654.

Face: late 13c., front of the head, from Old French: *face* (12c.) *face, countenance, look, appearance*, from Latin: *facies: appearance, form, figure*, and secondarily *visage, countenance*; probably related to *facere: to make*. Replaced Old English: *andwlita*.

All's Well That Ends Well, I 2 line 260; All's Well That Ends Well, I 3 line 388; All's Well That Ends Well, III 1 line 1450; All's Well That Ends Well, III 5 line 1663; All's Well That Ends Well, IV 3 line 2203; All's Well That Ends Well, IV 5 line 2551; All's Well That Ends Well, IV 5 line 2557.

Antony and Cleopatra, II 5 line 1095; Antony and Cleopatra, II 5 line 1177; Antony and Cleopatra, II 6 line 1279; Antony and Cleopatra, II 6 line 1335; Antony and Cleopatra, II 6 line 1336; Antony and Cleopatra, III 2 line 1655; Antony and Cleopatra, III 3 line 1698; Antony and Cleopatra, III 3 line 1726; Antony and Cleopatra, III 13 line 2249; Antony and Cleopatra, III 13 line 2375; Antony and Cleopatra, IV 9 line 2845; Antony and Cleopatra, IV 14 line 3069; Antony and Cleopatra, V 2 line 3414; Antony and Cleopatra, V 2 line 3485.

As You Like It, I 3 line 519; As You Like It, I 3 line 530; As You Like It, II 7 line 1044; As You Like It, II 7 line 1095; As You Like It, III 2 line 1205; As You Like It, III 2 line 1263; As You Like It, V 4 line 2612.

Comedy of Errors, I 2 line 255; Comedy of Errors, II 1 line 360; Comedy of Errors, II 2 line 524; Comedy of Errors, III 1 line 617; Comedy of Errors, III 1 line 709; Comedy of Errors, III 2 line 864; Comedy of Errors, IV 2 line 1077; Comedy of Errors, IV 4 line 1094; Comedy of Errors, IV 4 line 1312; Comedy of Errors, V 1 line 1618; Comedy of Errors, V 1 lines 1675, 1682; Comedy of Errors, V 1 line 1738; Comedy of Errors, V 1 line 1750; Comedy of Errors, V 1 line 1866.

Coriolanus, I 1 line 256; Coriolanus, I 4 line 530; Coriolanus, I 9 line 817; Coriolanus, I 9 line 844; Coriolanus, II 1 lines 971, 976; Coriolanus, II 2 line 1355; Coriolanus, II 3 line 1491; Coriolanus, IV 5 line 2824; Coriolanus, IV 5 lines 2924, 2925; Coriolanus, IV 6 line 3160; Coriolanus, V 3 line 3639; Coriolanus, V 4 line 3747.

Cymbeline, I 1 line, 16; Cymbeline, I 2 line 246; Cymbeline, IV 1 line 2305; Cymbeline, IV 2 line 2609; Cymbeline, IV 2 line 2685; Cymbeline, IV 2 line 2713; Cymbeline, IV 2 line 2770; Cymbeline, V 1 line 2979; Cymbeline, V 3 line 3045; Cymbeline, V 4 line 3183; Cymbeline, V 5 line 3395.

Hamlet, I 2 line 346; Hamlet, I 2 line 443; Hamlet, II 1 line 1049; Hamlet, II 2 line 1301; Hamlet, II 2 line 1501; Hamlet, II 2 line 1646;

Hamlet, III 1 line 1835; Hamlet, III 2 line 1963; Hamlet, III 2 line 2112; Hamlet, III 2 line 2145; Hamlet, III 4 line 2438; Hamlet, IV 7 line 3252; Hamlet, V 2 line 3946.
Henry IV, Part I, I 3 line 472; Henry IV, Part I, I 3 lines 533, 539; Henry IV, Part I, I 3 line 612; Henry IV, Part I, II 3 line 919; Henry IV, Part I, II 4 line 1119; Henry IV, Part I, II 4 line 1129; Henry IV, Part I, II 4 line 1140; Henry IV, Part I, II 4 line 1181; Henry IV, Part I, II 4 line 1241; Henry IV, Part I, II 4 line 1487; Henry IV, Part I, III 2 line 1905; Henry IV, Part I, III 3 line 2031; Henry IV, Part I, III 3 line 2035; Henry IV, Part I, III 3 lines 2038, 2041, 2044; Henry IV, Part I, III 3 line 2058; Henry IV, Part I, III 3 line 2086; Henry IV, Part I, IV 2 line 2398; Henry IV, Part I, IV 3 line 2541; Henry IV, Part I, V 1 line 2697; Henry IV, Part I, V 3 line 2900; Henry IV, Part I, V 4 line 3060.
Henry IV, Part II, I 2 lines 296r, 298; Henry IV, Part II, I 2 lines 479, 539; Henry IV, Part II, II 1 line 890; Henry IV, Part II, II 2 line 960; Henry IV, Part II, II 2 line 1042; Henry IV, Part II, II 4 line 1492; Henry IV, Part II, II 4 line 1585; Henry IV, Part II, II 4 line 1634; Henry IV, Part II, IV 1 line 2227; Henry IV, Part II, IV 3 line 2701; Henry IV, Part II, IV 5 line 3062; Henry IV, Part II, V 1 line 3225; Henry IV, Part II, V 2 line 3274.
Henry V, II 1 line 552; Henry V, II 1 line 588; Henry V, III 2 line1160r; Henry V, III 6 line 1567; Henry V, III 7 line 1717; Henry V, IV 0 lines 1796, 1822; Henry V, IV 1 line 2047; Henry V, IV 6 lines 2490, 2497; Henry V, V 2 line 2990; Henry V, V 2 line 3011r; Henry V, V 2 lines 3129, 3145; Henry V, V 2 lines 3214, 3225.
Henry VI, Part I, I 1 line 18; Henry VI, Part I, I 1 line 146; Henry VI, Part I, I 3 line 399; Henry VI Part I, III 3 line 1655; Henry VI, Part I, III 4 line 1731; Henry VI, Part I, IV 2 line 1993; Henry VI, Part I, II 4 line 1140; Henry IV, Part I, II 4 line 1181; Henry IV, Part I, IV 6 line 2204; Henry VI, Part I, IV 7 line 2337; Henry VI, Part I, V 3 line 2608.
Henry VI, Part II, I 1 line 25; Henry VI, Part II, I 1 line 150; Henry VI, Part II, I 2 line 282; Henry VI Part II, I 3 line 538; Henry VI, Part II, II 4 line 1168; Henry VI, Part II, III 1 line 1485; Henry VI, Part II, III 1 lines 1621, 1658; Henry VI, Part II, III 2 line 1755; Henry VI, Part II, III 2 line 1825; Henry VI, Part II, III 2 lines 1845, 1852;
Henry IV, Part II, III 2 line 2009; Henry IV, Part II, IV 1 line 2253; Henry VI, Part II, IV 4 line 2537; Henry VI, Part II, IV 8 line 2788; Henry VI, Part II, IV 10 line 2933; Henry VI, Part II, V 1 line 3069.
Henry VI, Part III, I 4 line 484; Henry VI, Part III, I 4 lines 556, 580; Henry VI, Part III, I 4 line 593; Henry VI Part III, II 1 line 687; Henry VI, Part III, II 2 lines 856, 869, 882; Henry VI, Part III, II 3 line 1063; Henry VI, Part III, II 5 line 1165; Henry VI, Part III, II 5 line 1187; Henry VI, Part III, II 5 line 1202; Henry VI, Part III, II 6 line 1292; Henry IV, Part III, III 1 line 1451; Henry IV, Part III, III 2 line 1674; Henry VI, Part III, IV 8 line 2576; Henry VI, Part III, V 1 line 2647.
Henry VIII, I 3 line 577; Henry VIII, II 1 line 838; Henry VIII, III 1 line 1785; Henry VIII, IV 1 line 2502; Henry VIII, IV 2 line 2650; Henry VIII, IV 2 lines 2671; Henry VIII, IV 2 line 2683; Henry VIII, V 3 line 3105r; Henry VIII, V 4 line 3311.

Julius Caesar, I 2 line 106; Julius Caesar, I 2 line 139; Julius Caesar, II 1 line 623; Julius Caesar, II 1 line 685; Julius Caesar, II 1 line 732; Julius Caesar, II 1 line 904; Julius Caesar, II 2 line 987; Julius Caesar, III 2 line 1732; Julius Caesar, IV 3 line 2221; Julius Caesar, V 1 line 2354; Julius Caesar, V 3 line 2608; Julius Caesar, V 5 line 2728.

King John, I 1 line 85; King John, I 1 line 91; King John, I 1 lines 98, 99, 100; King John, I 1 lines 147, 152; King John, I 1 lines 158, 159; King John, II 1 line 313; King John, II 1 line 359; King John, II 1 lines 391, 393; King John, II 1 line 560; King John, II 1 line 581; King John, II 1 line 700r; King John, II 1 line 728; King John, II 1 line 807; King John, II 1 line 880; King John, IV 2 line 1748; King John, IV 2 line 1977; King John, V 1 line 2244; King John, V 2 line 2368; King John, V 2 line 2441.

King Lear, I 1 line 287; King Lear, I 4 line 717; King Lear, I 5 line 896; King Lear, II 2 line 1160; King Lear, II 3 lines 1260, 1262; King Lear, III 1 line 1639; King Lear, III 4 line 1884; King Lear, III 7 line 2244; King Lear, IV 6 line 2727; King Lear, IV 7 line 2947; King Lear, V 3 line 3415.

Love's Labour's Lost, I 2 line 436; Love's Labour's Lost, II 1 line 614; Love's Labour's Lost, II 1 line 746; Love's Labour's Lost, III 1 line 829; Love's Labour's Lost, III 1 line 960; Love's Labour's Lost, IV 2 line 1147; Love's Labour's Lost, IV 3 line 1352; Love's Labour's Lost, IV 3 line 1516; Love's Labour's Lost, IV 3 line 1560; Love's Labour's Lost, IV 3 line 1597; Love's Labour's Lost, IV 3 line 1617; Love's Labour's Lost, IV 3 line 1621; Love's Labour's Lost, IV 3 lines 1645, 1653; Love's Labour's Lost, V 2 line 1913; Love's Labour's Lost, V 2 line 1926; Love's Labour's Lost, V 2 line 1961; Love's Labour's Lost, V 2 line 2013; Love's Labour's Lost, V 2 line 2032; Love's Labour's Lost, V 2 line 2093; Love's Labour's Lost, V 2 line 2095; Love's Labour's Lost, V 2 line 2182; Love's Labour's Lost, V 2 line 2310; Love's Labour's Lost, V 2 line 2317; Love's Labour's Lost, V 2 line 2550; Love's Labour's Lost, V 2 line 2554; Love's Labour's Lost, V 2 line 2555; Love's Labour's Lost, V 2 line 2557; Love's Labour's Lost, V 2 line 2563; Love's Labour's Lost, V 2 line 2564; Love's Labour's Lost, V 2 line 2584; Love's Labour's Lost, V 2 line 2770.

Lover's Complaint, lines 81, 284.

Macbeth, I 2 line 39; Macbeth, I 4 line 289; Macbeth, I 5 line 417; Macbeth, I 7 line 535; Macbeth, I 7 line 566; Macbeth, II 2 line 718; Macbeth, II 3 line 888; Macbeth, II 4 line 957; Macbeth, III 1 line 1138; Macbeth, III 2 line 1207; Macbeth, III 4 line 1287; Macbeth, III 4 line 1354; Macbeth, IV 2 line 1827; Macbeth, IV 3 line 1848;

Macbeth, V 3 line 2258; Macbeth, V 3 lines 2263, 2266; Macbeth, V 3 line 2268; Macbeth, V 7 line 2451.

Measure for Measure, I 4 lines 361, 362; Measure for Measure, II 1 line 535; Measure for Measure, II 1 lines 595, 597; Measure for Measure, II 1 line 601; Measure for Measure, II 1 lines 603, 604; Measure for Measure, V 1 line 2575; Measure for Measure, V 1 line 2576; Measure for Measure, V 1 line 2610; Measure for Measure, V 1 line 2613; Measure for Measure, V 1 line 2769.

Merchant of Venice, I 3 line 462; Merchant of Venice, II 2 line 663; Merchant of Venice, II 5 line 891; Merchant of Venice, II 7 line 1032; Merchant of Venice, II 8 line 1119; Merchant of Venice, IV 1 line 1948; Merchant of Venice, IV 2 line 2438; Merchant of Venice, V 1 line 2623.
Merry Wives of Windsor, I 1 line 153; Merry Wives of Windsor, I 4 line 425; Merry Wives of Windsor, II 3 line 1130; Merry Wives of Windsor, IV 2 line 2094; Merry Wives of Windsor, V 5 line 2613.
Midsummer Night's Dream, I 1 line 210; Midsummer Night's Dream, I 2 line 310; Midsummer Night's Dream, I 2 line 342; Midsummer Night's Dream, I 2 line 353; Midsummer Night's Dream, II 1 line 596; Midsummer Night's Dream, III 1 line 851; Midsummer Night's Dream, III 2 line 1263; Midsummer Night's Dream, III 2 line 1494; Midsummer Night's Dream, III 2 line 1498; Midsummer Night's Dream, IV 1 line 1568; Midsummer Night's Dream, V 1 line 2037.
Much Ado About Nothing, I 1 line 25; Much Ado About Nothing, I 1 line 122; Much Ado About Nothing, I 1 line 124; Much Ado About Nothing, II 1 line 410; Much Ado About Nothing, II 1 line 424; Much Ado About Nothing, II 3 line 863; Much Ado About Nothing, III 1 line 1139; Much Ado About Nothing, III 2 line 1248; Much Ado About Nothing, III 2 line 1259; Much Ado About Nothing, IV 1 line 1714; Much Ado About Nothing, IV 1 line 1810; Much Ado About Nothing, V 1 line 2373r; Much Ado About Nothing, V 4 line 2589; Much Ado About Nothing, V 4 line 2604.
Othello, II 1 line 1114; Othello, III 3 line 1681; Othello, III 3 line 2068; Othello, IV 1 line 2507; Othello, IV 2 line 2768; Othello, V 1 line 3243; Othello, V 2 line 3395.
Pericles, I 0 line 23; Pericles, I 1 line 61; Pericles, I 1 line 76; Pericles, I 2 line 293; Pericles, I 2 lines 315, 319; Pericles, IV 2 line 1712; Pericles, IV 3 line 1852; Pericles, IV 3 line 1868; Pericles, IV 4 line 1910; Pericles, IV 6 line 2080.
Rape of Lucrece, lines 103, 115, 123, 254, 364, 528, 598, 613, 733, 851, 880, 1274, 1305, 1386, 1405, 1440, 1447, 1448, 1459, 1478, 1496, 1555, 1569, 1577, 1583, 1590, 1642, 1764, 1795, 1826.
Richard II, I 1 line 17r; Richard II, I 1 line 114; Richard II, I 1 line 200; Richard II, I 3 line 482; Richard II, I 4 line 620; Richard II, II 1 lines 857, 863; Richard II, II 3 line 1252; Richard II, II 4 line 1340; Richard II, III 2 line 1459; Richard II, III 2 line 1486; Richard II, III 3 line 1738; Richard II, IV 1 line 1987; Richard II, IV 1 line 2255; Richard II, IV 1 lines 2269, 2272r, 2274, 2276r, 2277, 2281; Richard II, IV 1 line 2285; Richard II, V 2 line 2473; Richard II, V 3 line 2621; Richard II, V 3 line 2682; Richard II, V 5 line 2826.
Richard III, I 2 line 343; Richard III, I 3 line 509; Richard III, III 4 line 1957; Richard III, III 4 line 2009; Richard III, III 4 line 2010; Richard III, III 7 line 2337; Richard III, III 7 line 2444; Richard III, IV 1 line 2541; Richard III, IV 4 line 2989; Richard III, IV 4 lines 3043; Richard III, V 3 lines 3749, 3773; Richard III, V 5 line 3925.
Romeo and Juliet, I 2 line 363; Romeo and Juliet, I 3 line 426; Romeo and Juliet, I 3 line 440; Romeo and Juliet, I 3 line 466; Romeo and Juliet, I 4 line 605; Romeo and Juliet, I 5 line 678; Romeo and Juliet, II

2 line 888; Romeo and Juliet, II 2 line 934; Romeo and Juliet, II 4 lines 1261, 1262; Romeo and Juliet, II 5 line 1401; Romeo and Juliet, II 5 line 1417; Romeo and Juliet, III 2 line 1741; Romeo and Juliet, III 2 line 1795; Romeo and Juliet, III 5 line 2264; Romeo and Juliet, III 5 line 2270; Romeo and Juliet, IV 1 line 2393; Romeo and Juliet, IV 1 line 2394; Romeo and Juliet, IV 1 line 2399; Romeo and Juliet, IV 1 line 2400; Romeo and Juliet, IV 5 line 2700; Romeo and Juliet, V 3 line 2966; Romeo and Juliet, V 3 line 3019.

Sonnet III lines 1, 2; Sonnet XVII line 8; Sonnet XX line 1; Sonnet XXVII line 12; Sonnet XXXIII lines 3, 6; Sonnet XXXIV line 6; Sonnet LXII line 5; Sonnet XCIII line 10; Sonnet XCIV line 7; Sonnet C line 9; Sonnet CIII line 6; Sonnet CXXVII line 6; Sonnet CXXXI line 6; Sonnet CXXXI line 10; Sonnet CXXXII line 9; Sonnet CXXXVII line 12; Sonnet CXXXIX line 11; Sonnet CXLIII line 7.

Taming of the Shrew, Prologue 2 line 210; Taming of the Shrew, I 1 line 361; Taming of the Shrew, I 1 line 458; Taming of the Shrew, I 1 line 494; Taming of the Shrew, I 2 line 670; Taming of the Shrew, II 1 line 847; Taming of the Shrew, II 1 line 1084; Taming of the Shrew, II 1 line 1140; Taming of the Shrew, III 2 line 1535; Taming of the Shrew, IV 1 line 1701; Taming of the Shrew, IV 3 line 2088; Taming of the Shrew, IV 5 line 2300.

Tempest, I 2 line 205; Tempest, II 1 line 925; Tempest, III 1 1337; Tempest, IV 1 1908.

Timon of Athens, I 1 line 74; Timon of Athens, III 6 lines 1530, 1532; Timon of Athens, IV 2 1627; Timon of Athens, IV 3 line 1829; Timon of Athens, IV 3 line 1877; Timon of Athens, IV 3 line 2210.

Titus Andronicus, II 3 line 874; Titus Andronicus, II 3 line 1017; Titus Andronicus, II 4 lines 1092, 1095; Titus Andronicus, III 1 line 1147; Titus Andronicus, III 1 line 1341; Titus Andronicus, III 1 line 1362; Titus Andronicus, IV 2 line 1816; Titus Andronicus, V 1 line 2178; Titus Andronicus, V 3 line 2532; Titus Andronicus, V 3 line 2605; Titus Andronicus, V 3 line 2698.

Troilus and Cressida, II 3 line 1426; Troilus and Cressida, II 3 line 1450; Troilus and Cressida, III 3 line 1978; Troilus and Cressida, IV 1 line 2220; Troilus and Cressida, V 5 line 3507; Troilus and Cressida, V 6 line 3520.

Twelfth Night, I 1 line 31; Twelfth Night, I 5 line 458; Twelfth Night, I 5 line 518; Twelfth Night, I 5 line 520; Twelfth Night, I 5 line 586; Twelfth Night, III 2 line 1481; Twelfth Night, III 4 line 1618; Twelfth Night, IV 2 line 2111; Twelfth Night, V 1 line 2239; Twelfth Night, V 1 line 2277; Twelfth Night, V 1 line 2404; Twelfth Night, V 1 line 2415.

Two Gentlemen of Verona, II 1 line 526; Two Gentlemen of Verona, III 1 line 1174; Two Gentlemen of Verona, IV 4 line 1902; Two Gentlemen of Verona, IV 4 line 1995; Two Gentlemen of Verona, IV 4 line 2026; Two Gentlemen of Verona, V 2 line 2073; Two Gentlemen of Verona, V 2 line 2075; Two Gentlemen of Verona, V 4 line 2270.

Venus and Adonis, lines 21, 26, 82, 177, 206, 463, 507, 508, 561r, 576, 590, 652, 664, 795, 830, 894, 1005, 1089, 1098, 1115, 1131, 1144.

Winter's Tale, I 2 line 187; Winter's Tale, I 2 line 236; Winter's Tale, I 2 line 576; Winter's Tale, II 1 line 612; Winter's Tale, II 1 line 784; Winter's Tale, IV 3 line 1839; Winter's Tale, IV 4 line 1926; Winter's Tale, IV 4 line 2112; Winter's Tale, IV 4 line 2131; Winter's Tale, IV 4 line 2618.

Falcon: mid-13c., from Old France: *faucon* (12c.), probably from Latin: *falx: curved blade, pruning hook, sickle*; the bird said to be so called for the shape of its talons, legs, or beak, but also possibly from the shape of its spread wings. The other theory is that *falx* is of Germanic origin and means *grey bird*, which is supported by the antiquity of the word in Germanic but opposed by those who point out that falconry by all evidences was imported from the East, and the Germans got it from the Romans, not the other way around.
    As You Like It, III 3 line 1569.
    Hamlet, II 2 line 1508.
    Henry VI, Part II, II 1 line 726; Henry VI, Part II, line 731; Henry VI, Part II, II 1 line 738.
    Henry VI, Part III, I 4 line 479.
    Macbeth, II 4 line 961.
    Measure for Measure, III 1 line 1322.
    Rape of Lucrece, line 557.
    Richard II, I 3 line 357.
    Romeo and Juliet, II 2 line 1019.
    Taming of the Shrew, IV 1 line 1801.
    Troilus and Cressida, III 2 line 1704.
    Venus and Adonis, line 1049.
    Winter's Tale, IV 4 line 1872.

Fangs: canine tooth (1550s) probably developed from Old English: *fengtod*, literally, catching-or grasping-tooth.
    As You Like It, II 1 line 553.
    Hamlet, III 4 line 2608.
    Henry IV, Part II, IV 1 line 2425.
    King John, II 1 line 663.
    King Lear, III 7 line 2187.
    Merchant of Venice, III 3 line 1715.
    Timon of Athens, IV 3 line 1685.
    Twelfth Night, I 5 line 477.
    Venus and Adonis, line 684.

Farrow: Old English *fearh* young pig, Sense of a *litter of pigs* first recorded 1570s. As a verb, early 13c.
    Macbeth, IV 1 line 1621.

Fashions: a skin disease in horses, now called *farcy*.
    Taming of the Shrew, III 2 line 1412.

Fawn: a young deer; late Middle English: from Old French *faon*.
    As You Like It, II 7 line 1024.

Coriolanus, III 2 line 2246.
Henry VI, Part I, IV 4 line 2121.
Henry VI, Part III, IV 1 line 2050; Henry VI, Part III, IV 8 line 2571.
Julius Caesar, I 2 line 163; Julius Caesar, III 1 line 1249.
Love's Labour's Lost, V 2 line 1944.
Midsummer Night's Dream, II 1 line 579.
Richard II, I 3 line 467; Richard II, III 2 line 1540; Richard II, V 1 line 2367.
Richard III, I 3 line 757.
Sonnet CXLIX line 6.
Timon of Athens, III 4 line 1224.
Venus and Adonis, 898.

Feather: Old English: *feder*: feather, in plural, wings. The feather is absolute lightness, flight, the element of wind and air. To wear feathers is to assume the powers of the bird, and thus puts the wearer in touch with the knowledge of the bird. Can also mean emptiness, dryness, height, flight, soul/heart, charity, faith and justice. Three feathers often connotes power, divinity and Light. Crimson feathers are normally associated with fairies. A feather crown is a halo.

All's Well That Ends Well, IV 5 line 2561; All's Well That Ends Well, V 3 line 2945.
Antony and Cleopatra, III 2 line 1651.
Comedy of Errors, III 1 line 714; Comedy of Errors, III 1 lines 716, 717.
Cymbeline, I 6 line 818.
Hamlet, II 2 line 1391; Hamlet, III 2 line 2163.
Henry IV, Part I, IV 1 line 2332.
Henry IV, Part II, II 4 line 1354; Henry IV, Part II, IV 5 line2920.
Henry V, I 2 line 458; Henry V, IV 1 line 2048; Henry V, IV 3 line 2350.
Henry VI, Part II, III 1 line 1353; Henry VI, Part II, IV 8 line 2812.
Henry VI, Part III, II 1 line 798; Henry VI, Part III, III 1 line 1451; Henry VI, Part III, III 3 line 1858.
Henry VIII, I 3 line 601.
Julius Caesar, I 1 line 73.
King John, IV 2 line 1913.
King Lear, IV 6 line 2656; King Lear, V 3 line 3444.
Love's Labour's Lost, IV 1 line 1069.
Measure for Measure, IV 2 line 1912.
Merchant of Venice, II 2 line 726.
Othello, I 3 line 621.
Pericles, IV 0 line 1524: Pericles, V 2 line 2509.
Phoenix and the Turtle, line 11.
Rape of Lucrece, lines 1173, 1267.
Romeo and Juliet, I 1 line 204; Romeo and Juliet, I 4 line 516; Romeo and Juliet, III 2 line 1798.
Sonnet LXXVIII line 7; Sonnet CXLIII line 2.
Taming of the Shrew, III 2 line 1426; Taming of the Shrew, IV 3 line 2135.

Tempest, I 2 line 472.
Timon of Athens, I 1 line 126; Timon of Athens, II 1 line 658.
Twelfth Night, III 1 line 1298.
Venus and Adonis, lines 76, 322, 326.
Winter's Tale, II 3 line 1117.

Fell: skin or hide of an animal, Old English *fel*.
King Lear, V 3 line 3148.

Fells: rocky hill, c.1300, from Old Norse: *fiall*: mountain.
As You Like It, III 2 line 1168.

Fen: Old English: *fenn*: mud, mire, dirt; fen, marsh, moor.
Coriolanus, III 3 line 2493; Coriolanus, IV 3 line 2553.
Tempest, I 2 line 472; Tempest, II 1 line 752; Tempest, II 2 line 1083.

Fennel: Old English: *fenol, finul*, perhaps via (or influenced by) Old French: *fenoil*. Apparently so called from its hay-like appearance and sweet odour. This was generally considered as an inflammatory herb; one of the herbs distributed by Ophelia in her distraction is fennel which she offers either as a cordial or as an emblem of flattery.
Hamlet, IV 5 line 3056.
Henry IV, Part II, II 4 line 1528.

Fern-seed: Old English: *fearn*, related to *feather, wing*. Applied to the plant perhaps from the feather-like appearance of the fronds. The plant's ability to appear as if from nothing accounts for the ancient belief that fern seeds conferred invisibility, especially on Midsummer Eve. It was believed at one time to have neither flower nor seed; the seed, which lay on the back of the leaf, being so small as to escape the detection of the observer. On this account, probably, proceeding on the fantastic doctrine of signatures, our ancestors derived the notion that those who could obtain and wear this invisible seed would be themselves invisible.
Henry IV, Part I, II 1 line 730; Henry IV, Part I, II 1 line 732.

Fetlock: early 14c., *fetlak*, from a Germanic source.
Henry V, IV 7 line 2599.
Henry VI, Part III, II 3 line 1049.
Venus and Adonis, line 315.

Fico: a fig.
Merry Wives of Windsor, I 3 line 331.

Field: Old English: *feld*: plain, open land (as opposed to woodland), also a parcel of land marked off and used for pasture or tillage, probably related to Old English: *folde:* earth, land.
All's Well That Ends Well, II 3 line 1192; All's Well That Ends Well, III 1 line 1395.

Antony and Cleopatra, I 2 line 170; Antony and Cleopatra, I 4 line 505; Antony and Cleopatra, II 1 line 636; Antony and Cleopatra, II 6 line 1335; Antony and Cleopatra, II 6 line 1336; Antony and Cleopatra, II 1 line 643; Antony and Cleopatra, III 1 line 1585; Antony and Cleopatra, III 13 line 2462; Antony and Cleopatra, IV 6 line 2714.
As You Like It, III 2 line 1138; As You Like It, V 3 line 2377.
Comedy of Errors, III 2 line 800.
Coriolanus, I 2 line 331; Coriolanus, I 4 line 494; Coriolanus, I 6 line 671; Coriolanus, I 7 line 729; Coriolanus, I 9 lines 816; Coriolanus, II 2 lines 1344, 1368.
Cymbeline, IV 2 line 2368r; Cymbeline, V 3 line 3096; Cymbeline, V 4 line 3268.
Hamlet, V 2 line 4071.
Henry IV, Part I, I 1 lines 8, 25; Henry IV, Part I, I 3 line 640; Henry IV, Part I, II 3 line 899; Henry IV, Part I, III 1 line 1583; Henry IV, Part I, III 2 line 1925; Henry IV, Part I, IV 2 line 2444; Henry IV, Part I, V 4 line 2961; Henry IV, Part I, V 4 line 2985; Henry IV, Part I, V 4 line 3133; Henry IV, Part I, V 5 line 3158.
Henry IV, Part II, Prologue 1 lines 25, 35; Henry IV, Part II, I 1 line 67; Henry IV, Part II, I 1 line 74; Henry IV, Part II, I 1 line 183; Henry IV, Part II, II 3 line 1190; Henry IV, Part II, III 2 line 2048; Henry IV, Part II, IV 1 line 2227; Henry IV, Part II, IV 4 line 2748.
Henry V, Prologue 1 line 13; Henry V, I 2 line 274; Henry V, II 3 line 848; Henry V, II 4 line 900; Henry V, III 2 line 1136; Henry V, III 5 line 1429; Henry V, IV 2 lines 2193, 2200; Henry V, IV 2 line 2205; Henry V, IV 2 line 2225; Henry V, IV 3 line 2324; Henry V, IV 3 line 2339; Henry V, IV 5 line 2470 ; Henry V, IV 6 line 2478; Henry V, IV 6 line 2494; Henry V, IV 7 line 2577; Henry V, IV 7 lines 2593, 2603; Henry V, IV 7 line 2607; Henry V, IV 7 line 2612; Henry V, IV 8 line 2789.
Henry VI, Part I, I 1 line 77; Henry VI, Part I, I 4 line 541; Henry VI, Part I, II 2 line 785; Henry VI Part I, III 1 line 1332; Henry VI, Part I, III 2 line 1515; Henry VI, Part I, III 2 line 1551; Henry VI, Part I, IV 7 line 2317; Henry IV, Part I, V 3 line 2460; Henry IV, Part I, V 4 line 2700.
Henry VI, Part II, I 1 line 87; Henry VI, Part II, I 3 line 504; Henry VI, Part II, IV 2 line 2355; Henry VI, Part II, IV 7 line 2699; Henry VI, Part II, V 1 line 3023; Henry VI, Part II, V 1 line 3187.
Henry VI, Part III, I 1 line 97; Henry VI, Part III, I 1 line 110; Henry VI, Part III, I 1 line 278; Henry VI Part III, I 2 line 362; Henry VI, Part III, I 4 line 436; Henry VI, Part III, II 1 line 660; Henry VI, Part III, II 2 line 916; Henry VI, Part III, II 2 line 928; Henry VI, Part III, III 2 line 1471; Henry VI, Part III, IV 3 line 2177; Henry IV, Part III, V 1 line 2717; Henry IV, Part III, V 3 line 2797.
Henry VIII, III 1 line 1792; Henry VIII, V 5 line 3415.
Julius Caesar, V 1 line 2363; Julius Caesar, V 1 line 2417; Julius Caesar, V 3 line 2521; Julius Caesar, V 3 line 2625; Julius Caesar, V 4 line 2634; Julius Caesar, V 5 line 2694; Julius Caesar, V 5 line 2766.
King John, I 1 line 60; King John, II 1 line 601; King John, II 1 line 667; King John, II 1 line 890; King John, V 1 line 2266; King John, V 3

line 2473; King John, V 4 line 2492; King John, V 4 line 2533; King John, V 5 line 2559.
King Lear, III 2 line 1770; King Lear, III 4 line 2522.
Love's Labour's Lost, II 1 line 573; Love's Labour's Lost, II 1 line 583; Love's Labour's Lost, III 1 line 950; Love's Labour's Lost, IV 3 line 1711; Love's Labour's Lost, V 2 line 2265; Love's Labour's Lost, V 2 line 2491.
Macbeth, V 1 line 2130; Macbeth, V 8 line 2527.
Merchant of Venice, II 1 line 541.
Merry Wives of Windsor, II 3 line 1170; Merry Wives of Windsor, II 3 line 1177; Merry Wives of Windsor, V 5 line 2633.
Midsummer Night's Dream, II 1 line 465; Midsummer Night's Dream, II 1 line 613; Midsummer Night's Dream, III 2 line 1456; Midsummer Night's Dream, V 1 line 2266.
Othello, I 1 line 22; Othello, I 3 line 425; Othello, I 3 line 480.
Passionate Pilgrim, line 356.
Pericles, I 1 line 82.
Rape of Lucrece, lines 109, 123, 158, 1481.
Richard II, I 3 line 438; Richard II, IV 1 line 2076; Richard II, IV 1 line 2128.
Richard III, I 4 line 889; Richard III, II 1 lines 1237, 1240; Richard III, IV 3 line 2780; Richard III, IV 3 line 2788; Richard III, V 2 line 3436; Richard III, V 3 line 3456; Richard III, V 3 line 3532; Richard III, V 3 line 3801; Richard III, V 4 line 3885.
Romeo and Juliet, II 1 line 839; Romeo and Juliet, III 1 line 1556; Romeo and Juliet, IV 5 line 2686.
Sonnet, II line 2.
Taming of the Shrew, I 2 line 753; Taming of the Shrew, III 2 line 1597; Taming of the Shrew, IV 5 line 2290.
Timon of Athens, I 2 line 414; Timon of Athens, I 2 line 591.
Titus Andronicus, I 1 line 40; Titus Andronicus, I 1 line 220; Titus Andronicus, II 2 line 698; Titus Andronicus, IV 2 line 1857; Titus Andronicus, V 1 line 2146.
Troilus and Cressida, I 1 line 37; Troilus and Cressida, I 1 line 136; Troilus and Cressida, I 1 line 137; Troilus and Cressida, I 2 line 163; Troilus and Cressida, I 2 line 323; Troilus and Cressida, I 3 line 635; Troilus and Cressida, II 3 line 1383; Troilus and Cressida, III 1 line 1620; Troilus and Cressida, III 1 line 1634; Troilus and Cressida, III 2 line 1660; Troilus and Cressida, III 3 line 2064; Troilus and Cressida, III 3 line 2129; Troilus and Cressida, IV 1 line 2209; Troilus and Cressida, IV 4 line 2585; Troilus and Cressida, IV 4 line 2586; Troilus and Cressida, IV 5 line 2896; Troilus and Cressida, IV 5 line 2911; Troilus and Cressida, V 3 line 3354; Troilus and Cressida, V 5 line 3475; Troilus and Cressida, V 8 line 3615; Troilus and Cressida, V 10 line 3632; Troilus and Cressida, V 10 line 3638.
Twelfth Night, II 3 line 827.
Venus and Adonis, lines 28, 128, 475, 916.

Figs: early 13c., from Old French: *figue* (12c.). The insulting sense of the word in Shakespeare, etc. (*A fig for...*) is 1570s, in part from fig as *small, valueless thing*, but also from Greek and Italian use of their versions of the word as slang for vaginal opening; apparently because of how a ripe fig looks when split open. Formerly the term *fig* served as a common expression of contempt, and was used to denote a thing of the least importance.
> **Antony and Cleopatra**, I 2 line 111; Antony and Cleopatra, V 2 line 3685; Antony and Cleopatra, V 2 line 3817.
> **Henry IV, Part II**, V 3 line 3530.
> **Henry V**, III 6 line 1520.
> **Henry VI, Part II**, II 3 line 1116.
> **King John**, II 1 line 459.
> **Midsummer Night's Dream**, III 1 line 992.
> **Othello**, I 3 line 677.

Filberts: a cultivated hazel tree that bears edible oval nuts. Middle English *fylberd*, from Anglo-Norman French *philbert*, dialect French: *noix de filbert* (so named because it is ripe about 20 August, the feast day of St Philibert).
> **Tempest**, II 2 line 1257.

Fill-horse: a shaft or till horse.
> **Merchant of Venice**, II 2 line 660.

Finch: Old English: *finc*. Perhaps an imitation of the sound the bird makes.
> **Midsummer Night's Dream**, III 1 line 952.
> **Troilus and Cressida**, V 1 line 2966.

Finger: Old English: *fingor*.
> **All's Well That Ends Well**, III 2 line 1458; All's Well That Ends Well, IV 2 line 2074; All's Well That Ends Well, V 3 line 2799; All's Well That Ends Well, V 3 line 3033.
> **As You Like It**, I 1 line 24.
> **Comedy of Errors**, II 2 line 594; Comedy of Errors, IV 4 line 1396; Comedy of Errors, V 1 line 1714.
> **Coriolanus**, I 3 line 451; Coriolanus, IV 5 line 2923; Coriolanus, V 4 line 3734.
> **Cymbeline**, I 4 line 448; Cymbeline, II 3 line 991; Cymbeline, V 5 line 3538; Cymbeline, V 5 line 3592; Cymbeline, V 5 line 3939.
> **Hamlet**, I 5 line 942; Hamlet, III 2 line 1949; Hamlet, III 2 line 2238; Hamlet, III 4 line 2589; Hamlet, IV 7 line 3320; Hamlet, V 1 line 3601; Hamlet, V 2 line 3665.
>> **Henry IV, Part I**, I 3 line 361; Henry IV, Part I, II 3 line 951; Henry IV, Part I, IV 2 line 2442.
>> **Henry IV, Part II**, II 2 line 1075; Henry IV, Part II, IV 3 line 2741.
>> **Henry V**, II 2 line 738; Henry V, II 3 line 846; Henry V, IV 7 lines 2547, 2548.
>> **Henry VI, Part I**, II 4 line 972; Henry VI, Part I, V 3 line 2507.
>> **Henry VI, Part II**, III 2 line 1828; Henry VI, Part II, IV 10 line 2934.

Henry VI, Part III, I 2 line 326; Henry VI, Part III, I 4 line 493; Henry VI, Part III, V 1 line 2640.
Henry VIII, I 1 line 95; Henry VIII, III 2 line 1981; Henry VIII, IV 1 line 2481; Henry VIII, V 3 line 3181; Henry VIII, V 3 line 3210.
Julius Caesar, I 2 line 335; Julius Caesar, III 1 line 1420; Julius Caesar, IV 3 line 2003.
King John, III 4 line 1415; King John, III 4 line 1556; King John, V 7 line 2670.
Love's Labour's Lost, V 1 line 1805; Love's Labour's Lost, V 1 line 1830; Love's Labour's Lost, V 2 line 1995; Love's Labour's Lost, V 2 line 2827.
Macbeth, I 3 line 144; Macbeth, IV 1 line 1577.
Measure for Measure, V 1 line 2731.
Merchant of Venice, II 2 line 671; Merchant of VeniceIII 2 line 1554; Merchant of Venice, V 1 lines 2633, 2638; Merchant of Venice, V 1 line 2653.
Merry Wives of Windsor, I 4 line 487; Merry Wives of Windsor, II 3 line 1141; Merry Wives of Windsor, III 2 line 1384; Merry Wives of Windsor, V 5 line 2648.
Midsummer Night's Dream, III 1 line 881; Midsummer Night's Dream, III 1 line 1008; Midsummer Night's Dream, IV 1 line 1589; Midsummer Night's Dream, V 1 line 2021.
Othello, II 1 lines 961, 964; Othello, II 1 line 1019; Othello, III 4 line 2340; Othello, IV 2 line 2803.
Pericles, I 1 line 129; Pericles, IV 0 line 1524.
Rape of Lucrece, line 370.
Richard II, V 5 line 2802.
Richard III, I 2 line 392.
Romeo and Juliet, I 4 lines 566, 573; Romeo and Juliet, III 5 line 2272; Romeo and Juliet, IV 2 line 2499; Romeo and Juliet, IV 2 lines 2502, 2503; Romeo and Juliet, V 3 line 2967.
Sonnet XCVI line 5; Sonnet CXXVIII line 3, 11, 14.
Taming of the Shrew, Prologue 1 line 39; Taming of the Shrew, I 1 line 375; Taming of the Shrew, II 1 line 994; Taming of the Shrew, III 1 line 1331; Taming of the Shrew, IV 3 line 2108.
Tempest, III 2 line 1475; Tempest, IV 1 line 1986; Tempest, IV 1 line 1991.
Timon of Athens, II 1 line 652.
Titus Andronicus, II 3 line 973; Titus Andronicus, II 4 line 1106.
Troilus and Cressida, I 3 line 657; Troilus and Cressida, I 3 line 696; Troilus and Cressida, II 1 line 881; Troilus and Cressida, III 1 line 1637; Troilus and Cressida, V 2 line 3115; Troilus and Cressida, V 2 line 3231.
Twelfth Night, I 3 line 187; Twelfth Night, II 5 line 1180.
Two Gentlemen of Verona, I 2 line 259; Two Gentlemen of Verona, IV 4 line 1976.
Venus and Adonis, lines 248, 497.
Winter's Tale, I 2 line 190; Winter's Tale, II 3 line 1056.

Fire: c.1200, *furen*, figurative, *arouse, excite*; literal sense of *set fire to* is from late 14c., from fire. The Old English verb *fyrian: to supply* with fire apparently did not survive into Middle English. Fire consumes, warms, and illuminates, but can also bring pain and death; thus, its symbolic meaning varies wildly, depending upon the context of its use. It is often the symbol of inspiration, and yet it is also the predominant symbol of Hell; fire is the only one of the Four Elements that humans can produce themselves, so it bridges the connection between mortals and gods. Rituals often involve an eternal flame, and kindling a fire is equated with birth and resurrection.

All's Well That Ends Well, II 1 line 675; All's Well That Ends Well, III 2 line 1519; All's Well That Ends Well, III 7 line 1875; All's Well That Ends Well, IV 2 line 2009; All's Well That Ends Well, IV 5 lines 2504, 2505, 2511; All's Well That Ends Well, V 3 line 2680.

Antony and Cleopatra, I 3 line 375; Antony and Cleopatra, II 6 line 1361; Antony and Cleopatra, III 13 line 2429; Antony and Cleopatra, III 3 line 1726; Antony and Cleopatra, III 13 line 2249; Antony and Cleopatra, IV 10 line 2884; Antony and Cleopatra, V 2 line 3747.

As You Like It, I 2 line 184; As You Like It, III 2 line 1146.

Comedy of Errors, IV 3 line 1205r; Comedy of Errors, V 1 line 1506; Comedy of Errors, V 1 line 1606.

Coriolanus, I 1 line 174; Coriolanus, I 1 line 194; Coriolanus, I 4 line 562; Coriolanus, II 1 line 1205; Coriolanus, III 3 line 2431; Coriolanus, IV 6 line 3111; Coriolanus, IV 7 line 3272; Coriolanus, V 1 line 3293; Coriolanus, V 2 line 3378; Coriolanus, V 2 line 3418; Coriolanus, V 2 line 3445; Coriolanus, V 3 line 3702; Coriolanus, V 4 line 3779; Coriolanus, V 5 line 3810.

Cymbeline, I 1 line 91; Cymbeline, III 1 line 1445; Cymbeline, IV 4 line 2905; Cymbeline, V 5 line 3573.

Hamlet, I 1 line 134; Hamlet, I 1 line 176; Hamlet, I 3 line 607; Hamlet, I 5 line 828; Hamlet, II 2 line 1212; Hamlet, II 2 line 1396; Hamlet, II 2 line 1536; Hamlet, III 2 line 2153; Hamlet, III 4 line 2476; Hamlet, IV 7 line 3257; Hamlet, IV 7 line 3340; Hamlet, V 2 line 3913.

Henry IV, Part I, II 4 line 1301; Henry IV, Part I, II 4 line 1366; Henry IV, Part I, III 1 line 1566; Henry IV, Part I, III 1 line 1567; Henry IV, Part I, III 1 line 1817; Henry IV, Part I, III 3 lines 2038, 2042, 2047, 2055; Henry IV, Part I, IV 1 lines 2340, 2343.

Henry IV, Part II, I 1 line 131; Henry IV, Part II, I 1 lines 170, 172; Henry IV, Part II, I 1 line 200; Henry IV, Part II, I 3 line 618; Henry IV, Part II, II 1 line 814; Henry IV, Part II, II 2 line 1051; Henry IV, Part II, II 4 line 1446; Henry IV, Part II, IV 1 line 2327; Henry IV, Part II, V 5 line 3706.

Henry V, Prologue 1 line 2; Henry V, I 2 line 276; Henry V, II 0 line 464; Henry V, II 1 line 558; Henry V, II 3 line 872; Henry V, II 3 line 873; Henry V, III 2 line 1174; Henry V, III 6 lines 1569, 1570, 1571; Henry V, IV 0 lines 1795r, 1810.

Henry VI, Part I, I 1 line 16; Henry IV, Part I, IV 2 line 1977; Henry VI, Part I, IV 6 line 2202.

Henry VI, Part II, II 4 line 644; Henry VI, Part II, III 1 line 1587; Henry VI, Part II, IV 1 line 2253; Henry VI, Part II, IV 2 line 2263; Henry VI,

Part II, IV 2 line 2366; Henry VI, Part II, IV 6 lines 2618; Henry VI, Part II, V 2 line 3270.
Henry VI, Part III, II 1 line 710; Henry VI, Part III, III 2 line 1531; Henry VI, Part III, IV 8 line 2528; Henry VI, Part III, V 4 line 2877.
Henry VIII, I 1 lines 211, 216; Henry VIII, II 4 line 1434; Henry VIII, V 3 line 3190; Henry VIII, V 4 line 3314.
Julius Caesar, I 2 line 268; Julius Caesar, I 3 line 431; Julius Caesar, I 3 lines 439, 446; Julius Caesar, I 3 line 489; Julius Caesar, I 3 line 535; Julius Caesar, II 1 line 728; Julius Caesar, II 1 line 738; Julius Caesar, II 1 line 966; Julius Caesar, III 1 line 1241; Julius Caesar, III 1 line 1269; Julius Caesar, III 1 line 1392r; Julius Caesar, III 2 line 1660; Julius Caesar, III 2 line 1749; Julius Caesar, III 2 line 1800; Julius Caesar, III 2 line 1802; Julius Caesar, III 3 line 1855; Julius Caesar, IV 3 line 2099; Julius Caesar, IV 3 line 2155; Julius Caesar, V 3 line 2510; Julius Caesar, V 5 line 2741.
King John, II 1 line 528; King John, II 1 line 661; King John, II 1 line 774; King John, III 1 line 1202r; King John, III 1 line 1274; King John, IV 1 line 1649; King John, IV 1 line 1695; King John, IV 1 line 1709; King John, IV 2 line 1900; King John, V 1 line 2243r; King John, V 2 line 2365; King John, V 4 line 2513; King John, V 7 line 2665.
King Lear, I 4 line 641; King Lear, II 2 line 1144; King Lear, II 2 line 1175; King Lear, III 2 line 1681; King Lear, III 2 lines 1690, 1691; King Lear, III 2 line 1722; King Lear, III 4 line 1853; King Lear, III 4 lines 1906, 1908; King Lear, III 4 line 1945; King Lear, III 6 line 2057; King Lear, III 7 line 2190; King Lear, IV 7 line 2954; King Lear, IV 7 line 2963; King Lear, V 3 line 3147; King Lear, V 3 line 3281.
Love's Labour's Lost, I 1 line 150; Love's Labour's Lost, I 1 line 183; Love's Labour's Lost, III 1 line 822; Love's Labour's Lost, IV 2 line 1235; Love's Labour's Lost, IV 3 lines 1649, 1695; Love's Labour's Lost, V 2 line 2404.
Lover's Complaint, lines 296, 326.
Macbeth, I 4 line 332; Macbeth, II 2 line 648; Macbeth, III 4 line 1352; Macbeth, IV 1 line 1558; Macbeth, IV 1 line 1568; Macbeth, IV 1 line 1583.
Merchant of Venice, II 1 line 519; Merchant of Venice, II 6 line 920; Merchant of Venice, II 9 line 1195; Merchant of Venice, III 2 line 1395.
Merry Wives of Windsor, I 4 line 412; Merry Wives of Windsor, I 4 line 487; Merry Wives of Windsor, II 1 line 630; Merry Wives of Windsor, II 2 line 929; Merry Wives of Windsor, III 4 line 1736; Merry Wives of Windsor, V 5 line 2608; Merry Wives of Windsor, V 5 line 2648; Merry Wives of Windsor, V 5 line 2653; Merry Wives of Windsor, V 5 line 2662; Merry Wives of Windsor, V 5 line 2809.
Midsummer Night's Dream, I 1 line 180; Midsummer Night's Dream, II 1 line 372; Midsummer Night's Dream, II 2 line 762; Midsummer Night's Dream, III 1 lines 925, 926; Midsummer Night's Dream, V 1 line 2242.
Much Ado About Nothing, I 1 line 209; Much Ado About Nothing, II 1 line 635; Much Ado About Nothing, III 1 line 1155; Much Ado About Nothing, IV 1 line 1811.

Othello, I 1 line 79; Othello, II 1 line 858; Othello, III 3 line 2069; Othello, IV 1 line 2669; Othello, V 2 line 3466; Othello, V 2 line 3637.
Passionate Pilgrim, lines 28, 68, 98.
Pericles, I 1 line 99; Pericles, I 4 line 420; Pericles, I 4 line 506; Pericles, II 3 line 867; Pericles, II 4 line 959; Pericles, III 1 line 1229; Pericles, III 1 line 1254; Pericles, III 2 line 1286; Pericles, III 2 lines 1380, 1384, 1388, 1389; Pericles, IV 2 line 1809.
Rape of Lucrece, lines 56, 228, 232, 366, 406, 698, 935, 1405, 1526, 1542, 1574, 1603, 1604, 1607, 1608, 1655.
Richard II, I 1 line 21; Richard II, I 2 line 223; Richard II, I 3 line 595; Richard II, II 1 line 716; Richard II, III 2 line 1450; Richard II, III 3 lines 1693, 1695; Richard II, V 1 lines 2374, 2382; Richard II, V 5 line 2865; Richard II, V 6 line 2881.
Richard III, I 3 line 723.
Romeo and Juliet, I 1 line 104; Romeo and Juliet, I 1 line 204; Romeo and Juliet, I 1 line 218; Romeo and Juliet, I 2 line 319; Romeo and Juliet, I 2 line 366; Romeo and Juliet, I 5 line 647; Romeo and Juliet, I 6 line 1468; Romeo and Juliet, III 1 line 1632; Romeo and Juliet, III 3 line 2014; Romeo and Juliet, V 1 line 2875.
Sonnet XLV line 1; Sonnet LV line 7; Sonnet LXXIII line 9; Sonnet CXLIV line 14; Sonnet CLIII line 3; Sonnet CLIII line 5; Sonnet CLIII line 9; Sonnet CLIII line 14; Sonnet CLIV line 5; Sonnet CLIV line 10; Sonnet CLIV line 14.
Taming of the Shrew, I 2 line 759; Taming of the Shrew, II 1 lines 975, 977, 978; Taming of the Shrew, IV 1 lines 1623, 1626, 1627; Taming of the Shrew, IV 1 line 1634; Taming of the Shrew, IV 1 line 1644; Taming of the Shrew, IV 1 line 1650; Taming of the Shrew, IV 1 line 1652; Taming of the Shrew, IV 1 line 1655; Taming of the Shrew, V 2 line 2607.
Tempest, I 2 line 89; Tempest, I 2 line 309; Tempest, I 2 line 322; Tempest, I 2 line 333; Tempest, I 2 line 456; Tempest, II 2 line 1087; Tempest, IV 1 1759; Tempest, V 1 2066.
Timon of Athens, I 1 line 32; Timon of Athens, III 3 line 1345; Timon of Athens, IV 3 1824; Timon of Athens, IV 3 line 1871; Timon of Athens, IV 3 line 2151.
Titus Andronicus, I 1 line 144; Titus Andronicus, I 1 line 164; Titus Andronicus, V 1 line 2268; Titus Andronicus, V 1 line 2283.
Troilus and Cressida, I 2 line 295; Troilus and Cressida, I 3 line 755; Troilus and Cressida, II 2 line 1105; Troilus and Cressida, III 2 line 1712; Troilus and Cressida, III 3 line 2140; Troilus and Cressida, V 1 line 2998.
Twelfth Night, I 5 line 546; Twelfth Night, II 5 line 1078; Twelfth Night, III 2 lines 1422, 1424; Twelfth Night, V 1 line 2473.
Two Gentlemen of Verona, I 2 line 180; Two Gentlemen of Verona, I 3 line 383; Two Gentlemen of Verona, II 4 line 687; Two Gentlemen of Verona, II 7 lines 994, 995; Two Gentlemen of Verona, II 7 lines 996, 997.
Venus and Adonis, lines 55, 114, 216, 295, 354, 368, 408, 422, 515, 675, 1094, 1095, 1184.

Winter's Tale, II 3 line 933; Winter's Tale, II 3 line 1047; Winter's Tale, II 3 line 1073; Winter's Tale, II 3 lines 1095, 1103; Winter's Tale, III 2 line 1411; Winter's Tale, IV 4 line 1888; Winter's Tale, IV 4 line 1926.

Firmament: mid-13c., from Latin: *firmamentum: firmament*, literally *a support or strengthening*, from *firmus: firm*, a word used of both the vault of the sky and the floor of the earth.
   Hamlet, II 2 line 1395.
   Julius Caesar, III 1 line 1267.
   King Lear, I 2 line 454.
   Richard II, II 4 line 1351.
   Titus Andronicus, V 3 line 2545.
   Winter's Tale, III 3 line 1580.

Fish: Old English: *fisc*.
   All's Well That Ends Well, III 6 line 1811; All's Well That Ends Well, V 2 line 2621.
   Antony and Cleopatra, I 4 line 427; Antony and Cleopatra, II 5 line 1062.
   Comedy of Errors, II 1 line 290; Comedy of Errors, II 1 line 295; Comedy of Errors, III 1 line 635; Comedy of Errors, III 1 line 714; Comedy of Errors, III 1 line 717.
   Coriolanus, IV 7line 3252.
   Cymbeline, IV 2 line 2359; Cymbeline, IV 2 line 2517..
   Hamlet, IV 3 lines 2738, 2739.
   Henry IV, Part I, III 1 line 1696; Henry IV, Part I, III 3 line 2138.
   Henry IV, Part II, I 1 line 258.
   Henry VI, Part II, IV 8 line 2757.
   Henry VIII, I 2 line 409.
   King Lear, I 4 line 550.
   Merchant of Venice, I 1 line 98; Merchant of Venice, III 1 line 1287.
   Merry wives of Windsor, I 1 line 20r.
   Much Ado About Nothing, II 3 line 927; Much Ado About Nothing, III 1 line 1101.
   Pericles, II 1 lines 603, 605; Pericles, II 1 line 647; Pericles, II 1 line 650; Pericles, II 1 line 661; Pericles, II 1 line 695.
   Richard III, I 4 line 858.
   Romeo and Juliet, I 1 line 44; Romeo and Juliet, I 3 line 474; Romeo and Juliet, V 1 line 2853.
   Tempest, II 1 line 812; Tempest, II 2 lines 1109r, 1110r, 1112, 1113, 1121; Tempest, II 2 line 1247; Tempest, II 2 line 1267; Tempest, III 2 lines 1421, 1424; Tempest, V 1 line 2340.
   Timon of Athens, IV 3 line 2136; Timon of Athens, IV 3 line 2137.
   Titus Andronicus, IV 4 line 2105.
   Troilus and Cressida, IV 4 line 2539.
   Two Gentlemen of Verona, II 5 line 896.
   Venus and Adonis, line 1122.
   Winter's Tale, IV 4 lines 2160, 2165; Winter's Tale, V 2 line 3192.

Fishpond: not surprisingly, a pond for keeping fish. Pond: mid-13c., artificially banked body of water, variant of *pound: enclosed place*.
All's Well That Ends Well, V 2 line 2635.

Fitchew: see Polecat.
King Lear, IV 6 line 2730.
Othello, IV 1 line 2576.
Troilus and Cressida, V 1 line 2992.

Fives: a disease of horses.
Taming of the Shrew, III 2 line 1413.

Flame: mid-14c., from Anglo-French: *flaume*, Old French: *flamme* (10c.), from Latin: *flammula: small flame*. The meaning *a sweetheart* is attested from 1640s; the figurative sense of *burning passion* was in Middle English.
All's Well That Ends Well, I 2 line 301; All's Well That Ends Well, I 3 line 537; All's Well That Ends Well, II 3 line 978.
Coriolanus, IV 3 line 2682; Coriolanus, V 2 line 3418.
Cymbeline, II 2 line 1001.
Hamlet, I 5 line 737; Hamlet, II 2 line 1579; Hamlet, III 4 line 2522; Hamlet, IV 7 line 3258.
Henry IV, Part I, I 2 line 121.
Henry IV, Part II, Prologue 1 line 27; Henry IV, Part II, V 5 line 3620.
Henry V, III 3 line 1288; Henry V, III 6 line 1568; Henry V, IV 0 line 1795.
Henry VI, Part I, III 1 line 1426.
Henry VI, Part II, V 2 line 3258.
Henry VI, Part III, II 1 line 711.
Julius Caesar, I 2 line 203; Julius Caesar, I 3 line 437; Julius Caesar, III 2 line 1689.
King John, V 1 line 2200.
King Lear, II 4 line 1450; King Lear, III 4 line 1853.
Lover's Complaint, lines 192, 269, 289.
Macbeth, IV 1 line 1623.
Merry Wives of Windsor, V 5 line 2649; Merry Wives of Windsor, V 5 line 2664.
Othello, II 1 line 1026.
Passionate Pilgrim, line 98.
Pericles, I 1 line 66; Pericles, I 1 line 190; Pericles, II 2 line 790; Pericles, IV 1 line 1552; Pericles, IV 2 line 1802.
Phoenix and the Turtle, line 24.
Rape of Lucrece, lines 32, 57, 231.
Richard III, IV 4 line 3135.
Sonnet I line 6; Sonnet CIX line 2; Sonnet CXV line 4.
Tempest, I 2 lines 317, 319.
Timon of Athens, I 1 line 33.
Troilus and Cressida, III 2 line 1809; Troilus and Cressida, V 2 line 3239; Troilus and Cressida, V 6 line 3543.
Twelfth Night, I 3 line 240; Twelfth Night, I 5 line 554.

Flank: late Old English: *flanc: fleshy part of the side*, from Old French: *flanc*.
Venus and Adonis, lines 1075, 1137.

Flaw: a small wind or storm, early 16c.
Antony and Cleopatra, III 12 line 2238.
Coriolanus, V 3 line 3576.
Hamlet, V 1 line 3544.
Henry IV, Part II, IV 4 line 2783.
Henry VI, Part II, III 1 line 1640.
Henry VIII, I 1 line 145; Henry VIII, I 2 line 342.
King Lear, II 4 line 1586; King Lear, V 3 line 3355.
Love's Labour's Lost, V 2 line 2337.
Macbeth, III 4 line 1350.
Measure for Measure, II 3 line 976.
Pericles, III 1 line 1236.
Venus and Adonis, Line 477.
Winter's Tale, II 1 line 768.

Flax: Old English: *fleax: cloth made with flax, linen*.
Hamlet, IV 5 line 3071.
Henry VI, Part II, V 2 line 3271.
King Lear, III 7 line 2243.
Merry Wives of Windsor, V 5 line 2724.
Twelfth Night, I 3 line 208.
Winter's Tale, I 2 line 379.

Flea: Old English: *flea*, perhaps related to Old English:*fleon: to flee*, with a notion of the jumping parasite.
Henry IV, Part I, II 1 line 657; Henry IV, Part I, II 1 line 662.
Henry V, II 3 line 870; Henry V, III 7 line 1774.
Love's Labour's Lost, V 2 line 2632.
Merry Wives of Windsor, IV 2 line 2108.
Taming of the Shrew, IV 3 line 2072.
Twelfth Night, III 2 line 1464.

Fleece: Old English: *fleos*. The verb is 1530s in the literal sense of *to strip a sheep of fleece* and 1570s in the figurative meaning *to cheat, swindle*.
As You Like It, II 4 line 797.
Henry IV, Part I, II 2 line 825.
Henry VI, Part I, IV 7 line 2326.
Henry VI, Part II, III 1 line 1409.
Henry VI, Part III, II 5 line 1139; Henry VI, Part III, V 6 line 3003.
Merchant of Venice, I 1 line 177; Merchant of Venice, III 2 line 1616; Merchant of Venice, II 2 line 1617.
Rape of Lucrece, line 729.
Sonnet LXVIII line 8.
Titus Andronicus, II 3 line 767.

Flesh: 1520s, *to render (a hunting animal) eager for prey by rewarding it with flesh from a kill*. Old English: *flæsc: flesh, meat*, also *near kindred* (a sense now obsolete except in phrase flesh and blood). *Flesh-colour*, the hue of Caucasian skin, is first recorded 1610s, described as a tint composed of a light pink with a little yellow. An Old English poetry-word for body was *flæschama*, literally, *flesh-home*.

All's Well That Ends Well, I 3 line 350; All's Well That Ends Well, I 3 line 356; All's Well That Ends Well, I 3 lines 367r, 368, 369; All's Well That Ends Well, IV 3 line 2107; All's Well That Ends Well, IV 5 line 2474.

Antony and Cleopatra, I 2 line 98; Antony and Cleopatra, I 4 line 497; Antony and Cleopatra, V 2 line 3538.

As You Like It, III 2 line 1180; As You Like It, IV 3 line 2153.

Comedy of Errors, II 2 line 532; Comedy of Errors, III 1 line 635; Comedy of Errors, IV 1 line 1417.

Coriolanus, II 2 line 1364; Coriolanus, V 3 line 3537.

Cymbeline, I 4 line 450; Cymbeline, IV 2 line 2487; Cymbeline, V 5 line 3688.

Hamlet, I 2 line 333; Hamlet, I 5 line 758; Hamlet, III 1 line 1756; Hamlet, IV 3 line 2765; Hamlet, V 1 line 3573.

Henry IV, Part I, II 2 line 776; Henry IV, Part I, II 4 line 1228; Henry IV, Part I, III 3 line 2138; Henry IV, Part I, III 3 line 2176; Henry IV, Part I, V 4 line 3043; Henry IV, Part I, V 4 line 3067; Henry IV, Part I, V 4 line 3100.

Henry IV, Part II, I 1 line 207; Henry IV, Part II, I 1 line 230; Henry IV, Part II, II 4 line 1588; Henry IV, Part II, II 4 line 1659; Henry IV, Part II, IV 5 line 3028; Henry IV, Part II, V 3 line 3414.

Henry V, II 4 line 950; Henry V, III 3 line 1283.

Henry VI, Part I, I 1 line 45; Henry IV, Part I, III 1 line 1428; Henry VI, Part I, IV 7 line 2291; Henry VI, Part I, V 4 line 2688.

Henry VI, Part II, I 1 line 245; Henry VI, Part II, III 1 line 1586.

Henry VI, Part III, I 1 line 287; Henry VI, Part III, II 1 line 726.

Henry VIII, V 3 line 3070.

Julius Caesar, III 1 line 1272.

King John, II 1 line 664; King John, III 3 line 1321; King John, IV 2 line 1989; King John, V 1 line 2267.

King Lear, II 2 line 1115; King Lear, II 2 line 1191; King Lear, II 4 lines 1518, 1519; King Lear, III 4 lines 1872, 1873; King Lear, III 4 line 1937; King Lear, III 7 line 2187; King Lear, IV 2 line 2413; King Lear, IV 6 line 2845; King Lear, V 3 line 3148.

Love's Labour's Lost, I 1 line 191; Love's Labour's Lost, I 1 line 219; Love's Labour's Lost, III 1 line 897; Love's Labour's Lost, IV 3 line 1397; Love's Labour's Lost, IV 3 line 1559.

Macbeth, V 3 line 2284.

Measure for Measure, II 1 line 696; Measure for Measure, V 1 line 2749.

Merchant of Venice, I 3 line 478; Merchant of Venice, I 3 lines 493, 495; Merchant of Venice, II 2 line 657; Merchant of Venice, III 1 line 1270; Merchant of Venice, III 1 line 1272; Merchant of Venice, III 1 line

1273; Merchant of Venice, III 1 line 1286; Merchant of Venice, III 2 line 1663; Merchant of Venice, III 3 line 1744; Merchant of Venice, IV 1 line 1955; Merchant of Venice, IV 1 line 1973; Merchant of Venice, IV 1 line 2031; Merchant of Venice, IV 1 line 2044; Merchant of Venice, IV 1 line 2174; Merchant of Venice, IV 1 line 2200; Merchant of Venice, IV 1 line 2245; Merchant of Venice, IV 1 line 2248; Merchant of Venice, IV 1 lines 2253, 2254; Merchant of Venice, IV 1 lines 2272, 2274; Merchant of Venice, V 1 line 2634.
Merry Wives of Windsor, IV 4 line 2218; Merry Wives of Windsor, V 5 line 2651.
Much Ado About Nothing, IV 1 line 1792; Much Ado About Nothing, IV 2 line 2060.
Pericles, I 1 line 139; Pericles, I 1 line 182; Pericles, II 1 line 605; Pericles, II 1 line 660; Pericles, IV 6 line 1977; Pericles, V 1 line 2361; Pericles, V 3 line 2576r.
Rape of Lucrece, lines 763, 790.
Richard II, I 3 lines 493, 494; Richard II, III 2 lines 1578, 1582; Richard II, V 5 line 2869.
Richard III, IV 3 line 2732; Richard III, V 3 line 3683.
Romeo and Juliet, I 1 line 43; Romeo and Juliet, I 5 line 715; Romeo and Juliet, II 4 line 1198r; Romeo and Juliet, III 2 line 1804; Romeo and Juliet, V 1 line 2895; Romeo and Juliet, V 3 line 3058.
Sonnet XLIV line 1; Sonnet LI line 11; Sonnet CLI line 8.
Taming of the Shrew, Prologue 2 line 274; Taming of the Shrew, IV 1 line 1784.
Tempest, III 1 line 1352; Tempest, III 3 line 1618; Tempest, V 1 line 2103; Tempest, V 1 line 2147.
Timon of Athens, IV 3 line 1837; Timon of Athens, IV 3 line 2245.
Titus Andronicus, I 1 line 115; Titus Andronicus, III 2 line 1454; Titus Andronicus, IV 2 line 1773; Titus Andronicus, V 3 line 2596.
Troilus and Cressida, V 10 line 3682.
Twelfth Night, I 5 line 319; Twelfth Night, IV 1 line 1989; Twelfth Night, V 1 line 2220.
Venus and Adonis, lines 76, 162.
Winter's Tale, II 1 line 782; Winter's Tale, IV 4 line 2165; Winter's Tale, IV 4 line 2666; Winter's Tale, IV 4 lines 2670r, 2672.

Flies: plural of fly. Old English *flyge, fleoge*.
Antony and Cleopatra, III 13 line 2454; Antony and Cleopatra, V 2 line 3455.
Coriolanus, IV 6 line 3132.
Cymbeline, IV 2 line 2806; Cymbeline, V 4 line 3178.
Hamlet, III 2 line 2096.
Henry IV, Part II, III 1 line 1715.
Henry V, V 2 line 3292.
Henry VI, Part II, I 2 line 370.
Henry VI, Part III, II 6 lines 1258, 1257.
King Lear, IV 1 line 2289.
Love's Labour's Lost, V 2 line 2330.

Macbeth, IV 2 line 1777.
Othello, I 1 line 74; Othello, IV 2 line 2814.
Pericles, IV 3 line 1871.
Romeo and Juliet, II 4 line 1192; Romeo and Juliet, III 3 lines 1906, 1912.
Timon of Athens, II 2 line 864.
Troilus and Cressida, I 3 line 501; Troilus and Cressida, V 1 line 2964.
Venus and Adonis, line 336.
Winter's Tale, IV 4 line 2486; Winter's Tale, IV 4 line 2769.

Flint: from the Old English, meaning *flint-rock*.
All's Well That Ends Well, IV 4 line 2429.
Antony and Cleopatra, IV 9 line 2853.
Coriolanus, V 3 line 3551.
Cymbeline, III 6 line 2180; Cymbeline, V 4 line 3316.
Hamlet, V 1 line 3563.
Henry IV, Part II, IV 4 line 2781.
Henry VI, Part I, II 1 line 693.
Henry VI, Part II, II 4 line 1165; Henry VI, Part II, II 4 line 1194; Henry VI, Part II, III 2 line 1780; Henry VI, Part II, III 2 line 2011; Henry VI, Part II, V 1 line 3001.
Henry VI, Part III, I 4 line 582; Henry VI, Part III, II 1 line 830.
Julius Caesar, II 1 line 638; Julius Caesar, IV 3 line 2099.
King John, II 1 line 694.
Love's Labour's Lost, IV 2 line 1235.
Merchant of Venice, IV 1 line 1963.
Othello, I 3 line 579.
Pericles, IV 4 line 1924.
Rape of Lucrece, lines 227, 232.
Richard II, III 2 line 1621; Richard II, V 1 line 2336; Richard II, V 5 line 2768.
Richard III, I 3 line 603.
Romeo and Juliet, II 6 line 1476.
Timon of Athens, I 1 line 33; Timon of Athens, IV 3 line 2200.
Titus Andronicus, II 3 line 879; Titus Andronicus, V 3 line 2627.
Troilus and Cressida, III 3 line 2141.
Twelfth Night, I 5 line 579.
Venus and Adonis, lines 115, 219, 220.

Flock: *tuft of wool*, mid-13c., probably from Old French: *floc*, from Latin: *floccus: flock of wool, lock of hair*. Old English: *flocc: a group of persons, company, troop*. Extended c.1200 *to a number of animals of one kind moving or feeding together*; of domestic animals c.1300. Transferred to bodies of Christians, in relation to Christ or their local pastor, from mid-14c. The verb meaning to *gather, congregate* is from c.1300, from the noun.
As You Like it, I 1 line 100; As You Like it, II 4 line 810; As You Like it, II 4 line 806; As You Like it, II 4 line 810; As You Like it, III 5 line 1733.
Henry IV, Part I, II 1 line 647; Henry IV, Part I, II 4 line 1128.

Henry IV, Part II, I 1 line 267; Henry IV, Part II, IV 2 line 2446; Henry IV, Part II, V 1 line 3213.
Henry VI, Part II, II 2 line 1029; Henry VI, Part II, III 1 line 1542.
Henry VI, Part III, II 1 line 740; Henry VI, Part III, II 5 line 1133; Henry VI, Part III, IV 8 line 2526.
Henry VIII, I 4 line 757.
Merchant of Venice, IV 1 line 2047.
Midsummer Night's Dream, II 1 line 466.
Othello, II 3 line 1191.
Passionate Pilgrim, lines 246, 287, 359.
Richard III, IV 4 line 3335.
Twelfth Night, I 1 line 40.
Venus and Adonis, line 707.
Winter's Tale, IV 4 line 1936; Winter's Tale, IV 4 line 1986.

Flote: wave, sea.
Tempest, I 2 line 360.

Flow: in Scottish: a watery swamp or morass. Old English: *flowan: to flow, stream, issue; become liquid, melt; abound, overflow.*
All's Well That Ends Well, V 3 line 3047.
Antony and Cleopatra, II 7 line 1393; Antony and Cleopatra, V 2 line 3405.
As You Like It, II 7 line 967.
Coriolanus, V 3 line 3604.
Cymbeline, III 3 line 1701; Cymbeline, III 5 line 2139r.
Henry IV, Part I, I 2 lines 143, 149.
Henry IV, Part II, V 2 line 3381.
Henry V, IV 3 line 2290.
Henry VI, Part I, I 1 line 88; Henry VI, Part I, II 1 line 693.
Henry VI, Part II, III 1 line 1481.
Henry VI, Part III, IV 8 line 2578.
Henry VIII, I 0 line 4; Henry VIII, I 1 line 220; Henry VIII, II 2 line 1276; Henry VIII, III 2 line 1974.
King Lear, V 3 line 3142.
Love's Labour's Lost, IV 3 line 1349; Love's Labour's Lost, IV 3 line 1560.
Measure for Measure, I 3 line 344.
Much Ado About Nothing, IV 1 line 1902.
Othello, II 3 line 1190.
Pericles, IV 3 line 1845.
Rape of Lucrece, line 702, 1620.
Romeo and Juliet, II 4 line 1200; Romeo and Juliet, III 5 line 2240.
Sonnet XXX line 5.
Tempest, II 1 line 946; Tempest, V 1 line 2344.
Timon of Athens, I 2 line 394; Timon of Athens, I 2 line 395; Timon of Athens, II 2 line 670; Timon of Athens, II 2 line 830; Timon of Athens, II 2 line 853; Timon of Athens, II 2 line 913; Timon of Athens, V 4 line 2649.

Troilus and Cressida, II 3 line 1348; Troilus and Cressida, IV 4 line 2511; Troilus and Cressida, V 2 line 3092.
Winter's Tale, II 2 line 906.

Flower: c.1200, from Old French: *flor: flower, blossom; heyday, prime; fine flour; elite; innocence, virginity*. Also used from 13c. in sense of *finest part or product of anything* and from c.1300 in the sense of *virginity*. The flower and the blossom are both universal symbols of young life. Flowers are associated with the Sun because the arrangement of its petals is reminiscent of the shape of a star they may be innocent representatives of spring, or they may designate lust and the realm of the erotic. They are transitory, evoking a certain *joie de vivre*, or an understanding of the fragile quality of childhood. The flower is often a representative of beauty. The colour of the flower often has a great deal to do with the symbolism it carries; red is love and passion, white is innocence and blamelessness. Virtue, goodness and purity are three widely associated traits.

All's Well That Ends Well, V 3 line 3049.
Antony and Cleopatra, II 2 line 935; Antony and Cleopatra, IV 14 line 3042.
As You Like It, V 3 line 2387.
Coriolanus, I 6 line 653; Coriolanus, V 5 line 3810.
Cymbeline, I 5 line 491; Cymbeline, II 3 line 1010; Cymbeline, IV 2 lines 2606, 2609; Cymbeline, IV 2 lines 2683, 2686; Cymbeline, IV 2 line 2698; Cymbeline, V 4 line 3248.
Hamlet, III 2 line 2019; Hamlet, IV 5 line 2900; Hamlet, V 1 line 3578.
Henry IV, Part I, II 3 line 867.
Henry IV, Part II, IV 5 line 2967.
Henry V, II 3 line 846; Henry V, III 3 line 1286.
Henry VI, Part I, II 4 line 1067; Henry VI, Part I, II 5 line 1134; Henry VI, Part I, IV 1 line 1871.
Henry VI, Part II, III 1 line 1512.
Henry VI, Part III, II 1 line 698.
Henry VIII, III 1 line 1626; Henry VIII, IV 1 lines 2432, 2433; Henry VIII, IV 2 line 2769.
Julius Caesar, I 1 line 51.
Love's Labour's Lost, IV 2 line 1273; Love's Labour's Lost, IV 3 line 1725; Love's Labour's Lost, V 2 line 2249; Love's Labour's Lost, V 2 line 2596.
Lover's Complaint, lines 75, 148.
Macbeth, I 5 line 420; Macbeth, IV 3 line 2039; Macbeth, V 2 line 2242.
Measure for Measure, II 2 line 941.
Merry Wives of Windsor, V 5 lines 2627, 2635, 2638.
Midsummer Night's Dream, II 1 line 394; Midsummer Night's Dream, II 1 lines 538, 541; Midsummer Night's Dream, II 1 line 613; Midsummer Night's Dream, II 2 line 678; Midsummer Night's Dream, II 2 line 725; Midsummer Night's Dream, III 1 line 894; Midsummer Night's Dream, III 1 line 979; Midsummer Night's Dream, III 1 line 1024; Midsummer Night's Dream, III 2 line 1138; Midsummer Night's

Dream, III 2 line 1244; Midsummer Night's Dream, IV 1 lines 1600, 1621.
Passionate Pilgrim, lines 132, 172, 174, 178, 209, 364.
Pericles, I 1 line 185; Pericles, III 2 line 1398; Pericles, IV 1 line 1560; Pericles, IV 1 line 1562; Pericles, IV 1 line 1574.
Rape of Lucrece, lines 921, 1278, 1305, 1306.
Richard II, I 3 line 591; Richard II, II 1 line 818; Richard II, III 2 line 1427; Richard II, III 3 line 1738; Richard II, III 4 line 1903; Richard II, III 4 line 1908.
Richard III, II 4 line 1498; Richard III, IV 4 line 2802.
Romeo and Juliet, I 3 line 462; Romeo and Juliet, I 3 line 463r; Romeo and Juliet, II 2 line 973; Romeo and Juliet, II 3 lines 1066, 1081; Romeo and Juliet, II 4 line 1218; Romeo and Juliet, II 4 line 1220; Romeo and Juliet, II 5 line 1420; Romeo and Juliet, III 2 line 1795; Romeo and Juliet, IV 5 line 2682; Romeo and Juliet, IV 5 line 2696; Romeo and Juliet, IV 5 line 2748; Romeo and Juliet, V 3 line 2933; Romeo and Juliet, V 3 line 2941; Romeo and Juliet, V 3 line 2946r; Romeo and Juliet, V 3 line 3256.
Sonnet XVII line 7; Sonnet XXI line 7; Sonnet LXV line 4 Sonnet LXVIII line 2; Sonnet LXIX line 12; Sonnet XCIV line 9; Sonnet XCIV line 11; Sonnet XCVIII line 6; Sonnet XCVIX line 13; Sonnet CXIII line 6; Sonnet CXXIV line 4r.
Taming of the Shrew, Prologue 1 line 57; Taming of the Shrew, II 1 line 1096.
Tempest, IV 1 line 1789.
Titus Andronicus, II 3 line 947; Titus Andronicus, IV 4 line 2085; Titus Andronicus, 2146.
Troilus and Cressida, I 2 line 163; Troilus and Cressida, I 2 line 333; Troilus and Cressida, II 3 line 1488.
Twelfth Night, I 1 line 44; Twelfth Night, I 5 line 344; Twelfth Night, II 4 line 955r.
Two Gentlemen of Verona, II 4 line 821.
Venus and Adonis, lines 28, 85, 151, 172, 686, 968, 1077, 1101, 1190, 1193, 1199, 1210.
Winter's Tale, IV 4 line 1942; Winter's Tale, IV 4 line 1949; Winter's Tale, IV 4 line 1953; Winter's Tale, IV 4 lines 1980, 1983; Winter's Tale, IV 4 lines 1992, 1996; Winter's Tale, IV line 2012.

Flower-de-Luce: archaic name for the Iris or the Lily, from the Old French: *fleur de lis*.
    Henry V, V 2 line 3194.
    Henry VI, Part I, I 1 line 85; Henry VI, Part I, I 2 line 296.
    Henry VI, Part II, V 1 line 2987.
    Winter's Tale, IV 4 line 2006.

Flowerets: florets, especially of cauliflower and broccoli. floret: c.1400, *flourette*, from Old French: *florete: little flower; cheap silk material*.
    Henry IV, Part I, II 3 line 867.
    Midsummer Night's Dream, IV 1 line 1603.

Flowery*: from flower, meaning covered with flowers.
    All's Well That Ends Well, IV 5 line 2510.
    Measure for Measure, III 1 line 941.
    Midsummer Night's Dream, III 1 line 950; Midsummer Night's Dream, IV 1 line 1546.

Flux: late 14c., from Old French: *flus: flowing, rolling, bleeding*, or directly from Latin: *fluxus: flowing, loose, slack*. Originally *excessive flow* (of blood or excrement); an early name for dysentery. The verb is early 15c., from the noun.
    As You Like It, II 1 line 602; As You Like It, III 2 line 1181.

Fly: Old English: *fleoge: fly, winged insect*.
    Antony and Cleopatra, II 2 line 906; Antony and Cleopatra, III 1 line 1567.
    As You Like It, IV 1 line 1890.
    Cymbeline, IV 2 line 2593.
    Henry V, V 2 line 3297.
    King Lear, IV 6 line 2721.
    Othello, II 1 line 957.
    Pericles, IV 1 line 1633.
    Titus Andronicus, III 2 line 1499; Titus Andronicus, III 2 line 1505; Titus Andronicus, III 2 line 1509; Titus Andronicus, III 2 line 1513; Titus Andronicus, III 2 line 1523; Titus Andronicus, V 1 line 2277.
    Troilus and Cressida, II 3 line 1229.

Foal: Old English: *fola; young of an animal*. Also means to give birth.
    Midsummer Night's Dream, II 1 line 414.
    Timon of Athens, II 1 line 635.

Fog: thick, obscuring mist, 1540s, probably from a Scandinavian source akin to Danish: *fog: spray, shower, snowdrift*. Figurative phrase *in a fog at a loss what to do* first recorded c.1600. Fog illustrates obscurity, indistinction; in the Bible, it is an image preceding great revelations.
    Coriolanus, II 3 line 1453.
    Cymbeline, II 3 line 1133; Cymbeline III 2 line 1595.
    King Lear, I 4 line 828; King Lear, II 4 line 1452.
    Macbeth, I 1 line 14.
    Midsummer Night's Dream, II 1 line 459; Midsummer Night's Dream, III 2 line 1414.
    Titus Andronicus, III 1 line 1351.
    Twelfth Night, IV 2 line 2064.

Foggy: 1540s, perhaps from a Scandinavian source.
    As You Like It, III 5 line 1703.
    Henry V, III 5 line 1406.
    Macbeth, III 5 line 1486.
    Rape of Lucrece, line 822.

Foison: plentiful crop or harvest. Middle English *foisoun*, from Old French *foison*, from 1587.
    Antony and Cleopatra, II 7 line 1396.
    Macbeth, IV 3 line 1944.
    Measure for Measure, I 4 line 395.
    Sonnet LIII line 9.
    Tempest, II 1 line 873; Tempest, IV 1 line 1826.

Foot: stumbling has from the earliest period been considered ominous. Old English: *fot*. Of a bed, grave, etc., first recorded c.1300. Usually ambivalent. Direct contact with mother earth. Is phallic with the shoe as the vulva and the foot itself as a euphemism for genitals. Can connote dying, passing on as well as slow wandering. Bare feet is a sign of mourning and respect. Footprints have high relation to black magic; fairies have no footprints. Can also bring luck and prosperity.
    All's Well That Ends Well, II 3 line 1177; All's Well That Ends Well, III 4 line 1597; All's Well That Ends Well, IV 3 line 2246; All's Well That Ends Well, V 3 line 2722.
    Antony and Cleopatra, I 5 line 573; Antony and Cleopatra, III 7 line 2019r; Antony and Cleopatra, IV 10 line 2885; Antony and Cleopatra, V 2 line 3691.
    As You Like It, II 7 line 963; As You Like It, III 2 line 1400; As You Like It, III 2 line 1401; As You Like It, V 4 line 2551.
    Comedy of Errors, III 2 line 874.
    Coriolanus, I 2 line 340; Coriolanus, I 8 line 741; Coriolanus, II 2 line 1355; Coriolanus, III 1 line 2121; Coriolanus, IV 3 line 2584; Coriolanus, IV 5 line 2886; Coriolanus, IV 7 line 3224.
    Cymbeline, III 3 lines 1697, 1700; Cymbeline, III 5 line 2121; Cymbeline, IV 2 line 2712; Cymbeline, V 4 line 3267.
    Hamlet, I 2 line 442; Hamlet, II 2 line 1531; Hamlet, III 2 line 1957; Hamlet, IV 3 line 2768.
    Henry IV, Part I, I 2 line 148; Henry IV, Part I, I 3 line 524; Henry IV, Part I, I 3 line 615; Henry IV, Part I, II 1 line 716; Henry IV, Part I, II 2 lines 752, 753, 762, 766; Henry IV, Part I, II 2 line 776; Henry IV, Part I, II 2 line 787; Henry IV, Part I, II 2 line 820; Henry IV, Part I, II 3 line 947; Henry IV, Part I, II 4 line 1108; Henry IV, Part I, II 4 line 1203; Henry IV, Part I, II 4 line 1338r; Henry IV, Part I, II 4 line 1536; Henry IV, Part I, III 2 line 1919; Henry IV, Part I, III 3 line 2194; Henry IV, Part I, IV 1 line 2320; Henry IV, Part I, V 5 line 3162.
    Henry IV, Part II, I 3 line 642; Henry IV, Part II, II 1 line 917; Henry IV, Part II, III 1 line 1768; Henry IV, Part II, IV 2 line 2484; Henry IV, Part II, IV 3 line 2637; Henry IV, Part II, IV 4 line 2754.
    Henry V, I 2 line 357; Henry V, I 2 line 461; Henry V, II 1 line 572; Henry V, II 4 line 1047; Henry V, III 1 line 1123; Henry V, III 4 line 1377; Henry V, III 4 lines 1378, 1382, 1385; Henry V, III 6 line 1497; Henry V, III 7 line 1729.
    Henry VI, Part I, I 2 line 211; Henry IV, Part I, I 3 line 393; Henry VI, Part I, III 1 line 1402; Henry VI, Part I, III 2 line 1523; Henry IV, Part I,

III 3 line 1674; Henry VI, Part I, IV 1 line 1931; Henry VI, Part I, IV 6 line 2245.
Henry VI, Part II, II 4 line 1217; Henry VI, Part II, III 1 line 1345; Henry VI, Part II, III 2 line 1768; Henry VI, Part II, IV 1 line 2207; Henry VI, Part II, IV 7 line 2668; Henry VI, Part II, IV 10 line 2937; Henry VI, Part II, V 1 line 3199; Henry VI, Part II, V 2 line 3217; Henry VI, Part II, V 3 line 3324.
Henry VI, Part III, I 1 line 177; Henry VI, Part III, I 4 line 450; Henry VI, Part III, I 4 line 496; Henry VI, Part III, II 2 line 858; Henry VI, Part III, III 2 line 1626; Henry VI, Part III, V 7 lines 3109, 3113.
Henry VIII, III 1 line 1824; Henry VIII, V 2 line 3033; Henry VIII, V 3 line 3219; Henry VIII, V 4 line 3287.
Julius Caesar, I 3 line 547; Julius Caesar, II 1 line 871; Julius Caesar, II 1 line 965; Julius Caesar, III 1 line 1261; Julius Caesar, III 2 line 1806.
King John, I 1 line 152; King John, I 1 lines 189, 190, 224; King John, II 1 line 314; King John, III 3 line 1363; King John, III 4 line 1518; King John, III 4 line 1557; King John, IV 1 line 1575; King John, IV 2 line 1829; King John, IV 2 line 1909; King John, IV 3 line 2044; King John, IV 3 line 2121; King John, V 1 line 2262; King John, V 2 line 2356; King John, V 7 line 2750.
King Lear, I 4 line 615; King Lear, II 4 line 1510; King Lear, III 3 line 1788; King Lear, III 4 line 1890; King Lear, III 4 line 1914; King Lear, III 7 line 2171; King Lear, III 7 line 2197; King Lear, IV 1 line 2312; King Lear, IV 3 line 2508; King Lear, IV 6 line 2626; King Lear, IV 6 line 2824; King Lear, V 3 line 3285.
Love's Labour's Lost, I 2 line 464; Love's Labour's Lost, IV 1 line 1059; Love's Labour's Lost, IV 3 line 1516; Love's Labour's Lost, IV 3 line 1621; Love's Labour's Lost, V 2 line 2401; Love's Labour's Lost, V 2 line 2609; Love's Labour's Lost, V 2 line 2688.
Macbeth, II 3 line 917; Macbeth, III 1 line 1044; Macbeth, IV 3 line 2057.
Measure for Measure, IV 5 line 2348; Measure for Measure, V 1 line 2819.
Merchant of Venice, I 3 line 445; Merchant of Venice, II 4 line 840; Merchant of Venice, III 1 lines 1324, 1325; Merchant of Venice, V 1 line 2473.
Merry Wives of Windsor, I 3 line 360; Merry Wives of Windsor, II 1 line 683; Merry Wives of Windsor, III 3 line 1462; Merry Wives of Windsor, IV 6 line 2444.
Midsummer Night's Dream, II 1 line 420; Midsummer Night's Dream, III 2 line 1240; Midsummer Night's Dream, III 2 line 1265.
Much Ado About Nothing, II 1 line 411; Much Ado About Nothing, II 1 line 649; Much Ado About Nothing, II 3 line 829; Much Ado About Nothing, II 3 line 884; Much Ado About Nothing, III 2 line 1207.
Othello, II 1 line 853; Othello, II 3 line 1381; Othello, IV 3 line 3060.
Rape of Lucrece, lines 606, 715, 724, 1478, 1500.
Richard II, I 1 lines 68, 71; Richard II, I 1 line 140; Richard II, I 1 line 169; Richard II, II 2 line 1042; Richard II, III 4 line 1959.

Richard III, I 1 line 98; Richard III, I 2 line 215; Richard III, I 4 line 850; Richard III, III 4 line 2042; Richard III, IV 4 line 3256; Richard III, V 3 lines 3807, 3811; Richard III, V 4 line 3877.
Romeo and Juliet, I 1 line 99; Romeo and Juliet, I 5 line 644; Romeo and Juliet, II 1 line 818; Romeo and Juliet, II 2 line 887; Romeo and Juliet, II 2 line 1001; Romeo and Juliet, II 5 line 1418; Romeo and Juliet, II 6 line 1475; Romeo and Juliet, III 2 line 1719; Romeo and Juliet, V 2 line 2905; Romeo and Juliet, V 3 line 2939; Romeo and Juliet, V 3 line 2954.
Sonnet IXX line 6; Sonnet XLIV line 5; Sonnet LXV line 11; Sonnet CVI line 6.
Taming of the Shrew, II 1 line 873; Taming of the Shrew, II 1 line 1256; Taming of the Shrew, III 2 line 1428; Taming of the Shrew, IV 1 line 1643; Taming of the Shrew, IV 1 line 1748; Taming of the Shrew, IV 3 line 1973; Taming of the Shrew, IV 3 line 2144; Taming of the Shrew, V 2 line 2629; Taming of the Shrew, V 2 line 2685.
Tempest, I 2 line 541; Tempest, I 2 line 655; Tempest, II 2 lines 1091,1092; Tempest, II 2 line 1235; Tempest, II 2 line 1239; Tempest, IV 1 line 1860; Tempest, IV 1 line 1938; Tempest, IV 1 line 1962; Tempest, V 1 line 2055.
Timon of Athens, I 1 line 108; Timon of Athens, I 1 line 114; Timon of Athens, V 1 line 2519; Timon of Athens, V 4 line 2611.
Titus Andronicus, II 3 line 937; Titus Andronicus, IV 2 line 1714; Titus Andronicus, IV 3 line 1995; Titus Andronicus, V 2 line 2361.
Troilus and Cressida, I 2 line 226; Troilus and Cressida, I 3 line 588; Troilus and Cressida, I 3 line 609; Troilus and Cressida, II 1 line 882; Troilus and Cressida, II 2 line 1153; Troilus and Cressida, II 3 line 1219; Troilus and Cressida, III 2 line 1723; Troilus and Cressida, III 3 line 2016; Troilus and Cressida, IV 5 line 2062; Troilus and Cressida, V 5 line 3477.
Twelfth Night, I 4 line 263; Twelfth Night, II 5 line 1214; Twelfth Night, III 2 line 1464.
Two Gentlemen of Verona, V 2 line 2116; Two Gentlemen of Verona, V 3 line 2138.
Venus and Adonis, lines 165, 582, 701, 744.
Winter's Tale, I 1 line 4; Winter's Tale, I 2 line 391r; Winter's Tale, III 3 line 1605; Winter's Tale, IV 3 line 1790; Winter's Tale, IV 3 line 1791r; Winter's Tale, IV 3 line 1792; Winter's Tale, IV 4 line 2232; Winter's Tale, V 3 line 3407.

Forefinger: mid 15c, from *fore-*, meaning *first*, + *finger*.
    All's Well That Ends Well, II 2 line 846.
    Romeo and Juliet, I 4 line 556.

Forehead: Old English: *forheafod*, from fore- + *heafod*.
    All's Well That Ends Well, IV 3 line 2316.
    Antony and Cleopatra, III 3 line 1730.
    As You Like It, II 3 line 693; As You Like It, III 3 line 1552.
    Comedy of Errors, III 2 line 882.

Coriolanus, I 3 line 405; Coriolanus, II 1 line 966.
Hamlet, III 3 line 2345; Hamlet, III 4 line 2434.
Henry IV, Part II, I 3 line 612.
King John, V 2 line 2460.
Love's Labour's Lost, IV 3 line 1454.
Merry Wives of Windsor, IV 2 line 1991.
Much Ado About Nothing, I 1 line 217; Much Ado About Nothing, I 1 line 238.
Othello, III 3 line 1948.
Rape of Lucrece, line 1143.
Richard III, IV 4 line 2937.
Romeo and Juliet, II 1 line 816.
Tempest, IV 1 line 1990.
Troilus and Cressida, II 2 line 1203; Troilus and Cressida, III 1 line 1592.
Twelfth Night, II 3 line 857.
Two Gentlemen of Verona, IV 4 line 2034.
Winter's Tale, II 3 line 1053.

Forest: late 13c., *extensive tree-covered district*, especially one set aside for royal hunting and under the protection of the king, from Old French: *forest: forest, wood, woodland.* The forest is a mysterious place; in legends and fairy tales, they are usually inhabited by mysterious creatures, symbols of all of the dangers with which young people must contend if they are to become adults. It is a place of testing, a realm of death holding the secrets of nature which man must penetrate to find meaning.
As You Like It, I 1 line 100; As You Like It, I 3 line 514; As You Like It, II 4 line 733; As You Like It, II 6 line 883; As You Like It, II 7 line 906; As You Like It, III 2 line 1128; As You Like It, III 2 line 1232; As You Like It, III 2 line 1330; As You Like It, III 2 line 1397; As You Like It, III 2 line 1398; As You Like It, III 2 line 1427; As You Like It, III 2 line 1445; As You Like It, III 2 line 1501; As You Like It, III 3 line 1540; As You Like It, III 4 line 1622; As You Like It, IV 3 line 2078; As You Like It, IV 3 line 2103; As You Like It, V 1 line 2193; As You Like It, V 1 line 2209; As You Like It, V 4 lines 2433, 2438; As You Like It, V 4 line 2566.
Hamlet, III 2 line 2163.
Henry IV, Part II, IV 1 line 2201; Henry IV, Part II, IV 1 line 2202; Henry IV, Part II, IV 1 line 2222.
Henry VI, Part III, II 2 line 855; Henry VI, Part III, IV 6 line 2400; Henry VI, Part III, V 7 line 3107.
Julius Caesar, III 1 line 1429.
King Lear, I 1 line 64.
Macbeth, IV 1 line 1663; Macbeth, V 3 line 2317.
Merry Wives of Windsor, V 5 line 2573; Merry Wives of Windsor, V 5 line 2683.
Midsummer Night's Dream, II 1 line 391; Midsummer Night's Dream, II 1 line 452; Midsummer Night's Dream, II 2 line 722.
Richard II, III 1 line 1382.
Sonnet CIV line 4.

Timon of Athens, IV 3 line 2051.
Titus Andronicus, II 1 line 671; Titus Andronicus, II 3 line 794.
Two Gentlemen of Verona, V 1 line 2061; Two Gentlemen of Verona, V 2 line 2108.

Fountain: early 15c., *spring of water that collects in a pool*, from Old French: *fontaine: natural spring* (12c.). The extended sense of *artificial jet of water* (and the structures that make them) is first recorded c.1500.
    As You Like It, IV 1 line 1925.
    Julius Caesar, II 2 line 1058.
    Lover's Complaint, line 256.
    Macbeth, II 3 line 883.
    Midsummer Night's Dream, II 1 line 396; Midsummer Night's Dream, II 1 line 454; Midsummer Night's Dream, IV 1 line 1671.
    Othello, IV 2 line 2807.
    Rape of Lucrece, lines 628, 1758, 1785.
    Richard II, V 3 line 2639.
    Romeo and Juliet, I 1 line 105.
    Sonnet XXXV line 2; Sonnet CLIII line 4.
    Taming of the Shrew, V 2 line 2650.
    Titus Andronicus, II 4 line 1087; Titus Andronicus, III 1 lines 1252, 1256.
    Troilus and Cressida, III 2 line 1719; Troilus and Cressida, III 3 line 2189; Troilus and Cressida, III 3 line 2192.
    Venus and Adonis, line 254.

Fowl: Old English: *fugel: bird*, representing the general Germanic word for them. Originally *bird*; narrower sense of *domestic hen or rooster* is first recorded 1570s.
    Comedy of Errors, II 1 lines 290, 295; Comedy of Errors, III 1 line 714; Comedy of Errors, III 1 line 717.
    Cymbeline, I 4 line 406.
    Henry IV, Part I, IV 2 line 2387.
    Henry VI, Part II, II 1 line 776.
    Henry VI, Part III, V 6 line 3014.
    Measure for Measure, II 2 line 847; Measure for Measure, III 1 line 1322.
    Merry Wives of Windsor, V 5 line 2569.
    Midsummer Night's Dream, III 1 line 848; Midsummer Night's Dream, III 2 line 1050.
    Much Ado About Nothing, II 1 line 586; Much Ado About Nothing, II 3 line 912.
    Phoenix and the Turtle, line 10.
    Rape of Lucrece, lines 558, 562, 1387.
    Titus Andronicus, V 3 line 2606.
    Twelfth Night, IV 2 line 2069.

Fox: Old English: *fox*. Metaphoric extension to *clever person* is early 13c. In other contexts, it typically meant *drunk* (1610s).

All's Well That Ends Well, II 1 lines 670, 672; All's Well That Ends Well, III 6 line 1826.
Coriolanus, I 1 line 173.
Cymbeline, III 3 line 1644.
Hamlet, IV 2 line 2705.
Henry IV, Part I, III 3 line 2124; Henry IV, Part I, V 2 line 2779.
Henry IV, Part II, 1 2 line 473.
Henry V, IV 4 line 2382.
Henry VI, Part II, III 1 line 1332; Henry VI, Part II, III 1 lines 1537, 1541.
Henry VI, Part III, IV 7 line 2449.
Henry VIII, I 4 line 227.
King Lear, I 4 line 847; King Lear, III 4 line 1887; King Lear, III 6 line 2027; King Lear, III 7 line 2150; King Lear, V 3 line 3147.
Love's Labour's Lost, III 1 line 847; Love's Labour's Lost, III 1 line 851; Love's Labour's Lost, III 1 line 857.
Measure for Measure, III 2 line 1521; Measure for Measure, V 1 line 2714.
Merry Wives of Windsor, III 3 line 1555.
Much Ado About Nothing, II 3 line 857.
Taming of the Shrew, II 1 line 1257.
Timon of Athens, IV 3 lines 2029, 2030, 2031.
Troilus and Cressida, III 2 line 1844; Troilus and Cressida, V 4 line 3420.
Twelfth Night, I 5 line 369; Twelfth Night, II 5 line 1148.
Two Gentlemen of Verona, IV 4 line 1931.
Venus and Adonis, line 696.

Frank: feeding place for swine.
Henry IV, Part II, I 3 line 646.

Freckles: late 14c., also *frecken,* related to *scatter.* As a verb, from late 14c. (implied in *fracled:* spotted; freckle itself as a verb is recorded from 1610s.
Midsummer Night's Dream, II 1 line 380.

Freezing*: Old English: *freoseth*, of Germanic origin; related to Dutch *vriezen* and German *frieren*.
Cymbeline, III 3 line 1643.
Rape of Lucrece, line 1196.
Sonnet XCVII line 3.

Frog: Old English: *frogga*; frogs were extensively used for the purpose of divination.
Henry V, V 2 line 2119.
King Lear, III 4 line 1923.
Macbeth, IV 1 line 1561.

Frost: Old English: *forst: frost, a freezing, becoming frozen, extreme cold*, related to *freosan: to freeze.* Both forms of the word were common in English

till late 5c.; the triumph of frost may be due to its similarity to the forms in other Germanic languages.
    As You Like It, II 3 line 697.
    Coriolanus, V 3 line 3567.
    Hamlet, III 4 line 2479.
    Henry IV, Part I, II 3 line 877; Henry IV, Part I, IV 1 line 2355.
    Henry IV, Part II, I 3 line 646.
    Henry V, III 5 lines 1412, 1414.
    Henry VI, Part II, V 1 line 3157.
    Henry VIII, III 2 line 2259r.
    Love's Labour's Lost, I 1 line 104; Love's Labour's Lost, V 2 line 2743.
    Merchant of Venice, II 7 line 1064.
    Midsummer Night's Dream, II 1 line 476.
    Much Ado About Nothing, V 4 line 2590.
    Rape of Lucrece, lines 382, 406.
    Richard II, I 3 line 596.
    Romeo and Juliet, IV 5 line 2685.
    Sonnet V line 7.
    Taming of the Shrew, IV 1 line 1639; Taming of the Shrew, V 2 line 2647.
    Tempest, I 2 line 389.
    Titus Andronicus, III 1 line 1130; Troilus and Cressida, IV 4 line 2085; Titus Andronicus, V 3 line 2615.
    Venus and Adonis, line 56.

Frozen: mid-14c., see freezing. Figurative use is from 1570s
    Henry VI, Part II, V 2 line 3250.
    Love's Labour's Lost, V 2 line 2175; Love's Labour's Lost, V 2 line 2862.
    Rape of Lucrece, line 298.
    Richard II, I 1 line 67; Richard II, I 3 line 511; Richard II, II 1 line 801.
    Richard III, II 1 line 1241.
    Romeo and Juliet, I 4 line 603.
    Taming of the Shrew, IV 1 line 1651.
    Titus Andronicus, III 1 line 1392.
    Two Gentlemen of Verona, III 2 line 1460.
    Venus and Adonis, line 586.

Fruit: late 12c., from Old French: *fruit: fruit, fruit eaten as dessert; harvest; virtuous action* (12c.), from Latin: *fructus: an enjoyment, delight, satisfaction; proceeds, produce, fruit, crops*. Originally in English meaning vegetables as well. Modern narrower sense is from early 13c.
    As You Like It, II 7 line 995; As You Like It, III 2 line 1227; As You Like It, III 2 line 1229; As You Like It, III 2 line 1337.
    Coriolanus, IV 6 line 3140.
    Cymbeline, III 3 line 1666; Cymbeline, V 5 line 3686.
    Hamlet, II 2 line 1140; Hamlet, II 2 line 1243; Hamlet, III 2 line 2082.
    Henry IV, Part I, II 4 line 1411r.

Henry IV, Part II, I 3 line 644; Henry IV, Part II, V 4 line 3569.
Henry V, I 1 line 101; Henry V, III 5 line 1408.
Henry VI, Part I, V 4 line 2683; Henry VI, Part I, V 4 line 2734.
Henry VI, Part II, III 2 line 1900.
Henry VI, Part III, III 2 line 1540; Henry VI, Part III, III 2 line 1541; Henry VI, Part III, III 3 line 1822; Henry VI, Part III, IV 4 line 2266; Henry VI, Part III, V 6 line 3047; Henry VI, Part III, V 7 line 3127.
Henry VIII, V 1 line 2801.
King John, II 1 line 785.
Merchant of Venice, IV 1 line 2048.
Othello, II 3 line 1141; Othello, II 3 line 1530; Othello, V 1 line 3281.
Pericles, I 1 line 67; Pericles, I 1 line 74..
Rape of Lucrece, line 1115.
Richard II, II 1 line 840; Richard II, III 4 line 1929.
Richard III, II 1 line 1262; Richard III, III 7 line 2378.
Romeo and Juliet, II 1 line 834.
Sonnet XCVII line 10.
Titus Andronicus, V 1 lines 2176, 2181.
Troilus and Cressida, II 3 line 1338.
Twelfth Night, II 5 line 1223.

Fumitory: late Middle English: from Old French: *fumeterre*, from medieval Latin: *fumus terrae:* smoke of the earth (because of its greyish leaves).
    Henry V, V 2 line 3026.

Furze: Old English: *fyrs*. Similar to the Gorse: a shrub with yellow flowers.
    Tempest, I 1 line 80.

Gall: Old English: *galla: bile*. Also: *to make sore by chafing*, mid-15c., from gall. Earlier, *to have sores, be sore* (early 14c.). Figurative sense of *harass, irritate* is from 1570s.
    Cymbeline, I 1 line 120.
    Hamlet, I 2 line 339; Hamlet, III 2 line 2149.
    Henry V, IV 7 line 2621; Henry V, V 2 line 3017; Henry V, V 2 line 3366.
    Henry VI, Part I, I 6 line 634; Henry VI, Part I, II 4 line 923; Henry VI, Part I, II 4 line 1062.
    Henry VI, Part II, III 2 line 2016r.
    Henry VIII, I 1 line 220.
    King John, IV 3 line 2119; King John, IV 3 line 2120.
    King Lear, I 4 line 642; King Lear, I 4 line 796.
    Love's Labour's Lost, V 2 line 2137; Love's Labour's Lost, V 2 line 2138.
    Macbeth, I 5 line 398; Macbeth, IV 1 line 1574.
    Measure for Measure, I 3 line 328; Measure for Measure, II 2 line 866; Measure for Measure, III 2 line 1696.
    Othello, I 1 line 162; Othello, I 3 line 565; Othello, II 1 line 882.
    Passionate Pilgrim, line 271.
    Rape of Lucrece, line 940.
    Romeo and Juliet, I 1 line 221; Romeo and Juliet II, I 5 line 717.

Troilus and Cressida, I 3 line 646; Troilus and Cressida, II 2 line 1142; Troilus and Cressida, IV 5 line 2629; Troilus and Cressida, V 1 line 2965.
Twelfth Night, III 2 line 1450.

Gardens: 13c., *gardin,* from Old French; and Old English: *geard,* meaning, enclosure. Most commonly used as a reference to the Garden of Eden, a garden is typically an earthly paradise.
Antony and Cleopatra, III 5 line 1809.
Cymbeline, I 1 line 97.
Hamlet, II 2 line 1651; Hamlet, IV 7 line 3242.
Henry IV, Part I, I 2 lines 143, 149.
Henry IV, Part II, V 2 line 3381.
Henry V, IV 3 line 2290.
Henry VI, Part I, I 1 line 88; Henry VI, Part I, II 1 line 693.
Henry VI, Part II, III 1 line 1309; Henry IV, Part II, IV 10 line 2893; Henry IV, Part II, IV 10 line 2920; Henry IV, Part II, IV 10 line 2951.
Henry VIII, V 4 line 3270.
King Lear, IV 6 line 2803.
Love's Labour's Lost, I 1 line 246.
Measure for Measure, IV 1 line 1825; Measure for Measure, V 1 line 2618; Measure for Measure, V 1 line 2638.
Much Ado About Nothing, V 1 line 2254.
Richard II, III 4 line 1861; Richard II, III 4 line 1907; Richard II, III 4 line 1923; Richard II, III 4 line 1940; Richard II, III 4 line 1967.
Richard III, III 4 line 1984.
Sonnet XVI line 6.
Taming of the Shrew, I 1 line 297; Taming of the Shrew, IV 4 line 2257.
Twelfth Night, III 1 line 1327.
Venus and Adonis, line 85.
Winter's Tale, I 2 line 263; Winter's Tale, IV 4 line 1956; Winter's Tale, IV 4 line 1974.

Garlic: Old English: *garleac,* from *gar,* meaning, *spear.*
Coriolanus, IV 6 line 3136.
Henry IV, Part I, III 1 line 1707.
Measure for Measure, III 2 line 1691.
Midsummer Night's Dream, IV 2 line 1824.
Winter's Tale, IV 4 line 2048.

Gaskin: muscular part of the hind leg of a horse; late 16c.
Twelfth Night, I 5 line 316.

Geese: plural of *goose*. Old English *gos,* of Germanic origin; related to Dutch *gans* and German *Gans,* from an Indo-European root shared by Latin *anser* and Greek *khen.*
Coriolanus, I 1 line 173; Coriolanus, I 4 line 527.
Henry IV, Part I, II 4 line 1128.

Henry IV, Part II, V 1 line 3214.
King Lear, II 4 line 1324.
Love's Labour's Lost, I 1 line 99.
Macbeth, V 3 line 2261.
Merry Wives of Windsor, III 4 line 1673; Merry Wives of Windsor, V 1 line 2503.
Midsummer Night's Dream, III 2 line 1050.
Two Gentlemen of Verona, IV 4 line 1867.

Geld: late 13c., from Old Norse: *gelda*, meaning, *castrated*. Also, Old English, a royal tax in Medieval times: *gield*.
Henry VI, Part II, IV 2 line 2471.
Love's Labour's Lost, II 1 line 638.
Measure for Measure, II 1 line 673.
Pericles, IV 6 line 2068.
Richard II, II 1 line 928.
Winter's Tale, II 1 line 773; Winter's Tale, IV 4 line 2573.

Gelding: late 13c., from Old Norse: *geldingr*.
Henry IV, Part I, line 676; Henry IV, Part I, II 1 line 737; Henry IV, Part I, III 1 line 1653.
Merry Wives of Windsor, II 2 line 1091.

Germen**: seeds. Sometimes spelled as *germain*.
King Lear, III 2 line 1685.
Macbeth, IV 1 line 1611.

Gill: organ of breathing in fishes, early 14c., of unknown origin, perhaps from a Scandinavian source, e.g. Old Norse *giolnar* which perhaps means *gills*; Old Danish *-gæln* (in *fiske-gæln*: fish gill).
Venus and Adonis, line 1122.

Gillyver: cultivated wallflower. Its old name was *stock-gillofer* and *wall-gilloflower*.
Winter's Tale, IV 4 line 1954; Winter's Tale, IV 4 line 1974.

Ginger: mid 14c., from Old English: *gingifar*.
Henry IV, Part I, II 1 line 665.
Henry V, III 7 line 1660.
Measure for Measure, IV 3 lines 2121, 2123.
Merchant of Venice, III 1 line 1247.
Twelfth Night, II 3 line 817.
Winter's Tale, IV 3 line 1772.

Gib: male cat.
Hamlet, III 4 line 2594.
Henry IV, Part I, I 2 line 180.

Glowworm: early 14c., from Old English: *glowen* + *wurm*.

Hamlet, I 5 line 827.
Merry Wives of Windsor, V 5 line 2642.
Midsummer Night's Dream, III 1 line 995.
Pericles, II 3 line 866.
Venus and Adonis, line 642.

Gnats: Old English: *gnætt: gnat, midge, mosquito*, earlier *gneat*, used of various small, flying insects; literally, biting insect: *gnaw*.
    Antony and Cleopatra, III 13 line 2454.
    Comedy of Errors, II 2 line 424.
    Cymbeline, I 3 line 296.
    Henry VI, Part III, II 6 line 1259.
    King John, IV 1 line 1681.
    Love's Labour's Lost, IV 3 line 1497.
    Merchant of Venice, III 2 line 1492.
    Pericles, II 3 line 888.
    Rape of Lucrece, line 1065.
    Romeo and Juliet, I 4 line 564.
    Titus Andronicus, IV 4 line 2096.

Goats: Old English: *gat,* meaning: *she-goat.* It is curious that the harmless goat should have had an evil name, and been associated with devil-lore. There is a common superstition in England and Scotland that it is never seen for twenty-four hours together; and that once in this space, it pays a visit to the devil in order to have its beard combed. It was, formerly, too, a popular notion that the devil appeared frequently in the shape of a goat, which accounted for his horns and tail.
    As You Like It, III 3 line 1506; As You Like It, III 3 line 1510.
    Coriolanus, III 1 line 1946.
    Cymbeline, IV 4 line 2927.
    Henry IV, Part I, III 1 line 1582; Henry IV, Part I, IV 1 line 2329.
    Henry V, IV 4 line 2391; Henry V, V 1 line 2914; Henry V, V 1 line 2915.
    King Lear, I 2 line 450.
    Macbeth, IV 1 line 1574.
    Merchant of Venice, I 3 line 494.
    Merry Wives of Windsor, V 5 line 2712.
    Othello, III 3 line 1832 ; Othello, III 3 line 2085; Othello, IV 1 line 2710.
    Titus Andronicus, IV 2 line 1874.

Goss: fine cobwebs common in autumn, derived from *goose,* eaten in November.
    Tempest, IV 1 line 1915.

Goose: see *geese*.
    As You Like It, III 4 line 1632.
    Henry IV, Part I, III 1 line 1780.
    Henry VI, Part I, I 3 line 408.
    King Lear, II 2 line 1150.

Love's Labour's Lost, III 1 line 853; Love's Labour's Lost, III 1 line 859; Love's Labour's Lost, III 1 line 861; Love's Labour's Lost, III 1 lines 863, 864, 866; Love's Labour's Lost, III 1 line 870; Love's Labour's Lost, III 1 line 872; Love's Labour's Lost, III 1 line 883; Love's Labour's Lost, IV 3 line 1398.
Macbeth, II 3 line 801; Macbeth, V 3 line 2259.
Merchant of Venice, V 1 line 2562.
Merry Wives of Windsor, V 5 line 2567.
Midsummer Night's Dream, V 1 line 2074; Midsummer Night's Dream, V 1 line 2076; Midsummer Night's Dream, V 1 line 2078.
Romeo and Juliet, II 4 lines 1228, 1229, 1231; Romeo and Juliet, II 4 line 1233; Romeo and Juliet, II 4 line 1235; Romeo and Juliet, II 4 line 1238; Romeo and Juliet, II 4 line 1242r.
Tempest, II 2 line 1219.
Troilus and Cressida, V 10 line 3691.

Gooseberry: 1530s, perhaps from German *Krausebeere* or *Kräuselbeere*, related to Middle Dutch *croesel*.
Henry IV, Part II, 493.

Gorbellied: A person who is gorbellied is corpulent, with a protruding belly. It seems probable that it derives from Old English *gor* or *gore*, meaning at first dung or dirt; in the sixteenth century it shifted sense to our modern one of blood that has been shed as a result of violence.
Henry IV, Part I, II 2 line 827.

Gorge: mid-14c., throat, from Old French *gorge*: throat, bosom, from Late Latin *gurges* gullet, throat, jaws, of uncertain origin
Hamlet, V 1 line 3519.
Othello, II 1 line 1031.
Timon of Athens, IV 3 line 1703.
Venus and Adonis, line 78.
Winter's Tale, II 1 line 653.

Goujeres: the french disease.
King Lear, V 3 line 3148.

Grain: early 13c., scarlet dye made from insects, from Old French: *grain* (12c.) *seed, grain, particle, berry, scarlet dye*, from Latin: *granum: seed, a grain, small kernel*. As a collective singular meaning *seed of wheat and allied grasses used as food*, it is attested from early 14c. Extended from c.1300 to other objects (e.g. salt, sand). As a unit of weight, from 1540s. Used of wood (1560s), from the arrangement of fibres, which resemble seeds.
Antony and Cleopatra, II 7 line 1398.
Comedy of Errors, III 2 line 868.
Coriolanus, I 1 line 73; Coriolanus, I 1 line 200; Coriolanus, II 3 line 1686; Coriolanus, III 3 line 2458; Coriolanus, V 1 line 3308; Coriolanus, V1 lines 3310, 3312.
Henry V, II 4 line 1042.

Henry VIII, I 1 line 223.
King John, IV 1 line 1681.
Macbeth, I 3 line 160.
Measure for Measure, III 1 line 1242.
Merchant of Venice, I 1 line 123.
Othello, V 2 line 3491.

Grape: mid-13c., from Old French: *grape: bunch of grapes, grape* (12c.). The vine is not native to England. The word replaced Old English: *winberige: wine berry*.

All's Well That Ends Well, II 1 lines 670, 671; All's Well That Ends Well, II 3 line 998.
Antony and Cleopatra, II 7 line 1517; Antony and Cleopatra, V 2 line 3740.
As You Like It, V 1 lines 2220, 2221.
Coriolanus, V 4 line 3747.
Measure for Measure, II 1 line 578.
Midsummer Night's Dream, III 1 line 992.
Othello, II 1 line 1052.
Rape of Lucrece, line 266.
Timon of Athens, IV 3 line 2142.
Venus and Adonis, line 622.

Grass: Old English: *græs, gærs*: herb, plant, grass. As a colour name (especially grass-green, Old English: *græsgrene*) by c.1300. Grass is the symbol for usefulness; it might represent native land, or, when pulled, surrender or conquest of a land or territory. However, the usefulness is often humble. Commonness, submission, lower caste of people, sign of defeat. Evanescence; quick to grow but may soon be gone.

All's Well That Ends Well, IV 5 line 2482.
Comedy of Errors, II 2 line 590.
Hamlet, III 2 line 2224; Hamlet, IV 5 line 2891.
Henry IV, Part I, II 4 line 1294.
Henry V, I 1 line 104; Henry V, III 3 line 1284; Henry V, IV 2 line 2214.
Henry VI, Part II, III 2 line 2031; Henry IV, Part II, IV 2 line 2373; Henry IV, Part II, IV 10 line 2894; Henry IV, Part II, IV 10 line 2928.
Love's Labour's Lost, V 2 line 2076; Love's Labour's Lost, V 2 line 2078.
Merchant of Venice, I 1 line 19.
Midsummer Night's Dream, III 2 line 219; Midsummer Night's Dream, III 2 line 1380.
Othello, III 3 line 1948.
Rape of Lucrece, line 446.
Richard II, I 3 line 590; Richard II, III 3 line 1686; Richard II, III 3 line 1740.
Tempest, II 1 line 756; Tempest, IV 1 line 1783; Tempest, IV 1 line 1794.
Timon of Athens, IV 3 line 2135.
Titus Andronicus, IV 4 line 2086.

Venus and Adonis, lines 226, 494, 1050, 1077.

Grasshoppers: mid-14c. (late 13c. as a surname), earlier *greshoppe* (c. 1200), from Old English *gærshoppa*. Middle Swedish *gräshoppare*, German *Grashüpfer*. As a term of reproach, from Eccl. xii:5. Also recorded c.1300 as a name for the hare.
    Romeo and Juliet, I 4 line 560.

Gravel: early 13c., from Old French: *gravele: sand, gravel*; from: *grave: sand, seashore*.
    Henry VIII, I 1 line 223.
    Measure for Measure, IV 3 line 2180.
    Merchant of Venice, II 2 line 601.
    Troilus and Cressida, V 1 line 2949.

Green: Old English: *grene: green, young, immature*. The colour of jealousy at least since Shakespeare (1596); *Greensleeves*, ballad of an inconstant lady-love, is from 1570s. Meaning *of a field, grassy place* was in Old English. Sense of *of tender age, youthful* is from early 15c.; hence *gullible* (c.1600).
    Antony and Cleopatra, I 5 line 607; Antony and Cleopatra, III 2 line 1598; Antony and Cleopatra, IV 14 line 3051.
    As You Like It, II 7 line 1081; As You Like It, III 3 line 1575; As You Like It, IV 3 line 2111; As You Like It, V 3 line 2377.
    Hamlet, I 2 line 202; Hamlet, I 3 line 588; Hamlet, IV 5 line 2891; Hamlet, IV 5 line 2944.
    Henry IV, Part I, II 4 line 1207; Henry IV, Part I, II 4 line 1217.
    Henry IV, Part II, II 1 line 822; Henry IV, Part II, III 2 line 2023; Henry IV, Part II, IV 3 line 2689; Henry IV, Part II, IV 5 line 3089.
    Henry V, II 3 line 848; Henry V, II 4 line 1040; Henry V, V 1 line 2929; Henry V, V 2 line 3030; Henry V, V 2 line 3125.
    Henry VI, Part II, III 1 line 1572.
    King John, II 1 line 543; King John, II 1 line 784; King John, III 4 line 1533.
    King Lear, III 4 line 1926.
    Love's Labour's Lost, I 1 line 99; Love's Labour's Lost, I 2 line 384; Love's Labour's Lost, I 2 line 390; Love's Labour's Lost, IV 3 line 1398.
    Lover's Complaint, 214.
    Macbeth, I 7 line 514; Macbeth, II 2 line 727.
    Merchant of Venice, III 2 line 1477.
    Merry Wives of Windsor, I 4 line 450r; Merry Wives of Windsor, II 1 line 626; Merry Wives of Windsor, IV 4 line 2245; Merry Wives of Windsor, IV 6 line 2462; Merry Wives of Windsor, V 3 line 2528; Merry Wives of Windsor, V 5 line 2579; Merry Wives of Windsor, V 5 line 2601; Merry Wives of Windsor, V 5 line 2670; Merry Wives of Windsor, V 5 line 2771; Merry Wives of Windsor, V 5 line 2777.
    Midsummer Night's Dream, I 1 line 193; Midsummer Night's Dream, II 1 line 376; Midsummer Night's Dream, II 1 line 395; Midsummer Night's Dream, II 1 lines 463, 469; Midsummer Night's Dream, III 1 line

822; Midsummer Night's Dream, III 1 line 992; Midsummer Night's Dream, III 2 line 1450; Midsummer Night's Dream, V 1 line 2180.
Much Ado About Nothing, II 1 line 621.
Othello, II 1 line 1046; Othello, III 3 line 1817; Othello, IV 3 lines 3063, 3074.
Passionate Pilgrim, lines 44, 81, 136, 284.
Pericles, II 2 line 800; Pericles, IV 1 line 1562; Pericles, IV 6 line 1959.
Rape of Lucrece, line 445.
Richard II, III 3 line 1684; Richard II, V 2 line 2490.
Richard III, II 2 line 1400; Richard III, II 2 line 1408.
Romeo and Juliet, II 2 line 853; Romeo and Juliet, III 5 line 2263; Romeo and Juliet, III 5 line 2337; Romeo and Juliet, IV 3 line 2594; Romeo and Juliet, V 1 line 2855.
Sonnet XII line 7; Sonnet XXXIII line 3; Sonnet LXIII line 14; Sonnet LXVIII line 11; Sonnet CIV line 8; Sonnet CXXII line 4.
Taming of the Shrew, III 2 line 1577; Taming of the Shrew, IV 5 line 2314.
Tempest, II 1 line 756; Tempest, II 1 line 758; Tempest, IV 1 line 1851; Tempest, V 1 lines 2058, 2064.
Timon of Athens, IV 1 line 1571.
Titus Andronicus, II 2 line 698; Titus Andronicus, II 3 line 747.
Troilus and Cressida, I 2 line 300; Troilus and Cressida, II 3 line 1476; Troilus and Cressida, I 3 line 609; Troilus and Cressida, II 1 line 882; Troilus and Cressida, V 1 line 2961.
Twelfth Night, II 4 line 1014.
Venus and Adonis, lines 166, 548, 828, 1198.
Winter's Tale, I 2 line 238; Winter's Tale, III 2 line 1416; Winter's Tale, IV 4 line 1887; Winter's Tale, IV 4 line 2041.

Greenwood: a wood or forest in leaf. Often referred to as a Medieval outlaw hide.
As You Like It, II 5 line 820.

Greyhound: Old English: *grighund*, from *grig: bitch* + *hund: dog*. The name usually is said to have nothing to do with colour, and most are not grey.
Coriolanus, I 6 line 659.
Henry IV, Part I, I 3 line 587.
Henry IV, Part II, II 4 line 1353.
Henry V, III 1 line 1123.
Henry VI, Part III, II 5 line 1238.
King Lear, III 6 line 2069.
Love's Labour's Lost, V 2 line 2601.
Macbeth, III 1 line 1108.
Merry Wives of Windsor, I 1 line 81.
Much Ado About Nothing, V 2 line 2149.
Taming of the Shrew, Prologue 2 line 191; Taming of the Shrew, V 2 line 2544.
Timon of Athens, I 2 line 551.

Groin: 1590s, earlier *grine* (1530s), from Middle English: *grynde: groin* (c. 1400), originally *depression in the ground*, from Old English: *grynde: abyss*. Altered 16c. by influence of loin or obsolete *groin: snout*.
    Henry IV, Part II, II 4 line 1482.
    Venus and Adonis, 1138.

Ground: mid-13c., to put on the ground, to strike down to the ground. Of ships, *to run into the ground*, from mid-15c. Meaning *to base* (an argument, sermon, etc.) is late 14c. Old English: *grund: bottom, foundation, ground, surface of the earth*, especially *bottom of the sea* (a sense preserved in run aground). Sense of *reason, motive* first attested c.1200.
    All's Well That Ends Well, III 1 line 1385; All's Well That Ends Well, III 4 line 1565; All's Well That Ends Well, III 7 line 1849.
    Antony and Cleopatra, I 5 line 555.
    As You Like It, I 2 line 395; As You Like It, III 2 line 1342; As You Like It, IV 3 line 2118.
    Comedy of Errors, II 1 line 371.
    Coriolanus, II 2 line 1235; Coriolanus, III 1 line 2037; Coriolanus, IV 3 line 2577; Coriolanus, V 2 line 3393; Coriolanus, V 4 line 3748.
    Cymbeline, I 2 line 248; Cymbeline, I 2 line 252; Cymbeline, I 5 line 491; Cymbeline, III 5 line 2116; Cymbeline, III 6 line 2146; Cymbeline, IV 2 line 2504; Cymbeline, IV 2 line 2617; Cymbeline, IV 2 line 2627; Cymbeline, IV 2 line 2689; Cymbeline, V 2 line 3007; Cymbeline, V 4 line 3286; Cymbeline, V 5 line 3548; Cymbeline, V 5 line 3854.
    Hamlet, I 1 line 18; Hamlet, I 4 line 692; Hamlet, I 5 line 909; Hamlet, II 2 line 1678; Hamlet, III 2 line 2047; Hamlet, IV 4 line 2805; Hamlet, IV 5 line 2931; Hamlet, V 1 line 3419; Hamlet, V 1 line 3494; Hamlet, V 1 line 3625.
    Henry IV, Part I, I 2 line 315; Henry IV, Part I, I 3 line 535; Henry IV, Part I, II 2 line 766; Henry IV, Part I, II 2 line 773; Henry IV, Part I, II 4 line 1202; Henry IV, Part I, IV 1 line 2230; Henry IV, Part I, IV 1 line 2332; Henry IV, Part I, V 4 line 3066; Henry IV, Part I, V 4 line 3105.
    Henry IV, Part II, II 1 line 805; Henry IV, Part II, II 1 line 882; Henry IV, Part II, II 3 line 1209; Henry IV, Part II, III 1 line 1796; Henry IV, Part II, IV 1 line 2218; Henry IV, Part II, IV 1 line 2224; Henry IV, Part II, IV 1 line 2315; Henry IV, Part II, IV 4 line 2798.
    Henry V, I 2 line 251; Henry V, III 6 line 1628; Henry V, III 7 line 1757; Henry V, IV 7 line 2663.
    Henry VI, Part I, I 1 line 125; Henry IV, Part I, I 4 line 503; Henry VI, Part I, II 4 line 1021; Henry VI, Part I, II 5 line 1087; Henry IV, Part I, III 2 line 1457.
    Henry VI, Part II, I 2 line 298; Henry VI, Part II, I 2 line 355; Henry VI, Part II, II 1 line 921; Henry VI, Part II, II 3 line 1063; Henry VI, Part II, III 2 line 1989; Henry VI, Part II, III 2 line 2028; Henry VI, Part II, IV 1 line 2231; Henry VI, Part II, IV 10 line 2921.
    Henry VI, Part III, I 1 line 168; Henry VI, Part III, I 4 line 450; Henry VI, Part III, II 1 line 703; Henry VI, Part III, II 6 line 1266; Henry VI, Part III,

III 3 line 1698; Henry VI, Part III, III 3 line 1821; Henry IV, Part III, V 6 line 3059.
Henry VIII, I 2 line 484; Henry VIII, III 2 line 1980; Henry VIII, V 5 line 3447.
Julius Caesar, III 1 line 1413; Julius Caesar, IV 2 line 1973; Julius Caesar, IV 3 line 2214; Julius Caesar, V 3 line 2566.
King John, II 1 line 611; King John, II 1 line 709; King John, II 1 line 715; King John, II 1 line 891; King John, III 1 line 1001; King John, IV 1 line 1576; King John, IV 3 line 2017; King John, V 5 line 2554.
King Lear, II 4 line 1425; King Lear, IV 6 line 2599.
Love's Labour's Lost, I 1 line 238; Love's Labour's Lost, I 2 line 463; Love's Labour's Lost, IV 3 line 1569; Love's Labour's Lost, IV 3 lines 1645, 1648; Love's Labour's Lost, V 2 line 1917; Love's Labour's Lost, V 2 line 1999.
Lover's Complaint, line 64.
Macbeth, III 5 line 1475; Macbeth, V 8 line 2507.
Measure for Measure, I 2 line 192; Measure for Measure, II 2 line 943; Measure for Measure, V 1 line 2445.
Merchant of Venice, II 1 lines 669, 675; Merchant of Venice, IV 1 line 2049.
Merry Wives of Windsor, II 1 line 1005.
Midsummer Night's Dream, II 2 line 731; Midsummer Night's Dream, II 2 line 759; Midsummer Night's Dream, III 2 line 1464; Midsummer Night's Dream, III 2 line 1524; Midsummer Night's Dream, IV 1 line 1637; Midsummer Night's Dream, IV 1 line 1653; Midsummer Night's Dream, V 1 line 2018.
Much Ado About Nothing, III 1 line 1100.
Othello, I 1 line 29; Othello, V 2 line 3470.
Passionate Pilgrim, lines 124, 178, 280.
Pericles, I 2 line 299; Pericles, I 4 line 495; Pericles, II 4 line 980; Pericles, IV 6 line 2087; Pericles, V 1 line 2207.
Rape of Lucrece, lines 1125, 1250, 1897.
Richard II, I 1 line 13; Richard II, I 1 line 68; Richard II, I 3 line 607; Richard II, II 3 line 1249; Richard II, III 2 line 1496; Richard II, III 2 line 1550; Richard II, III 2 lines 1560, 1565; Richard II, IV 1 line 2121; Richard II, IV 1 line 2280; Richard II, V 2 line 2571; Richard II, V 3 line 2688; Richard II, V 5 line 2834.
Richard III, I 3 line 489; Richard III, I 3 line 530; Richard III, III 7 line 2250; Richard III, V 3 line 3796.
Romeo and Juliet, I 1 line 107; Romeo and Juliet, I 4 line 512; Romeo and Juliet, III 3 line 1915; Romeo and Juliet, III 3 line 1940; Romeo and Juliet, III 3 line 1961; Romeo and Juliet, V 1 line 2809; Romeo and Juliet, V 3 line 2937; Romeo and Juliet, V 3 lines 3141, 3148, 3149.
Sonnet LXII line 4; Sonnet LXXV line 2; Sonnet CXXX line 12; Sonnet CXXLII line 2; Sonnet CLIII line 4.
Taming of the Shrew, Prologue, 2 line 184; Taming of the Shrew, III 1 line 1340.

Tempest, I 1 line 6; Tempest, I 1 line 80; Tempest, II 1 line 757; Tempest, II 1 line 1072; Tempest, II 2 line 1152; Tempest, IV 1 line 1908.
Timon of Athens, IV 3 line 1729.
Titus Andronicus, II 1 line 599; Titus Andronicus, II 1 line 622; Titus Andronicus, II 2 line 729; Titus Andronicus, II 3 line 748.
Twelfth Night, II 3 line 850; Twelfth Night, III 4 line 1824; Twelfth Night, III 4 line 1850; Twelfth Night, V 1 line 2264; Twelfth Night, V 1 line 2565.
Two Gentlemen of Verona, I 1 line 102; Two Gentlemen of Verona, III 1 line 1184.
Venus and Adonis, lines 244, 945, 1005, 1068, 1189.
Winter's Tale, I 2 line 467; Winter's Tale, II 1 line 788; Winter's Tale, III 3 line 1629; Winter's Tale, IV 3 line 1776; Winter's Tale, IV 4 line 1873.

Grove: Old English: *graf: wood, copse or thicket.*
    Coriolanus, I 10 line 910.
    Henry IV, Part I, I 1 line 83.
    Henry VI, Part II, I 2 line 282; Henry VI, Part II, I 2 line 306; Henry VI, Part II, I 4 line 637; Henry VI, Part II, II 1 line 773; Henry VI, Part II, II 1 line 782; Henry VI, Part II, III 2 line 2017.
    Macbeth, V 5 line 2398.
    Midsummer Night's Dream, II 1 line 395; Midsummer Night's Dream, II 1 line 517; Midsummer Night's Dream, II 1 line 622; Midsummer Night's Dream, II 1 line 628; Midsummer Night's Dream, III 2 line 1035; Midsummer Night's Dream, III 2 line 1447; Midsummer Night's Dream, IV 1 line 1670.
    Passionate Pilgrim, line 378.
    Pericles, I 4 line 425.
    Rape of Lucrece, lines 1180, 1300.
    Romeo and Juliet, I 1 line 142.
    Taming of the Shrew, II 1 line 1108.
    Tempest, IV 1 line 1776; Tempest, V 1 line 2027; Tempest, V 1 line 2054.
    Titus Andronicus, II 3 line 793.
    Venus and Adonis, line 887.

Grow: Old English: *growan* (of plants): *to grow, flourish, increase, develop, get bigger.* Applied in Middle English: to human beings (c.1300) and animals (early 15c.) and their parts, supplanting Old English: *weaxan.*
    All's Well That Ends Well, I 2 line 297; All's Well That Ends Well, II 1 line 633; All's Well That Ends Well, II 3 line 1058; All's Well That Ends Well, V 1 line 2570.
    Antony and Cleopatra, I 3 lines 354, 355, 359; Antony and Cleopatra, I 5 line 557; Antony and Cleopatra, II 2 line 714; Antony and Cleopatra, II 7 line 1494; Antony and Cleopatra, III 6 line 1857; Antony and Cleopatra, III 7 line 2023; Antony and Cleopatra, III 13 line 2389; Antony and Cleopatra, IV 2 line 2567.

As You Like It, I 1 line 12; As You Like It, I 1 line 59; As You Like It, I 1 line 73; As You Like It, I 2 line 244; As You Like It, I 2 line 257; As You Like It, II 4 line 777; As You Like It, II 7 line 941; As You Like It, III 2 line 1313; As You Like It, IV 3 line 2109.

Comedy of Errors, II 2 line 465; Comedy of Errors, III 2 line 765; Comedy of Errors, IV 1 line 958; Comedy of Errors, IV 4 line 1376; Comedy of Errors, IV 1 line 1392.

Coriolanus, I 1 line 282; Coriolanus, I 9 line 818; Coriolanus, II 1 line 950; Coriolanus, III 1 line 1775; Coriolanus, III 2 line 2219; Coriolanus, IV 4 line 2742; Coriolanus, IV 6 line 3018; Coriolanus, V 4 line 3741.

Cymbeline, I 1 line 133; Cymbeline, I 3 line 313; Cymbeline, III 4 line 1778; Cymbeline, IV 1 line 2302; Cymbeline, IV 2 line 2393; Cymbeline, IV 2 line 2551; Cymbeline, IV 4 line 2922; Cymbeline, V 3 line 3075; Cymbeline, V 4 line 3297; Cymbeline, V 5 line 3910.

Hamlet, I 2 lines 340, 348; Hamlet, I 3 lines 495, 498; Hamlet, I 4 line 655; Hamlet, I 5 line 832; Hamlet, II 2 line 1339; Hamlet, II 2 line 1425; Hamlet, II 2 line 1434; Hamlet, III 2 line 2063r; Hamlet, III 2 line 2118; Hamlet, III 3 line 2282; Hamlet, IV 3 line 2716; Hamlet, IV 7 line 3261; Hamlet, V 1 line 3475; Hamlet, V 2 line 3712.

Henry IV, Part I, II 4 line 1122; Henry IV, Part I, II 4 line 1205; Henry IV, Part I, II 4 line 1384; Henry IV, Part I, III 1 line 1575; Henry IV, Part I, III 2 line 1980; Henry IV, Part I, V 4 line 2973; Henry IV, Part I, V 4 line 2978; Henry IV, Part I, V 4 lines 3137, 3138.

Henry IV, Part II, I 2 line 293; Henry IV, Part II, I 2 line 387; Henry IV, Part II, I 2 line 477; Henry IV, Part II, I 3 line 614; Henry IV, Part II, II 3 line 1216; Henry IV, Part II, II 4 line 1435; Henry IV, Part II, II 4 line 1567; Henry IV, Part II, III 1 line 1744; Henry IV, Part II, III 1 line 1795; Henry IV, Part II, III 2 line 2114; Henry IV, Part II, IV 1 line 2214; Henry IV, Part II, IV 1 line 2431.

Henry V, I 1 line 99; Henry V, II 1 line 560; Henry V, II 2 line 657; Henry V, III 3 line 1327; Henry V, IV 7 line 2621; Henry V, V 2 lines 3024, 3036, 3040; Henry V, V 2 line 3050; Henry V, V 2 line 3144.

Henry VI, Part I, I 1 line 165; Henry IV, Part I, II 4 line 1032; Henry VI, Part I, II 4 line 1062; Henry VI, Part I, III 1 line 1424; Henry IV, Part I, IV 1 line 1796; Henry VI, Part I, V 4 line 2824.

Henry VI, Part II, I 1 line 144; Henry VI, Part II, II 1 line 749; Henry VI, Part II, II 1 line 791; Henry VI, Part II, III 1 line 1309; Henry VI, Part II, III 1 line 1571; Henry VI, Part II, III 2 line 2031; Henry VI, Part II, IV 1 line 2239; Henry VI, Part II, V 1 line 3120.

Henry VI, Part III, II 2 line 1014; Henry VI, Part III, II 5 line 1104; Henry VI, Part III, III 1 line 1367; Henry VI, Part III, III 3 line 1731; Henry VI, Part III, IV 7 line 2488; Henry IV, Part III, IV 8 line 2587.

Henry VIII, I 2 line 452; Henry VIII, I 3 line 613; Henry VIII, I 4 line 790; Henry VIII, II 1 line 997; Henry VIII, II 3 line 1207; Henry VIII, III 1 line 1620; Henry VIII, III 1 lines 1719, 1722; Henry VIII, III 1 line 1784; Henry VIII, III 1 lines 1802, 1805; Henry VIII, III 2 line 2055; Henry VIII, IV 2 line 2765; Henry VIII, V 3 line 3266; Henry VIII, V 4 line 3340; Henry VIII, V 5 lines 3416, 3433.

Julius Caesar, I 1 line 73; Julius Caesar, I 2 line 241; Julius Caesar, I 2 line 390; Julius Caesar, I 3 line 503; Julius Caesar, II 1 line 635; Julius Caesar, II 1 line 725; Julius Caesar, II 1 line 819; Julius Caesar, II 4 line 1186; Julius Caesar, IV 3 line 2064.
King John, III 1 line 1201; King John, III 2 line 1280; King John, V 1 line 2247.
King Lear, I 2 line 354; King Lear, I 3 line 510; King Lear, I 3 line 529; King Lear, I 4 line 691; King Lear, I 4 line 727; King Lear, II 2 line 1232; King Lear, III 4 line 1937; King Lear, III 4 line 1958; King Lear, IV 4 lines 2520, 2522; King Lear, IV 6 line 2603; King Lear, V 3 line 3247.
Love's Labour's Lost, I 1 line 81; Love's Labour's Lost, I 1 line 98; Love's Labour's Lost, I 1 line 111; Love's Labour's Lost, I 2 line 311; Love's Labour's Lost, I 2 line 419; Love's Labour's Lost, II 1 line 540; Love's Labour's Lost, IV 1 line 1004; Love's Labour's Lost, IV 1 line 1122; Love's Labour's Lost, V 2 line 2130; Love's Labour's Lost, V 2 line 2162; Love's Labour's Lost, V 2 line 2571.
Macbeth, 1 3 line 160; Macbeth, I 4 line 309; Macbeth, I 4 line 313; Macbeth, III 4 line 1306; Macbeth, III 4 line 1417; Macbeth, IV 3 line 1931; Macbeth, IV 3 line 1941.
Measure for Measure, I 3 line 312; Measure for Measure, I 4 line 393; Measure for Measure, II 4 line 1025; Measure for Measure, III 1 line 1502; Measure for Measure, III 2 line 1779.
Merchant of Venice, I 1 line 71; Merchant of Venice, I 1 line 116; Merchant of Venice, I 2 line 242; Merchant of Venice, I 3 line 508; Merchant of Venice, II 2 line 582; Merchant of Venice, II 2 line 661; Merchant of Venice, III 2 line 1694; Merchant of Venice, III 5 line 1867.
Merry Wives of Windsor, I 1 line 71; Merry Wives of Windsor, I 1 line 230; Merry Wives of Windsor, IV 4 line 2244.
Midsummer Night's Dream, I 1 line 80; Midsummer Night's Dream, I 1 line 84; Midsummer Night's Dream, I 2 line 273; Midsummer Night's Dream, II 1 line 499; Midsummer Night's Dream, II 1 line 629; Midsummer Night's Dream, II 2 line 776; Midsummer Night's Dream, III 2 line 1118; Midsummer Night's Dream, III 2 line 1178; Midsummer Night's Dream, III 2 line 1248; Midsummer Night's Dream, III 2 line 1305. Midsummer Night's Dream, III 2 line 1342; Midsummer Night's Dream, V 1 line 1856.
Much Ado About Nothing, II 2 line 805; Much Ado About Nothing, V 1 line 2387.
Othello, I 3 line 490; Othello, II 1 line 987; Othello, II 3 line 1478; Othello, II 3 line 1529; Othello, IV 2 line 3013; Othello, V 1 line 3148; Othello, V 2 line 3316; Othello, V 2 line 3443.
Passionate Pilgrim, lines 76, 380.
Pericles, I 1 line 155; Pericles, I 2 lines 251, 267; Pericles, I 2 line 329; Pericles, IV 0 lines 1498, 1508; Pericles, IV 4 line 1893; Pericles, IV 6 line 1984.
Phoenix and the Turtle, line 42.
Rape of Lucrece, lines 101, 332, 349, 543, 1113, 1300.
Richard II, I 1 line 187; Richard II, I 4 line 657; Richard II, II 1 line 948; Richard II, III 2 line 1443; Richard II, III 2 line 1624; Richard II, III 3 line

1823; Richard II, III 4 line 1898; Richard II, III 4 line 1927; Richard II, III 4 line 1968; Richard II, V 3 line 2606; Richard II, V 3 line 2688; Richard II, V 6 line 2929.
Richard III, I 3 line 531; Richard III, II 2 line 1313; Richard III, II 4 line 1488; Richard III, II 4 line 1490; Richard III, II 4 line 1492; Richard III, II 4 lines 1494, 1496, 1497; Richard III, II 4 line 1504; Richard III, II 4 line 1509; Richard III, III 1 lines 1675, 1676; Richard III, IV 2 line 2616; Richard III, IV 2 line 2650.
Romeo and Juliet, I 1 line 174; Romeo and Juliet, I 3 line 480; Romeo and Juliet, I 5 line 647; Romeo and Juliet, II 6 line 1492; Romeo and Juliet, III 2 line 1733; Romeo and Juliet, III 3 line 2045; Romeo and Juliet, III 5 line 2132.
Sonnet XI line 1; Sonnet XII line 12; Sonnet XV line 1; Sonnet XVIII line 12; Sonnet XXXII line 10r; Sonnet XLV line 14; Sonnet LXIX line 14; Sonnet LXXXIII line 8; Sonnet LXXXVII line 12; Sonnet XCIII line 13; Sonnet XCIX line 11; Sonnet CII lines 8, 12; Sonnet CXV line 14r; Sonnet CXIX 12; Sonnet CXXIV line 12; Sonnet CXXVI lines 3, 4; Sonnet CXXX line 4; Sonnet CXL lines 8, 10; Sonnet CXLII line 11; Sonnet CLIV line 12.
Taming of the Shrew, Prologue 1 line 106; Taming of the Shrew, Prologue 1 line 146; Taming of the Shrew, I 1 line 332; Taming of the Shrew, I 2 line 564; Taming of the Shrew, I 2 line 602; Taming of the Shrew, II 1 line 860; Taming of the Shrew, II 1 line 977; Taming of the Shrew, III 1 line 1268; Taming of the Shrew, III 1 line 1329.
Tempest, I 2 line 206; Tempest, II 2 line 1253; Tempest, IV 1 line 1719; Tempest, IV 1 line 1828; Tempest, IV 1 line 1930.
Timon of Athens, I 1 line 6; Timon of Athens, II 2 line 915; Timon of Athens, IV 1 line 1603r; Timon of Athens, V 1 line 2494.
Titus Andronicus, I 1 line 175; Titus Andronicus, II 1 line 589; Titus Andronicus, II 1 line 594; Titus Andronicus, II 3 line 945; Titus Andronicus, III 1 line 1225; Titus Andronicus, V 1 line 2178.
Troilus and Cressida, I 3 lines 456, 459; Troilus and Cressida, I 3 line 588; Troilus and Cressida, I 3 line 598; Troilus and Cressida, I 3 line 641; Troilus and Cressida, I 3 line 724; Troilus and Cressida, II 3 line 1372; Troilus and Cressida, III 2 line 1772; Troilus and Cressida, III 3 line 2098; Troilus and Cressida, III 3 line 2137; Troilus and Cressida, IV 4 line 2502; Troilus and Cressida, V 3 line 3314; Troilus and Cressida, V 4 line 3426.
Twelfth Night, I 4 line 263; Twelfth Night, I 5 line 333; Twelfth Night, I 5 line 401; Twelfth Night, II 4 line 934; Twelfth Night, III 1 line 1258; Twelfth Night, III 1 line 1280; Twelfth Night, III 4 line 1925; Twelfth Night, V 1 line 2364.
Two Gentlemen of Verona, II 4 line 820; Two Gentlemen of Verona, IV 2 line 1645; Two Gentlemen of Verona, V 4 line 2157.
Venus and Adonis, lines 161, 186r, 547, 561, 1202.
Winter's Tale, I 2 line 559; Winter's Tale, I 2 line 561; Winter's Tale, IV 1 lines 1638, 1648, 1656; Winter's Tale, IV 2 line 1708; Winter's Tale, IV 4 line 1995; Winter's Tale, IV 4 line 2309; Winter's Tale, IV 4 line 2500.

Gudgeon: small freshwater fish, early 15c., from *goujon*, from Old French: *gojon* (14c.), from Latin: *gobionem*, alteration of *gobius*, from Greek: *kobios*, a kind of fish, of unknown origin. The figurative sense of a credulous is from 1580s. This being the bait for many of the larger fish, *to swallow a gudgeon*, was sometimes used for to be caught or deceived. More commonly, however, the allusion is to the easiness with which the gudgeon itself is caught.
    Merchant of Venice, I 1 line 108.

Gulf: throat.
    Comedy of Errors, II 2 line 515.
    Henry V, II 4 line 906.
    Henry VI, Part III, V 6 line 3020.
    Macbeth, IV 1 line 1570.
    Rape of Lucrece, line 608.
    Richard III, III 7 line 2339.

Gull: Shakespeare often uses this word as synonymous with fool; late Middle English: of Celtic origin; related to Welsh: *gwylan* and Breton: *gwelan*.
    Henry V, II 2 line 757; Henry V, III 6 line 1529.
    Much Ado About Nothing, II 3 line 936.
    Othello, V 2 line 3499.
    Richard III, I 3 line 800.
    Sonnet LXXXVI line 10.
    Timon of Athens, II 1 line 659.
    Twelfth Night, II 3 line 834; Twelfth Night, II 5 line 1212; Twelfth Night, III 2 line 1471; Twelfth Night, V 1 line 2404; Twelfth Night, V 1 line 2555.

Gurnet: Middle English, from Old French *gornart*, from *gronir*, to grunt (from its grunting when caught). Any of various widely distributed marine fishes of the family *Triglidae*, having large fanlike pectoral fins and a large armoured head and including the sea robins. The *gurnet*, of which there are several species, was probably thought a very bad and vulgar dish when soused or pickled.
    Henry IV, Part I, IV 2 line 2379.

Gusts: 1580s, possibly a dialectal survival from Old Norse: *gustr*: *a cold blast of wind*.
    Coriolanus, I 6 line 614.
    Henry VI, Part I, 2858.
    Henry VI, Part II, III 2 line 1769.
    Henry VI, Part III, II 6 line 1288; Henry VI, Part III, III 1 line 1455.
    Julius Caesar, I 2 line 190.
    Merchant of Venice, IV 1 line 2009.
    Rape of Lucrece, line 600.
    Sonnet XIII line 12; Sonnet CXIV line 11.
    Taming of the Shrew, II 1 line 978.
    Timon of Athens, III 5 line 1363.

Titus Andronicus, V 3 line 2607.
Twelfth Night, I 3 line 144.
Venus and Adonis, line 477.
Winter's Tale, I 2 line 314.

Habitation: late 14c., *act or fact of dwelling*; also *place of lodging, abode*, from Old French: *habitacion, abitacion: act of dwelling*(12c.).
Henry IV, Part II, I 3 line 696.
Measure for Measure, III 1 line 1232.
Merchant of Venice, I 3 line 354.
Midsummer Night's Dream, V 1 line 1847.
Sonnet XCV line 10.

Haggard: an older hawk, used for training. Mid 16th cent. (used in falconry): from French *hagard*; perhaps related to hedge.
Othello, III 3 line 1921.
Taming of the Shrew, IV 2 line 1865.
Twelfth Night, III 1 line 1298.

Hail: frozen rain, Old English: *hægl, hagol* (Mercian: *hegel*) also the name of the rune for *H*.
All's well That Ends Well, V 3 line 2712.
Antony and Cleopatra, II 5 line 1104; Antony and Cleopatra, III 13 line 2447.
Macbeth, I 3 line 201.

Hailstone: Old English: *hagolstan*.
Coriolanus, I 1 line 175.
Merry Wives of Windsor, I 3 line 379.

Hair: Old English: *hær*. Hair symbolises physical strength and virility; the virtues and properties of a person are said to be concentrated in his hair and nails. It is a symbol of instinct, of female seduction and physical attraction. Baldness may suggest sterility. Hair flowing depicts freedom and looseness; the unwilling removal of hair may be a castration symbol. Carries the context of magical power; witches had their hair shaven off, as well as in the Bible, in which Samson loses all his power when his locks are stripped. Heavy relations to fertility and even love (the quantity is related to love-potential). It can be thought of as the external soul.
All's Well That Ends Well, II 2 line 840; All's Well That Ends Well, V 3 line 2761.
Antony and Cleopatra, I 2 line 289; Antony and Cleopatra, II 5 line 1132; Antony and Cleopatra, II 5 line 1199; Antony and Cleopatra, II 7 line 1517; Antony and Cleopatra, III 3 line 1729; Antony and Cleopatra, III 11 line 2124.
As You Like It, II 1 line 589; As You Like It, III 4 line 1600; As You Like It, III 4 line 1603; As You Like It, III 5 line 1699; As You Like It, III 5 line 1785; As You Like It, IV 3 line 2109.

Comedy of Errors, II 2 line 464; Comedy of Errors, II 2 line 469; Comedy of Errors, II 2 line 472; Comedy of Errors, II 2 line 473; Comedy of Errors, II 2 line 474; Comedy of Errors, II 2 line 475; Comedy of Errors, II 2 line 490; Comedy of Errors, III 2 line 810; Comedy of Errors, IV 3 line 1221; Comedy of Errors, V 1 line 1608.
Coriolanus, I 3 line 393; Coriolanus, IV 6 line 3182.
Cymbeline, II 3 line 1008; Cymbeline, II 3 line 1137.
Hamlet, I 5 line 755; Hamlet, III 4 line 2520.
Henry IV, Part I, II 4 line 1129; Henry IV, Part I, II 4 line 1361; Henry IV, Part I, II 4 line 1451; Henry IV, Part I, III 1 line 1684; Henry IV, Part I, III 3 line 2066; Henry IV, Part I, III 3 line 2069; Henry IV, Part I, IV 1 line 2283; Henry IV, Part I, V 2 line 2789.
Henry IV, Part II, I 2 line 296; Henry IV, Part II, I 2 line 479; Henry IV, Part II, I 2 line 590; Henry IV, Part II, II 4 line 1535; Henry IV, Part II, V 5 line 3641.
Henry V, III 0 line 1075; Henry V, III 7 line 1654; Henry V, III 7 line 1699; Henry V, V 2 line 3050; Henry V, V 2 line 3024.
Henry VI, Part II, III 1 line 1654; Henry VI, Part II, III 2 lines 1856, 1859; Henry VI, Part II, III 2 line 2012; Henry VI, Part II, III 3 line 2129; Henry VI, Part II, V 1 line 3152.
Henry VI, Part III, II 5 line 1142; Henry IV, Part III, V 1 line 2650.
Henry VIII, III 2 line 2151; Henry VIII, IV 1 line 2432.
Julius Caesar, II 1 line 763; Julius Caesar, III 2 line 1679; Julius Caesar, IV 3 line 2309.
King John, III 4 line 1430; King John, III 4 line 1447; King John, III 4 line 1454; King John, III 4 line 1458; King John, IV 1 line 1681; King John, V 2 line 2415; King John, V 7 line 2689.
King Lear, II 3 line 1261; King Lear, III 1 line 1624; King Lear, III 4 line 1881; King Lear, III 7 line 2164.
Love's Labour's Lost, IV 3 line 1412; Love's Labour's Lost, IV 3 line 1470; Love's Labour's Lost, IV 3 line 1603; Love's Labour's Lost, IV 3 line 1689; Love's Labour's Lost, V 2 line 2168.
Lover's Complaint, lines 29, 205.
Macbeth, 1 3 line 248; Macbeth, IV 1 line 1685; Macbeth, IV 2 line 1832; Macbeth, V 5 line 2366; Macbeth, V 8 line 2533.
Merchant of Venice, I 2 line 202; Merchant of Venice, II 2 line 659; Merchant of Venice, II 2 line 662; Merchant of Venice, III 2 line 1489; Merchant of Venice, III 2 line 1680; Merchant of Venice, IV 1 line 2279; Merchant of Venice, V 1 line 2623.
Merry Wives of Windsor, I 1 line 44; Merry Wives of Windsor, II 3 line 1136; Merry Wives of Windsor, IV 2 line 1969.
Midsummer Night's Dream, I 1 line 37; Midsummer Night's Dream, I 2 line 353; Midsummer Night's Dream, II 2 line 683; Midsummer Night's Dream, IV 1 lines 1568, 1569; Midsummer Night's Dream, IV 1 line 1599; Midsummer Night's Dream, IV 1 line 2008; Midsummer Night's Dream, V 1 line 2035.
Much Ado About Nothing, II 1 line 649; Much Ado About Nothing, II 3 line 847; Much Ado About Nothing, II 3 line 961; Much Ado About Nothing, III 4 line 1502; Much Ado About Nothing, V 1 line 2138.

Othello, I 3 line 481; Othello, V 2 line 3392.
Pericles, III 3 line 1455; Pericles, IV 2 line 1723; Pericles, IV 2 line 1759; Pericles, IV 4 line 1908.
Rape of Lucrece, lines 451, 1032, 1180.
Richard II, III 2 line 1522.
Richard III, I 3 line 772; Richard III, I 4 line 896; Richard III, II 2 line 1304.
Romeo and Juliet, I 4 line 591; Romeo and Juliet, II 4 line 1249; Romeo and Juliet, III 1 lines 1515, 1516; Romeo and Juliet, III 3 line 1939.
Sonnet XCVIX line 7; Sonnet CXXX line 4.
Taming of the Shrew, IV 1 line 1695.
Tempest, I 2 line 120; Tempest, I 2 line 334r; Tempest, I 2 line 341; Tempest, IV 1 line 1980.
Titus Andronicus, II 3 line 767; Titus Andronicus, III 1 line 1401; Titus Andronicus, IV 4 line 2069.
Troilus and Cressida, I 1 line 72; Troilus and Cressida, I 1 line 84; Troilus and Cressida, I 2 line 182; Troilus and Cressida, I 2 line 263; Troilus and Cressida, I 2 line 289; Troilus and Cressida, I 2 line 299; Troilus and Cressida, I 2 line 300; Troilus and Cressida, I 2 line 304; Troilus and Cressida, I 2 lines 308, 309, 310; Troilus and Cressida, III 1 line 1628; Troilus and Cressida, III 2 line 1835; Troilus and Cressida, IV 2 line 2405.
Twelfth Night, I 3 line 204; Twelfth Night, I 3 line 205; Twelfth Night, III 1 line 1277.
Two Gentlemen of Verona, II 7 line 1019; Two Gentlemen of Verona, III 1 line 1265; Two Gentlemen of Verona, III 1 lines 1419, 1420; Two Gentlemen of Verona, III 1 line 1424; Two Gentlemen of Verona, III 1 lines 1425,1426; Two Gentlemen of Verona, III 1 line 1430; Two Gentlemen of Verona, IV 4 line 2030.
Venus and Adonis, lines 71, 167, 211, 326, 508, 646.
Winter's Tale, II 1 line 609; Winter's Tale, IV 4 line 2220; Winter's Tale, IV 4 line 2699.

Hand: Old English: *hond, hand: hand; side; power, control, possession.* Meaning *person who does something with his hands* is from 1580s. Clock and watch sense is from 1570s. The linear measure of 4 inches (originally 3) is from 1560s, now used only in giving the height of horses. The meaning *playing cards held in one player's hand* is from 1620s; that of *a round at a card game* is from 1620s. First hand, second hand, etc. (mid-15c.) are from the notion of something being passed down from hand to hand. Out of hand (1590s) is opposite of *in hand: under control* (c.1200). *Hand-to-mouth* is from c.1500. *Hand-in-hand* attested from c.1500 as *with hands clasped*; figurative sense of *concurrently* recorded from 1570s. In palmistry a moist one is said to denote an amorous constitution. A dry hand, however, has been supposed to denote age and debility. It was once supposed that little worms were bred in the fingers of idle servants. The hand is the most frequently symbolised part of the human body. It gives blessing, it is expressive. According to Aristotle, the hand is the *tool of tools*. In general it is strength, power and protection.

However, it can just as easily mean generosity, hospitality and stability; *lend a hand*. It is used in gestures of greeting and friendship (shake hands).

The right and left have different symbols related to each: right - the rational, conscious and logical, as well as aggressive and anxious, left - opposite of the right, weakness, decay, death. However, the two can be juxtaposed to symbolise balance and the middle

All's Well That Ends Well, I 2 line 282; All's Well That Ends Well, II 1 line 677; All's Well That Ends Well, II 1 line 805; All's Well That Ends Well, II 1 line 813; All's Well That Ends Well, II 2 lines 833, 834; All's Well That Ends Well, II 2 line 844; All's Well That Ends Well, II 3 line 922; All's Well That Ends Well, II 3 line 998; All's Well That Ends Well, II 3 line 1051; All's Well That Ends Well, II 3 line 1075; All's Well That Ends Well, II 3 line 1079; All's Well That Ends Well, II 3 line 1117; All's Well That Ends Well, II 5 line 1310; All's Well That Ends Well, III 2 line 1454; All's Well That Ends Well, III 2 line 1482; All's Well That Ends Well, III 5 line 1611; All's Well That Ends Well, III 6 line 1769; All's Well That Ends Well, III 6 line 1798; All's Well That Ends Well, IV 3 line 2276; All's Well That Ends Well, V 1 line 2602; All's Well That Ends Well, V 2 line 2656; All's Well That Ends Well, V 3 line 2871; All's Well That Ends Well, V 3 line 3063.

Antony and Cleopatra, I 2 line 89; Antony and Cleopatra, I 2 line 151; Antony and Cleopatra, I 2 line 220; Antony and Cleopatra, II 1 line 675; Antony and Cleopatra, II 2 line 860; Antony and Cleopatra, II 2 line 864; Antony and Cleopatra, II 2 line 935; Antony and Cleopatra, II 5 line 1085; Antony and Cleopatra, II 5 line 1158; Antony and Cleopatra, II 5 line 1187; Antony and Cleopatra, II 6 line 1271; Antony and Cleopatra, II 6 line 1306; Antony and Cleopatra, II 6 line 1333; Antony and Cleopatra, II 6 line 1335; Antony and Cleopatra, II 7 line 1504; Antony and Cleopatra, II 7 lines 1507, 1513r; Antony and Cleopatra, II 7 line 1530; Antony and Cleopatra, III 13 line 2340; Antony and Cleopatra, III 13 line 2348; Antony and Cleopatra, III 13 line 2373; Antony and Cleopatra, III 13 line 2405; Antony and Cleopatra, III 13 line 2421; Antony and Cleopatra, IV 2 line 2531; Antony and Cleopatra, IV 8 lines 2786, 2794; Antony and Cleopatra, IV 8 line 2811; Antony and Cleopatra, IV 8 line 2818; Antony and Cleopatra, IV 9 line 2871; Antony and Cleopatra, IV 12 line 2925; Antony and Cleopatra, IV 12 line 2956; Antony and Cleopatra, IV 14 line 3013; Antony and Cleopatra, IV 14 line 3042r; Antony and Cleopatra, IV 15 line 3225; Antony and Cleopatra, V 1 line 3304; Antony and Cleopatra, V 2 line 3403; Antony and Cleopatra, V 2 line 3428.

As You Like It, I 1 line 47; As You Like It, I 1 line 51; As You Like It, I 2 line 359; As You Like It, II 4 line 767; As You Like It, II 7 line 1100; As You Like It, III 1 line 1112; As You Like It, III 2 line 1165; As You Like It, III 2 line 1170; As You Like It, III 2 line 1173; As You Like It, III 2 line 1177; As You Like It, III 2 line 1472; As You Like It, III 2 line 1472; As You Like It, III 3 line 1565; As You Like It, IV 1 line 1817; As You Like It, IV 1 line 1890; As You Like It, IV 1 line 1902; As You Like It, IV 3 lines 2026r, 2027, 2028, 2029, 2031; As You Like It, IV 3 line 2082; As You

Like It, V 1 line 2224; As You Like It, V 4 line 2494; As You Like It, V 4 line 2507; As You Like It, V 4 line 2521.

Comedy of Errors, I 2 line 257; Comedy of Errors, II 1 line 317; Comedy of Errors, II 1 line 318; Comedy of Errors, II 1 line 322; Comedy of Errors, II 2 lines 505, 526; Comedy of Errors, III 1 line 623; Comedy of Errors, III 1 line 733; Comedy of Errors, III 2 line 833; Comedy of Errors, III 2 line 880; Comedy of Errors, IV 4 lines 1271; Comedy of Errors, IV 4 line 1280; Comedy of Errors, IV 4 line 1302; Comedy of Errors, IV 4 line 1303; Comedy of Errors, V 1 line 1526; Comedy of Errors, V 1 line 1737; Comedy of Errors, V 1 line 1873r.

Coriolanus, I 1 line 47; Coriolanus, I 3 line 398; Coriolanus, I 10 line 906; Coriolanus, II 1 line 938; Coriolanus, II 1 line 1127; Coriolanus, III 1 line 1948; Coriolanus, III 1 line 2006; Coriolanus, III 1 line 2013; Coriolanus, III 1 line 2072; Coriolanus, III 1 line 2078; Coriolanus, III 2 line 2254; Coriolanus, III 3 line 2434; Coriolanus, IV 1 line 2585; Coriolanus, IV 2 line 2620; Coriolanus, IV 5 line 2899; Coriolanus, IV 5 line 2915; Coriolanus, IV 5 line 2919; Coriolanus, IV 5 line 2965; Coriolanus, IV 6 line 3161; Coriolanus, V 1 line 3358; Coriolanus, V 3 line 3517; Coriolanus, V 3 line 3964.

Cymbeline, I 1 line 42; Cymbeline, I 1 line 214; Cymbeline, I 4 line 387; Cymbeline, I 4 line 479; Cymbeline, I 5 line 586; Cymbeline, I 6 lines 723, 729; Cymbeline, II 3 line 1054; Cymbeline, II 3 line 1081; Cymbeline, II 4 line 1243; Cymbeline, III 1 line 1454; Cymbeline, III 2 line 1511; Cymbeline, III 4 lines 1721, 1733; Cymbeline, III 4 line 1747; Cymbeline, III 4 line 1798; Cymbeline, III 4 lines 1800, 1802; Cymbeline, III 5 line 2099; Cymbeline, IV 1 line 2310; Cymbeline, IV 2 line 2450; Cymbeline, IV 2 line 2480; Cymbeline, IV 2 line 2712; Cymbeline, IV 4 line 2938; Cymbeline, V 3 line 3125; Cymbeline, V 4 line 3171; Cymbeline, V 5 line 3419; Cymbeline, V 5 line 3490; Cymbeline, V 5 line 3813; Cymbeline, V 5 line 3938; Cymbeline, V 5 line 3959.

Hamlet, I 1 line 119; Hamlet, I 2 line 249; Hamlet, I 2 line 421; Hamlet, I 4 line 715; Hamlet, I 4 line 721; Hamlet, I 5 lines 787r, 812; Hamlet, I 5 line 874; Hamlet, I 5 line 911; Hamlet, II 1 line 1048; Hamlet, II 2 line 1158; Hamlet, II 2 line 1342; Hamlet, II 2 line 1453; Hamlet, III 2 line 1886; Hamlet, III 2 line 2050; Hamlet, III 2 line 2147; Hamlet, III 3 lines 2324, 2339; Hamlet, III 4 line 2471; Hamlet, IV 5 line 2972; Hamlet, IV 5 line 3082; Hamlet, IV 7 line 3185; Hamlet, V 1 line 3265; Hamlet, V 1 line 3410; Hamlet, V 1 line 3550; Hamlet, V 1 line 3604; Hamlet, V 2 line 3861; Hamlet, V 2 line 3862; Hamlet, V 2 line 3899; Hamlet, V 2 line 3973.

Henry IV, Part I, I 1 line 42; Henry IV, Part I, I 3 line 335; Henry IV, Part I, I 3 line 424r; Henry IV, Part I, I 3 line 549; Henry IV, Part I, II 1 line 642; Henry IV, Part I, II 1 line 689; Henry IV, Part I, II 1 line 690; Henry IV, Part I, II 1 line 773; Henry IV, Part I, II 3 line 922; Henry IV, Part I, II 4 line 986; Henry IV, Part I, II 4 line 1008; Henry IV, Part I, II 4 line 1095; Henry IV, Part I, II 4 line 1203; Henry IV, Part I, II 4 line 1209; Henry IV, Part I, II 4 line 1218; Henry IV, Part I, III 2 line 1824; Henry IV, Part I, III 2 line 2004; Henry IV, Part I, III 3 line 2192; Henry

IV, Part I, IV 1 line 2364; Henry IV, Part I, V 1 lines 2659, 2690; Henry IV, Part I, V 4 line 3009; Henry IV, Part I, V 4 line 3047.

Henry IV, Part II, I 1 line 66; Henry IV, Part II, I 1 lines 204, 210; Henry IV, Part II, I 2 line 294; Henry IV, Part II, I 2 line 325; Henry IV, Part II, I 2 line 505; Henry IV, Part II, I 2 line 536; Henry IV, Part II, I 3 line 626; Henry IV, Part II, II 1 line 878; Henry IV, Part II, II 2 line 999; Henry IV, Part II, II 2 line 1023; Henry IV, Part II, II 4 line 1418; Henry IV, Part II, III 1 line 1815; Henry IV, Part II, III 2 lines 1818, 1819; Henry IV, Part II, III 2 line 1874; Henry IV, Part II, III 2 line 1923r; Henry IV, Part II, III 2 line 2132; Henry IV, Part II, IV 1 line 2248; Henry IV, Part II, IV 1 line 2307; Henry IV, Part II, IV 1 line 2435; Henry IV, Part II, IV 4 line 2779; Henry IV, Part II, IV 4 line 2833; Henry IV, Part II, IV 4 line 2855; Henry IV, Part II, IV 5 line 2888; Henry IV, Part II, IV 5 line 3087; Henry IV, Part II, V 1 line 3200; Henry IV, Part II, V 2 lines 3360, 3361, 3365, 3388; Henry IV, Part II, V 5 line 3625.

Henry V, I 1 line 118; Henry V, I 2 line 323; Henry V, I 2 line 443; Henry V, II 0 line 491; Henry V, II 1 line 537; Henry V, II 1 line 617; Henry V, II 2 line 668; Henry V, II 2 line 827; Henry V, II 3 line 855; Henry V, II 4 line 954; Henry V, III 2 lines 1218, 1222; Henry V, III 2 line 1240; Henry V, III 3 lines 1284, 1292, 1306; Henry V, III 4 line 1337; Henry V, III 4 line 1338; Henry V, III 4 line 1342; Henry V, III 4 line 1347; Henry V, III 4 line 1356; Henry V, III 4 line 1370; Henry V, III 4 line 1384; Henry V, III 6 line 1485; Henry V, III 6 line 1637; Henry V, III 7 line 1728; Henry V, IV 1 line 2062; Henry V, IV 1 line 2126; Henry V, IV 1 line 2149; Henry V, IV 2 line 2183; Henry V, IV 2 line 2211; Henry V, IV 4 line 2431; Henry V, IV 5 line 2464; Henry V, IV 6 line 2497; Henry V, V 1 line 2972; Henry V, V 2 line 3054; Henry V, V 2 line 3112; Henry V, V 2 line 3220; Henry V, V 2 line 3235.

Henry VI, Part I, I 1 line 20; Henry VI, Part I, I 2 line 244; Henry VI, Part I, I 2 line 303; Henry VI, Part I, I 2 line 308; Henry VI, Part I, I 4 lines 536, 546, 552; Henry VI, Part I, II 4 line 1005; Henry VI, Part I, III 1 line 1315; Henry VI, Part I, III 1 line 1357; Henry VI, Part I, III 1 line 1366r; Henry VI, Part I, III 2 line 1557; Henry VI, Part I, IV 1 line 1770; Henry VI, Part I, IV 1 line 1961; Henry VI, Part I, IV 2 line 1989; Henry VI, Part I, V 3 lines 2483, 2484; Henry VI, Part I, V 3 line 2497; Henry VI, Part I, V 3 line 2502; Henry VI, Part I, V 3 line 2506; Henry VI, Part I, V 3 line 2521; Henry VI, Part I, V 3 line 2579; Henry VI, Part I, V 3 line 2630; Henry VI, Part I, V 4 line 2773.

Henry VI, Part II, I 1 line 17; Henry VI, Part II, I 1 line 169; Henry VI, Part II, I 1 line 239; Henry VI, Part II, I 2 line 284; Henry VI, Part II, I 3 line 558; Henry VI, Part II, I 3 line 569; Henry VI, Part II, I 4 line 647; Henry VI, Part II, I 4 line 677; Henry VI, Part II, II 1 line 779; Henry VI, Part II, II 3 line 1089; Henry VI, Part II, II 4 line 1175; Henry VI, Part II, III 1 line 1425; Henry VI, Part II, III 1 line 1562; Henry VI, Part II, III 1 line 1603; Henry VI, Part II, III 1 line 1633; Henry VI, Part II, III 2 line 1684; Henry VI, Part II, III 2 line 1727; Henry VI, Part II, III 2 lines 1821, 1828; Henry VI, Part II, III 2 line 1841; Henry VI, Part II, III 2 line 1857; Henry VI, Part II, III 2 lines 2033, 2037; Henry VI, Part II, III 3 line 2142; Henry VI, Part II, IV 1 lines 2206, 2216; Henry VI, Part II, IV

1 line 2292; Henry VI, Part II, IV 2 line 2325; Henry VI, Part II, IV 2 line 2395; Henry VI, Part II, IV 7 line 2689; Henry VI, Part II, IV 7 line 2700; Henry VI, Part II, IV 7 line 2718; Henry VI, Part II, IV 10 line 2935; Henry VI, Part II, V 1 line 2983; Henry VI, Part II, V 1 lines 3080, 3085. **Henry VI, Part III**, I 1 line 3; Henry VI, Part III, I 3 line 376; Henry VI, Part III, I 3 line 412; Henry VI, Part III, I 4 line 495; Henry VI, Part III, I 4 lines 508, 534, 542; Henry VI, Part III, I 4 line 607; Henry VI, Part III, II 1 line 683; Henry VI, Part III, II 1 line 700r; Henry VI, Part III, II 1 line 780; Henry VI, Part III, II 2 line 855; Henry VI, Part III, II 2 line 915; Henry VI, Part III, II 2 line 949; Henry VI, Part III, II 3 line 1064; Henry VI, Part III, II 3 line 1072; Henry VI, Part III, II 4 lines 1093, 1094, 1096; Henry VI, Part III, II 5 lines 1160r, 1171, 1172; Henry VI, Part III, II 5 line 1241; Henry VI, Part III, II 6 line 1276; Henry VI, Part III, II 6 lines 1333, 1336; Henry VI, Part III, III 1 line 1366; Henry VI, Part III, III 2 line 1393; Henry VI, Part III, III 2 line 1634; Henry VI, Part III, III 3 line 1754; Henry VI, Part III, III 3 line 1846; Henry VI, Part III, III 3 lines 1950, 1951; Henry VI, Part III, III 3 line 1954; Henry VI, Part III, III 3 line 1955; Henry VI, Part III, IV 1 line 2055; Henry VI, Part III, IV 2 line 2140; Henry VI, Part III, IV 5 line 2284; Henry VI, Part III, IV 6 lines 2352, 2354r; Henry VI, Part III, IV 6 lines 2384, 2390; Henry VI, Part III, IV 7 line 2492; Henry VI, Part III, IV 8 line 2547; Henry VI, Part III, V 1 line 2605; Henry VI, Part III, V 1 line 2609; Henry VI, Part III, V 1 line 2619; Henry VI, Part III, V 1 line 2646; Henry VI, Part III, V 1 line 2650; Henry VI, Part III, V 1 line 2697; Henry VI, Part III, V 2 line 2757; Henry VI, Part III, V 4 line 2865.
Henry VIII, I 2 line 556; Henry VIII, I 3 line 639; Henry VIII, I 4 line 765; Henry VIII, II 2 line 1146; Henry VIII, II 2 line 1163; Henry VIII, II 2 line 1168; Henry VIII, II 4 line 1596; Henry VIII, III 1 line 1755; Henry VIII, III 2 line 1931; Henry VIII, III 2 lines 2063, 2065; Henry VIII, III 2 line 2117; Henry VIII, III 2 line 2136; Henry VIII, III 2 line 2182; Henry VIII, III 2 line 2196; Henry VIII, III 2 line 2360; Henry VIII, IV 1 line 2394; Henry VIII, IV 2 lines 2651, 2661; Henry VIII, V 1 line 2814; Henry VIII, V 1 line 2822; Henry VIII, V 1 line 2898; Henry VIII, V 1 line 2922; Henry VIII, V 3 line 3047; Henry VIII, V 3 line 3080; Henry VIII, V 4 line 3342; Henry VIII, V 5 line 3393.
Julius Caesar, I 2 line 122; Julius Caesar, I 2 line 305; Julius Caesar, I 2 line 314; Julius Caesar, I 2 line 338; Julius Caesar, I 2 line 412; Julius Caesar, I 3 lines 437, 439; Julius Caesar, I 3 line 529; Julius Caesar, I 3 line 545; Julius Caesar, I 3 line 568; Julius Caesar, II 1 line 663; Julius Caesar, II 1 line 730; Julius Caesar, II 1 line 766; Julius Caesar, II 1 line 873; Julius Caesar, II 1 line 949; Julius Caesar, II 1 line 951; Julius Caesar, II 2 line 1060; Julius Caesar, III 1 line 1232; Julius Caesar, III 1 line 1256; Julius Caesar, III 1 line 1283; Julius Caesar, III 1 line 1320; Julius Caesar, III 1 line 1379; Julius Caesar, III 1 lines 1387,1388; Julius Caesar, III 1 lines 1406,1408; Julius Caesar, III 1 line 1441; Julius Caesar, III 1 line 1475; Julius Caesar, III 1 lines 1487, 1497; Julius Caesar, III 1 line 1528; Julius Caesar, III 2 line 1577; Julius Caesar, IV 3 line 2059; Julius Caesar, IV 3 line 2106; Julius Caesar, V 1 line 2363; Julius Caesar, V 1 line 2364; Julius

Caesar, V 1 line 2406; Julius Caesar, V 1 lines 2429, 2438; Julius Caesar, V 5 line 2730.

King John, I 1 line 16; King John, I 1 line 59; King John, I 1 line 169; King John, I 1 line 277; King John, II 1 line 305; King John, II 1 line 323; King John, II 1 line 369; King John, II 1 line 396; King John, II 1 lines 452, 454; King John, II 1 line 537; King John, II 1 lines 609, 616; King John, II 1 lines 627, 630; King John, II 1 line 653; King John, II 1 line 806; King John, II 1 line 845; King John, II 1 line 846; King John, II 1 lines 904, 906; King John, III 1 line 936; King John, III 1 line 972; King John, III 1 line 1080; King John, III 1 1098; King John, III 1 line 1115; King John, III 1 line 1118; King John, III 1 line 1120; King John, III 1 lines 1151, 1159, 1164; King John, III 1 line 1186; King John, III 1 line 1187; King John, III 1 line 1256; King John, III 3 line 1315; King John, III 3 line 1326; King John, III 4 line 1457; King John, III 4 line 1523; King John, IV 4 line 1627; King John, IV 2 line 1811; King John, IV 2 line 1940; King John, IV 2 line 1949; King John, IV 2 line 1959; king John, IV 2 lines 1961, 1965; King John, IV 2 line 1984; King John, IV 2 lines 1995, 1996; King John, IV 3 lines 2078, 2079; King John, IV 3 lines 2080, 2082, 2091; King John, IV 3 line 2189; King John, V 1 line 2192; King John, V 1 line 2196; King John, V 1 line 2236; King John, V 2 line 2300; King John, V 2 lines 2338, 2345; King John, V 2 line 2355; King John, V 2 lines 2419, 2428; King John, V 2 lines 2453, 2457.

King Lear, I 1 line 104; King Lear, I 1 line 265; King Lear, I 2 line 390; King Lear, I 2 line 398; King Lear, II 4 line 1415; King Lear, II 4 line 1487; King Lear, II 4 line 1488; King Lear, III 1 line 1671; King Lear, III 2 line 1730; King Lear, III 4 line 1817; King Lear, III 4 line 1843; King Lear, III 4 lines 1887, 1890; King Lear, III 5 line 1996; King Lear, III 7 line 2164; King Lear, III 7 line 2172; King Lear, III 7 line 2202; King Lear, IV 2 line 2367; King Lear, IV 2 line 2411; King Lear, IV 5 line 2585; King Lear, IV 6 line 2629; King Lear, IV 6 line 2741; King Lear, IV 6 line 2765; King Lear, IV 6 line 2794; King Lear, IV 6 line 2838; King Lear, IV 6 line 2906; King Lear, IV 7 line 2972; King Lear, IV 7 line 2976; King Lear, V 2 line 3107; King Lear, V 2 lines 3114, 3116.

Love's Labour's Lost, I 1 line 23; Love's Labour's Lost, II 1 line 660; Love's Labour's Lost, III 1 line 781; Love's Labour's Lost, III 1 line 930; Love's Labour's Lost, IV 1 line 995; Love's Labour's Lost, IV 1 line 1118r; Love's Labour's Lost, IV 1 line 1120r; Love's Labour's Lost, IV 1 line 1132; Love's Labour's Lost, IV 2 lines 1281, 1290; Love's Labour's Lost, IV 3 line 1440; Love's Labour's Lost, IV 3 line 1516; Love's Labour's Lost, IV 3 line 1563; Love's Labour's Lost, IV 3 line 1720; Love's Labour's Lost, V 2 line 1939; Love's Labour's Lost, V 2 line 2113; Love's Labour's Lost, V 2 line 2114; Love's Labour's Lost, V 2 line 2222; Love's Labour's Lost, V 2 line 2242; Love's Labour's Lost, V 2 line 2333; Love's Labour's Lost, V 2 line 2752; Love's Labour's Lost, V 2 line 2757.

Lover's Complaint, lines 30, 41, 142, 226.

Macbeth, I 2 line 40; Macbeth, I 3 line 131r; Macbeth, I 4 line 335; Macbeth, I 5 line 420; Macbeth, I 6 line 467 Macbeth, I 7 line 483; Macbeth, II 1 line 613; Macbeth, II 2 line 676; Macbeth, II 2 line 707;

Macbeth, II 2 lines 722, 724r; Macbeth, II 2 line 729; Macbeth, II 3 line 888; Macbeth, II 3 line 924, Macbeth, III 1 line 1072; Macbeth, III 1 line 1093; Macbeth, III 1 line 1104; Macbeth, III 2 line 1224; Macbeth, III 4 line 1443; Macbeth, III 6 line 1544; Macbeth, IV 1 line 1650; Macbeth, IV 1 line 1728; Macbeth, IV 3 line 1892; Macbeth, IV 3 line 2004; Macbeth, V 1 line 2152; Macbeth, V 1 line 2154; Macbeth, V 1 line 2167; Macbeth, V 1 line 2175; Macbeth, V 1 line 2184; Macbeth, V 1 line 2189; Macbeth, V 2 line 2226; Macbeth, V 4 line 2324; Macbeth, V 8 line 2560.

Measure for Measure, I 1 line 76; Measure for Measure, I 4 line 406; Measure for Measure, II 1 line 612; Measure for Measure, III 1 line 1423; Measure for Measure, III 2 line 1558; Measure for Measure, IV 1 line 1856; Measure for Measure, IV 2 line 2096; Measure for Measure, V 1 lines 2400, 2404; Measure for Measure, V 1 line 2615; Measure for Measure, V 1 line 2871; Measure for Measure, V 1 line 2930; Measure for Measure, V 1 line 2937.

Merchant of Venice, I 3 line 419; Merchant of Venice, II 1 line 549; Merchant of Venice, II 2 lines 605, 607; Merchant of Venice, II 4 lines 813r, 815; Merchant of Venice, II 7 line 1011; Merchant of Venice, II 8 lines 1119, 1121; Merchant of Venice, II 9 line 1229; Merchant of Venice, III 1 line 1293; Merchant of Venice, III 2 line 1613; Merchant of Venice, III 4 line 1773; Merchant of Venice, III 4 line 1801; Merchant of Venice, III 4 line 1809; Merchant of Venice, IV 1 line 2106; Merchant of Venice, IV 1 line 2153; Merchant of Venice, IV 1 line 2210; Merchant of Venice, IV 1 line 2383; Merchant of Venice, V 1 line 2455; Merchant of Venice, V 1 line 2505; Merchant of Venice, V 1 line 2585; Merchant of Venice, V 1 line 2626; Merchant of Venice, V 1 line 2642.

Merry Wives of Windsor, I 4 line 428; Merry Wives of Windsor, I 4 line 501; Merry Wives of Windsor, I 4 line 543; Merry Wives of Windsor, II 1 line 644; Merry Wives of Windsor, II 1 line 755; Merry Wives of Windsor, II 1 line 773; Merry Wives of Windsor, II 2 line 817; Merry Wives of Windsor, II 2 line 1000; Merry Wives of Windsor, II 2 line 1033; Merry Wives of Windsor, II 2 line 1040; Merry Wives of Windsor, III 1 lines 1292, 1293; Merry Wives of Windsor, III 3 line 1518; Merry Wives of Windsor, III 5 line 1842; Merry Wives of Windsor, IV 2 line 2137; Merry Wives of Windsor, IV 4 line 2247; Merry Wives of Windsor, IV 6 lines 2458, 2465; Merry Wives of Windsor, V 1 lines 2508, 2509; Merry Wives of Windsor, V 5 line 2641r.

Midsummer Night's Dream, II 1 line 591; Midsummer Night's Dream, II 1 line 620; Midsummer Night's Dream, II 2 line 783; Midsummer Night's Dream, III 2 line 1148; Midsummer Night's Dream, III 2 line 1181; Midsummer Night's Dream, III 2 line 1248; Midsummer Night's Dream, III 2 line 1397; Midsummer Night's Dream, IV 1 line 1555; Midsummer Night's Dream, IV 1 line 1636; Midsummer Night's Dream, IV 1 line 1783; Midsummer Night's Dream, V 1 line 1868; Midsummer Night's Dream, V 1 line 1959; Midsummer Night's Dream, V 1 line 2183; Midsummer Night's Dream, V 1 line 2249r; Midsummer Night's Dream, V 1 line 2260; Midsummer Night's Dream, V 1 line 2289.

Much Ado About Nothing, I 1 line 144; Much Ado About Nothing, I 1 line 271; Much Ado About Nothing, I 3 line 375; Much Ado About Nothing, I 3 lines 383, 384; Much Ado About Nothing, II 1 line 503; Much Ado About Nothing, III 1 line 1192; Much Ado About Nothing, III 3 line 1374; Much Ado About Nothing, IV 1 line 1691; Much Ado About Nothing, IV 1 line 1762; Much Ado About Nothing, IV 1 line 1780; Much Ado About Nothing, IV 1 line 1842; Much Ado About Nothing, IV 1 lines 1951, 1952; Much Ado About Nothing, IV 1 line 1972; Much Ado About Nothing, IV 1 line 1976r; Much Ado About Nothing, IV 2 line 2046; Much Ado About Nothing, V 1 line 2126; Much Ado About Nothing, V 1 lines 2128, 2130; Much Ado About Nothing, V 1 line 2340; Much Ado About Nothing, V 2 line 2412; Much Ado About Nothing, V 4 line 2605; Much Ado About Nothing, V 4 line 2607; Much Ado About Nothing, V 4 line 2639; Much Ado About Nothing, V 4 line 2643; Much Ado About Nothing, V 4 line 2645.
Othello, I 2 line 302; Othello, I 3 line 521; Othello, II 1 line 864; Othello, II 1 line 1053; Othello, II 1 lines 1057, 1061; Othello, II 3 line 1244; Othello, II 3 line 1291; Othello, III 3 line 1813; Othello, III 3 line 2103; Othello, III 3 line 2119; Othello, III 3 line 2155; Othello, III 4 line 2213r; Othello, III 4 lines 2216, 2220; Othello, III 4 line 2223; Othello, III 4 lines 2224r, 2225; Othello, III 4 line 2103; Othello, IV 1 line 2566; Othello, IV 1 line 2606; Othello, IV 1 line 2614; Othello, IV 2 line 2909; Othello, IV 2 line 2978; Othello, IV 3 line 3064; Othello, V 1 line 3141; Othello, V 1 line 3142; Othello, V 2 line 3375; Othello, V 2 line 3543; Othello, V 2 line 3556; Othello, V 2 line 3713.
Passionate Pilgrim, line 238.
Pericles, I 1 line 125; Pericles, I 1 line 191; Pericles, I 4 line 437; Pericles, II 2 line 792; Pericles, II 4 line 962; Pericles, II 4 line 1009; Pericles, II 5 line 1088; Pericles, III 2 line 1416; Pericles, IV 1 line 1609; Pericles, IV 2 line 1738; Pericles, IV 2 line 1740.
Rape of Lucrece, lines 162, 304, 311r, 409, 421, 437, 444, 487, 488, 491, 514, 518, 689, 1050, 1081, 1261r, 1286, 1454, 1466, 1476, 1478, 1648, 1773, 1893.
Richard II, I 2 line 217; Richard II, I 2 line 234; Richard II, I 3 line 341; Richard II, I 3 line 348; Richard II, I 3 lines 455, 461; Richard II, I 3 line 476; Richard II, I 3 line 595; Richard II, I 4 line 660; Richard II, II 1 line 726; Richard II, II 1 lines 865, 867, 868; Richard II, II 1 line 874; Richard II, II 1 line 897; Richard II, II 2 line 1109; Richard II, II 3 line 1204; Richard II, III 1 lines 1365, 1389; Richard II, III 2 line 1409; Richard II, III 2 lines 1414, 1419; Richard II, III 2 line 1548; Richard II, III 3 line 1672; Richard II, III 3 lines 1718, 1720, 1730; Richard II, III 3 lines 1745, 1750; Richard II, III 3 line 1850; Richard II, IV 1 line 2031; Richard II, IV 1 line 2094; Richard II, IV 1 line 2147; Richard II, IV 1 line 2171; Richard II, IV 1 lines 2193, 2196; Richard II, IV 1 line 2228; Richard II, V 1 line 2417r; Richard II, V 2 line 2445; Richard II, V 2 line 2478; Richard II, V 2 line 2549; Richard II, V 3 line 2619; Richard II, V 3 line 2632; Richard II, V 3 line 2714; Richard II, V 5 lines 2836, 2837; Richard II, V 5 lines 2861, 2865, 2866; Richard II, V 6 line 2918; Richard II, V 6 line 2933.

Richard III, I 1 line 126; Richard III, I 2 lines 184, 187; Richard III, I 2 line 269; Richard III, I 2 line 378; Richard III, I 2 line 396; Richard III, I 3 line 558; Richard III, I 3 line 827; Richard III, I 4 line 927; Richard III, I 4 line 1018; Richard III, I 4 line 1026; Richard III, I 4 line 1104; Richard III, II 1 line 1127; Richard III, II 1 line 1130; Richard III II 1 line 1141; Richard III, II 2 line 1273; Richard III, II 2 line 1365; Richard III, II 3 line 1466; Richard III, III 1 line 1773; Richard III, III 2 line 1906; Richard III, III 5 line 2120; Richard III, III 6 line 2185; Richard III, III 6 line 2187; Richard III, III 7 lines 2146, 2148; Richard III, III 7 line 2309; Richard III, IV 1 line 2467; Richard III, IV 1 line 2526; Richard III, IV 1 line 2467; Richard III, IV 1 line 2538; Richard III, IV 2 line 2583; Richard III, IV 4 line 2831; Richard III, IV 4 line 2868r; Richard III, IV 4 line 3028; Richard III, IV 4 line 3153; Richard III, V 3 line 3583; Richard III, V 3 line 3828r.
Romeo and Juliet, Prologue 1 line 4; Romeo and Juliet, I 1 lines 106, 114; Romeo and Juliet, I 5 line 622; Romeo and Juliet, I 5 line 673; Romeo and Juliet, I 5 line 719; Romeo and Juliet, I 5 lines 723, 725r; Romeo and Juliet, I 5 line 729; Romeo and Juliet, II 1 lines 878, 879; Romeo and Juliet, II 2 line 887; Romeo and Juliet, II 2 line 1042; Romeo and Juliet, II 4 line 1266; Romeo and Juliet, II 5 line 1418; Romeo and Juliet, II 6 line 1464; Romeo and Juliet, III 1 lines 1669, 1678; Romeo and Juliet, II 6 line 1464; Romeo and Juliet, III 1 lines 1669, 1678; Romeo and Juliet, III 2 line 1757; Romeo and Juliet, III 2 line 1793; Romeo and Juliet, III 3 line 1875; Romeo and Juliet, III 3 line 1907; Romeo and Juliet, III 3 line 1983; Romeo and Juliet, III 3 line 1989; Romeo and Juliet, III 3 line 2054; Romeo and Juliet, III 5 line 2191; Romeo and Juliet, III 5 line 2331; Romeo and Juliet, III 5 line 2303; Romeo and Juliet, IV 1 lines 2421, 2422; Romeo and Juliet, IV 3 line 2560; Romeo and Juliet, V 1 line 2806; Romeo and Juliet, V 3 lines 3026, 3045; Romeo and Juliet, V 3 line 3124; Romeo and Juliet, V 3 line 3271.
Sonnet VI line 71; Sonnet XX line 1; Sonnet XXVIII line 6; Sonnet XLVIII line 4; Sonnet XLIX line 11; Sonnet LVIII 3; Sonnet LX line 14; Sonnet LXIII line 2; Sonnet LXV line 11; Sonnet LXXI line 6; Sonnet XCVIX line 6; Sonnet CIV line 9; Sonnet CVI line 6; Sonnet CXI line 7; Sonnet CXXVII line 5; Sonnet CXXVIII line 6; Sonnet CXLV line 1; Sonnet CLIV line 4; Sonnet CLIV line 7.
Taming of the Shrew, Prologue, 1 line 59; Taming of the Shrew, Prologue, 1 line 98; Taming of the Shrew, Prologue, 2 line 221; Taming of the Shrew, I 1 line 460; Taming of the Shrew, I 1 line 472; Taming of the Shrew, I 1 line 481; Taming of the Shrew, I 2 line 694; Taming of the Shrew, I 2 line 777; Taming of the Shrew, II 1 line 840; Taming of the Shrew, II 1 line 857; Taming of the Shrew, II 1 line 970; Taming of the Shrew, II 1 line 994; Taming of the Shrew, II 1 line 1165; Taming of the Shrew, II 1 line 1169; Taming of the Shrew, II 1 line 1201; Taming of the Shrew, III 2 line 1372; Taming of the Shrew, IV 1 line 1645r; Taming of the Shrew, IV 1 line 1696; Taming of the Shrew, IV 1 line 1716; Taming of the Shrew, IV 2 line 1826; Taming of the Shrew, IV 2

line 1854; Taming of the Shrew, V 1 line 2383; Taming of the Shrew, V 2 line 2593; Taming of the Shrew, V 2 lines 2660, 2685, 2687.

Tempest, I 1 line 29; Tempest, I 2 line 112; Tempest, I 2 line 538; Tempest, II 1 line 1035; Tempest, II 2 line 1130; Tempest, II 2 line 1211; Tempest, III 1 line 1384; Tempest, III 2 line 1442; Tempest, III 2 line 1463; Tempest, III 2 line 1507; Tempest, IV 1 line 1705; Tempest, IV 1 line 1963; Tempest, IV 1 line 1969; Tempest, V 1 line 2272; Tempest, V 1 line 2413.

Timon of Athens, I 1 line 87; Timon of Athens, I 1 line 107; Timon of Athens, I 1 line 184; Timon of Athens, I 1 line 202; Timon of Athens, I 2 line 475; Timon of Athens, II 1 line 626; Timon of Athens, II 1 line 647; Timon of Athens, II 2 line 667; Timon of Athens, II 2 line 827; Timon of Athens, IV 1 line 1575; Timon of Athens, IV 2 line 1638; Timon of Athens, IV 3 line 2065; Timon of Athens, V 1 line 2398; Timon of Athens, V 4 line 2583.

Titus Andronicus, I 1 line 185; Titus Andronicus, I 1 line 347; Titus Andronicus, I 1 line 467; Titus Andronicus, II 1 line 669; Titus Andronicus, II 3 lines 771, 778; Titus Andronicus, II 3 line 859; Titus Andronicus, II 3 line 909; Titus Andronicus, II 3 line 984; Titus Andronicus, II 3 line 990; Titus Andronicus, II 4 line 1062; Titus Andronicus, II 4 line 1068; Titus Andronicus, II 4 line 1069; Titus Andronicus, II 4 line 1072; Titus Andronicus, II 4 lines 1080, 1108; Titus Andronicus, III 1 lines 1196, 1197, 1202, 1208, 1209; Titus Andronicus, III 1 line 1236; Titus Andronicus, III 1 line 1260; Titus Andronicus, III 1 line 1284; Titus Andronicus, III 1 line 1291; Titus Andronicus, III 1 lines 1293, 1295; Titus Andronicus, III 1 lines 1298, 1302; Titus Andronicus, III 1 line 1305; Titus Andronicus, III 1 line 1307; Titus Andronicus, III 1 line 1315; Titus Andronicus, III 1 line 1320; Titus Andronicus, III 1 line 1325; Titus Andronicus, III 1 lines 1328, 1329; Titus Andronicus, III 1 line 1335; Titus Andronicus, III 1 line 1343; Titus Andronicus, III 1 line 1372; Titus Andronicus, III 1 lines 1374, 1376; Titus Andronicus, III 1 lines 1396, 1401; Titus Andronicus, III 1 lines 1421, 1423; Titus Andronicus, III 1 lines 1449, 1451; Titus Andronicus, III 2 line 1467; Titus Andronicus, III 2 lines 1470, 1471, 1474, 1477, 1478; Titus Andronicus, IV 1 line 1611; Titus Andronicus, IV 2 line 1786; Titus Andronicus, IV 3 line 1988; Titus Andronicus, IV 3 line 1996; Titus Andronicus, IV 4 line 2009; Titus Andronicus, V 1 line 2174; Titus Andronicus, V 1 line 2228; Titus Andronicus, V 1 lines 2246, 2250; Titus Andronicus, V 2 line 2324; Titus Andronicus, V 2 line 2333; Titus Andronicus, V 2 line 2384; Titus Andronicus, V 2 line 2324; Titus Andronicus, V 2 line 2333; Titus Andronicus, V 2 line 2384; Titus Andronicus, V 2 line 2471; Titus Andronicus, V 2 lines 2491, 2492, 2493, 2498; Titus Andronicus, V 3 line 2542; Titus Andronicus, V 3 line 2569. Titus Andronicus, V 3 line 2645; Titus Andronicus, V 3 lines 2672r, 2676r; Titus Andronicus, V 3 line 2678.

Troilus and Cressida, I 1 line 85; Troilus and Cressida, I 1 line 98; Troilus and Cressida, I 2 line 184; Troilus and Cressida, I 2 line 270; Troilus and Cressida, I 2 line 286; Troilus and Cressida, I 3 line 516; Troilus and Cressida, I 3 line 596; Troilus and Cressida, I 3 lines 653,

654, 661; Troilus and Cressida, I 3 line 765; Troilus and Cressida, II 2 line 1080; Troilus and Cressida, II 2 line 1162; Troilus and Cressida, III 1 line 1570; Troilus and Cressida, III 2 line 1849; Troilus and Cressida, III 3 line 2042; Troilus and Cressida, IV 1 line 2206; Troilus and Cressida, IV 1 line 2222; Troilus and Cressida, IV 2 lines 2357, 2362; Troilus and Cressida, IV 2 line 2366; Troilus and Cressida, IV 3 line 2418; Troilus and Cressida, IV 4 line 2549; Troilus and Cressida, IV 4 line 2577; Troilus and Cressida, IV 5 line 2698; Troilus and Cressida, IV 5 line 2715; Troilus and Cressida, IV 5 line 2745; Troilus and Cressida, IV 5 line 2779; Troilus and Cressida, IV 5 line 2827r; Troilus and Cressida, IV 5 line 2902; Troilus and Cressida, V 1 line 3024; Troilus and Cressida, V 3 line 3336; Troilus and Cressida, V 5 line 3491.

Twelfth Night, I 3 line 147; Twelfth Night, I 3 line 176; Twelfth Night, I 3 line 177; Twelfth Night, I 3 line 180; Twelfth Night, I 3 line 184; Twelfth Night, I 3 line 188; Twelfth Night, I 5 line 502; Twelfth Night, I 5 line 528; Twelfth Night, II 3 line 729; Twelfth Night, II 3 line 823; Twelfth Night, II 3 line 890; Twelfth Night, II 5 line 1092; Twelfth Night, II 5 lines 1111, 1113; Twelfth Night, II 5 lines 1165, 1169; Twelfth Night, III 1 line 1329; Twelfth Night, III 2 line 1426; Twelfth Night, III 2 line 1443; Twelfth Night, III 4 lines 1573, 1574; Twelfth Night, III 4 line 1578; Twelfth Night, IV 1 line 1971; Twelfth Night, IV 1 line 1987; Twelfth Night, IV 2 line 2099; Twelfth Night, IV 2 line 2126; Twelfth Night, V 1 line 2355; Twelfth Night, V 1 line 2475; Twelfth Night, V 1 line 2532; Twelfth Night, V 1 lines 2543, 2544; Twelfth Night, V 1 line 2559.

Two Gentlemen of Verona, I 2 line 264; Two Gentlemen of Verona, I 3 line 350; Two Gentlemen of Verona, II 2 line 574; Two Gentlemen of Verona, II 3 line 600; Two Gentlemen of Verona, III 1 lines 1301, 1303; Two Gentlemen of Verona, III 1 line 1343; Two Gentlemen of Verona, V 4 line 2220; Two Gentlemen of Verona, V 4 line 2272.

Venus and Adonis, lines 100, 163r, 178, 243, 371, 372, 373, 381, 393, 441, 654, 787, 792, 934, 1146.

Winter's Tale, I 1 line 29; Winter's Tale, I 2 line 176; Winter's Tale, I 2 line 576; Winter's Tale, II 3 line 1005; Winter's Tale, II 3 line 1024; Winter's Tale, II 3 line 1056; Winter's Tale, II 3 line 1087; Winter's Tale, II 3 line 1101; Winter's Tale, III 2 line 1347; Winter's Tale, III 3 line 1492; Winter's Tale, IV 3 lines 1794, 1795; Winter's Tale, IV 4 line 2037; Winter's Tale, IV 4 line 2101; Winter's Tale, IV 4 line 2168; Winter's Tale, IV 4 line 2261r; Winter's Tale, IV 4 line 2268; Winter's Tale, IV 4 line 2290; Winter's Tale, IV 4 line 2299; Winter's Tale, IV 4 line 2497; Winter's Tale, IV 4 line 2647; Winter's Tale, IV 4 line 2746; Winter's Tale, IV 4 line 2782; Winter's Tale, IV 4 line 2801; Winter's Tale, V 1 line 3005; Winter's Tale, V 2 line 3156; Winter's Tale, V 2 line 3212; Winter's Tale, V 2 line 3248; Winter's Tale, V 2 line 3264; Winter's Tale, V 2 lines 3272, 3274, 3276; Winter's Tale, V 3 line 3306; Winter's Tale, V 3 line 3341; Winter's Tale, V 3 line 3395; Winter's Tale, V 3 line 3419; Winter's Tale, V 3 line 3462.

Hare: long-eared mammal. Old English: *hara*, of Germanic origin: related to Dutch *haas* and German *Hase*. This was formerly esteemed a melancholy animal, and its flesh was supposed to engender melancholy in those who ate it.
>**As You Like It**, IV 3 line 2019.
>**Antony and Cleopatra**, IV 7 line 2773.
>**Coriolanus**, I 1 line 172; Coriolanus, I 8 line 745.
>**Cymbeline**, IV 4 line 2927.
>**Henry IV, Part I**, I 2 line 183; Henry IV, Part I, I 3 line 529 Henry IV, Part I, II 4 line 1420.
>**Henry VI, Part III**, II 5 line 1239.
>**King John**, II 1 line 433.
>**Macbeth**, I 2 line 56.
>**Merchant of Venice**, I 2 line 213.
>**Midsummer Night's Dream**, V 1 line 2262.
>**Romeo and Juliet**, II 4 lines 1285r, 1288, 1289, 1291.
>**Troilus and Cressida**, III 2 line 1739.
>**Twelfth Night**, III 4 line 1942.
>**Venus and Adonis**, lines 695, 701.

Harebell: also called a bluebell; pale flower on long stems, hanging like a bell. Middle English: probably so named because it is found growing in places frequented by hares.
>**Cymbeline**, IV 2 line 2610.

Harelip: mid 16th cent.: from a perceived resemblance to the mouth of a hare. It was popularly believed to be the mischievous act of an elf or malicious fairy.
>**King Lear**, III 4 line 1912.

Harlock: corruption of charlock. A wild mustard.
>**King Lear**, IV 4 line 2519.

Harvest: Old English: *hærfest*: autumn, period between August and November. The borrowing of autumn in a seasonal sense gradually focused the meaning of harvest to the *time of gathering crops* (mid-13c.), then to the action itself and the product of the action (after c.1300). Figurative use by 1530s. *Harvest home* (1590s) is the occasion of bringing home the last of the harvest.
>**Antony and Cleopatra**, II 7 line 1399.
>**As You Like It**, III 5 line 1758.
>**Coriolanus**, I 3 line 399.
>**Cymbeline**, I 1 line 52.
>**Henry IV, Part I**, I 3 line 360.
>**Henry VI, Part I**, III 2 line 1500.
>**Henry VI, Part II**, III 1 line 1670.
>**Henry VI, Part III**, V 7 line 3116.
>**Love's Labour's Lost**, IV 3 line 1671.
>**Macbeth**, I 4 line 314.

Merry Wives of Windsor, II 2 line 1060.
Much Ado About Nothing, I 3 line 53.
Pericles, IV 2 line 1804.
Rape of Lucrece, line 910.
Richard III, I 4 line 1071; Richard III, II 2 lines 1388, 1389; Richard III, V 2 line 3443.
Sonnet CXXVIII line 7.
Tempest, IV 1 line 1831.
Twelfth Night, III 1 line 1370.
Venus and Adonis, line 15.

Haunch: early 13c., from Old French:*hanche* (12c.) *hip, thigh; haunch.*
    As You Like It, II 1 line 573.
    Henry IV, Part II, IV 4 line 2842.
    Merry Wives of Windsor, V 5 line 2583.

Hawk: c.1300, *hauk*, earlier *havek* (c.1200), from Old English: *hafoc*. Also, *to clear one's throat*, 1580s, imitative. The diversion of catching game with hawks was very popular in Shakespeare's time, and hence, as might be expected, we find many scattered allusions to it throughout his plays. The training of a hawk for the field was an essential part of the education of a young Saxon nobleman; and the present of a well-trained hawk was a gift to be welcomed by a king.
    All's Well That Ends Well, I 1 line 95.
    As You Like It, V 3 line 2370.
    Hamlet, II 2 line 1461.
    Henry V, III 7 line 1656.
    Henry VI, Part I, II 4 line 931.
    Henry VI, Part II, I 2 line 332; Henry VI, Part II, II 1 line 736; Henry VI, Part II, II 1 line 785.
    Macbeth, II 4 line 962.
    Merry Wives of Windsor, III 3 line 1619.
    Much Ado About Nothing, III 4 line 1539.
    Rape of Lucrece, line 745.
    Sonnet XCI lines 4, 12.
    Taming of the Shrew, Prologue 2 line 187r; Taming of the Shrew, V 2 line 2565.

Hawthorn: Old English: *hagaþorn*, earlier *hæguþorn: hawthorn, white thorn*, from obsolete *haw: hedge or encompassing fence.*
    As You Like It, III 2 line 1447.
    Henry VI, Part III, II 5 line 1144.
    King Lear, III 4 line 1848; King Lear, III 4 line 1892.
    Merry Wives of Windsor, III 3 line 1470.
    Midsummer Night's Dream, I 1 line 193; Midsummer Night's Dream, III 1 line 823.

Hazel: Old English: *hæsl, hæsel*. Shakespeare was first to use it (in print) in the sense of reddish-brown colour of eyes (in reference to the color of ripe hazel-nuts).
Romeo and Juliet, III 1 line 1518.
Taming of the Shrew, II 1 line 1103.

Hazelnut: Old English: *hæselhnutu*.
Romeo and Juliet, I 4 line 567.
Taming of the Shrew, II 1 line 1105.

Head: Old English: *heafod: top of the body*, also, upper end of a slope, also chief person, leader, ruler; capital city. Of rounded tops of plants from late 14c. Meaning *origin of a river* is mid-14c. Meaning *foam on a mug of beer* is first attested 1540s. As a height measure of persons, from c.1300. According to the old writers on physiognomy, a round head denoted foolishness.
All's Well That Ends Well, I 1 line 67; All's Well That Ends Well, I 3 line 374; All's Well That Ends Well, I 3 line 494; All's Well That Ends Well, II 3 line 936; All's Well That Ends Well, III 2 line1428; All's Well That Ends Well, IV 3 line 2387; All's Well That Ends Well, IV 5 line 2561.
Antony and Cleopatra, II 2 line 686; Antony and Cleopatra, II 5 line 1132; Antony and Cleopatra, III 1 line 1559; Antony and Cleopatra, III 3 line 1690; Antony and Cleopatra, III 7 line 2000; Antony and Cleopatra, III 11 line 2161; Antony and Cleopatra, III 13 line 2265; Antony and Cleopatra, III 13 line 2268; Antony and Cleopatra, IV 1 line 2507; Antony and Cleopatra, IV 7 line 2762; Antony and Cleopatra, V 2 line 3691.
As You Like It, II 1 line 561; As You Like It, II 1 line 572; As You Like It, III 2 line 1310; As You Like It, III 5 line 1793; As You Like It, IV 1 line 1966; As You Like It, IV 2 line 1984; As You Like It, IV 3 lines 2113, 2119; As You Like It, V 1 lines 2204, 2205.
Comedy of Errors, II 1 line 353; Comedy of Errors, II 2 lines 430, 432; Comedy of Errors, III 2 line 874; Comedy of Errors, V 1 line 1503.
Coriolanus, I 1 line 108; Coriolanus, II 1 line 1128; Coriolanus, II 2 line 1320; Coriolanus, II 2 line 1335; Coriolanus, II 3 line 1440; Coriolanus, III 1 line 1726; Coriolanus, III 2 line 2173; Coriolanus, III 2 line 2258; Coriolanus, IV 3 line 2523; Coriolanus, IV 5 line 2768; Coriolanus, IV 6 line 3182; Coriolanus, V 6 line 3930.
Cymbeline, I 6 line 624; Cymbeline, III 4 line 1920; Cymbeline, III 5 line 1976; Cymbeline, IV 1 line 2303; Cymbeline, IV 2 line 2452; Cymbeline, IV 2 line 2470; Cymbeline, IV 2 line 2475; Cymbeline, IV 2 line 2477; Cymbeline, IV 2 lines 2500, 2505; Cymbeline, IV 2 line 2515; Cymbeline, IV 2 line 2544; Cymbeline, IV 2 line 2651; Cymbeline, IV 2 lines 2733, 2736; Cymbeline, V 4 line 3334; Cymbeline, V 5 line 3561; Cymbeline, V 5 line 3727; Cymbeline, V 5 line 3801.
Hamlet, I 1 line 123; Hamlet, I 2 line 248; Hamlet, I 2 line 427; Hamlet, I 2 line 442; Hamlet, I 3 line 508; Hamlet, I 5 line 817; Hamlet, II 1 line 1036; Hamlet, II 1 lines 1052, 1056; Hamlet, II 2 line 1143;

Hamlet, II 2 line 1256; Hamlet, II 2 line 1531; Hamlet, II 2 line 1552; Hamlet, II 2 line 1580; Hamlet, III 2 line 1995; Hamlet, III 2 line 2018; Hamlet, IV 5 line 2891; Hamlet, IV 5 line 2965; Hamlet, IV 7 line 3279; Hamlet, V 1 line 3511; Hamlet, V 1 lines 3584, 3591; Hamlet, V 2 line 3675; Hamlet, V 2 line 3748; Hamlet, V 2 line 3755; Hamlet, V 2 line 3823; Hamlet, V 2 line 4052.

Henry IV, Part I, I 2 line 269; Henry IV, Part I, I 3 line 431; Henry IV, Part I, I 3 line 455; Henry IV, Part I, I 3 line 491; Henry IV, Part I, I 3 line 622r; Henry IV, Part I, II 1 line 669; Henry IV, Part I, III 1 line 1607; Henry IV, Part I, III 1 line 1764; Henry IV, Part I, III 1 line 1779; Henry IV, Part I, III 1 line 1789; Henry IV, Part I, III 2 line 1926; Henry IV, Part I, III 2 lines 1956, 1967; Henry IV, Part I, III 2 line 1992; Henry IV, Part I, IV 1 line 2303; Henry IV, Part I, IV 2 line 2389; Henry IV, Part I, IV 3 line 2544; Henry IV, Part I, IV 3 line 2563; Henry IV, Part I, IV 4 line 2602; Henry IV, Part I, IV 4 line 2605; Henry IV, Part I, V 1 lines 2670, 2690; Henry IV, Part I, V 1 line 2711; Henry IV, Part I, V 2 line 2789; Henry IV, Part I, V 2 line 2821; Henry IV, Part I, V 3 line 2881; Henry IV, Part I, V 4 line 2978; Henry IV, Part I, V 4 line 2993; Henry IV, Part I, V 4 line 3122; Henry IV, Part I, V 4 line 3031.

Henry IV, Part II, Prologue 1 line 19; Henry IV, Part II, Prologue 1 line 33; Henry IV, Part II, I 1 lines 95, 98; Henry IV, Part II, I 1 line 153; Henry IV, Part II, I 1 line 206; Henry IV, Part II, I 1 line 226; Henry IV, Part II, I 2 line 517; Henry IV, Part II, I 2 line 548; Henry IV, Part II, I 3 line 621; Henry IV, Part II, I 3 line 676; Henry IV, Part II, I 3 line 710; Henry IV, Part II, II 1 line 744; Henry IV, Part II, II 1 line 768; Henry IV, Part II, II 1 line 815; Henry IV, Part II, II 4 line 1675; Henry IV, Part II, III 1 line 1727; Henry IV, Part II, III 1 line 1735; Henry IV, Part II, III 1 line 1781; Henry IV, Part II, III 2 line 1854; Henry IV, Part II, III 2 line 1873; Henry IV, Part II, III 2 lines 2182, 2191; Henry IV, Part II, IV 3 line 2640; Henry IV, Part II, IV 5 line 3010; Henry IV, Part II, IV 5 lines 3061, 3070; Henry IV, Part II, IV 5 line 3082; Henry IV, Part II, V 3 line 3515.

Henry V, I 2 line 242; Henry V, I 2 line 324; Henry V, II 2 line 653; Henry V, II 4 line 970; Henry V, II 4 line 1008; Henry V, III 1 line 1101; Henry V, III 2 line 1168; Henry V, III 2 line 1262; Henry V, III 3 line 1309; Henry V, III 7 line 1766; Henry V, III 7 line 1772; Henry V, IV 0 line 1819; Henry V, IV 1 line 1857; Henry V, IV 1 line 1982; Henry V, IV 1 line 2036; Henry V, IV 2 line 2212; Henry V, IV 3 line 2356.

Henry VI, Part I, I 3 line 446; Henry IV, Part I, I 4 line 562; Henry VI, Part I, I 5 line 625; Henry VI, Part I, II 5 line 1132; Henry IV, Part I, III 2 line 1589; Henry VI, Part I, IV 1 line 1759; Henry VI, Part I, IV 1 line 2019; Henry VI, Part I, V 3 lines 2468, 2471, 2478; Henry VI, Part I, V 3 line 2580.

Henry VI, Part II, I 1 lines 239, 258; Henry VI, Part II, I 2 lines 275, 283, 287; Henry VI, Part II, I 2 lines 302, 307, 311; Henry VI, Part II, I 3 line 454; Henry VI, Part II, I 3 line 531; Henry VI, Part II, I 3 line 596; Henry VI, Part II, II 1 line 917; Henry VI, Part II, II 1 line 935; Henry VI, Part II, II 3 line 1063; Henry VI, Part II, II 4 line 1182; Henry VI, Part II, III 1 lines 1443, 1446; Henry VI, Part II, III 1 line 1638; Henry VI, Part

II, IV 1 line 2167; Henry VI, Part II, IV 1 line 2208; Henry VI, Part II, IV 1 line 2222; Henry VI, Part II, IV 1 line 2301; Henry VI, Part II, IV 2 line 2466; Henry VI, Part II, IV 4 line 2522; Henry VI, Part II, IV 4 line 2527; Henry VI, Part II, IV 4 line 2541; Henry VI, Part II, IV 5 line 2596; Henry VI, Part II, IV 7 line 2711; Henry VI, Part II, IV 7 lines 2726, 2728; Henry VI, Part II, IV 7 line 2736; Henry VI, Part II, IV 7 line 2746; Henry VI, Part II, IV 8 line 2815; Henry VI, Part II, IV 8 line 2824; Henry VI, Part II, IV 10 line 2971; Henry VI, Part II, V 1 line 2978; Henry VI, Part II, V 1 line 3042; Henry VI, Part II, V 1 lines 3045, 3046; Henry VI, Part II, V 1 line 3047; Henry VI, Part II, V 1 line 3068; Henry VI, Part II, V 1 line 3079; Henry VI, Part II, V 1 line 3157.

Henry VI, Part III, I 1 line 19; Henry VI, Part III, I 1 line 23; Henry VI, Part III, I 1 line 121; Henry VI, Part III, I 1 line 122; Henry VI, Part III, I 1 line 250; Henry VI, Part III, I 4 lines 535, 543, 547, 609; Henry VI, Part III, I 4 line 623; Henry VI, Part III, II 1 line 692; Henry VI, Part III, II 1 line 769; Henry VI, Part III, II 1 line 781; Henry VI, Part III, II 1 line 825; Henry VI, Part III, II 2 line 844; Henry VI, Part III, II 2 line 897; Henry VI, Part III, II 2 line 927; Henry VI, Part III, II 2 line 974; Henry VI, Part III, II 6 lines 1305, 1306; Henry VI, Part III, II 6 line 1339; Henry IV, Part III, III 1 line 1339; Henry VI, Part III, III 1 line 1429; Henry VI, Part III, III 2 line 1660; Henry VI, Part III, IV 4 line 2269; Henry VI, Part III, IV 6 line 2337; Henry VI, Part III, IV 6 lines 2383, 2388; Henry VI, Part III, V 1 line 2637; Henry VI, Part III, V 1 line 2651; Henry VI, Part III, V 5 line 2896; Henry VI, Part III, V 5 line 2987; Henry VI, Part III, V 6 line 3048; Henry IV, Part III, V 7 line 3116.

Henry VIII, I 2 line 531; Henry VIII, II 1 line 945; Henry VIII, III 1 line 1630; Henry VIII, III 1 line 1793; Henry VIII, III 2 line 2149; Henry VIII, III 2 line 2209; Henry VIII, IV 1 lines 2430, 2432, 2438, 2440; Henry VIII, IV 2 lines 2649, 2653, 2657; Henry VIII, V 1 line 2975; Henry VIII, V 4 line 3277; Henry VIII, V 4 line 3291; Henry VIII, V 4 lines 3315, 3319; Henry VIII, V 4 line 3354; Henry VIII, V 4 line 3364; Henry VIII, V 5 line 3416.

Julius Caesar, I 2 line 376; Julius Caesar, II 1 lines 783, 802; Julius Caesar, II 1 line 870; Julius Caesar, III 1 line 1323; Julius Caesar, IV 1 line 1905; Julius Caesar, IV 3 line 1995; Julius Caesar, V 1 line 2442; Julius Caesar, V 4 line 2632.

King John, I 1 line 82; King John, II 1 line 707; King John, II 1 line 894; King John, III 1 line 934; King John, III 1 line 1077; King John, III 1 line 1116; King John, III 1 line 1247; King John, III 2 line 1278; King John, III 2 line 1282; King John, III 4 line 1487; King John, IV 1 lines 1623, 1627; King John, IV 1 line 1700; King John, IV 2 line 1869; King John, IV 2 line 1932; King John, IV 2 line 1975; King John, V 2 line 2393; King John, V 4 line 2504.

King Lear, I 4 line 738; King Lear, I 4 line 797; King Lear, I 5 line 905; King Lear, II 4 line 1284; King Lear, III 2 line 1683; King Lear, III 2 line 1699; King Lear, III 2 lines 1701r, 1703, 1704; King Lear, III 2 line 1727; King Lear, III 4 line 1833; King Lear, III 6 lines 2066, 2073; King Lear, III 7 line 2188; King Lear, IV 1 line 2328; King Lear, IV 2 line 2362; King Lear, IV 2 line 2396; King Lear, IV 6 line 2616; King Lear,

IV 6 line 2729; King Lear, IV 6 line 2753; King Lear, IV 6 line 2845; King Lear, V 3 line 3283; King Lear, V 3 line 3295.
Love's Labour's Lost, I 1 line 300; Love's Labour's Lost, IV 1 line 1015; Love's Labour's Lost, IV 1 line 1016; Love's Labour's Lost, IV 2 line 1151; Love's Labour's Lost, IV 3 line 1568; Love's Labour's Lost, IV 3 line 1681; Love's Labour's Lost, V 1 line 1776; Love's Labour's Lost, V 1 line 1782; Love's Labour's Lost, V 1 line 1826; Love's Labour's Lost, V 2 line 1970; Love's Labour's Lost, V 2 line 2484; Love's Labour's Lost, V 2 line 2553; Love's Labour's Lost, V 2 line 2575.
Lover's Complaint, line 8.
Macbeth, 1 2 line 42; Macbeth, II 3 line 883; Macbeth, III 1 line 1070; Macbeth, III 4 line 1303; Macbeth, III 4 line 1443; Macbeth, Iv 1 lines 1608, 1610; Macbeth, IV 1 line 1626; Macbeth, IV 1 line 1665; Macbeth, IV 3 line 1895; Macbeth, V 8 line 2541; Macbeth, V 8 line 2543.
Measure for Measure, I 2 line 159; Measure for Measure, I 2 line 264; Measure for Measure, II 1 lines 681, 683; Measure for Measure, II 4 line 1212; Measure for Measure, III 1 line 1287; Measure for Measure, III 1 line 1321; Measure for Measure, IV 2 line 1886; Measure for Measure, IV 2 lines 1888, 1889; Measure for Measure, IV 2 line 2029; Measure for Measure, IV 2 line 2073; Measure for Measure, IV 2 line 2077; Measure for Measure, IV 2 line 2080; Measure for Measure, IV 2 line 2111; Measure for Measure, IV 3 line 2191; Measure for Measure, IV 3 line 2212; Measure for Measure, IV 3 line 2224; Measure for Measure, IV 3 line 2242; Measure for Measure, IV 3 line 2270; Measure for Measure, IV 3 line 2283; Measure for Measure, V 1 line 2466; Measure for Measure, V 1 line 2505; Measure for Measure, V 1 line 2932; Measure for Measure, V 1 line 2979.
Merchant of Venice, II 2 line 719; Merchant of Venice, II 5 line 880; Merchant of Venice, II 7 line 1030; Merchant of Venice, II 9 line 1189;
Merchant of Venice, II 9 lines 1203, 1207; Merchant of Venice, III 1 line 1279; Merchant of Venice, III 2 line 1432; Merchant of Venice, III 2 line 1462; Merchant of Venice, III 3 line 1723; Merchant of Venice, IV 1 line 2100; Merchant of Venice, IV 1 line 2147; Merchant of Venice, IV 1 line 2153.
Merry Wives of Windsor, I 1 line 114; Merry Wives of Windsor, I 1 line 115; Merry Wives of Windsor, I 4 line 429; Merry Wives of Windsor, I 4 line 432; Merry Wives of Windsor, I 4 line 526; Merry Wives of Windsor, II 1 line 712; Merry Wives of Windsor, II 1 line 741; Merry Wives of Windsor, II 1 line 744; Merry Wives of Windsor, III 5 line 1849; Merry Wives of Windsor, IV 1 line 1906; Merry Wives of Windsor, IV 1 line 1907; Merry Wives of Windsor, IV 2 line 2039; Merry Wives of Windsor, IV 2 line 2246; Merry Wives of Windsor, IV 6 line 2463; Merry Wives of Windsor, V 1 line 2485; Merry Wives of Windsor, V 5 line 2676; Merry Wives of Windsor, V 5 line 2721.
Midsummer Night's Dream, I 1 line 111; Midsummer Night's Dream, I 1 line 177; Midsummer Night's Dream, II 2 line 694; Midsummer

Night's Dream, III 1 line 917; Midsummer Night's Dream, III 2 line 1047; Midsummer Night's Dream, III 2 line 1469; Midsummer Night's Dream, IV 1 line 1548; Midsummer Night's Dream, IV 1 line 1552; Midsummer Night's Dream, IV 1 line 1613; Midsummer Night's Dream, IV 1 line 1629; Midsummer Night's Dream, IV 1 line 1675; Midsummer Night's Dream, IV 1 line 1713; Midsummer Night's Dream, V 1 line 2081.

Much Ado About Nothing, I 1 line 102; Much Ado About Nothing, II 1 line 436; Much Ado About Nothing, II 1 line 500; Much Ado About Nothing, II 1 line 733; Much Ado About Nothing, III 2 line 1207; Much Ado About Nothing, V 1 line 2135; Much Ado About Nothing, V 1 line 2256.

Othello, I 3 line 420; Othello, I 3 lines 487, 490, 524; Othello, I 3 line 626; Othello, II 1 line 943; Othello, III 3 line 2048; Othello, IV 1 line 2481; Othello, IV 2 line 2753; Othello, IV 2 line 2797; Othello, IV 3 line 3053; Othello, IV 3 line 3064.

Passionate Pilgrim, line 304.

Pericles, I 1 line 157; Pericles, I 1 line 159; Pericles, I 1 line 198; Pericles, I 1 line 233; Pericles, I 4 line 440; Pericles, II 3 line 923; Pericles, II 4 line 987; Pericles, III 0 line 1154; Pericles, V 1 line 2456.

Rape of Lucrece, lines 419, 441, 572, 732, 828, 844, 1466, 1478, 1532, 1672, 1712.

Richard II, I 1 line 100; Richard II, I 2 line 221; Richard II, I 3 line 367; Richard II, II 1 line 785; Richard II, II 1 lines 806, 807; Richard II, II 1 line 904; Richard II, II 2 line 1100; Richard II, III 2 line 1536; Richard II, III 2 line 1548; Richard II, III 2 line 1552; Richard II, III 2 line 1582; Richard II, III 3 line 1640; Richard II, III 3 line 1643; Richard II, III 3 line 1649r; Richard II, III 3 line 1652; Richard II, III 3 line 1730; Richard II, III 3 line 1749; Richard II, III 3 lines 1799, 1801; Richard II, III 4 line 1898; Richard II, IV 1 line 1994; Richard II, IV 1 line 2192; Richard II, V 1 line 2393; Richard II, V 1 line 2404; Richard II, V 2 line 2446; Richard II, V 2 line 2471; Richard II, V 6 line 2888; Richard II, V 6 line 2895; Richard II, V 6 line 2919; Richard II, V 6 line 2927.

Richard III, I 4 line 1027; Richard III, II 1 line 1275; Richard III, III 1 line 1769; Richard III, III 2 line 1854; Richard III, III 2 line 1877; Richard III, III 3 line 1933; Richard III, III 4 line 1992; Richard III, III 4 line 2033; Richard III, III 4 line 2051; Richard III, III 4 line 2053; Richard III, III 4 line 2064; Richard III, III 5 line 2091; Richard III, III 5 line 2092; Richard III, IV 2 line 2724; Richard III, IV 4 line 3029; Richard III, IV 4 line 3046; Richard III, IV 4 line 3322; Richard III, IV 5 line 3378; Richard III, V 1 lines 3417, 3421; Richard III, V 3 line 3708; Richard III, V 3 line 3734; Richard III, V 3 line 3855; Richard III, V 3 line 3863.

Romeo and Juliet, I 1 line 37; Romeo and Juliet, I 1 line 38; Romeo and Juliet, I 1 line 39; Romeo and Juliet, I 1 line 132; Romeo and Juliet, II 2 line 863; Romeo and Juliet, II 2 line 874; Romeo and Juliet, II 3 line 1093; Romeo and Juliet, II 5 line 1425r; Romeo and Juliet, III 1 lines 1520, 1521; Romeo and Juliet, III 1 line 1532; Romeo and Juliet, III 1 line 1636; Romeo and Juliet, III 3 line 1893; Romeo and Juliet, III

5 line 2119; Romeo and Juliet, IV 4 line 2637; Romeo and Juliet, V 3 line 3002; Romeo and Juliet, V 3 line 3192; Romeo and Juliet, V 3 line 3282.
Sonnet XXVI line 14; Sonnet XXVII line 3; LXVIII line 7; Sonnet CXXX line 4; Sonnet CXLVIII line 1.
Taming of the Shrew, Prologue 1 line 49; Taming of the Shrew, Prologue 1 line 127; Taming of the Shrew, I 2 line 628; Taming of the Shrew, I 2 line 686; Taming of the Shrew, I 2 line 802; Taming of the Shrew, II 1 line 985; Taming of the Shrew, II 1 line 997; Taming of the Shrew, II 1 line 1260; Taming of the Shrew, IV 1 line 1633; Taming of the Shrew, IV 1 line 1693; Taming of the Shrew, V 2 lines 2531, 2532r; Taming of the Shrew, V 2 line 2655.
Tempest, II 1 line 818; Tempest, II 1 line 928; Tempest, II 2 line 1107; Tempest, III 2 line 1404; Tempest, III 2 line 1428; Tempest, III 2 line 1508; Tempest, III 3 line 1619; Tempest, V 1 line 2016; Tempest, V 1 line 2331.
Timon of Athens, I 1 line 93; Timon of Athens, I 1 line 114; Timon of Athens, II 2 line 825; Timon of Athens, II 2 line 858; Timon of Athens, II 2 line 897; Timon of Athens, III 4 line 1240; Timon of Athens, III 5 line 1335; Timon of Athens, IV 2 line 1635; Timon of Athens, IV 3 line 1696.
Titus Andronicus, I 1 line 210; Titus Andronicus, I 1 line 211; Titus Andronicus, II 3 line 772; Titus Andronicus, III 1 line 1338; Titus Andronicus, III 1 line 1372; Titus Andronicus, III 1 line 1395; Titus Andronicus, III 1 lines 1412, 1420; Titus Andronicus, IV 4 line 2077; Titus Andronicus, IV 4 line 2084; Titus Andronicus, V 1 lines 2237, 2250; Titus Andronicus, V 2 line 2359; Titus Andronicus, V 2 lines 2507, 2519.
Troilus and Cressida, I 2 line 284; Troilus and Cressida, I 3 line 641; Troilus and Cressida, I 3 line 675; Troilus and Cressida, I 3 line 677; Troilus and Cressida, II 1 line 882; Troilus and Cressida, II 1 line 931; Troilus and Cressida, II 3 line 1305; Troilus and Cressida, III 1 line 1561; Troilus and Cressida, III 3 line 2139; Troilus and Cressida, IV 2 line 2326; Troilus and Cressida, IV 4 line 2577; Troilus and Cressida, IV 5 line 2599; Troilus and Cressida, IV 5 line 2629; Troilus and Cressida, IV 5 line 2646; Troilus and Cressida, V 2 line 3263; Troilus and Cressida, V 6 line 3512.
Twelfth Night, I 3 line 204; Twelfth Night, III 4 line 1879; Twelfth Night, V 1 line 2375; Twelfth Night, V 1 line 2382; Twelfth Night, V 1 line 2617.
Two Gentlemen of Verona, II 4 line 720; Two Gentlemen of Verona, III 1 line 1087; Two Gentlemen of Verona, III 1 line 1265.
Venus and Adonis, lines 34, 138, 243, 316, 687, 1060, 1080, 1193.
Winter's Tale, I 2 line 275; Winter's Tale, III 3 line 1512; Winter's Tale, IV 4 line 2118; Winter's Tale, IV 4 line 2149; Winter's Tale, IV 4 line 2211; Winter's Tale, IV 4 line 2762; Winter's Tale, V 2 line 3223; Winter's Tale, V 3 line 3439.

Heart: Old English: *heorte: heart; breast, soul, spirit, will, desire; courage; mind, intellect.* The heart was esteemed the seat of the understanding. It is compassion and understanding, life-giving and complex. It is a symbol for love. Often known as the seat of emotions, the heart is synonymous with affection. In Egypt, represented life-essence, as the mummified had their heart preserved, first part of man to live, last to die. Hearts also carry senses of intellect and understanding, as well as connotations of the soul, along with come will and courage.

All's Well That Ends Well, I 1 line 47; All's Well That Ends Well, I 1 line 96r; All's Well That Ends Well, I 3 line 373; All's Well That Ends Well, I 3 line 405; All's Well That Ends Well, I 3 line 411; All's Well That Ends Well, II 1 line 601; All's Well That Ends Well, II 1 line 616; All's Well That Ends Well, II 3 line 1119; All's Well That Ends Well, II 3 line 1170; All's Well That Ends Well, II 3 line 1173; All's Well That Ends Well, II 5 line 1275; All's Well That Ends Well, III 2 line 1483; All's Well That Ends Well, III 4 line 1602; All's Well That Ends Well, III 5 line 1683; All's Well That Ends Well, III 6 line 1844; All's Well That Ends Well, IV 1 line 1931; All's Well That Ends Well, IV 3 line 2410; All's Well That Ends Well, V 3 line 2692; All's Well That Ends Well, V 3 line 2726; All's Well That Ends Well, V 3 line 3064.

Antony and Cleopatra, I 1 line 7; Antony and Cleopatra, I 2 line 146; Antony and Cleopatra, I 3 line 346; Antony and Cleopatra, I 3 lines 349, 357; Antony and Cleopatra, I 3 line 409; Antony and Cleopatra, I 5 line 568; Antony and Cleopatra, II 1 line 632; Antony and Cleopatra, II 2 line 836; Antony and Cleopatra, II 2 line 863; Antony and Cleopatra, II 2 line 867; Antony and Cleopatra, II 2 line 910; Antony and Cleopatra, II 2 line 951; Antony and Cleopatra, II 2 line 970; Antony and Cleopatra, II 6 line 1281; Antony and Cleopatra, II 6 line 1337; Antony and Cleopatra, III 2 line 1609; Antony and Cleopatra, III 2 line 1638; Antony and Cleopatra, III 2 lines 1649, 1650; Antony and Cleopatra, III 4 line 1792; Antony and Cleopatra, III 6 line 1909; Antony and Cleopatra, III 6 line 1914; Antony and Cleopatra, III 6 line 1926; Antony and Cleopatra, III 7 line 1949; Antony and Cleopatra, III 11 line 2174; Antony and Cleopatra, III 13 line 2406; Antony and Cleopatra, III 13 line 2445; Antony and Cleopatra, III 13 line 2461; Antony and Cleopatra, III 13 line 2467; Antony and Cleopatra, III 13 line 2490; Antony and Cleopatra, IV 2 line 2568; Antony and Cleopatra, IV 4 line 2629; Antony and Cleopatra, IV 6 line 2746; Antony and Cleopatra, IV 14 line 2996; Antony and Cleopatra, IV 14 line 3017; Antony and Cleopatra, IV 14 lines 3029, 3030; Antony and Cleopatra, IV 15 line 3267; Antony and Cleopatra, V 1 lines 3306, 3307; Antony and Cleopatra, V 1 lines 3329, 3333; Antony and Cleopatra, V 1 line 3346; Antony and Cleopatra, V 2 line 3516.

As You Like It, I 1 line 133; As You Like It, I 1 line 140; As You Like It, I 2 line 310; As You Like It, I 2 line 353; As You Like It, I 3 line 422; As You Like It, I 3 line 526; As You Like It, II 4 line 725; As You Like It, II 4 line 750; As You Like It, II 5 line 841; As You Like It, II 6 line 881; As You Like It, III 1 line 1115; As You Like It, III 2 lines 1257, 1263; As You Like It, III 2 lines 1124, 1128; As You Like It, III 2 line 1263; As You Like It, III 2 line 1316; As You Like It, III 2 line 1345; As You Like It, III 2 line 1369; As You Like It, III 2 line 1494; As You Like It, III 2 line 1502; As

You Like It, III 3 line 1543; As You Like It, III 4 line 1630; As You Like It, III 5 line 1654; As You Like It, III 5 line 1666; As You Like It, III 5 line 1791; As You Like It, III 5 line 1793; As You Like It, IV 1 line 1838; As You Like It, IV 3 line 2043; As You Like It, IV 3 line 2047; As You Like It, IV 3 line 2157; As You Like It, IV 3 line 2172; As You Like It, IV 3 line 2179; As You Like It, V 2 line 2267; As You Like It, V 2 line 2269; As You Like It, V 2 line 2288; As You Like It, V 2 line 2301; As You Like It, V 3 line 2363; As You Like It, V 4 line 2508; As You Like It, V 4 line 2525r.
Comedy of Errors, III 1 line 642; Comedy of Errors, III 2 line 775; Comedy of Errors, III 2 line 826r; Comedy of Errors, III 2 line 902; Comedy of Errors, IV 2 line 1077; Comedy of Errors, IV 2 line 1091; Comedy of Errors, IV 2 line 1101; Comedy of Errors, IV 2 line 1109; Comedy of Errors, IV 4 line 1336; Comedy of Errors, IV 4 line 1418; Comedy of Errors, V 1 line 1852.
Coriolanus, I 1 line 109; Coriolanus, I 1 line 133; Coriolanus, I 1 line 217; Coriolanus, I 4 lines 514, 515; Coriolanus, I 6 line 650; Coriolanus, I 6 line 681; Coriolanus, I 9 line 771; Coriolanus, I 9 line 807; Coriolanus, I 10 line 906; Coriolanus, II 1 line 1091; Coriolanus, II 1 line 1116; Coriolanus, II 1 line 1221; Coriolanus, II 2 line 1254; Coriolanus, II 2 line 1289; Coriolanus, II 3 line 1532; Coriolanus, II 3 line 1539; Coriolanus, II 3 line 1543; Coriolanus, II 3 line 1593; Coriolanus, II 3 line 1594; Coriolanus, II 3 line 1653; Coriolanus, III 1 line 2057; Coriolanus, III 2 line 2201; Coriolanus, III 2 line 2233; Coriolanus, III 2 line 2259; Coriolanus, III 2 line 2269; Coriolanus, III 2 line 2286; Coriolanus, III 2 line 2317; Coriolanus, III 2 line 2323; Coriolanus, III 3 line 2379; Coriolanus, III 3 line 2497; Coriolanus, III 3 line 2532; Coriolanus, IV 3 line 2548; Coriolanus, IV 3 line 2653; Coriolanus, IV 3 line 2683; Coriolanus, IV 3 line 2709; Coriolanus, IV 4 line 2734; Coriolanus, IV 5 line 2781; Coriolanus, IV 5 lines 2844, 2850; Coriolanus, IV 5 lines 2869, 2882; Coriolanus, V 1 line 3336; Coriolanus, V 3 line 3500; Coriolanus, V 3 line 3605; Coriolanus, V 6 line 3937; Coriolanus, V 6 line 3944.
Cymbeline, I 1 line 12; Cymbeline, I 1 line 18; Cymbeline, I 1 line 137; Cymbeline, I 4 line 417; Cymbeline, I 5 line 519; Cymbeline, I 6 line 632; Cymbeline, I 6 line 701; Cymbeline, I 6 line 744; Cymbeline, I 6 line 757; Cymbeline, I 6 line 797; Cymbeline, II 1 line 905; Cymbeline, II 3 line 1106; Cymbeline, II 4 line 1213; Cymbeline, II 4 line 1369; Cymbeline, III 4 line 1791; Cymbeline, III 4 lines 1803, 1809; Cymbeline, III 4 line 1904; Cymbeline, III 5 lines 2054, 2055; Cymbeline, III 5 line 2111; Cymbeline, IV 2 line 2360; Cymbeline, IV 2 line 2419; Cymbeline, IV 2 line 2726; Cymbeline, V 3 line 3030; Cymbeline, V 3 line 3072; Cymbeline, V 4 line 3212; Cymbeline, V 5 line 3366; Cymbeline, V 5 line 3383; Cymbeline, V 5 line 3443; Cymbeline, V 5 line 3465; Cymbeline, V 5 line 3507; Cymbeline, V 5 line 3552.
Hamlet, I 1 line 10; Hamlet, I 2 line 203; Hamlet, I 2 lines 241, 247; Hamlet, I 2 lines 298, 303; Hamlet, I 2 line 327; Hamlet, I 2 line 363; Hamlet, I 3 line 515; Hamlet, I 3 line 530; Hamlet, I 5 line 831; Hamlet,

I 5 line 865; Hamlet, I 5 lines 880, 881; Hamlet, II 2 line 1235; Hamlet, II 2 line 1660; Hamlet, III 1 line 1709; Hamlet, III 1 line 1755; Hamlet, III 1 line 1865; Hamlet, III 2 line 1952rr; Hamlet, III 2 line 2050; Hamlet, III 2 line 2243; Hamlet, III 2 line 2269; Hamlet, III 3 line 2352; Hamlet, III 4 line 2425; Hamlet, III 4 line 2559; Hamlet, IV 5 line 2862; Hamlet, IV 7 line 3132; Hamlet, IV 7 line 3190; Hamlet, IV 7 line 3252; Hamlet, V 2 line 3653; Hamlet, V 2 line 3847; Hamlet, V 2 line 4006; Hamlet, V 2 line 4021.

Henry IV, Part I, I 3 line 454; Henry IV, Part I, II 2 line 767; Henry IV, Part I, II 3 line 889; Henry IV, Part I, II 4 line 1036; Henry IV, Part I, II 4 line 1112; Henry IV, Part I, III 1 line 1672; Henry IV, Part I, III 1 line 1732; Henry IV, Part I, III 1 line 1772; Henry IV, Part I, III 1 line 1800; Henry IV, Part I, III 1 line 1820; Henry IV, Part I, III 2 line 1841; Henry IV, Part I, III 2 lines 1857, 1875; Henry IV, Part I, III 2 line 1976; Henry IV, Part I, III 3 line 2013; Henry IV, Part I, III 3 line 2059; Henry IV, Part I, IV 1 line 2227; Henry IV, Part I, IV 1 line 2307; Henry IV, Part I, IV 2 line 2388; Henry IV, Part I, IV 3 line 2462; Henry IV, Part I, IV 3 lines 2523, 2543; Henry IV, Part I, V 4 line 2982; Henry IV, Part I, V 4 line 3051; Henry IV, Part I, V 5 line 3167.

Henry IV, Part II, I 1 line 62; Henry IV, Part II, I 1 line 216; Henry IV, Part II, I 3 line 697; Henry IV, Part II, II 2 line 1001; Henry IV, Part II, II 3 line 1167; Henry IV, Part II, II 3 line 1200; Henry IV, Part II, II 4 line 1233; Henry IV, Part II, II 4 line 1256; Henry IV, Part II, II 4 line 1268; Henry IV, Part II, II 4 line 1447; Henry IV, Part II, II 4 line 1498; Henry IV, Part II, II 4 line 1561; Henry IV, Part II, II 4 line 1597; Henry IV, Part II, II 4 line 1691; Henry IV, Part II, II 4 line 1696; Henry IV, Part II, III 1 line 1745; Henry IV, Part II, III 2 line 1875; Henry IV, Part II, III 2 line 2057; Henry IV, Part II, IV 1 line 2215; Henry IV, Part II, IV 1 line 2362; Henry IV, Part II, IV 2 line 2462; Henry IV, Part II, IV 3 line 2704; Henry IV, Part II, IV 4 line 2806; Henry IV, Part II, IV 5 line 3003; Henry IV, Part II, IV 5 line 3047; Henry IV, Part II, V 1 line 3203; Henry IV, Part II, V 2 line 3301; Henry IV, Part II, V 3 line 3418; Henry IV, Part II, V 3 line 3424; Henry IV, Part II, V 3 line 3448; Henry IV, Part II, V 3 line 3557; Henry IV, Part II, V 5 line 3639.

Henry V, I 2 line 175; Henry V, I 2 line 274; Henry V, II 0 line 480; Henry V, II 1 line 592; Henry V, II 1 line 623; Henry V, II 1 line 629; Henry V, II 2 line 656; Henry V, II 2 line 662; Henry V, II 2 line 666; Henry V, II 2 line 794; Henry V, II 3 line 834; Henry V, II 4 line 1001; Henry V, III 3 line 1283; Henry V, III 5 line 1449; Henry V, III 6 line 1468; Henry V, III 6 line 1486; Henry V, IV 1 line 1879; Henry V, IV 1 lines 1890, 1893; Henry V, IV 1 line 1960; Henry V, IV 1 line 2082; Henry V, IV 1 lines 2139, 2142; Henry V, IV 3 line 2353; Henry V, IV 4 line 2438; Henry V, IV 7 line 2680; Henry V, IV 8 line 2755; Henry V, V 1 line 2908; Henry V, V 1 line 2938; Henry V, V 2 line 3022; Henry V, V 2 line 3085; Henry V, V 2 line 3088; Henry V, V 2 line 3156; Henry V, V 2 line 3183; Henry V, V 2 line 3219; Henry V, V 2 line 3274; Henry V, V 2 line 3342.

Henry VI, Part I, I 2 line 306; Henry VI, Part I, I 3 line 375; Henry VI, Part I, I 3 line 442; Henry VI, Part I, I 4 line 493; Henry VI, Part I, I 4 line 514; Henry VI, Part I, I 4 lines 568, 571; Henry VI, Part I, II 3 line 914; Henry VI, Part I, II 4 line 1019; Henry VI, Part I, III 1 line 1247; Henry VI, Part I, III 1 line 1292; Henry VI, Part I, III 1 line 1351; Henry VI, Part I, III 1 line 1367; Henry VI, Part I, III 2 line 1538; Henry VI, Part I, III 2 line 1552; Henry VI, Part I, III 2 line 1584; Henry VI, Part I, III 2 line 1600; Henry VI, Part I, III 3 line 1692; Henry VI, Part I, III 4 line 1716; Henry VI, Part I, IV 1 line 1839; Henry VI, Part I, IV 1 line 1872; Henry VI, Part I, IV 1 line 1952; Henry VI, Part I, IV 3 line 2052; Henry VI, Part I, IV 6 line 2203; Henry VI, Part I, IV 6 line 2235; Henry VI, Part I, IV 7 line 2262; Henry VI, Part I, V 3 line 2521; Henry VI, Part I, V 3 line 2652; Henry VI, Part I, V 4 line 2672; Henry VI, Part I, V 4 line 2730; Henry VI, Part I, V 5 line 2857.

Henry VI, Part II, I 1 line 24; Henry VI, Part II, I 1 line 35; Henry VI, Part II, I 1 line 39; Henry VI, Part II, I 1 line 61; Henry VI, Part II, I 1 line 133; Henry VI, Part II, I 1 line 165; Henry VI, Part II, I 1 line 207; Henry VI, Part II, I 1 line 247; Henry VI, Part II, I 3 line 443; Henry VI, Part II, I 3 line 472; Henry VI, Part II, I 3 line 618; Henry VI, Part II, II 1 line 746; Henry VI, Part II, II 1 line 792; Henry VI, Part II, II 1 line 913; Henry VI, Part II, II 1 line 930; Henry VI, Part II, II 2 line 1022; Henry VI, Part II, II 2 line 1034; Henry VI, Part II, II 3 line 1061; Henry VI, Part II, II 4 line 1228; Henry VI, Part II, III 1 line 1305; Henry VI, Part II, III 1 line 1380; Henry VI, Part II, III 1 lines 1435, 1438; Henry VI, Part II, III 1 line 1480; Henry VI, Part II, III 1 line 1553; Henry VI, Part II, III 1 lines 1622, 1631; Henry VI, Part II, III 2 line 1741; Henry VI, Part II, III 2 lines 1780, 1788, 1790, 1792; Henry VI, Part II, III 2 lines 1848, 1851; Henry VI, Part II, III 2 line 1884; Henry VI, Part II, III 2 line 1919; Henry VI, Part II, III 2 line 1995; Henry VI, Part II, III 2 line 2001; Henry VI, Part II, III 2 line 2014; Henry VI, Part II, III 2 line 2105; Henry VI, Part II, IV 1 line 2241; Henry VI, Part II, IV 4 line 2558; Henry VI, Part II, IV 7 line 2741; Henry VI, Part II, IV 8 line 2794; Henry VI, Part II,V 1 line 3072; Henry VI, Part II, V 1 line 3132; Henry VI, Part II, V 2 line 3267; Henry VI, Part II, V 2 line 3290; Henry VI, Part II, V 2 lines 3309, 3312.

Henry VI, Part III, I 1 line 66; Henry VI, Part III, I 1 line 76; Henry VI, Part III, I 1 line 135; Henry VI, Part III, I 1 line 170; Henry VI, Part III, I 1 line 192; Henry VI, Part III, I 1 line 240; Henry VI, Part III, I 1 line 288; Henry VI, Part III, I 2 line 328; Henry VI, Part III, I 3 line 406; Henry VI, Part III, I 4 line 493; Henry VI, Part III, I 4 line 526; Henry VI, Part III, I 4 line 577; Henry VI, Part III, I 4 line 608; Henry VI, Part III, I 4 line 618; Henry VI, Part III, II 1 lines 707, 708; Henry VI, Part III, II 1 line 763; Henry VI, Part III, II 1 line 829; Henry VI, Part III, II 2 line 846; Henry VI, Part III, II 2 line 883; Henry VI, Part III, II 2 line 922; Henry VI, Part III, II 2 line 956; Henry VI, Part III, II 2 line 988; Henry VI, Part III, II 2 line 995; Henry VI, Part III, II 3 line 1053; Henry VI, Part III, II 3 line 1064; Henry VI, Part III, II 4 line 1094; Henry VI, Part III, II 5 line 1181; Henry VI, Part III, II 5 lines 1192, 1193; Henry VI, Part III, II 5 lines 1221, 1222; Henry VI, Part III, II 5 line 1230; Henry VI, Part III, III 1 line 1405; Henry VI, Part III, III 1 line 1429; Henry VI, Part III, III 2 lines 1633, 1672; Henry VI, Part III, III 3 line 1702; Henry VI, Part III, III 3 line 1703; Henry VI, Part III, III 3 line 1755; Henry VI, Part III, III 3

line 1874; Henry VI, Part III, III 3 line 1875; Henry VI, Part III, IV 2 line 2139; Henry VI, Part III, IV 6 line 2353; Henry VI, Part III, IV 6 lines 2410, 2411; Henry VI, Part III, IV 8 line 2350; Henry VI, Part III, V 1 line 2702; Henry VI, Part III, V 2 line 2730; Henry VI, Part III, V 4 line 2870; Henry VI, Part III, V 5 lines 2959, 2960.
Henry VIII, I 1 line 157; Henry VIII, I 2 line 316; Henry VIII, I 2 line 341; Henry VIII, I 2 line 389; Henry VIII, I 2 line 520; Henry VIII, I 4 line 795; Henry VIII, II 1 line 899; Henry VIII, II 1 line 914; Henry VIII, II 1 line 965; Henry VIII, II 2 line 1060; Henry VIII, II 2 line 1067; Henry VIII, II 2 line 1154; Henry VIII, II 3 line 1212; Henry VIII, II 3 line 1235; Henry VIII, II 4 line 1473; Henry VIII, III 1 line 1633; Henry VIII, III 1 line 1741; Henry VIII, III 1 line 1785; Henry VIII, III 1 line 1803; Henry VIII, III 1 line 1821; Henry VIII, III 2 line 1969; Henry VIII, III 2 line 2033; Henry VIII, III 2 lines 2064, 2065; Henry VIII, III 2 line 2237; Henry VIII, III 2 line 2270; Henry VIII, III 2 line 2299; Henry VIII, III 2 line 2338; Henry VIII, III 2 line 2357; Henry VIII, IV 2 line 2714; Henry VIII, V 1 line 2802; Henry VIII, V 1 line 2853; Henry VIII, V 1 line 2965; Henry VIII, V 2 line 3020; Henry VIII, V 3 lines 3096, 3100; Henry VIII, V 3 line 3255; Henry VIII, V 3 line 3259; Henry VIII, V 5 line 3396.
Julius Caesar, I 1 line 37; Julius Caesar, I 2 line 199; Julius Caesar, I 2 line 300; Julius Caesar, I 2 line 366; Julius Caesar, I 3 line 590; Julius Caesar, II 1 line 795; Julius Caesar, II 1 line 918; Julius Caesar, II 1 line 936; Julius Caesar, II 1 line 966; Julius Caesar, II 2 line 1018; Julius Caesar, II 2 line 1020; Julius Caesar, II 2 line 1118; Julius Caesar, II 3 line 1132; Julius Caesar, II 4 line 1145; Julius Caesar, II 4 line 1183; Julius Caesar, III 1 line 1237; Julius Caesar, III 1 line 1337; Julius Caesar, III 1 lines 1390, 1395; Julius Caesar, III 1 line 1430; Julius Caesar, III 1 line 1513; Julius Caesar, III 2 line 1650; Julius Caesar, III 2 line 1667; Julius Caesar, III 2 line 1731; Julius Caesar, III 2 line 1760; Julius Caesar, III 3 line 1854; Julius Caesar, IV 1 line 1913; Julius Caesar, IV 3 line 2024; Julius Caesar, IV 3 line 2057; Julius Caesar, IV 3 line 2107; Julius Caesar, IV 3 line 2162; Julius Caesar, IV 3 line 2318; Julius Caesar, V 1 line 2380; Julius Caesar, V 3 line 2567; Julius Caesar, V 3 line 2602; Julius Caesar, V 5 line 2712.
King John, I 1 lines 273, 277, 278, 280; King John, II 1 line 293; King John, II 1 line 306; King John, II 1 line 576; King John, II 1 line 819; King John, III 4 line 1512; King John, III 4 line 1537; King John, III 4 1552; King John, IV 1 line 1623; King John, IV 1 line 1674; King John, IV 2 lines 1775, 1778; King John, IV 2 line 1921; King John, IV 2 line 1983; King John, V 2 lines 2325, 2333; King John, V 2 line 2370; King John, V 2 line 2439; King John, V 3 line 2470; King John, V 5 line 2567; King John, V 7 lines 2687, 2690.
King Lear, I 1 line 71; King Lear, I 1 line 94; King Lear, I 1 line 108; King Lear, I 1 line 119; King Lear, I 1 line 132; King Lear, I 1 lines 151, 159; King Lear, I 2 line 390; King Lear, I 2 line 398; King Lear, I 2 line 413; King Lear, I 2 line 430; King Lear, I 4 line 522; King Lear, I 4 line 784; King Lear, I 4 line 795; King Lear, I 4 line 861; King Lear, II 1 line 1027; King Lear, II 4 line 1333; King Lear, II 4 line 1398r; King Lear, II 4 line 1415; King Lear, II 4 line 1445; King Lear, II 4 lines 1575, 1585;

King Lear, III 1 line 1635; King Lear, III 2 line 1707; King Lear, III 2 line 1751; King Lear, III 4 line 1806; King Lear, III 4 line 1822; King Lear, III 4 line 1856; King Lear, III 4 line 1879; King Lear, III 4 lines 1881, 1882, 1887, 1890; King Lear, III 4 line 1907; King Lear, III 4 line 1924; King Lear, III 6 line 2056; King Lear, III 6 line 2065; King Lear, III 6 lines 2078, 2079; King Lear, III 7 line 2175; King Lear, III 7 line 2191; King Lear, IV 3 line 2481; King Lear, IV 3 line 2503; King Lear, IV 5 line 2563; King Lear, IV 6 line 2635; King Lear, IV 6 line 2750; King Lear, IV 6 line 2840; King Lear, IV 6 line 2882; King Lear, V 3 line 3230; King Lear, V 3 lines 3275, 3281, 3288; King Lear, V 3 line 3296; King Lear, V 3 line 3335; King Lear, V 3 line 3390; King Lear, V 3 line 3502.

Love's Labour's Lost, I 1 line 273; Love's Labour's Lost, II 1 line 665; Love's Labour's Lost, II 1 line 672; Love's Labour's Lost, II 1 line 676; Love's Labour's Lost, II 1 line 729; Love's Labour's Lost, II 1 line 736; Love's Labour's Lost, III 1 line 796; Love's Labour's Lost, III 1 line 797r; Love's Labour's Lost, III 1 line 798; Love's Labour's Lost, III 1 lines 801, 802r, 803, 804r; Love's Labour's Lost, III 1 line 949; Love's Labour's Lost, IV 1 lines 1005, 1007; Love's Labour's Lost, IV 1 line 1060; Love's Labour's Lost, IV 3 line 1385; Love's Labour's Lost, IV 3 line 1464; Love's Labour's Lost, IV 3 line 1484; Love's Labour's Lost, V 1 lines 1832, 1836; Love's Labour's Lost, V 2 line 1881; Love's Labour's Lost, V 2 line 1898; Love's Labour's Lost, V 2 line 2033; Love's Labour's Lost, V 2 line 2116; Love's Labour's Lost, V 2 line 2189; Love's Labour's Lost, V 2 line 2253; Love's Labour's Lost, V 2 line 2343; Love's Labour's Lost, V 2 line 2653; Love's Labour's Lost, V 2 line 2678; Love's Labour's Lost, V 2 line 2744; Love's Labour's Lost, V 2 line 2758; Love's Labour's Lost, V 2 line 2781.

Lover's Complaint, lines 143, 176, 192, 196, 204, 276, 311, 316, 327.

Macbeth, I 3 line 249; Macbeth, I 3 line 271; Macbeth, I 4 line 312; Macbeth, I 5 line 348; Macbeth, I 7 line 566; Macbeth, II 2 line 730; Macbeth, II 3 line 795; Macbeth, II 3 line 835; Macbeth, II 3 line 905; Macbeth, III 1 line 1121; Macbeth, III 2 line 1207; Macbeth, III 4 line 1273; Macbeth, III 4 line 1280; Macbeth, III 4 line 1282; Macbeth, III 6 line 1506; Macbeth, IV 1 line 1648; Macbeth, IV 1 line 1668; Macbeth, IV 1 line 1680; Macbeth, IV 1 line 1727; Macbeth, IV 3 line 2089; Macbeth, IV 3 line 2113; Macbeth, V 1 line 2176; Macbeth, V 1 line 2177; Macbeth, V 3 line 2255; Macbeth, V 3 line 2270; Macbeth, V 3 line 2300; Macbeth, V 4 line 2341.

Measure for Measure, I 1 line 52; Measure for Measure, I 4 line 385; Measure for Measure, II 1 line 698; Measure for Measure, II 2 line 810; Measure for Measure, II 2 line 904; Measure for Measure, II 4 line 1022; Measure for Measure, II 4 line 1040; Measure for Measure, III 1 line 1288; Measure for Measure, IV 3 line 2180; Measure for Measure, IV 3 line 2262; Measure for Measure, IV 3 line 2275; Measure for Measure, IV 3 line 2280; Measure for Measure, V 1 line 2390; Measure for Measure, V 1 line 2650; Measure for Measure, V 1 line 2806; Measure for Measure, V 1 line 2813; Measure for Measure, V 1 line 2916.

Merchant of Venice, I 1 line 88; Merchant of Venice, I 2 line 317; Merchant of Venice, I 3 line 428; Merchant of Venice, II 1 line 543; Merchant of Venice, II 2 line 578; Merchant of Venice, II 6 line 965; Merchant of Venice, II 7 line 1065; Merchant of Venice, II 9 line 1149; Merchant of Venice, III 1 line 1358; Merchant of Venice, III 2 line 1431; Merchant of Venice, III 2 line 1450; Merchant of Venice, III 2 line 1491; Merchant of Venice, III 2 line 1565; Merchant of Venice, III 4 line 1785; Merchant of Venice, III 4 line 1792; Merchant of Venice, IV 1 line 1963; Merchant of Venice, IV 1 line 2012; Merchant of Venice, IV 1 line 2083; Merchant of Venice, IV 1 line 2135; Merchant of Venice, IV 1 line 2153; Merchant of Venice, IV 1 line 2175; Merchant of Venice, IV 1 line 2185; Merchant of Venice, IV 1 line 2198; Merchant of Venice, IV 1 line 2226; Merchant of Venice, V 1 line 2610; Merchant of Venice, V 1 line 2630; Merchant of Venice, V 1 line 2655.

Merry Wives of Windsor, I 1 lines 75, 77r; Merry Wives of Windsor, I 1 line 247; Merry Wives of Windsor, II 1 line 781; Merry Wives of Windsor, II 2 line 863; Merry Wives of Windsor, II 2 line 884; Merry Wives of Windsor, II 2 line 888; Merry Wives of Windsor, II 2 line 899; Merry Wives of Windsor, II 2 line 1013; Merry Wives of Windsor, II 2 lines 1073, 1093, 1094; Merry Wives of Windsor, II 3 line 1127; Merry Wives of Windsor, III 1 line 1252; Merry Wives of Windsor, III 1 line 1295; Merry Wives of Windsor, III 1 line 1308; Merry Wives of Windsor, III 2 line 1387; Merry Wives of Windsor, III 2 line 1396; Merry Wives of Windsor, III 3 line 1615; Merry Wives of Windsor, III 3 line 1626; Merry Wives of Windsor, III 4 line 1687; Merry Wives of Windsor, III 4 lines 1735, 1736; Merry Wives of Windsor, III 5 line 1782; Merry Wives of Windsor, III 5 line 1786; Merry Wives of Windsor, IV 1 line 1902; Merry Wives of Windsor, IV 2 line 1979; Merry Wives of Windsor, IV 2 line 2031; Merry Wives of Windsor, IV 2 line 2113; Merry Wives of Windsor, IV 2 line 2172; Merry Wives of Windsor, IV 5 line 2404; Merry Wives of Windsor, IV 5 line 2417; Merry Wives of Windsor, IV 6 line 2472; Merry Wives of Windsor, V 3 line 2538; Merry Wives of Windsor, V 5 line 2582; Merry Wives of Windsor, V 5 line 2651; Merry Wives of Windsor, V 5 line 2664; Merry Wives of Windsor, V 5 line 2720; Merry Wives of Windsor, V 5 line 2781.

Midsummer Night's Dream, I 1 line 39; Midsummer Night's Dream, I 1 line 201; Midsummer Night's Dream, I 2 line 328; Midsummer Night's Dream, II 1 line 491; Midsummer Night's Dream, II 1 line 532; Midsummer Night's Dream, II 1 lines 570, 571; Midsummer Night's Dream, II 1 line 604; Midsummer Night's Dream, II 2 line 696; Midsummer Night's Dream, II 2 lines 701, 702; Midsummer Night's Dream, II 2 line 764; Midsummer Night's Dream, II 2 line 810; Midsummer Night's Dream, III 1 line 1004; Midsummer Night's Dream, III 1 line 1092; Midsummer Night's Dream, III 2 line 1193; Midsummer Night's Dream, III 2 line 1202; Midsummer Night's Dream, III 2 line 1209; Midsummer Night's Dream, III 2 line 1252; Midsummer Night's Dream, III 2 line 1331; Midsummer Night's Dream, III 2 line 1368; Midsummer Night's Dream, IV 1 line 1727; Midsummer Night's Dream, IV 1 line 1775; Midsummer Night's Dream, IV 2 line 1809; Midsummer

Night's Dream, V 1 line 1861; Midsummer Night's Dream, V 1 line 2063; Midsummer Night's Dream, V 1 line 2132; Midsummer Night's Dream, V 1 line 2142.

Much Ado About Nothing, I 1 lines 113, 114; Much Ado About Nothing, I 1 lines 134, 136; Much Ado About Nothing, I 1 line 295; Much Ado About Nothing, II 1 line 402; Much Ado About Nothing, II 1 line 561; Much Ado About Nothing, II 1 line 657; Much Ado About Nothing, II 1 line 660; Much Ado About Nothing, II 1 line 690; Much Ado About Nothing, II 1 line 693; Much Ado About Nothing, II 3 line 961; Much Ado About Nothing, II 3 line 1011; Much Ado About Nothing, III 1 line 1126; Much Ado About Nothing, III 1 line 1192; Much Ado About Nothing, III 2 lines 1210, 1211; Much Ado About Nothing, III 2 line 1285; Much Ado About Nothing, III 4 line 1513; Much Ado About Nothing, III 4 line 1544; Much Ado About Nothing, III 4 line 1555; Much Ado About Nothing, III 4 lines 1564, 1568; Much Ado About Nothing, III 5 line 1599; Much Ado About Nothing, IV 1 line 1746; Much Ado About Nothing, IV 1 line 1936; Much Ado About Nothing, IV 1 line 1937; Much Ado About Nothing, IV 1 line 1956; Much Ado About Nothing, V 1 line 2141; Much Ado About Nothing, V 1 line 2180; Much Ado About Nothing, V 1 line 2248; Much Ado About Nothing, V 1 line 2278; Much Ado About Nothing, V 1 line 2387; Much Ado About Nothing, V 2 line 2471r; Much Ado About Nothing, V 2 line 2502; Much Ado About Nothing, V 4 line 2577; Much Ado About Nothing, V 1 line 2645; Much Ado About Nothing, V 4 line 2672.

Othello, I 1 lines 51, 62, 64; Othello, I 1 line 92; Othello, I 3 line 497; Othello, I 3 lines 542, 543; Othello, I 3 line 568; Othello, I 3 line 602; Othello, I 3 line 631; Othello, I 3 line 661; Othello, I 3 line 725; Othello, II 1 line 893; Othello, II 1 line 993; Othello, II 1 line 1023; Othello, II 3 line 1361; Othello, II 3 line 1454; Othello, III 3 line 1768; Othello, III 3 line 1813; Othello, III 3 line 1922; Othello, III 3 line 2133; Othello, III 4 line 2215; Othello, III 4 line 2223; Othello, III 4 lines 2224, 2225; Othello, III 4 line 2259; Othello, III 4 line 2304; Othello, IV 1 line 2613; Othello, IV 1 line 2650; Othello, IV 2 line 2805; Othello, IV 2 line 2881; Othello, V 1 line 3179; Othello, V 2 line 3341; Othello, V 2 line 3376; Othello, V 2 line 3491; Othello, V 2 line 3512; Othello, V 2 line 3731; Othello, V 2 line 3742.

Passionate Pilgrim, lines 31, 49, 195, 204, 252, 268, 280, 429.

Pericles, I 1 line 233; Pericles, II 1 line 600; Pericles, II 3 line 847; Pericles, II 5 line 1094; Pericles, III 2 line 1375; Pericles, III 3 line 1426; Pericles, IV 0 line 1502; Pericles, IV 1 line 1582; Pericles, IV 1 line 1642; Pericles, V 1 line 2486; Pericles, V 3 line 2573.

Phoenix and the Turtle, line 29.

Rape of Lucrece, lines 89, 279, 321, 327, 344, 346, 365, 420, 484, 486, 490, 516, 522, 609, 641, 676, 810, 1029, 1188, 1260, 1290, 1443, 1446, 1691, 1767, 1833, 1835, 1879.

Richard II, I 1 lines 127, 152; Richard II, I 1 line 176; Richard II, I 3 line 383; Richard II, I 3 line 507; Richard II, I 3 line 558; Richard II, I 3 line 564; Richard II, I 4 line 625; Richard II, I 4 line 638; Richard II, II 1 line 894; Richard II, II 1 line 919; Richard II, II 1 lines 938, 939; Richard II,

II 2 line 1131; Richard II, II 2 line 1142; Richard II, II 3 line 1204; Richard II, II 3 line 1241; Richard II, III 2 line 1503; Richard II, III 2 line 1521; Richard II, III 2 line 1541r; Richard II, III 3 line 1674; Richard II, III 3 line 1758; Richard II, III 3 line 1782; Richard II, III 3 lines 1800, 1802; Richard II, III 3 line 1830; Richard II, III 3 lines 1840, 1842; Richard II, III 4 line 1868; Richard II, IV 1 line 2010; Richard II, IV 1 line 2021; Richard II, IV 1 line 2194; Richard II, IV 1 line 2329; Richard II, V 1 line 2362; Richard II, V 1 line 2417r; Richard II, V 1 lines 2427, 2431; Richard II, V 1 line 2433; Richard II, V 2 line 2476; Richard II, V 3 line 2631; Richard II, V 3 line 2636; Richard II, V 3 line 2667; Richard II, V 3 line 2686; Richard II, V 3 line 2704; Richard II, V 3 line 2720; Richard II, V 4 line 2744; Richard II, V 5 line 2805; Richard II, V 5 line 2827; Richard II, V 5 line 2849.

Richard III, I 2 line 188r; Richard III, I 2 line 258; Richard III, I 2 lines 354, 358; Richard III, I 2 line 381; Richard III, I 2 line 393; Richard III, I 2 line 408; Richard III, I 2 line 424; Richard III, I 3 line 603; Richard III I 3 line 613; Richard III, I 3 line 767; Richard III, I 3 line 823; Richard III, I 4 lines 1002, 1003; Richard III, II 1 lines 1129, 1130; Richard III, II 1 line 1137; Richard III, II 1 line 1165; Richard III, II 2 lines 1385, 1340; Richard III, II 4 line 1487; Richard III, III 1 lines 1577, 1580; Richard III, III 1 line 1684; Richard III, III 1 line 1722; Richard III, III 2 line 1899; Richard III, III 4 line 1958; Richard III, III 4 line 1986; Richard III, III 4 line 2009; Richard III, III 4 line 210; Richard III, III 5 line 2154; Richard III, III 7 line 2341; Richard III, III 7 line 2421; Richard III, IV 1 line 2469; Richard III, IV 1 line 2504; Richard III, IV 1 line 2549; Richard III, IV 1 line 2558; Richard III, IV 4 line 2927; Richard III, IV 4 line 3028, 3031; Richard III, IV 4 line 3064; Richard III, IV 4 line 3076; Richard III, IV 4 line 3078; Richard III, IV 4 line 3135; Richard III, IV 4 line 3172; Richard III, IV 4 line 3217; Richard III, IV 4 line 3251; Richard III, IV 5 line 3391; Richard III, V 1 line 3422; Richard III, V 3 line 3458; Richard III, V 3 line 3674; Richard III, V 3 line 3866.

Romeo and Juliet, I 1 line 80; Romeo and Juliet, I 1 line 210; Romeo and Juliet, I 1 line 211; Romeo and Juliet, I 2 line 286; Romeo and Juliet, I 4 line 531; Romeo and Juliet, I 5 line 674; Romeo and Juliet, I 5 lines 711, 713; Romeo and Juliet, I 5 line 796; Romeo and Juliet, II 2 line 966; Romeo and Juliet, II 2 line 975; Romeo and Juliet, II 3 line 1084; Romeo and Juliet, II 3 line 1128; Romeo and Juliet, II 4 line 1162; Romeo and Juliet, II 4 line 1173; Romeo and Juliet, II 4 line 1328; Romeo and Juliet, II 5 line 1428; Romeo and Juliet, III 2 line 1779; Romeo and Juliet, III 2 line 1795; Romeo and Juliet, III 3 line 1919; Romeo and Juliet, III 3 line 1944; Romeo and Juliet, III 5 lines 2188, 2189; Romeo and Juliet, III 5 line 2338; Romeo and Juliet, IV 1 lines 2421, 2424; Romeo and Juliet, IV 2 line 2544; Romeo and Juliet, IV 5 line 2655; Romeo and Juliet, IV 5 lines 2762r, 2763; Romeo and Juliet, IV 5 line 2764; Romeo and Juliet, IV 5 lines 2765, 2766; Romeo and Juliet, IV 5 line 2783.

Sonnet X line 12; Sonnet XX line 3; Sonnet XXII line 5; Sonnet XXII line 6; Sonnet XXII line 11; Sonnet XXII line 13; Sonnet XXIII line 4; Sonnet XXIV line 2; Sonnet XXXI line 1; Sonnet XLI line 2; Sonnet

XLVI line 3; Sonnet XLVI line 4; Sonnet XLVI line 5; Sonnet XLVI line 10; Sonnet XLVI line 12; Sonnet XLVI line 14; Sonnet XLVII line 1; Sonnet XLVII line 4; Sonnet XLVII line 6; Sonnet XLVII line 7; Sonnet XLVII line 14r; Sonnet LIII line 14; Sonnet LXII line 4; Sonnet LXIX line 2; Sonnet LXX line 14; Sonnet XC line 5; Sonnet XCIII line 4; Sonnet XCIIII line 7; Sonnet XCIII line 11; Sonnet XCV line 13; Sonnet CIX line 1; Sonnet CX line 7; Sonnet CXIII line 5; Sonnet CXIX line 5; Sonnet CXXII line 5; Sonnet CXXV line 9; Sonnet CXXXI line 3; Sonnet CXXXII line 2; Sonnet CXXXII line 10; Sonnet CXXXIII line 1r; Sonnet CXXXIII line 9; Sonnet CXXXIII line 10r; Sonnet CXXXIII line 11; Sonnet CXXXVII line 8; Sonnet CXXXVII line 9; Sonnet CXXXVII line 10; Sonnet CXXXVII line 13; Sonnet CXXXIX line 2; Sonnet CXL line 14; Sonnet CXLI line 3; Sonnet CXLI line 10; Sonnet CXLI line 12; Sonnet CXLII line 11; Sonnet CXLV line 5; Sonnet CL line 2; Sonnet CLIV line 2; Sonnet CLIV line 6.

Taming of the Shrew, Prologue 1 line 90; Taming of the Shrew, I 1 line 358; Taming of the Shrew, I 1 line 451; Taming of the Shrew, I 2 line 587; Taming of the Shrew, III 2 line 1372; Taming of the Shrew, IV 1 line 1626; Taming of the Shrew, IV 1 line 1758; Taming of the Shrew, IV 2 line 1835; Taming of the Shrew, IV 3 line 2011; Taming of the Shrew, IV 3 lines 2041, 2042; Taming of the Shrew, IV 4 line 2226; Taming of the Shrew, IV 5 line 2346; Taming of the Shrew, V 2 lines 2675, 2679.

Tempest, I 1 line 9r; Tempest, I 1 line 31; Tempest, I 2 line 93; Tempest, I 2 line 99; Tempest, I 2 line 162; Tempest, I 2 line 184; Tempest, I 2 line 447; Tempest, II 2 line 1243; Tempest, III 1 line 1354; Tempest, III 1 line 1383; Tempest, III 1 line 1385; Tempest, III 3 line 1658; Tempest, IV 1 line 1762; Tempest, V 1 line 2143; Tempest, V 1 line 2273.

Timon of Athens, I 1 line 73; Timon of Athens, I 1 line 268; Timon of Athens, I 1 line 321; Timon of Athens, I 2 line 342; Timon of Athens, I 2 line 393; Timon of Athens, I 2 line 413; Timon of Athens, I 2 line 414; Timon of Athens, I 2 line 415; Timon of Athens, I 2 line 423; Timon of Athens, I 2 line 430; Timon of Athens, I 2 line 558; Timon of Athens, I 2 line 585; Timon of Athens, I 2 line 606; Timon of Athens, II 2 line 858; Timon of Athens, II 2 lines 866, 869, 871; Timon of Athens, III 1 line 952; Timon of Athens, III 1 line 1000; Timon of Athens, III 2 line 1102; Timon of Athens, III 4 line 1188; Timon of Athens, III 4 line 1261; Timon of Athens, III 4 line 1271; Timon of Athens, III 5 line 1342; Timon of Athens, III 5 line 1431; Timon of Athens, III 6 line 1462; Timon of Athens, IV 2 line 1626; Timon of Athens, IV 2 line 1648; Timon of Athens, IV 3 line 1718; Timon of Athens, IV 3 line 1955; Timon of Athens, IV 3 line 2094; Timon of Athens, V 1 line 2439; Timon of Athens, V 4 line 2591; Timon of Athens, V 4 line 2613.

Titus Andronicus, I 1 line 188; Titus Andronicus, I 1 line 232; Titus Andronicus, I 1 line 236; Titus Andronicus, I 1 line 267; Titus Andronicus, I 1 line 354; Titus Andronicus, I 1 line 490; Titus Andronicus, I 1 line 532; Titus Andronicus, II 1 line 559; Titus Andronicus, II 3 line 771; Titus Andronicus, II 3 line 878; Titus

Andronicus, II 3 line 894; Titus Andronicus, II 3 line 931; Titus Andronicus, II 3 line 951; Titus Andronicus, II 3 line 960; Titus Andronicus, II 3 line 961; Titus Andronicus, II 3 line 964; Titus Andronicus, II 4 lines 1098, 1101; Titus Andronicus, III 1 line 1139; Titus Andronicus, III 1 line 1189; Titus Andronicus, III 1 line 1195; Titus Andronicus, III 1 line 1291; Titus Andronicus, III 1 line 1348; Titus Andronicus, III 1 line 1382; Titus Andronicus, III 1 line 1391; Titus Andronicus, III 2 lines 1453, 1458, 1462; Titus Andronicus, III 2 line 1500; Titus Andronicus, IV 1 line 1613; Titus Andronicus, IV 1 line 1671; Titus Andronicus, IV 2 line 1787; Titus Andronicus, IV 2 line 1808; Titus Andronicus, IV 4 line 2040; Titus Andronicus, IV 4 lines 2111, 2113; Titus Andronicus, V 1 lines 2248, 2251; Titus Andronicus, V 1 line 2278; Titus Andronicus, V 2 line 2427; Titus Andronicus, V 3 line 2538; Titus Andronicus, V 3 line 2566; Titus Andronicus, V 3 lines 2627, 2634; Titus Andronicus, V 3 line 2716.

Troilus and Cressida, I 1 line 36; Troilus and Cressida, I 1 line 65; Troilus and Cressida, I 1 line 83; Troilus and Cressida, I 2 line 230; Troilus and Cressida, I 2 line 351; Troilus and Cressida, I 2 lines 359, 364; Troilus and Cressida, I 2 line 446; Troilus and Cressida, I 3 line 507; Troilus and Cressida, I 3 line 696; Troilus and Cressida, I 3 line 815; Troilus and Cressida, II 2 line 1039; Troilus and Cressida, II 2 line 1155; Troilus and Cressida, II 3 line 1303; Troilus and Cressida, III 1 line 1524; Troilus and Cressida, III 2 line 1688; Troilus and Cressida, III 2 line 1704; Troilus and Cressida, III 2 line 1763; Troilus and Cressida, III 2 line 1846; Troilus and Cressida, III 3 line 2174; Troilus and Cressida, III 3 line 2180; Troilus and Cressida, IV 1 line 2213; Troilus and Cressida, IV 2 line 2321; Troilus and Cressida, IV 2 line 2406; Troilus and Cressida, IV 3 line 2420; Troilus and Cressida, IV 4 lines 2443, 2444r; Troilus and Cressida, IV 4 line 2484; Troilus and Cressida, IV 4 line 2490; Troilus and Cressida, IV 4 line 2496; Troilus and Cressida, IV 5 line 2698; Troilus and Cressida, IV 5 line 2715; Troilus and Cressida, IV 5 line 2793r; Troilus and Cressida, V 1 line 3033; Troilus and Cressida, V 2 line 3146; Troilus and Cressida, V 2 line 3147; Troilus and Cressida, V 2 line 3177; Troilus and Cressida, V 2 line 3192; Troilus and Cressida, V 2 line 3238; Troilus and Cressida, V 3 line 3402; Troilus and Cressida, V 8 line 3603.

Twelfth Night, I 1 lines 37, 41; Twelfth Night, I 3 line 181; Twelfth Night, I 3 line 242; Twelfth Night, I 5 line 477; Twelfth Night, I 5 line 485; Twelfth Night, I 5 line 516; Twelfth Night, I 5 line 532; Twelfth Night, I 5 line 579; Twelfth Night, II 2 line 687; Twelfth Night, II 3 line 717; Twelfth Night, II 3 line 803; Twelfth Night, II 4 line 923; Twelfth Night, II 4 line 989; Twelfth Night, II 4 line 994r; Twelfth Night, II 4 line 1006; Twelfth Night, II 5 line 1131; Twelfth Night, III 1 lines 1355, 1357; Twelfth Night, III 1 line 1397; Twelfth Night, III 1 line 1403; Twelfth Night, III 2 line 1422; Twelfth Night, III 4 line 1576; Twelfth Night, III 4 line 1648; Twelfth Night, III 4 line 1743; Twelfth Night, IV 1 line 2011; Twelfth Night, V 1 lines 2309, 2323.

Two Gentlemen of Verona, I 1 line 32; Two Gentlemen of Verona, I 1 line 72; Two Gentlemen of Verona, I 2 line 215; Two Gentlemen of

Verona, I 3 line 350; Two Gentlemen of Verona, I 3 line 396; Two Gentlemen of Verona, II 3 line 602; Two Gentlemen of Verona, II 4 lines 789, 792; Two Gentlemen of Verona, II 7 lines 1052, 1053; Two Gentlemen of Verona, III 1 line 1376; Two Gentlemen of Verona, III 2 line 1526; Two Gentlemen of Verona, IV 1 line 1603; Two Gentlemen of Verona, IV 2 line 1694; Two Gentlemen of Verona, IV 2 line 1696; Two Gentlemen of Verona, IV 2 line 1721; Two Gentlemen of Verona, IV 2 line 1754; Two Gentlemen of Verona, IV 3 lines 1802, 1815; Two Gentlemen of Verona, IV 4 line 1933; Two Gentlemen of Verona, V 4 line 2195; Two Gentlemen of Verona, V 4 line 2227; Two Gentlemen of Verona, V 4 line 2257.

Venus and Adonis, lines 17, 115, 177, 349, 355, 390r, 394, 395, 398, 408, 424, 443, 446, 452, 521, 523, 538, 601, 605, 668, 690, 801, 805, 807, 830, 851, 912, 964, 1046, 1064, 1094, 1095, 1208.

Winter's Tale, I 1 line 40; Winter's Tale, I 2 lines 185, 188; Winter's Tale, I 2 line 261; Winter's Tale, I 2 line 335; Winter's Tale, I 2 line 383; Winter's Tale, I 2 line 460; Winter's Tale, I 2 line 576; Winter's Tale, II 3 line 1094; Winter's Tale, II 3 line 1178; Winter's Tale, III 2 line 1212; Winter's Tale, III 2 line 1263; Winter's Tale, III 2 line 1380; Winter's Tale, III 2 line 1407; Winter's Tale, III 2 line 1431; Winter's Tale, III 2 line 1462; Winter's Tale, III 3 line 1503; Winter's Tale, IV 4 line 2000; Winter's Tale, IV 4 line 2063; Winter's Tale, III 3 line 1544; Winter's Tale, IV 3 line 1809; Winter's Tale, IV 3 line 1832; Winter's Tale, IV 3 line 2163; Winter's Tale, IV 4 line 2244; Winter's Tale, IV 4 line 2258; Winter's Tale, IV 4 line 2346; Winter's Tale, IV 4 line 2513; Winter's Tale, IV 4 line 2525; Winter's Tale, IV 4 line 2618; Winter's Tale, IV 4 line 2688; Winter's Tale, IV 4 line 2748; Winter's Tale, V 2 line 3186; Winter's Tale, V 2 line 3198.

Heath: Old English hæð untilled land, tract of wasteland, earlier *heather*, influenced by Old Norse heiðr field.
Macbeth, I 1 line 8; Macbeth, I 3 line 178.
Tempest, I 1 line 80.

Heaven: Old English: *heofon: home of God, earlier: sky, firmament.*
All's Well That Ends Well, I 1 line 65; All's Well That Ends Well, I 1 line 72; All's Well That Ends Well, I 1 line 219; All's Well That Ends Well, I 3 line 486; All's Well That Ends Well, I 3 line 506; All's Well That Ends Well, I 3 lines 518, 519; All's Well That Ends Well, I 3 line 577; All's Well That Ends Well, II 1 line 629; All's Well That Ends Well, II 1 lines 761, 763; All's Well That Ends Well, II 1 line 804; All's Well That Ends Well, II 3 line 915; All's Well That Ends Well, II 3 line 922; All's Well That Ends Well, II 3 line 960; All's Well That Ends Well, II 3 line 961; All's Well That Ends Well, II 4 line 1214; All's Well That Ends Well, III 4 line 1588; All's Well That Ends Well, IV 2 line 2079; All's Well That Ends Well, IV 2 line 2081; All's Well That Ends Well, IV 3 line 2142; All's Well That Ends Well, IV 4 line 2434; All's Well That Ends Well, IV 4 line 2442; All's Well That Ends Well, V 3 line 2753; All's Well That Ends Well, V 3 line 2846; All's Well That Ends Well, V 3 line 2872.

Antony and Cleopatra, I 1 line 21; Antony and Cleopatra, I 2 line 137; Antony and Cleopatra, I 3 line 341; Antony and Cleopatra, I 4 line 436; Antony and Cleopatra, I 5 line 588; Antony and Cleopatra, III 6 line 1876; Antony and Cleopatra, III 12 line 2214; Antony and Cleopatra, III 13 line 2447; Antony and Cleopatra, IV 8 line 2828; Antony and Cleopatra, V 2 line 3485; Antony and Cleopatra, V 2 line 3763.

As You Like It, I 2 line 309; As You Like It, I 2 line 406; As You Like It, I 3 line 511; As You Like It, II 4 line 799; As You Like It, II 5 line 849; As You Like It, II 7 line 913; As You Like It, III 2 lines 1252, 1253, 1262, 1265; As You Like It, III 5 line 1711; As You Like It, V 4 lines 2501, 2505.

Comedy of Errors, I 1 line 68; Comedy of Errors, II 1 line 288; Comedy of Errors, III 2 line 828r; Comedy of Errors, IV 4 line 1308; Comedy of Errors, V 1 line 1705.

Coriolanus, I 1 line 60; Coriolanus, I 3 line 409; Coriolanus, I 4 line 532; Coriolanus, IV 3 line 2533r; Coriolanus, IV 2 line 2619; Coriolanus, IV 2 line 2637; Coriolanus, V 3 line 3542; Coriolanus, V 3 line 3696; Coriolanus, V 4 line 3754.

Cymbeline, I 1 line 3; Cymbeline, I 1 line 189; Cymbeline, I 3 line 309; Cymbeline, I 6 line 692; Cymbeline, II 1 line 912; Cymbeline, II 2 lines 945, 973; Cymbeline, II 3 line 997; Cymbeline, III 3 lines 1604, 1608; Cymbeline, III 3 line 1611; Cymbeline, III 3 line 1612; Cymbeline, III 3 lines 1679, 1707; Cymbeline, III 5 line 2010; Cymbeline, III 4 line 2140; Cymbeline, III 6 line 2171; Cymbeline, IV 2 lines 2706, 2714; Cymbeline, IV 3 line 2828; Cymbeline, IV 3 line 2875; Cymbeline, IV 4 line 2934; Cymbeline, V 1 line 2972; Cymbeline, V 3 line 3027; Cymbeline, V 3 line 3071; Cymbeline, V 5 line 3436; Cymbeline, V 5 line 3448; Cymbeline, V 5 lines 3799, 3801; Cymbeline, V 5 line 3937.

Hamlet, I 1 line 48; Hamlet, I 1 line 62; Hamlet, I 1 line 141; Hamlet, I 2 lines 298, 304; Hamlet, I 2 line 330; Hamlet, I 2 lines 345, 346; Hamlet, I 2 line 388; Hamlet, I 3 line 532; Hamlet, I 3 line 601; Hamlet, I 4 line 670; Hamlet, I 4 line 722; Hamlet, I 4 line 729; Hamlet, I 5 line 792; Hamlet, I 5 line 824; Hamlet, I 5 lines 830, 892; Hamlet, I 5 line 854; Hamlet, I 5 line 863; Hamlet, I 5 line 867; Hamlet, I 5 line 919; Hamlet, II 1 line 1064; Hamlet, II 1 line 1074; Hamlet, II 2 line 1123; Hamlet, II 2 line 1505; Hamlet, II 2 lines 1557, 1569; Hamlet, II 2 line 1591; Hamlet, II 2 line 1659; Hamlet, III 1 line 1820; Hamlet, III 1 line 1826; III 1 line 1833; Hamlet, III 2 line 2010; Hamlet, III 2 line 2108; Hamlet, III 3 lines 2318, 2327; Hamlet, III 3 lines 2357, 2361, 2365, 2376; Hamlet, III 3 line 2381; Hamlet, III 4 line 2439; Hamlet, III 4 line 2451; Hamlet, III 4 line 2502; Hamlet, III 4 line 2552; Hamlet, III 4 line 2576; Hamlet, IV 3 line 2744; Hamlet, IV 5 line 3093; Hamlet, V 2 line 3701; Hamlet, V 2 line 3920r; Hamlet, V 2 line 3990; Hamlet, V 2 line 4003.

Henry IV, Part I, I 1 line 11; Henry IV, Part I, I 3 line 532; Henry IV, Part I, II 4 line 1390; Henry IV, Part I, III 1 line 1553; Henry IV, Part I, III 1 line 1556; Henry IV, Part I, III 1 line 1566; Henry IV, Part I, III 1 line 1567; Henry IV, Part I, III 1 line 1581; Henry IV, Part I, III 1 line 1749; Henry IV, Part I, III 1 line 1770; Henry IV, Part I, III 2 line 1833; Henry

IV, Part I, III 2 line 1873; Henry IV, Part I, V 2 line 2875; Henry IV, Part I, V 4 line 3063.
Henry IV, Part II, I 1 line 211; Henry IV, Part II, I 1 line 264; Henry IV, Part II, I 3 line 699; Henry IV, Part II, II 1 line 882; Henry IV, Part II, II 3 lines 1171, 1173; Henry IV, Part II, II 3 line 1216; Henry IV, Part II, II 4 line 1509; Henry IV, Part II, II 4 line 1671; Henry IV, Part II, III 2 line 1894; Henry IV, Part II, III 2 line 1914; Henry IV, Part II, IV 2 lines 2462, 2470; Henry IV, Part II, IV 4 line 2846; Henry IV, Part II, V 5 line 3633.
Henry V, Prologue 1 line 3; Henry V, I 2 line 329; Henry V, II 3 line 839; Henry V, II 4 line 982; Henry V, IV 1 line 1877; Henry V, IV 1 line 2150; Henry V, IV 3 line 2238; Henry V, IV 3 line 2339; Henry V, IV 6 line 2492.
Henry VI, Part I, I 1 line 5; Henry VI, Part I, I 1 line 58; Henry VI, Part I, I 2 line 191; Henry VI, Part I, I 2 line 246; Henry VI, Part I, I 2 line 271; Henry VI, Part I, I 4 lines 543, 545; Henry VI, Part I, I 5 line 590; Henry VI, Part I, II 1 line 718; Henry VI, Part I, III 2 line 1555; Henry VI, Part I, III 2 line 1573; Henry VI, Part I, III 2 line 1582; Henry VI, Part I, IV 5 line 2189; Henry VI, Part I, V 4 line 2724; Henry VI, Part I, V 4 line 2736.
Henry VI, Part II, I 2 line 287; Henry VI, Part II, II 1 line 743; Henry VI, Part II, II 1 line 745; Henry VI, Part II, II 1 line 938; Henry VI, Part II, III 1 line 1636; Henry VI, Part II, III 2 line 1717; Henry VI, Part II, III 2 line 2035; Henry VI, Part II, III 2 line 2055; Henry VI, Part II, III 3 line 2133; Henry VI, Part II, III 3 line 2141; Henry VI, Part II, IV 1 line 2282; Henry VI, Part II, IV 7 line 2694; Henry VI, Part II, IV 8 line 2818; Henry VI, Part II, IV 9 line 2847; Henry VI, Part II, IV 10 line 2665; Henry VI, Part II, V 1 lines 3087, 3088; Henry VI, Part II, V 1 line 3171; Henry VI, Part II,V 1 line 3206; Henry VI, Part II, V 2 line 3243; Henry VI, Part II, V 2 lines 3249, 3259; Henry VI, Part II, V 2 line 3296.
Henry VI, Part III, I 1 line 27; Henry VI, Part III, I 1 line 63; Henry VI, Part III, I 4 line 475; Henry VI, Part III, I 4 line 609; Henry VI, Part III, II 1 line 658; Henry VI, Part III, II 1 line 819; Henry VI, Part III, II 3 line 1032; Henry VI, Part III, II 3 lines 1068, 1071; Henry VI, Part III, II 5 line 1201; Henry VI, Part III, III 2 lines 1637, 1657; Henry VI, Part III, III 3 line 1770; Henry VI, Part III, III 3 line 1807; Henry VI, Part III, III 3 lines 1883, 1884; Henry VI, Part III, IV 6 line 2346; Henry VI, Part III, V 2 line 2772; Henry VI, Part III, V 4 line 2875; Henry VI, Part III, V 5 line 2922; Henry VI, Part III, V 5 line 2972; Henry VI, Part III, V 6 line 3076.
Henry VIII, I 1 line 108; Henry VIII, I 1 line 111; Henry VIII, I 1 line 287; Henry VIII, I 1 line 295; Henry VIII, I 2 line 347; Henry VIII, I 4 line 741; Henry VIII, I 4 line 795; Henry VIII, II 1 line 893; Henry VIII, II 1 line 923; Henry VIII, II 1 line 960; Henry VIII, II 2 lines 1058, 1062; Henry VIII, II 2 line 1183; Henry VIII, II 3 line 1243; Henry VIII, II 3 line 1271; Henry VIII, II 4 line 1378; Henry VIII, II 4 line 1558; Henry VIII, III 1 line 1736; Henry VIII, III 1 line 1768; Henry VIII, III 1 line 1785; Henry VIII, III 2 line 1996; Henry VIII, III 2 line 2007; Henry VIII, III 2 line 2010; Henry VIII, III 2 line 2055; Henry VIII, III 2 line 2294; Henry VIII, III 2 line 2367; Henry VIII, III 2 line 2375; Henry VIII, IV 1 line 2461; Henry

VIII, IV 1 line 2513; Henry VIII, IV 2 line 2590; Henry VIII, IV 2 line 2661; Henry VIII, IV 2 line 2686; Henry VIII, IV 2 lines 2732, 2737, 2751; Henry VIII, IV 2 line 2758; Henry VIII, V 1 line 2981; Henry VIII, V 2 line 3018; Henry VIII, V 3 line 3100; Henry VIII, V 3 line 3177; Henry VIII, V 3 line 3192; Henry VIII, V 5 line 3378; Henry VIII, V 5 line 3385; Henry VIII, V 5 line 3399, 3400, 3412, 3427, 3433, 3438; Henry VIII, V 5 line 3452.

Julius Caesar, I 3 line 432; Julius Caesar, I 3 line 470; Julius Caesar, I 3 line 476; Julius Caesar, I 3 lines 487, 495; Julius Caesar, II 2 line 973; Julius Caesar, II 2 line 1007; Julius Caesar, II 4 line 1184; Julius Caesar, IV 3 line 2057.

King John, I 1 line 46; King John, I 1 line 68; King John, I 1 line 76; King John, I 1 line 89; King John, I 1 line 90; King John, I 1 line 266; King John, II 1 line 325; King John, II 1 lines 380, 382; King John, II 1 lines 467, 468, 469; King John, II 1 line 471; King John, II 1 line 472; King John, II 1 line 553; King John, II 1 line 683; King John, II 1 line 717; King John, III 1 line 1016; King John, III 1 lines 1027, 1028; King John, III 1 line 1058; King John, III 1 line 1077; King John, III 1 lines 1161, 1167; King John, III 1 line 1191r; King John, III 1 line 1240; King John, III 3 line 1328; King John, III 3 line 1335; King John, III 3 line 1358; King John, III 4 line 1433; King John, III 4 lines 1463, 1473; King John, III 4 line 1546; King John, IV 1 line 1600; King John, IV 1 line 1637; King John, IV 1 line 1663; King John, IV 1 line 1680; King John, IV 1 line 1699; King John, IV 1 line 1723; King John, IV 2 line 1742; King John, IV 2 line 1960; King John, IV 3 line 2026; King John, IV 3 line 2105; King John, IV 3 lines 2175, 2189; King John, V 1 line 2223; King John, V 2 lines 2330, 2345; King John, V 5 line 2552; King John, V 6 line 2618; King John, V 7 line 2695; King John, V 7 line 2708.

King Lear, I 2 line 424; King Lear, I 2 line 445; King Lear, I 5 line 918; King Lear, II 2 line 1237; King Lear, II 4 line 1446; King Lear, II 4 line 1482; King Lear, II 4 line 1572; King Lear, III 4 line 1839; King Lear, III 4 line 1884; King Lear, III 5 line 1992; King Lear, III 7 line 2191; King Lear, III 7 line 2244; King Lear, IV 1 lines 2319, 2321; King Lear, IV 2 line 2391; King Lear, IV 3 line 2485; King Lear, IV 6 line 2841; King Lear, V 3 line 3146; King Lear, V 3 line 3373; King Lear, V 3 line 3400; King Lear, V 3 line 3436.

Love's Labour's Lost, I 1 lines 86, 90; Love's Labour's Lost, I 1 line 198; Love's Labour's Lost, III 1 line 961; Love's Labour's Lost, IV 1 line 1034; Love's Labour's Lost, IV 1 line 1134; Love's Labour's Lost, IV 2 line 1146; Love's Labour's Lost, IV 2 line 1265; Love's Labour's Lost, IV 3 line 1331; Love's Labour's Lost, IV 3 line 1342; Love's Labour's Lost, IV 3 lines 1383, 1389; Love's Labour's Lost, IV 3 line 1405; Love's Labour's Lost, IV 3 line 1410; Love's Labour's Lost, IV 3 line 1437; Love's Labour's Lost, IV 3 line 1560; Love's Labour's Lost, IV 3 lines 1565, 1571; Love's Labour's Lost, IV 3 line 1591; Love's Labour's Lost, IV 3 line 1600; Love's Labour's Lost, IV 3 line 1690; Love's Labour's Lost, V 1 line 1803; Love's Labour's Lost, V 2 line 2055; Love's Labour's Lost, V 2 line 2173; Love's Labour's Lost, V 2 line

2276; Love's Labour's Lost, V 2 line 2296; Love's Labour's Lost, V 2 line 2379; Love's Labour's Lost, V 2 lines 2707, 2709.
Lover's Complaint, lines 13, 216.
Macbeth, I 5 line 402; Macbeth, I 6 line 438; Macbeth, I 7 line 495; Macbeth, II 1 line 573; Macbeth, II 1 line 644; Macbeth, II 3 line 763; Macbeth, II 4 line 953; Macbeth, III 1 line 1165; Macbeth, III 6 line 1509; Macbeth, IV 2 line 1816; Macbeth, IV 3 line 1848; Macbeth, IV 3 line 2004; Macbeth, IV 3 lines 2012, 2020; Macbeth, IV 3 line 2086; Macbeth, IV 3 lines 2107, 2111; Macbeth, IV 3 lines 2115, 2119; Macbeth, V 1 line 2172.
Measure for Measure, I 1 line 39; Measure for Measure, I 1 line 83; Measure for Measure, I 2 line 101; Measure for Measure, I 2 line 212; Measure for Measure, II 1 line 493; Measure for Measure, II 1 line 522; Measure for Measure, II 1 line 524; Measure for Measure, II 2 line 788; Measure for Measure, II 2 line 795; Measure for Measure, II 2 line 805; Measure for Measure, II 2 line 825; Measure for Measure, II 2 line 847; Measure for Measure, II 2 lines 878, 879, 886; Measure for Measure, II 2 line 892; Measure for Measure, II 2 line 915; Measure for Measure, II 2 line 920; Measure for Measure, II 3 lines 1001, 1002; Measure for Measure, II 4 lines 1018, 1020; Measure for Measure, II 4 line 1040; Measure for Measure, II 4 line 1056; Measure for Measure, II 4 line 1067; Measure for Measure, II 4 line 1072; Measure for Measure, II 4 line 1095; Measure for Measure, II 4 line 1155; Measure for Measure, III 1 line 1281; Measure for Measure, III 1 line 1331; Measure for Measure, III 1 line 1378; Measure for Measure, III 2 line 1517; Measure for Measure, III 2 line 1758; Measure for Measure, III 2 line 1770; Measure for Measure, IV 2 line 1958; Measure for Measure, IV 3 line 2196; Measure for Measure, IV 3 line 2234; Measure for Measure, IV 3 line 2251; Measure for Measure, IV 4 line 2310; Measure for Measure, V 1 line 2480; Measure for Measure, V 1 line 2508; Measure for Measure, V 1 line 2520; Measure for Measure, V 1 line 2571; Measure for Measure, V 1 line 2634.
Merchant of Venice, I 3 line 419; Merchant of Venice, II 2 line 576; Merchant of Venice, II 2 line 600; Merchant of Venice, II 2 line 630; Merchant of Venice, II 4 line 838; Merchant of Venice, II 6 line 943; Merchant of Venice, II 7 lines 1031, 1034; Merchant of Venice, III 4 line 1776; Merchant of Venice, III 5 line 1871; Merchant of Venice, III 5 lines 1912, 1914, 1915; Merchant of Venice, IV 1 line 2009; Merchant of Venice, IV 1 line 2126; Merchant of Venice, IV 1 line 2169; Merchant of Venice, IV 1 line 2236; Merchant of Venice, V 1 line 2511; Merchant of Venice, V 1 line 2656; Merchant of Venice, V 1 line 2727.
Merry Wives of Windsor, I 1 line 173; Merry Wives of Windsor, I 1 line 227; Merry Wives of Windsor, I 4 line 434; Merry Wives of Windsor, I 4 line 532; Merry Wives of Windsor, I 4 line 541; Merry Wives of Windsor, II 1 line 595; Merry Wives of Windsor, II 2 line 850; Merry Wives of Windsor, III 1 line 1223; Merry Wives of Windsor, III 3 line 1444; Merry Wives of Windsor, III 3 line 1478; Merry Wives of Windsor, III 3 line 1505; Merry Wives of Windsor, III 3 line 1594; Merry Wives of Windsor, III 3 line 1600; Merry Wives of Windsor, III 4 line

1733; Merry Wives of Windsor, IV 2 line 2047; Merry Wives of Windsor, IV 2 line 2072; Merry Wives of Windsor, IV 2 line 2092; Merry Wives of Windsor, IV 5 line 2418; Merry Wives of Windsor, V 2 line 2523; Merry Wives of Windsor, V 5 line 2591; Merry Wives of Windsor, V 5 line 2645; Merry Wives of Windsor, V 5 line 2799; Merry Wives of Windsor, V 5 line 2803; Merry Wives of Windsor, V 5 line 2807.
Midsummer Night's Dream, I 1 line 11; Midsummer Night's Dream, I 1 line 152; Midsummer Night's Dream, I 1 line 215; Midsummer Night's Dream, II 1 line 619; Midsummer Night's Dream, III 2 line 1522; Midsummer Night's Dream, V 1 line 1843r.
Much Ado About Nothing, II 1 lines 437, 438, 410.
Othello, I 1 line 34; Othello, I 1 line 61; Othello, I 1 line 185; Othello, I 3 line 467; Othello, I 3 lines 486, 507; Othello, I 3 lines 613, 618; Othello, II 1 line 766; Othello, II 1 line 801; Othello, II 1 line 813; Othello, II 1 line 864; Othello, II 1 line 1000; Othello, II 2 line 1126; Othello, II 3 line 1317; Othello, II 3 line 1352; Othello, II 3 line 1415; Othello, II 3 line 1504; Othello, III 3 line 1750; Othello, III 3 line 1812; Othello, III 3 line 1826; Othello, III 3 line 1854; Othello, III 3 line 1940; Othello, III 3 line 1965; Othello, III 3 line 2049; Othello, III 3 line 2052; Othello, III 3 line 2130; Othello, III 3 line 2146; Othello, III 4 line 2267; Othello, III 4 line 2350; Othello, III 4 line 2358; Othello, IV 1 line 2419; Othello, IV 1 line 2430; Othello, IV 1 line 2483; Othello, IV 1 line 2588; Othello, IV 1 line 2721; Othello, IV 2 line 2753; Othello, IV 2 line 2782; Othello, IV 2 line 2785; Othello, IV 2 line 2786; Othello, IV 2 line 2795; Othello, IV 2 line 2826; Othello, IV 2 line 2831; Othello, IV 2 line 2840; Othello, IV 2 line 2896; Othello, IV 2 line 2902; Othello, IV 2 line 2908; Othello, IV 2 line 2919; Othello, IV 3 line 3092; Othello, IV 3 line 3093; Othello, IV 3 line 3132; Othello, V 1 line 3198; Othello, V 1 line 3226; Othello, V 1 line 3245; Othello, V 2 line 3323; Othello, V 2 line 3331; Othello, V 2 line 3336; Othello, V 2 line 3339; Othello, V 2 line 3373; Othello, V 2 line 3375; Othello, V 2 line 3467; Othello, V 2 line 3476; Othello, V 2 line 3495; Othello, V 2 line 3523; Othello, V 2 line 3559r; Othello, V 2 line 3563; Othello, V 2 line 3579; Othello, V 2 line 3582; Othello, V 2 lines 3631, 3635.
Passionate Pilgrim, lines 29, 35, 70, 108, 235, 344.
Pericles, I 0 line 25; Pericles, I 1 line 76; Pericles, I 1 line 94; Pericles, I 1 lines 121, 132; Pericles, I 1 line 149; Pericles, I 1 line 159; Pericles, I 2 line 294; Pericles, I 2 line 303; Pericles, I 4 line 412; Pericles, 1 4 line 449; Pericles, II 1 line 524; Pericles, II 1 line 580; Pericles, II 2 line 760; Pericles, II 4 line 958; Pericles, II 4 line 966; Pericles, III 1 line 1229; Pericles, III 2 line 1399; Pericles, III 2 line 1403; Pericles, III 3 line 1465; Pericles, IV 3 line 1836; Pericles, IV 3 line 1859; Pericles, IV 4 line 1922; Pericles, V 1 line 2441; Pericles, V 1 line 2452; Pericles, V 3 line 2614; Pericles, V 3 line 2627.
Rape of Lucrece, lines 64, 68, 163, 339, 389, 394, 407, 623, 649, 718, 1217, 1424, 1888.
Richard II, I 1 line 26; Richard II, I 1 lines 33, 41; Richard II, I 2 line 219; Richard II, I 3 line 308; Richard II, I 3 line 318; Richard II, I 3 line 329; Richard II, I 3 lines 335, 336; Richard II, I 3 line 576; Richard II, II

1 line 813; Richard II, II 2 line 1046; Richard II, II 2 line 1075; Richard II, II 4 line 1339; Richard II, III 1 line 1392; Richard II, III 2 lines 1437, 1438, 1439; Richard II, III 2 lines 1445, 1468, 1470; Richard II, III 2 line 1619; Richard II, III 3 line 1652; Richard II, III 3 line 1742; Richard II, IV 1 line 2039; Richard II, IV 1 line 2046r; Richard II, IV 1 line 2163; Richard II, IV 1 line 2225; Richard II, V 2 line 2478.

Richard III, I 1 line 76; Richard III, I 1 lines 125, 126; Richard III, I 1 line 154; Richard III, I 2 line 238; Richard III, I 2 line 283; Richard III, I 2 line 284; Richard III, I 2 line 369; Richard III, I 3 line 468; Richard III, I 3 line 567; Richard III, I 3 lines 655, 659; Richard III, I 3 line 681; Richard III, I 4 line 1077; Richard III, I 4 line 1108; Richard III, II 1 line 1125; Richard III, II 1 line 1129; Richard III, II 2 line 1207; Richard III, II 2 line 1366; Richard III, III 1 line 1608; Richard III, III 3 line 1943; Richard III, III 7 line 2298; Richard III, IV 4 line 2946; Richard III, IV 4 line 3043; Richard III, IV 4 line 3160; Richard III, IV 4 line 3214; Richard III, V 3 line 3798; Richard III, V 3 line 3827; Richard III, V 5 line 3900; Richard III, V 5 line 3912.

Romeo and Juliet, I 2 line 295; Romeo and Juliet, II 2 lines 860, 865; Romeo and Juliet, II 2 line 875; Romeo and Juliet, II 3 line 1133; Romeo and Juliet, II 4 line 1347; Romeo and Juliet, II 6 line 1459; Romeo and Juliet, III 1 line 1631; Romeo and Juliet, III 2 lines 1741, 1750; Romeo and Juliet, III 2 line 1761; Romeo and Juliet, III 2 line 1763; Romeo and Juliet, III 3 lines 1900, 1903; Romeo and Juliet, III 3 lines 1999, 2000; Romeo and Juliet, III 5 line 2119; Romeo and Juliet, III 5 line 2277; Romeo and Juliet, III 5 lines 2331, 2335, 2337; Romeo and Juliet, IV 3 line 2552; Romeo and Juliet, IV 5 lines 2725, 2726, 2729, 2731, 2733; Romeo and Juliet, IV 5 line 2753; Romeo and Juliet, V 3 line 2972; Romeo and Juliet, V 3 line 3004; Romeo and Juliet, V 3 line 3175; Romeo and Juliet, V 3 line 3236; Romeo and Juliet, V 3 line 3268.

Sonnet VII line 5; Sonnet XIV line 8; Sonnet XVII line 3; Sonnet XVII line 8; Sonnet XVIII line 5; Sonnet XXI line 3; Sonnet XXI line 8; Sonnet XXI line 12; Sonnet XXVIII line 10; Sonnet XVII line 3; Sonnet XIX line 3; Sonnet XIX line 12; Sonnet XXIII line 4; Sonnet XXIII line 14; Sonnet LXX line 4; Sonnet XCIII line 9; Sonnet XCIV line 5; Sonnet CX line 13; Sonnet CXXIX line 14; Sonnet CXXX line 13; Sonnet CXXXII line 5; Sonnet CXLV line 12; Sonnet CXLVIII line 12.

Taming of the Shrew, Prologue, 1 line 52; Taming of the Shrew, Prologue 2 line 158; Taming of the Shrew, I 2 line 590; Taming of the Shrew, I 2 line 754; Taming of the Shrew, III 1 line 1272; Taming of the Shrew, IV 5 lines 2299, 2300.

Tempest, I 2 line 156; Tempest, I 2 line 219; Tempest, I 2 line 265; Tempest, I 2 line 290; Tempest, I 2 line 598; Tempest, II 1 line 1074; Tempest, II 2 line 1224; Tempest, III 1 line 1358; Tempest, III 1 line 1367; Tempest, III 3 line 1584; Tempest, IV 1 line 1706; Tempest, IV 1 line 1718; Tempest, IV 1 line 1798; Tempest, V 1 line 2073; Tempest, V 1 line 2136; Tempest, V 1 line 2193.

Timon of Athens, I 1 line 266; Timon of Athens, I 2 line 622; Timon of Athens, II 2 line 855; Timon of Athens, IV 3 line 1691; Timon of Athens,

IV 3 line 1812; Timon of Athens, IV 3 line 1819; Timon of Athens, IV 3 line 1870; Timon of Athens, IV 3 line 1917; Timon of Athens, IV 3 line 2232; Timon of Athens, V 1 line 2322.

Titus Andronicus, I 1 line 369; Titus Andronicus, I 1 line 375; Titus Andronicus, I 1 line 441; Titus Andronicus, I 1 line 475; Titus Andronicus, I 1 line 525; Titus Andronicus, II 1 line 687; Titus Andronicus, II 3 line 774; Titus Andronicus, II 4 line 1112; Titus Andronicus, III 1 line 1308; Titus Andronicus, III 1 lines 1343, 1349; Titus Andronicus, III 1 line 1360; Titus Andronicus, III 2 line 1487; Titus Andronicus, IV 1 line 1573; Titus Andronicus, IV 1 line 1578; Titus Andronicus, IV 1 line 1617; Titus Andronicus, IV 1 lines 1668, 1674; Titus Andronicus, IV 2 line 1747; Titus Andronicus, IV 3 line 1921; Titus Andronicus, IV 3 line 1931; Titus Andronicus, IV 3 line 1962; Titus Andronicus, IV 3 line 1974; Titus Andronicus, IV 3 lines 1975, 1976; Titus Andronicus, IV 4 line 2022.

Troilus and Cressida, I 3 line 520; Troilus and Cressida, I 3 line 538; Troilus and Cressida, I 3 line 763; Troilus and Cressida, II 3 line 1243; Troilus and Cressida, II 3 line 1250; Troilus and Cressida, II 3 line 1462; Troilus and Cressida, III 2 line 1788; Troilus and Cressida, III 3 lines 2002, 2008; Troilus and Cressida, IV 1 line 2203; Troilus and Cressida, IV 4 line 2474; Troilus and Cressida, IV 4 line 2507; Troilus and Cressida, IV 4 line 2516; Troilus and Cressida, IV 4 line 2557; Troilus and Cressida, IV 5 line 2870; Troilus and Cressida, IV 5 line 2914; Troilus and Cressida, IV 4 line 2496; Troilus and Cressida, IV 5 line 2698; Troilus and Cressida, V 2 lines 3228, 3229, 3230; Troilus and Cressida, V 3 line 3292; Troilus and Cressida, V 3 line 3325; Troilus and Cressida, V 6 line 3543; Troilus and Cressida, V 10 line 3639.

Twelfth Night, I 5 line 360; Twelfth Night, I 5 line 362; Twelfth Night, II 1 line 628; Twelfth Night, II 4 line 921; Twelfth Night, III 1 line 1320; Twelfth Night, III 4 line 1589; Twelfth Night, III 4 line 1911; Twelfth Night, IV 2 line 2113; Twelfth Night, IV 3 line 2186; Twelfth Night, V 1 line 2288; Twelfth Night, V 1 line 2318.

Two Gentlemen of Verona, I 3 line 354; Two Gentlemen of Verona, II 4 line 802; Two Gentlemen of Verona, II 6 line 955; Two Gentlemen of Verona, II 7 line 1053; Two Gentlemen of Verona, II 7 line 1054; Two Gentlemen of Verona, III 1 lines 1226, 1238; Two Gentlemen of Verona, III 2 line 1524; Two Gentlemen of Verona, IV 2 line 1674; Two Gentlemen of Verona, IV 3 line 1814; Two Gentlemen of Verona, IV 4 line 1925; Two Gentlemen of Verona, IV 4 line 1945; Two Gentlemen of Verona, V 4 line 2185; Two Gentlemen of Verona, V 4 line 2210; Two Gentlemen of Verona, V 4 line 2234; Two Gentlemen of Verona, V 4 line 2266; Two Gentlemen of Verona, V 4 line 2275.

Venus and Adonis, lines 84, 213, 218, 288, 451, 514, 554, 563, 752, 753, 815.

Winter's Tale, I 1 line 31; Winter's Tale, I 2 line 138; Winter's Tale, I 2 line 422r; Winter's Tale, I 2 line 552; Winter's Tale, II 1 line 726; Winter's Tale, II 1 line 755; Winter's Tale, III 2 line 1373; Winter's Tale, III 3 line 1492; Winter's Tale, III 3 line 1548; Winter's Tale, IV 4 line

2274; Winter's Tale, IV 4 line 2473; Winter's Tale, V 1 line 2824; Winter's Tale, V 1 line 2871; Winter's Tale, V 1 line 2984; Winter's Tale, V 1 lines 3030, 3032; Winter's Tale, V 1 line 3067; Winter's Tale, V 3 line 3468.

Hebona: a herb
Hamlet, I 5 line 799.

Hedge: Old English: *hecg*: originally any fence, living or artificial. Figurative sense of *boundary, barrier* is from mid-14c. Prefixed to any word, it *notes something mean, vile, of the lowest class* (Johnson), from contemptuous attributive sense of *plying one's trade under a hedge* (hedge-priest, hedge-lawyer, hedge-wench, etc.), a usage attested from 1530s. Late 14c., *make a hedge*, also *surround with a barricade or palisade*; from hedge. The sense of *dodge, evade* is first recorded 1590s. That of *insure oneself against loss*, as in a bet, probably from an earlier use of hedge in meaning, to secure (a debt) by including it in a larger one which has better security (1610s).

All's Well That Ends Well, IV 1 line 1904.
Antony and Cleopatra, I 4 line 493.
Hamlet, IV 5 line 2993.
Henry IV, Part I, II 2 line 809; Henry IV, Part I, IV 2 line 2416.
Henry V, V 2 lines 3023, 3035.
Henry VI, Part I, I 1 line 124; Henry VI, Part I, IV 1 line 1803.
Henry VI, Part II, IV 2 line 2356.
Henry VIII, III 2 line 1877.
Julius Caesar, IV 3 line 2010.
King John, II 1 line 316.
Love's Labour's Lost, V 2 line 2475.
Merchant of Venice, II 1 line 532.
Merry Wives of Windsor, II 2 line 819.
Much Ado About Nothing, I 3 line 353.
Passionate Pilgrim, line 73.
Richard II, III 4 line 1909.
Taming of the Shrew, Prologue 1 line 20.
Troilus and Cressida, III 1 line 1552; Troilus and Cressida, III 3 line 2034 .
Venus and Adonis, line 1116.
Winter's Tale, IV 3 line 1728; Winter's Tale, IV 4 line 2802.

Hedgehog: mid-15c. (replacing Old English: *igl*), the second element a reference to its pig-like snout. The urchin or hedgehog, like the toad, for its solitariness, the ugliness of its appearance, and from a popular belief that it sucked or poisoned the udders of cows, was adopted into the demonologic system; and its shape was sometimes supposed to be assumed by mischievous elves.

Midsummer Night's Dream, II 2 line 660.
Richard III, I 2 line 280.
Tempest, II 2 line 1091.

Hedge-pig*: see Hedgehog.
    Macbeth, IV 1 line 1549.

Hedge-sparrow: a common European bird (*Prunella modularis, Accentor modularis*) that resembles a thrush, frequents hedges, and is reddish brown and ashen grey with the wing coverts tipped with white; called also *dunnock, hedge accentor.*
    King Lear, I 4 line 316.

Heel: back of the foot, Old English: *hela*. Meaning, back of a shoe or boot is c. 1400.
    All's Well That Ends Well, I 2 line 299; All's Well That Ends Well, III 4 line 1574; All's Well That Ends Well, IV 3 line 2192.
    Antony and Cleopatra, I 4 line 488; Antony and Cleopatra, II 2 line 874; Antony and Cleopatra, IV 5 line 2682.
    As You Like It, III 2 line 1315; As You Like It, III 2 line 1375.
    Comedy of Errors, I 2 line 258; Comedy of Errors, III 1 line 630; Comedy of Errors, V 1 line 1512.
    Coriolanus, I 4 line 551; Coriolanus, III 1 line 2131; Coriolanus, III 2 line 2164.
    Cymbeline, IV 4 line 2930; Cymbeline, V 3 line 3098.
    Hamlet, III 2 line 2212; Hamlet, III 3 line 2376; Hamlet, IV 5 line 2892; Hamlet, IV 7 line 3312; Hamlet, V 1 line 3476.
    Henry IV, Part I, II 4 line 1034; Henry IV, Part I, II 4 line 1420; Henry IV, Part I, III 2 line 1951; Henry IV, Part I, IV 3 line 2532.
    Henry IV, Part II, I 1 line 96; Henry IV, Part II, I 2 line 289; Henry IV, Part II, I 2 line 435; Henry IV, Part II, I 3 line 686; Henry IV, Part II, I 3 line 712.
    Henry V, Prologue 1 line 7; Henry V, II 0 line 470; Henry V, III 5 line 1424; Henry V, IV 7 line 2600; Henry V, IV 7 line 2692; Henry V, V 0 line 2865.
    Henry VI, Part I, I 4 line 571; Henry IV, Part I, IV 3 line 2513; Henry VI, Part I, IV 8 line 2821; Henry VI, Part I, IV 10 line 2969.
    Henry VI, Part II, I 1 line 144; Henry VI, Part II, II 1 line 749; Henry VI, Part II, II 1 line 791; Henry VI, Part II, III 1 line 1309; Henry VI, Part II, III 1 line 1571; Henry VI, Part II, III 2 line 2031; Henry VI, Part II, IV 1 line 2239; Henry VI, Part II, V 1 line 3120.
    Henry VIII, V 4 line 3354.
    Julius Caesar, II 4 line 1176; Julius Caesar, III 1 line 1336.
    King John, IV 2 line 1884; King John, IV 2 line 1913; King John, V 7 line 2716.
    King Lear, I 4 line 616; King Lear, I 5 line 886; King Lear, II 2 line 1099; King Lear, II 2 line 1233.
    Macbeth, I 2 line 49; Macbeth, I 6 line 458.
    Merchant of Venice, II 2 lines 574, 595.
    Merry Wives of Windsor, I 3 line 333; Merry Wives of Windsor, I 4 line 463; Merry Wives of Windsor, I 4 line 527; Merry Wives of Windsor, II 1 line 679; Merry Wives of Windsor, II 3 line 1188; Merry Wives of Windsor, III 2 line 1315; Merry Wives of Windsor, III 3 line

1507; Merry Wives of Windsor, III 5 line 1816; Merry Wives of Windsor, III 5 line 1849.
Midsummer Night's Dream, III 2 line 1481.
Much Ado About Nothing, III 4 line 1533; Much Ado About Nothing, III 4 line 1536; Much Ado About Nothing, V 4 line 2673.
Othello, I 2 line 250.
Richard II, V 3 line 2725.
Richard III, IV 1 line 2510.
Romeo and Juliet, I 2 line 297; Romeo and Juliet, I 4 line 532; Romeo and Juliet, III 1 line 1533.
Taming of the Shrew, IV 1 line 1633; Taming of the Shrew, IV 1 line 1732.
Timon of Athens, I 1 line 37; Timon of Athens, I 1 line 317.
Titus Andronicus, IV 3 line 1925.
Troilus and Cressida, II 1 line 904; Troilus and Cressida, II 2 line 1035; Troilus and Cressida, IV 4 line 2520; Troilus and Cressida, IV 4 line 2589; Troilus and Cressida, V 8 line 3596.
Twelfth Night, II 5 line 1158; Twelfth Night, III 4 line 1842.
Two Gentlemen of Verona, III 1 line 1392.
Venus and Adonis, line 332.
Winter's Tale, IV 4 line 2118; Winter's Tale, IV 4 line 2656.

Heifer: Old English: *heahfore*. Possibly, the first part meaning, *enclosure*; the second part meaning, *dweller*.
    Henry VI, Part II, II 2 line 1128; Henry VI, Part II, III 2 line 1873.
    Troilus and Cressida, III 2 line 1844.
    Winter's Tale, I 2 line 202.

Hemlock: poisonous parsley plant. The name has been got from *healm*, or *haulm*, straw, and *leac*, a plant, because of the dry hollow stalks which remain after flowering is done. Old English: *hymlice*, *hemlic*, of unknown origin.
    Henry V, V 2 line 3026.
    King Lear, IV 4 line 2519.
    Macbeth, IV 1 line 1572.

Hen: Old English: *henn*. *As wanton as a wet hen* is in Scots Proverbs (1813). Among Middle English proverbial expressions was *nice as a nonne*: over-refined, fastidiously wanton (c.1500); *to singen so hen in snowe*: sing miserably, sing like a hen in snow (c.1200).
    All's Well That Ends Well, II 3 line 1115.
    As You Like It, IV 1 line 1923.
    Coriolanus, V 3 line 3673.
    Henry IV, Part I, III 3 line 2061.
    Henry IV, Part II, II 4 line 1354; Henry IV, Part II, V 1 line 3169.
    Taming of the Shrew, II 1 line 1076.
    Winter's Tale, IV 4 line 2722.

Herb: c.1300, *erbe: non-woody plant*, from Old French: *erbe: grass, herb, plant* (12c).

All's Well That Ends Well, IV 5 lines 2477, 2478, 2480r.
Cymbeline, IV 2 line 2684.
Hamlet, IV 5 line 3057.
Henry IV, Part II, III 1 line 1310.
Merchant of Venice, V 1 line 2459.
Midsummer Night's Dream, II 1 lines 541, 545; Midsummer Night's Dream, II 1 line 558; Midsummer Night's Dream, III 2 line 1423.
Othello, I 3 line 681.
Pericles, IV 6 line 2024.
Richard II, III 4 line 1910; Richard II, III 4 line 1973.
Richard III, II 4 line 1497.
Romeo and Juliet, II 3 lines 1074, 1086.
Titus Andronicus, III 1 line 1309.
Venus and Adonis, lines 185, 1077.

Herb-of-Grace: or Herb Grace. A popular name for rue. The origin of the term is uncertain. Most probably it arose from the extreme bitterness of the plant, which, as it had always borne the name rue (to be sorry for anything), was not unnaturally associated with repentance. It was, therefore, the herb of repentance, and this was soon changed into *herb of grace*, repentance being the chief sign of grace.
    Hamlet, IV 5 line 3057.

Herblets: small herbs.
    Cymbeline, IV 2 line 2687.

Herd: *heord: herd, flock*, mid-13c., *to watch over or herd* (livestock); of animals, *to gather in a herd, to form a flock*, late 14c.
    All's Well That Ends Well, I 3 line 375.
    Antony and Cleopatra, III 13 line 2408.
    As You Like It, II 1 line 602.
    Coriolanus, I 4 line 524; Coriolanus, III 1 line 1768; Coriolanus, III 2 line 2205.
    Henry IV, Part I, III 1 line 1582.
    Henry VI, Part I, IV 2 line 2014.
    Henry VI, Part III, II 1 line 640; Henry VI, Part III, III 1 line 1373.
    Julius Caesar, I 2 line 357.
    Merchant of Venice, V 1 line 2527.
    Passionate Pilgrim, lines 72, 286.
    Sonnet XXII line 6.
    Tempest, II 1 line 1064.
    Troilus and Cressida, I 3 line 498.
    Twelfth Night, IV 5 line 5678.
    Venus and Adonis, lines 477, 711.
    Winter's Tale, IV 4 line 2570.

Herring: Old English: *hering* (Anglian), of unknown origin, perhaps related to or influenced in form by Old English: *har: grey, hoar*. The Battle of the

Herrings is the popular name for the battle at Rouvrai, Feb. 12, 1492, fought in defence of a convoy of provisions, mostly herrings and other *lenten stuffe*.
    Henry IV, Part I, II 4 line 1120.
    Henry VI, Part II, IV 2 line 2339.
    King Lear, III 6 line 2035.
    Merry Wives of Windsor, II 3 line 1111.
    Romeo and Juliet, II 4 line 1198.
    Troilus and Cressida, V 1 line 2993.
    Twelfth Night, I 5 line 413; Twelfth Night, III 1 line 1268.

Hill: Old English: *hyll.*
    Antony and Cleopatra, III 9 line 2052; Antony and Cleopatra, III 13 line 2407; Antony and Cleopatra, IV 10 line 2886.
    Coriolanus, III 2 line 2165.
    Cymbeline, III 3 line 1613.
    Hamlet, I 1 line 190; Hamlet, II 2 line 1570; Hamlet, III 4 line 2451.
    Henry IV, Part I, II 2 line 749; Henry IV, Part I, II 2 line 792; Henry IV, Part I, II 2 line 820; Henry IV, Part I, II 4 line 1228; Henry IV, Part I, II 4 line 1329; Henry IV, Part I, V 1 line 2622; Henry IV, Part I, V 5 line 3163.
    Henry IV, Part II, V 1 line 3182.
    Henry V, I 2 line 153; Henry V, III 3 line 1295; Henry V, IV 7 line 2575.
    Henry VI, Part III, II 5 line 1125; Henry VI, Part II, III 1 line 1371.
    Henry VIII, I 1 line 196.
    Julius Caesar, V 1 line 2347; Julius Caesar, V 3 line 2509; Julius Caesar, V 3 lines 2519, 2522; Julius Caesar, V 3 line 2565.
    King John, II 1 line 602.
    King Lear, II 1 line 1350; King Lear, III 4 line 1875; King Lear, IV 6 line 2597.
    Love's Labour's Lost, IV 1 line 973; Love's Labour's Lost, V 1 line 1811.
    Lover's Complaint, line 1.
    Macbeth, IV 1 line 1659; Macbeth, V 5 line 2392.
    Midsummer Night's Dream, II 1 line 369; Midsummer Night's Dream, II 1 line 452.
    Othello, II 1 line 978.
    Passionate Pilgrim, lines 122, 356.
    Pericles, I 1 line 150; Pericles, I 4 line 421.
    Rape of Lucrece, line 441.
    Richard II, II 3 line 1156.
    Romeo and Juliet, II 5 lines 1380, 1383.
    Sonnet, VII line 5.
    Taming of the Shrew, IV 1 line 1673; Taming of the Shrew, IV 2 line 1890.
    Timon of Athens, I 1 line 80; Timon of Athens, I 1 line 91.
    Tempest, V 1 line 2054.
    Titus Andronicus, II 1 line 555.
    Twelfth Night, I 5 line 563.
    Venus and Adonis, lines 253, 719, 880.

Hip: part of the body where pelvis and thigh join, Old English: *hype*. Seed pod (especially of wild rose), Old English: *heope, hiope: seed vessel of the wild rose*.
>**Comedy of Errors**, III 2 line 872r; Comedy of Errors, III 2 line 874r.
>**Henry IV, Part II**, III 1 line 1756.
>**Henry V**, IV 2 line 2212.
>**Measure for Measure**, I 2 line 151.
>**Merchant of Venice**, I 3 line 367; Merchant of Venice, IV 1 line 2282.
>**Midsummer Night's Dream**, II 1 line 422.
>**Much Ado About Nothing**, III 2 line 1233.
>**Othello**, II 1 line 1106.
>**Timon of Athens**, IV 3 line 2132.
>**Venus and Adonis**, line 64.

Hive: Old English: *hyf: beehive*. Figurative sense of swarming, busy place is from 1630s. As a verb, of bees, etc., to form themselves into a hive, c.1400; to put bees in a hive, mid-15c.
>**All's Well That Ends Well**, I 2 line 308.
>**Henry IV, Part II**, IV 5 line 2970.
>**Henry VI, Part I**, I 5 line 608.
>**Henry VI, Part II**, III 2 line 1807.
>**Lover's Complaint**, line 8.
>**Merchant of Venice**, II 5 line 896.
>**Rape of Lucrece**, lines 890, 1820.
>**Timon of Athens**, IV 3 line 1959.
>**Troilus and Cressida**, I 3 line 534.

Hobby-horse: late 13c., *hobyn: small horse*, pony, later mock horse used in the morris dance, and c.1550 child's toy riding horse, which led to hobby-horse in a transferred sense of favourite pastime or avocation. The connecting notion being activity that doesn't go anywhere. The original hobbyhorse was a *Tourney Horse*, a wooden or basketwork frame worn around the waist and held on with shoulder straps, with a fake tail and horse head attached, so the wearer appears to be riding a horse. These were part of church and civic celebrations at Midsummer and New Year's throughout England.
>**Hamlet**, III 2 lines 2013, 2014.
>**Love's Labour's Lost**, III 1 line 791; Love's Labour's Lost, III 1 line 792; Love's Labour's Lost, III 1 line 793.
>**Much Ado About Nothing**, III 2 line 1263.
>**Othello**, IV 1 line 2585.
>**Winter's Tale**, I 2 line 378.

Hog: late 12c. (implied in *hogaster*), swine reared for slaughter (usually about a year old), also used by stockmen for *young sheep* (mid-14c.) and for *horse older than one year*, suggesting the original sense may have had something to do with an age, not a type of animal. Figurative sense of *gluttonous person*, is first recorded early 15c.

As You Like It, I 1 line 33.
King Lear, III 4 line 1887.
Merchant of Venice, III 5 line 1863.
Merry Wives of Windsor, IV 1 line 1927; Merry Wives of Windsor, IV 1 line 1931.
Midsummer Night's Dream, III 1 lines 925, 927.
Richard III, I 3 line 692.

Hogshead: large cask or barrel, late 14c., presumably on some perceived resemblance to aw pig or boar. The original liquid measure was 63 old wine gallons (by a statute of 1423); later anywhere from 100 to 140 gallons.
Henry IV, Part I, II 4 line 989.
Henry IV, Part II, II 4 line 1308.
Love's Labour's Lost, IV 2 line 1233; Love's Labour's Lost, IV 2 line 1234.
Tempest, IV 1 line 1992.
Winter's Tale, III 3 line 1589.

Holy Thistle: *Carduus Benedictus*, called also *blessed thistle*, was so named, like other plants which bear the specific name of *blessed*, from its supposed power of counteracting the effect of poison.
Much Ado About Nothing, III 4 line 1560.

Honey: Old English: *hunig*. A term of endearment from at least mid-14c.
All's Well That Ends Well, I 2 line 307.
As You Like It, III 3 line 1529.
Hamlet, III 1 line 1847; Hamlet, III 4 line 2487.
Henry IV, Part I, I 2 line 152; Henry IV, Part I, I 2 line 263; Henry IV, Part I, III 2 line 1894.
Henry IV, Part II, II 1 line 773r; Henry IV, Part II, IV 5 line 2969.
Henry V, I 1 line 89; Henry V, I 2 lines 333, 345; Henry V, II 2 line 665; Henry V, II 3 line 833; Henry V, IV 1 line 1853.
Henry VIII, III 2 line 1853.
Julius Caesar, II 1 line 855; Julius Caesar, V 1 line 2385.
Love's Labour's Lost, V 2 line 2129; Love's Labour's Lost, V 2 line 2252; Love's Labour's Lost, V 2 line 2461.
Midsummer Night's Dream, III 1 line 993; Midsummer Night's Dream, IV 1 lines 1557, 1559, 1561.
Othello, II 1 line 1000.
Pericles, II 1 line 555; Pericles, II 1 line 628 .
Rape of Lucrece, lines 544, 891, 940.
Richard III, IV 1 line 2550.
Romeo and Juliet, II 5 line 1394; Romeo and Juliet, II 6 line 1469; Romeo and Juliet, V 3 line 3039 .
Sonnet LXV line 5.
Taming of the Shrew, IV 3 line 2012.
Tempest, IV 1 line 1790.
Titus Andronicus, II 3 line 869; Titus Andronicus, II 4 line 1089; Titus Andronicus, III 1 line 1242; Titus Andronicus, IV 4 line 2105.

Troilus and Cressida, I 3 line 536; Troilus and Cressida, II 2 line 1142; Troilus and Cressida, III 1 line 1557; Troilus and Cressida, III 1 line 1626; Troilus and Cressida, V 2 line 3068; Troilus and Cressida, V 10 lines 3679, 3681.
Two Gentlemen of Verona, I 2 line 265.
Venus and Adonis, lines 36, 473, 559.
Winter's Tale, II 2 line 885; Winter's Tale, IV 4 line 2762.

Honeycomb: Old English: *hunigcamb*: honey + comb. Probably the image is from wool combing. Transferred use, of structures of similar appearance, from 1520s.
Tempest, I 2 line 479.

Honey-stalks: red clover flowers containing a sweet nectar.
Titus Andronicus, IV 4 line 2105.

Honeysuckle: mid-13c., from Old English: *hunigsuge*, meaning perhaps honeysuckle, clover, or privet, literally, honey-suck. So called because *honey* can be sucked from it.
Henry IV, Part II, II 1 line 772.
Midsummer Night's Dream, IV 1 line 1587.
Much Ado About Nothing, III 1 line 1080.

Hoof: Old English: *hof*.
Henry IV, Part I, I 1 line 9; Henry IV, Part I, V 3 line 2927.
Henry V, Prologue 1 line 28; Henry V, III 7 line 1658.
Henry VI, Part II, IV 7 line 2698.
Lover's Complaint, line 166.
Merry Wives of Windsor, I 3 line 380.
Richard II, III 2 line 1415.
Venus and Adonis, lines 287, 315.

Horn: Old English, unchanged: *horn*. Horns are an animal's weapon, so it follows that as a symbol they function as representing strength and aggressiveness. Horns represent salvation and immortality as well, as the horn is extremely durable. Notions of protection and asylum are carried with the horn. Madness and rage are often associated with the horn, especially from that of a charging animal. Can be phallic in the sense of masculine penetration. Has unfavourable interpretations when in connection with the ox, which carries senses of castration and sacrifice; also negative in its connection to Satan, who is said to have horns. Can be fabulous, though, when thought of with the mystical unicorn.
All's Well That Ends Well, I 3 line 375; All's Well That Ends Well, II 2 line 848.
Antony and Cleopatra, I 3 line 82; Antony and Cleopatra, III 13 line 2408; Antony and Cleopatra, IV 12 line 2955.

As You Like It, III 3 lines 1545r, 1547, 1549, 1554; As You Like It, IV 1 line 1847; As You Like It, IV 2 line 1984; As You Like It, IV 2 lines 1990, 1993, 1997rr.
Coriolanus, I 1 line 219; Coriolanus, III 1 line 1850; Coriolanus, IV 6 line 3065.
Henry IV, Part II, I 2 line 332; Henry IV, Part II, IV 1 line 2300.
Henry V, III 7 line 1657.
Henry VI, Part I, II 3 line 892.
Henry VI, Part III, III 3 line 1859.
King John, I 1 line 226.
King Lear, I 3 line 515; King Lear, I 4 line 542; King Lear, I 5 line 906; King Lear, III 6 line 2076; King Lear, IV 6 line 2680.
Love's Labour's Lost, IV 1 lines 1093, 1094; Love's Labour's Lost, IV 1 line 1098; Love's Labour's Lost, IV 3 line 1683; Love's Labour's Lost, V 1 line 1782; Love's Labour's Lost, V 1 line 1783; Love's Labour's Lost, V 1 line 1795; Love's Labour's Lost, V 1 lines 1797, 1798; Love's Labour's Lost, V 2 line 2061; Love's Labour's Lost, V 2 line 2062.
Measure for Measure, II 4 line 1032.
Merchant of Venice, V 1 line 2499.
Merry Wives of Windsor, II 1 line 682; Merry Wives of Windsor, II 2 line 1066; Merry Wives of Windsor, III 5 line 1888; Merry Wives of Windsor, IV 4 line 2226; Merry Wives of Windsor, V 1 line 2484; Merry Wives of Windsor, V 2 line 2524; Merry Wives of Windsor, V 5 line 2563; Merry Wives of Windsor, V 5 line 2585; Merry Wives of Windsor, V 5 line 2686.
Midsummer Night's Dream, IV 1 line 1655; Midsummer Night's Dream, IV 1 line 1680; Midsummer Night's Dream, IV 1 lines 1693, 1694; Midsummer Night's Dream, V 1 lines 2080, 2081; Midsummer Night's Dream, V 1 line 2082, 2084.
Much Ado About Nothing, I 1 line 237; Much Ado About Nothing, II 1 line 419; Much Ado About Nothing, II 1 line 420; Much Ado About Nothing, II 1 line 436; Much Ado About Nothing, II 3 line 879; Much Ado About Nothing, V 1 line 2255; Much Ado About Nothing, V 4 line 2592; Much Ado About Nothing, V 4 line 2677.
Othello, IV 1 line 2485.
Passionate Pilgrim, line 122.
Taming of the Shrew, Prologue 1 line 15; Taming of the Shrew, IV 1 line 1643; Taming of the Shrew, V 2 line 2532.
Titus Andronicus, I 1 line 544; Titus Andronicus, II 2 line 706; Titus Andronicus, II 3 lines 781, 790; Titus Andronicus, II 3 line 798; Titus Andronicus, IV 3 line 1953; Titus Andronicus, IV 3 line 1956.
Troilus and Cressida, I 1 line 144; Troilus and Cressida, IV 5 line 2630; Troilus and Cressida, IV 5 line 2648; Troilus and Cressida, V 2 line 3161; Troilus and Cressida, V 7 line 3571.
Two Gentlemen of Verona, I 1 line 83r.
Venus and Adonis, lines 1047, 1055.
Winter's Tale, I 2 line 371.

Horse: Old English: *hors*. Used since at least late 14c. of various devices or appliances which suggest a horse (e.g. sawhorse). Although Shakespeare's allusions to the horse are most extensive, yet he has said little of the many widespread superstitions, legends, and traditional tales that have been associated from the earliest times with this brave and intellectual animal. Witches, too, have generally been supposed to harass the horse, using it in various ways for their fiendish purposes. Thus, there are numerous local traditions in which the horse at night-time has been ridden by the witches, and found in the morning in an almost prostrate condition, bathed in sweat. It was a current notion that a horse hair dropped into corrupted water would soon become an animal. A horse is said to have *a cloud in his face*, when he has a dark coloured spot in his forehead between his eyes. This gives him a sour look, and, being supposed to indicate an ill-temper, is generally considered a great blemish

All's Well That Ends Well, II 1 line 771; All's Well That Ends Well, II 5 line 1288; All's Well That Ends Well, II 5 line 1358; All's Well That Ends Well, III 3 line 1543; All's Well That Ends Well, III 6 line 1775; All's Well That Ends Well, IV 3 line 2218; All's Well That Ends Well, IV 3 line 2236; All's Well That Ends Well, IV 3 line 2375; All's Well That Ends Well, IV 5 line 2514; All's Well That Ends Well, V 1 line 2609.

Antony and Cleopatra, I 4 line 492; Antony and Cleopatra, I 5 lines 545, 546, 547; Antony and Cleopatra, III 1 line 1584; Antony and Cleopatra, III 2 line 1618; Antony and Cleopatra, III 6 line 1872; Antony and Cleopatra, III 7 lines 1944, 1945, 1946; Antony and Cleopatra, III 7 line 2010; Antony and Cleopatra, III 7 line 2026; Antony and Cleopatra, III 10 line 2104; Antony and Cleopatra, IV 14 line 2988.

As You Like It, I 1 line 9; As You Like It, III 3 line 1568; As You Like It, III 4 line 1614; As You Like It, III 4 line 1631; As You Like It, V 3 line 2374; As You Like It, V 4 line 2498.

Comedy of Errors, III 1 line 645; Comedy of Errors, III 2 line 848.

Coriolanus, I 4 line 480; Coriolanus, I 4 line 485; Coriolanus, I 9 line 800; Coriolanus, II 1 line 1036; Coriolanus, II 1 line 1149; Coriolanus, III 2 line 2164; Coriolanus, V 4 line 3745.

Cymbeline, II 3 line 1008; Cymbeline, III 2 line 1559; Cymbeline, III 2 line 1586; Cymbeline, III 4 line 1720; Cymbeline, III 4 line 1834; Cymbeline, III 5 line 1974; Cymbeline, IV 1 line 2309; Cymbeline, IV 4 line 2904; Cymbeline, IV 4 line 2928.

Hamlet, II 2 line 1529; Hamlet, IV 7 lines 3224, 3226; Hamlet, V 1 line 3426; Hamlet, V 2 line 3792; Hamlet, V 2 line 3804.

Henry IV, Part I, I 1 line 61; Henry IV, Part I, I 1 line 64; Henry IV, Part I, I 2 line 233; Henry IV, Part I, I 2 line 277; Henry IV, Part I, I 2 line 279; Henry IV, Part I, II 1 line 645; Henry IV, Part I, II 2 line 742; Henry IV, Part I, II 2 lines 751, 770, 771; Henry IV, Part I, II 2 line 780; Henry IV, Part I, II 2 line 809; Henry IV, Part I, II 2 line 819; Henry IV, Part I, II 2 line 839; Henry IV, Part I, II 2 line 848; Henry IV, Part I, II 3 line 928; Henry IV, Part I, II 3 line 929; Henry IV, Part I, II 3 line 930; Henry IV, Part I, II 3 line 939r; Henry IV, Part I, II 3 line 957; Henry IV, Part I, II 3 line 965; Henry IV, Part I, II 4 line 1098; Henry IV, Part I, II 4 line 1181; Henry IV, Part I, II 4 line 1227; Henry IV, Part I, II 4 line 1329; Henry IV,

Part I, II 4 line 1338; Henry IV, Part I, II 4 line 1519; Henry IV, Part I, III 1 line 1705; Henry IV, Part I, III 1 line 1819; Henry IV, Part I, III 3 line 2016; Henry IV, Part I, III 3 line 2046; Henry IV, Part I, III 3 line 2195; Henry IV, Part I, III 3 line 2206r; Henry IV, Part I, IV 1 line 2335; Henry IV, Part I, IV 1 lines 2345, 2348r; Henry IV, Part I, IV 3 lines 2476, 2478, 2481; Henry IV, Part I, IV 3 line 2482.
Henry IV, Part II, Prologue 1 line 5; Henry IV, Part II, I 1 line 56; Henry IV, Part II, I 1 lines 90, 95; Henry IV, Part II, I 1 line 113; Henry IV, Part II, I 2 line 345; Henry IV, Part II, I 2 line 346; Henry IV, Part II, II 1 line 917; Henry IV, Part II, II 4 line 1427; Henry IV, Part II, V 1 line 3206; Henry IV, Part II, V 3 line 3534; Henry IV, Part II, V 3 line 3548.
Henry V, Prologue 1 line 27; Henry V, II 0 line 468; Henry V, II 3 line 885; Henry V, III 7 line 1645; Henry V, III 7 line 1646; Henry V, III 7 line 1649; Henry V, III 7 line 1652; Henry V, III 7 line 1664; Henry V, III 7 line 1666; Henry V, III 7 line 1674; Henry V, III 7 line 1683; Henry V, III 7 line 1694; Henry V, III 7 line 1697; Henry V, III 7 line 1704; Henry V, III 7 line 1713; Henry V, IV 1 line 2120; Henry V, IV 2 line 2164; Henry V, IV 2 line 2179r; Henry V, IV 2 line 2210; Henry V, IV 2 line 2223; Henry V, IV 7 line 2575; Henry V, IV 7 line 2606; Henry V, V 2 line 3122.
Henry VI, Part I, I 1 line 126; Henry VI, Part I, I 4 line 571; Henry VI, Part I, I 5 line 616; Henry VI, Part I, II 4 line 934; Henry VI, Part I, IV 1 line 1931; Henry VI, Part I, IV 2 line 2011; Henry VI, Part I, IV 3 line 2038; Henry VI, Part I, IV 4 line 2119; Henry VI, Part I, IV 4 line 2126; Henry VI, Part I, IV 5 line 2143; Henry VI, Part I, IV 6 line 2239; Henry VI, Part I, V 5 line 2907.
Henry VI, Part II, I 4 line 714; Henry VI, Part II, IV 3 line 2513; Henry VI, Part II, IV 4 line 2578; Henry VI, Part II, IV 7 line 2670; Henry VI, Part II, V 1 line 3029; Henry VI, Part II, V 3 line 3327.
Henry VI, Part III, I 1 line 4; Henry VI, Part III, I 4 line 567; Henry VI, Part III, II 3 line 1052; Henry VI, Part III, IV 5 line 2291; Henry VI, Part III, IV 5 line 2299.
Henry VIII, I 1 line 45; Henry VIII, I 1 line 198; Henry VIII, II 2 line 1017; Henry VIII, V 3 line 3079.
Julius Caesar, II 2 line 998; Julius Caesar, IV 1 line 1892; Julius Caesar, IV 2 line 1942; Julius Caesar, IV 2 line 1948; Julius Caesar, V 3 line 2513; Julius Caesar, V 3 line 2529.
King John, II 1 line 590.
King Lear, I 4 line 746; King Lear, I 4 line 776; King Lear, I 4 line 783; King Lear, I 4 line 868; King Lear, I 5 line 907; King Lear, I 5 line 920; King Lear, II 2 line 1077; King Lear, II 4 line 1283; King Lear, II 4 line 1313; King Lear, II 4 line 1402; King Lear, II 4 line 1603; King Lear, III 4 line 1856; King Lear, III 4 line 1929; King Lear, III 6 line 2023; King Lear, III 7 line 2140; King Lear, IV 1 line 2312; King Lear, IV 6 line 2741; King Lear, IV 6 line 2790; King Lear, V 3 line 3495.
Love's Labour's Lost, I 2 line 356; Love's Labour's Lost, III 1 line 810; Love's Labour's Lost, III 1 line 813; Love's Labour's Lost, IV 1 line 972; Love's Labour's Lost, IV 2 line 1276.
Lover's Complaint, lines 107, 111.

Macbeth, I 7 line 495; Macbeth, II 3 line 942; Macbeth, II 4 line 963; Macbeth, III 1 line 1031; Macbeth, III 1 line 1041; Macbeth, III 1 line 1044; Macbeth, III 3 line 1244; Macbeth, III 3 line 1249; Macbeth, IV 1 line 1719; Macbeth, V 3 line 2288.
Measure for Measure, I 2 line 252.
Merchant of Venice, I 2 line 234; Merchant of Venice, I 2 line 250; Merchant of Venice, II 2 line 660; Merchant of Venice, II 6 line 919.
Merry Wives of Windsor, II 1 line 657; Merry Wives of Windsor, III 5 line 1858; Merry Wives of Windsor, IV 3 line 2183; Merry Wives of Windsor, IV 3 line 2189; Merry Wives of Windsor, IV 5 line 2357; Merry Wives of Windsor, IV 5 line 2370; Merry Wives of Windsor, V 5 line 2689.
Midsummer Night's Dream, II 1 line 413; Midsummer Night's Dream, III 1 line 909; Midsummer Night's Dream, III 1 line 915; Midsummer Night's Dream, III 1 lines 925, 928.
Much Ado About Nothing, I 1 line 62; Much Ado About Nothing, I 1 line 127; Much Ado About Nothing, I 1 line 240; Much Ado About Nothing, III 4 line 1539; Much Ado About Nothing, III 5 line 1614.
Othello, I 1 line 122.
Pericles, I 4 line 512; Pericles, III 0 line 1148.
Rape of Lucrece, line 979.
Richard II, II 1 line 990r; Richard II, II 1 line 991; Richard II, III 2 line 1415; Richard II, IV 1 line 2055; Richard II, V 2 line 2522; Richard II, V 2 line 2566; Richard II, V 3 line 2593; Richard II, V 5 lines 2831, 2832; Richard II, V 5 lines 2841, 2843.
Richard III, I 1 lines 154, 168; Richard III, I 3 line 585; Richard III, II 2 line 1401; Richard III, III 2 line 1795; Richard III, III 4 line 2042; Richard III, V 3 line 3679; Richard III, V 3 lines 3802, 3807, 3811, 3814; Richard III, V 3 line 3858; Richard III, V 4 line 3877; Richard III, V 4 line 3881rr; Richard III, V 4 line 3882; Richard III, V 4 line 3887rr.
Romeo and Juliet, I 4 line 589; Romeo and Juliet, V 1 line 2832; Romeo and Juliet, V 1 line 2841.
Sonnet LI line 9; Sonnet XCI line 4; Sonnet XCI line 12.
Taming of the Shrew, Prologue, 1 line 62; Taming of the Shrew, Prologue 2 line 185; Taming of the Shrew, I 1 line 433; Taming of the Shrew, I 2 line 629; Taming of the Shrew, III 2 line 1409; Taming of the Shrew, III 2 line 1424; Taming of the Shrew, III 2 line 1436; Taming of the Shrew, III 2 line 1440; Taming of the Shrew, III 2 line 1451; Taming of the Shrew, III 2 line 1571; Taming of the Shrew, III 2 line 1572; Taming of the Shrew, III 2 line 1598; Taming of the Shrew, IV 1 line 1662; Taming of the Shrew, IV 1 line 1676; Taming of the Shrew, IV 1 line 1678; Taming of the Shrew, IV 1 lines 1680, 1681, 1683, 1684, 1686; Taming of the Shrew, IV 1 line 1696; Taming of the Shrew, IV 1 line 1720; Taming of the Shrew, IV 1 line 1728; Taming of the Shrew, IV 3 line 2144; Taming of the Shrew, IV 3 line 2150; Taming of the Shrew, IV 5 line 2275.
Timon of Athens, I 1 line 280; Timon of Athens, I 2 line 521; Timon of Athens, I 2 line 543; Timon of Athens, II 1 lines 633, 634, 636; Timon of Athens, IV 3 line 1829; Timon of Athens, IV 3 lines 2040, 2041.

Titus Andronicus, II 2 line 718; Titus Andronicus, II 2 line 726; Titus Andronicus, II 2 line 728.
Troilus and Cressida, I 3 line 492; Troilus and Cressida, I 3 line 664; Troilus and Cressida, II 1 line 874; Troilus and Cressida, III 3 line 2002; Troilus and Cressida, III 3 line 2037; Troilus and Cressida, III 3 line 2187; Troilus and Cressida, V 5 line 3453; Troilus and Cressida, V 5 line 3476; Troilus and Cressida, V 6 line 3521; Troilus and Cressida, V 8 line 3614; Troilus and Cressida, V 10 line 3637.
Twelfth Night, II 3 line 866; Twelfth Night, II 3 line 867; Twelfth Night, III 4 line 1832; Twelfth Night, III 4 lines 1836, 1839.
Two Gentlemen of Verona, III 1 lines 1340, 1349, 1350.
Venus and Adonis, lines 50, 278, 313, 342, 400, 410, 699.
Winter's Tale, III 1 line 1207; Winter's Tale, IV 3 line 1790; Winter's Tale, IV 3 line 1793.

Horse-piss: horse + piss, late 13c., from Old French: *pissier: urinate* (12c).
    Tempest, IV 1 line 1942.

Hound: Old English: *hund: dog*. Meaning narrowed 12c. to dog used for hunting. Sense of *pursue relentlessly* is first recorded c.1600.
    Comedy of Errors, IV 2 line 1114.
    Coriolanus, V 6 line 3954.
    Henry V, Prologue 1 line 8; Henry V, II 1 line 578.
    Henry VI, Part I, IV 2 line 2019.
    Julius Caesar, II 1 line 794; Julius Caesar, V 1 line 2392.
    King Lear, III 6 line 2070.
    Love's Labour's Lost, IV 2 line 1275.
    Macbeth, III 1 line 1108.
    Midsummer Night's Dream, III 1 lines 924, 927; Midsummer Night's Dream, III 2 line 1097; Midsummer Night's Dream, IV 1 lines 1660, 1666; Midsummer Night's Dream, IV 1 line 1669; Midsummer Night's Dream, IV 1 line 1674.
    Othello, II 3 line 1517.
    Passionate Pilgrim, line 123.
    Rape of Lucrece, line 745.
    Sonnet XCI line 4.
    Taming of the Shrew, Prologue 1 line 16; Taming of the Shrew, Prologue 1 line 62; Taming of the Shrew, Prologue 2 line 189; Taming of the Shrew, V 2 line 2565.
    Tempest, IV 1 line 1997.
    Titus Andronicus, I 1 line 544; Titus Andronicus, II 2 line 707; Titus Andronicus, II 2 line 728; Titus Andronicus, II 3 lines 750, 760; Titus Andronicus, II 3 line 798; Titus Andronicus, II 3 line 805.
    Troilus and Cressida, V 1 line 3036.
    Twelfth Night, I 1 line 24.
    Venus and Adonis, line 935.

Human: mid-15c., *humain, humaigne*, from Old French: *humain, umain: of or belonging to man* (12c.), from Latin: *humanus: of man, human*, also humane, philanthropic, kind, gentle, polite; learned, refined, civilized, probably related to homo (*hominis*) man, and to *humus: earth*, on notion of earthly beings, as opposed to the gods.

All's Well That Ends Well, V 3 line 2807.
Antony and Cleopatra, V 1 line 3319.
As You Like It, V 2 line 2306.
Comedy of Errors, V 1 line 1625.
Coriolanus, I 1 line 16; Coriolanus, II 1 line 1158; Coriolanus, II 1 line 1196; Coriolanus, III 1 line 1902; Coriolanus, III 1 line 2146.
Cymbeline, I 5 line 514; Cymbeline, III 2 line 1522.
Hamlet, III 2 line 1912.
Henry IV, Part II, IV 3 line 2714.
Henry V, II 2 line 730; Henry V, IV 1 line 1952.
Henry VI, Part I, I 1 line 127; Henry VI, Part I, II 3 line 884; Henry VI, Part I, III 2 line 1602.
Henry VI, Part III, I 4 line 595.
King Lear, IV 2 line 2393.
Macbeth, I 5 line 361; Macbeth, III 4 line 1367.
Measure for Measure, I 3 line 344.
Merchant of Venice, IV 1 line 1934; Merchant of Venice, IV 1 line 1957; Merchant of Venice, IV 1 line 2069.
Midsummer Night's Dream, II 1 line 470; Midsummer Night's Dream, II 2 line 711; Midsummer Night's Dream, II 2 line 778.
Othello, I 3 line 674; Othello, II 1 line 1039; Othello, III 3 line 1921; Othello, V 1 line 3215.
Passionate Pilgrim, line 109.
Rape of Lucrece, lines 246, 622.
Richard III, 1 2 line 234.
Tempest, I 2 line 401; Tempest, I 2 line 420; Tempest, I 2 line 498; Tempest, III 3 line 1510: Tempest, IV 1 line 1929; Tempest, V 1 line 2038.
Timon of Athens, I 1 line 319; Timon of Athens, III 6 line 1546; Timon of Athens, IV 3 line 1872; Timon of Athens, IV 3 line 2002; Timon of Athens, V 4 line 2646.
Titus Andronicus, V 2 line 2494; Titus Andronicus, V 3 line 2539.
Troilus and Cressida, II 2 line 1173; Troilus and Cressida, IV 1 line 2220.
Winter's Tale, III 2 line 1241; Winter's Tale, III 2 line 1397; Winter's Tale, V 1 line 2867.

Humble-bee: Middle English: *humbylbee*.
All's Well That Ends Well, IV 5 line 2470.
Love's Labour's Lost, III 1 line 847; Love's Labour's Lost, III 1 line 851; Love's Labour's Lost, III 1 line 857.
Midsummer Night's Dream, III 1 993; Midsummer Night's Dream, IV 1 line 1556.
Troilus and Cressida, V 10 line 3678.

Husbandry: c.1300, management of a household; late 14c. as farm management, from husband, in a now-obsolete sense of peasant farmer (early 13c.).
    As You Like It, II 3 line 709.
    Coriolanus, IV 7 line 3240.
    Cymbeline, III 3 line 1701.
    Hamlet, IV 1 line 563.
    Henry V, IV 1 line 1849; Henry V, V 2 line 3020.
    Henry VI, Part II, III 1 line 1310.
    Macbeth, II 1 line 573.
    Measure for Measure, I 4 line 396.
    Merchant of Venice, III 4 line 1774.
    Pericles, III 2 line 1309.
    Sonnet III line 6; Sonnet XIII line 10.
    Timon of Athens, II 2 line 845.
    Troilus and Cressida, I 2 line 161.

Husks: late 14c., *huske: dry, outer skin of certain fruits and seeds*, of unknown origin.
    As You Like It, I 1 line 33.
    Henry IV, Part I, IV 2 line 2403.
    Henry V, IV 2 line 2182.
    Tempest, I 2 line 645.
    Troilus and Cressida, IV 5 line 2788.

Hyen: hyena, mid-14c., from Old French: *hiene*, from Latin: *hyaena*. So called for its bristles. Applied to cruel, treacherous, and greedy persons.
    As You Like It, IV 1 line 1926.

Ice: c.1400, *ysen*.
    All's Well That Ends Well, II 3 line 992.
    As You Like It, III 4 line 1608.
    Coriolanus, I 1 line 174.
    Hamlet, I 1 line 79; Hamlet, III 1 line 1828.
    Henry V, IV 1 line 2047.
    King John, IV 2 line 1740.
    Measure for Measure, II 1 line 495; Measure for Measure, III 1 line 1358.
    Midsummer Night's Dream, V 1 line 1896.
    Richard III, IV 2 line 2605.
    Taming of the Shrew, I 2 line 820; Taming of the Shrew, IV 1 line 1632.
    Timon of Athens, IV 3 line 1914.
    Troilus and Cressida, III 3 line 2095.
    Two Gentlemen of Verona, III 2 line 1458.

Icicles: Middle English: from ice + dialect: *ickle: icicle* (from Old English gicel).
    Henry V, III 5 line 1413.

Love's Labour's Lost, V 2 line 2859.
Merchant of Venice, II 1 line 519.

Iris: late 14c., flowering plant; also prismatic rock crystal, from Latin: *iris*. The eye region was so called (early 15c. in English) for being the coloured part; the Greek word was used of any brightly coloured circle.
All's Well That Ends Well, I 3 line 471.
Henry VI, Part II, III 2 line 2103.

Island: 1590s, earlier *yland* (c.1300), from Old English: *igland: island*, from *ieg: island*. Spelling modified 15c. by association with similar but unrelated isle. Also, *ealand: river-land, watered place, meadow by a river*. In place names, Old English: *ieg* is often used of slightly raised dry ground offering settlement sites in areas surrounded by marsh or subject to flooding.
Antony and Cleopatra, V 2 line 3499.
Henry V, III 7 line 1769; Henry V, IV 2 line 2304.
Henry VI, Part II, III 1 line 1429; Henry VI, Part II, III 3 line 2117; Henry VI, Part II, IV 1 line 2293.
Henry VI, Part III, IV 8 line 2541.
King John, I 1 line 12; King John, II 1 line 315; King John, V 2 line 2383.
Othello, II 3 line 1258; Othello, II 3 line 1277; Othello, III 3 line 1943.
Pericles, V 1 line 2234.
Rape of Lucrece, line 1791.
Tempest, I 2 line 286; Tempest, I 2 line 417; Tempest, I 2 line 482; Tempest, I 2 line 552; Tempest, I 2 line 591; Tempest, I 2 line 635; Tempest, II 1 line 740; Tempest, II 1 line 790; Tempest, II 1 line 793; Tempest, II 1 line 1075; Tempest, II 2 line 1122; Tempest, II 2 line 1235; Tempest, III 2 line 1399; Tempest, III 2 line 1437; Tempest, III 3 lines 1596, 1597; Tempest, III 3 line 1632; Tempest, IV 1 line 1960; Tempest, V 1 line 2224; Tempest, V 1 line 2411.
Troilus and Cressida, III 1 line 1640; Troilus and Cressida, III 3 line 2090.
Two Gentlemen of Verona, I 3 line 312.

Ivory: mid 13c., Anglo-French: *ivorie*. As a colour, especially in reference to human skin, it is attested from 1580s.
Merchant of Venice, III 1 line 1274.
Rape of Lucrece, lines 458, 515, 1285.
Taming of the Shrew, II 1 line 1203.
Timon of Athens, I 1 line 87.
Venus and Adonis, lines 250, 383.

Ivy: Old English: *ifig*. Perhaps referring to some species producing poisonous figs. It was formerly the general custom in England, as it is still in France and the Netherlands, to hang a bush of ivy at the door of a vintner. Ivy is an evergreen, and by this connection stands for eternity and life, for immortality. It also may represent dependence and attachment, which can be seen in the way it climbs trees and buildings to get sunlight. The ivy leaf is also phallic,

depicting the male trinity, but it can also be a female symbol denoting a force in need of protection. Conversely, however, its malevolent, poison feature can cause it to be seen often as ingratitude.
    Comedy of Errors, II 2 line 567.
    Midsummer Night's Dream, IV 1 line 1588.
    Passionate Pilgrim, line 366.
    Tempest, I 2 line 186.
    Winter's Tale, III 3 line 1562.

Jade: an old worn out horse; Middle English. Late 16th century: from French *le jade* (earlier *l'ejade*), from Spanish *piedra de ijada*: stone of the flank (i.e. stone for colic, which it was believed to cure).
    All's Well That Ends Well, II 3 line 1186; All's Well That Ends Well, IV 5 line 2517.
    Antony and Cleopatra, III 1 line 1585.
    Hamlet, III 2 line 2135.
    Henry IV, Part I, II 1 line 648; Henry IV, Part I, II 1 line 652.
    Henry IV, Part II, I 1 line 97; Henry IV, Part II, II 4 line 1428.
    Henry V, III 5 line 1409; Henry V, III 7 line 1664; Henry V, III 7 line 1698; Henry V, IV 2 line 2211.
    Henry VI, Part II, IV 1 line 2154; Henry VI, Part II, IV 1 line 2205.
    Henry VIII, III 2 line 2174.
    Julius Caesar, IV 2 line 1945.
    King John, II 1 line 695.
    Measure for Measure, II 1 line 697.
    Much Ado About Nothing, I 1 line 130.
    Rape of Lucrece, line 757.
    Richard II, III 3 line 1821; Richard II, V 5 line 2836.
    Sonnet LI line 12.
    Taming of the Shrew, I 2 line 802; Taming of the Shrew, II 1 line 1049; Taming of the Shrew, IV 1 line 1621.
    Troilus and Cressida, II 1 line 876.
    Twelfth Night, II 5 line 1187.
    Two Gentlemen of Verona, III 1 line 1341.
    Venus and Adonis, line 411.

Jawbone: 15c.
    Hamlet, V 1 line 3419.

Jaws: late Middle English: from Old French: *joe: cheek, jaw*, of unknown origin.
    Antony and Cleopatra, II 5 line 1063.
    Hamlet, I 4 line 679; Hamlet, IV 2 line 2694.
    Henry IV, Part I, III 2 line 1925.
    Henry V, II 4 line 1008.
    Henry VI, Part II, IV 1 line 2157.
    King John, V 2 line 2396.
    Midsummer Night's Dream, I 1 line 154.
    Sonnet XIX line 3.

Troilus and Cressida, I 3 line 526.
Twelfth Night, III 4 line 1914.

Jay: c.1300, common European bird (Garrulus glandarinus). Applied to humans in sense of *impertinent chatterer, flashy dresser* from 1620s. From its gaudy plumage, this bird has been used for a loose woman.
Cymbeline, III 4 line 1771.
Merry Wives of Windsor, III 3 line 1442.
Taming of the Shrew, IV 3 line 2134.
Tempest, II 2 line 1255.
Winter's Tale, IV 3 line 1733.

Jelly: late 14c., from Old French: *gelee: a frost; jelly*.
Hamlet, I 2 line 414.
King Lear, III 7 line 2216.
Winter's Tale, I 2 line 544.

Jennet: small Spanish horse, mid-15c., from French *genet*, from Spanish *jinete:* a light horseman, perhaps from Arabic *Zenata*, name of a Barbary tribe. Sense transferred in English and French from the rider to the horse.
Venus and Adonis, line 280.

Jet: semi-precious variety of lignite. Middle English: from Old French: *jaiet*, from Latin: *Gagates*, from Greek: *gagatēs* from *Gagai*, a town in Asia Minor.
Henry VI, Part II, II 1 line 858; Henry VI, Part II, II 1 line 859; Henry VI, Part II, II 1 line 860.
Lover's Complaint, line 37.
Merchant of Venice, III 1 line1274.
Pericles, I 4 line 442.
Titus Andronicus, V 2 line 2356.

Jewel: late 13c., article of value used for adornment, from Anglo-French: *juel*, Old French: *jouel: ornament, jewel* (12c.). Sense of *precious stone* developed early 14c. Meaning *beloved person, admired woman* is late 14c. Colloquial, *jewel* as *testicle* dates to late 15c.
All's Well That Ends Well, IV 2 line 2058; All's Well That Ends Well, V 3 line 2673; All's Well That Ends Well, V 3 line 3013.
Antony and Cleopatra, IV 15 line 3260; Antony and Cleopatra, V 2 line 3559.
As You Like It, I 3 line 542; As You Like It, II 1 line 571: As You Like It, III 2 line 1200.
Comedy of Errors, II 1 line 383; Comedy of Errors, V 1 line 1578.
Coriolanus, I 4 line 559.
Cymbeline, I 1 line 109; Cymbeline, I 4 line 467r; Cymbeline, I 6 line 821; Cymbeline, II 3 line 1145; Cymbeline, II 4 line 1294; Cymbeline, V 5 line 3545.
Henry IV, Part II, I 2 line 292; Henry IV, Part II, II 4 line 1290.
Henry VI, Part I, I 6 line 653; Henry IV, Part I, V 1 line 2403.
Henry VI, Part II, III 2 line 1787; Henry VI, Part II, III 2 line 2106.

Henry VIII, II 2 line 1052; Henry VIII, IV 1 line 2546; Henry VIII, V 1 line 2818.
King John, V 1 line 2235.
King Lear, I 1 line 292; King Lear, IV 6 line 2630.
Love's Labour's Lost, II 1 line 743; Love's Labour's Lost, IV 2 line 1145; Love's Labour's Lost, V 2 line 2382; Love's Labour's Lost, V 2 line 2383.
Lover's Complaint, line 155.
Macbeth, III 1 line 1077; Macbeth, IV 3 line 1935.
Measure for Measure, II 1 line 477.
Merchant of Venice, II 4 line 836; Merchant of Venice, II 8 line 1091; Merchant of Venice, III 1 lines 1323, 1324; Merchant of Venice, V 1 line 2692.
Merry Wives of Windsor, II 2 line 1006; Merry Wives of Windsor, III 2 line 1444.
Midsummer Night's Dream, III 1 line 978; Midsummer Night's Dream, IV 1 line 1750.
Much Ado About Nothing, I 1 line 162.
Othello, I 3 line 544; Othello, III 3 line 1806; Othello, IV 2 line 2959; Othello, IV 2 line 2971; Othello, V 1 line 3152.
Pericles, II 1 line 735; Pericles, II 2 line 761; Pericles, III 1 line 1263; Pericles, III 2 line 1403; Pericles, III 4 line 1473; Pericles, IV 6 line 2097; Pericles, V 1 line 2306; Pericles, V 3 line 2548.
Rape of Lucrece, lines 85, 1242.
Richard II, I 1 line 185; Richard II, I 3 line 568; Richard II, I 3 line 571; Richard II, III 3 line 1789.
Richard III, I 4 line 860.
Romeo and Juliet, I 5 line 668.
Sonnet XXVII line 11; Sonnet XLVIII line 5; Sonnet LII line 8; Sonnet LXV line 10; Sonnet XCVI line 6; Sonnet CXXXI line 4.
Taming of the Shrew, I 2 line 665.
Tempest, III 1 1342.
Timon of Athens, I 1 line 1; Timon of Athens, I 1 line 12; Timon of Athens, I 1 line 26; Timon of Athens, I 1 line 203; Timon of Athens, I 1 line 213; Timon of Athens, I 1 line 249; Timon of Athens, I 2 line 511; Timon of Athens, I 2 line 526; Timon of Athens, III 2 line 1030; Timon of Athens, III 4 line 1186; Timon of Athens, III 4 line 1190; Timon of Athens, III 6 lines 1554, 1555.
Titus Andronicus, III 1 line 1333.
Twelfth Night, II 4 line 1025; Twelfth Night, II 5 line 1088; Twelfth Night, III 4 line 1750.
Two Gentlemen of Verona, II 4 line 829; Two Gentlemen of Verona, III 1 line 1160; Two Gentlemen of Verona, IV 4 line 1882.
Venus and Adonis, lines 183, 846.
Winter's Tale, V 1 line 2967; Winter's Tale, V 2 line 3142.

Joint: late 13c., a part of a body where two bones meet and move in contact with one another, from Old French: *joint: joint of the body. Out of joint* in the figurative sense is from early 15c. (literally, of bone displacement, late 14c.).

Hamlet, I 5 line 943.
Henry IV, Part I, IV 1 line 2306.
Henry IV, Part II, I 1 lines 198, 204; Henry IV, Part II, II 4 line 1654; Henry IV, Part II, V 1 line 3169; Henry IV, Part II, V 2 line 3303; Henry IV, Part II, V 4 line 3560.
Henry V, IV 3 line 2361.
Henry VI, Part II, III 2 line 2013.
Love's Labour's Lost, V 1 line 1855.
Measure for Measure, V 1 line 2728r.
Rape of Lucrece, 278, 504.
Richard II, III 2 line 1524; Richard II, III 3 line 1716; Richard II, V 3 line 2664; Richard II, V 3 line 2680; Richard II, V 3 line 2687.
Romeo and Juliet, III 5 line 2260; Romeo and Juliet, IV 3 line 2603; Romeo and Juliet, IV 5 line 2683; Romeo and Juliet, V 3 line 2972r.
Tempest, III 3 line 1694; Tempest, IV 1 line 2003.
Timon of Athens, I 1 line 290.
Titus Andronicus, II 3 line 959.
Troilus and Cressida, I 2 line 183r; Troilus and Cressida, I 3 line 694; Troilus and Cressida, II 3 line 1322; Troilus and Cressida, IV 1 line 2229; Troilus and Cressida, IV 5 line 2663; Troilus and Cressida, IV 5 line 2859r.
Venus and Adonis, lines 663, 1083.

June: c.1100, from Latin: *Iuniusi;* probably a variant of *Iunonius: sacred to Juno.*
Antony and Cleopatra, III 10 line 2079.
Henry VI, Part I, II 4 line 1345; Henry VI, Part I, III 2 line 1878.
Sonnet CIV line 7.

Kecksies: In Kent and Essex, the Hemlock is called Kecksies, and the stalks are spoken of as *Hollow Kecksies*. It has been suggested that *kecksies* may be a mistaken form of the plural *kex*; and that *kex* may have been formed from *keck*, something so dry that the eater would *keck* at it, or be unable to swallow it. The word is probably derived from the Welsh *cecys*, which is applied to several plants of the umbelliferous kind.
Henry V, V 2 line 3033.

Kernel: Old English: *cyrnel: seed, kernel, pip*. Figurative sense of *centre or things,* is from 1550s.
All's Well That Ends Well, II 3 line 1160; All's Well That Ends Well, II 5 line 1305.
Taming of the Shrew, II 1 line 1105.
Tempest, II 1 line 792.
Troilus and Cressida, II 1 line 960.
Winter's Tale, I 2 line 241.

Kibe: an ulcerated chilblain, usually on the heel. Middle English, origin unknown.
Hamlet, V 1 line 3477.

King Lear, I 5 line 887.
Merry Wives of Windsor, I 3 line 334.
Tempest, II 1 line 1014.

Kidney: early 14c., of unknown origin, originally *kidenere*.
Henry VI, Part I, II 2 line 746.
Merry Wives of Windsor, III 5 line 1852.

Kite: Middle English, from Old English *cyta*; akin to Middle High German *kuze:* owl. This bird was considered by the ancients to be unlucky. A person who preys on others.
Antony and Cleopatra, III 13 line 2360.
Coriolanus, IV 5 line 2799; Coriolanus, IV 5 line 2800.
Hamlet, II 2 line 1652.
Henry V, II 1 line 581.
Henry VI, Part II, III 1 line 1533; Henry VI, Part II, III 2 line 1878; Henry VI, Part II, III 2 line 1881; Henry VI, Part II, V 2 line 3220.
Julius Caesar, V 1 line 2441.
King Lear, I 4 line 788.
Macbeth, III 4 line 1361; Macbeth, IV 3 line 2100.
Richard III, I 1 line 140.
Taming of the Shrew, IV 1 line 1806.
Winter's Tale, II 3 line 1152; Winter's Tale, IV 3 line 1746.

Kitten: late Middle English *kitoun, ketoun*, from an Anglo-Norman French variant of Old French *chitoun*, diminutive of *chat cat*.
Henry VI, Part I, III 1 line 1561; Henry VI, Part I, III 1 line 1673.

Knee: early 13c., to bend the knee, kneel, from Old English: *cneowian*, from *cneow*.
All's Well That Ends Well, I 3 line 518.
Antony and Cleopatra, II 3 line 982.
As You Like It, III 5 line 1710.
Coriolanus, I 1 line 66; Coriolanus, I 3 line 410; Coriolanus, II 2 line 1342; Coriolanus, III 2 line 2256; Coriolanus, III 2 line 2306; Coriolanus, IV 6 line 3034; Coriolanus, V 1 line 3283; Coriolanus, V 3 line 3546; Coriolanus, V 3 line 3557; Coriolanus, V 3 line 3578; Coriolanus, V 3 line 3680.
Cymbeline, IV 2 line 2688; Cymbeline, V 4 line 3242; Cymbeline, V 5 line 3390; Cymbeline, V 5 line 3778.
Hamlet, II 1 line 1038; Hamlet, III 2 line 1940; Hamlet, III 3 line 2351.
Henry VI, Part I, I 3 line 580; Henry VI, Part I, II 4 line 1314; Henry VI, Part I, II 4 line 1315; Henry VI, Part I, III 3 line 2162; Henry VI, Part I, IV 3 line 2527.
Henry IV, Part II, II 4 line 1503.
Henry V, II 3 line 856; Henry V, IV 1 line 2101; Henry V, IV 3 line 2369; Henry V, IV 4 line 2429.

Henry VI, Part I, III 1 line 1402; Henry VI, Part I, III 3 line 1690; Henry VI, Part I, IV 5 line 2166; Henry VI, Part I, IV 7 line 2256; Henry VI, Part I, V 1 line 2418.
Henry VI, Part II, I 1 line 14; Henry VI, Part II, I 3 line 601; Henry VI, Part II, III 1 lines 1288, 1293; Henry VI, Part II, III 2 line 1906; Henry VI, Part II, IV 1 line 2281; Henry VI, Part II, IV 10 line 2945; Henry VI, Part II, V 1 line 3093; Henry VI, Part II, V 1 lines 3151, 3163.
Henry VI, Part III, II 2 line 932; Henry VI, Part III, II 3 line 1057; Henry VI, Part III, II 3 lines 1061, 1063; Henry VI, Part III, III 1 line 1385; Henry VI, Part III, V 1 line 2618.
Julius Caesar, I 1 line 53; Julius Caesar, II 1 line 897; Julius Caesar, II 2 line 1033; Julius Caesar, II 2 line 1062.
King John, I 1 line 88; King John, III 1 line 1235; King John, III 1 line 1237; King John, V 7 line 2740.
King Lear, II 4 line 1509.
Love's Labour's Lost, V 2 line 2484.
Macbeth, IV 3 line 1968.
Measure for Measure, III 1 line 1410; Measure for Measure, V 1 line 2640; Measure for Measure, V 1 line 2863; Measure for Measure, V 1 line 2875.
Merry Wives of Windsor, V 5 line 2637.
Midsummer Night's Dream, IV 1 line 1677.
Much Ado About Nothing, II 1 line 422; Much Ado About Nothing, II 3 line 960.
Othello, I 1 line 46; Othello, II 1 line 863; Othello, IV 2 line 2775; Othello, IV 3 line 3064.
Pericles, I 2 line 284; Pericles, IV 6 line 1955; Pericles, V 1 line 2434.
Rape of Lucrece, lines 410, 1897.
Richard II, I 3 line 342; Richard II, I 4 line 646; Richard II, II 3 line 1241; Richard II, III 3 line 1673; Richard II, III 3 line 1713; Richard II, III 3 line 1755; Richard II, III 3 lines 1838, 1843; Richard II, V 3 line 2606; Richard II, V 3 line 2675; Richard II, V 3 line 2679; Richard II, V 3 line 2688; Richard II, V 3 line 2716.
Richard III, I 2 line 364; Richard III, II 1 line 1250; Richard III, III 2 line 1378; Richard III, III 7 line 2279.
Romeo and Juliet, I 4 line 572; Romeo and Juliet, III 1 line 1673; Romeo and Juliet, III 5 line 2266.
Taming of the Shrew, I 1 line 461.
Timon of Athens, I 1 line 77; Timon of Athens, I 1 line 107; Timon of Athens, III 6 line 1537; Timon of Athens, IV 3 line 1700; Timon of Athens, IV 3 line 1889.
Titus Andronicus, I 1 line 523; Titus Andronicus, II 3 line 1041; Titus Andronicus, V 3 line 2706.
Troilus and Cressida, I 3 line 500; Troilus and Cressida, III 3 line 1916; Troilus and Cressida, IV 2 line 2386; Troilus and Cressida, V 3 line 3338.
Two Gentlemen of Verona, III 1 lines 1300, 1303.
Winter's Tale, I 2 line 275; Winter's Tale, II 3 line 1112; Winter's Tale, III 2 line 1447.

Knot-grass: a common Eurasian plant of the dock family, with jointed creeping stems and small pink flowers; weed, low, straggling, and many-jointed, hence its name of Knot-grass.It has the supposed power of hindering the growth of any child or animal, when taken in an infusion.
Midsummer Night's Dream, III 2 line 1380.

Labras: lips
Merry Wives of Windsor, I 1 line 147.

Ladybird: sweetheart, 1590s.
Romeo and Juliet, I 3 line 383.

Lady-smocks: This plant is so-called from the resemblance of its white flowers to little smocks hung out to dry. According to another explanation, the lady's smock is a corruption of *Our Lady's Smock*, so called from its first flowering about Lady-tide.
Love's Labour's Lost, V 2 line 2843.

Lake: body of water, early 12c., from Old French: *lack* and directly from Latin: *lacus: pond, lake*, also *basin, tank*. In Middle English, lake, as a descendant of the Old English word, also could mean *stream; river gully; ditch; marsh; grave; pit of hell*, and this might have influenced the form of the borrowed word. Also, *deep red colouring matter*, 1610s, from French: *laque*, from which it was obtained. Taking into consideration its reflecting power, it symbolises a mirror for self-contemplation as well as a chance for revelation.
Henry IV, Part II, II 4 line 1417.
Henry VI, Part II, I 4 line 672.
Henry VI, Part III, I 3 line 406.
King Lear, III 6 line 2014.
Rape of Lucrece, line 1728.
Tempest, IV 1 line 1918; Tempest, V 1 line 2054.
Titus Andronicus, IV 3 line 1924.

Lamb: Old English: *lamb;* plural was *lomberu*. Although meaning a new born sheep, it was also applied to persons (especially young Church members, gentle souls, etc.) from late Old English. Also sometimes used ironically for cruel or rough characters. Lamb's-wool is from 1550s. In Christianity, the lamb represents Christ as both suffering and triumphant; it is typically a sacrificial animal, and may also symbolise gentleness, innocence, and purity. When depicted with the lion, the pair can mean a state of paradise. In addition, the lamb symbolises sweetness, forgiveness and meekness.
As You Like It, III 2 line 1189; As You Like It, III 2 line 1193.
Comedy of Errors, IV 1 line 3456.
Coriolanus, II 1 line 924; Coriolanus, II 1 line 927; Coriolanus, II 1 line 928.
Cymbeline, I 6 line 657; Cymbeline, III 4 line 1820.
Henry V, III 7 line 1671.
Henry VI, Part I, I 2 line 273; Henry VI, Part I, V 4 line 2700.

Henry VI, Part II, III 1 line 1332; Henry VI, Part II, III 1 line 1349; Henry VI, Part II, III 1 line 1355; Henry VI, Part II, IV 2 line 2381.
Henry VI, Part III, I 1 line 260; Henry VI, Part III, I 4 line 440; Henry VI, Part III, IV 2 line 2381; Henry VI, Part III, II 5 line 1179; Henry VI, Part III, IV 8 lines 2571, 2572.
Julius Caesar, IV 3 line 2098.
King John, IV 1 line 1665.
Love's Labour's Lost, II 1 line 717; Love's Labour's Lost, IV 1 line 1065.
Macbeth, IV 3 line 1859; Macbeth, IV 3 line 1905.
Measure for Measure, III 2 line 1521; Measure for Measure, V 1 line 2714.
Merchant of Venice, I 3 line 414; Merchant of Venice, IV 1 line 2006.
Much Ado About Nothing, I 1 line 13; Much Ado About Nothing, III 3 line 1387.
Rape of Lucrece, lines 218, 728, 788, 929.
Richard II, II 1 line 861.
Richard III, IV 4 line 2814; Richard III, IV 4 line 2848; Richard III, IV 4 line 3032 .
Romeo and Juliet, I 3 line 383; Romeo and Juliet, II 5 line 1421; Romeo and Juliet, III 2 line 1798; Romeo and Juliet, IV 5 line 2654.
Sonnet XCVI line 9; Sonnet XCVI line 11.
Taming of the Shrew, III 2 line 1519.
Timon of Athens, IV 3 line 2030.
Titus Andronicus, II 3 line 970; Titus Andronicus, IV 2 line 1828.
Troilus and Cressida, III 2 line 1845; Troilus and Cressida, IV 4 line 2450.
Twelfth Night, V 1 line 2322.
Two Gentlemen of Verona, IV 4 line 1931.
Venus and Adonis, line 1120.
Winter's Tale, I 2 line 132.

Lambkin: used to describe a very young lamb, or a child, affectionately.
    Henry IV, Part II, V 3 line 3528.
    Henry V, II 1 line 632.

Land: Old English: *land, lond: ground, soil,* also *definite portion of the earth's surface, home region of a person or a people, territory marked by political boundaries.*
    All's Well That Ends Well, I 3 line 364.
    Antony and Cleopatra, I 4 line 510; Antony and Cleopatra, II 2 line 880; Antony and Cleopatra, II 6 line 1239; Antony and Cleopatra, II 6 line 1241; Antony and Cleopatra, II 6 line 1325; Antony and Cleopatra, II 6 line 1327; Antony and Cleopatra, II 6 line 1331; Antony and Cleopatra, II 6 line 1332; Antony and Cleopatra, III 6 line 1881; Antony and Cleopatra, III 7 line 1987; Antony and Cleopatra, III 7 line 1990; Antony and Cleopatra, III 7 line 2002; Antony and Cleopatra, III 7 line 2009; Antony and Cleopatra, III 7 line 2026; Antony and Cleopatra, III 7 line 2030; Antony and Cleopatra, III 8 line 2046; Antony and Cleopatra,

III 10 line 2057; Antony and Cleopatra, III 11 line 2111; Antony and Cleopatra, III 13 line 2458; Antony and Cleopatra, IV 2 line 2523; Antony and Cleopatra, IV 5 line 2678; Antony and Cleopatra, IV 10 line 2882; Antony and Cleopatra, IV 11 line 2893.

As You Like It, I 1 line 90; As You Like It, III 1 line 1111; As You Like It, III 1 line 1119; As You Like It, IV 1 line 1816; As You Like It, V 4 line 2559; As You Like It, V 4 lines 2562, 2565; As You Like It, V 4 line 2585.

Comedy of Errors, II 2 line 578; Comedy of Errors, IV 1 line 1045; Comedy of Errors, IV 2 line 1113.

Coriolanus, V 4 line 3792.

Cymbeline, I 2 line 247; Cymbeline, I 6 line 640; Cymbeline, II 1 line 915; Cymbeline, II 4 line 1202; Cymbeline, III 3 line 1711; Cymbeline, III 4 line1936.

Hamlet, I 1 line 88; Hamlet, I 1 lines 105, 120, 124; Hamlet, I 2 line 223; Hamlet, V 1 line 3412; Hamlet, V 1 lines 3445, 3450; Hamlet, V 2 line 3742.

Henry IV, Part I, I 1 line 49; Henry IV, Part I, II 4 line 1344; Henry IV, Part I, II 4 line 1396; Henry IV, Part I, III 1 line 1621; Henry IV, Part I, III 1 line 1642; Henry IV, Part I, III 1 line 1681; Henry IV, Part I, III 3 line 2212; Henry IV, Part I, IV 3 line 2503; Henry IV, Part I, IV 4 line 2605; Henry IV, Part I, V 5 line 3184.

Henry IV, Part II, I 1 line 274; Henry IV, Part II, III 1 line 1816; Henry IV, Part II, III 2 line 2195; Henry IV, Part II, IV 1 lines 2412, 2417; Henry IV, Part II, IV 3 line 2710; Henry IV, Part II, IV 5 line 3136; Henry IV, Part II, V 3 line 3535.

Henry V, I 1 line 46; Henry V, I 2 lines 184, 185, 189, 196, 201; Henry V, I 2 line 296; Henry V, II 4 line 1047; Henry V, III 5 line 1412; Henry V, III 5 line 1438; Henry V, V 0 line 2851.

Henry VI, Part I, IV 3 line 2082.

Henry VI, Part II, I 1 line 84; Henry VI, Part II, I 1 line 186; Henry VI, Part II, I 1 line 215; Henry VI, Part II, I 1 line 216; Henry VI, Part II, I 1 line 243; Henry VI, Part II, I 3 line 406; Henry VI, Part II, I 3 line 477; Henry VI, Part II, I 3 line 573; Henry VI, Part II, II 4 lines 1189, 1203; Henry VI, Part II, III 1 line 1427; Henry VI, Part II, III 2 line 1789; Henry VI, Part II, III 2 line 2052; Henry VI, Part II, V 1 line 3029.

Henry VI, Part III, II 6 line 1345; Henry VI, Part III, III 1 lines 1381, 1382; Henry VI, Part III, III 2 lines 1473, 1474; Henry VI, Part III, III 2 line 1493; Henry VI, Part III, III 2 line 1508; Henry VI, Part III, III 2 line 1519; Henry VI, Part III, III 2 line 1521; Henry VI, Part III, III 3 line 1536; Henry VI, Part III, III 2 line 1553; Henry VI, Part III, III 2 line 1604; Henry VI, Part III, III 3 line 1907; Henry VI, Part III, IV 6 line 2335; Henry VI, Part III, IV 6 line 2355; Henry VI, Part III, IV 6 line 2369; Henry VI, Part III, V 2 line 2747.

Henry VIII, I 3 line 639; Henry VIII, II 4 line 1417; Henry VIII, II 4 line 1575; Henry VIII, III 2 line 1893; Henry VIII, III 2 line 2147; Henry VIII, III 2 line 2245; Henry VIII, IV 1 line 2539; Henry VIII, V 1 line 2831; Henry VIII, V 5 line 3403.

Julius Caesar, I 3 line 513.

King John, I 1 line 76; King John, I 1 line 79; King John, I 1 line 97; King John, I 1 line 99; King John, I 1 line 103; King John, I 1 lines 116, 121; King John, I 1 line 135; King John, I 1 lines 141, 143; King John, I 1 line 150; King John, I 1 line 155; King John, I 1 line 157; King John, I 1 line 170; King John, I 1 line 190; King John, I 1 line 257; King John, II 1 line 315; King John, II 1 lines 350, 357; King John, IV 2 line 1734; King John, IV 2 line 1843; King John, IV 2 line 1878; King John, IV 2 line 1989; King John, IV 3 line 2189; King John, V 1 line 2214; King John, V 1 line 2262; King John, V 2 line 2310; King John, V 2 lines 2369, 2374; King John, V 7 line 2714; King John, V 7 line 2739.
King Lear, I 2 line 349; King Lear, I 2 line 502; King Lear, I 4 line 660; King Lear, I 4 line 667; King Lear, II 1 line 991; King Lear, II 1 line 1019; King Lear, IV 2 line 2401; King Lear, V 1 line 3052.
Love's Labour's Lost, IV 2 line 1148; Love's Labour's Lost, V 2 line 2223.
Lover's Complaint, line 139.
Macbeth, I 3 line 132; Macbeth, IV 2 line 1739; Macbeth, IV 3 line 1934; Macbeth, V 3 line 2307.
Merchant of Venice, IV 1 line 2256.
Merry Wives of Windsor, V 5 line 2800.
Midsummer Night's Dream, II 1 line 434; Midsummer Night's Dream, II 1 line 459; Midsummer Night's Dream, II 1 lines 492, 502; Midsummer Night's Dream, IV 1 line 1609.
Othello, I 2 line 263; Othello, I 3 line 738; Othello, II 1 line 768.
Pericles, I 2 line 260; Pericles, I 2 line 334; Pericles, I 3 line 402; Pericles, II 1 lines 608, 613; Pericles, II 1 line 627.
Rape of Lucrece, lines 387, 490.
Richard II, I 1 line 99; Richard II, I 3 line 487; Richard II, I 3 line 494; Richard II, I 3 line 553; Richard II, II 1 lines 731, 739r; Richard II, II 1 lines779, 787, 794, 795; Richard II, II 1 line 898; Richard II, II 1 line 931; Richard II, II 2 line 1042; Richard II, II 2 line 1079; Richard II, II 2 line 1097; Richard II, II 3 line 1233; Richard II, III 2 line 1521; Richard II, III 2 line 1561; Richard II, III 3 line 1679; Richard II, III 3 line 1684; Richard II, III 3 line 1735; Richard II, III 3 line 1803; Richard II, III 4 line 1907; Richard II, III 4 line 1923; Richard II, IV 1 line 1999; Richard II, IV 1 line 2072; Richard II, IV 1 line 2127; Richard II, IV 1 line 2214; Richard II, V 3 line 2706; Richard II, V 5 line 2867; Richard II, V 6 line 2919; Richard II, V 6 line 2932.
Richard III, II 3 line 1444; Richard III, II 3 line 1452; Richard III, II 3 line 1463; Richard III, III 1 line 1610; Richard III, III 7 line 2327; Richard III, III 7 line 2353; Richard III, III 7 line 2408; Richard III, III 7 line 2434; Richard III, IV 3 line 2729; Richard III, IV 4 line 3221; Richard III, V 2 line 3431; Richard III, V 3 lines 3837, 3850.
Sonnet XLIV line 7.
Taming of the Shrew, II 1 line 960; Taming of the Shrew, II 1 line 964; Taming of the Shrew, II 1 line 968; Taming of the Shrew, II 1 line 1223; Taming of the Shrew, II 1 lines 1225, 1226; Taming of the Shrew, V 1 line 2423; Taming of the Shrew, V 2 line 2657.

Tempest, II 1 line 823; Tempest, II 1 line 861; Tempest, III 3 line 1564; Tempest, IV 1 line 1851; Tempest, V 1 lines 2279, 2282.
Timon of Athens, I 2 line 590; Timon of Athens, I 2 line 592; Timon of Athens, II 2 line 834; Timon of Athens, II 2 line 840; Timon of Athens, III 5 line 1432; Timon of Athens, V 4 line 2600.
Titus Andronicus, IV 3 line 1890.
Troilus and Cressida, II 2 line 1084.
Twelfth Night, II 4 line 980.
Two Gentlemen of Verona, II 7 line 2997.
Venus and Adonis, line 15.
Winter's Tale, III 3 line 1498; Winter's Tale, III 3 line 1578; Winter's Tale, IV 3 line 1822; Winter's Tale, IV 4 line 1864; Winter's Tale, V 1 line 2997.

Lapwing: Several interesting allusions are made by Shakespeare to this eccentric bird. It was a common notion that the young lapwings ran out of the shell with part of it sticking on their heads, in such haste were they to be hatched. Old English: *hleapewince*, from *hleapan*: to leap and a base meaning, move from side to side (whence also wink); so named because of the way it flies. The lapwing, like the partridge, is also said to draw pursuers from her nest by fluttering along the ground in an opposite direction or by crying in other places. Through alluring intruders from its nest, the lapwing became a symbol of insincerity.
    Comedy of Errors, IV 2 line 1100.
    Hamlet, V 2 line 3823.
    Measure for Measure, I 4 line 384.
    Much Ado About Nothing, III 1 line 1099.

Lark: songbird, early 14c., earlier *lauerche* (c.1200), from *lawerce*. Some Old English and Old Norse forms suggest a compound meaning *treason-worker*, but there is no folk tale to explain or support this.
    All's Well That Ends Well, II 5 line 1269.
    Cymbeline, II 3 line 997; Cymbeline, III 6 line 2260.
    Henry V, III 7 line 1671.
    Henry VIII, II 3 line 1316; Henry VIII, III 3 line 2177.
    King Lear, IV 6 line 2665.
    Love's Labour's Lost, V 2 line 2851.
    Merchant of Venice, V 1 line 2559.
    Merry Wives of Windsor, II 1 line 345.
    Midsummer Night's Dream, I 1 line 192; Midsummer Night's Dream, III 1 line 952; Midsummer Night's Dream, IV 1 line 1645.
    Passionate Pilgrim, line 199.
    Richard II, III 3 line 1825.
    Richard III, V 3 line 3521.
    Romeo and Juliet, III 5 line 2099; Romeo and Juliet, III 5 line 2103; Romeo and Juliet, III 5 line 2118.
    Sonnet XXIX line 11.
    Taming of the Shrew, Prologue 2 line 188; Taming of the Shrew, IV 3 line 2134.

Titus Andronicus, III 1 line 1289.
Troilus and Cressida, IV 2 line 2297.
Venus and Adonis, line 875.
Winter's Tale, IV 3 line 1732.

Laund: lawn.
  Henry VI, Part III, III 1 line 1368.
  Venus and Adonis, line 835.

Laurel: From the very earliest times this classical plant has been regarded as symbolical of victory, and used for crowns. c.1300, *lorrer*, from Old French: *laurier* (12c.), from Latin: *laurus*: laurel tree.
  Antony and Cleopatra, I 3 line 415.
  Henry VI, Part III, IV 6 line 2348.
  Titus Andronicus, I 1 line 90.
  Troilus and Cressida, I 3 line 560.

Lavender: fragrant plant of the mint family, c.1300, from Anglo-French: *lavendre*, Old French: *lavendre*, from Middle Latin: *lavendula* lavender (10c.), perhaps from Latin: *lividus: bluish, livid*. Associated with French: *lavande*, Italian: *lavanda*: a washing (from Latin: *lavare*: to wash) because it was used to scent washed fabrics and as a bath perfume.
  Winter's Tale, IV 4 line 1981.

Lawn: turf, stretch of grass, 1540s, *laune: glade, open space between woods*, from Middle English: *launde* (c.1300), from Old French: *lande: heath, moor, barren land; clearing* (12c.).
  Othello, IV 3 line 3101.
  Rape of Lucrece, lines 309, 310.
  Venus and Adonis, line 611.
  Winter's Tale, IV 4 line 2109.

Lea: Old English: *leah: open field, meadow, piece of untilled ground*, earlier *læch*.
  Henry V, V 2 line 3025.
  Tempest, IV 1 line 1770.
  Timon of Athens, IV 3 line 1880.

Leather-coat: type of apple.
  Henry IV, Part II, V 3 line 3441.

Leaf: Old English: *leaf*, of Germanic origin; related to Dutch: *loof* and German: *Laub*. Leaves also connote people by way of their vast number, and relate back to dress in context with Adam, who covered himself with a leaf after first learning the shame of human nakedness. They often give a scary feeling, as the rustling of nearby leaves can mean evil is lurking near.
  All's Well That Ends Well, IV 1 line 2458.

Antony and Cleopatra, III 12 line 2208; Antony and Cleopatra, V 2 lines 3833, 3834.
Cymbeline, II 2 line 924; Cymbeline, II 2 line 978; Cymbeline, III 3 line 1668; Cymbeline, IV 2 line 2611.
Hamlet, IV 7 line 3316.
Henry IV, Part I, V 1 line 2626.
Henry IV, Part II, I 1 line 116.
Henry VI, Part I, IV 1 line 1857.
Henry VI, Part II, III 1 line 1369; Henry VI, Part II, V 1 line 3196.
Henry VI, Part III, III 3 line 1822.
Henry VIII, III 2 line 2258.
Julius Caesar, IV 3 line 2301.
Love's Labour's Lost, IV 3 line 1363; Love's Labour's Lost, IV 3 line 1434.
Macbeth, V 3 line 2274; Macbeth, V 6 line 2417.
Much Ado About Nothing, II 2 line 621; Much Ado About Nothing, II 3 line 893.
Passionate Pilgrim, lines 232, 365.
Pericles, V 1 line 2233.
Rape of Lucrece, line 1219.
Richard II, I 2 line 233; Richard II, III 4 lines 1914, 1915.
Richard III, II 2 line 1314; Richard III, II 3 line 1466.
Romeo and Juliet, I 1 line 172; Romeo and Juliet, I 2 line 325.
Sonnet V line 7; Sonnet XII line 5; Sonnet XXV line 5; Sonnet LXXIII line 2; Sonnet LXXVII line 3; Sonnet XCVII line 14.
Timon of Athens, IV 3 line 1797; Timon of Athens, IV 3 line 1958.
Titus Andronicus, II 3 line 747; Titus Andronicus, II 3 line 946; Titus Andronicus, IV 1 line 1584; Titus Andronicus, IV 1 line 1646.
Venus and Adonis, lines 436, 820, 836, 1077.

Leek: culinary herb, usually associated with Wales. The first of March is observed by the Welsh in honour of St David, their patron saint, when, as a sign of their patriotism, they wear a leek. Much doubt exists as to the origin of this custom. According to the Welsh, it is because St David ordered his Britons to place leeks in their caps, that they might be distinguished in fight from their Saxon foes. Old English: *læc* (Mercian), *leac* (W.Saxon).
Henry V, IV 1 line 1900; Henry V, IV 7 lines 2621r, 2624; Henry V, V 1 line 2886; Henry V, V 1 line 2896; Henry V, V 1 line 2907; Henry V, V 1 line 2910; Henry V, V 1 line 2925r; Henry V, V 1 line 2927; Henry V, V 1 line 2933; Henry V, V 1 line 2936r; Henry V, V 1 line 2940; Henry V, V 1 line 2943; Henry V, V 1 line 2947.
Midsummer Night's Dream, V 1 line 2180.

Leg: late 13c., from a Scandinavian source akin to Old Norse: *leggr: leg, bone of the arm or leg*. To be on (one's) last legs: *at the end of one's life* is from 1590s.
All's Well That Ends Well, II 2 lines 833, 834; All's Well That Ends Well, II 2 line 887.
Antony and Cleopatra, V 2 line 3490.

As You Like It, I 2 line 321; As You Like It, III 5 line 1773.
Coriolanus, I 1 line 110; Coriolanus, II 1 line 983; Coriolanus, IV 3 line 2583.
Cymbeline, III 3 line 1614; Cymbeline, IV 2 line 2711; Cymbeline, V 3 line 3126.
Hamlet, III 2 line 1999.
Henry IV, Part I, I 2 line 223; Henry IV, Part I, II 1 line 820; Henry IV, Part I, II 4 line 1371; Henry IV, Part I, IV 2 line 2408; Henry IV, Part I, V 1 line 2757.
Henry IV, Part II, I 2 line 508; Henry IV, Part II, II 3 line 1177; Henry IV, Part II, II 4 lines 1527, 1531; Henry IV, Part II, V 1 line 3169; Henry IV, Part II, V 5 lines 3725, 3735.
Henry V, III 6 line 1616; Henry V, IV 1 line 1981; Henry V, IV 7 line 2682; Henry V, V 2 line 3143.
Henry VI, Part I, II 3 line 869; Henry VI, Part I, IV 1 line 1774.
Henry VI, Part II, II 1 line 879; Henry VI, Part II, II 1 line 893; Henry VI, Part II, III 1 line 1471; Henry VI, Part II, IV 10 line 2936; Henry VI, Part II, V 1 line 3144.
Henry VI, Part III, II 2 line 947; Henry VI, Part III, III 2 line 1648; Henry VI, Part III, V 6 line 3069.
Henry VIII, I 3 line 581; Henry VIII, IV 2 line 2560.
Julius Caesar, I 2 line 228.
King John, I 1 line 146; King John, I 1 line 250.
King Lear, II 2 line 1224; King Lear, II 4 line 1285r.
Love's Labour's Lost, IV 2 line 1250; Love's Labour's Lost, IV 3 line 1517; Love's Labour's Lost, V 2 line 2111; Love's Labour's Lost, V 2 line 2493; Love's Labour's Lost, V 2 line 2580.
Macbeth, II 3 line 802; Macbeth, IV 1 line 1564.
Merchant of Venice, II 2 line 570.
Merry Wives of Windsor, V 5 line 2619.
Midsummer Night's Dream, II 2 line 671; Midsummer Night's Dream, III 2 line 1398; Midsummer Night's Dream, III 2 line 1422; Midsummer Night's Dream, III 2 line 1520.
Much Ado About Nothing, II 1 line 411; Much Ado About Nothing, II 1 line 567; Much Ado About Nothing, V 2 line 2428.
Othello, II 3 line 1333; Othello, III 3 line 2106; Othello, V 1 line 3167; Othello, V 1 line 3225.
Pericles, IV 6 line 1969; Pericles, IV 6 line 2113.
Rape of Lucrece, line 1478.
Richard II, II 3 line 1248; Richard II, III 3 line 1817; Richard II, III 4 line 1867.
Richard III, I 4 line 921.
Romeo and Juliet, I 4 line 530; Romeo and Juliet, I 4 line 559; Romeo and Juliet, II 1 line 818; Romeo and Juliet, II 5 line 1417.
Taming of the Shrew, Prologue 2 line 156; Taming of the Shrew, Prologue 2 line 203; Taming of the Shrew, I 1 line 360; Taming of the Shrew, III 2 line 1415; Taming of the Shrew, III 2 line 1424; Taming of the Shrew, IV 1 line 1695.

Tempest, II 2 line 1119; Tempest, II 2 lines 1151, 1152; Tempest, II 2 line 1156; Tempest, II 2 line 1178; Tempest, II 2 line 1192r.
Timon of Athens, I 2 lines 604, 606.
Titus Andronicus, IV 2 line 1792.
Troilus and Cressida, I 2 line 173; Troilus and Cressida, II 3 line 1323r; Troilus and Cressida, IV 5 line 2746; Troilus and Cressida, V 1 line 2988.
Twelfth Night, I 3 line 209; Twelfth Night, I 3 line 238; Twelfth Night, I 3 line 243; Twelfth Night, II 3 line 721; Twelfth Night, II 3 line 856; Twelfth Night, II 5 line 1190; Twelfth Night, III 1 line 1313; Twelfth Night, III 1 lines 1314, 1315; Twelfth Night, III 4 line 1572; Twelfth Night, III 4 line 1711; Twelfth Night, V 1 line 2251.
Two Gentlemen of Verona, IV 4 line 1842, 1870; Two Gentlemen of Verona, V 2 line 2068.
Venus and Adonis, lines 317, 720, 727.

Leprosy: a state of corruption and decay; mid 16th cent. (superseding Middle English: *lepry*).
Antony and Cleopatra, III 10 line 2076.
Timon of Athens, IV 1 line 1594; Timon of Athens, IV 3 line 1699; Timon of Athens, IV 3 line 2063.

Leviathan: late 14c., *sea monster, sea serpent*, but also the whale and sometimes the crocodile; also regarded as a form of Satan, from Hebrew: *livyathan: dragon, serpent, huge sea animal*, of unknown origin, perhaps related to *liwyah: wreath*. Of powerful persons or things from c.1600.
Henry V, III 3 line 1298.
Midsummer Night's Dream, II 1 line 546.
Two Gentlemen of Verona, III 2 line 1532.

Libbard: leopard.
Love's Labour's Lost, V 2 line 2484.

Life: Old English: *life: existence, lifetime, way of life, condition of being a living thing, opposite of death*. Meaning, property which distinguishes living from non-living matter is from 1560s. Sense of vitality, energy is from 1580s.
All's Well That Ends Well, I 1 line 64; All's Well That Ends Well, I 3 line 579; All's Well That Ends Well, II 1 line 603; All's Well That Ends Well, II 1 line 673; All's Well That Ends Well, II 1 line 785; All's Well That Ends Well, II 1 lines 790r, 791; All's Well That Ends Well, II 2 line 876; All's Well That Ends Well, II 3 line 910; All's Well That Ends Well, II 3 line 977; All's Well That Ends Well, II 3 line 1138; All's Well That Ends Well, III 6 line 1733; All's Well That Ends Well, III 6 line 1755; All's Well That Ends Well, III 7 line 1894; All's Well That Ends Well, IV 1 line 1971; All's Well That Ends Well, IV 1 line 1984; All's Well That Ends Well, IV 2 line 2065; All's Well That Ends Well, IV 3 line 2158; All's Well That Ends Well, IV 3 line 2254; All's Well That Ends Well, IV 3 line 2324; All's Well That Ends Well, IV 3 line 2373; All's Well That Ends Well, IV 4 line 2428; All's Well That Ends Well, V 3 lines 2777,

2779; All's Well That Ends Well, V 3 line 2849; All's Well That Ends Well, V 3 line 3008.

Antony and Cleopatra, I 1 line 43; Antony and Cleopatra, I 2 line 111; Antony and Cleopatra, I 2 lines 285, 288; Antony and Cleopatra, I 3 line 390; Antony and Cleopatra, I 5 line 559; Antony and Cleopatra, III 3 line 1711; Antony and Cleopatra, III 12 line 2224; Antony and Cleopatra, III 13 line 2450; Antony and Cleopatra, IV 2 line 2573; Antony and Cleopatra, IV 6 line 2751; Antony and Cleopatra, IV 9 line 2851; Antony and Cleopatra, IV 14 line 3017; Antony and Cleopatra, V 1 lines 3289, 3293; Antony and Cleopatra, V 1 line 3357; Antony and Cleopatra, V 2 line 3378; Antony and Cleopatra, V 2 line 3748; Antony and Cleopatra, V 2 line 3766.

As You Like It, I 1 line 128; As You Like It, I 2 line 249; As You Like It, I 2 line 398; As You Like It, II 1 lines 549, 562; As You Like It, II 1 line 605; As You Like It, II 4 line 816; As You Like It, II 7 line 903; As You Like It, II 7 line 1084; As You Like It, III 1 line 1116; As You Like It, III 2 line 1125; As You Like It, III 2 line 1133; As You Like It, III 2 lines 1134r, 1136, 1138; As You Like It, III 2 line 1241; As You Like It, III 5 line 1696; As You Like It, IV 1 line 1929; As You Like It, V 1 line 2237; As You Like It, V 2 line 2309; As You Like It, V 3 line 2388; As You Like It, V 4 line 2560; As You Like It, V 4 line 2577.

Comedy of Errors, I 1 line 121; Comedy of Errors, I 1 line 139; Comedy of Errors, I 1 line 153; Comedy of Errors, I 2 line 167; Comedy of Errors, I 2 line 260; Comedy of Errors, II 2 line 554; Comedy of Errors, III 2 line 831; Comedy of Errors, III 2 line 913; Comedy of Errors, V 1 lines 1513, 1516; Comedy of Errors, V 1 line 1615; Comedy of Errors, V 1 line 1630; Comedy of Errors, V 1 line 1722; Comedy of Errors, V 1 line 1735; Comedy of Errors, V 1 line 1753; Comedy of Errors, V 1 line 1758; Comedy of Errors, V 1 line 1764; Comedy of Errors, V 1 line 1835.

Coriolanus, I 6 line 700; Coriolanus, II 2 line 1387; Coriolanus, III 1 line 1914; Coriolanus, III 2 line 2292; Coriolanus, III 3 line 2483; Coriolanus, IV 5 line 2845; Coriolanus, V 3 line 3600; Coriolanus, V 3 line 3671; Coriolanus, V 4 line 3766; Coriolanus, V 5 line 3808; Coriolanus, V 6 line 3987.

Cymbeline, I 4 line 345; Cymbeline, II 4 line 1265; Cymbeline, II 4 line 1345; Cymbeline, III 3 lines 1624, 1629; Cymbeline, III 3 lines 1632, 1633; Cymbeline, III 3 line 1705; Cymbeline, III 4 line 1748; Cymbeline, III 4 line 1859; Cymbeline, III 4 line 1866; Cymbeline, III 5 line 1991; Cymbeline, III 6 line 2144; Cymbeline, IV 2 line 2642; Cymbeline, IV 3 line 2828; Cymbeline, IV 3 line 2838; Cymbeline, IV 4 line 2885; Cymbeline, IV 4 line 2915; Cymbeline, V 1 line 2977; Cymbeline, V 1 line 2972; Cymbeline, V 3 line 3027; Cymbeline, V 3 line 3071; Cymbeline, V 4 lines 3159, 3160, 3164; Cymbeline, V 4 line 3303; Cymbeline, V 5 line 3403; Cymbeline, V 5 line 3405; Cymbeline, V 5 line 3421; Cymbeline, V 5 line 3428; Cymbeline, V 5 line 3487; Cymbeline, V 5 line 3491; Cymbeline, V 5 line 3635; Cymbeline, V 5 line 3675; Cymbeline, V 5 line 3879.

Hamlet, I 1 line 105; Hamlet, I 1 line 155; Hamlet, I 1 line 193; Hamlet, I 2 line 458; Hamlet, I 4 line 698; Hamlet, I 5 line 776; Hamlet, I 5 line 813; Hamlet, II 1 line 1317rr; Hamlet, II 2 line 1644; Hamlet, III 1 lines 1762, 1770; Hamlet, III 2 line 2011; Hamlet, III 2 line 2150; Hamlet, III 3 line 2288; Hamlet, III 4 line 2520; Hamlet, III 4 line 2602r; III 4 line 2620; Hamlet, IV 1 line 2650; Hamlet, IV 5 line 3021; Hamlet, IV 5 line 3038; Hamlet, IV 5 line 3084; Hamlet, IV 7 line 3135; Hamlet, IV 7 line 3146; Hamlet, IV 7 line 3233; Hamlet, V 1 line 3363; Hamlet, V 1 line 3551; Hamlet, V 2 line 3672; Hamlet, V 2 line 3720; Hamlet, V 2 line 3728; Hamlet, V 2 line 3972; Hamlet, V 2 line 4040.

Henry IV, Part I, I 2 line 201; Henry IV, Part I, I 2 line 208; Henry IV, Part I, I 3 line 614; Henry IV, Part I, II 4 lines 1004, 1009; Henry IV, Part I, II 4 line 1096; Henry IV, Part I, II 4 line 1107; Henry IV, Part I, II 4 line 1259; Henry IV, Part I, II 4 line 1360; Henry IV, Part I, III 1 line 1585; Henry IV, Part I, III 2 line 1831; Henry IV, Part I, III 2 line 1982; Henry IV, Part I, III 3 line 2031; Henry IV, Part I, III 3 line 2098; Henry IV, Part I, IV 1 line 2250; Henry IV, Part I, IV 3 lines 2463, 2464; Henry IV, Part I, IV 3 line 2551; Henry IV, Part I, V 1 line 2647; Henry IV, Part I, V 1 line 2739; Henry IV, Part I, V 2 line 2825; Henry IV, Part I, V 2 lines 2856, 2858; Henry IV, Part I, V 3 line 2922; Henry IV, Part I, V 3 line 2946; Henry IV, Part I, V 4 line 3004; Henry IV, Part I, V 4 lines 3041, 3044r; Henry IV, Part I, V 4 line 3068; Henry IV, Part I, V 4 lines 3083, 3086, 3088.

Henry IV, Part II, I 1 line 113; Henry IV, Part II, I 1 line 168; Henry IV, Part II, I 1 line 199; Henry IV, Part II, I 1 line 240; Henry IV, Part II, I 1 line 266; Henry IV, Part II, I 2 line 446; Henry IV, Part II, II 3 line 1214; Henry IV, Part II, II 4 line 1578; Henry IV, Part II, III 1 line 1768; Henry IV, Part II, III 1 line 1789; Henry IV, Part II, IV 1 line 2271; Henry IV, Part II, IV 1 line 2332; Henry IV, Part II, IV 1 line 2407; Henry IV, Part II, IV 2 line 2451; Henry IV, Part II, IV 3 line 2613; Henry IV, Part II, IV 4 line 2870; Henry IV, Part II, IV 5 lines 3000, 3004, 3011; Henry IV, Part II, IV 5 line 3058; Henry IV, Part II, IV 5 line 3133; Henry IV, Part II, V 2 line 3252.

Henry V, I 1 line 90; Henry V, I 2 line 194; Henry V, II 2 line 644; Henry V, II 2 line 685; Henry V, III 6 line 1469; Henry V, III 6 line 1510; Henry V, IV 1 line 1891; Henry V, IV 1 line 2020; Henry V, IV 2 lines 2219, 2220r; Henry V, IV 4 line 2415; Henry V, IV 5 line 2474; Henry V, IV 7 line 2545r; Henry V, V 0 line 2843.

Henry VI, Part I, I 1 line 38; Henry VI, Part I, I 1 line 71; Henry VI, Part I, I 2 line 219; Henry VI, Part I, I 4 line 481; Henry VI, Part I, I 4 line 548; Henry VI, Part I, II 5 line 1196; Henry VI, Part I, II 5 line 1205; Henry VI, Part I, III 1 line 1242; Henry VI, Part I, III 1 line 1272; Henry VI, Part I, III 2 line 1567; Henry VI, Part I, III 2 line 1567; Henry VI, Part I, IV 2 line 2021; Henry VI, Part I, IV 4 line 2111; Henry VI, Part I, IV 4 line 2124; Henry VI, Part I, IV 5 line 2167; Henry VI, Part I, IV 5 line 2187; Henry VI, Part I, IV 6 line 2197; Henry VI, Part I, IV 6 line 2229; Henry VI, Part I, IV 6 lines 2235, 2237; Henry VI, Part I, IV 6 line 2247; Henry VI, Part I, IV 7 line 2252; Henry VI, Part I, IV 7 line 2303; Henry

VI, Part I, IV 7 line 2305; Henry VI, Part I, IV 7 line 2338; Henry VI, Part I, V 4 line 2685.

Henry VI, Part II, I 1 line 23; Henry VI, Part II, II 1 line 803; Henry VI, Part II, II 1 line 844; Henry VI, Part II, II 1 line 849; Henry VI, Part II, II 1 line 862; Henry VI, Part II, II 1 line 922; Henry VI, Part II, II 3 line 1053; Henry VI, Part II, III 1 line 1323; Henry VI, Part II, III 1 lines 1428, 1441, 1448; Henry VI, Part II, III 1 line 1490; Henry VI, Part II, III 1 lines 1523, 1524; Henry VI, Part II, III 1 line 1582; Henry VI, Part II, III 2 line 1736; Henry VI, Part II, III 2 line 1742; Henry VI, Part II, III 2 line 1821; Henry VI, Part II, III 2 line 1837; Henry VI, Part II, III 2 line 1842; Henry VI, Part II, III 2 line 1858; Henry VI, Part II, III 2 line 1960; Henry VI, Part II, III 2 line 1990; Henry VI, Part II, III 2 line 2050; Henry VI, Part II, III 2 line 2059; Henry VI, Part II, III 3 line 2119; Henry VI, Part II, III 3 line 2144; Henry VI, Part II, IV 1 line 2174; Henry VI, Part II, IV 1 line 2301; Henry VI, Part II, IV 2 line 2334; Henry VI, Part II, IV 7 line 2686; Henry VI, Part II, IV 7 line 2723; Henry VI, Part II, IV 7 line 2733; Henry VI, Part II, IV 9 line 2846; Henry VI, Part II, IV 10 line 2891.

Henry VI, Part III, I 1 line 180; Henry VI, Part III, I 1 line 263; Henry VI, Part III, I 2 line 305; Henry VI, Part III, I 3 line 379; Henry VI, Part III, I 4 lines 443, 461, 462; Henry VI, Part III, I 4 line 490; Henry VI, Part III, I 4 line 545; Henry VI, Part III, I 4 line 578; Henry VI, Part III, I 4 line 611; Henry VI, Part III, II 3 line 1083; Henry VI, Part III, II 5 lines 1123, 1143; Henry VI, Part III, II 5 lines 1163, 1171, 1172; Henry VI, Part III, II 5 lines 1189, 1197, 1198; Henry VI, Part III, II 6 line 1316; Henry VI, Part III, II 6 line 1333; Henry VI, Part III, III 2 line 1477; Henry VI, Part III, IV 4 line 2258; Henry VI, Part III, IV 6 line 2357; Henry VI, Part III, V 5 line 2904; Henry VI, Part III, V 6 lines 3020, 3024; Henry VI, Part III, V 6 lines 3063, 3085.

Henry VIII, I 1 line 81; Henry VIII, I 1 line 307; Henry VIII, I 2 line 316; Henry VIII, I 2 line 357; Henry VIII, I 2 line 396; Henry VIII, I 4 line 673; Henry VIII, II 1 line 850; Henry VIII, II 1 line 903; Henry VIII, II 1 lines 953, 970; Henry VIII, II 3 line 1204; Henry VIII, II 3 line 1318; Henry VIII, II 4 line 1562; Henry VIII, II 4 line 1600; Henry VIII, III 1 line 1664; Henry VIII, III 1 line 1704; Henry VIII, III 1 line 1822; Henry VIII, III 2 line 2138; Henry VIII, III 2 line 2171; Henry VIII, III 2 line 2190; Henry VIII, IV 2 line 2751; Henry VIII, V 3 line 3091; Henry VIII, V 3 line 3149; Henry VIII, V 3 line 3184; Henry VIII, V 5 line 3379; Henry VIII, V 5 line 3393.

Julius Caesar, I 2 line 184; Julius Caesar, I 3 line 483; Julius Caesar, I 3 line 522; Julius Caesar, III 1 line 1315; Julius Caesar, IV 3 line 2047; Julius Caesar, IV 3 line 2231; Julius Caesar, V 1 line 2464; Julius Caesar, V 3 line 2525; Julius Caesar, V 3 line 2541; Julius Caesar, V 5 lines 2712, 2718; Julius Caesar, V 5 line 2727; Julius Caesar, V 5 line 2759.

King John, II 1 line 303; King John, II 1 line 451; King John, III 1 line 946; King John, III 1 line 1053; King John, III 1 line 1101; King John, III 1 line 1266; King John, III 2 line 1280; King John, III 4 line 1490; King John, III 4 line 1496; King John, III 4 line 1520; King John, III 4 line

1532; King John, III 4 line 1548; King John, IV 1 line 1676; King John, IV 2 line 1821; King John, IV 2 line 1836; King John, IV 2 line 1954; King John, IV 3 line 2085; King John, IV 3 lines 2111, 2112; King John, IV 3 line 2132r; King John, V 1 line 2335; King John, V 4 line 2511; King John, V 7 line 2628; King John, V 7 line 2688.

King Lear, I 1 line 58; King Lear, I 1 line 157; King Lear, I 1 line 161; King Lear, I 1 line 162; King Lear, I 2 line 413; King Lear, I 3 line 523; King Lear, I 4 line 825; King Lear, II 1 line 1028; King Lear, II 2 line 1129; King Lear, II 2 line 1204; King Lear, II 4 line 1510; King Lear, II 4 line 1568; King Lear, III 2 line 1734; King Lear, III 4 line 1960; King Lear, III 6 line 2094; King Lear, III 7 line 2145; King Lear, IV 1 line 2260; King Lear, IV 2 line 2438; King Lear, IV 4 line 2536; King Lear, IV 5 line 2565; King Lear, IV 6 line 2650r; King Lear, IV 6 line 2661; King Lear, IV 6 line 2718; King Lear, IV 6 line 2810; King Lear, IV 6 line 2859; King Lear, IV 6 line 2891; King Lear, IV 7 line 2911; King Lear, IV 7 line 2957; King Lear, V 3 lines 3416, 3419; King Lear, V 3 line 3487; King Lear, V 3 lines 3494, 3495; King Lear, V 3 line 3509.

Love's Labour's Lost, II 1 line 682; Love's Labour's Lost, IV 2 line 1293; Love's Labour's Lost, IV 2 line 1311; Love's Labour's Lost, V 2 line 2377; Love's Labour's Lost, V 2 line 2660; Love's Labour's Lost, V 2 line 2741.

Lover's Complaint, line 115.

Macbeth, I 3 line 217; Macbeth, I 4 line 283; Macbeth, I 7 line 480; Macbeth, I 7 line 518; Macbeth, II 2 lines 697, 699; Macbeth, II 3 line 841; Macbeth, II 3 line 878; Macbeth, II 3 line 891; Macbeth, II 4 line 984; Macbeth, III 1 line 1122; Macbeth, III 1 line 1137; Macbeth, III 2 line 1194; Macbeth, IV 3 line 1989; Macbeth, V 1 line 2145; Macbeth, V 3 line 2273; Macbeth, V 5 line 2368; Macbeth, V 5 line 2382; Macbeth, V 8 line 2489; Macbeth, V 8 line 2561.

Measure for Measure, I 1 line 34; Measure for Measure, I 2 line 282; Measure for Measure, I 3 line 298; Measure for Measure, I 4 line 419; Measure for Measure, I 4 line 426; Measure for Measure, II 1 line 467; Measure for Measure, II 1 line 472; Measure for Measure, II 1 line 528; Measure for Measure, II 2 line 908; Measure for Measure, II 3 line 1012; Measure for Measure, II 4 line 1069; Measure for Measure, II 4 line 1075; Measure for Measure, II 4 lines 1086, 1088; Measure for Measure, II 4 line 1094; Measure for Measure, II 4 line 1114; Measure for Measure, II 4 line 1186; Measure for Measure, III 1 lines 1227, 1228, 1262r; Measure for Measure, III 1 line 1266; Measure for Measure, III 1 line 1293; Measure for Measure, III 1 line 1304; Measure for Measure, III 1 line 1318; Measure for Measure, III 1 line 1337; Measure for Measure, III 1 line 1352; Measure for Measure, III 1 line 1364; Measure for Measure, III 1 line 1370; Measure for Measure, III 1 line 1376; Measure for Measure, III 1 line 1412; Measure for Measure, III 1 line 1474; Measure for Measure, III 2 line 1537; Measure for Measure, III 2 line 1625; Measure for Measure, III 2 line 1651; Measure for Measure, III 2 line 1755; Measure for Measure, III 2 line 1764; Measure for Measure, IV 2 line 1974; Measure for Measure, IV 2 line 2085; Measure for Measure, IV 4 line 2338; Measure for

Measure, V 1 lines 2815, 2821r; Measure for Measure, V 1 line 2832; Measure for Measure, V 1 line 2848; Measure for Measure, V 1 lines 2863, 2864; Measure for Measure, V 1 line 2926.
Merchant of Venice, II 2 lines 722, 726; Merchant of Venice, II 7 line 1056; Merchant of Venice, II 9 line 1142; Merchant of Venice, III 2 line 1394; Merchant of Venice, III 2 line 1398; Merchant of Venice, III 2 line 1554; Merchant of Venice, III 2 line 1641; Merchant of Venice, III 3 line 1731; Merchant of Venice, III 5 line 1910; Merchant of Venice, IV 1 line 2064; Merchant of Venice, IV 1 lines 2228, 2229, 2230; Merchant of Venice, IV 1 lines 2300, 2304, 2309; Merchant of Venice, IV 1 line 2318; Merchant of Venice, IV 1 lines 2323, 2325; Merchant of Venice, V 1 line 2682; Merchant of Venice, V 1 line 2757.
Merry Wives of Windsor, I 1 line 37; Merry Wives of Windsor, I 3 line 323; Merry Wives of Windsor, II 2 lines 882, 883; Merry Wives of Windsor, II 2 line 908; Merry Wives of Windsor, III 3 line 1512; Merry Wives of Windsor, IV 5 line 2352; Merry Wives of Windsor, V 1 line 2502; Merry Wives of Windsor, V 5 line 2760.
Midsummer Night's Dream, I 1 line 77; Midsummer Night's Dream, I 1 line 95; Midsummer Night's Dream, I 1 line 126; Midsummer Night's Dream, II 2 line 715; Midsummer Night's Dream, II 2 line 717; Midsummer Night's Dream, III 1 lines 856, 858; Midsummer Night's Dream, III 2 line 1286; Midsummer Night's Dream, III 2 line 1292; Midsummer Night's Dream, III 2 line 1324; Midsummer Night's Dream, IV 1 line 1765; Midsummer Night's Dream, IV 2 line 1803; Midsummer Night's Dream, V 1 line 2047; Midsummer Night's Dream, V 1 line 2070.
Much Ado About Nothing, II 1 line 454; Much Ado About Nothing, II 1 line 622; Much Ado About Nothing, II 2 line 777; Much Ado About Nothing, II 3 line 924; Much Ado About Nothing, III 2 line 1265; Much Ado About Nothing, IV 1 line 1775; Much Ado About Nothing, IV 1 line 1847; Much Ado About Nothing, IV 1 lines 1876, 1878, 1880, 1894; Much Ado About Nothing, IV 2 line 2048; Much Ado About Nothing, V 3 line 2514; Much Ado About Nothing, V 4 line 2649; Much Ado About Nothing, V 4 line 2668.
Othello, I 1 line 169; Othello, I 2 line 225; Othello, I 3 line 463; Othello, I 3 line 474; Othello, I 3 lines 530, 531; Othello, I 3 line 652; Othello, II 3 line 1205; Othello, II 3 line 1410; Othello, III 3 line 2044; Othello, IV 2 line 2806; Othello, IV 2 line 2929; Othello, IV 2 line 2989; Othello, V 1 line 3155; Othello, V 1 line 3288; Othello, V 2 line 3359; Othello, V 2 line 3372.
Passionate Pilgrim, lines 29, 35, 70, 108, 235, 344.
Pericles, I 0 line 16; Pericles, I 1 lines 92, 101; Pericles, I 1 line 136; Pericles, I 2 line 249; Pericles, I 2 line 282; Pericles, I 2 line 297; Pericles, I 2 lines 351, 354; Pericles, I 3 line 398; Pericles, I 4 line 462; Pericles, 1 4 line 515; Pericles, II 1 line 704; Pericles, II 2 line 773; Pericles, II 3 line 903; Pericles, II 5 line 1017; Pericles, II 5 line 1060; Pericles, II 5 line 1112; Pericles, III 0 line 1177; Pericles, III 1 line 1223; Pericles, III 2 line 1384; Pericles, IV 0 line 1505; Pericles, IV 1 line

1630; Pericles, IV 1 line 1645; Pericles, IV 4 line 1886; Pericles, V 1 line 2468.

Rape of Lucrece, lines 11, 175, 192, 196, 284, 436, 453, 454, 457r, 567, 712, 738, 831, 926, 1096, 1106, 1122, 1206, 1237, 1259r, 1369, 1398, 1426r, 1507, 1780, 1851, 1855.

Richard II, I 1 lines 90, 102, 111; Richard II, I 1 line 140; Richard II, I 1 line 170; Richard II, I 1 lines 187, 188; Richard II, I 2 line 216; Richard II, I 2 lines 229, 241, 244, 248; Richard II, I 2 line 268; Richard II, I 3 line 439; Richard II, I 3 line 450; Richard II, I 3 line 499; Richard II, I 3 line 542; Richard II, II 1 line 697; Richard II, II 1 line 749; Richard II, II 1 line 829; Richard II, II 1 line 837; Richard II, II 1 line 962; Richard II, II 2 line 996; Richard II, II 2 line 1067; Richard II, II 3 line 1193; Richard II, II 3 line 1313; Richard II, III 2 line 1577; Richard II, V 2 line 2526; Richard II, V 2 line 2532; Richard II, V 2 line 2533; Richard II, V 3 lines 2649, 2650; Richard II, V 6 line 2908.

Richard III, I 2 line 185; Richard III, I 2 line 310; Richard III, I 2 line 311; Richard III, I 2 line 446; Richard III, I 3 line 744; Richard III, I 4 line 876; Richard III, I 4 line 1057; Richard III, I 4 line 1092; Richard III, II 1 line 1225; Richard III, II 1 lines 1256, 1257; Richard III, II 4 line 1545; Richard III, III 1 line 1659; Richard III, III 2 lines 1863, 1864; Richard III, IV 1 line 2468; Richard III, IV 1 line 2546; Richard III, IV 4 lines 2828, 2819; Richard III, IV 4 line 2872; Richard III, IV 4 line 2998; Richard III, IV 4 line 3016; Richard III, IV 4 line 3017; Richard III, IV 4 line 3027; Richard III, IV 4 line 3158; Richard III, IV 4 line 3185; Richard III, V 3 line 3502; Richard III, V 3 line 3821; Richard III, V 4 line 3883.

Romeo and Juliet, Prologue 1 line 6; Romeo and Juliet, I 4 line 612; Romeo and Juliet, I 5 line 747; Romeo and Juliet, II 2 line 926; Romeo and Juliet, II 4 line 1166; Romeo and Juliet, III 1 line 1530; Romeo and Juliet, III 1 line 1684; Romeo and Juliet, III 1 line 1697; Romeo and Juliet, III 1 line 1703; Romeo and Juliet, III 5 line 2140; Romeo and Juliet, IV 1 line 2467; Romeo and Juliet, IV 3 line 2567; Romeo and Juliet, IV 5 line 2675; Romeo and Juliet, IV 5 line 2684; Romeo and Juliet, IV 5 line 2699; Romeo and Juliet, IV 5 line 2717r; Romeo and Juliet, IV 5 line 2729; Romeo and Juliet, V 1 line 2811; Romeo and Juliet, V 1 line 2873; Romeo and Juliet, V 3 line 2962; Romeo and Juliet, V 3 line 3242.

Sonnet XVIII line 14; Sonnet XLV line 9; Sonnet LXIII line 12; Sonnet LXXI line 12; Sonnet LXXIV line 3; Sonnet LXXIV line 9; Sonnet LXXV line 1; Sonnet LXXXI line 5; Sonnet LXXXIII line 12; Sonnet LXXXIII line 13; Sonnet XCII line 3; Sonnet XCII line 4; Sonnet XCII line 6; Sonnet XCII line 10; Sonnet C line 13; Sonnet CXI line 3; Sonnet CXLV line 14.

Taming of the Shrew, Prologue, 2 line 153; Taming of the Shrew, Prologue 2 line 217; Taming of the Shrew, Prologue 2 line 283; Taming of the Shrew, I 1 lines 522, 528; Taming of the Shrew, I 2 line 665; Taming of the Shrew, I 2 line 742; Taming of the Shrew, III 1 line 1314; Taming of the Shrew, III 2 line 1385; Taming of the Shrew, IV 1 line 1740; Taming of the Shrew, IV 2 line 1909; Taming of the Shrew, IV 2 line 1913; Taming of the Shrew, IV 2 line 1914; Taming of the Shrew, IV 2 line 1937; Taming of the Shrew, IV 2 line 1948; Taming of the Shrew, IV 3 line 1957; Taming of the Shrew, IV 3 line 2117; Taming of the Shrew, V 1 line 2393; Taming of the Shrew, V 2 line 2504; Taming of the Shrew, V 2 line 2614; Taming of the Shrew, V 2 line 2654.

Tempest, I 2 line 403; Tempest, II 1 line 753; Tempest, II 1 line 980; Tempest, II 1 line 1047; Tempest, III 2 line 1416; Tempest, III 3 line 1658; Tempest, III 3 line 1667; Tempest, IV 1 line 1702; Tempest, IV 1 line 1725; Tempest, IV 1 line 1869; Tempest, IV 1 line 1888; Tempest, V 1 line 2249; Tempest, V 1 line 2348; Tempest, V 1 line 2382; Tempest, V 1 line 2391.

Timon of Athens, I 1 line 47; Timon of Athens, I 1 line 51; Timon of Athens, I 2 line 479; Timon of Athens, III 2 line 1094; Timon of Athens, III 5 line 1344; Timon of Athens, III 5 line 1371; Timon of Athens, III 5 line 1394; Timon of Athens, IV 2 line 1658; Timon of Athens, IV 3 line 2186; Timon of Athens, V 1 line 2324; Timon of Athens, V 1 line 2491.

Titus Andronicus, I 1 line 215; Titus Andronicus, I 1 line 279; Titus Andronicus, I 1 line 461; Titus Andronicus, I 1 line 501; Titus Andronicus, I 1 line 511; Titus Andronicus, II 3 line 784; Titus Andronicus, II 3 line 850; Titus Andronicus, II 3 line 910; Titus Titus Andronicus, II 3 line 1034; Titus Andronicus, II 4 line 1111; Titus Andronicus, III 1 line 1204; Titus Andronicus, III 1 lines 1387, 1388, 1389; Titus Andronicus, III 1 line 1433; Andronicus, III 2 line 1467; Titus Andronicus, III 2 line 1470; Titus Andronicus, III 2 line 1496; Titus Andronicus, IV 2 line 1813; Titus Andronicus, IV 3 line 1970; Titus Andronicus, IV 3 line 1985; Titus Andronicus, IV 4 lines 2037, 2048; Titus Andronicus, V 2 line 2438; Titus Andronicus, V 3 line 2686; Titus Andronicus, V 3 line 2734; Titus Andronicus, V 3 line 2744.

Troilus and Cressida, I 3 line 514; Troilus and Cressida, I 3 line 848; Troilus and Cressida, II 2 line 1157; Troilus and Cressida, II 2 line 1192; Troilus and Cressida, III 1 line 1542; Troilus and Cressida, III 1 line 1574; Troilus and Cressida, IV 1 line 2217; Troilus and Cressida, IV 1 line 2221; Troilus and Cressida, IV 1 line 2274; Troilus and Cressida, IV 2 line 2312; Troilus and Cressida, IV 4 line 2551; Troilus and Cressida, IV 5 line 2815; Troilus and Cressida, IV 5 line 2877; Troilus and Cressida, V 3 line 3307; Troilus and Cressida, V 6 line 3521; Troilus and Cressida, V 6 line 3546; Troilus and Cressida, V 8 line 3589; Troilus and Cressida, V 8 line 3598; Troilus and Cressida, V 10 line 3670.

Twelfth Night, I 3 line 117; Twelfth Night, I 3 line 192; Twelfth Night, I 3 line 216; Twelfth Night, I 5 line 555; Twelfth Night, II 3 line 709; Twelfth Night, II 3 line 735; Twelfth Night, II 3 line 737; Twelfth Night, II 4 line 913; Twelfth Night, II 5 line 1111; Twelfth Night, II 5 line 1132; Twelfth Night, II 5 line 1135; Twelfth Night, III 4 line 1775; Twelfth Night, IV 1 line 1995; Twelfth Night, V 1 line 2269; Twelfth Night, V 1 lines 2238, 2241; Twelfth Night, V 1 line 2382; Twelfth Night, V 1 line 2463.

Two Gentlemen of Verona, I 3 line 349; Two Gentlemen of Verona, II 4 line 785; Two Gentlemen of Verona, III 1 line 1186; Two Gentlemen

of Verona, III 1 line 1241; Two Gentlemen of Verona, III 1 line 1260; Two Gentlemen of Verona, III 1 line 1319 Two Gentlemen of Verona, V 4 line 2170; Two Gentlemen of Verona, V 4 line 2186.
Venus and Adonis, lines 32, 217, 231, 309, 433, 495, 517, 518, 762, 788.
Winter's Tale, I 1 line 40; Winter's Tale, I 2 line 136; Winter's Tale, I 2 line 411; Winter's Tale, I 2 line 591; Winter's Tale, II 1 line 657; Winter's Tale, II 1 line 713; Winter's Tale, II 1 line 753; Winter's Tale, II 3 line 960; Winter's Tale, II 3 line 1082; Winter's Tale, II 3 line 1098; Winter's Tale, II 3 lines 1124, 1127; Winter's Tale, III 2 line 1228; Winter's Tale, III 2 lines 1245, 1253, 1254; Winter's Tale, III 2 line 1296; Winter's Tale, III 2 lines 1310, 1311, 1326; Winter's Tale, III 2 line 1383; Winter's Tale, III 3 line 1537; Winter's Tale, IV 3 line 1753; Winter's Tale, IV 3 line 1825; Winter's Tale, V 1 line 2869; Winter's Tale, V 1 line 2999; Winter's Tale, V 2 line 3222; Winter's Tale, V 2 line 3262; Winter's Tale, V 3 line 3295; Winter's Tale, V 3 line 3308; Winter's Tale, V 3 line 3329r; Winter's Tale, V 3 line 3366; Winter's Tale, V 3 line 3414; Winter's Tale, V 3 line 3427.

Light: brightness, radiant energy, Old English: *leht*, earlier *leoht*: *light, daylight; luminous, beautiful*.
All's Well That Ends Well, I 1 line 89; All's Well That Ends Well, II 1 line 683; All's Well That Ends Well, II 5 line 1305; All's Well That Ends Well, III 4 line 1593; All's Well That Ends Well, IV 2 line 2009; All's Well That Ends Well, IV 5 line 2477.
Antony and Cleopatra, I 2 line 271; Antony and Cleopatra, II 2 line 903; Antony and Cleopatra, III 2 line 1675; Antony and Cleopatra, V 2 line 3487.
As You Like It, II 3 line 712.
Comedy of Errors, I 1 lines 68, 82; Comedy of Errors, III 2 line 814; Comedy of Errors, III 2 line 859; Comedy of Errors, IV 3 lines 1201, 1203, 1204, 1205, 1206; Comedy of Errors, V 1 lines 1513, 1516; Comedy of Errors, V 1 line 1503.
Coriolanus, I 4 line 523; Coriolanus, II 1 line 1115.
Cymbeline, I 4 line 406; Cymbeline, I 6 line 731; Cymbeline, II 2 line 943; Cymbeline, III 1 line 1457; Cymbeline, V 4 line 3162; Cymbeline, V 4 line 3320r.
Hamlet, I 3 line 605; Hamlet, II 1 line 1059; Hamlet, II 2 line 1359; Hamlet, II 2 line 1480; Hamlet, II 2 line 1530; Hamlet, III 2 line 2108; Hamlet, III 2 line 2156; Hamlet, III 2 line 2157rr; Hamlet, III 4 line 2451; Hamlet, IV 6 line 3119; Hamlet, V 2 line 4017.
Henry IV, Part I, I 1 line 64; Henry IV, Part I, II 2 line 801; Henry IV, Part I, II 3 line 870; Henry IV, Part I, III 2 line 1961; Henry IV, Part I, III 3 lines 2044, 2049, 2053; Henry IV, Part I, III 3 line 2071; Henry IV, Part I, V 1 line 2641.
Henry IV, Part II, I 2 line 333; Henry IV, Part II, I 2 line 486; Henry IV, Part II, II 2 line 1021; Henry IV, Part II, II 3 line 1173; Henry IV, Part II, II 4 line 1390; Henry IV, Part II, II 4 line 1404; Henry IV, Part II, II 4 line

1587; Henry IV, Part II, IV 1 line 2402; Henry IV, Part II, IV 5 line 2921; Henry IV, Part II, V 5 line 3721.
Henry V, II 2 line 725; Henry V, II 2 line 822; Henry V, IV 8 line 2729; Henry V, IV 8 line 2770.
Henry VI, Part I, I 4 line 528; Henry VI, Part I, IV 2 line 2011; Henry VI, Part I, V 3 line 2495.
Henry VI, Part II, I 3 line 481; Henry VI, Part II, II 1 line 804; Henry VI, Part II, II 4 line 1200; Henry VI, Part II, III 1 line 1342; Henry VI, Part II, IV 8 line 2789.
Henry VI, Part III, II 1 line 657; Henry VI, Part III, II 5 line 1104; Henry VI, Part III, II 6 line 1252; Henry VI, Part III, V 6 line 3082.
Henry VIII, I 1 line 43; Henry VIII, I 1 line 46; Henry VIII, III 2 line 1863; Henry VIII, V 1 line 2991.
Julius Caesar, I 1 line 55; Julius Caesar, II 1 line 608; Julius Caesar, II 1 line 649; Julius Caesar, III 1 line 1491; Julius Caesar, V 3 line 2528; Julius Caesar, V 3 line 2531.
King John, I 1 line 269; King John, III 1 line 1129; King John, III 1 line 1221; King John, IV 3 line 2081.
King Lear, II 1 line 958; King Lear, III 1 line 1673; King Lear, III 4 line 1867; King Lear, III 4 line 1888; King Lear, III 6 line 2112; King Lear, IV 6 line 2755.
Love's Labour's Lost, I 1 lines 77, 78rrr, 79, 80, 84; Love's Labour's Lost, I 2 line 420; Love's Labour's Lost, II 1 line 691; Love's Labour's Lost, II 1 line 692r; Love's Labour's Lost, IV 3 line 1328; Love's Labour's Lost, IV 3 line 1352; Love's Labour's Lost, IV 3 line 1575; Love's Labour's Lost, IV 3 line 1601; Love's Labour's Lost, IV 3 line 1613; Love's Labour's Lost, IV 3 line 1730; Love's Labour's Lost, V 2 lines 1895, 1898; Love's Labour's Lost, V 2 line 1899; Love's Labour's Lost, V 2 line 1900; Love's Labour's Lost, V 2 line 1901; Love's Labour's Lost, V 2 line 1902; Love's Labour's Lost, V 2 line 1905; Love's Labour's Lost, V 2 line 1906; Love's Labour's Lost, V 2 line 2297r; Love's Labour's Lost, V 2 line 2571.
Lover's Complaint, line 86.
Macbeth, I 4 line 334; Macbeth, II 3 line 941; Macbeth, II 4 line 958; Macbeth, III 2 line 1225; Macbeth, III 3 line 1245; Macbeth, III 3 line 1253r; Macbeth, III 3 line 1263; Macbeth, V 1 line 2147; Macbeth, V 1 line 2148; Macbeth, V 5 line 2379.
Measure for Measure, III 2 line 1685; Measure for Measure, IV 1 line 1798; Measure for Measure, IV 3 line 2275; Measure for Measure, V 1 line 2634; Measure for Measure, V 1 line 2694.
Merchant of Venice, II 2 line 644; Merchant of Venice, II 6 line 953; Merchant of Venice, III 1 line 1330; Merchant of Venice, IV 1 line 1970; Merchant of Venice, IV 1 line 2276; Merchant of Venice, V 1 line 2546; Merchant of Venice, V 1 lines 2594r, 2595.
Merry Wives of Windsor, II 1 line 574; Merry Wives of Windsor, V 2 line 2513; Merry Wives of Windsor, V 2 line 2522; Merry Wives of Windsor, V 3 line 2542.
Midsummer Night's Dream, III 1 line 995; Midsummer Night's Dream, III 2 line 1171; Midsummer Night's Dream, III 2 line 1228; Midsummer

Night's Dream, III 2 line 1443; Midsummer Night's Dream, III 2 line 1487; Midsummer Night's Dream, V 1 line 2092; Midsummer Night's Dream, V 1 line 2147; Midsummer Night's Dream, V 1 lines 2241, 2244.
Much Ado About Nothing, II 1 line 425; Much Ado About Nothing, III 4 line 1524; Much Ado About Nothing, III 4 line 1533; Much Ado About Nothing, IV 1 line 1756; Much Ado About Nothing, V 1 line 2306; Much Ado About Nothing, V 4 line 2646.
Othello, I 1 line 156r; Othello, I 2 line 232; Othello, I 3 line 525; Othello, I 3 line 761; Othello, II 3 line 1320; Othello, II 3 line 1398; Othello, III 3 line 1995; Othello, III 3 line 2152; Othello, IV 1 line 2531; Othello, IV 1 line 2718; Othello, IV 2 line 2919; Othello, IV 3 line 3092; Othello, IV 3 line 3093; Othello, V 1 line 3174; Othello, V 1 line 3193; Othello, V 1 line 3194; Othello, V 1 line 3227; Othello, V 1 line 3243; Othello, V 2 line 3300; Othello, V 2 lines 3308r, 3310, 3311, 3314.
Pericles, I 1 line 124; Pericles, I 1 line 188; Pericles, I 2 line 355; Pericles, I 3 line 390; Pericles, II 3 lines 864, 867; Pericles, II 3 line 939; Pericles, II 5 line 1031; Pericles, III 1 line 1254; Pericles, IV 2 line 1738.
Rape of Lucrece, lines 156, 215, 241, 242, 279, 367r, 426, 450, 512, 698, 724, 725, 796, 844, 834, 858, 991, 1134r, 1142, 1282, 1430, 1485, 1531, 1678.
Richard II, I 1 line 85; Richard II, I 3 line 473; Richard II, I 3 line 521; Richard II, I 3 line 594; Richard II, I 4 line 657; Richard II, II 1 line 720; Richard II, III 2 lines 1446, 1451; Richard II, III 4 line 1953; Richard II, III 4 line 1959; Richard II, V 6 line 2927.
Richard III, I 2 line 195; Richard III, III 1 line 1690; Richard III, III 1 line 1691; Richard III, III 4 line 2051; Richard III, IV 4 line 3215; Richard III, V 3 line 3682.
Romeo and Juliet, I 1 line 157; Romeo and Juliet, I 2 line 295; Romeo and Juliet, I 4 line 508; Romeo and Juliet, I 4 line 516; Romeo and Juliet, I 4 line 531; Romeo and Juliet, I 4 line 542; Romeo and Juliet, I 5 line 646; Romeo and Juliet, I 5 line 712r; Romeo and Juliet, II 2 line 847; Romeo and Juliet, II 2 line 915; Romeo and Juliet, II 2 lines 948, 954; Romeo and Juliet, II 2 line 1013; Romeo and Juliet, II 3 line 1060; Romeo and Juliet, II 6 lines 1475, 1479; Romeo and Juliet, III 2 line 2002; Romeo and Juliet, III 4 line 2092; Romeo and Juliet, III 5 lines 2109r, 2112; Romeo and Juliet, III 5 line 2132r; Romeo and Juliet, III 5 line 2133r; Romeo and Juliet, IV 2 line 2545; Romeo and Juliet, V 3 line 2962; Romeo and Juliet, V 3 line 3031; Romeo and Juliet, V 3 line 3076; Romeo and Juliet, V 3 line 3558.
Sonnet VII line 1; Sonnet XXXVIII line 8; Sonnet LXIII line 7; Sonnet LX line 5; Sonnet LXXXVIII line 1; Sonnet C line 4.
Taming of the Shrew, I 1 line 406; Taming of the Shrew, I 1 line 422; Taming of the Shrew, I 2 line 716; Taming of the Shrew, II 1 line 1052; Taming of the Shrew, II 1 line 1123.
Tempest, I 2 lines 486, 491; Tempest, I 2 lines 629, 630; Tempest, I 2 line 681; Tempest, II 2 line 1231; Tempest, II 2 line 1237; Tempest, III 2 line 1410; Tempest, IV 1 line 1723; Tempest, IV 1 line 1810.

Timon of Athens, I 2 line 597r; Timon of Athens, II 2 line 891; Timon of Athens, IV 3 line 1738; Timon of Athens, IV 3 line 2054; Timon of Athens, IV 3 line 2082; Timon of Athens, V 1 line 2304.
Titus Andronicus, IV 2 line 1815; Titus Andronicus, V 2 line 2339.
Troilus and Cressida, I 1 line 68; Troilus and Cressida, I 2 line 162; Troilus and Cressida, I 3 line 478; Troilus and Cressida, II 3 line 1490; Troilus and Cressida, V 1 line 3000; Troilus and Cressida, V 1 line 3003.
Twelfth Night, II 4 line 895; Twelfth Night, III 3 line 1535; Twelfth Night, IV 2 line 2123; Twelfth Night, IV 2 line 2127; Twelfth Night, II 5 line 1111; Twelfth Night, II 5 line 1132; Twelfth Night, IV 2 line 2134; Twelfth Night, V 1 line 2548.
Two Gentlemen of Verona, I 2 line 239; Two Gentlemen of Verona, II 1 line 466; Two Gentlemen of Verona, II 4 line 872; Two Gentlemen of Verona, III 1 line 1117; Two Gentlemen of Verona, III 1 line 1199; Two Gentlemen of Verona, III 1 line 1247r.
Venus and Adonis, lines 170, 175, 183, 512, 554, 587, 778, 848, 882, 886, 1050, 1061, 1073, 1156, 1214.
Winter's Tale, II 3 line 1031; Winter's Tale, IV 4 line 2069.

Lightning: late 13c., from *lightnen*: *make bright*, extended form of Old English: *lihting*. A superstitious notion prevailed among the ancients, that those who were stricken with lightning were honoured by Jupiter, and therefore to be accounted holy. The bodies of such were supposed not to putrify; and, after having been exhibited for a certain time to the people, were not buried in the usual manner, but interred on the spot where the lightning fell, and a monument erected over them. The ground, too, that had been smitten by a thunderbolt was accounted sacred, and afterwards enclosed; nor did anyone even presume to walk on it. Such spots were, therefore, consecrated to the gods, and could not in future become the property of anyone.

Antony and Cleopatra, III 13 line 2486.
Cymbeline, IV 2 line 2669; Cymbeline, V 4 line 3239; Cymbeline, V 5 line 3850.
Henry VI, Part II, I 4 line 674.
Henry VI, Part III, II 1 line 757.
Julius Caesar, I 3 line 420; Julius Caesar, I 3 line 476; Julius Caesar, II 2 line 971.
King John, I 1 line 26.
King Lear, IV 7 line 2951.
Love's Labour's Lost, IV 2 line 1262.
Macbeth, I 1 line 1; Macbeth, I 1 line 3.
Midsummer Night's Dream, I 1 line 151.
Passionate Pilgrim, line 67.
Richard II, I 3 line 374.
Richard III, I 2 line 238.
Romeo and Juliet, II 2 line 970; Romeo and Juliet, III 1 line 1689; Romeo and Juliet, V 3 lines 3036, 2037.
Tempest, I 1 line 1; Tempest, III 1 line 1295; Tempest, III 3 line 1626.

Titus Andronicus, II 1 line 550.
Venus and Adonis, line 378.

Lilies: Old English: *lilie*, from Latin: *lilia: a lily*, cognate with Greek: *leirion*. As an adjective, 1530s, white, pure, lovely; later pale, colourless (1580s). 1605, *cowardly: lily-livered* (in its colour sense of pale, bloodless, which was a supposed seat of love and passion). A healthy liver is typically dark reddish-brown. Although so many pretty legends and romantic superstitions have clustered round this popular flower, Shakespeare, has simply made it typify elegance and beauty, and be the symbol of purity and whiteness.
    Cymbeline, II 2 line 937; Cymbeline, IV 2 line 2582.
    Henry VIII, III 1 line 1791; Henry VIII, V 5 line 3446.
    King John, III 1 line 968; King John, IV 2 line 1738.
    Love's Labour's Lost, V 2 line 2272.
    Passionate Pilgrim, line 90.
    Rape of Lucrece, lines 122, 437, 529.
    Richard II, IV 5 line 1234.
    Richard III, V 2 line 3456.
    Romeo and Juliet, II 4 line 1200.
    Sonnet XCIV line 14; Sonnet XCVIII line 9; Sonnet XCVIX line 6.
    Titus Andronicus, II 4 line1108; Titus Andronicus, III 1 line 1243.
    Two Gentlemen of Verona, II 3 line 613.
    Venus and Adonis, lines 248, 382, 1075.
    Winter's Tale, IV 4 line 2005.

Limb: part or member, Old English: *lim: limb, joint, main branch of a tree*. In Old and Middle English, and until lately in dialects, it could mean any visible body part. Hence, *limb-lifter: fornicator* (1570s). *Life and limb* in reference to the body inclusively is from c.1200.
    All's Well That Ends Well, III 2 line1514; All's Well That Ends Well, V 1 line 2569.
    As You Like It, I 1 line 109; As You Like It, II 3 line 685.
    Coriolanus, II 2 line 1327; Coriolanus, III 1 line 2109.
    Cymbeline, II 4 line 1361.
    Hamlet, II 2 line 1185; Hamlet, II 2 line 1588.
    Henry IV, Part I, IV 1 line 2264; Henry IV, Part I, V 1 line 2636.
    Henry IV, Part II, I 1 line 201; Henry IV, Part II, III 2 line 1950; Henry IV, Part II, III 2 line 2122; Henry IV, Part II, IV 1 line 2430; Henry IV, Part II, V 2 line 3383.
    Henry V, III 1 line 1117; Henry V, IV 7 line 2597; Henry V, V 1 line 2970.
    Henry VI, Part I, II 3 line 849; Henry VI, Part I, II 5 line 1079; Henry VI, Part I, IV 4 line 2104; Henry VI, Part I, IV 5 line 2138.
    Henry VI, Part II, II 3 line 1087; Henry VI, Part II, IV 10 line 2934r.
    Henry VI, Part III, I 3 line 392.
    Henry VIII, I 1 line 87; Henry VIII, I 1 line 302; Henry VIII, II 3 line 1245; Henry VIII, V 4 line 3333.
    Julius Caesar, I 3 line 507; Julius Caesar, II 1 lines 783, 785; Julius Caesar, III 1 line 1491.

King John, I 1 line 249; King John, III 1 line 1050; King John, III 1 line 1052; King John, III 1 line 1054 King John, III 1 line 1122; King John, IV 3 line 2021.
Love's Labour's Lost, IV 3 line 1518; Love's Labour's Lost, V 1 line 1855.
Measure for Measure, III 1 line 1249.
Merchant of Venice, II 7 line 1060.
Merry Wives of Windsor, III 1 line 1266.
Much Ado About Nothing, IV 1 line 1849.
Richard II, III 2 line 1597; Richard II, IV 1 line 2053.
Richard III, II 2 line 1330; Richard III, III 7 line 2336.
Romeo and Juliet, II 3 line 1098; Romeo and Juliet, V 3 line 2973.
Sonnet XXVII lines 2, 13.
Timon of Athens, IV 1 line 1588.
Titus Andronicus, I 1 line 114; Titus Andronicus, I 1 line 146; Titus Andronicus, I 1 line 163; Titus Andronicus, II 3 line 799; Titus Andronicus, V 3 line 2610.
Troilus and Cressida, I 3 lines 817, 819; Troilus and Cressida, IV 5 line2866r.
Twelfth Night, I 5 line 586.
Venus and Adonis, line 1089.

Line-grove: probably, a grove of lime trees.
    Tempest, V 1 line 2027.

Lion: late 12c., from Old French: *lion: lion*, figuratively *hero*, from Latin: *leonem*: lion; the constellation leo, from Greek: *leon*. Used figuratively from c. 1200 in an approving sense, one who is fiercely brave,and a disapproving one, tyrannical leader, greedy devourer. The traditions and stories of the darker ages abounded with examples of the lion's generosity.
    All's Well That Ends Well, I 1 line 92; All's Well That Ends Well, III 2 line 1527.
    Antony and Cleopatra, III 13 line 2368; Antony and Cleopatra, IV 14 line 2980; Antony and Cleopatra, V 1 line 3298.
    As You Like It, V 2 line 2270.
    Coriolanus, I 1 line 172; Coriolanus, I 1 line 249.
    Cymbeline, V 3 line 3064; Cymbeline, V 4 line 3292; Cymbeline, V 5 lines 3905, 3913.
    Hamlet, I 4 line 719.
    Henry IV, Part I, I 2 line 181; Henry IV, Part I, I 3 line 529; Henry IV, Part I, II 4 lines 1256, 1260; Henry IV, Part I, II 4 line 1285; Henry IV, Part I, III 1 line 1698; Henry IV, Part I, III 1 line 1712; Henry IV, Part I, III 2 line 1926; Henry IV, Part I, III 3 line 2156; Henry IV, Part I, III 3 line 2157; Henry IV, Part I, III 3 line 2158.
    Henry IV, Part II, I 2 line 524; Henry IV, Part II, IV 1 line 2425.
    Henry V, I 2 line 254; Henry V, I 2 line 269; Henry V, II 2 line 758; Henry V, III 7 line 1774; Henry V, IV 3 line 2331.
    Henry VI, Part I, I 2 line 220; Henry VI, Part I, I 5 lines 613, 614; Henry VI, Part I, III 2 line 1538; Henry VI, Part I, IV 7 line 2258.

Henry VI, Part II, III 1 line 1296; Henry VI, Part II, V 3 line 3320.
Henry VI, Part III, I 3 line 389; Henry VI, Part III, II 1 line 640; Henry VI, Part III, II 2 line 853; Henry VI, Part III, II 5 line 1178; Henry VI, Part III, IV 8 line 2571; Henry VI, Part III, V 2 line 2735; Henry VI, Part III, V 7 line 3106.
Henry VIII, III 2 line 2091.
Julius Caesar, I 3 line 441; Julius Caesar, I 3 line 501; Julius Caesar, I 3 line 534; Julius Caesar, II 1 line 830; Julius Caesar, II 2 line 1024.
King John, I 1 line 60; King John, I 1 line 91; King John, I 1 line 142; King John, I 1 line 263; King John, I 1 lines 276, 279; King John, II 1 line 293; King John, II 1 line 302; King John, II 1 line 434; King John, II 1 lines 437, 438; King John, II 1 lines 594, 595; King John, II 1 line 598; King John, II 1 line 763; King John, II 1 line 771; King John, III 1 line 1049; King John, III 1 line 1184; King John, V 1 line 2252; King John, V 2 line 2355.
King Lear, III 1 line 1630; King Lear, III 4 line 1888.
Love's Labour's Lost, IV 1 line 1063; Love's Labour's Lost, V 2 line 2517; Love's Labour's Lost, V 2 line 2565.
Macbeth, I 2 line 56; Macbeth, IV 1 line 1656.
Measure for Measure, I 3 line 312; Measure for Measure, I 4 line 418.
Merchant of Venice, II 1 line 545; Merchant of Venice, V 1 line 2452.
Midsummer Night's Dream, I 2 line 322; Midsummer Night's Dream, I 2 line 324; Midsummer Night's Dream, I 2 line 327; Midsummer Night's Dream, II 1 line 554; Midsummer Night's Dream, III 1 line 843; Midsummer Night's Dream, III 1 lines 846, 848; Midsummer Night's Dream, III 1 line 850; Midsummer Night's Dream, III 1 lines 852, 857; Midsummer Night's Dream, IV 2 lines 1821, 1823; Midsummer Night's Dream, V 1 line 1969; Midsummer Night's Dream, V 1 lines 1982, 1986, 1993; Midsummer Night's Dream, V 1 line 1995; Midsummer Night's Dream, V 1 line 1996; Midsummer Night's Dream, V 1 line 1997; Midsummer Night's Dream, V 1 line 2061; Midsummer Night's Dream, V 1 line 2062; Midsummer Night's Dream, V 1 lines 2063, 2066, 2068r, 2069; Midsummer Night's Dream, V 1 line 2073; Midsummer Night's Dream, V 1 line 2103; Midsummer Night's Dream, V 1 line 2105; Midsummer Night's Dream, V 1 line 2109; Midsummer Night's Dream, V 1 line 2110; Midsummer Night's Dream, V 1 line 2111; Midsummer Night's Dream, V 1 lines 2133, 2134; Midsummer Night's Dream, V 1 line 2195; Midsummer Night's Dream, V 1 line 2220.
Othello, II 3 line 1429.
Rape of Lucrece, lines 472, 1007.
Richard II, I 1 line 179; Richard II, II 1 line 860; Richard II, V 1 lines 2363, 2368.
Sonnet XIX line 1.
Taming of the Shrew, I 2 line 780.
Tempest, II 1 line 1059; Tempest, II 1 line 1064.
Timon of Athens, III 5 line 1358; Timon of Athens, IV 3 lines 2029, 2031, 2043.
Titus Andronicus, II 3 line 890; Titus Andronicus, IV 1 line 1642.

Troilus and Cressida, I 2 line 175; Troilus and Cressida, II 3 line 1303; Troilus and Cressida, III 2 line 1739; Troilus and Cressida, III 3 line 2105; Troilus and Cressida, IV 1 line 2219; Troilus and Cressida, V 3 line 3319.
Twelfth Night, III 1 line 1366.
Two Gentlemen of Verona, II 1 line 426; Two Gentlemen of Verona, V 4 line 2182.
Venus and Adonis, lines 649, 906, 1115.

Lioness: from 13c., *leoness*.
As You Like It, IV 3 line 2117; As You Like It, IV 3 line 2130; As You Like It, IV 3 line 2135; As You Like It, IV 3 line 2153.
Julius Caesar, II 2 line 992.
King John, II 4 line 56.
Titus Andronicus, IV 2 line 1829.

Lip: Old English: *lippa*. Transferred sense of *edge or margin of a cup*, etc. is from 1590s. Slang sense: *move the lip* (1570s) utter even the slightest word (against someone). To bite (one's) lip: show vexation, is from early 14c.
All's Well That Ends Well, II 2 line 834; All's Well That Ends Well, II 2 line 849.
Antony and Cleopatra, I 3 line 339; Antony and Cleopatra, II 1 line 641; Antony and Cleopatra, II 5 line 1086; Antony and Cleopatra, III 13 line 2351; Antony and Cleopatra, III 13 line 2463; Antony and Cleopatra, IV 8 line 2811; Antony and Cleopatra, IV 14 line 3017; Antony and Cleopatra, IV 15 line 3190; Antony and Cleopatra, IV 15 line 3212; Antony and Cleopatra, V 2 line 3567; Antony and Cleopatra, V 2 lines 3740, 3749, 3752.
As You Like It, I 3 line 486; As You Like It, III 2 line 1174; As You Like It, III 4 line 1607; As You Like It, III 5 line 1775; As You Like It, V 1 lines 2220, 2221.
Coriolanus, I 1 line 278; Coriolanus, II 1 line 1033; Coriolanus, II 2 line 1339; Coriolanus, III 2 line 2306; Coriolanus, IV 5 line 2987; Coriolanus, V 1 line 3335; Coriolanus, V 3 line 3543.
Cymbeline, I 6 lines 723, 728; Cymbeline, I 6 line 769; Cymbeline, V 5 line 3418; Cymbeline, V 5 line 3719.
Hamlet, I 5 line 942; Hamlet, V 1 line 3519.
Henry IV, Part I, I 1 line 7; Henry IV, Part I, II 3 line 955; Henry IV, Part I, II 4 line 1142; Henry IV, Part I, II 4 line 1388.
Henry V, II 3 line 877; Henry V, III 6 line 1569; Henry V, III 7 line 1774; Henry V, IV 6 line 2501; Henry V, V 2 line 3241; Henry V, V 2 line 3259.
Henry VI, Part I, II 5 line 1116.
Henry VI, Part II, I 2 line 366; Henry VI, Part II, III 2 line 1824; Henry VI, Part II, III 2 lines 2089, 2092; Henry VI, Part II, IV 1 line 2231.
Henry VI, Part III, II 2 line 963; Henry VI, Part III, V 2 line 2758, 2761; Henry VI, Part III, V 7 line 3124.
Henry VIII, III 2 line 1979.

Julius Caesar, I 2 line 212; Julius Caesar, I 2 line 343; Julius Caesar, III 1 line 1489.
King John, II 1 line 847; King John, III 4 line 1554; King John, IV 2 line 1780; King John, V 7 line 2673.
King Lear, IV 3 line 2474; King Lear, IV 6 line 2775; King Lear, IV 7 line 2942; King Lear, V 3 line 3499.
Love's Labour's Lost, II 1 line 717; Love's Labour's Lost, II 2 line 722; Love's Labour's Lost, IV 1 line 1059; Love's Labour's Lost, IV 1 line 1122.
Lover's Complaint, line 87.
Macbeth, I 3 line 145; Macbeth, I 7 line 485; Macbeth, IV 1 line 1576.
Measure for Measure, II 2 line 839; Measure for Measure, III 1 line 1436; Measure for Measure, III 2 line 1645; Measure for Measure, IV 1 line 1795.
Merchant of Venice, I 1 line 100; Merchant of Venice, III 2 line 1487.
Merry Wives of Windsor, I 1 lines 211, 212.
Midsummer Night's Dream, II 1 line 417; Midsummer Night's Dream, III 2 line 1178; Midsummer Night's Dream, V 1 line 2034; Midsummer Night's Dream, V 1 line 2045; Midsummer Night's Dream, V 1 line 2175; Midsummer Night's Dream, V 1 line 2262.
Othello, I 1 line 68; Othello, II 1 line 866; Othello, II 1 line 1059; Othello, III 3 line 2106; Othello, IV 1 line 2459; Othello, IV 1 line 2495; Othello, IV 2 lines 2798, 2811; Othello, IV 3 line 3061; Othello, V 2 line 3351; Othello, V 2 line 3668.
Passionate Pilgrim, lines 92, 152, 153.
Pericles, II 3 line 874; Pericles, II 5 line 1107; Pericles, V 3 line 2570.
Rape of Lucrece, lines 471, 731, 1093, 1457, 1715, 1835.
Richard II, I 3 line 464; Richard II, IV 1 line 2006.
Richard III, I 1 line 99; Richard III, I 2 line 357; Richard III, I 3 line 753; Richard III, IV 2 line 2611; Richard III, IV 3 line 2738.
Romeo and Juliet, I 4 line 574; Romeo and Juliet, I 5 line 721; Romeo and Juliet, I 5 line 727; Romeo and Juliet, I 5 line 728; Romeo and Juliet, I 5 line 729; Romeo and Juliet, I 5 line 731; Romeo and Juliet, I 5 line 733; Romeo and Juliet, I 5 line 734; Romeo and Juliet, I 5 line 735; Romeo and Juliet, II 1 line 817; Romeo and Juliet, III 3 line 1881; Romeo and Juliet, III 3 line 1908; Romeo and Juliet, IV 1 line 2465; Romeo and Juliet, IV 5 line 2684; Romeo and Juliet, V 1 line 2812; Romeo and Juliet, V 3 lines 3041, 3059; Romeo and Juliet, V 3 line 3127, 3131.
Sonnet CVI line 6; Sonnet CXVI line 9; Sonnet CXXVIII line 7; Sonnet CXXVIII line 12; Sonnet CXXVIII line 14; Sonnet CXXX line 2; Sonnet CXLII line 5; Sonnet CXLV line 1.
Taming of the Shrew, I 1 line 465; Taming of the Shrew, II 2 line 1098; Taming of the Shrew, III 2 line 1540; Taming of the Shrew, IV 1 line 1625.
Timon of Athens, I 1 line 45; Timon of Athens, III 2 line 1086; Timon of Athens, III 6 line 1501; Timon of Athens, IV 3 line 1734; Timon of Athens, IV 3 line 1736; Timon of Athens, V 1 line 2482; Timon of Athens, V 1 line 2509.

Titus Andronicus, II 4 line 1088; Titus Andronicus, III 1 line 1250; Titus Andronicus, IV 2 line 1871; Titus Andronicus, V 3 line 2696; Titus Andronicus, V 3 line 2701.
Troilus and Cressida, I 1 line 57; Troilus and Cressida, I 3 line 525; Troilus and Cressida, I 3 line 696; Troilus and Cressida, I 3 line 731; Troilus and Cressida, III 1 line 1625; Troilus and Cressida, III 3 line 2138; Troilus and Cressida, IV 4 line 2455; Troilus and Cressida, IV 4 line 2465; Troilus and Cressida, IV 5 line 2623; Troilus and Cressida, IV 5 line 2661; Troilus and Cressida, IV 5 line 2887.
Twelfth Night, I 4 line 279; Twelfth Night, I 5 line 297; Twelfth Night, I 5 line 535; Twelfth Night, II 5 line 1094; Twelfth Night, II 5 line 1122; Twelfth Night, III 1 line 1385; Twelfth Night, V 1 line 2356.
Venus and Adonis, lines 39, 66, 68, 109, 110, 135r, 140r, 147, 227, 253, 498, 526, 532r, 537, 570r, 573, 593, 621, 654, 747, 1145.
Winter's Tale, I 2 line 389; Winter's Tale, I 2 line 491; Winter's Tale, II 3 line 1052; Winter's Tale, III 2 line 1443; Winter's Tale, V 1 line 2883; Winter's Tale, V 3 line 3366; Winter's Tale, V 3 line 3385.

Liver: secreting organ of the body, Old English: *lifer*. Formerly believed to be the body's blood-producing organ; in medieval times it rivalled the heart as the supposed seat of love and passion. By a popular notion the liver was anciently supposed to be the seat of love, a superstition to which Shakespeare frequently alludes.
Antony and Cleopatra, I 2 line 103.
As You Like It, III 2 line 1504.
Cymbeline, III 3 line 1610; Cymbeline, III 4 line 1880; Cymbeline, V 5 line 3383.
Henry IV, Part I, II 4 line 1308.
Henry IV, Part II, I 2 line 494; Henry IV, Part II, IV 3 line 2699; Henry IV, Part II, V 5 line 3620.
Henry VIII, II 3 line 1224.
Macbeth, IV 1 line 1573.
Merchant of Venice, I 1 line 87; Merchant of Venice, III 2 line 1453.
Merry Wives of Windsor, II 1 line 678.
Much Ado About Nothing, IV 1 line 1883.
Rape of Lucrece, line 98.
Romeo and Juliet, I 5 line 632.
Tempest, IV 1 line 1763.
Troilus and Cressida, II 2 line 1032; Troilus and Cressida, V 1 line 2950; Troilus and Cressida, V 3 line 3296.
Twelfth Night, I 1 line 41; Twelfth Night, II 4 line 997; Twelfth Night, II 5 line 1119; Twelfth Night, III 2 line 1422; Twelfth Night, III 2 line 1463.
Winter's Tale, I 2 line 410.

Lizard: It was a common superstition in the time of Shakespeare that lizards were venomous, a notion which probably originated in their singular form. Late 14c., *lusarde*, from Anglo-French: *lusard*, Old French: *laisarde: lizard*.
Henry VI, Part II, III 2 line 2019.
Henry VI, Part III, II 2 line 983.

Macbeth, IV 1 line 1564.
Troilus and Cressida, V 1 line 2992.

Loach: small edible European fish, mid-14c., from Old French: *loche* (13c.), also, in dialect, slug, of unknown origin.
Henry IV, Part I, II 1 line 663.

Lode-star: pole star.
Midsummer Night's Dream, I 1 line 191.
Rape of Lucrece, line 230.

Lodged: laid flat by wind and rain.
Henry VI, Part II, III 2 line 1860.
Macbeth, IV 1 line 1607.

Loins: early 14c., side of the body of an animal used for food, from Old French: *loigne: hip, haunch, lumbar region*. In reference to the living human body, it is attested from late 14c. In Biblical translations, often used for that part of the body that should be covered and about which the clothes are bound (1520s).
Coriolanus, III 3 line 2485.
Cymbeline, V 5 line 3778.
Hamlet, II 2 line 1582.
Henry VI, Part III, III 2 line 1615.
Julius Caesar, II 1 line 955.
King Lear, II 3 line 1261; King Lear, II 4 line 1284.
Measure for Measure, III 1 line 1252.
Much Ado About Nothing, IV 1 line 1784.
Richard III, I 3 line 696.
Romeo and Juliet, Prologue 1 line 5.
Troilus and Cressida, IV 1 line 2267.

Long Purples: This plant mentioned by Shakespeare as forming part of the nosegay of Ophelia, is generally considered to be the early purple orchis, which blossoms in April or May. It grows in meadows and pastures, and is about ten inches high. He also refers to it as, *Dead Men's Fingers*, from the pale colour and hand-like shape of the palmate tubers.
Hamlet, IV 7 line 3318.

Louse: parasitic insect infecting human hair and skin, Old English: *lus*.
Troilus and Cressida, V 1 line 2996.

Love-in-idleness: also known as *heartsease:* a wild European pansy which typically has purple and yellow flowers. It has given rise to hybrids from which most garden pansies. Late Middle English: origin uncertain, the term being applied by herbalists to both the pansy and the wallflower in the 16c. Flowers, and pansies especially, were used as love-philtres, or for the object of casting a spell over people in Shakespeare's day.
Midsummer Night's Dream, II 1 line 540.

Lowing: early 13c., make a noise like a cow.
>**Henry VI, Part II**, III 1 line 1496.
>**Tempest**, IV 1 line 1915.

Lubber: leopard.
>**Henry IV, Part II**, II 1 line 744.

Luce: a pike.
>**Merry Wives of Windsor,** I 1 line 20.

Luna: late 14c. moon, also an alchemical name for silver; from Latin: *luna: moon, goddess of the moon.*
>**Love's Labour's Lost**, IV 2 line 1183.

Lungs: human respiratory organ, c.1300, from Old English: *lungen.*
>**As You Like It**, II 7 line 924.
>**Coriolanus**, I 1 line 100; Coriolanus, III 1 line 1825.
>**Cymbeline**, I 6 line 683.
>**Hamlet**, II 2 line 1413; Hamlet, II 2 line 1649.
>**Henry IV, Part II**, IV 5 line 3112; Henry IV, Part II, V 3 line 3554; Henry IV, Part II, V 5 line 3596.
>**Henry V**, II 1 line 554.
>**Love's Labour's Lost**, III 1 line 839.
>**Lover's Complaint**, lines 229, 328.
>**Merchant of Venice**, IV 1 line 2075.
>**Merry Wives of Windsor**, IV 5 line 2309.
>**Pericles**, IV 6 line 2110.
>**Tempest**, II 1 line 751; Tempest, II 1 line 885.
>**Troilus and Cressida**, IV 5 line 2602; Troilus and Cressida, V 1 line 2951.

Lym: a bloodhound, so called because it was held by a *lym* or leash.
>**King Lear**, III 6 line 2070.

Mace: spice made from dry outer husk of nutmeg, late 14c., from Old French: *macis* (in English taken as a plural and stripped of its -s), of uncertain origin, sometimes said to be a scribal error for Latin: *macir*, the name of a red spicy bark from India.
>**Winter's Tale**, IV 3 line 1771.

Mackerel: edible fish, c.1300, from Old French: *maquerel: mackerel*, of unknown origin but apparently identical with Old French: *maquerel: pimp, procurer, broker, agent, intermediary.* Medieval people had imaginative notions about the erotic habits of beasts, including, mackerel. The fish approach the shore in shoals in summertime to spawn.
>**Henry IV, Part I**, II 4 line 1344.

Magot-pie: Magpie; probably from the Old French: *magot*, a monkey, because the bird chatters and plays droll tricks like a monkey. It has generally been regarded as a mysterious bird, and regarded with superstitious awe.
   Macbeth, III 4 line 1428.

Mallard: Middle English: from Old French: *wild drake*, from *masle*: *male*.
   Antony and Cleopatra, III 10 line 2086.

Malt: mid-15c., to convert grain to malt; to *make with malt* is from c.1600. Old English *malt* (Anglian), *mealt* (West Saxon).
   King Lear, III 2 line 1763.

Malt-horse: heavy, slow brewer's horse; so, a drudge, an idiot.
   Comedy of Errors, III 1 line 645.
   Taming of the Shrew, IV 1 line 1728.

Malt-worm: a tippler; a drunkard, after a worm in the beer.
   Henry IV, Part I, II 1 line 717.
   Henry IV, Part II, II 4 line 1635.

Mammets: a woman's breasts.
   Henry IV, Part I, II 3 line 955.

Mandrake: narcotic plant, early 14c., *mondrake*, from *mandragora*, from Latin: *mandragoras*, from Greek: *mandragoras*. The word was in late Old English in its Latin form; folk etymology associated the second element with *dragoun* and substituted native *drake* in its place. The forked root is thought to resemble a human body and is said to shriek when pulled from the ground. No plant, perhaps, has had, at different times, a greater share of folk-lore attributed to it than the mandrake; partly owing probably to the fancied resemblance of its root to the human figure, and the accidental circumstance of man being the first syllable of the word. An inferior degree of animal life was assigned to it; and it was commonly supposed that, when torn from the ground, it uttered groans of so pernicious a character, that the person who committed the violence either went mad or died. Some formed little idols of the roots of the mandrake, which were regularly dressed every day, and consulted as oracles, their repute being such that they were manufactured in great numbers and sold in cases. They were, also, imported into this country during the time of Henry VIII., it being pretended that they would; with the assistance of some mystic words, increase whatever money was placed near them. In order, too, to enhance the value of these so-called miracle workers, it was said that the roots of this plant were produced from the flesh of criminals which fell from the gibbet, and that it only grew in such a situation.
   Henry IV, Part II, I 2 line 288; Henry IV, Part II, III 2 line 2185; Henry IV, Part II, III 2 line 2004.
   Romeo and Juliet, IV 3 line 2589.

Mandragora: see, mandrake.
   Antony and Cleopatra, I 5 line 524.

Othello, III 3 line 2005.

Mane: Old English: *manu*.
    Othello, II 1 line 776.
    Troilus and Cressida, III 3 line 2105.
    Venus and Adonis, lines 291, 318, 325.

Marble: type of stone much used in sculpture, monuments, etc., early 14c., by dissimilation from *marbra* (mid-12c.), from Old French: *marbre*, from Latin: *marmor*, from or cognate with Greek: *marmaros*: marble, *gleaming stone*, of unknown origin, perhaps originally an adjective meaning sparkling, which would connect it with *marmairein*: *to shine*. The Latin word was taken directly into Old English as *marma*.
    Comedy of Errors, II 1 line 367.
    Cymbeline, V 4 line 3243; Cymbeline, V 4 line 3272.
    Hamlet, I 4 line 679.
    Henry VI, Part III, III 1 line 1405; Henry VI, Part III, III 2 line 1530.
    Henry VIII, III 2 line 2347.
    Macbeth, III 4 line 1298.
    Measure for Measure, III 1 line 1471; Measure for Measure, V 1 line 2642.
    Othello, III 3 line 2146.
    Rape of Lucrece, lines 611, 1291, 1292.
    Richard II, IV 5 line 1234.
    Richard III, V 2 line 3456.
    Romeo and Juliet, II 4 line 1200.
    Sonnet LV line 1.
    Titus Andronicus, II 3 line 882.
    Winter's Tale, V 2 line 3198.

Mare: female horse, Old English: *mere* (Mercian), *myre* (West Saxon), fem. of *mearh*: *horse*. As the name of a throw in wrestling, it is attested from c.1600. *Mare's nest*: *illusory discovery, excitement over something which does not exist* is from 1610s.
    Antony and Cleopatra, III 7 lines 1944, 1945.
    Henry IV, Part II, II 1 line 765; Henry IV, Part II, II 1 line 800; Henry IV, Part II, II 1 line 804; Henry IV, Part II, II 4 line 1529.
    Henry V, II 1 line 531.
    Midsummer Night's Dream, III 2 line 1540.
    Venus and Adonis, line 404.

Marigold: late 14c., *marygolde*, from Mary (probably a reference to the Virgin) + gold, for colour. The Old English: name for the flower was simply *golde*. This flower was a great favourite with our old writers, from a curious notion that it always opened or shut its flowers at the sun's bidding.
    Pericles, IV 1 line 1563.
    Rape of Lucrece, line 448.
    Sonnet XXV line 6.
    Winter's Tale, IV 4 line 1982.

Marjoram: late 14c., from Old French: *majorane*, of uncertain origin, probably ultimately from India with form influenced by Latin: *major: greater*.
    All's Well That Ends Well, IV 5 line 2478.
    King Lear, IV 6 line 2703.
    Sonnet XCVIX line 7.
    Winter's Tale, IV 4 line 1981.

Marmoset: small monkey, late 14c., from Old French: *marmoset: grotesque figurine; fool, jester* (late 13c.), perhaps a variant of *marmote: long-tailed monkey, ape*, then, as a term of endearment, *little child*; said to be from *marmonner, marmotter: to mutter, mumble*, probably of imitative origin. Some French authorities suggest a derivation of marmoset from *marmor: marble*, as if little marble figurine.
    Tempest, II 2 line 1256.

Marrow: late 14c., from Old English: *mearg: marrow*, earlier *mærh*. Figurative sense of *inmost or central part* is attested from c.1400.
    All's Well That Ends Well, II 3 line 1183.
    Hamlet, I 4 line 650.
    Henry VI, Part III, III 2 line 1614.
    Macbeth, III 4 line 1389.
    Timon of Athens, IV 1 line 1590; Timon of Athens, IV 3 line 1880; Timon of Athens, V 4 line 2565.
    Venus and Adonis, lines 162, 763.

Mars: Roman god of war, also the name of the bright red planet, late 14c., from Latin: *Mars* (*Mawort*), the Roman god of war, of unknown origin, apparently from earlier *Mavors*. He also had agricultural attributes, and might ultimately have been a Spring-Dionysus. The planet was so named by the Romans, no doubt for its blood-like colour.
    All's Well That Ends Well, I 1 line 194; All's Well That Ends Well, I 1 line 195; All's Well That Ends Well, I 1 line 196; All's Well That Ends Well, I 1 line 197; All's Well That Ends Well, II 1 line 645; All's Well That Ends Well, II 3 line 1185; All's Well That Ends Well, III 3 line 1554; All's Well That Ends Well, IV 1 line 1932.
    Antony and Cleopatra, I 1 line 5; Antony and Cleopatra, I 5 line 542; Antony and Cleopatra, II 2 line 687; Antony and Cleopatra, II 5 line 1203; Antony and Cleopatra, IV 14 line 3039.
    Coriolanus, I 4 line 492; Coriolanus, IV 5 line 2885; Coriolanus, IV 5 line 2962; Coriolanus, V 6 line 3940.
    Cymbeline, V 4 line 3179.
    Hamlet, II 2 line 1564; Hamlet, III 4 line 2449.
    Henry IV, Part I, III 2 line 1936; Henry IV, Part I, IV 1 line 2342.
    Henry V, Prologue 1 line 7; Henry V, IV 2 line 2208.
    Henry VI, Part I, I 2 line 191.
    Henry VI, Part III, IV 8 line 2586.
    Henry VIII, III 2 line 1852.

Love's Labour's Lost, V 2 line 2585; Love's Labour's Lost, V 2 line 2592.
Macbeth, II 3 line 793.
Merchant of Venice, III 2 line 1452.
Merry Wives of Windsor, I 3 line 402.
Othello, V 1 line 3139.
Passionate Pilgrim, line 146.
Richard II, II 1 line 723; Richard II, II 3 line 1258.
Sonnet LV line 7.
Tempest, IV 1 line 1811.
Timon of Athens, IV 3 line 2088.
Troilus and Cressida, II 1 line 910; Troilus and Cressida, II 3 line 1467; Troilus and Cressida, III 3 line 2067; Troilus and Cressida, IV 5 line 2801; Troilus and Cressida, IV 5 line 2822; Troilus and Cressida, IV 5 line 2884; Troilus and Cressida, V 2 line 3238; Troilus and Cressida, V 3 line 3336.

Martlet: late Middle English (denoting a swift): from Old French: *merlet*, influenced by *martinet*.
    Macbeth, I 6 line 437.
    Merchant of Venice, II 9 line 1157.

Mary-bud: budding blossom of the common marsh marigold.
    Cymbeline, II 3 line 1000.

Mastiff: large, powerful breed of dog, early 14c., from Old French *mastin* (Modern French *mâtin*) or Provençal **mastis**, both from Vulgar Latin: *mansuetinus*: domesticated, tame, from Latin *mansuetus*: tame, gentle. Probably originally meaning a dog that stays in the house, thus a guard-dog. Form in English perhaps influenced by Old French *mestif*: mongrel.
    Henry V, III 7 line 1769; Henry V, III 7 line 1776.
    King Lear, III 6 line 2069.
    Troilus and Cressida, I 3 line 855.

May: fifth month, early 12c., from Old French: *mai* and directly from Latin: *Majus, Maius mensis: month of May*, possibly from *Maja, Maia*, a Roman earth goddess (wife of Vulcan) whose name is of unknown origin. Replaced Old English *primilce*, month in which cows can be milked three times a day. May marriages have been considered unlucky at least since Roman times.
    As You Like It, IV 1 line 1920.
    Hamlet, III 3 line 2364; Hamlet, IV 5 line 3035.
    Henry IV, Part I, IV 1 line 2327.
    Henry VI, Part II, I 1 line 55.
    Henry VIII, V 5 line 3283.
    Love's Labour's Lost, IV 3 line 1431.
    Merry Wives of Windsor, III 2 line 1377.
    Midsummer Night's Dream, IV 1 line 1688.
    Much Ado About Nothing, I 1 line 173; Much Ado About Nothing, V 1 line 2151.

Passionate Pilgrim, lines 229, 376.
Pericles, I 0 line 15.
Richard II, V 1 line 4114.
Sonnet XVIII line 3.
Troilus and Cressida, I 2 line 321.
Twelfth Night, III 4 line 1685.

Maw: jaws or mouth, usually of a voracious animal. Old English: *maga* (in the sense stomach), of Germanic origin; related to Dutch: *maag* and German *Magen*: *stomach*.
Comedy of Errors, I 2 line 231.
Henry V, II 1 line 554.
King John, V 7 line 2670.
Macbeth, III 4 line 1361; Macbeth, IV 1 line 1570.
Measure for Measure, III 2 line 1533.
Romeo and Juliet, V 3 line 2983.
Timon of Athens, III 4 line 1226.
Venus and Adonis, line 623.

Meacock: An uxorious, effeminate, or spiritless man.
Taming of the Shrew, II 1 line 1154.

Mead: Old English: *mæd: meadow, pasture*.
Henry V, V 2 lines 3029, 3035.
King Lear, I 1 line 65.
Merry Wives of Windsor, III 3 line 1416; Merry Wives of Windsor, III 3 line 1524.
Midsummer Night's Dream, II 1 line 452.
Rape of Lucrece, line 1269.
Taming of the Shrew, V 2 line 2647.
Tempest, IV 1 line 1773.
Titus Andronicus, II 4 line 1118.
Venus and Adonis, line 657.

Meadow: Old English: *mædwe: meadow, pasture*, originally *land covered in grass which is mown for hay.*
Love's Labour's Lost, V 2 line 2845.
Merry Wives of Windsor, V 5 line 2630.
Sonnet XXXIII line 3.
Titus Andronicus, III 1 line 1255

Medlar: This fruit, which Shakespeare describes as only fit to be eaten when rotten, is applied by Lucio to a woman of loose character. A small fruit-bearing tree, mid 14c. (in reference to the fruit itself), from Old French: *medler*, variant of *mesple*, from Latin: *mespila: fruit of the medlar*, from Greek: *mespilion*, a foreign word of unknown origin. The Old English name was *openærs*, literally, *open-arse.*
As You Like It, III 2 line 1229.
Measure for Measure, IV 3 line 2301.

Romeo and Juliet, II 1 lines 833, 835.
Timon of Athens, IV 3 line 2006; Timon of Athens, IV 3 line 2009.

Metal: mid-13c., from Old French: *metal: metal; material, substance, stuff* (12c.), from Latin: *metallum: metal; mine, quarry, mineral, what is got by mining*, from Greek: *metallon: metal*, probably from *metalleuein: to mine, to quarry*, of unknown origin, but related somehow to *metallan: to seek after*.
    All's Well That Ends Well, I 1 line 133; All's Well That Ends Well, II 1 line 637; all's Well That Ends Well, III 6 line 1762.
    Comedy of Errors, IV 1 line 1035.
    Hamlet, III 2 line 1990; Hamlet, IV 1 line 2653.
    Henry IV, Part I, I 2 line 315.
    Henry IV, Part II, I 1 line 174.
    Henry VIII, III 2 line 2128.
    Julius Caesar, I 1 line 62; Julius Caesar, I 2 line 405.
    King John, V 2 line 2294.
    King Lear, I 1 line 70.
    Love's Labour's Lost, III 1 line 818.
    Lover's Complaint, line 206.
    Measure for Measure, I 1 line 56; Measure for Measure, II 4 line 1070.
    Merchant of Venice, I 3 line 460; Merchant of Venice, IV 1 line 2059.
    Much Ado About Nothing, II 1 line 450.
    Pericles, III 2 line 1327.
    Richard II, I 2 line 236.
    Richard III, IV 1 line 2530; Richard III, IV 4 line 3194.
    Tempest, II 1 line 862; Tempest, II 1 line 893.
    Timon of Athens, III 3 line 1114.
    Titus Andronicus, IV 3 line 1928.
    Troilus and Cressida, I 3 line 472.
    Twelfth Night, II 5 line 1041.

Meteor: late 15c., any atmospheric phenomenon, *meteore* (13c.) and directly from Greek: *ta meteora: the celestial phenomena, things in heaven above*. Specific sense of, fireball, shooting star, is attested from 1590s. Atmospheric phenomena were formerly classified as aerial meteors (wind), aqueous meteors (rain, snow, hail), luminous meteors (aurora, rainbows), and igneous meteors (lightning, shooting stars).
    Comedy of Errors, IV 2 line 1077.
    Henry IV, Part I, I 1 line 11; Henry IV, Part I, II 4 line 1304; Henry IV, Part I, V 1 line 2642.
    Henry VIII, V 4 line 3320.
    King John, III 4 line 1545; King John, V 2 line 2331.
    Merry Wives of Windsor, II 2 line 1065.
    Richard II, II 4 line 1339.
    Romeo and Juliet, III 5 line 2110.

Mice: *mys*, plural of *mouse*.
    Henry IV, Part I, I 2 line 202.

King Lear, III 4 line 1931; King Lear, IV 6 line 2618.
Measure for Measure, I 4 line 418.
Midsummer Night's Dream, II 2 line 653.

Milch: a cow or deer or other domesticated animal kept for milk. Middle English: from Old English: *milce*, only in *thrimilce:* May (when cows could be milked three times a day).
Hamlet, II 2 line 1591.
Merry Wives of Windsor, IV 4 line 2228.
Taming of the Shrew, II 1 line 1210.
Venus and Adonis, line 897.

Milk: Old English: *meoluc* (West Saxon), *milc* (Anglian).
All's Well That Ends Well, IV 3 line 2196.
Antony and Cleopatra, IV 15 line 3256.
As You Like It, II 4 line 766.
Coriolanus, V 4 line 3758.
Hamlet, I 5 line 807; Hamlet, II 2 line 1552.
Henry IV, Part I, II 3 line 892; Henry IV, Part I, V 4 line 2697.
Henry IV, Part II, I 1 line 256.
King Lear, I 1 line 86; King Lear, I 4 line 873; King Lear, IV 2 line 2395.
Love's Labour's Lost, V 2 line 2129; Love's Labour's Lost, V 2 line 2862.
Macbeth, I 5 line 361; Macbeth, I 5 line 398; Macbeth, I 7 line 534; Macbeth, IV 3 line 1954.
Measure for Measure, I 2 line 265.
Merchant of Venice, III 2 line 1453.
Midsummer Night's Dream, II 1 line 403; Midsummer Night's Dream, II 1 line 539; Midsummer Night's Dream, V 1 line 2183.
Passionate Pilgrim, line 120.
Pericles, IV 0 line 1514.
Richard III, V 3 line 3640.
Romeo and Juliet, III 3 line 1926.
Tempest, II 1 line 1025.
Timon of Athens, I 2 line 543; Timon of Athens, III 1 line 1000; Timon of Athens, IV 3 line 1795.
Titus Andronicus, II 3 line 882; Titus Andronicus, V 1 line 2163.
Twelfth Night, I 5 line 453.
Two Gentlemen of Verona, III 1 line 1324; Two Gentlemen of Verona, III 1 line 1342; Two Gentlemen of Verona, III 1 line 1372.
Venus and Adonis, line 924.
Winter's Tale, III 2 line 1317; Winter's Tale, IV 4 line 2131; Winter's Tale, IV 4 line 2374.

Minnow: small freshwater fish, early 15c., probably related to Old English: *myne*.
Coriolanus, III 1 line 1842.
Love's Labour's Lost, I 1 line 247.

Mint: aromatic herb, Old English: *minte* (8c.), a borrowing from Latin: *menta, mentha*, from Greek: *minthe*, personified as a nymph transformed into an herb by *Proserpine*, probably a loan-word from a lost Mediterranean language.
    Love's Labour's Lost, I 1 line 170; Love's Labour's Lost, V 2 line 2597.
    Troilus and Cressida, I 3 line 646.
    Twelfth Night, III 2 line 1424.
    Winter's Tale, IV 4 line 1981.

Minx: 1540s, *mynx: pet dog*, later a *young, pert, wanton girl* (1590s), of uncertain origin, perhaps a shortening of *minikin: girl, woman*.
    Othello, III 3 line 2167; Othello, IV 1 line 2584.
    Twelfth Night, III 4 line 1664.

Mistletoe: This plant, which from the earliest times has been an object of interest to naturalists, on account of its curious growth, deriving its subsistence entirely from the branch to which it annexes itself, has been the subject of wide-spread superstition. Old English: *mistiltan*.
    Titus Andronicus, II 3 line 831.

Mite: tiny animal, minute arachnid, Old English: *miton*, originally meaning perhaps *the cutter*, in reference to its bite.
    All's Well That Ends Well, I 1 line 143.
    Pericles, II 4 line 538.

Mole: spot on skin, Old English: *mal: spot, mark, blemish*, especially on cloth or linen. Specifically of dark marks on human skin from late 14c. These have from time immemorial been regarded as ominous, and special attention has been paid by the superstitious to their position on the body.
    Comedy of Errors, III 2 line 899.
    Cymbeline, II 2 line 961; Cymbeline, II 4 line 1344; Cymbeline, V 5 line 3816.
    King John, III 1 line 962.
    Midsummer Night's Dream, V 1 line 2262.
    Twelfth Night, V 1 line 2443.

Mole: type of small burrowing mammal, mid-14c., probably from obsolete *moldwarp*, literally, earth-thrower. Metaphoric use for *one who works in darkness* is from c.1600. spot on skin, Old English: *mal: spot, mark, blemish*, especially on cloth or linen. Specifically of dark marks on human skin from late 14c.
    Hamlet, I 4 line 652; Hamlet, I 5 line 915.
    Pericles, I 1 line 149.
    Tempest, IV 1 line 1937.
    Winter's Tale, IV 4 line 2811.

Molehill: small mound of earth, mid 15c.
    Coriolanus, V 3 line 3424.

Henry VI, Part III, I 4 line 506; Henry VI, Part III, II 5 line 1116.

Mongrel: late 15c., mixed-breed dog, from obsolete *mong*: mixture, from Old English *gemong*: mingling, from Proto-Germanic *mangjan*: to knead together. Meaning, person not of pure race, is from 1540s. As an adjective from 1570s.
  King Lear, I 4 line 582; King Lear, II 2 line 1093; King Lear, III 6 line 2069.
  Macbeth, III 1 line 1108.
  Troilus and Cressida, II 1 line 869; Troilus and Cressida, V 4 line 3422.

Monkey: 1520s, likely from an unrecorded derivation of an Old French form of the name is *Monequin*, which could be a diminutive of some personal name, or it could be from the general Romanic word, which may be ultimately from Arabic: *maimun: monkey*, literally, *auspicious*, a euphemistic usage because the sight of apes was held by the Arabs to be unlucky. Monkey has been used affectionately for child since c.1600.
  As You Like It, IV 1 line 1927.
  Cymbeline, I 6 line 646.
  Henry IV, Part II, III 2 line 2184.
  King Lear, II 4 line 1284.
  Macbeth, IV 2 line 1802.
  Merchant of Venice, III 1 line 1351; Merchant of Venice, III 1 line 1354.
  Midsummer Night's Dream, II 1 line 555.
  Othello, III 3 line 2085; Othello, IV 1 line 2559; Othello, IV 1 line 2710.
  Tempest, III 2 line 1439.
  Timon of Athens, I 1 line 294.

Moon: Old English: *mona*. The *man in the moon* is mentioned since early 14c.; he carries a bundle of thorn-twigs and is accompanied by a dog. Apart from his sundry allusions to the *pale-faced, silver moon*, Shakespeare has referred to many of the superstitions associated with it, several of which still linger on in country nooks. A widespread legend of great antiquity informs us that the moon is inhabited by a man with a bundle of sticks on his back, who has been exiled thither for many centuries, and who is so far off that he is beyond the reach of death. This tradition, which has given rise to many superstitions, is still preserved under various forms in most countries; but it has not been decided who the culprit originally was, and how he came to be imprisoned in his lonely abode. From the very earliest times the moon has not only been an object of popular superstition, but been honoured by various acts of adoration. In Europe, in the fifteenth century, it was a matter of complaint that some still worshipped the new moon with bended knee, or hood or hat removed. And to this day we may still see a hat raised to her, half in conservatism and half in jest. It is with deference to silver as the lunar metal that money is turned when the act of adoration is performed, while practical peasant wit dwells on the ill luck of having no piece of silver when the new moon is first seen. Shakespeare often incidentally alludes to this form of superstition. In many places it is customary for young women to appeal to the moon to tell them of their future prospects in matrimony. As in the case of the sun, an eclipse of the moon was formerly considered ominous. By a popular astrological doctrine the moon was supposed to exercise great influence over agricultural operations, and also over many of the minor concerns of life, such as the gathering of herbs, the killing of animals for the table, and other matters of a like nature.

Antony and Cleopatra, III 12 line 2203; Antony and Cleopatra, III 13 line 2370; Antony and Cleopatra, III 13 line 2438; Antony and Cleopatra, IV 9 line 2842; Antony and Cleopatra, IV 12 line 2955; Antony and Cleopatra, IV 15 line 3246; Antony and Cleopatra, V 2 line 3486; Antony and Cleopatra, V 2 line 3692.

As You Like It, III 2 line 1484; as You Like It, V 2 line 2347.

Coriolanus, I 1 line 219; Coriolanus, I 1 line 281; Coriolanus, II 1 line 1014; Coriolanus, IV 5 line 2876; Coriolanus, V 1 line 3314; Coriolanus, V 3 line 3566.

Cymbeline, III 1 line 1456.

Hamlet, I 3 line 521; Hamlet, I 4 line 682; Hamlet, III 2 line 2048; Hamlet, III 2 line 2052; Hamlet, III 4 line 2614; Hamlet, IV 7 line 3292.

Henry IV, Part I, I 2 line 125; Henry IV, Part I, I 2 lines 138, 140; Henry IV, Part I, I 3 line 533; Henry IV, Part I, II 4 line 1013; Henry IV, Part I, III 1 line 1643; Henry IV, Part I, III 1 line 1686.

Henry IV, Part II, IV 3 line 2639.

Henry V, IV 0 line 1814; Henry V, V 2 line 3147r.

Henry VI, Part II, III 1 line 1439.

Henry VIII, III 2 line 1984; Henry VIII, III 2 line 2003.

Julius Caesar, IV 3 line 2006.

King John, IV 2 line 1925; King John, IV 2 line 1928.

King Lear, I 2 line 429; King Lear, I 2 line 444; King Lear, II 1 line 969; King Lear, II 2 line 1101; King Lear, IV 6 line 2627; King Lear, IV 6 line 2680; King Lear, V 3 line 3142.

Love's Labour's Lost, IV 2 line 1183; Love's Labour's Lost, IV 2 line 1184; Love's Labour's Lost, IV 2 line 1192; Love's Labour's Lost, IV 3 line 1350; Love's Labour's Lost, IV 3 line 1574; Love's Labour's Lost, V 2 line 2095; Love's Labour's Lost, V 2 line 2097; Love's Labour's Lost, V 2 line 2105; Love's Labour's Lost, V 2 line 2107; Love's Labour's Lost, V 2 line 2108.

Macbeth, II 1 line 570; Macbeth, III 5 line 1473; Macbeth, IV 1 line 1570.

Measure for Measure, III 1 line 1247.

Merchant of Venice, V 1 line 2444; Merchant of Venice, V 1 line 2549; Merchant of Venice, V 1 line 2566; Merchant of Venice, V 1 line 2607.

Midsummer Night's Dream, I 1 lines 4, 5; Midsummer Night's Dream, I 1 line 10; Midsummer Night's Dream, I 1 line 78; Midsummer Night's Dream, I 1 line 88; Midsummer Night's Dream, II 1 line 374; Midsummer Night's Dream, II 1 line 472; Midsummer Night's Dream, II 1 lines 528, 534; Midsummer Night's Dream, III 1 line 864; Midsummer Night's Dream, III 1 line 1023; Midsummer Night's Dream, III 2 line 1086; Midsummer Night's Dream, IV 1 line 1649; Midsummer Night's Dream, V 1 line 2079; Midsummer Night's Dream, V 1 line 2080;

Midsummer Night's Dream, V 1 lines 2084, 2085; Midsummer Night's Dream, V 1 line 2088; Midsummer Night's Dream, V 1 line 2095; Midsummer Night's Dream, V 1 line 2097r; Midsummer Night's Dream, V 1 line 2100; Midsummer Night's Dream, V 1 line 2107r; Midsummer Night's Dream, V 1 lines 2114, 2115; Midsummer Night's Dream, V 1 line 2149; Midsummer Night's Dream, V 1 line 2221.
Othello, I 3 line 424; Othello, III 3 line 1830; Othello, IV 2 line 2826; Othello, V 2 line 3421; Othello, V 2 line 3434.
Passionate Pilgrim, line 208.
Pericles, II 5 line 1023; Pericles, III 0 line 1159; Pericles, III 1 line 1243; Pericles, IV 3 line 1817.
Rape of Lucrece, line 1058.
Richard II, I 3 line 519; Richard II, II 4 line 1340.
Richard III, II 2 line 1341.
Romeo and Juliet, II 2 line 849; Romeo and Juliet, II 2 line 956; Romeo and Juliet, II 2 line 958r.
Sonnet XXI line 6; Sonnet XXXV line 3; Sonnet CVII line 5.
Taming of the Shrew, IV 5 line 2268; Taming of the Shrew, IV 5 line 2269; Taming of the Shrew, IV 5 line 2270; Taming of the Shrew, IV 5 line 2273; Taming of the Shrew, IV 5 line 2279; Taming of the Shrew, IV 5 line 2282; Taming of the Shrew, IV 5 line 2283; Taming of the Shrew, IV 5 line 2287.
Tempest, II 1 line 894; Tempest, II 2 line 982; Tempest, II 2 lines 1225, 1226; Tempest, II 2 line 1233; Tempest,V 1 line 2344.
Timon of Athens, IV 3 lines 1738, 1739; Timon of Athens, IV 3 lines 2150, 2153.
Titus Andronicus, II 3 line 978; Titus Andronicus, IV 3 line 1949.
Troilus and Cressida, III 2 line 1827; Troilus and Cressida, V 1 line 3039.
Twelfth Night, I 5 line 493.
Venus and Adonis, line 513.
Winter's Tale, I 2 line 554; Winter's Tale, II 1 line 610; Winter's Tale, III 3 line 1557; Winter's Tale, IV 3 line 1739; Winter's Tale, IV 4 line 2061.

Moonbeam*: 1580s, moon + beam.
    Midsummer Night's Dream, III 1 line 998.

Moonlight: light of the moon, mid 14c. From moon + light.
    Merchant of Venice, V 1 line 2508.
    Midsummer Night's Dream, I 1 line 34; Midsummer Night's Dream, I 2 line 357; Midsummer Night's Dream, II 1 line 374; Midsummer Night's Dream, II 1 line 429; Midsummer Night's Dream, II 1 line 511; Midsummer Night's Dream, III 1 lines 862, 863.
    Taming of the Shrew, IV 5 line 2269.

Moonshine: c.1500, moonlight, from moon + shine. In figurative use, implying *appearance without substance*, from late 15c.; perhaps connected in that sense with notion of *moonshine in water*.
    King Lear, I 2 line 338; King Lear, II 2 line 1102.

Love's Labour's Lost, V 2 line 2100.
Merry Wives of Windsor, V 5 line 2602; Merry Wives of Windsor, V 5 line 2669.
Midsummer Night's Dream, III 1 line 866r; Midsummer Night's Dream, V 1 line 1980.
Romeo and Juliet, I 4 line 562.
Tempest, V 1 line 2058.

Moon-calf: also *mooncalf: abortive, shapeless, fleshy mass*, 1560s, attributed to the influence of the. In later 16c., deformed creature, monster.
Tempest, II 2 line 1194; Tempest, II 2 line 1199; Tempest, II 2 line 1222; Tempest, III 2 lines 1416, 1417.

Morning: mid-13c., *morn, morewen*, on pattern of evening. Originally the time just before sunrise. As an adjective from 1530s.
All's Well That Ends Well, IV 3 line 2166; All's Well That Ends Well, IV 3 line 2183.
Antony and Cleopatra, II 2 line 779; Antony and Cleopatra, IV 4 line 2657; Antony and Cleopatra, IV 5 line 2681; Antony and Cleopatra, IV 5 line 2683.
As You Like It, II 2 line 627; As You Like It, II 7 line 1044; As You Like It, III 4 line 1610.
Comedy of Errors, V 1 line 1798.
Coriolanus, II 1 line 967; Coriolanus, V 1 line 3339; Coriolanus, V 4 line 3793.
Cymbeline, II 3 line 985; Cymbeline, II 3 line 988; Cymbeline, II 3 line 1045; Cymbeline, II 3 line 1149; Cymbeline, III 3 line 1605; Cymbeline, IV 2 line 2396.
Hamlet, I 1 line 197; Hamlet, I 2 line 429; Hamlet, I 5 line 796; Hamlet, II 2 line 1470; Hamlet, IV 5 line 2911.
Henry IV, Part I, I 2 line 146; Henry IV, Part I, I 2 line 229; Henry IV, Part I, II 4 line 1149; Henry IV, Part I, II 4 line 1321; Henry IV, Part I, II 4 lines 1534, 1539; Henry IV, Part I, IV 3 line 2530.
Henry V, III 7 line 1647; Henry V, III 7 line 1719; Henry V, III 7 line 1725; Henry V, IV 0 lines 1803, 1812; Henry V, IV 1 line 1934; Henry V, IV 2 line 2305.
Henry VI, Part II, I 2 line 297.
Henry VI, Part III, II 1 line 647; Henry VI, Part III, II 5 line 1103; Henry VI, Part III, IV 7 line 2510.
Henry VIII, III 2 line 1937; Henry VIII, III 2 line 1987; Henry VIII, V 1 line 2836; Henry VIII, V 1 line 2905; Henry VIII, V 1 line 2955; Henry VIII, V 4 line 3283.
Julius Caesar, II 1 line 845; Julius Caesar, II 1 line 863; Julius Caesar, II 1 line 890; Julius Caesar, V 1 line 2440.
King John, IV 3 line 2036.
King Lear, III 6 line 2084.
Love's Labour's Lost, III 1 line 923; Love's Labour's Lost, IV 3 line 1347.
Macbeth, III 4 line 1430; Macbeth, III 5 line 1466.

Measure for Measure, II 1 line 489; Measure for Measure, IV 2 line 1891; Measure for Measure, IV 2 line 1996; Measure for Measure, IV 1 line 2078; Measure for Measure, IV 3 line 2160; Measure for Measure, IV 3 line 2189; Measure for Measure, IV 3 line 2238.
Merchant of Venice, I 2 line 276; Merchant of Venice, II 5 line 873; Merchant of Venice, III 2 line 1654; Merchant of Venice, IV 1 line 2413; Merchant of Venice, V 1 line 2500; Merchant of Venice, V 1 line 2768.
Merry Wives of Windsor, II 2 line 866; Merry Wives of Windsor, II 2 line 891; Merry Wives of Windsor, II 2 line 940; Merry Wives of Windsor, III 3 line 1617; Merry Wives of Windsor, III 5 line 1786; Merry Wives of Windsor, III 5 line 1865.
Midsummer Night's Dream, III 2 line 1446; Midsummer Night's Dream, IV 1 line 1645; Midsummer Night's Dream, IV 1 line 1676; Midsummer Night's Dream, IV 1 line 1740.
Much Ado About Nothing, II 1 line 422; Much Ado About Nothing, III 2 line 1238; Much Ado About Nothing, III 3 line 1471; Much Ado About Nothing, III 5 line 1623; Much Ado About Nothing, IV 2 line 2038; Much Ado About Nothing, V 1 line 2243; Much Ado About Nothing, V 1 line 2360; Much Ado About Nothing, V 1 line 2402.
Othello, I 3 line 632; Othello, I 3 line 732; Othello, II 3 line 1481; Othello, II 3 line 1531.
Passionate Pilgrim, line 195.
Rape of Lucrece, lines 40, 75, 796, 829, 1158.
Richard III, I 4 line 911; Richard III, V 3 line 3491; Richard III, V 3 line 3560; Richard III, V 3 line 3740; Richard III, V 3 line 3816.
Romeo and Juliet, I 1 lines 151, 152; Romeo and Juliet, II 2 line 1040; Romeo and Juliet, III 5 line 2116; Romeo and Juliet, IV 1 line 2473; Romeo and Juliet, IV 2 line 2521; Romeo and Juliet, IV 3 line 2573; Romeo and Juliet, IV 5 line 2700; Romeo and Juliet, V 3 line 2960; Romeo and Juliet, V 3 line 3161; Romeo and Juliet, V 3 line 3281.
Sonnet XXXIII line 1; Sonnet CXXXII line 5.
Taming of the Shrew, Prologue 2 line 188; Taming of the Shrew, I 1 line 425; Taming of the Shrew, II 1 line 1018; Taming of the Shrew, III 2 line 1470.
Tempest, III 1 line 1318; Tempest, V 1 line 2094.
Timon of Athens, II 2 line 700; Timon of Athens, IV 3 line 1915.
Titus Andronicus, II 3 line 947.
Troilus and Cressida, I 2 line 201; Troilus and Cressida, I 3 line 685; Troilus and Cressida, II 1 line 981; Troilus and Cressida, II 2 line 1072; Troilus and Cressida, III 2 line 1791; Troilus and Cressida, IV 3 line 2411; Troilus and Cressida, IV 4 line 2583; Troilus and Cressida, V 3 line 3357.
Twelfth Night, III 4 line 1650; Twelfth Night, III 4 line 1685; Twelfth Night, V 1 line 2398; Twelfth Night, V 1 line 2491.
Two Gentlemen of Verona, II 2 line 474; Two Gentlemen of Verona, IV 2 line 1767.
Venus and Adonis, lines 877, 888.

Morn: contracted from Middle English: *morwen*, from Old English (Mercian) *margen*, earlier *morgen: morning, forenoon, sunrise*.
> **Antony and Cleopatra**, II 5 line 1073; Antony and Cleopatra, IV 4 line 2654; Antony and Cleopatra, IV 9 line 2835.
> **As You Like It**, II 2 line 627; As You Like It, II 7 line 1044; As You Like It, III 4 line 1610.
> **Cymbeline**, I 3 line 307; Cymbeline, III 6 line 2260; Cymbeline, IV 2 line 2350.
> **Hamlet**, I 1 line 173; Hamlet, I 1 line 189; Hamlet, I 3 line 525.
> **Henry V**, III 1 line 1111.
> **Henry VI, Part I**, V 4 line 2694.
> **Henry VI, Part II**, III 1 line 1290.
> **Love's Labour's Lost**, V 2 line 2595.
> **Macbeth**, IV 3 line 1846.
> **Measure for Measure**, II 4 line 1096; Measure for Measure, IV 1 line 1798; Measure for Measure, IV 4 line 2322; Measure for Measure, V 1 line 2503.
> **Midsummer Night's Dream**, I 1 line 173; Midsummer Night's Dream, V 1 line 2212.
> **Othello**, III 3 lines 1695, 1696.
> **Passionate Pilgrim**, lines 72, 118, 160.
> **Pericles**, V 3 line 2546.
> **Rape of Lucrece**, line 993.
> **Richard III**, IV 4 line 2808; Richard III, V 3 line 3713.
> **Romeo and Juliet**, II 3 line 1059; Romeo and Juliet, III 5 line 2103; Romeo and Juliet, III 5 line 2218.
> **Sonnet** XXXIII line 9; Sonnet LXIII line 4.
> **Taming of the Shrew**, II 1 line 1145.
> **Tempest**, V 1 line 2384.
> **Titus Andronicus**, II 1 line 552; Titus Andronicus, II 2 line 697.
> **Troilus and Cressida**, IV 2 line 2286.
> **Two Gentlemen of Verona**, IV 2 line 1770.
> **Venus and Adonis**, lines 22, 174, 474, 505, 516.

Moth: Until 16c. used mostly of the larva and usually in reference to devouring clothes. In the minds of most people it stands for an insect either contemptible from its size and inertness, or positively obnoxious from its attacks on many articles of clothing. Shakespeare, employs the expression *moth* to denote something trifling or extremely minute.
> **Coriolanus**, I 3 line 450.
> **Merchant of Venice**, II 9 line 1212.

Mouldwarp: mole. Middle English: probably from Middle Low German: *moldewerp*.
> **Henry IV, Part I**, III 1 line 1694.

Mountain: c.1200, from Old French: *montaigne*.
> **Antony and Cleopatra**, IV 14 line 2982.
> **As You Like It**, III 2 line 1293.

Comedy of Errors, IV 4 line 1417.
Coriolanus, II 3 line 1553.
Cymbeline, III 3 line 1613; Cymbeline, III 3 line 1680; Cymbeline, III 6 line 2148; Cymbeline, IV 2 line 2546; Cymbeline, IV 4 line 2893; Cymbeline, V 5 line 3710.
Hamlet, III 4 line 2448; Hamlet, IV 1 line 2656; Hamlet, IV 5 line 2896; Hamlet, V 1 line 3590; Hamlet, V 1 line 3624.
Henry IV, Part I, I 3 line 414; Henry IV, Part I, I 3 line 489; Henry IV, Part I, II 4 line 1211; Henry IV, Part I, III 1 line 1582.
Henry IV, Part II, I 3 line 1752; Henry IV, Part II, IV 1 line 2395.
Henry V, II 4 line 956r; Henry V, IV 2 line 2194; Henry V, IV 4 line 2391; Henry V, V 1 line 2923.
Henry VI, Part I, II 5 line 1184.
Henry VI, Part II, III 2 line 2030; Henry VI, Part II, V 1 line 3195.
Henry VI, Part III, I 4 line 507; Henry VI, Part III, III 2 line 1646.
Henry VIII, III 1 line 1624; Henry VIII, V 5 line 3437.
Julius Caesar, II 4 line 1145.
King John, II 1 line 763; King John, II 1 line 770; king John, III 4 line 1565.
Love's Labour's Lost, V 1 line 1810; Love's Labour's Lost, V 1 line 1812.
Merchant of Venice, IV 1 line 2007.
Merry Wives of Windsor, I 1 line 145; Merry Wives of Windsor, II 2 line 820; Merry Wives of Windsor, III 5 line 1763.
Midsummer Night's Dream, IV 1 line 1664.
Much Ado About Nothing, II 1 line 737.
Othello, II 1 line 771.
Passionate Pilgrim, line 357.
Pericles, I 4 line 422; Pericles, II 4 line 538.
Rape of Lucrece, lines 599, 1128.
Romeo and Juliet, III 5 line 2107.
Sonnet XXXIII line 2; Sonnet CXIII line 11.
Taming of the Shrew, II 2 line 983.
Tempest, I 2 line 699; Tempest, IV 1 line 1772; Tempest, IV 1 line 1999; Tempest, IV 1 line 2007.
Timon of Athens, I 1 line 106.
Titus Andronicus, IV 2 line 1829.
Troilus and Cressida, I 3 line 490.
Twelfth Night, IV 1 line 1998.
Two Gentlemen of Verona, V 2 line 2116.
Venus and Adonis, lines 252, 772.
Winter's Tale, III 2 line 1449.

Mouse: Old English: *mus*, (plural) *mys*, of Germanic origin; related to Dutch muis and German Maus, from an Indo-European root shared by Latin and Greek *mus*.

Coriolanus, I 6 line 667.
Hamlet, I 1 line 12; Hamlet, III 4 line 2587.
Henry IV, Part II, III 2 line 2013.

Henry V, I 2 line 317.
King Lear, IV 6 line 2699.
Love's Labour's Lost, V 2 line 1899.
Midsummer Night's Dream, V 1 line 2064; Midsummer Night's Dream, V 1 line 2236.
Pericles, IV 1 line 1633.
Rape of Lucrece, line 606.
Romeo and Juliet, I 4 line 536; Romeo and Juliet, III 1 line 1605; Romeo and Juliet, III 3 line 1902.
Twelfth Night, I 5 line 354.

Mouth: Old English: *muþ: mouth, opening, door, gate*. In the sense of, outfall of a river, it is attested from late Old English; as the opening of anything with capacity (a bottle, cave, etc.) it is recorded from c.1200.

All's Well That Ends Well, I 3 line 376; All's Well That Ends Well, II 2 line 850; All's Well That Ends Well, II 3 line 955; All's Well That Ends Well, IV 1 line 1944.
Antony and Cleopatra, I 3 line 333.
As You Like It, I 2 line 222; As You Like It, II 7 line 1051; As You Like It, III 1 line 1113; As You Like It, III 2 lines 1305r, 1308; As You Like It, IV 3 lines 1327, 1328; As You Like It, IV 3 line 2113; As You Like It, V 1 line 2220.
Coriolanus, I 1 line 213; Coriolanus, III 1 line 1753; Coriolanus, III 1 line 1772; Coriolanus, III 1 line 2057; Coriolanus, III 1 line 2077; Coriolanus, IV 6 line 3094.
Cymbeline, IV 2 line 2421; Cymbeline, V 5 line 3705.
Hamlet, I 2 line 249; Hamlet, III 2 line 1884; Hamlet, III 2 line 2238; Hamlet, IV 2 line 2695; Hamlet, IV 4 line 2839; Hamlet, V 1 line 3627; Hamlet, V 2 line 4039; Hamlet, V 2 line 4060.
Henry IV, Part I, I 3 line 422; Henry IV, Part I, I 3 line 482; Henry IV, Part I, III 1 line 1807; Henry IV, Part I, III 2 line 1876; Henry IV, Part I, III 2 line 1940; Henry IV, Part I, III 3 line 2118.
Henry IV, Part II, I 2 line 330; Henry IV, Part II, II 4 line 1319; Henry IV, Part II, IV 5 line 2969.
Henry V, I 2 lines 377, 379; Henry V, II 1 line 555; Henry V, II 3 line 888; Henry V, II 4 line 971; Henry V, III 0 line 1089; Henry V, III 7 line 1771; Henry V, IV 2 line 2214; Henry V, IV 3 line 2287; Henry V, IV 7 line 2560; Henry V, V 0 line 2849; Henry V, V 2 line 3256.
Henry VI, Part I, I 2 line 201; Henry VI, Part I, II 4 line 932; Henry VI, Part I, III 1 line 1432; Henry VI, Part I, IV 1 line 1895.
Henry VI, Part II, III 2 line 2092; Henry VI, Part II, IV 1 line 2229; Henry VI, Part II, IV 7 line 2627; Henry VI, Part II, IV 7 line 2629; Henry VI, Part II, IV 7 line 2634.
Henry VI, Part III, V 5 line 2912.
Henry VIII, I 1 line 182; Henry VIII, I 1 line 203; Henry VIII, I 2 line 388; Henry VIII, I 3 line 642; Henry VIII, II 2 line 1025; Henry VIII, II 3 line 1307; Henry VIII, II 4 line 1472; Henry VIII, III 2 line 2124; Henry VIII, III 2 line 2233; Henry VIII, V 3 line 3081.

Julius Caesar, I 2 line 236; Julius Caesar, I 2 line 346; Julius Caesar, III 1 line 1489; Julius Caesar, III 2 line 1769.
King John, I 1 line 23; King John, II 1 line 692; King John, II 1 line 713; King John, II 1 line 725; King John, II 1 line 760; King John, II 1 line 769; King John, III 1 line 1074; King John, III 1 line 1225; King John, III 1 line 1233; King John, III 3 line 1338; King John, III 4 line 1423; King John, IV 2 line 1898; King John, IV 2 lines 1931, 1939; King John, V 2 line 2457.
King Lear, I 1 line 94; King Lear, III 2 line 1710; King Lear, III 4 lines 1813, 1817; King Lear, III 6 line 2047; King Lear, III 6 line 2067; king Lear, V 3 line 3306.
Love's Labour's Lost, II 1 line 753.
Macbeth, IV 1 line 1617; Macbeth, V 3 line 2278.
Measure for Measure, II 4 line 1020; Measure for Measure, II 4 line 1204; Measure for Measure, III 2 line 1690; Measure for Measure, V 1 line 2560; Measure for Measure, V 1 line 2718; Measure for Measure, V 1 line 2723.
Merchant of Venice, I 2 line 244; Merchant of Venice, I 3 line 384.
Merry Wives of Windsor, I 1 lines 211, 213.
Midsummer Night's Dream, III 2 line 1278; Midsummer Night's Dream, IV 1 line 1678; Midsummer Night's Dream, V 1 line 1986.
Much Ado About Nothing, I 3 line 361; Much Ado About Nothing, II 1 line 409; Much Ado About Nothing, II 1 line 688; Much Ado About Nothing, V 2 line 2419; Much Ado About Nothing, V 4 line 2651.
Othello, II 3 line 1339; Othello, II 3 line 1370; Othello, II 3 line 1444; Othello, II 3 line 1457; Othello, IV 1 line 2475; Othello, V 2 line 3389.
Passionate Pilgrim, lines 92, 152, 153.
Pericles, I 4 line 450; Pericles, II 1 line 612; Pericles, III 0 line 1125; Pericles, IV 2 line 1765.
Richard II, I 3 line 389; Richard II, I 3 lines 452, 463; Richard II, II 3 line 1247; Richard II, V 1 line 2430; Richard II, V 3 line 2607; Richard II, V 3 line 2684; Richard II, V 3 line 2701; Richard II, V 6 line 2920.
Richard III, I 2 line 230; Richard III, I 2 line 425; Richard III, IV 4 line 2793.
Romeo and Juliet, IV 3 line 2586; Romeo and Juliet, V 3 line 3190.
Sonnet LXXVII line 6; Sonnet LXXXI line 14.
Taming of the Shrew, Prologue 1 line 18; Taming of the Shrew, I 1 line 531; Taming of the Shrew, IV 1 line 1629.
Tempest, I 1 line 62; Tempest, II 2 lines 1171, 1173; Tempest, II 2 line 1183; Tempest, II 2 line 1185; Tempest, III 1 line 1352; Tempest, IV 1 line 1959; Tempest, V 1 line 2170; Tempest, V 1 line 2282.
Timon of Athens, II 2 line 759; Timon of Athens, II 2 line 836; Timon of Athens, III 6 line 1527; Timon of Athens, IV 3 line 1956.
Titus Andronicus, II 3 line 925; Titus Andronicus, II 3 line 945; Titus Andronicus, II 3 line 983; Titus Andronicus, II 3 line 1025; Titus Andronicus, IV 1 lines 1613, 1619; Titus Andronicus, V 1 line 2286; Titus Andronicus, V 2 line 2474; Titus Andronicus, V 2 line 2479; Titus Andronicus, V 2 line 2484; Titus Andronicus, V 3 line 2719.

Troilus and Cressida, III 2 line 1783; Troilus and Cressida, V 1 line 3036; Troilus and Cressida, V 5 line 3493.
Twelfth Night, II 3 line 818; Twelfth Night, II 3 line 830; Twelfth Night, III 4 line 1731; Twelfth Night, V 1 line 2267.
Two Gentlemen of Verona, II 3 line 639; Two Gentlemen of Verona, III 1 line 1396.
Venus and Adonis, lines 268, 416, 563, 717, 923, 942.
Winter's Tale, I 2 line 573; Winter's Tale, II 2 line 885; Winter's Tale, III 2 line 1317; Winter's Tale, IV 4 line 2087; Winter's Tale, IV 4 line 2807.

Mow: Old English: *mawan*: *to mow, to cut down grass or grain with a sickle or scythe*. Also, *stack of hay*, Old English: *muga, muwa: a heap, swath of corn, crowd of people*.
Coriolanus, I 3 line 399; Coriolanus, IV 5 line 2972.
Cymbeline, I 6 line 648.
Hamlet, II 2 line 1447.
Henry V, III 3 line 1285.
Henry VI, Part II, III 1 line 1345.
Henry VI, Part III, V 7 line 3099.
Henry VIII, V 4 line 3292.
King Lear, IV 1 line 2317.
Sonnet LX line 12.
Tempest, II 2 line 1090; Tempest, III 3 line 1663; Tempest, IV 1 line 1751.
Troilus and Cressida, V 5 line 3481.

Mud: mid-14c. Meaning *lowest or worst of anything* is from 1580s.
All's Well That Ends Well, V 2 line 2616; All's Well That Ends Well, V 2 line 2636.
Antony and Cleopatra, II 7 line 1402; Antony and Cleopatra, V 2 line 3454.
Hamlet, II 2 line 1641; Hamlet, IV 5 line 2942; Hamlet, IV 7 line 3331.
Henry IV, Part I, II 1 line 738.
Henry IV, Part II, II 4 line 1279; Henry IV, Part II, II 4 line 1298.
Henry VI, Part II, III 1 line 1381.
Henry VIII, II 3 line 1313.
Lover's Complaint, line 46.
Merchant of Venice, I 1 line 2518.
Merry Wives of Windsor, III 3 line 1416.
Midsummer Night's Dream, II 1 line 467; Midsummer Night's Dream, III 2 line 1177.
Rape of Lucrece, lines 628, 901.
Richard II, V 3 line 2640.
Sonnet XXXV line 2.
Taming of the Shrew, V 2 line 2651.
Tempest, III 3 line 1685; Tempest, V 1 line 2110; Tempest, V 1 line 2195.
Titus Andronicus, V 2 line 2487.
Winter's Tale, I 2 line 434.

Mulberry: late 14c., developed from 13c. *morberie*.
    Coriolanus, III 2 line 2260.
    Midsummer Night's Dream, III 1 line 992; Midsummer Night's Dream, V 1 line 1991.
    Venus and Adonis, line 1125.

Mule: offspring of donkey and horse, from Old English: *mul*, Old French: *mul: mule, hinny* (12c) both from Latin: *mulus*: a mule, probably from a pre-Latin Mediterranean language.
    All's Well That Ends Well, IV 1 line 1945.
    Antony and Cleopatra, IV 6 line 2734.
    Coriolanus, II 1 line 1194.
    Henry VI, Part I, I 2 line 200.
    Henry VI, Part II, IV 1 line 2207.
    Henry VIII, IV 2 line 2575.
    Merchant of Venice, IV 1 line 2023.
    Troilus and Cressida, V 1 line 2992.

Muscles: late 14c., from French: *muscle: muscle, sinew* (14c.) and directly from Latin: *musculus: a muscle*, literally, *little mouse*, diminutive of *mus: mouse*. So called because the shape and movement of some muscles (notably biceps) were thought to resemble mice.
    Tempest, I 2 line 645.

Muset: a small hole or gap through which a wild animal passes.
    Venus and Adonis, line 705.

Mushroom: mid-15c., *muscheron, musseroun*. Used figuratively for something or someone that makes a sudden appearance in full form from 1590s. There is a superstition that sheep will not eat the grass that grows on fairy rings.
    Tempest, V 1 line 2060.

Musk: late 14c., from Old French *musc* (13c.) and directly from Late Latin *muscus*, from Late Greek *moskhos*, from Persian *mushk*, from Sanskrit *muska-s:* testicle, from *mus:* mouse (so called, presumably, for resemblance). The deer gland was thought to resemble a scrotum. German has *moschos*, from a Medieval Latin form of the Late Greek word. Spanish has *almizcle*, from Arabic *al misk*: the musk, from Persian. Applied to various plants and animals of similar smell.
    Merry Wives of Windsor, II 2 line 860.

Musk-cat: civet; an animal producing musk.
    All's Well That Ends Well, V 2 line 2634.

Musk-rose: a rambling rose with large, musk scented, flowers.
    Midsummer Night's Dream, II 1 line 631; Midsummer Night's Dream, II 2 line 652; Midsummer Night's Dream, IV 1 line 1548.

Mustard: late 13c., from Old French: *mostarde: mustard, mustard plant*, from *moust: must*, from Latin: *mustum: new wine*.; so called because it was originally prepared by adding must to the ground seeds of the plant to make a paste.
    As You Like It, I 2 lines 199, 201; As You Like It, I 2 line 212.
    Henry IV, Part II, II 4 line 1522.
    Taming of the Shrew, IV 3 line 1979; Taming of the Shrew, IV 3 line 1981; Taming of the Shrew, IV 3 line 1982; Taming of the Shrew, IV 3 line 1983; Taming of the Shrew, IV 3 line 1986.

Mutton: flesh of sheep used as food, late 13c., from Old French: *moton: mutton; ram, wether, sheep* (12c). Transferred slang sense of: food for lust, loose women, prostitutes. (1510s).
    As You Like It, III 2 line 1171.
    Henry IV, Part II, II 4 line 1654; Henry IV, Part II, V 1 line 3169.
    Love's Labour's Lost, I 1 line 294.
    Measure for Measure, III 2 line 1688.
    Merchant of Venice, I 3 line 495.
    Taming of the Shrew, IV 1 line 1764.

    Twelfth Night, I 3 line 227.
    Two Gentlemen of Verona, I 1 lines 98, 99r, 100; Two Gentlemen of Verona, I1 line 101.

Myrtle: c.1400, from Old French: *mirtile*. Associated with, love.
    Antony and Cleopatra, III 12 line 2208.
    Measure for Measure, II 2 line 882.
    Passionate Pilgrim, lines 145, 365, 378.
    Venus and Adonis, line 887.

Nag: an old horse, in poor heath. Origin unknown.
    Antony and Cleopatra, III 10 line 2075.
    Henry IV, Part I, III 1 line 1679.
    Henry IV, Part II, II 4 line 1457.

Nail: Old English: *nægl*: fingernail (*handnægl*), toenail. To bite one's nails as a sign of anxiety is attested from 1570s. To hit the nail on the head say or do just the right thing is first recorded 1520s. The nail is most often associated in the Christian tradition with the crucifixion of Christ, and thus symbolise his passion. The nail also represents the *Cosmic Axis*, or *Axis Mundi*, around which the heavens rotate.
    All's Well That Ends Well, V 2 line 2645.
    Antony and Cleopatra, IV 12 line 2947; Antony and Cleopatra, V 2 line 3667.
    Comedy of Errors, IV 3 line 1220; Comedy of Errors, IV 4 line 1355.
    Henry V, III 4 line 1345; Henry V, III 4 lines 1346, 1347; Henry V, III 4 line 1357; Henry V, III 4 line 1372; Henry V, III 4 line 1373; Henry V, III 4 line 1384; Henry V, IV 1 line 2441.

Henry VI, Part I, I 4 line 503; Henry VI, Part I, III 1 line 1331.
Henry VI, Part II, I 3 line 537.
Henry VI, Part III, II 5 line 1105.
King Lear, I 4 line 836; King Lear, III 7 line 2185.
Love's Labour's Lost, V 2 line 2861.
Midsummer Night's Dream, III 2 line 1346; Midsummer Night's Dream, IV 2 line 1822.
Rape of Lucrece, lines 790, 1523, 1615.
Richard II, V 5 line 2767.
Richard III, I 2 line 306; Richard III, IV 4 line 3035.
Taming of the Shrew, I 1 line 404.
Tempest, II 2 line 1254.
Troilus and Cressida, II 1 line 963; Troilus and Cressida, IV 5 line 2648.
Twelfth Night, IV 2 line 2148.
Winter's Tale, II 3 line 1056.

Nature: late 13c., restorative powers of the body, bodily processes; powers of growth; from Old French: *nature*, from Latin: *natura: course of things, natural character, the universe*. From late 14c. as *creation, the universe*; also *heredity, birth, hereditary circumstance; essential qualities, innate disposition* (e.g. human nature); *nature personified*, Mother Nature.
All's Well That Ends Well, I 1 line 20; All's Well That Ends Well, I 1 line 130; All's Well That Ends Well, I 1 lines 138, 143; All's Well That Ends Well, I 1 line 224; All's Well That Ends Well, I 2 line 261; All's Well That Ends Well, I 2 line 318; All's Well That Ends Well, I 3 lines 446, 449; All's Well That Ends Well, I 3 line 464; All's Well That Ends Well, II 1 line 727; All's Well That Ends Well, II 3 line 1033; All's Well That Ends Well, II 5 line 1308; All's Well That Ends Well, III 1 line 1388; All's Well That Ends Well, III 2 line 1494; All's Well That Ends Well, III 2 line 1529; All's Well That Ends Well, IV 3 line 2095; All's Well That Ends Well, IV 3 line 2140; All's Well That Ends Well, IV 3 line 2239; All's Well That Ends Well, IV 3 line 2326; All's Well That Ends Well, IV 5 line 2472; All's Well That Ends Well, IV 5 line 2517; All's Well That Ends Well, V 3 line 2699; All's Well That Ends Well, V 3 line 2754; All's Well That Ends Well, V 3 line 2793; All's Well That Ends Well, V 3 line 2913.
Antony and Cleopatra, I 2 line 87; Antony and Cleopatra, I 2 line 178; Antony and Cleopatra, I 3 line 315; Antony and Cleopatra, II 2 line 925; Antony and Cleopatra, II 2 line 943; Antony and Cleopatra, V 1 line 3314; Antony and Cleopatra, V 2 lines 3507, 3509; Antony and Cleopatra, V 2 line 3753.
As You Like It, I 1 line 16; As You Like It, I 2 lines 179, 181; As You Like It, I 2 lines 183, 184; As You Like It, I 2 lines 187, 188r; As You Like It, I 2 line 190; As You Like It, II 4 line 772r; As You Like It, III 1 line 1118; As You Like It, III 2 line 1150; As You Like It, III 2 lines 1253, 1256; As You Like It, III 5 line 1697; As You Like It, IV 3 line 2133.
Comedy of Errors, I 1 line 36; Comedy of Errors, II 2 line 465; Comedy of Errors, II 2 line 491.

Coriolanus, I 1 line 34; Coriolanus, I 1 line 284; Coriolanus, II 1 line 922; Coriolanus, II 3 line 1634; Coriolanus, II 3 line 1643; Coriolanus, II 3 line 1716; Coriolanus, III 1 line 1895; Coriolanus, III 1 line 2055; Coriolanus, III 1 line 2126; Coriolanus, III 2 line 2180; Coriolanus, III 2 line 2241; Coriolanus, IV 6 line 3128; Coriolanus, IV 7 line 3227; Coriolanus, IV 7 lines 3253, 3259; Coriolanus, V 3 lines 3519, 3527; Coriolanus, V 6 line 3847.
Cymbeline, I 4 line 361; Cymbeline, I 5 line 536; Cymbeline, I 6 line 638; Cymbeline, I 6 line 751; Cymbeline, II 4 line 1277; Cymbeline, III 3 lines 1687, 1693; Cymbeline, III 4 line 1764; Cymbeline, III 6 line 2164; Cymbeline, IV 2 lines 2345, 2347; Cymbeline, IV 2 line 2541; Cymbeline, IV 2 line 2768; Cymbeline, V 2 line 2997; Cymbeline, V 4 line 3185; Cymbeline, V 4 line 3195; Cymbeline, V 5 line 3556; Cymbeline, V 5 line 3676; Cymbeline, V 5 line 3820.
Hamlet, I 2 line 205; Hamlet, I 2 line 275; Hamlet, I 2 lines 290, 305; Hamlet, I 2 line 340; Hamlet, I 3 line 489; Hamlet, I 3 line 495; Hamlet, I 4 lines 652, 654, 660; Hamlet, I 4 line 683; Hamlet, I 5 line 748; Hamlet, I 5 line 819; Hamlet, II 1 line 1065; Hamlet, III 2 lines 1899, 1901, 1910; Hamlet, III 2 line 2269; Hamlet, III 3 line 2312; Hamlet, III 3 line 2344; Hamlet, III 4 line 2571; Hamlet, IV 5 line 2875; Hamlet, IV 7 line 3138; Hamlet, IV 7 line 3337; Hamlet, V 2 line 3713; Hamlet, V 2 line 3723; Hamlet, V 2 line 3819; Hamlet, V 2 line 3868; Hamlet, V 2 line 3882.
Henry IV, Part I, I 1 line 12; Henry IV, Part I, III 1 line 1569; Henry IV, Part I, IV 3 line 2501.
Henry IV, Part II, I 1 line 117; Henry IV, Part II, I 1 line 211; Henry IV, Part II, II 3 line 1178; Henry IV, Part II, III 1 line 1710; Henry IV, Part II, III 1 line 1786; Henry IV, Part II, III 2 line 2199; Henry IV, Part II, IV 2 line 2536; Henry IV, Part II, IV 4 line 2875; Henry IV, Part II, IV 5 line 2927; Henry IV, Part II, IV 5 line 2958; Henry IV, Part II, V 2 line 3249.
Henry V, I 2 line 334; Henry V, II 4 line 959; Henry V, II 4 line 983; Henry V, III 1 line 1099; Henry V, III 7 line 1680; Henry V, V 2 line 3036; Henry V, V 2 line 3315.
Henry VI, Part I, III 1 line 1238; Henry VI, Part I, III 3 line 1669; Henry VI, Part I, V 3 line 2513.
Henry VI, Part II, III 1 line 1542; Henry VI, Part II, V 3 line 3342.
Henry VI, Part III, III 2 line 1644; Henry VI, Part III, III 3 line 1799; Henry VI, Part III, IV 6 line 2388; Henry VI, Part III, V 1 line 2682.
Henry VIII, I 1 line 163; Henry VIII, I 2 line 380; Henry VIII, I 2 line 448; Henry VIII, II 4 line 1559; Henry VIII, III 1 line 1693; Henry VIII, III 2 line 2020; Henry VIII, III 2 line 2331; Henry VIII, IV 2 line 2734; Henry VIII, V 1 line 2780; Henry VIII, V 1 line 2794; Henry VIII, V 3 line 3069; Henry VIII, V 3 line 3207.
Julius Caesar, I 3 line 493; Julius Caesar, II 1 line 614; Julius Caesar, II 1 line 676; Julius Caesar, IV 3 line 2203; Julius Caesar, IV 3 line 2239; Julius Caesar, V 5 line 2760.
King John, II 1 line 468; King John, III 1 lines 967, 968; King John, III 4 line 1542; King John, IV 2 line 1965; King John, IV 2 line 2000.

King Lear, I 1 line 53; King Lear, I 1 line 183; King Lear, I 1 line 230; King Lear, I 1 line 256; King Lear, I 2 lines 334, 344; King Lear, I 2 lines 430, 432, 437; King Lear, I 2 line 499; King Lear, I 4 line 794; King Lear, I 4 line 802; King Lear, I 5 line 907; King Lear, II 1 line 1055; King Lear, II 2 line 1124; King Lear, II 2 line 1143; King Lear, II 2 line 1166; King Lear, II 4 line 1385; King Lear, II 4 line 1429; King Lear, II 4 lines 1457, 1464; King Lear, II 4 lines 1567r, 1570; King Lear, III 2 line 1685; King Lear, III 2 line 1724; King Lear, III 4 line 1803; King Lear, III 4 line 1869; King Lear, III 5 line 1985; King Lear, III 6 line 2078; King Lear, III 6 line 2099; King Lear, III 7 line 2219; King Lear, IV 2 line 2376; King Lear, IV 4 line 2528; King Lear, IV 6 line 2697; King Lear, IV 6 line 2743; King Lear, IV 6 line 2815; King Lear, IV 7 line 2926; King Lear, V 3 line 3417.
Love's Labour's Lost, II 1 line 494; Love's Labour's Lost, V 2 line 2298.
Lover's Complaint, lines 80, 211, 221, 313.
Macbeth, I 2 line 30; Macbeth, I 5 line 250; Macbeth, I 5 line 360; Macbeth, I 5 lines 395, 400; Macbeth, I 7 line 549; Macbeth, II 1 line 577; Macbeth, II 1 line 629; Macbeth, II 2 line 655; Macbeth, II 2 line 698; Macbeth, II 3 line 901; Macbeth, II 4 line 965; Macbeth, II 4 line 982; Macbeth, III 1 line 1059; Macbeth, III 1 line 1101; Macbeth, III 1 line 1113; Macbeth, III 2 line 1212; Macbeth, III 4 line 1304; Macbeth, III 4 line 1445; Macbeth, IV 1 line 1611; Macbeth, IV 1 line 1667; Macbeth, IV 3 line 1864; Macbeth, IV 3 line 1921; Macbeth, IV 3 line 1983; Macbeth, V 1 line 2135.
Measure for Measure, I 1 line 12; Measure for Measure, I 1 line 42; Measure for Measure, I 1 line 90; Measure for Measure, I 2 line 219; Measure for Measure, I 3 line 333; Measure for Measure, II 2 line 958; Measure for Measure, II 3 line 971; Measure for Measure, II 4 line 1065; Measure for Measure, III 1 line 1298; Measure for Measure, III 1 line 1366; Measure for Measure, III 1 line 1371; Measure for Measure, III 1 line 1404.
Merchant of Venice, I 1 line 54; Merchant of Venice, II 9 line 1192; Merchant of Venice, III 2 line 1457; Merchant of Venice, IV 1 line 2116; Merchant of Venice, V 1 line 2538.
Merry Wives of Windsor, III 3 line 1464.
Midsummer Night's Dream, II 2 line 763; Midsummer Night's Dream, V 1 line 2133; Midsummer Night's Dream, V 1 line 2260.
Much Ado About Nothing, III 1 line 1126; Much Ado About Nothing, III 1 line 1141; Much Ado About Nothing, III 3 line 1336; Much Ado About Nothing, IV 1 line 1777.
Othello, I 3 line 391; Othello, I 3 line 400; Othello, I 3 lines 437, 442; Othello, I 3 line 687; Othello, I 3 line 756; Othello, II 1 line 848; Othello, II 1 line 1014; Othello, II 1 line 1032; Othello, II 1 line 1090; Othello, II 3 line 1265; Othello, III 3 line 1795; Othello, III 3 line 1851; Othello, III 3 line 1885; Othello, III 3 line 1889; Othello, III 3 line 1999; Othello, III 4 line 2339; Othello, IV 1 line 2457; Othello, IV 1 line 2713; Othello, V 2 line 3312; Othello, V 2 line 3703.

Pericles, I 1 line 54; Pericles, II 1 line 583; Pericles, II 2 line 754; Pericles, III 2 line 1291; Pericles, III 2 line 1315; Pericles, III 2 line 1329; Pericles, III 2 line 1383; Pericles, III 3 line 1448; Pericles, IV 2 line 1802; Pericles, V 0 line 2149.
Phoenix and the Turtle, line 39.
Rape of Lucrece, lines 590, 748, 1426.
Richard II, I 2 line 227; Richard II, II 1 line 725.
Richard III, I 1 line 20; Richard III, I 2 line 325; Richard III, I 2 line 427; Richard III, I 3 line 694; Richard III, IV 3 line 2744; Richard III, IV 4 line 3160.
Romeo and Juliet, II 1 line 824; Romeo and Juliet, II 3 line 1067; Romeo and Juliet, II 4 line 1245; Romeo and Juliet, III 2 line 1802; Romeo and Juliet, IV 5 lines 2741, 2742.
Sonnet IV line 3, Sonnet IV line 11; Sonnet XI line 9; Sonnet XVIII line 8; Sonnet XX line 1; Sonnet XX line 10; Sonnet LX line 11; Sonnet LXVII line 9; Sonnet LXVIII line 13; Sonnet XCIV line 6; Sonnet CIX line 9; Sonnet CXI line 6; Sonnet CXXVI line 5; Sonnet CXXVII line 5.
Taming of the Shrew, I 1 line 410.
Tempest, I 2 line 194; Tempest, I 2 line 513; Tempest, I 2 line 695; Tempest, II 1 lines 869, 872; Tempest, IV 1 line 1927; Tempest, V 1 line 2105; Tempest, V 1 line 2308.
Timon of Athens, I 1 line 50; Timon of Athens, I 1 line 72; Timon of Athens, I 1 line 82; Timon of Athens, I 1 line 196; Timon of Athens, II 2 line 904; Timon of Athens, II 2 line 915; Timon of Athens, III 1 line 1007; Timon of Athens, III 3 line 1145; Timon of Athens, IV 3 lines 1669, 1671, 1682, 1708; Timon of Athens, IV 3 line 1862; Timon of Athens, IV 3 line 1890; Timon of Athens, IV 3 line 1917, 1920; Timon of Athens, IV 3 line 1963; Timon of Athens, IV 3 line 2133; Timon of Athens, IV 3 line 2209; Timon of Athens, V 1 line 2321; Timon of Athens, V 1 line 2350; Timon of Athens, V 1 line 2490; Timon of Athens, V 1 line 2515; Timon of Athens, V 4 line 2595; Timon of Athens, V 4 line 2651.
Titus Andronicus, I 1 line 134; Titus Andronicus, I 1 line 414; Titus Andronicus, I 1 line 415; Titus Andronicus, II 3 line 857; Titus Andronicus, IV 1 line 1597; Titus Andronicus, IV 1 line 1598; Titus Andronicus, V 1 line 2161; Titus Andronicus, V 2 line 2479; Titus Andronicus, V 2 line 2484; Titus Andronicus, V 3 line 2693; Titus Andronicus, V 3 line 2712.
Troilus and Cressida, I 2 line 177; Troilus and Cressida, I 3 line 593; Troilus and Cressida, I 3 line 632; Troilus and Cressida, II 2 lines 1170, 1174, 1182; Titus Andronicus, II 3 line 1464; Titus Andronicus, III 3 line 1875; Titus Andronicus, III 3 line 2003; Titus Andronicus, III 3 line 2052; Titus Andronicus, IV 2 line 2370; Titus Andronicus, IV 4 line 2510; Titus Andronicus, V 1 line 2936; Titus Andronicus, V 1 line 2964; Titus Andronicus, V 2 line 3222.
Twelfth Night, I 2 line 72; Twelfth Night, I 2 line 97; Twelfth Night, I 3 line 141; Twelfth Night, I 3 line 206; Twelfth Night, I 5 line 561; Twelfth Night, II 4 line 984; Twelfth Night, III 3 line 1520; Twelfth Night, III 4 line

1766; Twelfth Night, III 4 line 1921; Twelfth Night, V 1 line 2427; Twelfth Night, V 1 line 2461.
Two Gentlemen of Verona, II 3 line 597; Two Gentlemen of Verona, V 4 line 2209.
Venus and Adonis, lines 31, 191, 311, 751, 756, 766, 975.
Winter's Tale, I 2 line 233; Winter's Tale, I 2 line 322; Winter's Tale, II 2 line 917; Winter's Tale, II 3 line 1057; Winter's Tale, III 2 line 1481; Winter's Tale, IV 4 line 1955; Winter's Tale, IV 4 line 1962; Winter's Tale, IV 4 lines 1964, 1965, 1966, 1970, 1971; Winter's Tale, IV 4 line 2411; Winter's Tale, IV 4 line 2724; Winter's Tale, V 2 line 3146; Winter's Tale, V 2 line 3207.

Neat: cow, ox or bullock or other domestic bovine animal. Old English.
Cymbeline, I 1 line 190.
Henry IV, Part I, II 4 line 1230.
Henry VI, Part III, II 1 line 640.
Julius Caesar, I 1 line 27.
Merchant of Venice, I 1 line 118.
Taming of the Shrew, IV 3 line 1973.
Tempest, II 2 line 1161.
Winter's Tale, I 2 line 203; Winter's Tale, IV 4 line 2219.

Neb: beak or bill of a bird, Old English *nebb*: beak, nose; face, countenance; beak-shaped thing.
Winter's Tale, I 2 line 270.

Neck: Old English: *hnecca: neck, nape, back of the neck* (a fairly rare word). The more usual Old English word: *hals*.
Antony and Cleopatra, III 13 line 2410; Antony and Cleopatra, III 13 line 2449; Antony and Cleopatra, IV 8 line 2800; Antony and Cleopatra, IV 14 line 3069.
As You Like It, I 1 line 126; As You Like It, I 2 line 245; As You Like It, I 2 line 357; As You Like It, III 2 line 1289; As You Like It, III 5 line 1655; As You Like It, IV 3 line 2110.
Comedy of Errors, III 2 line 900; Comedy of Errors, V 1 line 1434; Comedy of Errors, V 1 line 1696.
Coriolanus, I 3 line 411; Coriolanus, II 1 line 953; Coriolanus, II 1 line 1069; Coriolanus, II 1 line 1147; Coriolanus, III 3 line 2380; Coriolanus, IV 7 line 3243; Coriolanus, V 4 line 3764.
Cymbeline, III 3 line 1701; Cymbeline, V 4 line 3325; Cymbeline, V 5 line 3816.
Hamlet, III 2 line 2020; Hamlet, III 4 lines 2589, 2600.
Henry IV, Part I, II 1 line 704; Henry IV, Part I, IV 3 line 2552.
Henry IV, Part II, II 3 line 1198.
Henry V, III 4 line 1361; Henry V, IV 1 line 1963; Henry V, IV 6 line 2500; Henry V, IV 8 line 2752; Henry V, V 2 line 3163.
Henry VI, Part I, II 3 line 897; Henry VI, Part I, II 5 line 1114; Henry VI, Part I, V 4 line 2762.

Henry VI, Part II, I 2 line 340; Henry VI, Part II, III 2 line 1787; Henry VI, Part II, IV 2 line 2410; Henry VI, Part II, IV 8 line 2779; Henry VI, Part II, IV 9 line 2843; Henry VI, Part II, IV 9 line 2845.
Henry VI, Part III, III 3 line 1707.
Henry VIII, II 2 line 1053.
Julius Caesar, V 1 line 2395.
King Lear, II 4 line 1284; King Lear, II 4 line 1349; King Lear, V 3 line 3373.
Love's Labour's Lost, IV 1 line 1032; Love's Labour's Lost, IV 1 line 1094.
Macbeth, IV 3 line 2016.
Measure for Measure, III 2 line 1551.
Merchant of Venice, II 2 line 578; Merchant of Venice, II 5 line 878.
Midsummer Night's Dream, III 1 line 852.
Much Ado About Nothing, I 1 line 180; Much Ado About Nothing, II 1 line 574.
Othello, IV 1 line 2566; Othello, V 2 line 3507.
Richard II, II 2 line 1071; Richard II, III 1 line 1377; Richard II, V 2 line 2460; Richard II, V 5 line 2839.
Richard III, IV 4 lines 2906, 2907.
Romeo and Juliet, I 1 line 20; Romeo and Juliet, I 4 line 582.
Sonnet CXXXI line 11.
Taming of the Shrew, II 1 line 1159; Taming of the Shrew, III 2 line 1539; Taming of the Shrew, IV 1 line 1634.
Tempest, I 2 line 643.
Timon of Athens, IV 3 line 2223.
Titus Andronicus, IV 4 line 2060; Titus Andronicus, V 1 line 2267.
Troilus and Cressida, III 3 line 2104; Troilus and Cressida, III 3 line 2143; Troilus and Cressida, IV 2 line 2375; Troilus and Cressida, V 4 line 3446.
Twelfth Night, I 5 line 537; Twelfth Night, II 5 line 1214.
Venus and Adonis, lines 119, 283, 560, 613, 614, 648, 894.
Winter's Tale, I 2 line 415; Winter's Tale, I 2 line 457; Winter's Tale, V 2 line 3142; Winter's Tale, V 3 line 3426.

Nectar: 1550s, from Latin: *nectar*, from Greek: *nektar*, name of the drink of the gods, which is said to be a compound of *nek*: death (necro-) + *-tar*: overcoming. Meaning *sweet liquid in flowers* first recorded c.1600.
    Troilus and Cressida, III 2 line 1671.
    Two Gentlemen of Verona, II 4 line 831.
    Venus and Adonis, line 593.

Nest: Old English: *nest: bird's nest, snug retreat*, also *young bird, brood*. Used since Middle English in reference to various accumulations of things. *Nest egg*: originally a real or artificial egg left in a nest to induce the hen to go on laying there (c.1600).
    All's Well That Ends Well, IV 3 line 2367.
    As You Like It, IV 1 line 1968.
    Comedy of Errors, IV 2 line 1100.

Cymbeline, III 3 line 1631; Cymbeline, III 4 line 1879.
Henry IV, Part I, V 1 line 2684.
Henry V, I 2 line 315; Henry V, II 0 line 483.
Henry VI, Part II, II 1 line 936; Henry VI, Part II, III 2 line 1767; Henry VI, Part II, III 2 line 1876.
Henry VI, Part III, II 2 line 873.
King John, V 2 line 2433.
Macbeth, IV 2 line 1751.
Midsummer Night's Dream, I 1 line 88.
Much Ado About Nothing, II 1 line 604; Much Ado About Nothing, II 1 line 612.
Phoenix and the Turtle, line 57.
Rape of Lucrece, line 1662.
Richard III, I 3 line 737; Richard III, IV 4 line 3238.
Romeo and Juliet, II 5 line 1452; Romeo and Juliet, V 3 line 3111.
Tempest, II 2 line 1255.
Titus Andronicus, I 1 line 420.
Venus and Adonis, line 553.
Winter's Tale, II 3 line 1030; Winter's Tale, IV 4 line 2763.

Nettle: Old English: *netele*.
Coriolanus, II 1 line 1122r.
Hamlet, IV 7 line 3318.
Henry IV, Part I, I 3 line 575; Henry IV, Part I, II 3 line 867.
Henry V, I 1 line 99.
Henry VI, Part III, III 3 line 1871.
King Lear, IV 4 line 2519.
Othello, I 3 line 680.
Richard II, III 2 line 1426.
Tempest, II 1 line 852.
Titus Andronicus, II 3 line 1024.
Troilus and Cressida, I 2 line 320.
Winter's Tale, I 2 line 438.

Newt: early 15c., misdivision of *an ewte*, from Middle English: *evete*.
King Lear, III 4 line 1924.
Macbeth, IV 1 line 1561.
Midsummer Night's Dream, II 2 line 671.
Timon of Athens, IV 3 line 1869.

Night: Old English: *niht*. Throughout the 16th and 17th centuries, the boundaries of the night were driven back and simultaneously the associations of darkness were enriched and transformed. The schedule of the day changed. The traditional two-part, segmented sleep (with a waking interval) of rural communities was replaced in cities with a single phase of sleep. The schedule of the urban day slipped back, so rising, mealtimes and sleep occurred later. But the meaning of the night also changed, its symbolisms and associations were re-imagined and re-invented.

All's Well That Ends Well, III 2 line 1537; All's Well That Ends Well, III 6 line 1830; All's Well That Ends Well, III 7 line 1890; All's Well That Ends Well, IV 2 line 2075; All's Well That Ends Well, IV 3 line 2106; All's Well That Ends Well, IV 3 line 2190; All's Well That Ends Well, IV 4 line 2448; All's Well That Ends Well, V 1 line 2556; All's Well That Ends Well, V 1 line 2568; All's Well That Ends Well, V 1 line 2592; All's Well That Ends Well, V 2 line 2667.
Antony and Cleopatra, I 1 lines 64, 66; Antony and Cleopatra, I 4 line 428; Antony and Cleopatra, I 4 line 437; Antony and Cleopatra, II 2 line 903; Antony and Cleopatra, II 3 lines 984, 987, 988; Antony and Cleopatra, II 3 line 989; Antony and Cleopatra, II 5 line 1072; Antony and Cleopatra, II 7 lines 1521, 1527; Antony and Cleopatra, III 10 line 2099; Antony and Cleopatra, III 13 line 2472; Antony and Cleopatra, IV 2 line 2571; Antony and Cleopatra, IV 3 line 2578; Antony and Cleopatra, IV 3 line 2582; Antony and Cleopatra, IV 3 line 2583; Antony and Cleopatra, IV 3 line 2586r; Antony and Cleopatra, IV 9 line 2833; Antony and Cleopatra, IV 9 line 2839; Antony and Cleopatra, IV 9 line 2850.
As You Like It, II 3 line 666; As You Like It, III 2 line 1123; As You Like It, III 2 line 1148; As You Like It, IV 1 line 1882; As You Like It, V 1 line 2568.
Comedy of Errors, III 2 line 820; Comedy of Errors, IV 2 line 1141; Comedy of Errors, IV 4 line 1414; Comedy of Errors, V 1 line 1647; Comedy of Errors, V 1 line 1753.
Coriolanus, I 3 line 458; Coriolanus, II 1 line 966; Coriolanus, IV 4 line 2728; Coriolanus, IV 5 line 2992.
Cymbeline, I 4 line 374; Cymbeline, I 6 line 832; Cymbeline, II 2 line 930; Cymbeline, II 2 line 972; Cymbeline, II 3 line 1150; Cymbeline, II 4 line 1226; Cymbeline, III 3 line 1667; Cymbeline, III 4 line 1876; Cymbeline, III 5 line 2034; Cymbeline, III 6 line 2145; Cymbeline, III 6 line 2222; Cymbeline, III 6 line 2260; Cymbeline, IV 2 line 2684; Cymbeline, IV 2 line 2696; Cymbeline, IV 2 line 2756.
Hamlet, I 1 line 13; Hamlet, I 1 line 20; Hamlet, I 1 line 24; Hamlet, I 1 line 36; Hamlet, I 1 line 43; Hamlet, I 1 line 46; Hamlet, I 1 line 59; Hamlet, I 1 lines 88, 94; Hamlet, I 1 lines 183, 185; Hamlet, I 2 line 270; Hamlet, I 2 line 396; Hamlet, I 2 lines 405, 407, 417; Hamlet, I 2 line 477; Hamlet, I 3 line 555; Hamlet, I 4 line 684; Hamlet, I 5 line 746; Hamlet, I 5 line 917; Hamlet, II 2 line 1177; Hamlet, II 2 lines 1182r, 1183; Hamlet, II 2 line 1530; Hamlet, II 2 line 1611; Hamlet, II 2 line 1617; Hamlet, III 1 line 1705; Hamlet, III 2 line 2109; Hamlet, III 2 line 2264; Hamlet, III 4 lines 2562, 2573, 2580; Hamlet, III 4 lines 2618, 2622; Hamlet, IV 5 lines 2933r, 2935r; Hamlet, V 1 line 3642; Hamlet, V 2 line 3896; Hamlet, V 2 line 4021.
Henry IV, Part I, I 1 line 88; Henry IV, Part I, I 2 line 135; Henry IV, Part I, I 2 line 145; Henry IV, Part I, I 2 line 235; Henry IV, Part I, I 2 line 294; Henry IV, Part I, I 3 line 514; Henry IV, Part I, I 3 line 525; Henry IV, Part I, II 1 line 699; Henry IV, Part I, II 1 line 732; Henry IV, Part I, II 4 line 1512; Henry IV, Part I, III 1 line 1625; Henry IV, Part I, III 1 line 1686; Henry IV, Part I, III 1 line 1701; Henry IV, Part I, III 1 line

1769; Henry IV, Part I, III 3 lines 2046, 2051; Henry IV, Part I, III 3 line 2108; Henry IV, Part I, IV 2 line 2426; Henry IV, Part I, V 1 line 2658; Henry IV, Part I, V 2 line 2846.
Henry IV, Part II, I 1 line 129; Henry IV, Part II, I 2 line 466; Henry IV, Part II, II 1 line 800; Henry IV, Part II, II 4 line 1676; Henry IV, Part II, II 4 line 1678; Henry IV, Part II, III 1 lines 1715, 1732; Henry IV, Part II, III 2 line 2047; Henry IV, Part II, III 2 line 2151; Henry IV, Part II, III 2 line 2189; Henry IV, Part II, IV 5 lines 2913, 2916; Henry IV, Part II, IV 5 line 3021; Henry IV, Part II, V 1 line 3172; Henry IV, Part II, V 3 line 3544; Henry IV, Part II, V 5 line 3606; Henry IV, Part II, V 5 line 3687; Henry IV, Part II, V 5 line 3748.
Henry V, I 1 line 104; Henry V, II 2 line 706; Henry V, II 4 line 1049; Henry V, III 6 line 1638; Henry V, III 7 line 1651; Henry V, IV 0 lines 1791, 1798, 1807, 1835, 1844; Henry V, IV 1 line 1923; Henry V, IV 1 line 1962; Henry V, IV 1 lines 2117, 2119, 2125; Henry V, IV 3 line 2323; Henry V, IV 7 line 2647; Henry V, IV 8 line 2759; Henry V, V 2 line 3179.
Henry VI, Part I, I 1 line 5; Henry VI, Part I, I 2 line 329; Henry VI, Part I, II 1 line 676; Henry VI, Part I, II 1 line 703; Henry VI, Part I, II 1 line 740; Henry VI, Part I, II 2 line 760; Henry VI, Part I, II 2 lines 787, 791; Henry VI, Part I, II 4 line 1064.
Henry VI, Part II, I 1 line 30; Henry VI, Part II, I 2 line 295; Henry VI, Part II, I 3 line 592; Henry VI, Part II, I 4 lines 643rr, 644; Henry VI, Part II, I 4 line 723; Henry VI, Part II, II 1 line 826; Henry VI, Part II, II 1 line 948; Henry VI, Part II, II 4 line 1200; Henry VI, Part II, III 1 lines 1390, 1391r; Henry VI, Part II, III 2 line 2029; Henry VI, Part II, IV 1 line 2155; Henry VI, Part II, IV 7 line 2751.
Henry VI, Part III, I 1 line 35; Henry VI, Part III, II 1 line 758; Henry VI, Part III, II 5 line 1106; Henry VI, Part III, II 5 line 1163; Henry VI, Part III, IV 2 lines 2144, 2153; Henry VI, Part III, IV 3 line 2185; Henry VI, Part III, IV 7 line 2462; Henry VI, Part III, IV 7 line 2509; Henry VI, Part III, V 4 line 2876; Henry VI, Part III, V 5 line 2920; Henry VI, Part III, V 6 line 3040; Henry VI, Part III, V 7 line 3112.
Henry VIII, I 1 line 66; Henry VIII, I 2 line 566; Henry VIII, I 3 line 635; Henry VIII, I 3 line 652; Henry VIII, I 4 line 660; Henry VIII, I 4 line 755; Henry VIII, IV 2 line 2585; Henry VIII, V 1 line 2839; Henry VIII, V 1 line 2840; Henry VIII, V 1 line 2868; Henry VIII, V 1 line 2870.
Julius Caesar, I 2 line 285; Julius Caesar, I 2 line 347; Julius Caesar, I 2 line 411; Julius Caesar, I 3 line 447; Julius Caesar, I 3 line 460; Julius Caesar, I 3 line 468; Julius Caesar, I 3 line 469; Julius Caesar, I 3 line 473; Julius Caesar, I 3 line 499; Julius Caesar, I 3 line 555; Julius Caesar, I 3 line 568; Julius Caesar, II 1 line 691; Julius Caesar, II 1 line 703; Julius Caesar, II 1 line 716; Julius Caesar, II 1 line 823; Julius Caesar, II 1 line 892; Julius Caesar, II 2 line 972; Julius Caesar, II 2 line 1102; Julius Caesar, IV 2 line 1947; Julius Caesar, IV 3 line 2238; Julius Caesar, IV 3 line 2242; Julius Caesar, IV 3 lines 2249, 2250; Julius Caesar, IV 3 line 2252; Julius Caesar, IV 3 line 2257; Julius Caesar, IV 3 line 2258; Julius Caesar, IV 3 lines 2297, 2300;

Julius Caesar, V 3 line 2627; Julius Caesar, V 5 lines 2693, 2694; Julius Caesar, V 5 line 2719.

King John, I 1 line 171; King John, I 1 line 179; King John, III 3 line 1340; King John, III 4 line 1411; King John, IV 1 line 1592; King John, IV 1 line 1607; King John, V 3 line 2478; King John, V 4 lines 2521, 2524; King John, V 5 line 2557; King John, V 5 line 2571; King John, V 6 line 2592; King John, V 6 line 2597; King John, V 6 line 2600; King John, V 6 line 2620; King John, V 7 line 2696.

King Lear, I 1 line 114; King Lear, I 2 line 473; King Lear, I 3 line 507; King Lear, II 1 line 930; King Lear, II 1 lines 949, 951; King Lear, II 1 line 1061; King Lear, II 2 line 1101; King Lear, II 2 line 1206r; King Lear, II 2 line 1249; King Lear, II 4 line 1277; King Lear, II 4 line 1365; King Lear, II 4 line 1606; King Lear, II 4 line 1615; King Lear, III 1 line 1629; King Lear, III 2 line 1689; King Lear, III 2 lines 1718, 1719; King Lear, III 2 line 1760; King Lear, III 3 line 1786; King Lear, III 4 line 1802; King Lear, III 4 lines 1819, 1821; King Lear, III 4 line 1876; King Lear, III 4 line 1905; King Lear, III 4 line 1943; King Lear, III 4 line 1963; King Lear, III 7 line 2189; King Lear, IV 1 line 2285; King Lear, IV 3 line 2483; King Lear, IV 5 line 2565; King Lear, IV 7 line 2953; King Lear, IV 7 line 2987; King Lear, V 3 line 3405.

Love's Labour's Lost, I 1 lines 45, 47, 48; Love's Labour's Lost, I 1 line 92; Love's Labour's Lost, III 1 line 939; Love's Labour's Lost, IV 1 line 1124; Love's Labour's Lost, IV 3 line 1349; Love's Labour's Lost, IV 3 line 1577; Love's Labour's Lost, IV 3 line 1599; Love's Labour's Lost, V 2 line 2595; Love's Labour's Lost, V 2 lines 2865, 2872.

Macbeth, I 3 lines 117, 120; Macbeth, I 5 line 400; Macbeth, I 5 lines 423, 424; Macbeth, II 1 line 569; Macbeth, II 1 line 593; Macbeth, II 2 line 651; Macbeth, II 2 line 739; Macbeth, II 3 line 798; Macbeth, II 3 lines 823, 829; Macbeth, II 3 line 831; Macbeth, II 4 line 950; Macbeth, II 4 lines 955, 956; Macbeth, III 1 line 1032; Macbeth, III 1 line 1042; Macbeth, III 1 line 1048; Macbeth, III 2 line 1191; Macbeth, III 2 line 1217; Macbeth, III 2 lines 1221, 1228; Macbeth, III 4 line 1418; Macbeth, III 4 line 1421; Macbeth, III 4 line 1423; Macbeth, III 4 line 1429; Macbeth, III 5 line 1469; Macbeth, III 6 line 1526; Macbeth, IV 1 line 1553; Macbeth, IV 3 line 2125; Macbeth, V 1 line 2128; Macbeth, V 1 line 2131; Macbeth, V 1 line 2184; Macbeth, V 1 line 2200; Macbeth, V 1 line 2203; Macbeth, V 5 line 2366.

Measure for Measure, I 4 line 446; Measure for Measure, II 1 lines 584, 585; Measure for Measure, III 1 line 1333; Measure for Measure, III 1 line 1504; Measure for Measure, IV 1 line 1832; Measure for Measure, IV 1 line 1859; Measure for Measure, IV 2 line 1965; Measure for Measure, IV 3 line 2157; Measure for Measure, IV 3 line 2159; Measure for Measure, IV 3 line 2168; Measure for Measure, V 1 line 2538; Measure for Measure, V 1 line 2638; Measure for Measure, V 1 line 2715.

Merchant of Venice, II 6 line 945; Merchant of Venice, II 6 line 959; Merchant of Venice, III 1 line 1342; Merchant of Venice, III 2 line 1654; Merchant of Venice, V 1 line 2355; Merchant of Venice, V 1 lines 2444, 2446, 2449; Merchant of Venice, V 1 line 2450; Merchant of Venice, V

1 line 2454; Merchant of Venice, V 1 line 2458; Merchant of Venice, V 1 line 2461; Merchant of Venice, V 1 line 2465; Merchant of Venice, V 1 line 2469; Merchant of Venice, V 1 line 2472; Merchant of Venice, V 1 line 2475; Merchant of Venice, V 1 line 2510; Merchant of Venice, V 1 line 2542; Merchant of Venice, V 1 line 2587; Merchant of Venice, V 1 line 2688; Merchant of Venice, V 1 line 2698; Merchant of Venice, V 1 line 2732; Merchant of Venice, V 1 line 2775.

Merry Wives of Windsor, I 4 line 411; Merry Wives of Windsor, II 1 line 583; Merry Wives of Windsor, II 1 line 683; Merry Wives of Windsor, II 2 line 1051; Merry Wives of Windsor, II 2 lines 1068, 1070; Merry Wives of Windsor, IV 4 line 2235; Merry Wives of Windsor, V 2 line 2522; Merry Wives of Windsor, V 3 line 2544; Merry Wives of Windsor, V 5 line 2601; Merry Wives of Windsor, V 5 line 2630; Merry Wives of Windsor, V 5 line 2805.

Midsummer Night's Dream, I 1 lines 8, 9; Midsummer Night's Dream, I 1 line 151; Midsummer Night's Dream, I 1 line 170; Midsummer Night's Dream, I 1 line 217; Midsummer Night's Dream, I 1 line 258; Midsummer Night's Dream, I 2 line 271; Midsummer Night's Dream, I 2 line 355; Midsummer Night's Dream, II 1 line 406; Midsummer Night's Dream, II 1 line 411; Midsummer Night's Dream, II 1 line 446; Midsummer Night's Dream, II 1 line 471; Midsummer Night's Dream, II 1 line 494; Midsummer Night's Dream, II 1 line 592; Midsummer Night's Dream, II 1 lines 596, 597; Midsummer Night's Dream, II 1 line 632; Midsummer Night's Dream, II 2 lines 655, 569; Midsummer Night's Dream, II 2 line 714; Midsummer Night's Dream, II 2 line 726; Midsummer Night's Dream, III 1 line 864; Midsummer Night's Dream, III 1 line 867; Midsummer Night's Dream, III 1 line 994; Midsummer Night's Dream, III 2 line 1035; Midsummer Night's Dream, III 2 line 1217; Midsummer Night's Dream, III 2 line 1227; Midsummer Night's Dream, III 2 line 1320r; Midsummer Night's Dream, III 2 line 1330; Midsummer Night's Dream, III 2 line 1412; Midsummer Night's Dream, III 2 lines 1436, 1444; Midsummer Night's Dream, III 2 line 1504r; Midsummer Night's Dream, IV 1 line 1616; Midsummer Night's Dream, IV 1 line 1647; Midsummer Night's Dream, V 1 line 1851; Midsummer Night's Dream, V 1 line 1853; Midsummer Night's Dream, V 1 line 1983; Midsummer Night's Dream, V 1 lines 2013r, 2014, 2015r; Midsummer Night's Dream, V 1 line 2212, 2214, 2216; Midsummer Night's Dream, V 1 line 2228; Midsummer Night's Dream, V 1 line 2288.

Much Ado About Nothing, I 1 line 3; Much Ado About Nothing, I 2 line 314; Much Ado About Nothing, II 1 line 534; Much Ado About Nothing, II 1 line 731; Much Ado About Nothing, II 1 line 743; Much Ado About Nothing, II 2 line 775; Much Ado About Nothing, II 2 line 799; Much Ado About Nothing, II 3 line 830; Much Ado About Nothing, II 3 line 901; Much Ado About Nothing, II 3 line 904; Much Ado About Nothing, II 3 line 946; Much Ado About Nothing, III 2 line 1300; Much Ado About Nothing, III 3 line 1382; Much Ado About Nothing, III 3 line 1391; Much Ado About Nothing, III 3 lines 1399, 1401; Much Ado About Nothing, III 3 line 1460; Much Ado About Nothing, III 3 lines 1468, 1473; Much Ado

About Nothing, III 4 line 1507; Much Ado About Nothing, IV 1 line 1734; Much Ado About Nothing, IV 1 line 1797; Much Ado About Nothing, IV 1 line 1798; Much Ado About Nothing, V 1 line 2243; Much Ado About Nothing, V 1 line 2306; Much Ado About Nothing, V 3 line 2519; Much Ado About Nothing, V 3 line 2530.
Othello, I 1 line 79; Othello, I 1 line 134; Othello, I 1 line 199; Othello, I 2 line 241; Othello, I 2 line 250; Othello, I 2 line 319; Othello, I 3 line 643; Othello, I 3 line 760; Othello, II 1 line 854; Othello, II 1 line 1108; Othello, II 3 lines 1137, 1143; Othello, II 3 line 1150; Othello, II 3 line 1174; Othello, II 3 line 1342; Othello, II 3 line 1364; Othello, II 3 line 1484; Othello, III 3 lines 1695, 1696; Othello, III 3 line 2017; Othello, III 4 line 2371; Othello, III 4 line 2403; Othello, IV 1 line 2492; Othello, IV 1 lines 2635, 2637; Othello, IV 2 lines 2986, 2987; Othello, IV 2 line 3013; Othello, IV 3 line 3021; Othello, IV 3 line 3036; Othello, IV 3 line 3055; Othello, IV 3 line 3082; Othello, IV 3 line 3132r; Othello, V 1 line 3188; Othello, V 1 line 3297.
Passionate Pilgrim, lines 182, 183, 201, 202, 206, 210r, 211, 313.
Pericles, I 1 line 187; Pericles, I 2 line 240; Pericles, I 2 line 326; Pericles, II 3 line 866; Pericles, II 5 line 1041; Pericles, III 1 line 1202; Pericles, III 2 line 1287; Pericles, III 2 line 1288; Pericles, IV 3 line 1831; Pericles, V 1 line 2218; Pericles, V 3 line 2605.
Phoenix and the Turtle, line 39.
Rape of Lucrece, lines 30, 37, 66, 168, 174, 213, 358, 407, 411, 447, 500, 536, 563, 605, 726, 731, 749, 780, 792, 798, 814, 815, 822, 835, 836r, 839, 850, 976, 993, 1016, 1021, 1064, 1075, 1126, 1131, 1132, 1136, 1143, 1283, 1313, 1431, 1622, 1681.
Richard II, I 3 line 478; Richard II, I 3 line 522; Richard II, I 3 line 528; Richard II, II 3 line 1319; Richard II, III 2 lines 1453, 1456; Richard II, III 2 line 1631; Richard II, III 3 line 1826; Richard II, V 1 lines 1374, 2377; Richard II, V 6 line 2926.
Richard III, I 1 line 77; Richard III, I 2 line 311; Richard III, I 4 lines 835, 838; Richard III, I 4 line 880; Richard III, I 4 line 911r; Richard III, II 1 line 1243; Richard III, II 3 line 1467; Richard III, II 4 line 1484; Richard III, II 4 line 1493; Richard III, III 2 line 1785; Richard III, IV 3 line 2770; Richard III, IV 4 line 2808; Richard III, IV 4 line 2913; Richard III, IV 4 line 3110; Richard III, IV 4 line 3215; Richard III, V 3 line 3490; Richard III, V 3 line 3500; Richard III, V 3 line 3504; Richard III, V 3 line 3529; Richard III, V 3 line 3546; Richard III, V 3 line 3552.
Romeo and Juliet, I 1 line 160; Romeo and Juliet, I 2 lines 290, 294, 299; Romeo and Juliet, I 3 lines 402, 406; Romeo and Juliet, I 3 line 465; Romeo and Juliet, I 3 line 493; Romeo and Juliet, I 4 lines 570r, 589; Romeo and Juliet, I 4 line 611; Romeo and Juliet, I 5 lines 667, 675; Romeo and Juliet, I 5 line 685; Romeo and Juliet, I 5 line 753; Romeo and Juliet, II 1 line 830; Romeo and Juliet, II 1 line 838; Romeo and Juliet, II 2 line 867; Romeo and Juliet, II 2 line 874; Romeo and Juliet, II 2 line 900; Romeo and Juliet, II 2 line 924; Romeo and Juliet, II 2 lines 934, 955; Romeo and Juliet, II 2 lines 971, 974r; Romeo and Juliet, II 2 lines 992, 993; Romeo and Juliet, II 2 line 996; Romeo and Juliet, II 2 line 1011; Romeo and Juliet, II 2 line 1026; Romeo and

Juliet, II 2 lines 1049r, 1051; Romeo and Juliet, II 3 lines 1059, 1064; Romeo and Juliet, II 4 line 1206; Romeo and Juliet, II 4 line 1344; Romeo and Juliet, II 5 line 1454; Romeo and Juliet, III 2 lines 1722, 1723, 1728r, 1735r, 1736, 1738r, 1742, 1747; Romeo and Juliet, III 2 line 1864; Romeo and Juliet, III 3 lines 2048, 2054; Romeo and Juliet, III 4 line 2067; Romeo and Juliet, III 4 line 2095; Romeo and Juliet, III 5 line 2101; Romeo and Juliet, III 5 line 2106; Romeo and Juliet, III 5 line 2111; Romeo and Juliet, III 5 line 2289; Romeo and Juliet, IV 1 line 2447; Romeo and Juliet, IV 1 lines 2457, 2482; Romeo and Juliet, IV 3 lines 2559; Romeo and Juliet, IV 3 line 2562; Romeo and Juliet, IV 3 lines 2589, 2596; Romeo and Juliet, IV 4 line 2622; Romeo and Juliet, IV 4 line 2624; Romeo and Juliet, IV 5 line 2657; Romeo and Juliet, V 3 lines 2948, 2951, 2956; Romeo and Juliet, V 3 line 3054; Romeo and Juliet, V 3 line 3222.

Sonnet XII line 2; Sonnet XV line 12; Sonnet XXVII line 11; Sonnet XXVII line 12; Sonnet XXVII lines 12, 13, 14; Sonnet XXVIII line 3; Sonnet XXVIII line 4r; Sonnet XXVIII line 11; Sonnet XXVIII line 14r; Sonnet XXX line 6; Sonnet XLIII line 11; Sonnet XLIII line 13; Sonnet XLIII line 14; Sonnet LXI line 2; Sonnet LXIII line 5; Sonnet LXXIII line 7; Sonnet LXXXVI line 7; Sonnet LXXXVI line 10; Sonnet XC line 7; Sonnet CII line 10; Sonnet CXIII line 11; Sonnet CXX line 9; Sonnet CXLV line 11.

Taming of the Shrew, Prologue 2 line 266; Taming of the Shrew, II 1 line 1152; Taming of the Shrew, III 2 line 1553; Taming of the Shrew, IV 1 line 1786; Taming of the Shrew, IV 1 lines 1809, 1715; Taming of the Shrew, IV 4 line 2215; Taming of the Shrew, V 2 line 2658; Taming of the Shrew, V 2 line 2695.

Tempest, I 2 line 477; Tempest, I 2 line 487; Tempest, III 1 line 1319; Tempest, IV 1 line 1732; Tempest, IV 1 line 1760; Tempest, V 1 line 2094; Tempest, V 1 line 2380.

Timon of Athens, I 1 line 147; Timon of Athens, II 2 line 857; Timon of Athens, III 1 line 1001; Timon of Athens, IV 1 line 1581; Timon of Athens, IV 3 line 1916; Timon of Athens, IV 3 line 1994; Timon of Athens, V 1 line 2303.

Titus Andronicus, II 2 line 705; Titus Andronicus, II 3 lines 833, 835; Titus Andronicus, II 3 line 979; Titus Andronicus, III 1 line 1130; Titus Andronicus, IV 3 line 1909; Titus Andronicus, V 1 line 2199; Titus Andronicus, V 1 line 2268; Titus Andronicus, V 2 line 2340; Titus Andronicus, V 3 line 2622.

Troilus and Cressida, I 1 line 43; Troilus and Cressida, I 3 line 624; Troilus and Cressida, III 2 line 1764; Troilus and Cressida, IV 2 line 2298; Troilus and Cressida, IV 2 line 2300; Troilus and Cressida, IV 4 line 2505; Troilus and Cressida, V 1 line 2976; Troilus and Cressida, V 1 line 3009; Troilus and Cressida, V 1 line 3011; Troilus and Cressida, V 1 line 3012; Troilus and Cressida, V 1 line 3013; Troilus and Cressida, V 1 line 3016; Troilus and Cressida, V 1 line 3018; Troilus and Cressida, V 1 line 3023; Troilus and Cressida, V 1 line 3029; Troilus and Cressida, V 2 line 3078; Troilus and Cressida, V 2 line 3082; Troilus and Cressida, V 2 line 3097; Troilus and Cressida, V 2

line 3135; Troilus and Cressida, V 2 line 3174; Troilus and Cressida, V 3 line 3288; Troilus and Cressida, V 8 line 3596; Troilus and Cressida, V 8 line 3609; Troilus and Cressida, V 10 line 3633.
Twelfth Night, I 3 line 119; Twelfth Night, I 3 line 130; Twelfth Night, I 5 line 562; Twelfth Night, II 3 line 724; Twelfth Night, II 3 line 759; Twelfth Night, II 3 line 790; Twelfth Night, II 3 line 873; Twelfth Night, II 3 line 876; Twelfth Night, II 4 line 893; Twelfth Night, II 4 line 936; Twelfth Night, III 1 line 1387; Twelfth Night, III 3 line 1510; Twelfth Night, V 1 line 2286; Twelfth Night, V 1 line 2474.
Two Gentlemen of Verona, I 1 line 33; Two Gentlemen of Verona, II 1 line 480; Two Gentlemen of Verona, II 4 line 789; Two Gentlemen of Verona, II 6 line 963; Two Gentlemen of Verona, III 1 line 1079; Two Gentlemen of Verona, III 1 line 1102; Two Gentlemen of Verona, III 1 line 1180; Two Gentlemen of Verona, III 1 line 1182; Two Gentlemen of Verona, III 1 line 1194; Two Gentlemen of Verona, III 1 lines 1212, 1223; Two Gentlemen of Verona, III 1 line 1251; Two Gentlemen of Verona, III 2 lines 1535, 1537; Two Gentlemen of Verona, IV 2 line 1734; Two Gentlemen of Verona, IV 2 line 1769; Two Gentlemen of Verona, IV 2 line 1777.
Venus and Adonis, lines 142, 174, 502, 513, 552, 555, 556, 558, 604, 739, 742, 749, 753, 777, 795, 838, 843, 847, 863, 869, 1063, 1208.
Winter's Tale, I 2 line 70; Winter's Tale, I 2 line 533; Winter's Tale, II 3 line 926; Winter's Tale, III 2 line 1233; Winter's Tale, III 3 line 1510; Winter's Tale, IV 3 line 1729.

Night-bird: any bird associated with night: owl; nightingale; nighthawk; etc.
Pericles, IV 0 line 1518.

Night-crow: the night-heron, Ardea nycti-corax, or according to some, the owl; according to others, the night-jar.
Henry VI, Part III, V 6 line 3040.

Nightingale: Old English: *næctigalæ, nihtegale*. A bird that carries both literary and poetic symbolism. The nightingale sings of love, but it is also a symbol of the connection between love and death. In *Romeo and Juliet* the nightingale's song signifies that the lovers will remain together, but that both are in danger of death. Associate with the rape of Philomel, featured in Ovid. Early Greek sources have it that Philomela was turned into a swallow, which has no song; Procne turns into a nightingale, singing a beautiful but sad song in remorse.
Antony and Cleopatra, IV 8 line 2806.
King Lear, III 3 line 2034.
Merchant of Venice, V 1 line 2561.
Midsummer Night's Dream, I 2 line 340.
Passionate Pilgrim, line 382.
Romeo and Juliet, III 5 line 2099; Romeo and Juliet, III 5 line 2104.
Taming of the Shrew, Prologue 2 180; Taming of the Shrew, II 1 line 1016.
Twelfth Night, III 4 line 1580.

Two Gentlemen of Verona, III 1 line 1252; Two Gentlemen of Verona V 4 line 2153.

Nose: Old English: *nosu*. Used to indicate *something obvious* from 1590s.
All's Well That Ends Well, II 3 line 1153; All's Well That Ends Well, IV 5 line 2480; All's Well That Ends Well, V 2 line 2623; All's Well That Ends Well, V 2 line 2626.
Antony and Cleopatra, I 2 line 136; Antony and Cleopatra, III 13 line 2291.
As You Like It, II 1 line 588; As You Like It, II 7 line 1057.
Comedy of Errors, III 2 lines 891, 894.
Coriolanus, I 9 line 821; Coriolanus, IV 6 line 3118; Coriolanus, V 1 line 3309.
Cymbeline, III 1 line 1426; Cymbeline, III 1 line 1449.
Hamlet, II 2 line 1648; Hamlet, IV 3 line 2746.
Henry IV, Part I, I 3 line 364; Henry IV, Part I, II 3 line 956; Henry IV, Part I, II 4 line 1294; Henry IV, Part I, III 3 line 2033; Henry IV, Part I, III 3 line 2087; Henry IV, Part I, IV 2 line 2415.
Henry IV, Part II, II 1 line 754; Henry IV, Part II, II 4 line 1627.
Henry V, II 3 line 847; Henry V, II 3 line 872; Henry V, III 6 lines 1569, 1571.
Henry VI, Part II, III 2 line 1714.
Henry VI, Part III, IV 7 line 2449.
Henry VIII, I 3 line 579; Henry VIII, III 2 line 1900; Henry VIII, V 4 lines 3312, 3315.
King Lear, III 2 line 1682.
Love's Labour's Lost, IV 2 line 1255.
Measure for Measure, II 2 line 881.
Midsummer Night's Dream, I 1 line 38; Midsummer Night's Dream, V 1 line 2176.
Much Ado About Nothing, V 1 line 2194.
Othello, I 3 line 758; Othello, III 1 line 1551; Othello, IV 1 line 2459; Othello, IV 1 line 2572; Othello, IV 2 line 2826.
Rape of Lucrece, line 1467.
Romeo and Juliet, I 4 lines 558, 567, 570.
Taming of the Shrew, V 1 line 2468.
Tempest, IV 1 line 1913; Tempest, IV 1 line 1943.
Timon of Athens, IV 3 line 1838.
Titus Andronicus, II 1 line 648.
Troilus and Cressida, I 2 line 258; Troilus and Cressida, III 1 line 1613; Troilus and Cressida, V 5 line 3491.
Twelfth Night, II 3 line 728; Twelfth Night, II 3 line 757; Twelfth Night, II 3 line 862; Twelfth Night, IV 1 line 1959.
Venus and Adonis, line 496.
Winter's Tale, I 2 line 199; Winter's Tale, I 2 line 388; Winter's Tale, II 1 line 615; Winter's Tale, II 1 line 779; Winter's Tale, II 3 line 1052; Winter's Tale, IV 3 line 1766; Winter's Tale, IV 4 line 2112; Winter's Tale, IV 4 line 2648; Winter's Tale, IV 4 line 2710; Winter's Tale, IV 4 line 2781.

Nostril: Old English: *nospyrl, nosðirl*, literally, the hole of the nose, from *nosu: nose*.
>**Cymbeline**, V 5 line 3951.
>**Henry V**, III 1 line 1116.
>**Henry VI, Part II**, III 2 line 1856.
>**Merry Wives of Windsor**, III 5 line 1830.
>**Pericles**, III 2 line 1360.
>**Tempest**, II 2 line 1154.
>**Venus and Adonis**, lines 293, 316.
>**Winter's Tale**, I 2 line 547.

Nut: Old English: *hnutu*. The nut that goes onto a bolt is first recorded 1610s, used of other small mechanical pieces since early 15c.
>**All's Well That Ends Well**, II 5 line 1305.
>**As You Like It**, III 2 lines 1220, 1221; As You Like It, III 4 line 1616.
>**Comedy of Errors**, IV 3 line 1222.
>**Midsummer Night's Dream**, IV 1 line 1580.
>**Romeo and Juliet**, III 1 line 1517.
>**Troilus and Cressida**, II 1 line 960.

Nutmeg: hard aromatic seed of the East Indies, c.1300, from Anglo-French: *noiz mugue*, from Old French: *nois muguete*, unexplained alteration of *nois muscade: nut smelling like musk*, from *nois*: nut. A gilt nutmeg was formerly a common gift at Christmas and on other festive occasions.
>**Henry V**, III 7 line 1659.
>**Love's Labour's Lost**, V 2 line 2587.
>**Winter's Tale**, IV 3 line 1772.

Nutshell: c.1200, *nute-scalen*; nut + shell. Figurative use with reference to great condensation (1570s) supposedly originally is a reference to a copy of the *Iliad*, mentioned by Pliny, which was so small it could fit into the shell of a nut.
>**Hamlet**, II 2 line 1354.
>**Tempest**, I 1 line 56.

Oak: Old English: *ac*. A crown of oak was considered by the Romans worthy of the highest emulation of statesmen and warriors. Oak is usually thought of as masculine, strength, protection, durability, and/or the human body.
>**As You Like It**, II 1 line 580; As You Like It, IV 3 line 2107.
>**Coriolanus**, I 1 line 183; Coriolanus, I 3 line 377; Coriolanus, II 1 line 1043; Coriolanus, II 1 line 1082; Coriolanus, II 2 line 1345; Coriolanus, V 2 line 3487; Coriolanus, V 3 line 3664.
>**Cymbeline**, IV 2 line 2666.
>**Henry VI, Part III**, II 1 line 682.
>**Julius Caesar**, I 3 line 427.
>**King Lear**, III 2 line 1682.
>**Love's Labour's Lost**, IV 2 line 1254.
>**Measure for Measure**, II 2 line 881.

Merry Wives of Windsor, IV 1 line 2226; Merry Wives of Windsor, IV 4 line 2235; Merry Wives of Windsor, IV 4 line 2238; Merry Wives of Windsor, IV 6 line 2441; Merry Wives of Windsor, V 1 line 2490; Merry Wives of Windsor, V 3 line 2541; Merry Wives of Windsor, V 3 line 2551r; Merry Wives of Windsor, V 5 line 2640.
Midsummer Night's Dream, I 2 line 364.
Much Ado About Nothing, II 1 line 621.
Othello, II 1 line 771; Othello, III 3 line 1864.
Passionate Pilgrim, line 60.
Rape of Lucrece, line 1001.
Taming of the Shrew, V 1 line 2468.
Tempest, I 2 line 432; Tempest, V 1 line 2066.
Timon of Athens, IV 3 line 1959; Timon of Athens, IV 3 line 2131.
Troilus and Cressida, I 3 line 500.
Winter's Tale, II 3 line 1041.

Oaten: cereal plant, with loose clusters of florets. Old English: *ate*, plural *atan*, of unknown origin. Unlike other names of cereals (such as wheat, barley, etc.), oat is not a mass noun and may originally have denoted the individual grain, which may imply that oats were eaten in grains and not as meal.
Henry IV, Part I, II 1 line 654.
King Lear, V 3 line 3164.
Love's Labour's Lost, V 2 line 2851.
Midsummer Night's Dream, IV 1 line 1577.
Taming of the Shrew, III 2 line 1572.
Tempest, IV 1 line 1771.

Ocean: late 13c., from Old French: *occean* (12c.), from Latin: *oceanus*, from Greek: *okeanos*, the great river or sea surrounding the disk of the Earth (as opposed to the Mediterranean), of unknown origin. Personified as Oceanus, son of Uranus and Gaia and husband of Tethys. In early times, when the only known land masses were Eurasia and Africa, the ocean was an endless river that flowed around them. Until c.1650, commonly ocean sea, translating Latin: *mare oceanum*. Application to individual bodies of water began 14c.; there are usually reckoned to be five of them, but this is arbitrary; also occasionally applied to smaller subdivisions. The ocean can also be seen as a symbol of stability, as it can exist largely unchanged for centuries. The ocean is considered to be boundless, a place where one can easily be lost, and can therefore be seen to represent the boundless span of life, and the way one can get lost on the journey through life.
Antony and Cleopatra, II 6 line 1234; Antony and Cleopatra, II 7 line 1456; Antony and Cleopatra, V 2 line 3490.
Comedy of Errors, I 2 line 200.
Cymbeline, I 2 line 249.
Hamlet, IV 5 line 2963.
Henry IV, Part II, III 1 line 1755.
Henry V, Prologue 1 line 23; Henry V, III 1 line 1105.
Henry VI, Part II, III 2 line 1826.
Henry VI, Part III, IV 8 line 2541.

Julius Caesar, I 3 line 428.
King John, II 1 line 314; King John, II 1 line 650; King John, IV 3 line 2161; King John, V 4 line 2545.
Lover's Complaint, line 257.
Macbeth, II 2 line 724.
Merchant of Venice, I 1 line 9.
Merry Wives of Windsor, II 2 line 929.
Rape of Lucrece, lines 640, 706, 1282.
Richard II, II 2 line 1146.
Richard III, I 1 line 5.
Sonnet LVI line 9; Sonnet LXIV line 5; Sonnet LXXX line 5.
Titus Andronicus, II 1 line 453; Titus Andronicus, IV 2 line 1791; Titus Andronicus, IV 2 line 1830; Titus Andronicus, IV 3 line 1888.
Two Gentlemen of Verona, II 7 line 1007; Two Gentlemen of Verona, II 7 line 1044.
Venus and Adonis, line 516.

Offal: late 14c., waste parts, refuse, from off + fall; the notion being that which *falls off* the butcher's block
    Hamlet, II 2 line 1654.
    Julius Caesar, I 3 line 537.
    Merry Wives of Windsor, III 5 line 1751.

Oil: late 12c., olive oil, from Anglo-French from Old French: *oile*. It meant olive oil exclusively till c.1300, when meaning began to be extended to any fatty, greasy substance. Use for petroleum first recorded 1520s, but not common until 19c. The artist's oils (1660s), short for oil-colour (1530s), are paints made by grinding pigment in oil.
    All's Well That Ends Well, I 2 line 301; All's Well That Ends Well, V 3 line 2680.
    Comedy of Errors, IV 1 line 1043.
    Henry IV, Part I, I 3 line 329.
    Henry VI, Part I, I 1 line 88.
    Henry VI, Part II, II 5 line 1083; Henry VI, Part II, V 2 line 3272.
    Henry VIII, IV 1 line 2517.
    King Lear, II 2 line 1144.
    Merry Wives of Windsor, II 1 line 627; Merry Wives of Windsor, V 5 line 2596.
    Tempest, II 1 line 862.
    Timon of Athens, I 2 line 480.
    Troilus and Cressida, I 1 line 91.
    Venus and Adonis, line 778.
    Winter's Tale, III 2 line 1412.

Olives: c.1200, olive tree, from Old French: *olive*, from Latin: *oliva: olive, olive tree*. Applied to the fruit or berry of the tree in English from late 14c. Olive branch as a token of peace is from early 13c. This plant ever famous from its association with the return of the dove to the oak, has been considered typical of peace.

Antony and Cleopatra, IV 6 line 2711.
As You Like It, III 5 line 1728; As You Like It, IV 3 line 2079.
Henry IV, Part II, IV 4 line 2836.
Henry VI, Part III, IV 6 line 2348.
Sonnet CVII line 8.
Timon of Athens, V 4 line 2656.
Twelfth Night, I 5 line 501.

Onion: early 12c., from Anglo-French: *union*, Old French: *oignon* (formerly also *oingnon*), one, unity; sense connection is the successive layers of an onion, in contrast with garlic or cloves.
All's Well That Ends Well, V 3 line 3041.
Antony and Cleopatra, I 2 line 264.
Midsummer Night's Dream, IV 2 line 1823.
Taming of the Shrew, Prologue 1 line 133.

Onion-eyed: having eyes full of tears.
Antony and Cleopatra, IV 2 line 2563.

Opal: 1590s, from French: *opalle*, from Latin: *opalus* (Pliny), supposedly gem, precious stone. Used in Middle English in Latin form (late 14c).
Lover's Complaint, line 216.
Twelfth Night, II 4 line 970.

Orange: c.1300, from Old French: *orenge* (12c.). The tree's original range probably was northern India. The Persian orange, grown widely in southern Europe after its introduction in Italy 11c., was bitter; sweet oranges were brought to Europe 15c. from India by Portuguese traders and quickly displaced the bitter variety, but only Modern Greek still seems to distinguish the bitter (*nerantzi*) from the sweet (*portokali: Portuguese*) orange. Portuguese, Spanish, Arab, and Dutch sailors planted citrus trees along trade routes to prevent scurvy. On his second voyage in 1493, Christopher Columbus brought the seeds of oranges, lemons and citrons to Haiti and the Caribbean. Introduced in Florida (along with lemons) in 1513 by Spanish explorer Juan Ponce de Leon. Not used as the name of a colour until 1540s.
Coriolanus, II 1 line 985.
Midsummer Night's Dream, I 2 line 349; Midsummer Night's Dream, III 1 line 947.
Much Ado About Nothing, II 1 line 672; Much Ado About Nothing, IV 1 line 1672.
Winter's Tale, IV 4 line 2191.

Orchard: Old English: *orceard: fruit garden*, (the word also meant, vegetable garden, until 15c.)
As You Like It, I 1 line 36.
Hamlet, I 5 line 772; Hamlet, I 5 line 797.
Henry IV, Part II, I 1 line 49; Henry IV, Part II, V 3 line 3395.
Julius Caesar, III 2 line 1793.
King John, V 7 line 2638.

Lover's Complaint, line 173.
Much Ado About Nothing, I 2 line 311; Much Ado About Nothing, II 3 line 817; Much Ado About Nothing, III 1 line 1077; Much Ado About Nothing, III 3 line 1463; Much Ado About Nothing, V 1 line 2309.
Romeo and Juliet, II 1 line 803; Romeo and Juliet, II 2 line 912.
Taming of the Shrew, II 1 line 955.
Troilus and Cressida, III 2 line 1665.
Twelfth Night, III 2 line 1411; Twelfth Night, III 4 line 1716; Twelfth Night, III 4 line 1768.

Organs: Old English: *organe*, and Old French: *orgene* (12c.), both meaning musical instrument, from Greek: organon: *implement, musical instrument, organ of the body*, literally, that with which one works. Applied vaguely in late Old English to musical instruments; sense narrowed by late 14c. to the musical instrument now known by that name (involving pipes supplied with wind by a bellows and worked by means of keys), though Augustine (c.400) knew this as a specific sense of Latin: *organa*. The meaning *body part adapted to a certain function* is attested from late 14c.
    All's Well That Ends Well, II 1 line 787.
    Antony and Cleopatra, II 7 line 1422.
    Hamlet, II 2 line 1679; Hamlet, III 2 line 2248; Hamlet, IV 7 line 3208.
    Henry V, IV 1 line 1864.
    King Lear, I 4 line 806.
    Merchant of Venice, III 1 line 1293.
    Merry Wives of Windsor, V 5 line 2616.
    Much Ado About Nothing, IV 1 line 1878.
    Troilus and Cressida, V 2 line 3195.
    Twelfth Night, I 4 line 281.

Osier: species of willow used in basket-work, c.1300, from Old French: *osier: willow twig*.
    As You Like It, IV 3 line 2081.
    Love's Labour's Lost, IV 2 line 1256.
    Passionate Pilgrim, lines 60, 76.
    Romeo and Juliet, II 3 line 1065.

Osprey: This bird, also called the sea-eagle, has a destructive power of devouring fish. Fishing hawk, mid-15c., from Anglo-French: *ospriet*, a generic term apparently confused with this specific bird in Old French on its similarity to *ossifrage*.
    Coriolanus, IV 7 line 3252.

Ostrich: early 13c., from Old French: *ostruce,* from Latin: *avis: bird*, from Greek: *strouthion: ostrich*, from *strouthos megale: big sparrow*. The Greeks also knew the bird as *strouthokamelos: camel-sparrow*, for its long neck. Among its proverbial peculiarities are indiscriminate voracity (especially a habit of swallowing iron and stone to aid digestion), want of regard for its eggs, and a tendency to hide its head in the sand when pursued. The

extraordinary digestion of this bird is said to be shown by its swallowing iron and other hard substances.
    Henry VI, Part II, IV 10 line 2916.

Otter: Old English: o*tr, otor.*
    Henry IV, Part I, III 3 line 2136; Henry IV, Part I, III 3 line 2137r.

Ounce: wildcat or tiger c.1300, from Old French *once*: lynx (13c.)
    Midsummer Night's Dream, II 2 line 683.

Ousel: similar to a blackbird; ale of the species. Od English: *osle*.
    Henry IV, Part II, III 2 line 1827.
    Midsummer Night's Dream, III 1 line 946.

Owl: The dread attached to this unfortunate bird is frequently spoken of by Shakespeare, who has alluded to several of the superstitions associated with it. At the outset, many of the epithets ascribed to it show the prejudice with which it was regarded; being in various places stigmatised. From the earliest period it has been considered a bird of ill-omen, and Pliny tells how, on one occasion, even Rome itself underwent a lustration, because one of them strayed into the city. He represents it also as a funereal bird, a monster of the night, the very abomination of human kind. Virgil describes its death-howl from the top of the temple by night, a circumstance introduced as a precursor of Dido's death. Ovid, too, constantly speaks of this bird's presence as an evil omen; and indeed the same notions respecting it may be found among the writings of most of the classical poets. This superstitious awe in which the owl is held may be owing to its peculiar look, its occasional and uncertain appearance, its loud and dismal cry, as well as to its being the bird of night. It has generally been associated with calamities and deeds of darkness. From Old English: *ule*.
    Comedy of Errors, II 2 line 579.
    Cymbeline, III 6 line 2260.
    Hamlet, IV 5 line 2904.
    Henry VI, Part I, IV 2 line 1981.
    Henry VI, Part III, V 4 line 2860; Henry VI, Part III, V 6 line 3039.
    Love's Labour's Lost, IV 1 line 1124; Love's Labour's Lost, V 2 line 2832; Love's Labour's Lost, V 2 line 2839.
    Macbeth, II 2 line 650; Macbeth, II 2 line 666; Macbeth, II 4 line 962; Macbeth, IV 2 line 1751.
    Midsummer Night's Dream, II 2 line 655.
    Richard III, IV 4 line 3337.
    Tempest, V 1 line 2120.
    Titus Andronicus, II 3 line 833.
    Troilus and Cressida, II 1 line 949; Troilus and Cressida, V 1 line 2993.
    Venus and Adonis, line 552.

Ox: said to be from root *uks: to sprinkle*, related to *ugw: wet, moist*. The animal word, then, is literally, besprinkler.

As You Like It, I 1 line 9; As You Like It, III 3 line 1568.
Henry IV, Part I, II 4 line 1435.
Henry VI, Part II, IV 2 line 2331.
Love's Labour's Lost, V 2 line 2159.
Merry Wives of Windsor, V 5 line 2695.
Midsummer Night's Dream, II 1 line 462.
Taming of the Shrew, III 2 line 1598.
Troilus and Cressida, V 1 lines 2990, 2991r.

Oxen: plural of ox.
Henry IV, Part I, V 2 line 2784.
Henry VI, Part I, I 5 line 616; Henry VI, Part I, V 5 line 2907.
Henry VI, Part II, IV 3 line 2503; Henry VI, Part I, V 1 line 3004.
Taming of the Shrew, II 1 line 1211.
Twelfth Night, III 2 line 1461.

Oxlips: woodland primula. Old English: *oxanslyppe*.
Midsummer Night's Dream, II 1 line 629.
Winter's Tale, IV 4 line 2004.

Oyster: mid-14c., from Old French: *oistre*.
Antony and Cleopatra, I 5 line 572.
As You Like It, V 4 line 2464.
King Lear, I 5 line 901.
Merry Wives of Windsor, II 2 line 797.
Much Ado About Nothing, II 3 lines 837, 838.
Richard II, I 4 line 644.
Taming of the Shrew, IV 2 line 1935.

Paddock: see *toad*.
Hamlet, III 4 line 2894.
Macbeth, I 1 line 11.

Palm: tropical tree, Old English: *palma*, Old French: *palme*, both from Latin: *palma: palm tree*, originally *palm of the hand*; the tree so called from the shape of its leaves, like fingers of a hand. In ancient times, a leaf or frond was carried or worn as a symbol of victory or triumph, or on feast days; hence figurative use of palm for victory, triumph (late 14c.).
As You Like It, III 2 line 1284.
Coriolanus, V 2 line 3415.
Winter's Tale, I 2 line 190.

Parasite:
Parasites exist in huge variety and include animals, plants, and microorganisms. They may live as ectoparasites on the surface of the host (e.g. arthropods such as ticks, mites, lice, fleas, and many insects infesting plants) or as endoparasites in the gut or tissues (e.g. many kinds of worm), and cause varying degrees of damage or disease to the host. 1530s, a hanger-on,

a toady: *person who lives on others*, from Greek: *parasitos: person who eats at the table of another.*
>   **Coriolanus**, I 9 line 818.
>   **Richard II**, II 2 line 1066.
>   **Timon of Athens**, III 6 line 1534.
>   **Venus and Adonis**, line 870.
>   **Winter's Tale**, I 2 line 251.

Pard: archaic form of leopard, c.1300, from Latin: *pardus*, from Greek: *pardos: male panther*, from the same source, probably Iranian.
>   **As You Like It**, II 7 line 1048.
>   **Midsummer Night's Dream**, II 2 line 683.
>   **Tempest**, IV 1 line 2007.
>   **Troilus and Cressida**, III 2 line 1845.

Park: mid-13c., enclosed preserve for beasts of the chase, from Old French: *parc*. Evidence suggests a West Germanic word that is pre-4c. and originally meant the fencing, not the place enclosed. Found also in Medieval Latin as *parricus: enclosure, park* (8c.), which is likely the direct source of the Old French word.
>   **Cymbeline**, III 1 line 1432.
>   **Henry IV, Part I**, II 3 line 934.
>   **Henry VI, Part I**, I 1 line 88.
>   **Henry VI, Part III**, IV 5 line 2282; Henry VI, Part III, V 2 line 2746.
>   **Love's Labour's Lost**, I 1 line 210; Love's Labour's Lost, I 1 line 239; Love's Labour's Lost, I 2 line 416; Love's Labour's Lost, I 2 line 427; Love's Labour's Lost, III 1 line 926; Love's Labour's Lost, IV 3 line 1719.
>   **Merchant of Venice**, III 4 line 1837.
>   **Merry Wives of Windsor**, I 4 line 511; Merry Wives of Windsor, III 3 line 1612; Merry Wives of Windsor, IV 4 line 2213; Merry Wives of Windsor, V 1 line 2490; Merry Wives of Windsor, V 3 line 2531.
>   **Midsummer Night's Dream**, II 1 line 371.
>   **Richard II**, III 1 line 1382.
>   **Taming of the Shrew**, IV 1 line 1729.
>   **Titus Andronicus**, III 1 line 1218.
>   **Venus and Adonis**, lines 251, 259.

Partridge: Middle English: *partrich*, from Old French: *pertriz, perdriz*, from Latin: *perdix*. probably related to Greek: *perdesthai: to break wind*, in reference to the whirring noise of the bird's wings.
>   **Henry VI, Part II**, III 2 line 1876.
>   **Much Ado About Nothing**, II 1 line 533.

Parrot: 1520s, replacing *popinjay*. To repeat without understanding, 1590s. Supposedly restless before rain.
>   **As You Like It**, IV 1 line 1925.
>   **Comedy of Errors**, IV 4 line 1291.
>   **Henry IV, Part I**, II 4 line 1090.
>   **Henry IV, Part II**, II 4 line 1548.

Merchant of Venice, I 1 line 57; Merchant of Venice, III 5 line 1884.
Much Ado About Nothing, I 1 line 125.
Othello, II 3 line 1433.
Troilus and Cressida, V 2 line 3270.

Pasture: c.1300, from Old French: *pasture: grass eaten by cattle*.
Antony and Cleopatra, I 4 line 495.
As You Like It, II 1 line 603; As You Like It, II 4 line 806; As You Like It, II 4 line 810; As You Like It, III 2 line 1147.
Cymbeline, V 4 line 3137.
Henry V, II 0 line 468; Henry V, III 1 line 1118.
Love's Labour's Lost, II 1 line 718; Love's Labour's Lost, II 1 line 719.
Richard II, III 3 line 1740.
Timon of Athens, IV 3 line 1675.
Two Gentlemen of Verona, I 1 line 101.

Pate: top of the head, late 12c., perhaps a shortened form of Old French: *patene*.
All's Well That Ends Well, II 1 line 665.
Comedy of Errors, I 2 line 230; Comedy of Errors, I 2 line 246; Comedy of Errors, II 1 line 351; Comedy of Errors, II 2 line 462; Comedy of Errors, II 2 line 608; Comedy of Errors, III 1 line 707.
Cymbeline, II 1 line 856.
Hamlet, II 2 line 1644; Hamlet, V 1 line 3420; Hamlet, V 1 line 3448; Hamlet, V 1 line 3626.
Henry IV, Part I, II 2 line 670; Henry IV, Part I, V 3 line 2915.
Henry V, IV 1 line 1900; Henry V, V 1 line 2928; Henry V, V 1 line 2944; Henry V, V 1 line 2951; Henry V, V 2 line 3144.
Henry VI, Part I, III 1 line 1309.
Henry VI, Part II, V 1 line 3124.
King John, II 1 line 883.
Merry Wives of Windsor, II 1 line 746.
Othello, II 1 line 915.
Romeo and Juliet, IV 5 line 2777.
Taming of the Shrew, I 2 line 563; Taming of the Shrew, II 1 line 998.
Tempest, IV 1 line 1985.
Timon of Athens, IV 3 line 1682.
Winter's Tale, I 2 line 319.

Pea: early or mid-17c., false singular from Middle English *pease* (plural *pesen*), which was both single and collective (e.g. wheat, corn) but the *s* sound was mistaken for the plural inflection. From Old English *pise* (West Saxon), *piose* (Mercian) pea, from Late Latin: *pisa*, variant of Latin *pisum* from Greek *pison*: *the pea*, perhaps of Thracian or Phrygian origin.
Midsummer Night's Dream, IV 1 line 1581.

Peach: late 12c., from Old French: *pesche*, from *persica: peach, peach tree*.
Henry IV, Part I, II 2 line 784.

Peaches**: used as a verb *peaches* as a quibble on the *peach-coloured satin* and as a familiar form of *impeaches*.
    Measure for Measure, IV 3 line 2127.

Peacock: c.1300, *poucock*, from Middle English: *po: peacock*. Used as the type of a vainglorious person from late 14c. Its flesh superstitiously believed to be incorruptible. This bird was as proverbially used for a proud, vain fool as the *lapwing* for a silly one.
    Comedy of Errors, IV 3 line 1229.
    Henry V, IV 1 line 2048.
    Henry VI, Part 1, III 3 line 1611.
    Tempest, IV 1 line 1784.
    Troilus and Cressida, III 3 line 2135.

Pear: Old English: *pere, peru*. In his few notices of the pear, Shakespeare only mentions two by name, the *warden* and the *poperin*, the former was chiefly used for roasting or baking.
    All's Well That Ends Well, I 2 lines 163, 164, 165.
    Henry V, IV 8 line 2744.
    Merry Wives of Windsor, IV 5 line 2393.
    Romeo and Juliet, II 1 line 837.

Pearl: mid-13c., from Old French: *perle* (13c.), Latin: *perna* in Sicily, *pearl*, earlier *sea-mussel*, so called for the shape of the mollusk shells. Another theory connects it with the root of pear, also somehow based on shape. The pearl is a symbol of perfection and incorruptibility; it is a symbol of long life and fertility, and because of its lustre it is often considered to be associated with the Moon. Buried within the oyster shell, the pearl represents hidden knowledge, and it is highly feminine. Also, a cataract of the eye.
    Antony and Cleopatra, I 5 line 568; Antony and Cleopatra, II 5 line 1105.
    As You Like It, V 4 line 2462.
    Hamlet, V 2 line 3930.
    Henry IV, Part II, II 4 line 1291.
    Henry V, IV 1 line 2107.
    Henry VIII, IV 1 line 2443.
    King John, II 1 line 467.
    King Lear, IV 3 line 2470.
    Love's Labour's Lost, IV 2 line 1235; Love's Labour's Lost, V 2 line 1935; Love's Labour's Lost, V 2 line 2385.
    Lover's Complaint, line 199.
    Macbeth, V 8 line 2544.
    Merchant of Venice, III 2 line 1515.
    Merry Wives of Windsor, V 5 line 2636.
    Midsummer Night's Dream, I 1 line 219; Midsummer Night's Dream, II 1 line 382; Midsummer Night's Dream, IV 1 line 1601.
    Much Ado About Nothing, III 4 line 1509.
    Othello, V 2 line 3714.

Passionate Pilgrim, line 134.
Rape of Lucrece, lines 1264, 1604.
Richard III, I 4 line 859; Richard III, IV 4 line 3129.
Sonnet XXXIV line 13.
Taming of the Shrew, Prologue 2 line 186; Taming of the Shrew, II 1 line 1206; Taming of the Shrew, V 1 line 2415.
Tempest, I 2 line 561.
Titus Andronicus, II 1 line 565; Titus Andronicus, V 1 line 2175.
Troilus and Cressida, I 1 line 130; Troilus and Cressida, II 2 line 1073.
Twelfth Night, IV 3 line 2153.
Two Gentlemen of Verona, II 4 line 830; Two Gentlemen of Verona, III 1 line 1298; Two Gentlemen of Verona, V 2 lines 2076, 2077; Two Gentlemen of Verona, V 2 line 2078.
Venus and Adonis, line 1002.

Peas: 17c., false singular from Middle English: *pease* (pl. *pesen*), which was both single and collective (e.g. wheat, corn) but was mistaken for a plural, from Old English: *pise* (W.Saxon), *piose* (Mercian). A practice called *peascod wooing* was formerly a common mode of divination in love affairs. The cook, when shelling green peas, would, if she chanced to find a pod having nine, lay it on the lintel of the kitchen door, and the first man who entered was supposed to be her future husband. Another way of divination by *peascod* consisted in the lover selecting one growing on the stem, snatching it away quickly, and if the good omen of the peas remaining in the husk were preserved, in then presenting it to the lady of his choice.
Henry IV, Part I, II 1 line 651.
Midsummer Night's Dream, IV 1 line 1581.

Peascod: 14c., the pod of a pea plant.
As You Like It, II 4 line 768.
Henry IV, Part II, II 4 line 1696.
King Lear, I 4 line 721.
Midsummer Night's Dream, III 1 line 1012.
Twelfth Night, I 5 line 449.

Pease: see, pea.
Love's Labour's Lost, V 2 line 2233.
Tempest, IV 1 line 1771.

Pebble: late 13c., from Old English: *papolstan*: pebblestone, of unknown origin.
Coriolanus, V 3 line 3558.
Hamlet, V 1 line 3563.
Henry VI, Part I, III 1 line 1307.
Henry VIII, V 4 line 3328.
King Lear, IV 6 line 2621.
Merry Wives of Windsor, IV 1 line 1920.
Two Gentlemen of Verona, II 3 line 602.

Pebbled: adjective of pebble.
Sonnet LX line 1.

Pelican: There are several allusions by Shakespeare to the pelican's piercing her own breast to feed her young. According to another idea, pelicans are hatched dead, but the cock pelican then wounds his breast, and lets one drop of blood fall upon each, and this quickens them.
Hamlet, IV 5 line 3021.
King Lear, III 4 line 1874.
Richard II, II 1 line 810.

Pepper: Old English *pipor*, from an early West Germanic borrowing of Latin *piper*, from Greek *piperi*, probably (via Persian) from Middle Indic *pippari*, from Sanskrit *pippali*: long pepper. The Latin word is the source of German *Pfeffer*, Italian *pepe*, French *poivre*, Old Church Slavonic *pipru*, Lithuanian *pipiras*, Old Irish *piobhar*, Welsh *pybyr*, etc. Application to fruits of the capsicum family (unrelated, originally native of tropical America) is 16c.
Henry VI, Part I, II 4 line 1178; Henry VI, Part I, III 1 line 1808; Henry VI, Part I, V 3 line 2920.
Romeo and Juliet, III 1 line 1604.
Twelfth Night, III 4 line 1687.

Pepper-box: pepper + box, from 1540s.
Merry Wives of Windsor, III 5 line 1884.

Peppercorn: Old English, the dried berry of the climbing vine.
Henry IV, Part I, III 3 line 2016.

Pestilence: c.1300, from Old French: *pestilence*, from Latin: *pestilentia*: plague, noun of action from *pestilentem*: infected, unwholesome, noxious, from *pestis*: deadly disease, plague.
Antony and Cleopatra, II 5 line 1126; Antony and Cleopatra, III 10 line 2074.
Coriolanus, IV 3 line 2535.
Hamlet, V 1 line 3510.
Henry VIII, V 1 line 2830.
Much Ado About Nothing, I 1 line 75.
Othello, II 3 line 1508.
Richard II, I 3 line 585; Richard II, III 3 line 1728.
Romeo and Juliet, V 2 line 2910.
Troilus and Cressida, IV 2 line 2312.
Twelfth Night, I 1 line 22.
Two Gentlemen of Verona, II 1 line 420.
Venus and Adonis, line 762.

Pettitoes: pig's trotters; or human toes, especially those of a child. First use: 1555. Old French: *petite oye:* goose giblets.
Winter's Tale, IV 4 line 2568.

Pheasant: late 13c., from Anglo-French: *fesaunt*, Old French: *faisan* (13c.), from Latin: *phasianus*, from Greek: *phasianos: a pheasant*, from Phasis, river flowing into the Black Sea in Colchis, where the birds were said to have been numerous.
    Winter's Tale, IV 4 line 2720; Winter's Tale, IV 4 line 2722.

Pia-mater: membrane that covers the brain.
    Troilus and Cressida, II 1 line 928.
    Twelfth Night, I 5 line 407.

Pig: probably from Old English: *picg*. Originally, young pig (the word for adults was swine). Another Old English: word for pig was *fearh*, related to *furh: furrow*. Synonyms grunter, porker are from sailors' and fishermen's euphemistic avoidance of uttering the word pig at sea, a superstition perhaps based on the fate of the Gadarene swine, who drowned. The meaning *oblong piece of metal* is first attested 1580s, on the notion of a large mass.
    Comedy of Errors, I 2 line 209; Comedy of Errors, II 1 line 339.
    Henry IV, Part II, II 4 line 1507.
    Henry V, IV 7 line 2531; Henry V, IV 7 line 2533r.
    Macbeth, IV 1 line 1549.
    Merchant of Venice, IV 1 lines 1979, 1986.
    Romeo and Juliet, I 4 line 589.
    Titus Andronicus, IV 2 line 1838.

Pigeon: early 13c., from Old French: *pijon: young dove*. As carriers these birds have been used from a very early date.
    As You Like It, I 2 line 223; As You Like It, III 3 line 1569; As You Like It, IV 1 line 1923.
    Hamlet, II 2 line 1651.
    Henry IV, Part II, V 1 line 3157; Henry IV, Part II, V 1 line 3168.
    Love's Labour's Lost, V 1 line 1802; Love's Labour's Lost, V 2 line 2233.
    Merchant of Venice, II 6 line 914.
    Titus Andronicus, IV 3 line 1961; Titus Andronicus, IV 3 line 1973; Titus Andronicus, IV 3 line 1977; Titus Andronicus, IV 3 line 1981; Titus Andronicus, IV 3 line 1987; Titus Andronicus, IV 3 line 1995; Titus Andronicus, IV 4 line 2055.

Pigmies: late 14c., *Pigmei: member of a fabulous race of dwarfs*, described by Homer and Herodotus and said to inhabit Egypt or Ethiopia and India. Believed in 17c. to refer to chimpanzees or orangutans.
    King John, V 2 line 2417.
    Much Ado About Nothing, II 1 line 650.

Pignut: almond flavoured tuber, favoured by pigs.
    Tempest, II 2 line 1254.

Pilchard: fish of the herring family, 1540s, earlier *pilcher* (1520s), of unknown origin.
Twelfth Night, III 1 line 1267.

Pin and Web: a disease of the eye.
Winter's Tale, I 2 line 394.

Pin-buttock: narrow buttocks.
All's Well That Ends Well, II 2 line 841.

Pinch-spotted: bruised due to pinching the flesh.
Tempest, IV 1 line 2006.

Pine: Old English: *pintreow*. Also, Old English *pinian* to torture, torment, afflict, cause to suffer, from *pine* pain, torture, punishment, possibly ultimately from Latin *poena:* punishment, penalty, from Greek *poine*. Intransitive sense of to languish, waste away, the main modern meaning, is first recorded early 14c.
Antony and Cleopatra, IV 12 line 2899; Antony and Cleopatra, IV 12 line 2928.
Cymbeline, IV 2 line 2546.
Henry VI, Part I, II 5 line 1135.
Henry VI, Part II, II 3 line 1090.
Love's Labour's Lost, I 1 line 27; Love's Labour's Lost, I 1 line 33.
Lover's Complaint, line 278.
Macbeth, I 3 line 120; Macbeth, III 6 line 1529.
Merchant of Venice, IV 1 line 2007.
Pericles, I 2 line 266.
Rape of Lucrece, lines 846, 956, 1166r, 1218.
Richard II, III 2 line 1450; Richard II, III 2 line 1621; Richard II, .
Sonnet LXXV line 13; Sonnet CXXXXVI lines 3, 10.
Taming of the Shrew, I 1 line 446.
Tempest, I 2 line 413; Tempest, I 2 line 430; Tempest, V 1 line 2069.
Troilus and Cressida, I 3 line 458.
Venus and Adonis, line 623.
Winter's Tale, II 1 line 642.

Pip: shortened form of *pipin: seed of a fleshy fruit* (c.1300), from Old French: *pepin* (13c). Also, a disease of birds, (15c).
Taming of the Shrew, I 2 line 584.

Pippins: from coveted varieties of apple that were raised from seed (so called since early 15c).
Henry IV, Part II, V 3 line 3396.
Merry Wives of Windsor, I 2 line 282.

Pioned: abounding with marsh marigolds.
Tempest, IV 1 line 1774.

Pismire: An ancient name for the ant, probably a Danish word, from *paid* and *myre*, signifying such ants as live in hillocks.
>**Henry IV, Part I**, I 3 line 575.

Pizzle: penis of a bull, usually used for flogging; late 15th cent.: from Low German *pesel* or Flemish: *pezel*.
>**Henry IV, Part I**, II 4 line 1230.

Plain: Middle English: from Old French: *plain*, from Latin: *planus*, from a base meaning, flat.
>**Henry IV, Part I**, I 1 line 71.
>**Henry V**, IV 6 line 2484.
>**Henry VI, Part II**, I 4 line 669; Henry VI, Part II, I 4 line 706.
>**Henry VIII**, V 5 line 3438.
>**King John**, II 1 line 599.
>**King Lear**, II 2 line 1150.
>**Passionate Pilgrim**, line 291.
>**Richard II**, III 3 line 1687.
>**Richard III**, V 3 line 3804.
>**Titus Andronicus**, II 2 line 727.
>**Troilus and Cressida**, I 0 line 13; Troilus and Cressida, I 3 line 532; Troilus and Cressida, V 10 line 3656.
>**Venus and Adonis**, line 256.

Plantain: banana from 1550s. Also, weed of the genus *Plantago*, mid-13c., from Anglo-French: *plaunteyne*, Old French: *plantain*. The leaves of this plant were carefully valued by our forefathers for their supposed efficacy in healing wounds. It was also considered as a preventive of poison.
>**Love's Labour's Lost**, III 1 lines 836r, 837; Love's Labour's Lost, III 1 line 870.
>**Romeo and Juliet**, I 2 line 325.

Plants: Old English: *plante: young tree or shrub, herb newly planted*, from Latin: *planta: sprout, shoot, cutting*, perhaps from *plantare: to drive in with the feet, push into the ground with the feet*, from *planta: sole of the foot*.
>**Antony and Cleopatra**, II 7 line 1373.
>**As You Like It**, III 2 line 1446.
>**Coriolanus**, V 6 line 3845.
>**Henry IV, Part I**, I 1 line 83; Henry IV, Part I, I 3 line 506.
>**Henry VI, Part III**, V 5 line 2962.
>**Henry VIII**, III 1 line 1626.
>**Julius Caesar**, III 2 line 1793.
>**Love's Labour's Lost**, IV 2 line 1170.
>**Lover's Complaint**, line 172.
>**Passionate Pilgrim**, lines 263, 380.
>**Pericles**, I 2 line 294.
>**Richard II**, III 4 line 1968.
>**Richard III**, IV 4 line 3208.
>**Romeo and Juliet**, II 3 lines 1074, 1087.

Sonnet XV line 4.
Tempest, IV 1 line 1829.
Venus and Adonis, line 185.

Plum: Old English: *plume*.
Hamlet, II 2 line 1303.
Henry VI, Part II, II 1 line 840.
King John, II 1 line 459.
Passionate Pilgrim, line 136.
Venus and Adonis, line 548.

Polecat: early 14c., first element is probably Anglo-French: *pol*, from Old French: *poule: fowl, hen*, so called because it preys on poultry. The other alternative is that the first element is from Old French: *pulent: stinking*, for obvious reasons. This animal is supposed to be very amorous; and hence its name.
Merry Wives of Windsor, IV 1 line 1915r; Merry Wives of Windsor, IV 2 line 2141.

Poll: to cut, trim, late 14c., to cut short the hair (of an animal or person). Of trees or plants from 1570s.
All's Well That Ends Well, IV 3 line 2255.
Coriolanus, III 1 line 1893; Coriolanus, IV 5 line 2972.
Hamlet, IV 5 line 3071.
Henry IV, Part II, II 4 line 1547.
Love's Labour's Lost, V 2 line 2518.

Pomewater: a kind of sweet, species evidently of a juicy nature, and hence of high esteem in Shakespeare's time.
Love's Labour's Lost, IV 2 line 1145.

Pomegranate: early 14c., *poumgarnet*, from Old French: *pome grenate*, from *pomum granatum*, literally, apple with many seeds, from *pome: apple, fruit* + *grenate: having grains*, from Latin: *granata*.
All's Well That Ends Well, II 3 line 1160.
Romeo and Juliet, III 5 line 2101.

Pond: mid-13c., artificially banked body of water, variant of *pound: enclosed place*.
All's Well That Ends Well, V 2 line 2635.
Cymbeline, I 4 line 406.
Henry IV, Part II, I 1 line 258.
Measure for Measure, III 1 line 1324.
Merchant of Venice, I 1 line 95.
Winter's Tale, I 2 line 286.

Pool: small body of water, Old English: *pol*.
Cymbeline, III 4 line 1879.
Henry VI, Part II, IV 1 line 2226r.

King Lear, III 4 line 1927.
Tempest, IV 1 line 1918; Tempest, IV 1 line 1951.

Poor-John: salted hake.
Tempest, II 2 line 1112.

Poperin: a sort of pear from Poperingue, a town in French Flanders.

Romeo and Juliet, II 1 line 837.

Popinjay: late 13c., a parrot, from Old French *papegai* (12c.), from Spanish *papagayo*, possibly formed in an African or other non-Indo-European language and imitative of its cry. Ending probably assimilated in Western European languages to *jay* words (Old French jai, etc.). Used of people in a complimentary sense (in allusion to beauty and rarity) from early 14c.; meaning *vain, talkative person* is first recorded 1520s. Obsolete figurative sense of *a target to shoot at*.
Henry IV, Part I, I 2 line 157.

Poppy: Old English: *popæg*.
Othello, III 3 line 2005.

Pork: early 13c., flesh of a pig as food, from Latin: *porcus: pig, tame swine*.
Merchant of Venice, I 3 line 345; Merchant of Venice, III 5 line 1863; Merchant of Venice, III 5 line 1874.

Porpentine: see Porcupine.
Comedy of Errors, III 1 line 753; Comedy of Errors, III 2 line 929; Comedy of Errors, IV 1 line 1002; Comedy of Errors, V 1 line 1659; Comedy of Errors, V 1 line 1713.
Henry VI, Part II, III 1 line 1650.
Troilus and Cressida, II 1 line 881.

Porpus: Also called *porpoise*. According to sailors the playing of porpoises round a ship is a certain prognostic of a violent gale of wind.
Pericles, II 1 line 604.

Posies: Meaning, flower, bouquet, first recorded 1570s, from notion of the language of flowers.
Hamlet, III 2 line 2042.
Merchant of Venice, V 1 line 2613; Merchant of Venice, V 1 line 2616.
Merry Wives of Windsor, III 1 line 1210, 1216.
Passionate Pilgrim, line 363.

Potatoes: 1560s, from Spanish: *patata*, from Carib (Haiti) *batata: sweet potato*. Sweet potatoes were first to be introduced to Europe; in cultivation in Spain by mid-16c. Early 16c. Portuguese traders carried the crop to all their shipping ports and the sweet potato was quickly adopted from Africa to India and Java. The name later (1590s) was extended to the common white potato,

from Peru, which was at first (mistakenly) called Virginia potato, or, because at first it was of minor importance compared to the sweet potato, bastard potato. Spanish invaders in Peru began to use white potatoes as cheap food for sailors 1530s. The first potato from South America reached Pope Paul III in 1540; grown in France at first as an ornamental plant. According to popular tradition, introduced to Ireland 1565 by John Hawkins. Brought to England from Colombia by Sir Thomas Herriot, 1586. Spoken of continually as having some powerful effect upon the human frame, in exciting the desires and passions.
    Merry Wives of Windsor, V 5 line 2579.
    Troilus and Cressida, V 2 line 3115.

Porcupine: also known as a *Porpentine*. According to a popular error, the porcupine could dart his quills. They are easily detached, very sharp, and slightly barbed, and may easily stick to a person's legs, when he is not aware that he is near enough to touch them. c.1400, *porke despyne*, from Old French: *porc-espin* (early 13c.), literally, spiny pig.
    Hamlet, I 5 line 756.

Pox: late 15c., spelling alteration of *pockes*, plural of *pocke*. Especially (after c.1500) of syphilis.
    All's Well That Ends Well, III 6 line 1772; All's Well That Ends Well, IV 3 line 2345; All's Well That Ends Well, IV 3 line 2357.
    Cymbeline, II 1 line 869.
    Hamlet, III 2 line 2144.
    Henry IV, Part I, I 2 line 157.
    Henry IV, Part II, I 2 line 577; Henry VI, Part II, I 2 lines 591, 592; Henry VI, Part II, II 4 line 1279.
    Henry V, III 7 line 1749.
    Love's Labour's Lost, V 2 line 1927.
    Measure for Measure, IV 3 line 2141; Measure for Measure, V 1 line 2768.
    Othello, I 3 line 717.
    Pericles, IV 6 line 1959; Pericles, IV 6 line 1961.
    Romeo and Juliet, II 4 line 1187.
    Tempest, I 1 line 50; Tempest, II 1 line 778; Tempest, III 2 line 1473.
    Timon of Athens, IV 3 line 1831.
    Twelfth Night, III 4 line 1826.
    Two Gentlemen of Verona, III 1 line 1445.

Pregnant: Meaning with child is early 15c., from Latin: *praegnantem*: with child, before birth.
    Antony and Cleopatra, II 1 line 670.
    Cymbeline, IV 2 line 2728r.
    Hamlet, II 2 line 1310; Hamlet, II 2 line 1642; Hamlet, III 2 line 1941.
    King Lear, II 1 line 1009; King Lear, IV 6 line 2838.
    Measure for Measure, I 1 line 14; Measure for Measure, II 1 line 476; Measure for Measure, IV 4 line 2328.
    Othello, II 1 line 1035.

Pericles, IV 0 line 1536.
Timon of Athens, I 1 line 112.
Troilus and Cressida, IV 4 line 2521.
Twelfth Night, II 2 line 685; Twelfth Night, III 1 line 1323; Twelfth Night, III 1 line 1325.
Winter's Tale, V 2 line 3139.

Pricket: late Middle English, a young male fallow deer having straight, unbranched horns.
Love's Labour's Lost, IV 2 line 1153; Love's Labour's Lost, IV 2 line 1162; Love's Labour's Lost, IV 2 line 1193; Love's Labour's Lost, IV 2 line 1196; Love's Labour's Lost, IV 3 lines 1201, 1206.

Primrose: early 15c., *primerose*, from Old French: *primerose* (12c.), from *prima rosa*, literally, first rose, so called because it blooms early in spring. Although the early primrose has always been such a popular and favourite flower, yet it seems to have been associated with sadness.
Cymbeline, I 5 line 593; Cymbeline, IV 2 line 2609.
Hamlet, I 3 line 534.
Henry VI, Part II, III 2 line 1744.
Macbeth, II 3 line 776.
Midsummer Night's Dream, I 1 line 223.
Venus and Adonis, line 171.
Winter's Tale, IV 4 line 2001.

Promontory: 1540s, from Latin: *promunturium: mountain ridge, headland*, probably related to *prominere: jut out*.
Antony and Cleopatra, IV 14 line 2982.
Hamlet, II 2 line 1394.
Henry VI, Part III, III 2 line 1624.
Midsummer Night's Dream, II 1 line 520.
Tempest, V 1 line 2067.
Titus Andronicus, II 2 line 725.

Prune: mid-14c., from Old French: *pronne: plum*.
Cymbeline, V 4 line 3269.
Henry IV, Part I, I 1 line 99; Henry IV, Part I, III 3 line 2123.
Henry IV, Part II, II 4 line 1404.
Henry V, V 2 line 3023.
Love's Labour's Lost, IV 2 line 1159.
Measure for Measure, II 1 line 541; Measure for Measure, II 1 line 552; Measure for Measure, II 1 line 559.
Merry Wives of Windsor, I 1 line 265.
Winter's Tale, IV 3 line 1773.

Puddle: early 14c., small pool of dirty water, frequentative or diminutive of Old English: *pudd: ditch*. Originally used of pools and ponds as well. The verb, to dabble in water, poke in mud (mid-15c).
Antony and Cleopatra, I 4 line 492.

Comedy of Errors, V 1 line 1608.
Henry VI, Part II, IV 1 line 2227.
Othello, III 4 line 2338.
Rape of Lucrece, lines 708, 709.

Pullet: a young hen, especially one less than one year old, late Middle English: from Old French *poulet*, diminutive of *poule*, from the feminine of Latin *pullus: chicken, young animal*.
Merry Wives of Windsor, III 5 line 1776.

Pulse: a throb, a beat, early 14c., from Old French: *pous* (late 12c). Also, peas, beans, lentils, c.1300, from Old French: *pols*, from Latin: *puls: thick gruel*.
All's Well That Ends Well, I 3 line 491.
Comedy of Errors, IV 4 line 1302; Comedy of Errors, V 1 line 1684.
Hamlet, III 4 line 2543.
King John, IV 2 line 1821.
Pericles, V 1 line 2362.
Romeo and Juliet, IV 1 line 2462.
Tempest, V 1 line 2133; Tempest, V 1 line 2146.
Venus and Adonis, line 497.

Puppy: late 15c., woman's small pet dog, from *poupée:* doll, toy. Meaning shifted from *toy dog* to *young dog* (1590s), replacing *whelp*. Also used about that time in sense of vain young man.
Cymbeline, I 2 line 249.
Henry IV, Part II, II 4 line 1353.
Henry V, III 2 line 1203.
Henry VIII, I 1 line 250; Henry VIII, V 4 line 3299.
King John, II 1 line 772.
Merry Wives of Windsor, III 5 line 1756.
Othello, I 3 line 695.
Tempest, II 2 line 1241.
Two Gentlemen of Verona, IV 4 line 1836.
Winter's Tale, IV 4 line 2683.

Purples-long: the purple orchis: *orchis mascula*.
Hamlet, IV 7 line 3318.

Purr: 1600c., imitative.
All's Well That Ends Well, V 2 line 2633.
King Lear, III 6 line 2049.

Puttock: various birds of prey.
Cymbeline, I 1 line 177.
Henry VI, Part II, III 2 line 1876.
Troilus and Cressida, V 1 line 2993.

Quagmire: 1570s, from obsolete *quag: bog, marsh* + *mire*.

Henry VI, Part I, I 4 line 572.
King Lear, III 4 line 1854.

Quail: c.1300, *quabyle*, from Old French: *quaille*, perhaps via Latin: *quanccula*, imitative of the bird's cry. The quail was thought to be an amorous bird; and hence was metaphorically used to denote people of a loose character.
   Antony and Cleopatra, II 3 line 1023; Antony and Cleopatra, V 2 line 3493.
   As You Like It, II 2 line 641.
   Cymbeline, V 5 line 3553.
   Henry IV, Part I, IV 1 line 2260.
   Henry VI, Part III, II 3 line 1082.
   Midsummer Night's Dream, V 1 line 2129.
   Troilus and Cressida, V 1 line 2983.

Quarry: heap of slaughtered game, literally: what is hunted, early 14c., *quirre* entrails of deer placed on the hide and given to dogs of the chase as a reward, from Anglo-French *quirreie*, Old French *cuiriee*: the spoil, quarry. Sense of *anything chased in hunt* is first recorded 1610s; earlier *bird targeted by a hawk or other raptor* (late 15c.).
   Coriolanus, I 1 line 203.
   Hamlet, V 2 line 4029.
   Macbeth, IV 3 line 2084.

Quarter: c.1300, one-fourth of anything; one of four parts or divisions of a thing; often in reference to the four parts into which a slaughtered animal is cut, from Old French *quartier, cartier* (12c.), from Latin *quartarius* fourth part, from *quartus*: fourth. One of the earliest dated references in English is to parts of the body as dismembered during execution (c.1300). Used of the phases of the moon from early 15c. The use of quarter of an hour is attested from mid-15c. In Middle English quarter also meant one of the four divisions of a 12-hour night (late 14c.), and the quarter of the night meant nine o'clock p.m. (early 14c.). From late 14c. as one of the four quadrants of the heavens; hence, from the notion of the winds, *a side, a direction* (c.1400). In heraldry from mid-14c. as one of the four divisions of a shield or coat of arms. The word's connection with four loosened in Middle English and by 15c. expressions such as six-quartered for six-sided are found. Meaning region, locality, area, place is from c.1400. Meaning portion of a town (identified by the class or race of people who live there) is first attested 1520s.
   All's Well That Ends Well, III 6 line 1791.
   Antony and Cleopatra, IV 3 line 2613; Antony and Cleopatra, IV 14 line 3051.
   Comedy of Errors, II 1 line 382; Comedy of Errors, III 2 lines 870, 871.
   Coriolanus, I 1 line 203.
   Cymbeline, IV 4 line 2905.
   Hamlet, IV 4 line 2831.
   Henry IV, Part I, II 4 line 1002; Henry IV, Part I, III 3 line 2024.

Henry IV, Part II, V 1 line 3191.
Henry V, I 2 line 361.
Henry VI, Part I, II 1 line 735; Henry VI, Part I, II 1 line 741; Henry VI, Part I, IV 2 line 1977.
Henry VIII, V 4 line 3323.
Julius Caesar, III 1 line 1497; Julius Caesar, IV 2 line 1947.
King John, II 1 lines 819, 821; King John, V 5 line 2573.
Macbeth, I 3 line 114; Macbeth, V 1 line 2155.
Measure for Measure, III 2 line 1710.
Merry Wives of Windsor, I 1 line 21; Merry Wives of Windsor, I 1 line 23; Merry Wives of Windsor, I 1 line 25; Merry Wives of Windsor, IV 4 line 2199.
Much Ado About Nothing, V 2 line 2483.
Othello, II 3 line 1326.
Richard III, V 3 line 3494.
Romeo and Juliet, III 1 line 1530.
Taming of the Shrew, IV 3 line 2072r.
Timon of Athens, V 4 line 2627.
Winter's Tale, IV 3 line 1806; Winter's Tale, IV 4 line 2763.

Quat: a pimple.
Othello, V 1 line 3147.

Quatch-buttock: squat or flat buttock.
All's Well That Ends Well, III 2 line 841.

Rabbit: late 14c., young of the coney, from French dialect. this animal is used as a term of reproach, a sense in which it was known in Shakespeare's day.
Henry IV, Part I, II 4 line 1420.
Henry IV, Part II, II 2 line 1047.
Love's Labour's Lost, III 1 line 781.
Taming of the Shrew, IV 4 line 2257.

Rabbit-sucker: a weasel.
Henry IV, Part I, II 4 line 1420.

Rack: cut of animal meat and bones, 1560s, of unknown origin. Also, to stretch out for drying, also to torture on the rack, early 15c. Of other pains from 1580s. Clouds driven before the wind, c.1300, also rush of wind, collision, crash, originally a northern word, possibly from Old English *racu* cloud. The distinction is that rack is *driven clouds*; wrack is seaweed cast up on shore. Also, type of gait of a horse, 1580s, from rack: move with a fast, lively gait 1520s in this sense (implied in racking), of unknown origin; perhaps from French *racquassure* racking of a horse in his pace, itself of unknown origin.
Antony and Cleopatra, IV 14 line 2989.
Hamlet, II 2 line 1558.
Sonnet XXXIII line 6.

Radish: late Old English: *rædic*, from Latin: *radicem*: *root*.
>   **Henry IV, Part I**, II 4 line 1174.
>   **Henry IV, Part II**, III 2 line 2181.

Rain: Old English: *regnian*, usually contracted to *rinan*. Transferred and figurative use of other things that fall as rain (blessings, tears, etc.) is recorded from c.1200. Phrase to *rain cats and dogs* is (variation rain dogs and polecats is from 1650s), of unknown origin, despite intense speculation. One of the less likely suggestions is pets sliding off sod roofs when the sod got too wet during a rainstorm. Probably rather an extension of cats and dogs as proverbial for *strife, enmity* (1570s).
>   **Antony and Cleopatra**, I 2 line 246; Antony and Cleopatra, V 2 line 3758.
>   **As You Like It**, III 2 line 1146; As You Like It, III 5 line 1704; As You Like It, IV 1 line 1925.
>   **Coriolanus**, IV 5 line 2981.
>   **Cymbeline**, III 3 line 1641.
>   **Hamlet**, III 3 line 2327.
>   **Henry IV, Part II**, II 3 line 1215; Henry IV, Part II, IV 5 line 2897.
>   **Henry VI, Part I**, II 1 line 670; Henry VI, Part I, III 2 line 1512; Henry VI, Part I, IV 1 line 1962.
>   **Henry VI, Part II**, III 2 line 2035.
>   **Henry VI, Part III**, I 4 line 586; Henry VI, Part III, III 2 line 1529.
>   **King John**, II 1 line 422; King John, II 1 line 773.
>   **King Lear**, II 4 line 1355; King Lear, III 1 line 1627; King Lear, III 2 line 1688; King Lear, III 2 lines 1690, 1691; King Lear, III 2 line 1723; King Lear, III 2 lines 1755, 1757; King Lear, III 7 line 2191; King Lear, IV 3 line 2472; King Lear, IV 6 line 2709.
>   **Love's Labour's Lost**, IV 3 line 1614; Love's Labour's Lost, V 2 line 2751.
>   **Lover's Complaint**, line 7.
>   **Macbeth**, I 1 line 3; Macbeth, III 3 line 1257.
>   **Measure for Measure**, III 2 line 1561.
>   **Merchant of Venice**, IV 1 line 2126.
>   **Merry Wives of Windsor**, V 5 line 2578.
>   **Midsummer Night's Dream**, I 1 line 136.
>   **Much Ado About Nothing**, III 3 line 1420.
>   **Pericles**, II 1 line 581.
>   **Rape of Lucrece**, lines 611, 1323, 1729, 1839, 1841.
>   **Richard II**, I 2 line 221; Richard II, III 3 line 1696.
>   **Richard III**, I 2 line 348.
>   **Romeo and Juliet**, III 5 line 2235.
>   **Sonnet** XIV line 6; Sonnet XXXIV line 6; Sonnet CXXXV line 9.
>   **Taming of the Shrew**, Prologue 1 line 133.
>   **Tempest**, III 1 line 1367.
>   **Timon of Athens**, I 1 line 100.
>   **Titus Andronicus**, II 3 line 879; Titus Andronicus, III 1 line 1142.
>   **Troilus and Cressida**, IV 4 line 2483.

Twelfth Night, III 1 line 1320; Twelfth Night, V 1 lines 2604, 2606, 2610, 2614, 2618.
Venus and Adonis, lines 91, 220, 258, 380, 821, 981, 987.

Rainbow: Old English: *renboga*. Secondary rainbows, the watery appearance in the sky accompanying the rainbow, are in many places termed *water-galls*.
King John, IV 2 line 1741.
Merry Wives of Windsor, IV 5 line 2408.
Rape of Lucrece, line 1638
Winter's Tale, IV 4 line 2095.

Rainy: Old English: *renig*.
Henry V, IV 3 line 2339.
Richard II, III 2 line 1556.
Sonnet XC line 7;
Titus Andronicus, V 1 line 2252.

Raisins: c.1300, from Anglo-French: *raycin* (late 13c.), Old French: *raisin*: *grape, raisin*.
Winter's Tale, IV 3 line 1774.

Ram: Old English: *ramm: male sheep*, earlier *rom: male sheep*.
Antony and Cleopatra, II 5 line 1079; Antony and Cleopatra, III 2 line 1628.
As You Like It, III 2 line 1191; As You Like It, III 2 line 1194; As You Like It, V 2 line 2276.
Henry VIII, IV 1 line 2505.
Merchant of Venice, I 3 line 407; Merchant of Venice, I 3 line 421.
Othello, I 1 line 94.
Passionate Pilgrim, line 248.
Rape of Lucrece, line 515.
Titus Andronicus, IV 3 line 1956.
Troilus and Cressida, I 3 line 659.
Winter's Tale, IV 4 line 1888.

Rascal: a deer too lean to be hunted.
As You Like It, III 3 line 1554.

Rat: Old English: *ræt*, of uncertain origin. Middle English common form was *ratton*, from augmented Old French form *raton*. Sense of *one who abandons his associates* (1620s) is from belief that rats leave a ship about to sink or a house about to fall and led to meaning, traitor, informant. The fanciful idea, that rats were commonly rhymed to death, in Ireland, is said to have arisen from some metrical charm or incantation, used there for that purpose.
As You Like It, III 2 line 1285.
Coriolanus, I 1 line 270.
Cymbeline, V 5 line 3666.
Hamlet, III 4 line 2410; Hamlet, IV 1 line 2636r.

King Lear, II 2 line 1141; King Lear, III 4 lines 1927, 1932; King Lear, V 3 line 3495.
Macbeth, I 3 line 107.
Measure for Measure, I 2 line 220.
Merchant of Venice, IV 1 line 1976.
Merry Wives of Windsor, II 1 line 783.
Richard III, V 3 line 3846.
Romeo and Juliet, III 1 line 1605.
Tempest, I 2 line 256.

Raven: Old English: *hræfn* (Mercian). The common raven is easily tamed, but is mischievous and thievish, and has been popularly regarded as a bird of evil omen and mysterious character. Old English: also used *hræmn*, *hremm*. The raven standard was the flag of the Danish Vikings. Perhaps no bird is so universally unpopular as the raven, its hoarse croak in most countries being regarded as ominous. Hence, as might be expected, Shakespeare often refers to it, in order to make the scene he depicts all the more vivid and graphic. It seems that the superstitious dread attaching to this bird has chiefly arisen from its supposed longevity. There are references to the notion that it was a constant attendant on a house infected with the plague. Like the crow, the raven is a generally negative symbol, although appearing occasionally in the Bible as a wise messenger. Once ravens' feathers were formerly used by witches, from an old superstition that the wings of this bird carried with them contagion wherever they went.

As You Like It, II 3 line 687.
Cymbeline, II 2 line 972.
Hamlet, III 2 line 2145.
Henry IV, Part I, III 1 line 1697.
Henry VI, Part II, III 2 line 1353; Henry VI, Part II, III 2 line 1721.
Henry VI, Part III, V 6 line 3042.
Julius Caesar, V 1 line 2441.
King John, IV 3 line 2183.
Love's Labour's Lost, IV 3 line 1413.
Macbeth, I 5 line 388.
Merry Wives of Windsor, I 3 line 336.
Midsummer Night's Dream, II 2 line 773.
Much Ado About Nothing, II 3 line 901.
Othello, IV 1 line 2432.
Rape of Lucrece, line 1000.
Romeo and Juliet, III 2 line 1737; Romeo and Juliet, III 2 line 1798.
Sonnet CXXVII line 9.
Tempest, I 2 line 472.
Titus Andronicus, II 3 line 818; Titus Andronicus, II 3 line 833; Titus Andronicus, II 3 lines 888, 892; Titus Andronicus, III 1 line 1289.
Troilus and Cressida, II 3 line 1434; Troilus and Cressida, V 2 line 3268.
Twelfth Night, V 1 line 2323.
Winter's Tale, II 3 line 1152.

Reap: to cut grain with a hook or sickle, Old English: *reopan*, Mercian form of *ripan*. Related to *ripe*, meaning, ready to be eaten.
    All's Well That Ends Well, II 1 line 756.
    Antony and Cleopatra, III 7 line 1982; Antony and Cleopatra, V 2 line 3496.
    As You Like It, III 2 line 1218; As You Like It, III 5 line 1758.
    Coriolanus, V 3 line 3654; Coriolanus, V 6 line 3859.
    Cymbeline, II 4 line 1280.
    Henry IV, Part I, I 3 line 360.
    Henry VI, Part II, III 1 line 1669.
    Henry VI, Part III, I 4 line 607; Henry VI, Part III, V 7 line 3117.
    Henry VIII, III 2 line 2089.
    Love's Labour's Lost, IV 3 line 1728.
    Measure for Measure, IV 1 line 1883.
    Richard II, I 3 line 518.
    Richard III, II 2 line 1389; Richard III, V 2 line 3443.
    Romeo and Juliet, II 4 line 1200.
    Sonnet CXXVIII line 7.
    Tempest, IV 1 line 1861.
    Twelfth Night, III 1 line 1371.

Reed: Old English: *hreod*. As part of the mouthpiece of a musical instrument is from 1520s. Among the uses to which the reed was formerly applied were the thatching of houses, and the making of shepherds' pipes.
    Antony and Cleopatra, II 7 line 1384.
    Cymbeline, IV 2 line 2666.
    Henry IV, Part I, I 3 line 431.
    Merchant of Venice, III 4 line 1820.
    Tempest, I 2 line 334; Tempest, V 1 line 2034.

Rere-mice: archaic for *bat*. Old English: *hreremus*, probably from *hreran*: move.
    Midsummer Night's Dream, II 2 line 653.

Rib: Old English: *ribb*, literally a covering (of the chest). Also, from 1580, a reference to a woman or wife (Adam's rib).
    As You Like It, I 2 line 250; As You Like It, I 2 line 258.
    Henry IV, Part I, II 4 line 1102; Henry IV, Part I, IV 2 line 2443.
    Henry IV, Part II, II 3 line 1210.
    King John, II 1 line 694; King John, III 3 line 1308.
    Love's Labour's Lost, I 1 line 29.
    Macbeth, I 3 line 249.
    Merchant of Venice, I 1 line 30; Merchant of Venice, II 2 line 682; Merchant of Venice, II 6 line 927; Merchant of Venice, II 7 line 1037.
    Much Ado About Nothing, IV 1 line 1801.
    Othello, I 2 line 207; Othello, II 1 line 771.
    Richard II, III 3 line 1669; Richard II, V 5 line 2768.
    Troilus and Cressida, I 3 line 630.

Rice: mid-13c., from Old French: *ris*.
    Richard III, IV 5 line 3386.
    Winter's Tale, IV 3 lines 1763, 1764.

Rind: Old English: *rinde*: *bark, crust*, later peel of a fruit or vegetable (c.1400).
    As You Like It, III 2 line 1220.
    Romeo and Juliet, II 3 line 1081.

Rivage: shore.
    Henry V, III 0 line 1065.

River: c.1300, from Old French: *riviere*.
    Antony and Cleopatra, II 2 line 911; Antony and Cleopatra, II 5 line 1061.
    Coriolanus, I 1 line 132.
    Cymbeline, IV 2 line 2359.
    Hamlet, I 2 line 283.
    Henry IV, Part I, III 1 line 1641.
    Henry IV, Part II, IV 4 line 2878.
    Henry V, I 2 line 208; Henry V, III 5 line 1391; Henry V, III 6 line 1639; Henry V, IV 7 lines 2543, 2544, 2547.
    Henry VI, Part III, IV 8 line 2529.
    Henry VIII, III 2 line 2078.
    King John, I 1 line 210; King John, III 1 line 928; King John, IV 3 line 2136; King John, V 7 line 2671.
    King Lear, I 1 line 65.
    Lover's Complaint, lines 38, 285.
    Measure for Measure, I 2 line 181.
    Merry Wives of Windsor, III 1 line 1207; Merry Wives of Windsor, III 1 line 1222; Merry Wives of Windsor, III 5 line 1755; Merry Wives of Windsor, IV 4 line 2215.
    Midsummer Night's Dream, II 1 line 460.
    Passionate Pilgrim, line 360.
    Rape of Lucrece, line 1789.
    Richard II, III 2 line 1517.
    Richard III, I 3 line 640.
    Titus Andronicus, II 4 line 1086.
    Troilus and Cressida, III 2 line 1706; Troilus and Cressida, V 4 line 3429.
    Two Gentlemen of Verona, II 3 line 645.
    Venus and Adonis, lines 91, 351.

Rheum: watery fluid that drips from nose and eyes; late Middle English: from Old French: *reume*, via Latin from Greek *rheuma*: *stream* (from *rhein: to flow*).
    Antony and Cleopatra, III 2 line 1664.
    Comedy of Errors, III 2 line 887.
    Coriolanus, V 6 line 3871.
    Hamlet, II 2 line 1580.
    Henry V, III 5 line 1442.

Julius Caesar, II 1 line 893.
King John, III 1 line 937; King John, IV 1 line 1613; King John, IV 3 line 2134.
Measure for Measure, III 1 line 1254.
Merchant of Venice, I 3 line 444.
Much Ado About Nothing, V 2 line 2484.
Othello, III 4 line 2229.
Richard II, I 4 line 621.
Troilus and Cressida, V 3 line 3398.
Winter's Tale, IV 4 line 2311.

Roan: horse, 1520s, from French: *roan: reddish brown*.
Henry IV, Part I, II 3 line 930; Henry IV, Part I, II 3 line 932; Henry IV, Part I, II 4 line 1097.
Richard II, V 5 line 2829.

Robin-Redbreast: (mid-15c.), from personal name *Robin*. It ousted the native *ruddock*, which is related to red. According to a pervading notion, this little bird is said to cover with leaves any dead body it may chance to find unburied.
Two Gentlemen of Verona, II 1 line 419.

Rock: Old English: *rocc* (in *stanrocc*: stone rock or obelisk), of uncertain origin, sometimes said to be from Celtic. It seems to have been used in Middle English principally for rock formations as opposed to individual stones. A rock is the ultimate embodiment of permanence, stability, and reliability. It is cold and hard, yet eternal; thus, they often symbolise the divine, the immortal.
All's Well That Ends Well, II 1 line 674.
Antony and Cleopatra, IV 14 line 2981.
Comedy of Errors, I 1 line 103.
Coriolanus, III 1 line 1992; Coriolanus, III 1 line 2007; Coriolanus, III 1 line 2071; Coriolanus, III 2 line 2165; Coriolanus, III 3 line 2439r; Coriolanus, III 3 line 2472; Coriolanus, V 2 line 3486.
Cymbeline, III 1 lines 1433, 1442; Cymbeline, III 3 line 1609; Cymbeline, III 3 line 1677; Cymbeline, IV 2 line 2516; Cymbeline, IV 2 line 2531; Cymbeline, V 5 line 3683.
Hamlet, III 2 line 2120.
Henry IV, Part II, II 4 line 1465; Henry IV, Part II, III 1 line 1723; Henry IV, Part II, IV 1 line 2395.
Henry V, III 1 line 1103.
Henry VI, Part II, III 2 lines 1771, 1777; Henry VI, Part II, V 1 line 3001.
Henry VI, Part III, II 2 line 847; Henry VI, Part III, V 4 lines 2814, 2827, 2831, 2836.
Henry VIII, I 1 line 167; Henry VIII, I 1 line 227; Henry VIII, III 2 line 2077.
Julius Caesar, V 5 line 2671.
King John, II 1 line 764; King John, II 1 line 770.
Lover's Complaint, line 293.
Macbeth, III 4 line 1298.

Merchant of Venice, I 1 line 33; Merchant of Venice, I 3 line 347; Merchant of Venice, III 2 line 1646.
Midsummer Night's Dream, I 2 line 291; Midsummer Night's Dream, IV 1 line 1637.
Much Ado About Nothing, III 1 line 1112.
Othello, I 3 line 486; Othello, II 1 line 845; Othello, II 3 line 1262.
Passionate Pilgrim, line 358.
Pericles, II 1 line 584.
Rape of Lucrece, lines 313, 386, 641.
Richard II, II 1 line 744.
Richard III, IV 4 line 3038.
Romeo and Juliet, V 3 line 3066.
Sonnet LXV line 7.
Tempest, I 2 line 494; Tempest, I 2 line 515; Tempest, II 2 line 1258; Tempest, IV 1 line 1779.
Titus Andronicus, III 1 line 1223.
Troilus and Cressida, III 2 line 1729.
Two Gentlemen of Verona, I 2 line 280; Two Gentlemen of Verona, II 4 line 831.
Venus and Adonis, line 1208.

Roe: fish eggs, c.1400, corresponding to Old Norse: *hrogn*.
Also, small deer, Old English: *ra*, from *raha*.
Love's Labour's Lost, V 2 line 2223.
Romeo and Juliet, II 4 line 1198.
Taming of the Shrew, Prologue 2 line 192.
Troilus and Cressida, V 1 line 2993.
Venus and Adonis, lines 582, 697.

Rooks: crow, Old English: *hroc*, possibly imitative of its raucous voice. Used as a disparaging term for persons since at least c.1500, and extended by 1570s to mean a *cheat*, especially at cards or dice. The verb: *to defraud by cheating* (originally especially in a game) is first attested 1580s. Formerly the nobles of England prided themselves in having a rookery in the neighbourhood of their castles, because rooks were regarded as fowls of good omen. On this account no one was permitted to kill them, under severe penalties. When rooks desert a rookery it is said to foretell the downfall of the family on whose property it is.
Henry VI, Part III, V 6 line 3042.
Love's Labour's Lost, V 2 line 2853.
Macbeth, III 4 line 1428.

Rooky**: to express *abounding in rooks; with trees in which the rooks build; where there is a rookery*.
Macbeth, III 2 line 1226.

Root: underground part of a plant, late Old English: *rot*. The usual Old English words for *roots* were *wyrttruma* and *wyrtwala*. Figurative use is from c.1200. Of teeth, hair, etc., from early 13c. Mathematical sense is from 1550s. fixed or firmly attached by roots (often figurative), late 14c., from root; sense of to pull up by the root. Also, *dig with the snout*, 1530s, from Old English: *wrotan*.

All's Well That Ends Well, IV 5 line 2475; All's Well That Ends Well, V 1 line 2571.

Antony and Cleopatra, II 7 line 1374; Antony and Cleopatra, V 2 line 3516.

As You Like It, II 1 line 560.

Coriolanus, II 1 line 1116; Coriolanus, III 2 line 2234; Coriolanus, IV 5 line 2870.

Cymbeline, I 1 line 34; Cymbeline, I 6 line 793; Cymbeline, IV 2 line 2380; Cymbeline, IV 2 line 2391; Cymbeline, IV 2 line 2395; Cymbeline, V 4 line 3273.

Henry IV, Part II, III 1 line 1796; Henry IV, Part II, IV 1 line 2414.

Henry V, II 4 line 936; Henry V, V 2 line 3026.

Henry VI, Part I, II 4 line 1016.

Henry VI, Part II, III 1 line 1308.

Henry VI, Part III, I 1 line 52; Henry VI, Part III, I 3 line 409; Henry VI, Part III, II 2 line 1010; Henry VI, Part III, II 6 line 1302; Henry VI, Part III, III 3 line 1821; Henry VI, Part III, V 4 line 2876.

Henry VIII, I 2 line 417; Henry VIII, I 2 line 428; Henry VIII, III 2 line 2260; Henry VIII, V 1 line 2837; Henry VIII, V 1 line 2921.

Macbeth, I 3 line 186; Macbeth, III 1 line 1006; Macbeth, IV 1 line 1572; Macbeth, IV 1 line 1664; Macbeth, IV 3 line 1941; Macbeth, V 3 line 2296.

Merry Wives of Windsor, IV 1 line 1937.

Much Ado About Nothing, I 3 line 350.

Othello, III 3 line 2104.

Pericles, I 2 line 278; Pericles, IV 6 line 2024; Pericles, V 1 line 2284.

Rape of Lucrece, lines 716, 874, 921.

Richard II, I 2 lines 226, 231; Richard II, III 4 line 1900; Richard II, III 4 line 1917.

Richard III, I 3 line 692; Richard III, II 2 line 1313.

Sonnet LV line 6; Sonnet CXLII line 11.

Tempest, I 2 line 645; Tempest, III 2 line 1490.

Timon of Athens, I 2 line 411; Timon of Athens, I 2 line 480; Timon of Athens, IV 3 lines 1685, 1690; Timon of Athens, IV 3 lines 1873, 1879; Timon of Athens, IV 3 line 1981; Timon of Athens, IV 3 line 1983; Timon of Athens, IV 3 line 2130; Timon of Athens, V 1 line 2337; Timon of Athens, V 1 line 2411; Timon of Athens, V 1 line 2447.

Titus Andronicus, IV 1 line 1589; Titus Andronicus, IV 2 line 1873.

Troilus and Cressida, IV 4 line 2484.

Two Gentlemen of Verona, II 4 line 821; Two Gentlemen of Verona, V 4 line 2258.

Venus and Adonis, line 657r.

Winter's Tale, I 1 line 22; Winter's Tale, II 3 line 1040.

Rose: from Latin: *rosa.* Used of a colour since 1530. In English civil wars of 15c., the white rose was the badge of the House of York, the red of its rival

Lancaster. *Rose-water* is attested from late 14c. In the figurative sense, bed of roses is from 1590s. As might be expected, the rose is the flower most frequently mentioned by Shakespeare; denoting, in many cases the symbol of all that is fair and lovely. In days gone by the rose entered largely into the customs and superstitions of most nations, and even now there are extensive meanings associated with it. It appears that in Shakespeare's time one of the fashions of the day was the wearing of enormous roses on the shoes, of which full-length portraits afford striking examples. Also reference to the court fashion of sticking roses in the ear. Shakespeare also mentions the use of the rose in rose-cakes and rose-water. The trailing white dog-rose is commonly considered to have been the one chosen by the house of York.

All's Well That Ends Well, I 3 line 446; All's Well That Ends Well, IV 2 line 2026.

Antony and Cleopatra, III 13 line 2269; Antony and Cleopatra, III 13 line 2291.

As You Like It, I 2 lines 163, 164; As You Like It, I 3 line 478; As You Like It, III 2 line 1221.

Hamlet, III 1 line 1843; Hamlet, III 4 line 2133; Hamlet, IV 5 line 2914; Hamlet, IV 5 line 3035.

Henry IV, Part I, I 3 line 505; Henry IV, Part I, II 1 line 655; Henry IV, Part I, V 4 line 3119.

Henry IV, Part II, II 4 line 1259.

Henry V, V 2 line 3281.

Henry VI, Part I, II 4 line 952; Henry VI, Part I, II 4 line 955; Henry VI, Part I, II 4 line 957; Henry VI, Part I, II 4 line 959; Henry VI, Part I, II 4 line 963; Henry VI, Part I, II 4 line 971; Henry VI, Part I, II 4 line 973; Henry VI, Part I, II 4 line 982; Henry VI, Part I, II 4 line 986; Henry VI, Part I, II 4 line 988; Henry VI, Part I, II 4 line 993; Henry VI, Part I, II 4 line 996; Henry VI, Part I, II 4 line 997; Henry VI, Part I, II 4 line 1001; Henry VI, Part I, II 4 line 1041; Henry VI, Part I, II 4 lines 1060, 1063; Henry VI, Part I, IV 1 line 1856; Henry VI, Part I, IV 1 lines 1916, 1917.

Henry VI, Part II, I 1 line 267.

Henry VI, Part III, I 1 line 148; Henry VI, Part III, I 2 line 327; Henry VI, Part III, II 5 lines 1202, 1206; Henry VI, Part III, V 1 line 2685.

Henry VIII, I 2 line 495; Henry VIII, IV 1 lines 2511, 2514.

Julius Caesar, III 2 line 1552.

King John, I 1 line 148; King John, III 1 line 969.

Love's Labour's Lost, I 1 line 109; Love's Labour's Lost, IV 3 line 1347; Love's Labour's Lost, V 2 line 2207; Love's Labour's Lost, V 2 lines 2209, 2211.

Lover's Complaint, line 288.

Measure for Measure, I 4 line 367.

Merry Wives of Windsor, III 1 line 1209.

Midsummer Night's Dream, I 1 line 80; Midsummer Night's Dream, I 1 line 135; Midsummer Night's Dream, II 1 line 477; Midsummer Night's Dream, II 1 line 631; Midsummer Night's Dream, II 2 line 653; Midsummer Night's Dream, III 1 line 907; Midsummer Night's Dream, IV 1 line 1548; Midsummer Night's Dream, IV 1 line 1687.

Much Ado About Nothing, I 3 line 353.

Othello, IV 2 line 2811; Othello, V 2 line 3314.
Passionate Pilgrim, lines 56, 132, 362.
Pericles, IV 6 line 1978r; Pericles, V 0 line 2150.
Rape of Lucrece, lines 122, 309, 310, 530, 543, 1333.
Richard II, V 1 line 2342.
Richard III, IV 3 line 2738; Richard III, V 5 line 3911.
Romeo and Juliet, II 2 line 890; Romeo and Juliet, IV 1 line 2465; Romeo and Juliet, V 1 line 2855.
Sonnet I line 2; Sonnet XXXV line 2; Sonnet LIV line 3; Sonnet LIV line 6; Sonnet LIV line 11; Sonnet LXVII line 8r; Sonnet XCV line 2; Sonnet XCVIII line 10; Sonnet XCVIX line 8; Sonnet CIX line 14; Sonnet CXXX line 5; Sonnet CXXX line 6.
Taming of the Shrew, Prologue 1 line 57; Taming of the Shrew, II 1 line 1018; Taming of the Shrew, III 2 line 1528.
Timon of Athens, IV 3 line 1761.
Titus Andronicus, II 4 line 1090.
Troilus and Cressida, I 2 line 162.
Twelfth Night, II 4 line 931; Twelfth Night, III 1 line 1388.
Two Gentlemen of Verona, IV 4 line 1994.
Venus and Adonis, lines 23, 30, 131, 595, 611, 958.
Winter's Tale, IV 4 line 2111.

Rosemary: mid-15c., earlier *rosmarine* (c.1300), from Latin: *rosmarinus*, literally, dew of the sea, from *ros*: *dew* + marinus. Perhaps so called because it grew near coasts. This plant was formerly in very high esteem, and was devoted to various uses. It was supposed to strengthen the memory, hence it was regarded as a symbol of remembrance, and on this account was often given to friends. Besides being used at weddings, it was also in request at funerals, probably for its odour, and as a token of remembrance of the deceased. Rosemary, too, was one of the evergreens with which dishes were anciently garnished during Christmas.
Hamlet, IV 5 line 3053.
King Lear, II 3 line 1267.
Pericles, IV 6 line 2093.
Romeo and Juliet, II 4 line 1360; Romeo and Juliet, II 4 line 1365; Romeo and Juliet, IV 5 line 2738.
Winter's Tale, IV 4 line 1943.

Rubies: c.1300, from Old French: *rubi* (12c).
Comedy of Errors, III 2 line 892.
Cymbeline, II 2 line 939.
Lover's Complaint, line 199.
Measure for Measure, II 4 line 1127.
Midsummer Night's Dream, II 1 line 379.

Rubious**: From the Latin word *rubeus: ruddy*, and from the gem called *ruby*. To convey the sense of *ruddy; ruby red*.
Twelfth Night, I 4 line 280.

Ruddock: archaic for the songbird, *robin*.
    Cymbeline, IV 2 line 2612.

Rue: an evergreen shrub. Middle English: from Old French, via Latin from Greek: *rhute*.
    Hamlet, IV 5 lines 3056, 3059.
    Richard II, III 4 lines 1973, 1974.
    Winter's Tale, IV 4 line 1943.

Rural: early 15c., from Old French: *rural* (14c.), from Latin: *ruralis*: *of the countryside*. There is usually little or no difference between the meanings of rural and rustic, but in later use the tendency is to employ rural when the idea of locality (country scenes, etc.) is prominent, and rustic when there is a suggestion of the more primitive qualities or manners naturally attaching to country life.
    Antony and Cleopatra, V 2 line 3683.
    Winter's Tale, IV 4 line 2360.

Rushes: plant growing in marshy ground, Old English: *resc*, earlier *risc*. Old French: *rusche* probably is from a Germanic source. Used for making torches and finger rings, also strewn on floors when visitors arrived; it was attested a type of something of no value, from c.1300.
    As You Like It, III 2 line 1454.
    Coriolanus, I 1 line 183; Coriolanus, I 4 line 505.
    Cymbeline, II 2 line 935.
    Henry IV, Part I, III 1 line 1763.
    Henry IV, Part II, V 5 line 3587; Henry IV, Part II, V 5 line 3588.
    Rape of Lucrece, line 369.
    Romeo and Juliet, I 4 line 532.
    Taming of the Shrew, IV 1 line 1656.

Rust: early 13c., decay, redness. As a plant disease, attested from mid-14c.
    All's Well That Ends Well, IV 3 line 2417.
    Coriolanus, IV 5 line 2989.
    Henry IV, Part II, I 2 line 554.
    Henry V, V 2 line 3027.
    Henry VI, Part II, III 2 line 1883.
    Henry VI, Part III, I 3 line 432.
    King John, IV 1 line 1648.
    Love's Labour's Lost, I 2 line 476.
    Othello, I 2 line 279.
    Pericles, II 2 line 811.
    Richard II, III 3 line 1758.
    Romeo and Juliet, V 3 line 3137.
    Venus and Adonis, line 789.
    Winter's Tale, III 2 line 1403.

Rustic: mid-15c., from Latin *rusticus*, from *rus* open land, country. Noun meaning *a country person, peasant* is from mid-16c. In early examples, there

is usually little or no difference between the meanings of rural and rustic, but in later use the tendency is to employ rural when the idea of locality (country scenes, etc.) is prominent, and rustic when there is a suggestion of the more primitive qualities or manners naturally attaching to country life(OED).
    As You Like It, V 4 line 2572.
    Cymbeline, IV 2 line 2453.
    Winter's Tale, IV 4 line 1956.

Rye: Old English: *ryge.*
    As You Like It, V 3 line 2382.
    Tempest, IV 1 line 1771.

Sable: fur or pelt of the animal, mid-14c., *black* as a heraldic colour, commonly identified with sable, but the animal's fur is brown and this may be a different word of unknown origin; it may reflect a medieval custom (unattested) of dyeing sable fur black. As an adjective from late 14c.
    Hamlet, I 2 line 459; **Hamlet**, II 2 line 1529; **Hamlet**, III 2 line 2010; **Hamlet**, IV 7 line 3220.
    Pericles, V 0 line 2162.
    Phoenix and the Turtle, line 18.
    Rape of Lucrece, lines 168, 1125.
    Sonnet XII line 4.

Saffron: c.1200, from Old French: *safran* (12c.), ultimately from Arabic: *za'faran*, of unknown origin.
    All's Well That Ends Well, IV 5 line 2466.
    Comedy of Errors, IV 4 line 1312.
    Tempest, IV 1 line 1789.
    Winter's Tale, IV 3 line 1770.

Salad: late 14c., from Old French: *salade* (14c).
    All's Well That Ends Well, IV 5 line 2477; **All's Well That Ends Well**, IV 5 line 2479.
    Antony and Cleopatra, I 5 line 607.

Salt: Old English: *sealt* (noun and adjective). Salt was long regarded as having power to repel spiritual and magical evil. Many metaphoric uses reflect that this was once a rare and important resource. Belief that spilling salt brings bad luck is attested from 16c. To be above (or below) the salt (1590s) refers to customs of seating at a long table according to rank or honour, and placing a large salt-cellar in the middle of the dining table.
    All's Well That Ends Well, I 3 line 494.
    Antony and Cleopatra, II 1 line 641; **Antony and Cleopatra**, II 5 line 1069.
    Comedy of Errors, III 2 line 887.
    Coriolanus, IV 3 line 2544; **Coriolanus**, V 6 line 3930.
    Cymbeline, III 1 line 1498.
    Hamlet, I 2 line 359; **Hamlet**, III 2 line 2047; **Hamlet**, IV 5 line 3032.
    Henry IV, Part II, I 2 line 397.

Henry V, I 2 line 355; Henry V, V 1 line 2894.
Henry VI, Part I, I 1 line 54.
Henry VI, Part II, III 2 line 1777; Henry VI, Part II, III 1 line 1826.
King John, V 7 line 2679.
King Lear, IV 6 line 2802.
Love's Labour's Lost, V 1 line 1790.
Macbeth, IV 1 line 1571.
Measure for Measure, V 1 line 2827.
Merry Wives of Windsor, I 1 line 20; Merry Wives of Windsor, II 2 line 1063; Merry Wives of Windsor, II 3 line 1143.
Midsummer Night's Dream, II 2 line 751; Midsummer Night's Dream, III 2 line 1450.
Much Ado About Nothing, IV 1 line 1792.
Othello, II 1 line 1040; Othello, III 3 line 2086; Othello, III 4 line 2229; Othello, IV 3 line 3068.
Rape of Lucrece, lines 701, 1282.
Richard II, IV 1 line 2234.
Richard III, I 2 line 338.
Romeo and Juliet, II 3 line 1131; Romeo and Juliet, III 5 line 2241.
Tempest, I 2 line 266; Tempest, I 2 line 386; Tempest, II 1 line 767.
Timon of Athens, IV 3 line 2152; Timon of Athens, IV 3 line 2152; Timon of Athens, V 1 line 2505.
Titus Andronicus, III 2 line 1465.
Troilus and Cressida, I 2 line 404; Troilus and Cressida, I 3 line 834; Troilus and Cressida, IV 4 line 2477.
Twelfth Night, III 4 line 1939; Twelfth Night, V 1 line 2257.
Two Gentlemen of Verona, III 1 lines 1426r, 1427.
Venus and Adonis, line 1093.

Saltpetre: potassium nitrate, (early 14c.), from Old French: *salpetre*, from Latin: *sal*: salt (see salt) + *petra*, rock, stone. So called because it looks like salt encrusted on rock.
Henry IV, Part I, I 3 line 385.

Sampire: a plant.
King Lear, IV 6 line 2615.

Sand: Old English, metaphoric for innumerable.
Cymbeline, III 1 line 1434; Cymbeline, III 2 line 1587; Cymbeline, V 5 line 3514.
Henry V, III 7 line 1673; Henry V, IV 1 line 1945.
Henry VI, Part I, IV 2 line 2002.
Henry VI, Part II, I 4 line 669; Henry VI, Part II, I 4 line 707; Henry VI, Part II, III 2 line 1778; Henry VI, Part II, IV 1 line 2161.
Henry VI, Part III, I 4 line 461; Henry VI, Part II, V 4 lines 2834, 2840.
King Lear, IV 6 line 2892.
Merchant of Venice, I 1 lines 27, 29; Merchant of Venice, III 2 line 1450.
Midsummer Night's Dream, II 1 line 496.

Pericles, V 2 line 2495.
Rape of Lucrece, line 386.
Richard II, II 2 line 1146.
Tempest, I 2 line 537; Tempest, V 1 line 2055.
Titus Andronicus, IV 1 line 1609; Titus Andronicus, IV 1 line 1649.
Troilus and Cressida, III 2 line 1843.
Two Gentlemen of Verona, II 4 line 830; Two Gentlemen of Verona, III 2 line 1533; Two Gentlemen of Verona, IV 3 line 1816.
Venus and Adonis, line 168.

Sanguine: early 14c., type of red cloth, from Old French *sanguin*, from Latin *sanguineus*: of blood, also bloody, bloodthirsty, from *sanguis*. Meaning: blood-red, is recorded from late 14c. Meaning: cheerful, hopeful, confident, first attested c.1500, because these qualities were thought in medieval physiology to spring from an excess of blood as one of the four humours.
    Cymbeline, V 5 line 3816.
    Henry IV, Part I, II 4 line 1226.
    Henry VI, Part I, IV 1 line 1857.
    Titus Andronicus, IV 2 line 1787.

Sap: liquid in a plant, Old English: *sæp*.
    Antony and Cleopatra, III 13 line 2482.
    Comedy of Errors, II 2 line 570; Comedy of Errors, V 1 line 1751.
    Henry VI, Part I, II 5 line 1086; Henry VI, Part I, IV 5 line 2138.
    Henry VIII, I 1 line 214; Henry VIII, I 2 line 429.
    King Lear, IV 2 line 2378.
    Rape of Lucrece, lines 1001, 1219.
    Richard II, III 4 line 1925.
    Richard III, II 2 line 1314; Richard III, IV 4 line 3083.
    Sonnet XV line 7; Sonnet V line 7.
    Troilus and Cressida, I 3 line 457.
    Venus and Adonis, lines 185, 1198.
    Winter's Tale, IV 4 line 2415.

Sapling: early 15c., see Sap.
    Pericles, IV 2 line 1751.
    Richard III, III 4 line 2026.
    Titus Andronicus, III 2 line 1495.

Sapphire: late 13c., from Old French: *saphir* (12c.), from Latin: *sapphirus*, from Greek: *sappheiros*: *blue stone* (the gem meant apparently was not the one that now has the name, but perhaps rather *lapis lazuli*. In Renaissance lapidaries, it was said to cure anger and stupidity.
    Comedy of Errors, III 2 line 892.
    Lover's Complaint, line 216.
    Merry Wives of Windsor, V 5 line 2636.

Saturn: Old English: *Sætern: Italic god*, also, *most remote planet* (then known), from Latin: *Saturnus*, Italic god of agriculture, possibly from Etruscan. Also the alchemical name for lead (late 14c.)
    Cymbeline, II 5 line 1382.
    Henry IV, Part II, II 4 line 1553.
    Much Ado About Nothing, I 3 line 339.
    Sonnet XCVIII line 4.
    Titus Andronicus, II 3 line 764; Titus Andronicus, IV 3 line 1938.

Savage: c.1300, wild, undomesticated, untamed (of animals and places), from Old French *sauvage, salvage* wild, savage, untamed, from Late Latin *salvaticus*, alteration of *silvaticus* wild, *literally of the woods*, from *silva*: forest, grove. Of persons, the meaning: reckless, ungovernable, is attested from c. 1400, earlier in sense *indomitable, valiant* (c.1300). Implications of ferocity are attested from 1570s, earlier of animals (c.1400).
    Antony and Cleopatra, I 4 line 492.
    Hamlet, II 1 line 983.
    Henry V, II 2 line 730; Henry V, III 5 line 1397; Henry V, V 2 line 3039.
    Henry VI, Part II, IV 1 line 2293.
    King Lear, III 3 line 1783.
    Love's Labour's Lost, IV 3 line 1566; Love's Labour's Lost, IV 3 line 1692; Love's Labour's Lost, V 2 line 2094.
    Merchant of Venice, V 1 line 2533.
    Much Ado About Nothing, I 1 line 234; Much Ado About Nothing, I 1 line 236; Much Ado About Nothing, IV 1 line 1702; Much Ado About Nothing, V 1 line 2255; Much Ado About Nothing, V 4 line 2591.
    Othello, IV 1 line 2476; Othello, IV 1 line 2620.
    Richard III, I 4 line 1088; Richard III, III 5 line 2153.
    Romeo and Juliet,V 3 line 2974.
    Sonnet C XXIX line 4.
    Tempest, I 2 line 508; Tempest, II 2 line 1149.
    Timon of Athens, V 1 line 2447.
    Titus Andronicus, IV 5 line 4567.
    Troilus and Cressida, II 3 line 1345; Troilus and Cressida, V 3 line 3332.
    Winter's Tale, II 3 line 1154; Winter's Tale, III 3 line 1537.

Savoury: aromatic mint, late 14c., perhaps an alteration of Old English: *sæperie*, which is ultimately from Latin: *satureia*: *savoury*. But early history of the word suggests transmission via Old French: *savereie*.
    Winter's Tale, IV 4 line 1981.

Scamel: shellfish, or rock hopping bird. Origin unknown
    Tempest, II 2 line 1258.

Scion: c.1300, a shoot or twig, from Old French: *sion, cion*.
    Henry V, III 5 line 1397.
    Othello, I 3 line 691.
    Winter's Tale, IV 4 line 1968.

Screech-owl: imitative, also know as the Barn Owl, with it's large black eyes and heart-shaped face.
>   **Henry VI, Part II**, I 4 line 645; Henry VI, Part II, III 2 line 2021.
>   **Henry VI, Part III**, II 6 line 1309.
>   **Midsummer Night's Dream**, V 1 line 2225.
>   **Troilus and Cressida**, V 10 line 3649.

Scull: shoal of fish.
>   **Troilus and Cressida**, V 5 line 3478.

Sea: Old English: *sæ: lake, body of water.* The expression, *sea change* is first seen in Shakespeare, 1610.
>   **All's Well That Ends Well**, II 1 line 749.
>   **Antony and Cleopatra**, I 2 line 280; Antony and Cleopatra, I 4 line 463; Antony and Cleopatra, I 4 line 478; Antony and Cleopatra, I 4 line 510; Antony and Cleopatra, II 1 line 627; Antony and Cleopatra, II 2 line 881; Antony and Cleopatra, II 6 line 1239; Antony and Cleopatra, II 6 line 1255; Antony and Cleopatra, II 6 line 1322; Antony and Cleopatra, II 6 line 1330; Antony and Cleopatra, III 6 line 1881; Antony and Cleopatra, III 7 line 1965; Antony and Cleopatra, III 7 line 1972; Antony and Cleopatra, III 7 line 1973; Antony and Cleopatra, III 7 line 1986; Antony and Cleopatra, III 7 line 1988r; Antony and Cleopatra, III 7 line 1997; Antony and Cleopatra, III 7 line 2014; Antony and Cleopatra, III 7 line 2029; Antony and Cleopatra, III 8 line 2047; Antony and Cleopatra, III 10 line 2093; Antony and Cleopatra, III 12 line 2209; Antony and Cleopatra, IV 2 line 2523; Antony and Cleopatra, IV 10 line 2881; Antony and Cleopatra, IV 10 line 2887.
>   **As You Like It**, II 7 line 967; As You Like It, III 2 line 1302.
>   **Comedy of Errors**, I 1 line 92; Comedy of Errors, II 1 lines 289, 293; Comedy of Errors, IV 1 line 986; Comedy of Errors, V 1 line 1446; Comedy of Errors, V 1 line 1478; Comedy of Errors, V 1 line 1801.
>   **Coriolanus**, II 2 line 1346; Coriolanus, IV 3 line 2527; Coriolanus, V 4 line 3792.
>   **Cymbeline**, I 6 line 640; Cymbeline, I 6 line 837; Cymbeline, III 1 line 1440; Cymbeline, III 4 line 1935; Cymbeline, IV 2 line 2358; Cymbeline, IV 2 line 2516; Cymbeline, IV 2 line 2741; Cymbeline, V 5 line 3726.
>   **Hamlet**, I 1 line 176; Hamlet, I 4 lines 704, 710; Hamlet, III 1 line 1752; Hamlet, III 1 line 1863; Hamlet, IV 1 line 2633; Hamlet, IV 6 line 2633.
>   **Henry IV, Part I**, I 2 line 139; Henry IV, Part I, I 2 line 143r; Henry IV, Part I, III 1 line 1587.
>   **Henry IV, Part II**, I 1 line 239; Henry IV, Part II, III 1 line 1754; Henry IV, Part II, V 2 line 3379; Henry IV, Part II, V 5 line 3630.
>   **Henry V**, I 2 line 309; Henry V, I 2 line 356; Henry V, II 0 line 501; Henry V, II 2 line 829; Henry V, III 0 line 1064; Henry V, III 7 line 1673; Henry V, IV 1 line 1995; Henry V, V 0 lines 2847, 2849.
>   **Henry VI, Part I**, III 1 line 1414; Henry VI, Part I, III 4 line 1736; Henry VI, Part I, IV 1 line 1854; Henry VI, Part I, IV 7 line 2265; Henry VI,

Part I, V 1 line 2406; Henry VI, Part I, V 3 line 2665; Henry VI, Part I, V 5 line 2943.
Henry VI, Part II, I 3 line 519; Henry VI, Part II, III 2 lines 1763, 1775, 1777, 1789; Henry VI, Part II, IV 1 line 2149; Henry VI, Part II, IV 1 line 2153; Henry VI, Part II, IV 8 line 2801.
Henry VI, Part III, I 1 line 221; Henry VI, Part III, I 1 line 256; Henry VI, Part III, II 2 line 986; Henry VI, Part III, II 5 lines 1107, 1109; Henry VI, Part III, II 5 line 1211; Henry VI, Part III, II 6 lines 1343, 1350; Henry VI, Part III, III 2 line 1627; Henry VI, Part III, III 3 line 1939; Henry VI, Part III, IV 1 line 2018; Henry VI, Part III, IV 7 line 2428; Henry VI, Part III, IV 8 line 2524; Henry VI, Part III, IV 8 line 2579; Henry VI, Part III, V 4 lines 2812, 2829; Henry VI, Part III, V 6 line 3019.
Henry VIII, II 4 line 1570; Henry VIII, III 1 line 1630; Henry VIII, III 2 line 2264; Henry VIII, IV 1 line 2500.
Julius Caesar, I 3 line 513; Julius Caesar, IV 3 line 2233.
King John, I 1 line 111; King John, II 1 line 761; King John, II 1 line 770; King John, II 1 line 800.
King Lear, III 1 line 1622; King Lear, III 4 line 1812; King Lear, III 7 line 2188; King Lear, IV 4 line 2517; King Lear, IV 6 line 2601; King Lear, IV 6 line 2681.
Love's Labour's Lost, IV 3 line 1560.
Macbeth, I 3 line 132; Macbeth, II 2 line 726; Macbeth, IV 2 line 1762.
Measure for Measure, I 2 line 105; Measure for Measure, III 1 line 1453; Measure for Measure, III 1 line 1458.
Merchant of Venice, I 1 line 12; Merchant of Venice, I 1 line 26; Merchant of Venice, I 1 line 184; Merchant of Venice, II 2 line 726; Merchant of Venice, II 8 line 1100; Merchant of Venice, III 1 line 1241; Merchant of Venice, III 1 line 1277; Merchant of Venice, III 2 line 1465; Merchant of Venice, V 1 line 2456.
Merry Wives of Windsor, II 1 line 654.
Midsummer Night's Dream, II 1 lines 454, 458; Midsummer Night's Dream, II 1 lines 523, 525.
Much Ado About Nothing, II 3 line 884; Much Ado About Nothing, IV 1 line 1789.
Othello, I 2 line 232; Othello, II 1 line 764; Othello, II 1 line 770; Othello, II 1 line 794; Othello, II 1 line 815; Othello, II 1 line 824; Othello, II 1 line 844; Othello, II 1 line 872; Othello, II 1 line 978; Othello, III 3 line 2139; Othello, V 2 line 3733.
Pericles, I 3 lines 401, 402; Pericles, I 4 line 450; Pericles, II 1 line 562; Pericles, II 1 line 584; Pericles, II 1 line 607; Pericles, II 1 line 629; Pericles, II 1 line 637; Pericles, II 1 line 638; Pericles, II 1 line 711; Pericles, II 1 line 734; Pericles, II 3 line 910; Pericles, II 3 line 914; Pericles, II 4 line 995; Pericles, III 0 lines 1171, 1187; Pericles, III 1 line 1244; Pericles, III 1 line 1248; Pericles, III 2 line 1303; Pericles, III 2 line 1344; Pericles, III 2 line 1350; Pericles, III 2 line 1354; Pericles, III 2 line 1380; Pericles, III 3 lines 1435, 1437; Pericles, III 4 line 1477; Pericles, IV 1 line 1610; Pericles, IV 1 line 1662; Pericles, IV 4 lines 1876, 1884, 1910; Pericles, IV 6 line 1988; Pericles, V 0 line 2156; Pericles, V 1 line 2366; Pericles, V 1 line 2367; Pericles, V 1

lines 2408, 2413, 2414; Pericles, V 1 line 2466; Pericles, V 3 line 2525; Pericles, V 3 line 2577.
Rape of Lucrece, lines 703, 708, 709, 1151.
Richard II, I 1 line 21; Richard II, II 1 lines 729, 744; Richard II, III 2 line 1411; Richard II, III 2 line 1461.
Richard III, I 4 line 861; Richard III, I 4 line 874; Richard III, III 7 line 2373; Richard III, IV 1 line 2512; Richard III, IV 2 line 2636; Richard III, IV 4 line 3286; Richard III, IV 4 line 3287; Richard III, IV 4 line 3296; Richard III, V 3 line 3843.
Romeo and Juliet, I 1 line 219; Romeo and Juliet, I 3 line 474; Romeo and Juliet, II 2 line 932; Romeo and Juliet, III 5 line 984; Romeo and Juliet, III 5 lines 2238, 2239; Romeo and Juliet, V 3 line 2976.
Sonnet XXI line 6; Sonnet XLIV line 7; Sonnet LXV line 1; Sonnet CXIII line 11; Sonnet CXXXV line 9.
Taming of the Shrew, I 2 line 623; Taming of the Shrew, I 2 line 751; Taming of the Shrew, II 1 line 1181; Taming of the Shrew, V 2 line 2657.
Tempest, I 1 line 22; Tempest, I 1 line 59; Tempest, I 1 line 79; Tempest, I 2 lines 88, 95; Tempest, I 2 lines 254, 258; Tempest, I 2 line 266; Tempest, I 2 line 442; Tempest, II 1 line 765; Tempest, II 1 line 792; Tempest, II 2 lines 1131r, 1144; Tempest, III 2 line 1408; Tempest, III 3 line 1563; Tempest, III 3 lines 1631, 1649, 1652; Tempest, V 1 line 2064; Tempest, V 1 line 2227; Tempest, V 1 line 2287; Tempest, V 1 line 2394.
Timon of Athens, IV 3 line 2151.
Titus Andronicus, III 1 line 1198; Titus Andronicus, III 1 line 1224; Titus Andronicus, III 1 lines 1361, 1364, 1366; Titus Andronicus, IV 3 line 1889; Titus Andronicus, V 2 line 2363.
Troilus and Cressida, I 3 line 484; Troilus and Cressida, I 3 line 550; Troilus and Cressida, II 2 lines 1078, 1095; Troilus and Cressida, III 2 line 1729.
Twelfth Night, I 1 line 12; Twelfth Night, I 2 line 61; Twelfth Night, II 1 line 631; Twelfth Night, II 4 line 971; Twelfth Night, II 4 line 999; Twelfth Night, V 1 line 2267.
Two Gentlemen of Verona, I 2 line 283; Two Gentlemen of Verona, I 3 line 384; Two Gentlemen of Verona, II 4 line 830; Two Gentlemen of Verona, III 1 line 1298; Two Gentlemen of Verona, III 1 line 1357; Two Gentlemen of Verona, IV 3 line 1816.
Venus and Adonis, line 409.
Winter's Tale, I 2 line 554; Winter's Tale, III 3 lines 1578, 1579; Winter's Tale, III 3 lines 1593, 1595, 1597; Winter's Tale, IV 4 lines 2425, 2433.

Sea-marge: shore, mid 16c., from French, from Latin: *margo: margin.*
    Tempest, IV 1 line 1779.

Season: c.1300, a period of the year, with reference to weather or work, from Old French: *seison*: a *sowing, planting,* from Latin: *sationem.* Applied to timber by 1540s. In 16c., it also meant to copulate with.

All's Well That Ends Well, I 1 line 45; All's Well That Ends Well, I 1 line 68; All's Well That Ends Well, I 1 lines 138, 143; All's Well That Ends Well, I 1 line 224; All's Well That Ends Well, V 3 line 2711.
Antony and Cleopatra, V 1 line 3336.
As You Like It, II 2 line 553; As You Like It, III 2 line 1344.
Comedy of Errors, I 2 line 233; Comedy of Errors, II 2 line 441; Comedy of Errors, IV 2 line 1139.
Coriolanus, III 3 line 2426.
Cymbeline, I 6 line 610; Cymbeline, II 3 line 1029; Cymbeline, III 4 line 1917; Cymbeline, IV 3 line 2851; Cymbeline, V 5 line 3861.
Hamlet, I 1 line 181; Hamlet, I 2 line 400; Hamlet, I 3 line 567; Hamlet, I 4 line 631; Hamlet, II 1 line 977; Hamlet, III 2 line 2101; Hamlet, III 2 line 2148; Hamlet, III 3 line 2369.
Henry IV, Part I, III 1 line 1560; Henry IV, Part I, IV 1 line 2223.
Henry IV, Part II, III 1 line 1812; Henry IV, Part II, IV 2 line 2524; Henry IV, Part II, IV 4 line 2876.
Henry VI, Part II, II 4 line 1160.
Julius Caesar, II 1 line 726.
King John, IV 2 line 1747.
King Lear, II 1 line 1061; King Lear, III 4 line 1835.
Love's Labour's Lost, I 1 line 111; Love's Labour's Lost, V 2 line 1945.
Lover's Complaint, line 18.
Macbeth, III 4 line 1445; Macbeth, IV 2 line 1758.
Measure for Measure, II 2 line 847; Measure for Measure, II 2 line 942.
Merchant of Venice, III 2 line 1443; Merchant of Venice, IV 1 line 2029; Merchant of Venice, IV 1 line 2137; Merchant of Venice, V 1 line 2564r.
Merry Wives of Windsor, II 2 line 960; Merry Wives of Windsor, III 3 line 1550.
Midsummer Night's Dream, II 1 line 467; Midsummer Night's Dream, II 2 line 776.
Much Ado About Nothing, I 3 line 351; Much Ado About Nothing, II 2 line 775; Much Ado About Nothing, IV 1 line 1791.
Rape of Lucrece, lines 217, 632, 846, 930.
Richard II, III 2 line 1516.
Richard III, I 4 line 895; Richard III, I 4 line 910; Richard III, III 7 line 2360; Richard III, V 3 line 3559.
Romeo and Juliet, II 3 line 1132.
Sonnet XIV line 4; Sonnet XX line 6; Sonnet LXXV line 2; Sonnet CIV line 6.
Tempest, I 2 line 367.
Timon of Athens, III 6 line 1486; Timon of Athens, IV 3 line 1760.
Troilus and Cressida, I 2 line 404; Troilus and Cressida, I 3 line 540.
Twelfth Night, I 1 line 34.
Venus and Adonis, line 347.
Winter's Tale, IV 4 line 1953.

Sedge: grass-like plant with triangular stems and inconspicuous flowers, growing typically in wet ground. Old English: *secg*, of Germanic origin, from an Indo-European root shared by Latin *secare: to cut*.
    Much Ado About Nothing, II 1 line 586.
    Taming of the Shrew, Prologue 2 lines 196, 198.
    Tempest, IV 1 line 1850.
    Two Gentlemen of Verona, II 7 line 1004.

Seed: Old English: *sed, sæd,* meaning progeny, offspring. To produce seed, late 14c.; to sow with seed, mid-15c.
    All's Well That Ends Well, I 3 line 465.
    Antony and Cleopatra, II 7 line 1397.
    Hamlet, I 2 line 340.
    Henry IV, Part I, II 1 line 730; Henry IV, Part I, II 1 line 732.
    Henry IV, Part II, II 1 line 773r; Henry IV, Part II, II 1 line 781; Henry IV, Part II, III 1 lines 1789, 1795.
    Henry V, II 4 line 958.
    Macbeth, I 3 line 159; Macbeth, III 1 line 1078.
    Measure for Measure, I 2 line 188; Measure for Measure, I 4 line 394.
    Merchant of Venice, II 9 line 1176.
    Pericles, IV 6 line 2024.
    Rape of Lucrece, line 654.
    Romeo and Juliet, V 1 line 2854.
    Tempest, I 2 line 520; Tempest, II 1 line 852.
    Troilus and Cressida, I 3 line 778; Troilus and Cressida, IV 5 line 2741.
    Venus and Adonis, line 187r.
    Winter's Tale, IV 4 line 2412.

Seedness: the sowing of the seed.
    Measure for Measure, I 4 line 394.

Serpent: c.1300, limbless reptile, from Old French: *sarpent*, from Latin: *serpentem*
    All's Well That Ends Well, I 3 line 460.
    Antony and Cleopatra, I 2 line 289; Antony and Cleopatra, I 5 line 560; Antony and Cleopatra, II 5 line 1153; Antony and Cleopatra, II 7 line 1400; Antony and Cleopatra, II 7 line 1402; Antony and Cleopatra, II 7 line 1427; Antony and Cleopatra, IV 15 line 3196.
    Coriolanus, I 8 line 740.
    Hamlet, I 5 lines 773, 776.
    Henry VI, Part II, III 2 line 1728; Henry VI, Part II, III 2 lines 1949, 1956; Henry VI, Part II, III 2 line 2021.
    Henry VI, Part III, II 2 line 857.
    Julius Caesar, II 1 line 633.
    King John, III 1 line 1183; King John, III 3 line 1362.
    King Lear, I 4 line 814; King Lear, II 4 line 1445; King Lear, V 3 line 3219.
    Love's Labour's Lost, V 2 line 2532.

Macbeth, I 5 line 421; Macbeth, III 4 line 1306.
Merchant of Venice, IV 1 line 2001.
Midsummer Night's Dream, II 2 lines 807, 810; Midsummer Night's Dream, III 2 line 1106; Midsummer Night's Dream, III 2 line 1304; Midsummer Night's Dream, V 1 line 2285.
Much Ado About Nothing, V 1 line 2165.
Othello, IV 2 line 2753.
Pericles, I 1 line 184.
Rape of Lucrece, line 413.
Richard II, III 4 line 1942; Richard II, V 3 line 2636.
Romeo and Juliet, III 2 line 1795; Romeo and Juliet, IV 1 line 2446.
Troilus and Cressida, V 1 line 3035.
Venus and Adonis, line 37.

Serpigo: a sort of skin eruption.
Measure for Measure, III 1 line 1253.
Troilus and Cressida, II 3 line 1287.

Shadow: Old English: *sceadwe, sceaduwe*, oblique cases of *sceadu*. Also, late Old English: *sceadwian: to protect as with covering wings.* Meaning *to follow like a shadow* is from c.1600 in an isolated instance.
All's Well That Ends Well, V 3 line 3027.
Antony and Cleopatra, IV 2 line 2551; Antony and Cleopatra, V 2 line 3510.
As You Like It, IV 1 line 1978.
Coriolanus, I 1 line 285.
Cymbeline, V 4 line 3247.
Hamlet, II 2 line 1357; Hamlet, II 2 line 1358; Hamlet, II 2 line 1360r; Hamlet, II 2 line 1362.
Henry IV, Part I, III 2 line 1923; Henry IV, Part I, V 4 line 2983.
Henry IV, Part II, I 1 line 251; Henry IV, Part II, II 2 line 1131; Henry IV, Part II, III 2 line 1980; Henry IV, Part II, III 2 line 1986; Henry IV, Part II, IV 2 line 2456.
Henry VI, Part I, II 3 line 866; Henry VI, Part I, II 3 line 876; Henry VI, Part I, II 3 line 881; Henry VI, Part I, II 3 line 895; Henry VI, Part I, V 4 line 2808.
Henry VI, Part II, I 1 line 18.
Henry VI, Part III, I 4 line 508; Henry VI, Part III, IV 3 line 2224; Henry VI, Part III, IV 6 line 2363.
Henry VIII, I 1 line 308.
Julius Caesar, I 2 line 146; Julius Caesar, V 1 line 2442.
King John, II 1 line 304; King John, II 1 lines 810, 811, 812.
King Lear, I 1 line 64; King Lear, I 4 line 753; King Lear, III 4 line 1857; King Lear, V 2 line 3107.
Macbeth, III 4 line 1402; Macbeth, IV 1 line 1681; Macbeth, V 4 line 2330; Macbeth, V 5 line 2381.
Measure for Measure, III 1 line 1488.

Merchant of Venice, I 2 line 254; Merchant of Venice, II 1 line 516; Merchant of Venice, II 9 lines 1198, 1199; Merchant of Venice, III 2 lines 1496, 1497; Merchant of Venice, V 1 line 2452.
Merry Wives of Windsor, II 2 line 999.
Midsummer Night's Dream, I 1 line 150; Midsummer Night's Dream, III 2 line 1404; Midsummer Night's Dream, V 1 line 2056; Midsummer Night's Dream, V 1 line 2275.
Othello, II 3 line 1435; Othello, IV 1 line 2457.
Passionate Pilgrim, line 192.
Pericles, IV 2 line 1776; Pericles, IV 4 line 1895.
Rape of Lucrece, lines 321, 511, 1022, 1048, 1467, 1508.
Richard II, II 2 lines 1007, 1016; Richard II, III 4 line 1888; Richard II, IV 1 lines 2284, 2285; Richard II, IV 1 lines 2287, 2290.
Richard III, I 1 line 27; Richard III, I 2 line 457; Richard III, I 4 line 886; Richard III, IV 4 line 2878; Richard III, V 3 line 3719; Richard III, V 3 line 3720.
Romeo and Juliet, II 5 line 1380; Romeo and Juliet, V 1 line 2816.
Sonnet XXVII line 10; Sonnet XXXVII line 10; Sonnet XLIII lines 5r, 6; Sonnet LIII lines 2, 4, 10; Sonnet LXI line 4; Sonnet LXVII line 8; Sonnet XCVIII line 14.
Tempest, IV 1 line 1777.
Timon of Athens, II 2 line 735; Timon of Athens, V 4 line 2563.
Titus Andronicus, I 1 line 117; Titus Andronicus, I 1 line 143; Titus Andronicus, II 1 line 688; Titus Andronicus, II 3 line 748; Titus Andronicus, II 4 line 1083; Titus Andronicus, III 2 line 1527; Titus Andronicus, IV 4 line 2099.
Twelfth Night, II 5 line 1044.
Two Gentlemen of Verona, III 1 line 1250; Two Gentlemen of Verona, IV 2 lines 1759, 1760; Two Gentlemen of Verona, IV 2 line 1763; Two Gentlemen of Verona, IV 2 line 1766; Two Gentlemen of Verona, IV 4 line 1960; Two Gentlemen of Verona, IV 4 line 2038r; Two Gentlemen of Verona, V 4 line 2150.
Venus and Adonis, lines 182, 196, 211, 335, 554, 728, 1023, 1121.
Winter's Tale, II 3 line 967.

Shale: husks, shells. Middle English schale: shell, husk, pod (late 14c.), also fish scale, from Old English *scealu*.
    Henry V, IV 2 line 2182.

Shard: wing cases.
    Antony and Cleopatra, III 2 line 1615.
    Cymbeline, III 3 line 1622.
    Macbeth, III 2 line 1216.

Shark: 1560s, of uncertain origin; apparently the word and the first specimen were brought to London by Capt. John Hawkins's second expedition. The meaning *dishonest person who preys on others*, though only attested from 1599 (sharker in this sense is from 1594), may be the original sense, later applied to the large, voracious marine fish.

Hamlet, I 1 line 114.
Macbeth, IV 1 line 1571.

Sheaved: made of straw, 1570s.
Lover's Complaint, line 30.

Sheep: Old English: *sceap, scep*. The more usual word for the animal is represented by ewe. As a type of timidity, from Old English; the meaning *stupid, timid person* is attested from 1540s. The image of the wolf in sheep's clothing was in Old English; that of separating the sheep from the goats is also Biblical in origin. Sheep's eyes: *loving looks* is attested from 1520s.
As You Like It, II 4 line 802; As You Like It, III 2 line 1147; As You Like It, III 2 line 1177; As You Like It, III 2 line 1496; As You Like It, IV 3 line 2079.
Comedy of Errors, IV 1 line 1047.
Coriolanus, II 1 line 1205.
Hamlet, V 1 line 3454; Hamlet, V 1 line 3456.
Henry VI, Part I, I 3 line 410; Henry VI, Part I, I 5 lines 614, 615; Henry VI, Part I, V 5 line 2907.
Henry VI, Part II, IV 2 line 2366; Henry VI, Part II, IV 3 line 2503; Henry VI, Part II, V 1 line 3004.
Henry VI, Part III, II 5 line 1145; Henry VI, Part III, V 6 line 3003.
Julius Caesar, I 3 line 533.
King John, IV 1 line 1594.
King Lear, II 3 line 1270; King Lear, III 4 line 1899; King Lear, III 6 lines 2046, 2048.
Love's Labour's Lost, II 1 line 715; Love's Labour's Lost, II 1 line 717; Love's Labour's Lost, II 1 line 718; Love's Labour's Lost, IV 3 line 1325r; Love's Labour's Lost, V 1 line 1784; Love's Labour's Lost, V 1 line 1789.
Measure for Measure, V 1 line 2769.
Merchant of Venice, I 3 line 397.
Much Ado About Nothing, II 3 line 878.
Taming of the Shrew, III 2 line 1416.
Tempest, IV 1 line 1772.
Timon of Athens, IV 3 line 2151.
Titus Andronicus, IV 4 line 2105.
Troilus and Cressida, III 3 line 2194.
Twelfth Night, II 5 line 1033.
Two Gentlemen of Verona, I 1 line 77; Two Gentlemen of Verona, I 1 line 78; Two Gentlemen of Verona, I 1 line 81; Two Gentlemen of Verona, I 1 line 84; Two Gentlemen of Verona, I 1 line 85; Two Gentlemen of Verona, I 1 lines 89r, 91; Two Gentlemen of Verona, I 1 lines 92, 93, 95.
Venus and Adonis, lines 553, 707.
Winter's Tale, III 3 line 1560; Winter's Tale, III 3 line 1620; Winter's Tale, IV 3 line 1762; Winter's Tale, IV 3 line 1841; Winter's Tale, IV 3 lines 1845, 1847; Winter's Tale, IV 4 line 1858; Winter's Tale, IV 4 line

1934; Winter's Tale, IV 4 line 2341; Winter's Tale, IV 4 lines 2754, 2758.

Shin: Old English: *scinu.*
    As You Like It, II 4 line 774.
    Love's Labour's Lost, III 1 line 833; Love's Labour's Lost, III 1 line 868; Love's Labour's Lost, III 1 line 874; Love's Labour's Lost, III 1 line 878; Love's Labour's Lost, III 1 line 880.
    Merry Wives of Windsor, I 1 line 263; Merry Wives of Windsor, V 5 line 2619.
    Romeo and Juliet, I 2 line 327.
    Tempest, IV 1 line 1917.
    Timon of Athens, IV 3 line 1833.

Shotten-herring: one that shed it's roe.
    Henry IV, Part I, II 4 line 1120.

Shore: c.1300, land bordering a large body of water, and according to etymologists originally with a sense of division between land and water, and thus related to Old English: *sceran: shear, to cut*. But if the word originated on the North Sea coast of the continent, it may as well have meant *land cut off from the mainland by tidal marshes*. Old English: words for *coast, shore* were *strand, warop, ofer*. General application to country near a seacoast is attested from 1610s.
    Antony and Cleopatra, II 7 line 1476; Antony and Cleopatra, II 7 line 1529; Antony and Cleopatra, II 7 line 1536; Antony and Cleopatra, II 6 line 1255; Antony and Cleopatra, II 6 line 1322; Antony and Cleopatra, IV 15 line 3179.
    Comedy of Errors, III 2 line 907.
    Cymbeline, I 3 line 271.
    Henry IV, Part I, III 1 line 1619; Henry IV, Part I, IV 3 lines 2518, 2536.
    Henry V, III 3 line 1299; Henry V, IV 1 line 2111; Henry V, V 2 line 3331.
    Henry VI, Part II, III 2 lines 1768, 1771, 1776, 1783; Henry VI, Part II, IV 1 line 2162.
    Henry VI, Part III, III 2 line 1625.
    Henry VIII, I 1 line 227.
    Julius Caesar, I 1 line 48; Julius Caesar, I 1 line 60; Julius Caesar, I 2 line 191.
    King John, I 1 line 111; King John, II 1 line 313; King John, II 1 line 648; King John, II 1 line 754; King John, V 2 line 2315.
    Measure for Measure, III 2 line 1761.
    Merchant of Venice, III 2 line 1464.
    Merry Wives of Windsor, I 3 line 378; Merry Wives of Windsor, II 1 line 627; Merry Wives of Windsor, III 5 line 1760.
    Midsummer Night's Dream, V 1 line 2184.
    Much Ado About Nothing, II 3 line 884.
    Othello, II 1 line 774; Othello, II 1 line 794; Othello, II 1 line 862; Othello, II 1 line 1084; Othello, V 2 line 3547.

Pericles, I 4 line 477; Pericles, II 1 line 575; Pericles, II 1 line 585r; Pericles, II 1 line 685; Pericles, II 3 line 911; Pericles, II 3 line 915; Pericles, III 2 line 1344; Pericles, III 2 line 1356; Pericles, III 3 line 1463; Pericles, IV 4 line 1925; Pericles, IV 6 line 2116; Pericles, V 1 line 2197; Pericles, V 1 line 2298; Pericles, V 1 line 2299; Pericles, V 1 line 2409; Pericles, V 1 line 2482; Pericles, V 1 line 2486; Pericles, V 3 line 2530; Pericles, V 3 line 2547.
Rape of Lucrece, lines 1165, 1491.
Richard II, II 1 line 744; Richard II, II 1 line 979; Richard II, III 2 line 1517.
Richard III, IV 4 lines 3250, 3255; Richard III, IV 4 line 3305; Richard III, IV 4 line 3356.
Romeo and Juliet, II 1 line 932.
Sonnet LVI line 10; Sonnet LX line 1; Sonnet LXIV line 6.
Taming of the Shrew, I 1 line 335; Taming of the Shrew, I 1 line 525.
Tempest, I 2 line 270; Tempest, I 2 line 296; Tempest, I 2 line 338; Tempest, II 1 line 820; Tempest, II 2 line 1132; Tempest, II 2 line 1212; Tempest, II 2 line 1216; Tempest, III 2 line 1409; Tempest, III 3 line 1643; Tempest, V 1 line 2110; Tempest, V 1 line 2177; Tempest, V 1 line 2205; Tempest, V 1 line 2281.
Titus Andronicus, I 1 line 104.
Troilus and Cressida, I 3 lines 558, 565; Troilus and Cressida, II 2 line 1057; Troilus and Cressida, II 3 line 1471.
Twelfth Night, V 1 line 2477.
Two Gentlemen of Verona, I 1 line 144.
Venus and Adonis, line 839.
Winter's Tale, III 3 line 1584; Winter's Tale, IV 4 line 2134; Winter's Tale, IV 4 line 2518; Winter's Tale, IV 4 line 2812; Winter's Tale, V 1 line 3020.

Shough: a rough, shaggy dog.
    Macbeth, III 1 line 1109.

Shoulder: Old English: *sculdor*. The verb is first attested c.1300 with sense *to push with the shoulder*; meaning *take a burden* first recorded 1580s.
    Antony and Cleopatra, III 11 line 2119.
    As You Like It, II 7 line 971; As You Like It, IV 1 line 1837.
    Comedy of Errors, I 2 line 247; Comedy of Errors, II 1 line 346; ; Comedy of Errors, II 2 line 432; Comedy of Errors, III 2 line 900; Comedy of Errors, IV 2 line 1112; Comedy of Errors, IV 4 line 1285.
    Coriolanus, II 1 line 1065.
    Cymbeline, IV 1 line 2303; Cymbeline, V 3 line 3109.
    Hamlet, I 3 line 542; Hamlet, II 1 line 1056; Hamlet, II 2 line 1256.
    Henry IV, Part I, I 2 line 269; Henry IV, Part I, II 4 line 1137; Henry IV, Part I, IV 2 line 2411.
    Henry IV, Part II, II 4 line 1390; Henry IV, Part II, II 4 line 1488; Henry IV, Part II, V 1 line 3225; Henry IV, Part II, V 4 line 3559.
    Henry V, IV 1 line 2072.

Henry VI, Part I, I 5 line 592; Henry VI, Part I, II 5 line 1085; Henry VI, Part I, IV 1 line 1958.
Henry VI, Part II, IV 7 line 2737; Henry VI, Part II, V 2 line 3279.
Henry VI, Part III, II 1 line 817; Henry VI, Part III, II 6 line 1354; Henry VI, Part III, V 7 line 3118.
Henry VIII, I 2 line 313; Henry VIII, III 2 line 2290.
Julius Caesar, I 2 line 203.
King John, I 1 line 255; King John, II 1 line 442.
King Lear, II 2 line 1161.
Love's Labour's Lost, IV 3 line 1416; Love's Labour's Lost, V 1 line 1831; Love's Labour's Lost, V 2 line 1990.
Measure for Measure, I 2 line 265.
Merchant of Venice, III 1 line 1331.
Merry Wives of Windsor, III 3 line 1414; Merry Wives of Windsor, III 5 line 1837; Merry Wives of Windsor, IV 2 line 2067; Merry Wives of Windsor, V 5 line 2584; Merry Wives of Windsor, V 5 line 2919; Merry Wives of Windsor, V 5 line 2721.
Much Ado About Nothing, I 1 line 102; Much Ado About Nothing, I 1 line 233.
Othello, I 3 line 490.
Richard II, I 1 line 82; Richard II, II 1 line 807.
Richard III, I 2 line 275; Richard III, III 1 line 1704; Richard III, III 2 line 1824; Richard III, III 7 line 2339.
Taming of the Shrew, III 2 line 1415; Taming of the Shrew, IV 1 line 1633.
Troilus and Cressida, III 2 line 1663; Troilus and Cressida, III 3 line 2015.
Venus and Adonis, line 1080.
Winter's Tale, III 3 line 1591; Winter's Tale, IV 3 line 1799; Winter's Tale, IV 4 line 1926.

Shower: Old English: *scur:* short fall of rain, fall of missiles or blows. As a verb from 1570.
Antony and Cleopatra, I 2 line 246; Antony and Cleopatra, II 5 line 1104; Antony and Cleopatra, III 2 line 1645.
Coriolanus, II 1 line 1217.
Hamlet, IV 5 line 2902.
Henry IV, Part I, V 1 line 2670.
Henry VI, Part II, III 1 line 1623.
Henry VI, Part III, I 4 line 585; Henry VI, Part III, II 2 line 1002; Henry VI, Part III, II 5 line 1190.
Henry VIII, I 4 line 746; Henry VIII, III 1 line 1627; Henry VIII, III 2 line 2045; Henry VIII, V 4 line 3327.
King John, V 2 line 2328.
Merry Wives of Windsor, III 2 line 1345.
Midsummer Night's Dream, I 1 line 256.
Pericles, IV 4 line 1906.
Rape of Lucrece, line 847.
Richard II, II 1 line 717; Richard II, III 3 line 1680.

Romeo and Juliet, III 5 line 2237.
Sonnet LXXV line 2; Sonnet CXXIV line 12.
Taming of the Shrew, Prologue 1 line 133.
Tempest, IV 1 line 1790.
Timon of Athens, II 2 line 893; Timon of Athens, V 1 line 2332.
Titus Andronicus, III 1 line 1144; Titus Andronicus, V 3 line 2705.
Troilus and Cressida, II 3 line 1348.
Venus and Adonis, line 86.

Shrew: small mammal, Old English: *screawa: shrew-mouse*, unknown outside English. Alternative word for it was *scirfemus*, from *sceorfan*: to *gnaw*. The meaning *peevish, malignant, clamorous, spiteful, vexatious, turbulent woman*, is late 14c., from earlier sense of spiteful person (male or female), mid-13c., traditionally said to derive from some supposed malignant influence of the animal, which was once believed to have a venomous bite and was held in superstitious dread.
    Comedy of Errors, IV 1 line 1004.
    Henry IV, Part II, V 3 line 3433.
    Merchant of Venice, III 1 line 1331.
    Taming of the Shrew, II 1 line 1164; Taming of the Shrew, III 2 line 1393; Taming of the Shrew, IV 1 line 1638; Taming of the Shrew, IV 1 line 1689; Taming of the Shrew, IV 1 line 1820; Taming of the Shrew, IV 2 line 1886; Taming of the Shrew, V 2 line 2556.
    Twelfth Night, I 3 line 159.

Shrimp: early 14c., kind of slender shellfish, probably from Old Norse: *skreppa: thin person*. The meaning *puny person*, is attested from late 14c.
    Henry VI, Part I, II 3 line 851.
    Love's Labour's Lost, V 2 line 2531.

Shrub: Old English: *scrybb*: *brushwood, shrubbery*, a rare and late word, possibly from a Scandinavian source.
    Henry VI, Part III, III 2 line 1644; Henry VI, Part III, V 2 line 2737.
    Rape of Lucrece, lines 715, 716.
    Tempest, II 2 line 1101; Tempest, IV 1 line 1792.
    Titus Andronicus, IV 3 line 1926.

Simple: a medicinal herb.
    As You Like It, IV 1 line 1811.

Sinew: Old English: *seonowe*.
    Antony and Cleopatra, III 13 line 2467.
    Coriolanus, V 6 line 3870.
    Cymbeline, III 3 line 1701.
    Hamlet, I 5 line 832; Hamlet, III 3 line 2353; Hamlet, IV 7 line 3142.
    Henry IV, Part I, IV 4 line 2594.
    Henry IV, Part II, IV 1 line 2378.
    Henry V, I 2 line 370; Henry V, II 2 line 671; Henry V, III 1 line 1098.
    Henry VI, Part I, II 3 line 896; Henry VI, Part I, III 1 line 1428.

Henry VI, Part III, II 3 line 1029; Henry VI, Part III, II 6 line 1345.
Julius Caesar, I 2 line 198.
King John, V 2 line 2342; King John, V 7 2724.
Measure for Measure, III 1 line 1460.
Tempest, III 1 line 1308; Tempest, IV 1 line 2005.
Troilus and Cressida, I 3 line 576; Troilus and Cressida, I 3 line 596; Troilus and Cressida, II 1 line 958; Troilus and Cressida, III 1 line 1639; Troilus and Cressida, III 3 line 2185; Troilus and Cressida, IV 5 line 2746; Troilus and Cressida, V 3 line 3314; Troilus and Cressida, V 8 line 3603.
Twelfth Night, II 5 line 1100.
Two Gentlemen of Verona, III 2 line 1530.
Venus and Adonis, line 925.

Sinewy: late 14c.
    All's Well That Ends Well, II 1 line 657.
    As You Like It, II 2 line 635.
    Love's Labour's Lost, IV 3 line 1653.
    Troilus and Cressida, II 3 line 1469.
    Venus and Adonis, line 119.

Skin: c.1200, animal hide (usually dressed and tanned), from Old Norse: *skinn: animal hide*. Meaning, epidermis of a living animal or person is attested from mid-14c.; extended to fruits, vegetables, etc. late 14c. late 14c., to remove the skin from (originally of circumcision), from skin (n.). As, to have (a particular kind of) skin, from c.1400.
    All's Well That Ends Well, II 2 line 850.
    As You Like It, IV 2 line 1991.
    Comedy of Errors, II 2 line 524; Comedy of Errors, III 1 line 624; Comedy of Errors, IV 3 line 1168.
    Hamlet, III 4 line 2449.
    Henry IV, Part I, III 3 line 2010.
    Henry V, IV 3 line 2331; Henry V, V 1 line 2939.
    Henry VI, Part II, III 1 line 1355; Henry VI, Part II, III 1 line 1585; Henry VI, Part II, IV 2 line 2328; Henry VI, Part II, IV 2 line 2381.
    King John, IV 3 line 2103.
    King Lear, III 4 line 1809.
    Lover's Complaint, line 94.
    Macbeth, II 3 line 900.
    Measure for Measure, II 2 line 903.
    Merry Wives of Windsor, III 1 line 1295.
    Midsummer Night's Dream, II 1 line 634.
    Much Ado About Nothing, III 5 line 1591.
    Othello, V 2 line 3305.
    Rape of Lucrece, line 470.
    Richard II, III 4 line 1924.
    Romeo and Juliet, V 1 line 2852.
    Taming of the Shrew, IV 3 line 2136.
    Tempest, IV 1 line 1975.

Titus Andronicus, V 1 line 2263.

Sky: early 13c., a cloud, from Old Norse: *sky*: *cloud*. Meaning, upper regions of the air is attested from c.1300; replaced native *heofon* in this sense. In Middle English, the word can still mean both cloud and heaven, as still in the skies, originally, the clouds.
    All's Well That Ends Well, I 1 line 219.
    Antony and Cleopatra, II 7 line 1456.
    As You Like It, II 7 line 1085; As You Like It, IV 1 line 1922.
    Comedy of Errors, II 1 line 289.
    Cymbeline, V 4 line 3246; Cymbeline V 5 line 3549.
    Hamlet, V 1 line 3592.
    Henry IV, Part II, IV 3 line 2638.
    Henry V, III 7 line 1710.
    Henry VI, Part I, I 1 line 7; Henry VI, Part I, IV 7 line 2273.
    Henry VI, Part II, III 2 line 1785.
    Henry VI, Part III, II 1 line 654.
    Julius Caesar, I 3 line 460.
    King John, II 1 line 707; King John, III 2 line 1281; King John, III 4 line 1541; King John, IV 2 line 1839.
    King Lear, II 3 line 1263.
    Love's Labour's Lost, IV 2 line 1146; Love's Labour's Lost, IV 3 line 1403.
    Macbeth, I 2 line 76.
    Measure for Measure, I 4 line 386; Measure for Measure, III 1 line 1231.
    Merry Wives of Windsor, V 5 line 2578.
    Midsummer Night's Dream, III 2 line 1053; Midsummer Night's Dream, III 2 line 1143; Midsummer Night's Dream, V 1 line 2147.
    Rape of Lucrece, lines 63, 1281, 1458, 1638.
    Richard II, I 1 line 44; Richard II, I 3 line 427; Richard II, III 2 line 1604.
    Richard III, I 3 line 754; Richard III, V 3 line 3795.
    Romeo and Juliet, II 4 line 1200.
    Sonnet XV line 7.
    Taming of the Shrew, II 5 line 456.
    Tempest, I 2 line 87; Tempest, IV 1 line 1780.
    Titus Andronicus, I 1 line 164; Titus Andronicus, IV 2 line 1779.
    Troilus and Cressida, V 2 line 3223.
    Two Gentlemen of Verona, V 1 line 2049.
    Venus and Adonis, lines 173, 204, 369, 507, 837.
    Winter's Tale, I 2 line 265; Winter's Tale I 2 line 397; Winter's Tale, III 3 line 1580.

Skull: early 13c., probably from Old Norse: *skalli:* bald head, skull; a general Scandinavian word, probably related to Old English: *scealu*: husk.
    Coriolanus, II 3 line 1444.

Hamlet, V 1 line 3417; Hamlet, V 1 line 3418; Hamlet, V 1 line 3439; Hamlet, V 1 line 3440; Hamlet, V 1 line 3506r; Hamlet, V 1 lines 3511, 3512; Hamlet, V 1 line 3515; Hamlet, V 1 line 3530.
Merchant of Venice, III 2 line 1463.
Richard II, IV 1 line 2052; Richard II, IV 1 line 2028.
Richard III, I 4 line 862.
Romeo and Juliet, IV 1 line 2449; Romeo and Juliet, V 3 line 3077.
Tempest, III 2 line 1485; Tempest, V 1 line 2089.
Twelfth Night, I 5 line 405.

Smoke: late Old English: *smoca*, related to *smeocan*: *give off smoke*. Old English verb: *smocian: to produce smoke*. Meaning, to drive out or away or into the open by means of smoke, is attested from 1590s. Meaning, to cure (bacon, fish, etc.) by exposure to smoke, is first attested 1590s. In connection with tobacco, the verb is first recorded 1604 in James I's *Counterblast to Tobacco*.

All's Well That Ends Well, III 6 line 1827; All's Well That Ends Well, IV 1 line 1929.
As You Like It, I 2 line 404; As You Like It, IV 1 line 1935.
Cymbeline, V 5 line 3859; Cymbeline, V 5 line 3951.
Henry IV, Part I, I 5 line 607.
Henry VI, Part I, II 2 line 787.
Julius Caesar, III 1 line 1380.
King John, II 1 line 435; King John, II 1 line 530; King John, II 1 line 764; King John, V 4 line 2522.
King Lear, V 3 line 3389.
Love's Labour's Lost, III 1 line 823.
Macbeth, I 2 line 37; Macbeth, I 5 line 401.
Pericles, I 1 line 190.
Rape of Lucrece, lines 363, 850, 1078, 1093.
Romeo and Juliet, I 1 line 217.
Sonnet XXXIV line 4.
Timon of Athens, III 6 line 1527; Timon of Athens, IV 3 line 1824.
Titus Andronicus, I 1 line 165; Titus Andronicus, IV 2 line 1801.
Twelfth Night, V 1 line 2241.
Venus and Adonis, line 576.

Snail: *snægl*, from Old English: *snaca: snake*, literally, *creeping thing*. Also formerly used of slugs. Symbolic of slowness since at least c.1000; *snail's pace* is attested from c.1400. A common amusement among children consisted of charming snails, in order to induce them to put out their horns.

As You Like It, II 7 line 1044; As You Like It, IV 1 line 1841; As You Like It, IV 1 line 1842; As You Like It, IV 1 line 1843.
Comedy of Errors, II 2 line 583.
King Lear, I 5 line 903.
Love's Labour's Lost, IV 3 line 1683.
Merchant of Venice, II 5 line 895.
Midsummer Night's Dream, II 2 line 673.
Richard III, IV 3 line 2785.

Troilus and Cressida, V 5 line 3474.
Venus and Adonis, line 1055.

Snake: see Snail. Meaning, treacherous person, first recorded 1590. There is an old notion that the snake, in the casting of its slough or skin annually, is supposed to regain new vigour and fresh youth.
Antony and Cleopatra, II 5 line 1098; Antony and Cleopatra, II 5 line 1176.
As You Like It, IV 3 line 2070; As You Like It, IV 3 line 2111.
Henry IV, Part II, V 5 line 3627.
Henry VI, Part II, III 1 line 1512; Henry VI, Part II, III 1 line 1629.
Love's Labour's Lost, V 1 line 1861; Love's Labour's Lost, V 1 line 1864.
Macbeth, III 2 line 1184; Macbeth, IV 1 line 1559.
Midsummer Night's Dream, II 1 line 634; Midsummer Night's Dream, II 2 line 659.
Richard II, III 2 line 1541.
Titus Andronicus, II 3 line 746; Titus Andronicus, II 3 line 836; Titus Andronicus, III 1 line 1392.

Snaky: in appearance or characteristics of a snake.
Merchant of Venice, III 2 line 1459.

Snout: early 13c., trunk or projecting nose of an animal.
Venus and Adonis, lines 643, 1127.

Snow: Old English: *snaw.* c.1300, replacing Old English: *sniwan*, which would have yielded, *snew* (which existed as a parallel form until 17c. and, in Yorkshire, even later).
All's Well That Ends Well, IV 3 line 2255.
Antony and Cleopatra, I 4 line 495.
Comedy of Errors, V 1 line 1751.
Coriolanus, V 3 line 3567.
Cymbeline, II 5 line 1384.
Hamlet, III 1 line 1828; Hamlet, III 3 line 2328; Hamlet, IV 5 line 2896; Hamlet, IV 5 line 3070.
Henry V, III 5 line 1440.
Henry VI, Part II, III 1 line 1507.
King John, III 4 line 1564.
King Lear, II 2 line 1144; King Lear, IV 6 line 2727.
Love's Labour's Lost, I 1 line 110; Love's Labour's Lost, I 1 line 242; Love's Labour's Lost, IV 2 line 1281; Love's Labour's Lost, V 2 line 2871
Macbeth, IV 3 line 1904.
Merchant of Venice, III 2 line 1395.
Merry Wives of Windsor, III 5 line 1767; Merry Wives of Windsor, V 5 line 2580.
Midsummer Night's Dream, III 2 line 1179; Midsummer Night's Dream, IV 1 line 1724; Midsummer Night's Dream, V 1 line 1896.

Othello, V 2 line 3305.
Pericles, IV 6 line 2084.
Rape of Lucrece, lines 247, 471, 1062, 1269.
Richard II, I 3 line 599; Richard II, IV 1 line 2249.
Richard III, I 4 line 1071; Richard III, V 3 line 3841.
Romeo and Juliet, I 5 line 670; Romeo and Juliet, III 2 line 1737.
Sonnet V line 8; Sonnet CXXX line 3.
Tempest, IV 1 line 1762.
Timon of Athens, IV 3 line 2090.
Titus Andronicus, II 3 line 811; Titus Andronicus, III 1 line 1146.
Two Gentlemen of Verona, II 7 line 994.
Venus and Adonis, lines 374, 382, 772.
Winter's Tale, IV 4 line 2109; Winter's Tale, IV 4 line 2264.

Snow-broth: a mixture of snow and water, or snow just melted. Often refers to a person who is cold-blooded.
Measure for Measure, I 4 line 412.

Soil: the earth or ground, c.1300, from Anglo-French: *soil: piece of ground, place* (13c.), from Latin: *solium: seat*, meaning confused with that of Latin: *solum: soil, ground*. Meaning, mould, earth, dirt (especially that which plants grow in) is attested from mid-15c.
Antony and Cleopatra, I 4 line 449.
As You Like It, II 4 line 816.
Cymbeline, II 3 line 1121.
Hamlet, I 3 line 499; Hamlet, I 4 line 649; Hamlet, II 1 line 992.
Henry IV, Part I, I 1 line 6; Henry IV, Part I, I 1 line 65.
Henry IV, Part II, IV 4 line 2802; Henry IV, Part II, IV 5 line 3085.
Henry VI, Part I, I 5 line 614.
Henry VI, Part II, I 1 line 252; Henry VI, Part II, IV 10 line 2912.
Henry VIII, I 2 line 347.
Julius Caesar, I 2 line 130.
King John, V 1 line 2267.
King Lear, IV 6 line 2731.
Love's Labour's Lost, II 1 lines 533, 534; Love's Labour's Lost, IV 2 line 1148.
Measure for Measure, II 4 line 1186; Measure for Measure, V 1 line 2545.
Much Ado About Nothing, III 2 line 1203.
Richard II, I 3 line 422; Richard II, I 3 line 607; Richard II, III 4 line 1903; Richard II, IV 1 line 2005.
Richard III, IV 4 line 3119.
Sonnet LXIV line 7.
Timon of Athens, III 5 line 1323.
Troilus and Cressida, II 2 line 1063; Troilus and Cressida, II 2 line 1146; Troilus and Cressida, V 2 line 3208.

Sore: Old English: *sar:* bodily injury, sickness, disease, pain, suffering.
All's Well That Ends Well, III 6 line 1770.

Antony and Cleopatra, II 5 line 1054; Antony and Cleopatra, IV 6 line 2727.
As You Like It, II 7 line 962.
Comedy of Errors, III 1 line 696.
Coriolanus, II 1 line 1198: Coriolanus, III 1 line 2028.
Cymbeline, III 6 line 2156; Cymbeline, IV 1 line 2310; Cymbeline, IV 2 line 2612.
Hamlet, I 1 line 91; Hamlet, V 1 line 3504; Hamlet, V 2 line 3867.
Henry IV, Part I, IV 2 line 2394.
Henry IV, Part II, IV 3 line 2672.
Henry V, I 2 line 169; Henry V, I 2 line 432.
Henry VI, Part II, IV 7 line 2628.
Henry VI, Part III, IV 6 line 2405.
Henry VIII, IV 2 line 2573.
King John, V 2 line 2290; King John, V 4 line 2492.
King Lear, II 4 line 1519; King Lear, II 4 line 1607; King Lear, III 5 line 2002.
Love's Labour's Lost, IV 2 lines 1202r, 1203, 1204r, 1205rrr, 1206, 1207.
Macbeth, II 2 line 697; Macbeth, II 4 line 950; Macbeth, V 1 line 2176.
Merchant of Venice, V 1 line 2779.
Much Ado About Nothing, IV 1 line 1905.
Othello, IV 2 line 2797.
Passionate Pilgrim, line 127.
Pericles, I 1 line 147; Pericles, IV 2 line 1699.
Rape of Lucrece, lines 256, 879, 1619.
Richard II, I 3 line 604; Richard II, II 1 line 956.
Richard III, I 4 line 875.
Romeo and Juliet, I 4 line 515.
Taming of the Shrew, III 2 line 1460.
Tempest, II 1 line 843; Tempest, III 1 line 1288; Tempest, V 1 line 2363.
Timon of Athens, IV 3 line 1669.
Troilus and Cressida, III 1 line 1604; Troilus and Cressida, IV 4 line 2586; Troilus and Cressida, V 1 line 2962; Troilus and Cressida, V 5 line 3469.
Two Gentlemen of Verona, I 1 line 32; Two Gentlemen of Verona, II 4 line 789.
Venus and Adonis, lines 453, 725, 938.
Winter's Tale, V 1 line 2840; Winter's Tale, V 3 line 3344.

Sorel: a male deer in his third year, 15c.
    Love's Labour's Lost, IV 2 lines 1204, 1206, 1208.

Sow: Old English: *sawan:* to scatter seed upon the ground or plant it in the earth. Also, sugu, su: female of the swine. Related to *swine.* As a term of abuse for a woman, attested from c.1500
    Coriolanus, III 1 line 1816; Coriolanus, IV 5 line 2971.
    Cymbeline, IV 2 line 2552.

Henry IV, Part II, I 2 line 285; Henry IV, Part II, V 1 line 3155.
Henry V, III 7 line 1700.
Henry VI, Part II, III 1 line 1666.
Henry VIII, III 1 line 1799.
Love's Labour's Lost, IV 3 line 1728.
Macbeth, IV 1 line 1620.
Measure for Measure, IV 1 line 1883.
Othello, I 3 line 680.
Tempest, II 1 line 792; Tempest, II 1 line 852.
Timon of Athens, IV 1 line 1593; Timon of Athens, IV 3 line 1832.
Twelfth Night, V 1 line 2363.
Winter's Tale, IV 3 line 1743.

Spaniel: 13c., as a surname meaning, Spaniard; as a name for a breed of dog of Spanish origin, late 14c.
Antony and Cleopatra, IV 12 line 2925.
Henry VIII, V 3 line 3204.
Julius Caesar, III 1 line 1247.
King Lear, III 6 line 2070.
Macbeth, III 1 line 1108.
Midsummer Night's Dream, II 1 lines 578, 580.
Pericles, IV 6 line 2069.
Taming of the Shrew, IV 1 line 1753.
Two Gentlemen of Verona, III 1 line 1344; Two Gentlemen of Verona, IV 2 line 1644.

Sparrow: small brownish-grey bird, Old English: *spearwa*. A popular name for the common sparrow was, *philip*, perhaps from its note, *phip, phip*.
As You Like It, II 3 line 688.
Hamlet, V 2 line 3854.
Henry IV, Part I, II 4 line 1332; Henry IV, Part I, II 4 line 1334; Henry IV, Part I, V 1 line 2686.
King John, I 1 line 240.
King Lear, I 4 line 737.
Macbeth, I 2 line 56.
Measure for Measure, III 2 line 1682.
Midsummer Night's Dream, III 1 line 952.
Rape of Lucrece, line 900.
Tempest, IV 1 line 1813.
Troilus and Cressida, II 1 lines 928, 929; Troilus and Cressida, III 2 line 1685; Troilus and Cressida, V 7 line 3570.

Spear grass: perhaps the common reed.
Henry IV, Part I, II 4 line 1294.

Spice: early 13c., from Old French: *espice*. Early druggists recognized four types of spices: saffron, clove, cinnamon, nutmeg. Figurative sense of, slight touch or trace of something, is recorded from 1530s. The verb, to season with spices, is first recorded early 14c.

Coriolanus, IV 7 line 3263.
Henry VIII, II 3 line 1233.
Merchant of Venice, I 1 line 34.
Midsummer Night's Dream, II 1 line 494.
Pericles, III 1 line 1262; Pericles, III 2 line 1364.
Richard III, IV 4 line 3238.
Romeo and Juliet, IV 4 line 2613.
Timon of Athens, IV 3 line 1704.
Troilus and Cressida, I 2 line 404.
Winter's Tale, I 2 line 422; Winter's Tale, III 2 line 1418; Winter's Tale, IV 3 line 1840; Winter's Tale, IV 3 line 1844.

Spider: *spiþra*. In literature, often a figure of cunning, skill, and industry as well as poisonous predation. Another word for the creature was *gangewifre: a weaver as he goes*. The spider's symbolism is partly related to the Greek myth of Arachne, who challenged Athene, Zeus' daughter, to a weaving contest, and hanged herself when the goddess destroyed her web. Athene then changed her into a spider, condemned for eternity to hang at the end of her thread: an example of the danger of excessive ambition.
Cymbeline, IV 2 line 2439.
Henry VI, Part II, III 1 line 1625.
Henry VIII, I 1 line 105.
King John, IV 3 line 2157.
Measure for Measure, III 2 line 1784.
Merchant of Venice, III 2 line 1490.
Midsummer Night's Dream, II 2 line 670.
Richard II, III 2 line 1422.
Richard III, I 2 line 191; Richard III, I 3 line 709; Richard III, IV 4 line 2876.
Romeo and Juliet, I 4 lines 559, 561.
Troilus and Cressida, II 3 line 1230.
Winter's Tale, II 1 lines 649, 655.

Spinner: see spider.
Midsummer Night's Dream, II 2 line 670.

Spleen: c.1300, from Old French: *esplen*. Regarded in medieval physiology as the seat of morose feelings and bad temper. Hence figurative sense of violent ill-temper (1590s). This was once supposed to be the cause of laughter.
As You Like It, IV 1 line 1974.
Coriolanus, IV 5 line 2856.
Henry IV, Part I, II 3 line 941; Henry IV, Part I, III 2 line 1949; Henry IV, Part I, V 2 line 2789.
Henry VI, Part I, IV 6 line 2205.
Henry VI, Part II, III 2 line 1810.
Henry VI, Part III, II 1 line 752.
Henry VIII, I 2 line 518; Henry VIII, II 4 line 1452; Henry VIII, II 4 line 1475; Henry VIII, III 2 line 1961.

Julius Caesar, IV 3 line 2029.
King John, II 1 line 356; King John, II 1 line 759; King John, IV 3 line 2122; King John, V 7 line 2685.
King Lear, I 4 line 809.
Love's Labour's Lost, III 1 line 839; Love's Labour's Lost, V 2 line 2001.
Measure for Measure, II 2 line 887.
Midsummer Night's Dream, I 1 line 152.
Othello, IV 1 line 2513.
Passionate Pilgrim, line 77.
Richard III, II 4 line 1552; Richard III, V 3 line 3869.
Romeo and Juliet, III 1 line 1674.
Taming of the Shrew, Prologue 1 line 144; Taming of the Shrew, III 2 line 1373.
Timon of Athens, III 5 line 1429.
Titus Andronicus, II 3 line 934.
Troilus and Cressida, I 3 line 629; Troilus and Cressida, II 2 line 1125; Troilus and Cressida, II 2 line 1194.
Twelfth Night, III 2 line 1470.
Venus and Adonis, line 929.

Sponge: Old English: *sponge*, *spunge*, from Latin: *spongia*.
Hamlet, IV 2 line 2689; Hamlet, IV 2 line 2691; Hamlet, IV 2 line 2697.
Merchant of Venice, I 2 line 289.

Spring: Old English, source of a stream or river, from spring, on the notion of the water bursting forth from the ground. Figurative sense of source or origin of something is attested from early 13c. Season following winter, 1540s, earlier springing time (late 14c.), spring-time (late 15c.), spring of the year (1520s), which had replaced Old English Lent by late 14c.
Antony and Cleopatra, III 2 line 1644.
As You Like It, V 3 lines 2379, 2381, 2385, 2389, 2393.
Comedy of Errors, III 2 line 765r; Comedy of Errors, III 2 line 817.
Coriolanus, II 3 line 1670.
Cymbeline, I 1 line 63; Cymbeline, II 2 line 969; Cymbeline, II 3 line 999.
Hamlet, I 3 line 523; Hamlet, I 4 line 636; Hamlet, IV 5 line 2937; Hamlet, IV 7 line 3151; Hamlet, V 1 line 3573.
Henry IV, Part I, I 2 line 261; Henry IV, Part I, V 2 line 2793.
Henry IV, Part II, I 3 line 642; Henry IV, Part II, IV 4 line 2783.
Henry V, II 4 line 938.
Henry VI, Part I, II 4 line 1016; Henry VI, Part I, III 1 line 1398; Henry VI, Part I, III 1 line 1409.
Henry VI, Part II, III 1 line 1308; Henry VI, Part II, III 1 line 1381; Henry VI, Part II, III 1 line 1622; Henry VI, Part II, IV 1 line 2228.
Henry VI, Part III, II 2 line 1008; Henry VI, Part III, II 3 line 1075; Henry VI, Part III, II 6 line 1303; Henry VI, Part III, III 2 line 1615; Henry VI, Part III, III 3 line 1701; Henry VI, Part III, III 3 line 1760; Henry VI, Part III, IV 8 line 2579.

Henry VIII, III 1 line 1628.
King Lear, I 1 line 199; King Lear, I 4 line 807; King Lear, IV 4 line 2534.
Love's Labour's Lost, I 1 line 99; Love's Labour's Lost, I 1 line 105; Love's Labour's Lost, IV 3 line 1649; Love's Labour's Lost, V 2 lines 2838, 2842.
Macbeth, I 2 line 46; Macbeth, II 3 line 883.
Midsummer Night's Dream, II 1 lines 451, 480.
Passionate Pilgrim, lines 133, 282, 380.
Pericles, I 1 line 58; Pericles, IV 4 line 1917; Pericles, V 1 line 2209.
Rape of Lucrece, lines 100, 382, 655, 920, 1001, 1128, 1506, 1808.
Richard II, I 1 line 100; Richard II, I 2 line 226; Richard II, I 3 line 514; Richard II, III 3 line 1749; Richard II, III 4 line 1913; Richard II, V 2 line 2490.
Richard III, II 2 line 1340; Richard III, III 1 line 1665.
Romeo and Juliet, III 2 line 1826; Romeo and Juliet, V 3 line 3192.
Sonnet I line 10; Sonnet LIII line 9; Sonnet LXIII line 8; Sonnet XCVIII line 1; Sonnet CII line 5; Sonnet CIV line 5.
Taming of the Shrew, II 1 line 1096.
Tempest, I 2 line 489; Tempest, II 2 line 1246; Tempest, IV 1 line 1830.
Timon of Athens, IV 3 line 2131.
Titus Andronicus, III 1 line 1146; Titus Andronicus, V 2 line 2487; Titus Andronicus, V 2 line 2487; Titus Andronicus, V 3 line 2711.
Troilus and Cressida, I 2 line 320.
Twelfth Night, III 1 line 1388.
Two Gentlemen of Verona, I 3 line 389.
Venus and Adonis, lines 147, 161, 187, 279.

Spur: roots of trees. Old English: *spura, spora: urging on*. Also refers to an outcrop of land or a mountain.
Tempest, V 1 line 2068.
Winter's Tale, I 2 line 168.

Squash: gourd, fruit, from 1600s.
Twelfth Night, I 5 line 449.
Winter's Tale, I 2 line 242.

Squirrel: early 14c., from Anglo-French: *esquirel*, Old French: *escurel*.
Midsummer Night's Dream, IV 1 line 1580.
Romeo and Juliet, I 4 line 568.
Two Gentlemen of Verona, IV 4 line 1889.
Stag: late 1200c, probably from Old English: *stagga*.
Antony and Cleopatra, I 4 line 495.
As You Like It, II 1 line 582.
Henry VI, Part I, IV 2 line 2018.
Merry Wives of Windsor, V 5 line 2572.
Richard III, III 2 line 1872.
Taming of the Shrew, Prologue 2 line 192.
Titus Andronicus, II 3 line 806.

Staniel: kestrel or windhover.
  Twelfth Night, II 5 line 1138.

Star: Old English: *steorra*. Astrological sense of influence of planets and zodiac on human affairs, is recorded from mid-13c.
  All's Well That Ends Well, I 1 line 87; All's Well That Ends Well, I 1 line 183; All's Well That Ends Well, I 1 line 193; All's Well That Ends Well, I 3 line 404; All's Well That Ends Well, I 3 line 577; All's Well That Ends Well, II 1 line 653; All's Well That Ends Well, II 5 line 1343; All's Well That Ends Well, III 2 line 1450; All's Well That Ends Well, V 3 line 2945.
  Antony and Cleopatra, III 2 line 1675; Antony and Cleopatra, III 13 line 2428; Antony and Cleopatra, IV 14 line 3113; Antony and Cleopatra, V 1 line 3333; Antony and Cleopatra, V 2 line 3771.
  Coriolanus, V 3 line 3559.
  Cymbeline, III 2 line 1537; Cymbeline, V 4 line 3254; Cymbeline, V 5 line 3801; Cymbeline, V 5 line 3816.
  Hamlet, I 1 line 47; Hamlet, I 1 lines 134, 135; Hamlet, I 4 line 659; Hamlet, I 5 line 783; Hamlet, II 2 line 1212; Hamlet, II 2 line 1239; Hamlet, IV 7 line 3147; Hamlet, V 1 line 3595; Hamlet, V 2 line 3896.
  Henry IV, Part I, I 2 line 125; Henry IV, Part I, V 4 line 3023.
  Henry IV, Part II, II 4 line 1452.
  Henry V, III 7 line 1707; Henry V, III 7 line 1708; Henry V, V 2 line 3365.
  Henry VI, Part I, I 1 line 9; Henry VI, Part I, I 1 line 59; Henry VI, Part I, I 2 line 343; Henry VI, Part I, IV 5 line 2140.
  Henry VI, Part II, III 1 line 1488.
  Henry VI, Part III, IV 6 line 2336; Henry VI, Part III, IV 6 line 2343.
  Henry VIII, IV 1 line 2475; Henry VIII, V 5 line 3330.
  Julius Caesar, I 2 line 231; Julius Caesar, II 1 line 601; Julius Caesar, III 1 line 1265.
  King John, III 1 line 1047; King John, V 7 line 2710.
  King Lear, I 2 lines 444, 450, 454; King Lear, I 5 line 909; King Lear, III 1 line 1641; KIng Lear, III 4 line 1858; King Lear, IV 3 lines 2488, 2489.
  Love's Labour's Lost, I 1 line 90; Love's Labour's Lost, III 1 line 840; Love's Labour's Lost, IV 3 line 1575; Love's Labour's Lost, V 2 line 2097; Love's Labour's Lost, V 2 line 2316.
  Macbeth, I 4 line 323; Macbeth, I 4 line 333.
  Measure for Measure, IV 2 line 2107.
  Merry Wives of Windsor, I 1 line 2; Merry Wives of Windsor, I 3 line 390.
  Midsummer Night's Dream, I 1 line 191; Midsummer Night's Dream, II 1 line 523; Midsummer Night's Dream, III 2 line 413; Midsummer Night's Dream, III 2 line 1470.
  Much Ado About Nothing, II 1 line 631; Much Ado About Nothing, II 1 line 711; Much Ado About Nothing, III 4 line 1542.
  Othello, V 2 line 3303; Othello, V 2 line 3627.

Pericles, I 1 line 82; Pericles, I 4 line 528; Pericles, II 3 line 862; Pericles, V 3 line 2529; Pericles, V 3 line 2614.
Phoenix and the Turtle, line 51.
Rape of Lucrece, lines 64, 215, 230, 1059, 1576.
Richard II, II 4 line 1339; Richard II, II 4 line 1350; Richard II, IV 1 line 2003.
Richard III, II 2 line 1375; Richard III, III 7 line 2383; Richard III, IV 4 line 3019.
Romeo and Juliet, Prologue 1 line 6; Romeo and Juliet, I 2 line 295; Romeo and Juliet, I 4 line 609; Romeo and Juliet, II 2 lines 860, 864; Romeo and Juliet, III 2 line 1740; Romeo and Juliet, V 1 line 2830; Romeo and Juliet, V 3 line 3057.
Sonnet XIV line 1; Sonnet XIV line 10; Sonnet XV line 4; Sonnet XXV line 1; Sonnet XXVI line 9; Sonnet XXVIII line 12; Sonnet CXVI line 7; Sonnet CXXXII line 7.
Taming of the Shrew, IV 5 line 2273; Taming of the Shrew, IV 5 line 2299; Taming of the Shrew, IV 5 line 2307.
Tempest, I 2 line 298.
Timon of Athens, V 1 line 2324.
Titus Andronicus, IV 2 line 1717.
Troilus and Cressida, II 2 line 1037; Troilus and Cressida, IV 4 line 2474.
Twelfth Night, I 3 line 238; Twelfth Night, II 1 line 613; Twelfth Night, II 5 lines 1165, 1193, 1196.
Two Gentlemen of Verona, II 6 line 939; Two Gentlemen of Verona, II 7 line 1049; Two Gentlemen of Verona, III 1 line 1228.
Venus and Adonis, lines 837, 883, 1054.
Winter's Tale, I 2 line 50; Winter's Tale, I 2 line 109; Winter's Tale, I 2 line 477; Winter's Tale, I 2 line 552; Winter's Tale, III 2 line 1316; Winter's Tale, V 1 line 2902r; Winter's Tale, V 1 line 3071.

Starlight: compounded in the late 14c.
   Merry Wives of Windsor, V 5 line 2659.
   Midsummer Night's Dream, II 1 line 395; Midsummer Night's Dream, V 1 line 2159.

Starling: This was one of the birds that was trained to speak. Old English: *stærlinc*.
   Henry IV, Part I, I 3 line 559.

Steed: Old English: *steda: stallion, stud horse*.
   All's Well That Ends Well, II 3 line 1185.
   Antony and Cleopatra, I 5 line 576.
   Coriolanus, I 1 line 110; Coriolanus, I 9 line 778; Coriolanus, I 9 line 835; Coriolanus, I 9 line 846.
   Cymbeline, II 3 line 999.
   Henry IV, Part I, II 3 line 908.
   Henry V, V 0 line 1797r; Henry V, IV 2 line 2171; Henry V, IV 7 line 2598.

Henry VI, Part II, V 2 line 3218.
Henry VI, Part III, II 1 line 811; Henry VI, Part III, II 3 line 1048; Henry VI, Part III, II 6 line 1262; Henry VI, Part III, IV 2 line 2152.
Lover's Complaint, 113.
Othello, III 3 line 2028.
Richard II, III 3 line 1757; Richard II, V 2 lines 2448, 2460.
Richard III, I 1 line 11.
Romeo and Juliet, III 2 line 1719.
Taming of the Shrew, I 2 line 756.
Tempest, IV 1 line 1730.
Titus Andronicus, II 3 line 811.
Troilus and Cressida, IV 5 line 2810; Troilus and Cressida, V 5 line 3454.
Venus and Adonis, lines 33, 59, 283, 310.

Steer: young ox, Old English: *steor*: bullock.
Henry IV, Part II, I 3 line 2556.
Winter's Tale, I 2 line 202.

Stigmatic: branded with deformity, c.1600, from Medieval Latin *stigmaticus*.
Comedy of Errors, IV 2 line 1095.
Henry VI, Part II, V 1 line 3205.
Henry VI, Part III, II 2 line 981.

Stomach: c.1300, internal pouch into which food is digested, from Old French: *estomac*, from Latin: *stomachus*: stomach, throat, also: pride, inclination, indignation (which were thought to have their origin in that organ), from Greek: *stomachos*: throat, gullet, esophagus, literally, mouth, opening, from *stoma*: mouth. Applied to the openings of various internal organs, especially the stomach, then to the stomach itself. Some 16c. anatomists tried to correct the sense back to *esophagus* and introduce ventricle for what we call the stomach. Meaning, belly, midriff, part of the body that contains the stomach, is from late 14c. The verb meaning, to tolerate, put up with, is from 1570s; earlier sense was opposite: to be offended at, resent.
All's Well That Ends Well, I 1 line 145; All's Well That Ends Well, III 2 line 1413; All's Well That Ends Well, III 6 line 1789.
Antony and Cleopatra, II 2 line 691; Antony and Cleopatra, III 4 line 1764.
As You Like It, III 2 line 1141.
Comedy of Errors, I 2 line 213, 214.
Cymbeline, III 4 line 1809; Cymbeline, III 4 line 1936; Cymbeline, III 6 line 2178; Cymbeline, V 4 line 3138.
Hamlet, I 1 line 116.
Henry IV, Part I, II 3 line 900.
Henry IV, Part II, I 1 line 186; Henry IV, Part II, IV 4 lines 2857, 2859.
Henry V, II 0 line 503; Henry V, III 2 line 1184; Henry V, III 7 line 1781; Henry V, IV 3 line 2270.
Henry VI, Part I, I 3 line 451; Henry VI, Part I, II 3 line 913; Henry VI, Part I, IV 1 line 1906.
Henry VI, Part II, II 1 line 791; Henry VI, Part II, IV 10 line 2895.

Henry VIII, III 2 line 2179; Henry VIII, IV 2 line 2594.
Julius Caesar, I 2 line 396; Julius Caesar, V 1 line 2418.
King John, I 1 line 198.
King Lear, V 3 line 3207.
Love's Labour's Lost, I 2 line 446; Love's Labour's Lost, IV 3 line 1639.
Merchant of Venice, III 5 line 1885; Merchant of Venice, III 5 line 1924.
Midsummer Night's Dream, II 2 line 798.
Much Ado About Nothing, I 1 line 46; Much Ado About Nothing, I 3 line 342; Much Ado About Nothing, II 1 line 754; Much Ado About Nothing, II 3 line 1061.
Othello, III 4 line 2294; Othello, V 2 line 3393.
Pericles, III 2 line 1350; Pericles, IV 1 line 1576.
Richard II, I 1 line 20.
Taming of the Shrew, I 1 line 331; Taming of the Shrew, I 2 line 743; Taming of the Shrew, IV 1 line 1762; Taming of the Shrew, V 2 line 2497; Taming of the Shrew, V 2 line 2684.
Tempest, I 2 line 267; Tempest, Ii 1 line 807; Tempest, II 2 line 1202; Tempest, III 3 line 1612.
Timon of Athens, IV 3 line 1997.
Titus Andronicus, III 1 line 1372; Titus Andronicus, V 3 line 2561.
Troilus and Cressida, II 1 line 982; Troilus and Cressida, III 3 line 2101; Troilus and Cressida, IV 5 line 2894.
Two Gentlemen of Verona, I 2 line 223.
Winter's Tale, IV 4 line 2115.

Stone: Old English: *stan*, used of common rocks, precious gems, concretions in the body, memorial stones. Slang sense of *testicle* is from mid-12c. The British measure of weight (usually equal to 14 pounds) is from late 14c., originally a specific stone.
All's Well That Ends Well, II 1 line 673.
Antony and Cleopatra, II 2 line 818; Antony and Cleopatra, III 13 line 2448.
As You Like It, II 1 line 574; As You Like It, II 4 line 764.
Coriolanus, I 1 line 212; Coriolanus, III 2 line 2256; Coriolanus, IV 4 line 2720; Coriolanus, V 4 line 3731.
Cymbeline, I 4 line 394; Cymbeline, I 6 line 641; Cymbeline, II 4 line 1221; Cymbeline, II 4 line 1228; Cymbeline, IV 2 line 2670; Cymbeline, V 5 line 3631; Cymbeline, V 5 line 3656.
Hamlet, III 4 line 2525; Hamlet, IV 5 line 2892; Hamlet, IV 7 line 3152.
Henry IV, Part II, Prologue 1 line 35; Henry IV, Part II, I 1 line 263; Henry IV, Part II, III 2 line 2198.
Henry V, I 2 line 432; Henry V, II 3 lines 856, 857, 859; Henry V, III 6 line 1490; Henry V, III 6 line 1497; Henry V, IV 7 line 2579.
Henry VI, Part I, I 4 line 503; Henry VI, Part I, III 1 line 1307; Henry VI, Part I, III 1 line 1317.
Henry VI, Part II, IV 6 line 2602; Henry VI, Part II, IV 6 line 2604; Henry VI, Part II, V 2 line 3266.

Henry VI, Part III, III 1 line 1430; Henry VI, Part III, V 1 line 2688; Henry VI, Part III, V 1 line 2712.
Henry VIII, V 3 line 3178.
Julius Caesar, I 1 line 36; Julius Caesar, I 3 line 475; Julius Caesar, III 2 line 1687; Julius Caesar, III 2 line 1774.
King John, II 1 line 517; King John, IV 1 line 1662; King John, IV 3 line 2025.
King Lear, III 2 line 1742; King Lear, V 3 line 3349; King Lear, V 3 lines 3434, 3439.
Lover's Complaint, lines 211, 217.
Macbeth, II 1 line 637; Macbeth, III 4 line 1426; Macbeth, IV 1 line 1553.
Measure for Measure, I 3 line 344; Measure for Measure, II 1 line 559; Measure for Measure, II 2 line 918.
Merchant of Venice, I 1 line 31; Merchant of Venice, II 8 lines 1091r, 1093; Merchant of Venice, II 8 line 1095; Merchant of Venice, V 1 line 2536.
Merry Wives of Windsor, I 4 line 514r; Merry Wives of Windsor, IV 1 line 1918; Merry Wives of Windsor, IV 1 line 1919.
Midsummer Night's Dream, V 1 line 2004; Midsummer Night's Dream, V 1 line 2025; Midsummer Night's Dream, V 1 lines 2034, 2035.
Othello, IV 1 line 2614; Othello, IV 3 line 3068; Othello, V 2 line 3376; Othello, V 2 line 3582.
Pericles, III 2 line 1327.
Rape of Lucrece, lines 228, 643, 644, 1010, 1029r, 1781.
Richard II, I 2 line 282; Richard II, II 1 line 727; Richard II, III 2 line 1432; Richard II, III 3 line 1663.
Richard III, I 3 line 828; Richard III, I 4 line 860; Richard III, I 4 line 1068; Richard III, III 7 line 2226; Richard III, III 7 line 2436; Richard III, IV 1 line 2572; Richard III, IV 4 line 3031; Richard III, V 3 line 3757.
Romeo and Juliet, I 3 line 438; Romeo and Juliet, I 4 line 555; Romeo and Juliet, II 3 line 1074; Romeo and Juliet, V 3 line 2947.
Sonnet LII line 7; Sonnet LV line 4; Sonnet LXV line 1; Sonnet XCIV line 3.
Taming of the Shrew, Prologue 2 line 233.
Tempest, II 1 line 946; Tempest, V 1 line 2344.
Timon of Athens, II 2 line 793; Timon of Athens, III 6 line 1562; Timon of Athens, IV 3 line 2073; Timon of Athens, IV 3 line 2074; Timon of Athens, IV 3 line 2083; Timon of Athens, V 1 line 2508; Timon of Athens, V 4 line 2637.
Titus Andronicus, III 1 line 1156; Titus Andronicus, III 1 lines 1164, 1172r, 1173; Titus Andronicus, V 3 line 2673.
Troilus and Cressida, I 2 line 293; Troilus and Cressida, III 2 line 1837; Troilus and Cressida, IV 5 line 2848; Troilus and Cressida, V 10 line 3651.
Twelfth Night, I 2 line 375; Twelfth Night, II 5 line 1074; Twelfth Night, III 4 line 1743.

Two Gentlemen of Verona, I 1 line 135; Two Gentlemen of Verona, I 2 line 270; Two Gentlemen of Verona, II 3 line 602r; Two Gentlemen of Verona, II 7 line 1004; Two Gentlemen of Verona, III 2 line 1531.
Venus and Adonis, lines 220, 231.
Winter's Tale, I 2 line 474; Winter's Tale, II 3 line 1042; Winter's Tale, IV 4 line 2558; Winter's Tale, IV 4 line 2756; Winter's Tale, IV 4 line 2783; Winter's Tale, V 3 line 3316; Winter's Tale, V 3 lines 3331, 3332, 3336; Winter's Tale, V 3 line 3355; Winter's Tale, V 3 line 3410.

Storm: Old English, of Germanic origin; related to Dutch *storm* and German *Sturm*.

Antony and Cleopatra, I 2 line 244; Antony and Cleopatra, III 13 line 2453; Antony and Cleopatra, Iv 4 line 2638.
Comedy of Errors, I 1 line 81.
Cymbeline, III 3 line 1668.
Hamlet, II 2 line 1557.
Henry IV, Part II, I 1 line 223.
Henry VI, Part II, III 1 line 1436; Henry VI, Part II, III 1 line 1637; Henry VI, Part II, III 2 line 1784; Henry VI, Part II, V 1 line 3188; Henry VI, Part II, V 1 line 3196.
Henry VI, Part III, III 3 line 1729; Henry VI, Part III, III 3 line 1740; Henry VI, Part III, IV 1 line 2013; Henry VI, Part III, IV 6 line 2416; Henry VI, Part III, IV 7 line 2471; Henry VI, Part III, V 3 line 2790.
Henry VIII, I 1 line 139; Henry VIII, III 1 line 1805; Henry VIII, IV 2 line 2581.
Julius Caesar, V 1 line 2421.
King John, V 1 line 2213; King John, V 2 line 2333.
King Lear, II 4 line 1357; King Lear, II 4 line 1558; King Lear, II 4 line 1589; King Lear, II 4 line 1616; King Lear, III 1 line 1669; King Lear, III 4 line 1808; King Lear, III 4 line 1832; King Lear, III 4 line 1832; King Lear, III 4 line 1862; King Lear, III 4 line 1895; King Lear, III 4 line 1955; King Lear, III 7 line 2188; King Lear, IV 1 line 2285; King Lear, IV 3 line 2483.
Lover's Complaint, lines 6, 102.
Macbeth, I 2 line 45.
Merchant of Venice, I 3 line 464.
Midsummer Night's Dream, I 2 line 287.
Much Ado About Nothing, V 4 line 2590.
Othello, I 3 line 601.
Pericles, III 0 line 1179; Pericles, III 1 line 1197; Pericles, III 1 line 1212; Pericles, III 2 line 1287; Pericles, IV 1 line 1567.
Rape of Lucrece, lines 166, 1017, 1569, 1640.
Richard II, II 1 line 717; Richard II, II 1 line 955; Richard II, II 4 line 1353; Richard II, III 2 line 1516.
Richard III, II 3 line 1468; Richard III, II 3 line 1477.
Romeo and Juliet, I 5 line 682; Romeo and Juliet, III 2 line 1786.
Sonnet XIII line 12; Sonnet XXXIV line 6.
Taming of the Shrew, I 1 line 463; Taming of the Shrew, III 2 line 1534; Taming of the Shrew, V 2 line 2658.

Tempest, I 1 line 20; Tempest, I 2 line 292; Tempest, II 2 lines 1102, 1125, 1129; Tempest, II 2 lines 1198, 1200.
Timon of Athens, IV 3 line 1961.
Titus Andronicus, I 1 line 175; Titus Andronicus, II 1 line 562; Titus Andronicus, II 3 line 756; Titus Andronicus, II 4 line 1108; Titus Andronicus, III 1 line 1404; Titus Andronicus, IV 2 line 1830; Titus Andronicus, IV 4 line 2085.
Troilus and Cressida, I 1 line 68; Troilus and Cressida, I 3 line 497.
Venus and Adonis, line 987.
Winter's Tale, III 2 line 1450; Winter's Tale, III 3 line 1540.

Stover: dried leaves and stalks of cereal crops, Middle English. This word, which is often found in the writings of Shakespeare's day, denotes fodder and provision of all sorts for cattle. Stover was used as a thatch for cart-lodges and other buildings that required but cheap coverings.
Tempest, IV 1 line 1773.

Straw: Old English: *streaw: stems or stalks of certain cereals*, literally, that which is scattered or strewn.
All's Well That Ends Well, IV 3 line 2340.
Hamlet, IV 4 line 2813; Hamlet, IV 4 line 2843; Hamlet, IV 5 line 2863.
Henry IV, Part II, V 5 line 3678.
Henry V, II 3 line 881.
Henry VI, Part III, II 2 line 989.
Julius Caesar, I 3 line 536.
King John, III 4 line 1516.
King Lear, III 2 line 1748; King Lear, III 4 line 1845; King Lear, IV 6 line 2772; King Lear, IV 7 line 2956.
Love's Labour's Lost, V 2 line 2851.
Lover's Complaint, line 8.
Measure for Measure, IV 3 line 2150.
Midsummer Night's Dream, I 2 line 348.
Passionate Pilgrim, lines 98, 99, 366.
Rape of Lucrece, line 1072.
Richard III, III 5 line 2075.
Taming of the Shrew, V 2 line 2681.
Tempest, IV 1 line 1758; Tempest, IV 1 line 1858.
Titus Andronicus, II 3 line 861.
Troilus and Cressida, V 5 line 3480.
Venus and Adonis, line 1165.
Winter's Tale, III 2 line 1327.

Strawberries: Old English: *streawberige*, from *streaw*: straw + *berige*. The reason for the name is uncertain, but perhaps it is in reference to the tiny chaff-like external seeds which cover the fruit. A cognate Old English name was *eoroberge: earth-berry*.
Henry V, I 1 line 99.
Othello, III 3 line 2119.
Richard III, III 4 line 1984; Richard III, III 4 line 2003.

Stream: Old English: a course of water. Meaning, current in the sea, is recorded from late 14c. The verb is attested from early 13c. *Streamer*: flag that streams in the air is recorded from late 13c.
> **All's Well That Ends Well**, II 3 line 973; All's Well That Ends Well, IV 3 line 2116.
> **Antony and Cleopatra**, I 4 line 473.
> **As You Like It**, II 1 line 596; As You Like It, III 2 line 1494; As You Like It, IV 3 line 2081.
> **Comedy of Errors**, I 1 line 88
> **Coriolanus**, II 3 line 1720.
> **Cymbeline**, IV 2 line 2557.
> **Hamlet**, IV 7 line 3316.
> **Henry IV, Part I**, II 3 line 918.
> **Henry IV, Part II**, IV 1 line 2275; Henry IV, Part II, V 2 line 3281.
> **Henry V**, I 2 line 355; Henry V, III 0 line 1058.
> **Henry VI, Part I**, III 3 line 1665; Henry VI, Part I, V 3 line 2522.
> **Henry VIII**, III 2 line 2268; Henry VIII, IV 1 line 2490.
> **Julius Caesar**, I 1 line 59; Julius Caesar, III 1 line 1423.
> **King John**, II 1 line 754.
> **Lover's Complaint**, line 287.
> **Macbeth**, III 2 line 1206.
> **Measure for Measure**, III 2 line 1651.
> **Merchant of Venice**, I 1 line 35; Merchant of Venice, III 2 lines 1411.
> **Midsummer Night's Dream**, III 2 line 1450.
> **Much Ado About Nothing**, III 1 line 1102.
> **Othello**, II 3 line 1195; Othello, III 3 line 2069; Othello, IV 3 line 3066.
> **Rape of Lucrece**, lines 700, 1129, 1638, 1825.
> **Richard II**, I 1 line 106; Richard II, IV 1 line 2077; Richard II, V 3 line 2640.
> **Richard III**, V 5 line 3929.
> **Romeo and Juliet**, II 2 line 866.
> **Sonnet** XXXIII line 4.
> **Timon of Athens**, IV 1 line 1592; Timon of Athens, V 4 line 2727.
> **Titus Andronicus**, II 1 line 691.
> **Troilus and Cressida**, II 3 line 1386.
> **Twelfth Night**, IV 1 line 2012.
> **Two Gentlemen of Verona**, II 7 line 1009.
> **Venus and Adonis**, line 794.

Sugar: late 13c., *sugre*, from Old French: *sucre* (12c.). Its Old World home was India (Alexander the Great's companions marvelled at the honey without bees) and it remained exotic in Europe until the Arabs began to cultivate it in Sicily and Spain; not until after the Crusades did it begin to rival honey as the West's sweetener. The Spaniards in the West Indies began raising sugar cane in 1506; first grown in Cuba 1523; first cultivated in Brazil 1532. Also, early 15c., to sweeten with sugar, also figuratively, to make more pleasing, mitigate the harshness of.
> **As You Like It**, III 3 line 1529.

Hamlet, III 1 line 1738.
Henry IV, Part I, II 4 lines 1007, 1015; Henry VI, Part I, II 4 line 1043; Henry VI, Part I, II 4 line 1453; Henry VI, Part I, III 3 line 2169.
Henry V, V 2 line 3262.
Henry VI, Part I, III 3 line 1623.
Henry VI, Part II, III 2 line 1726.
Love's Labour's Lost, V 2 line 2129.
Merchant of Venice, III 2 line 1488.
Merry Wives of Windsor, II 2 line 862.
Othello, I 3 line 565.
Rape of Lucrece, line 944.
Richard II, II 3 line 1158.
Richard III, I 3 line 709; Richard III, III 1 line 1579.
Timon of Athens, IV 3 line 1954.
Winter's Tale, IV 3 line 1763.

Sulphur: also sulphur, c.1300, from Old French *soufre* (13c.), from Late Latin *sulfur*, from Latin sulphur, probably from a root meaning *to burn*.
Coriolanus, V 3 line 3663.
Cymbeline, V 4 line 3266; Cymbeline, V 5 line 3656.
King Lear, IV 6 line 2737.
Measure for Measure, II 2 line 880.
Othello, III 3 line 2002; Othello, V 2 line 3636.
Pericles, III 1 line 1196.
Tempest, I 2 line 323.

Summer: Old English: *sumor*. The verb meaning, to pass the summer, is recorded from mid-15c. Horizontal bearing beam, late 13c., from Anglo-French: *sumer*, Old French: *somer: main beam*, originally *pack horse*.
All's Well That Ends Well, IV 4 line 2457.
As You Like It, IV 1 line 1882.
Comedy of Errors, I 1 line 134.
Coriolanus, IV 6 line 3131.
Cymbeline, III 4 line 1731; Cymbeline, IV 2 line 2607; Cymbeline, IV 4 line 2917.
Henry IV, Part I, I 2 line 261; Henry IV, Part I, III 1 line 1709; Henry IV, Part I, III 1 line 1758; Henry IV, Part I, IV 1 line 2328.
Henry IV, Part II, III 2 line 1985; Henry IV, Part II, IV 4 line 2841.
Henry V, I 1 line 104; Henry V, I 2 line 231; Henry V, I 2 line 340; Henry V, III 6 line 1526; Henry V, IV 8 line 2730; Henry V, V 2 line 3292; Henry V, V 2 line 3296.
Henry VI, Part I, I 2 line 330.
Henry VI, Part II, I 1 line 88; Henry VI, Part II, II 4 line 1158; Henry VI, Part II, III 2 line 1861.
Henry VI, Part III, II 2 line 1009; Henry VI, Part III, II 6 lines 1258, 1267; Henry VI, Part III, V 7 line 3113.
Henry VIII, III 2 line 2264; Henry VIII, IV 2 line 2617.
Julius Caesar, III 2 line 1717.
King John, V 7 line 2662.

Love's Labour's Lost, I 1 line 106; Love's Labour's Lost, V 2 line 2207; Love's Labour's Lost, V 2 line 2330; Love's Labour's Lost, V 2 line 2854.
Macbeth, I 6 line 436; Macbeth, III 4 line 1410; Macbeth, IV 3 line 1942.
Merchant of Venice, II 9 line 1229; Merchant of Venice, III 1 line 1297; Merchant of Venice, V 1 line 2734.
Merry Wives of Windsor, II 1 line 684.
Midsummer Night's Dream, I 2 line 343; Midsummer Night's Dream, II 1 lines 451, 479, 480; Midsummer Night's Dream, III 1 line 975.
Much Ado About Nothing, II 3 line 893.
Othello, IV 2 line 2814.
Passionate Pilgrim, lines 160, 161
Pericles, I 4 line 455; Pericles, II 5 line 1052; Pericles, IV 1 line 1565.
Rape of Lucrece, line 888.
Richard II, I 2 line 233; Richard II, II 3 line 437; Richard II, I 3 line 600; Richard II, III 3 line 1680; Richard II, III 3 line 1793.
Richard III, I 1 line 3; Richard III, III 1 line 1665; Richard III, IV 3 line 2739; Richard III, V 2 line 3436.
Romeo and Juliet, I 2 line 280; Romeo and Juliet, I 3 line 462; Romeo and Juliet, II 6 line 1478.
Sonnet V line 5; Sonnet V line 9; Sonnet VI line 2; Sonnet XII line 7; Sonnet XVIII line 1; Sonnet XVIII line 4; Sonnet XVIII line 9; Sonnet LIV line 8; Sonnet LVI line 14; Sonnet LXV line 5; Sonnet LXVIII line 11; Sonnet XCIV line 9r; Sonnet XCVII line 5; Sonnet XCVII line 10; Sonnet XCVIII line 7; Sonnet CII line 7; Sonnet CII line 9; Sonnet CIV line 4; Sonnet CIV line 14.
Tempest, V 1 line 2122.
Timon of Athens, III 6 line 1464; Timon of Athens, III 6 line 1467.
Titus Andronicus, II 3 line 830; Titus Andronicus, III 1 line 1145; Titus Andronicus, V 1 line 2145; Titus Andronicus, V 2 line 2488.
Troilus and Cressida, III 3 line 1951.
Twelfth Night, I 5 line 312; Twelfth Night, III 4 line 1597.
Two Gentlemen of Verona, II 4 line 821.
Venus and Adonis, lines 43, 111, 824.
Winter's Tale, I 1 line 6; Winter's Tale, IV 3 line 1734; Winter's Tale, IV 4 line 1951; Winter's Tale, IV 4 line 1983; Winter's Tale, V 3 line 3346.

Sumpter: a horse that carries provisions on a journey
    King Lear, II 4 line 1510.

Sun: 1510s, *to set something in the sun*, from *sun*. Meaning, to expose oneself to the sun, is recorded from c.1600. Old English: *sunne*. According to the old philosophy, the sun was accounted a planet, and thought to be whirled round the earth by the motion of a solid sphere, in which it was fixed. Supposing this sphere consumed, the sun must wander in endless space, and, as a natural consequence, the earth be involved in endless night. By a popular fancy, the sun was formerly said to dance at its rising on Easter morning. A cloudy rising of the sun has generally been regarded as ominous.

From the earliest times an eclipse of the sun was looked upon as an omen of coming calamity; and was oftentimes the source of extraordinary alarm as well as the occasion of various superstitious ceremonies. In 1597, during an eclipse of the sun, it is stated that at Edinburgh, men and women thought the day of judgment was come.

All's Well That Ends Well, I 3 line 517; All's Well That Ends Well, II 1 line 771.

Antony and Cleopatra, II 7 line 1403; Antony and Cleopatra, IV 8 line 2784; Antony and Cleopatra, IV 12 line 2924; Antony and Cleopatra, IV 15 line 3176; Antony and Cleopatra, V 2 line 3486.

As You Like It, I 3 line 505; As You Like It, II 5 line 855; As You Like It, II 7 line 909; As You Like It, III 2 line 1148.

Comedy of Errors, I 1 line 29; Comedy of Errors, I 1 line 90; Comedy of Errors, I 2 line 169; Comedy of Errors, II 1 line 373; Comedy of Errors, II 2 line 424; Comedy of Errors, III 2 line 818.

Coriolanus, I 1 line 175; Coriolanus, II 2 line 1320; Coriolanus, V 3 line 3560; Coriolanus, V 4 lines 3779, 3786.

Cymbeline, I 4 line 332; Cymbeline, I 6 line 706; Cymbeline, II 5 line 1384; Cymbeline, III 1 line 1455; Cymbeline, III 2 line 1580r; Cymbeline, III 3 line 1608; Cymbeline, IV 2 line 2657; Cymbeline, IV 4 lines 2924, 2931; Cymbeline, V 5 line 3945.

Hamlet, I 1 line 135; Hamlet, I 2 line 269; Hamlet, II 2 line 1213; Hamlet, II 2 line 1286; Hamlet, II 2 line 1289; Hamlet, III 2 line 2052; Hamlet, IV 1 line 2656; Hamlet, IV 5 line 2927.

Henry IV, Part I, I 2 line 118; Henry IV, Part I, I 2 line 300; Henry IV, Part I, II 4 line 1113; Henry IV, Part I, II 4 lines 1391, 1393; Henry IV, Part I, III 2 line 1900; Henry IV, Part I, IV 1 line 2328; Henry IV, Part I, IV 1 line 2337; Henry IV, Part I, V 1 line 2621.

Henry IV, Part II, II 3 line 1172.

Henry V, I 2 line 231; Henry V, I 2 line 310; Henry V, II 4 line 957; Henry V, III 5 line 1407; Henry V, III 7 line 1707; Henry V, IV 0 line 1830; Henry V, IV 1 line 2047; Henry V, IV 2 line 2163; Henry V, IV 2 line 2228; Henry V, IV 3 line 2338; Henry V, V 2 lines 3130, 3146, 3147.

Henry VI, Part I, I 1 line 18; Henry VI, Part I, I 2 line 274; Henry VI, Part I, I 4 line 544; Henry VI, Part I, V 3 line 2522; Henry VI, Part I, V 4 line 2758.

Henry VI, Part II, II 4 line 1199; Henry VI, Part II, III 1 line 1507; Henry VI, Part II, III 1 line 1641; Henry VI, Part II, III 2 line 2024; Henry VI, Part II, IV 1 line 2254.

Henry VI, Part III, II 1 line 648; Henry VI, Part III, II 1 line 651; Henry VI, Part III, II 1 lines 652r, 657; Henry VI, Part III, II 1 line 666; Henry VI, Part III, II 1 line 719; Henry VI, Part III, II 3 line 1033; Henry VI, Part III, II 6 line 1259; Henry VI, Part III, III 3 line 1822; Henry VI, Part III, IV 7 line 2510; Henry VI, Part III, IV 8 line 2585; Henry VI, Part III, V 2 line 2739; Henry VI, Part III, V 3 line 2782; Henry VI, Part III, V 6 line 3018.

Henry VIII, I 1 line 42; Henry VIII, I 1 line 71; Henry VIII, I 1 line 310; Henry VIII, II 3 line 1206; Henry VIII, III 1 line 1627; Henry VIII, III 2 lines 2323, 2328; Henry VIII, IV 2 line 2672; Henry VIII, V 5 line 3433.

Julius Caesar, II 1 line 724; Julius Caesar, V 3 lines 2570, 2573.
King John, II 1 line 784; King John, II 1 line 812; King John, III 1 line 996; King John, III 1 line 1254; King John, III 3 line 1335; King John, V 4 line 2523; King John, V 5 line 2552.
King Lear, I 1 line 113; King Lear, I 2 line 429; King Lear, I 2 line 444; King Lear, II 2 line 1238; King Lear, IV 6 line 2748.
Love's Labour's Lost, I 1 line 85; Love's Labour's Lost, IV 3 line 1346; Love's Labour's Lost, IV 3 line 1393; Love's Labour's Lost, IV 3 line 1418; Love's Labour's Lost, IV 3 line 1590.
Lover's Complaint, Line 9.
Macbeth, I 1 line 6; Macbeth, I 2 line 44; Macbeth, I 5 line 416; Macbeth, V 5 line 2410.
Measure for Measure, II 2 line 921; Measure for Measure, II 2 line 940; Measure for Measure, IV 3 line 2208.
Merchant of Venice, I 1 line 176; Merchant of Venice, II 1 line 516; Merchant of Venice, V 1 line 2589; Merchant of Venice, V 1 line 2593.
Merry Wives of Windsor, I 3 line 361; Merry Wives of Windsor, IV 4 line 2201; Merry Wives of Windsor, V 5 line 2710.
Midsummer Night's Dream, III 2 line 1083; Midsummer Night's Dream, V 1 line 2114; Midsummer Night's Dream, V 1 line 2234.
Much Ado About Nothing, III 1 lines 1010, 1011.
Othello, II 3 line 1529; Othello, III 4 line 2201; Othello, III 4 line 2255; Othello, V 2 line 3421.
Passionate Pilgrim, lines 38, 72, 82, 209.
Pericles, II 2 line 771; Pericles, II 3 line 863; Pericles, IV 2 line 1777; Pericles, IV 3 line 1817.
Rape of Lucrece, lines 76, 423, 826, 1269, 1275, 1277, 1281, 1888.
Richard II, I 3 line 442; Richard II, II 1 line 694; Richard II, II 4 line 1352; Richard II, III 3 line 1704; Richard II, IV 1 line 2017; Richard II, IV 1 line 2037r; Richard II, IV 1 line 2250; Richard II, IV 1 line 2275.
Richard III, I 1 lines 3, 27; Richard III, I 2 line 309; Richard III, I 2 line 454; Richard III, I 3 line 732; Richard III, I 3 line 733; Richard III, II 3 line 1467; Richard III, V 3 line 3479; Richard III, V 3 line 3788; Richard III, V 3 line 3794.
Romeo and Juliet, I 1 line 139; Romeo and Juliet, I 1 line 154; Romeo and Juliet, I 1 line 173; Romeo and Juliet, I 2 line 369; Romeo and Juliet, I 3 line 412; Romeo and Juliet, II 2 lines 848, 849; Romeo and Juliet, II 3 line 1063; Romeo and Juliet, II 3 line 1133; Romeo and Juliet, II 5 lines 1379, 1383; Romeo and Juliet, III 1 line 1523; Romeo and Juliet, III 2 line 1743; Romeo and Juliet, III 5 line 2110; Romeo and Juliet, III 5 line 2233; Romeo and Juliet, V 3 line 3282.
Sonnet XXI line 6; Sonnet XXV line 6; Sonnet XXXIII line 9; Sonnet XXXIII line 14r; Sonnet XXXV line 3; Sonnet LIX line 7; Sonnet LXXVI line 13; Sonnet CXXX line 1; Sonnet CXXXII line 5; Sonnet CXLVIII line 12.
Taming of the Shrew, Prologue 2 line 267; Taming of the Shrew, IV 3 line 2132; Taming of the Shrew, IV 3 line 2155; Taming of the Shrew, IV 5 line 2269; Taming of the Shrew, IV 5 line 2271; Taming of the

Shrew, IV 5 line 2279; Taming of the Shrew, IV 5 line 2284; Taming of the Shrew, IV 5 lines 2285, 2286; Taming of the Shrew, IV 5 line 2313.
Tempest, II 1 line 981; Tempest, II 2 line 1082; Tempest, III 1 line 1302; Tempest, V 1 line 2063.
Timon of Athens, I 2 line 490; Timon of Athens, III 4 line 1177; Timon of Athens, III 4 line 1200; Timon of Athens, IV 3 line 1664; Timon of Athens, IV 3 line 1740; Timon of Athens, IV 3 lines 2149, 2151; Timon of Athens, V 1 line 2408; Timon of Athens, V 1 line 2512.
Titus Andronicus, II 1 line 552; Titus Andronicus, II 3 line 746; Titus Andronicus, II 3 line 832; Titus Andronicus, III 1 line 1290; Titus Andronicus, III 1 line 1351; Titus Andronicus, IV 4 line 2096; Titus Andronicus, V 3 line 2545; Titus Andronicus, V 3 line 2546.
Troilus and Cressida, I 1 line 68; Troilus and Cressida, I 2 line 162; Troilus and Cressida, I 3 line 833; Troilus and Cressida, II 1 line 979; Troilus and Cressida, III 2 line 1828; Troilus and Cressida, III 3 line 1997; Troilus and Cressida, III 3 line 2116; Troilus and Cressida, IV 1 line 2227; Troilus and Cressida, V 1 line 3038; Troilus and Cressida, V 2 line 3247; Troilus and Cressida, V 8 lines 3595, 3597.
Twelfth Night, II 4 line 938; Twelfth Night, II 5 line 1044; Twelfth Night, III 1 line 1271; Twelfth Night, IV 3 line 2152.
Two Gentlemen of Verona, I 3 line 391; Two Gentlemen of Verona, II 6 line 940; Two Gentlemen of Verona, III 1 line 1158; Two Gentlemen of Verona, IV 4 line 1993; Two Gentlemen of Verona, V 1 line 2049.
Venus and Adonis, lines 21, 206, 210, 213, 214, 218, 504, 506, 754, 773, 822, 878, 1104, 1106, 1107.
Winter's Tale, I 2 line 132; Winter's Tale, IV 3 line 1774; Winter's Tale, IV 4 line 1982; Winter's Tale, IV 4 line 2368; Winter's Tale, IV 4 line 2424; Winter's Tale, IV 4 line 2768; Winter's Tale, V 1 line 2940.

Sunbeams: compound sun + beam.
Cymbeline, IV 4 line 2760.
Love's Labour's Lost, V 2 lines 2058, 2059.

Sunburnt: sunburn is from the 1520s, from sun + burn. Sunburnt (c.1400)
Much Ado About Nothing, II 1 line 696.
Tempest, IV 1 line 1856.
Troilus and Cressida, I 3 line 742.

Sunrise: mid-15c., from sun + rise; perhaps evolved from a 14c. subjunctive, e.g. *before the sun rise*.
Richard III, V 3 line 3528.

Sunset: late 14c.
Henry VI, Part III, II 2 line 961.
Sonnet LXXIII line 6.
King John, III 1 line 1020.
Romeo and Juliet, III 5 line 2234.
Sonnet LXXIII line 6.

Sunshine: mid 13c.
    All's Well That Ends Well, V 3 line 2712.
    Henry IV, Part II, IV 2 line 2452.
    Henry VI, Part III, II 1 line 815; Henry VI, Part III, II 2 line 1001; Henry VI, Part III, II 2 line 1008.
    King Lear, IV 3 line 2472.
    Love's Labour's Lost, V 2 line 2093.
    Richard II, IV 1 line 2209.
    Venus and Adonis, line 821.

Swallow: migratory bird. The etymological sense is disputed. Popularly regarded as a harbinger of summer; swallows building nests on or near a house is considered good luck. Old English: *swealwe*.
    Antony and Cleopatra, IV 12 line 2904.
    Henry IV, Part II, IV 3 line 2617.
    Henry VI, Part II, IV 10 line 2916.
    King Lear, III 4 line 1925.
    Timon of Athens, III 6 line 1464.
    Titus Andronicus, II 2 line 727; Titus Andronicus, IV 2 line 1868.
    Winter's Tale, IV 4 line 1998.

Swan: In classical mythology, sacred to Apollo and to Venus. According to a romantic notion, dating from antiquity, the swan is said to sing sweetly just before its death, many pretty allusions to which we find scattered here and there throughout Shakespeare's plays. The singing of swans before death was alluded to by Chaucer (late 14c.).
    Antony and Cleopatra, III 2 line 1650.
    As You Like It, I 3 line 479.
    Cymbeline, III 4 line 1879.
    Henry VI, Part I, V 3 line 2515.
    Henry VI, Part III, I 4 line 454.
    King John, V 7 line 2651.
    Merchant of Venice, III 2 line 1409.
    Merry Wives of Windsor, V 5 line 2565.
    Othello, V 2 line 3599.
    Phoenix and the Turtle, line 15.
    Rape of Lucrece, lines 1062, 1662.
    Romeo and Juliet, I 2 line 364.
    Titus Andronicus, IV 2 line 1792.

Swarth: quantity of grass cut down by one sweep of the scythe.
    Titus Andronicus, II 3 line 807.
    Twelfth Night, II 3 line 848.

Sweat: Old English: *swætan*. Meaning, to be worried, vexed, is recorded from c.1400.
    Antony and Cleopatra, I 3 line 408; Antony and Cleopatra, I 4 line 445.

As You Like It, II 3 lines 703, 705; As You Like It, III 2 lines 1170, 1171.
Comedy of Errors, III 2 line 865.
Coriolanus, I 4 line 518; Coriolanus, IV 3 line 2542; Coriolanus, V 3 line 3710.
Cymbeline, III 3 line 1702; Cymbeline, III 6 line 2177.
Hamlet, I 1 line 93; Hamlet, III 1 line 1770; Hamlet, III 4 line 2486.
Henry IV, Part I, II 2 line 852; Henry IV, Part I, II 3 line 917.
Henry IV, Part II, I 2 line 545; Henry IV, Part II, II 4 line 1492; Henry IV, Part II, II 4 line 1669; Henry IV, Part II, IV 3 line 2591r; Henry IV, Part II, V 5 line 3610; Henry IV, Part II, V 5 line 3743.
Henry V, III 5 line 1415; Henry V, IV 1 line 2117.
Henry VI, Part I, IV 4 line 2104.
Henry VIII, I 0 line 28; Henry VIII, I 1 line 63; Henry VIII, II 1 line 855.
Julius Caesar, I 2 line 338; Julius Caesar, IV 1 line 1884; Julius Caesar, V 1 line 2399.
King John, II 1 line 386; King John, V 2 line 2382.
King Lear, V 3 line 3183.
Love's Labour's Lost, V 2 line 2492.
Macbeth, II 3 line 756; Macbeth, IV 1 line 1621.
Measure for Measure, I 2 line 172.
Merchant of Venice, III 2 lines 1573, 1574; Merchant of Venice, IV 1 line 2027.
Merry Wives of Windsor, III 3 line 1484.
Midsummer Night's Dream, II 1 line 463.
Othello, II 3 line 1215; Othello, III 4 line 2219.
Rape of Lucrece, lines 447, 1433.
Richard III, III 1 line 1592; Richard III, V 3 line 3761.
Taming of the Shrew, I 2 line 752.
Tempest, II 1 line 870.
Timon of Athens, III 2 line 1036.
Titus Andronicus, II 3 line 959.
Troilus and Cressida, V 10 line 3692.
Venus and Adonis, lines 45, 195, 816.

Tail: hindmost part of an animal, Old English: *tægl, tægel*, the word was applied to the hairless tails of worms, bees, etc. Another Old English word for *tail* was *steort*; that of, backside of a person, buttocks, is recorded from c. 1300; slang sense of, *pudenda*, is from mid-14c. To *turn tail: take flight* (1580s) originally was a term in falconry.
All's Well That Ends Well, IV 3 line 2362; All's Well That Ends Well, IV 5 line 2470.
Cymbeline, IV 2 line 2505.
Henry VI, Part I, III 3 line 1611.
Henry VI, Part II, V 1 line 3144.
Henry VI, Part III, I 1 line 205; Henry VI, Part III, I 1 line 252.
King Lear, I 2 line 451.
Macbeth, I 3 line 107.

Merchant of Venice, II 2 line 660; Merchant of Venice, II 2 lines 661, 662.
Merry Wives of Windsor, III 4 line 1678.
Othello, II 1 line 943; Othello, III 1 line 1555.
Richard III, I 4 line 980.
Romeo and Juliet, I 4 line 579.
Taming of the Shrew, II 1 line 1063; Taming of the Shrew, II 1 line 1067; Taming of the Shrew, IV 1 line 1696.
Tempest, III 2 line 1406.
Troilus and Cressida, V 8 line 3614; Troilus and Cressida, V 10 line 3637; Troilus and Cressida, V 10 line 3680.
Two Gentlemen of Verona, II 3 line 643; Two Gentlemen of Verona, II 5 line 910.
Venus and Adonis, lines 318, 325, 334, 945.
Winter's Tale, I 2 line 438.

Talons: c.1400, *talounz*: claws of a bird or beast, probably originally from Old French: *talon*: heel or hinder part of the foot of a beast, or of a man, or of a shoe.
Henry VI, Part I, II 4 line 1316.
Henry VI, Part II, III 2 line 1881.
Henry VI, Part III, I 4 line 479.
Pericles, IV 3 line 1869.

Tassel-Gentle: The male of the Goshawk was so called on account of its tractable disposition, and the facility with which it was tamed.
Romeo and Juliet, II 2 line 1020.

Tears: water from the eye. Old English *tear*, of Germanic origin; related to German *Zähre*, from an Indo-European root shared by Old Latin *dacruma* (Latin *lacrima*) and Greek *dakru*.
All's Well That Ends Well, I 1 line 44; All's Well That Ends Well, I 1 line 81; All's Well That Ends Well, I 3 line 494; All's Well That Ends Well, III 4 line 2103; All's Well That Ends Well, IV 3 line 2155.
Antony and Cleopatra, I 2 line 243; Antony and Cleopatra, I 2 line 264; Antony and Cleopatra, I 3 line 387; Antony and Cleopatra, II 7 line 1428; Antony and Cleopatra, IV 8 line 2790; Antony and Cleopatra, V 1 line 3329.
As You Like It, I 1 line 131; As You Like It, I 2 line 348; As You Like It, II 1 lines 587, 592; As You Like It, III 2 line 1486; As You Like It, III 4 line 1596; As You Like It, IV 3 line 2146; As You Like It, V 2 line 2322.
Comedy of Errors, III 2 line 788; Comedy of Errors, V 1 line 1547.
Coriolanus, I 9 line 765; Coriolanus, II 1 line 1077; Coriolanus, III 2 line 2304; Coriolanus, IV 3 line 2522; Coriolanus, IV 3 line 2545; Coriolanus, V 6 line 3936; Coriolanus, V 6 line 3941.
Cymbeline, V 5 line 3695.
Hamlet, I 2 lines 353, 358; Hamlet, II 2 line 1593; Hamlet, II 2 lines 1628, 1635; Hamlet, III 4 line 2529; Hamlet, IV 5 line 3032; Hamlet, IV 7 line 3336.

Henry IV, Part I, II 4 line 1374; Henry IV, Part I, II 4 line 1377; Henry IV, Part I, II 4 line 1399; Henry IV, Part I, IV 3 line 2522.
Henry IV, Part II, III 1 line 1772; Henry IV, Part II, IV 5 line 2925; Henry IV, Part II, IV 5 line 2977; Henry IV, Part II, IV 5 line 3009; Henry IV, Part II, IV 5 line 3034; Henry IV, Part II, V 2 line 3308.
Henry V, II 4 line 1009; Henry V, IV 1 line 2146; Henry V, IV 2 line 2176; Henry V, IV 6 line 2508.
Henry VI, Part I, I 1 line 54; Henry VI, Part I, I 1 line 87; Henry VI, Part I, III 1 line 1220; Henry VI, Part I, III 1 line 1339; Henry VI, Part I, III 2 line 1484; Henry VI, Part I, III 3 line 1666.
Henry VI, Part II, I 1 line 125; Henry VI, Part II, I 3 line 429; Henry VI, Part II, II 3 line 1061; Henry VI, Part II, II 4 line 1193; Henry VI, Part II, II 4 line 1248; Henry VI, Part II, III 1 line 1407; Henry VI, Part II, III 1 line 1500; Henry VI, Part II, III 2 line 1741; Henry VI, Part II, III 2 line 1777; Henry VI, Part II, III 2 line 1826; Henry VI, Part II, III 2 line 2034; Henry VI, Part II, III 2 line 2080; Henry VI, Part II, IV 7 line 2688; Henry VI, Part II, V 2 line 3269.
Henry VI, Part III, I 4 line 587; Henry VI, Part III, I 4 line 592; Henry VI, Part III, I 4 lines 597, 599, 602, 603; Henry VI, Part III, I 4 line 615; Henry VI, Part III, II 1 lines 711, 713; Henry VI, Part III, II 1 line 732; Henry VI, Part III, II 5 line 1175; Henry VI, Part III, II 5 line 1182; Henry VI, Part III, II 5 line 1211; Henry VI, Part III, III 1 lines 1405, 1408; Henry VI, Part III, III 2 line 1672; Henry VI, Part III, III 3 line 1702; Henry VI, Part III, III 3 line 1855; Henry VI, Part III, IV 4 line 2265; Henry VI, Part III, IV 8 line 2566; Henry VI, Part III, V 2 line 2760; Henry VI, Part III, V 4 line 2881; Henry VI, Part III, V 6 line 3061.
Henry VIII, II 4 line 1433; Henry VIII, III 2 line 2311; Henry VIII, IV 2 line 2588; Henry VIII, V 1 line 2969; Henry VIII, V 3 line 3259.
Julius Caesar, I 1 line 58; Julius Caesar, III 2 line 1560; Julius Caesar, III 2 line 1714; Julius Caesar, V 3 line 2619.
King John, II 1 line 610; King John, IV 1 line 1615; King John, IV 1 line 1645; King John, IV 3 line 2070; King John, V 2 line 2325; King John, V 7 line 2677; King John, V 7 line 2746.
King Lear, I 4 line 812; King Lear, I 4 line 827; King Lear, III 1 line 1624; King Lear, III 4 line 1904; King Lear, III 6 line 2062; King Lear, IV 3 line 2472; King Lear, IV 4 line 2534; King Lear, IV 4 line 2545; King Lear, IV 7 line 2963; King Lear, IV 7 line 2991.
Love's Labour's Lost, IV 3 lines 1352, 1356, 1359; Love's Labour's Lost, IV 3 line 1486; Love's Labour's Lost, IV 3 line 1538; Love's Labour's Lost, V 2 line 2002; Love's Labour's Lost, V 2 line 2750.
Lover's Complaint, lines 18, 298.
Macbeth, I 7 line 489; Macbeth, II 3 line 915.
Measure for Measure, III 1 lines 1467, 1471.
Merchant of Venice, II 3 line 785; Merchant of Venice, II 8 line 1118; Merchant of Venice, III 1 line 1331.
Midsummer Night's Dream, I 1 line 161; Midsummer Night's Dream, I 2 line 285; Midsummer Night's Dream, II 2 line 751; Midsummer Night's Dream, III 2 line 1161; Midsummer Night's Dream, III 2 line

1195; Midsummer Night's Dream, IV 1 line 1603; Midsummer Night's Dream, V 1 line 1906; Midsummer Night's Dream, V 1 line 2138.
Much Ado About Nothing, I 1 line 23; Much Ado About Nothing, II 3 line 961; Much Ado About Nothing, IV 1 line 1804; Much Ado About Nothing, V 1 line 2368.
Othello, I 3 line 501; Othello, IV 1 line 2687; Othello, IV 1 line 2702; Othello, IV 2 line 2790; Othello, IV 3 line 3068; Othello, V 2 line 3323; Othello, V 2 line 3717.
Passionate Pilgrim, lines 97, 390.
Pericles, I 4 line 434; Pericles, I 4 line 470; Pericles, I 4 line 509; Pericles, III 3 lines 1467, 1468; Pericles, IV 4 lines 1906, 1911; Pericles, V 3 line 2565.
Rape of Lucrece, lines 482, 553, 611, 620, 639, 645, 733, 736, 849, 1178, 1322, 1326, 1371, 1519, 1600, 1611, 1615, 1643, 1765, 1869.
Richard II, I 4 line 618; Richard II, II 2 line 1009; Richard II, III 1 line 1373; Richard II, III 2 line 1417; Richard II, III 2 line 1518; Richard II, III 3 line 1696; Richard II, III 3 lines 1803, 1807; Richard II, III 3 line 1851; Richard II, IV 1 line 2176; Richard II, IV 1 line 2195; Richard II, IV 1 line 2233; Richard II, IV 1 line 2329; Richard II, V 1 line 2344; Richard II, V 2 line 2473; Richard II, V 3 line 2683; Richard II, V 5 lines 2803, 2806.
Richard III, I 2 line 338; Richard III, I 2 line 404; Richard III, I 2 line 425; Richard III, I 3 line 828; Richard III, II 2 line 1335; Richard III, II 2 line 1342; Richard III, II 2 line 1359; Richard III, IV 4 line 3028; Richard III, IV 4 line 3202; Richard III, V 3 line 3796.
Romeo and Juliet, I 1 line 152; Romeo and Juliet, I 1 line 219; Romeo and Juliet, I 2 line 366; Romeo and Juliet, III 1 line 1712; Romeo and Juliet, III 2 line 1826; Romeo and Juliet, III 2 line 1854; Romeo and Juliet, III 3 line 1961; Romeo and Juliet, III 3 line 1991; Romeo and Juliet, III 5 line 2174; Romeo and Juliet, III 5 lines 2236, 2240, 2242; Romeo and Juliet, IV 1 lines 2371, 2375; Romeo and Juliet, IV 1 line 2394; Romeo and Juliet, IV 1 line 2395; Romeo and Juliet, IV 1 line 2397; Romeo and Juliet, IV 5 lines 2737, 2741; Romeo and Juliet, V 3 line 2949.
Sonnet XXXIV line 13; Sonnet XLIV line 14; Sonnet CXIX line 1; Sonnet CXLVIII lines 10, 13.
Taming of the Shrew, Prologue 1 lines 138, 143; Taming of the Shrew, Prologue 2 line 205; Taming of the Shrew, Prologue 2 line 209.
Tempest, V 1 line 2033.
Timon of Athens, IV 3 line 2153; Timon of Athens, V 1 line 2438.
Titus Andronicus, I 1 lines 91, 92; Titus Andronicus, I 1 lines 122, 123; Titus Andronicus, I 1 lines 181, 183; Titus Andronicus, I 1 line 435; Titus Andronicus, II 3 line 878; Titus Andronicus, II 3 line 903; Titus Andronicus, II 3 line 1042; Titus Andronicus, II 4 line 1118; Titus Andronicus, III 1 lines 1131, 1139, 1140, 1145, 1152; Titus Andronicus, III 1 line 1169; Titus Andronicus, III 1 lines 1236, 1241; Titus Andronicus, III 1 line 1258; Titus Andronicus, III 1 line 1266; Titus Andronicus, III 1 line 1276; Titus Andronicus, III 1 line 1345; Titus Andronicus, III 1 line 1367; Titus Andronicus, III 1 line 1410; Titus

Andronicus, III 2 lines 1462, 1464; Titus Andronicus, III 2 line 1481; Titus Andronicus, III 2 lines 1495, 1496; Titus Andronicus, V 1 line 2251; Titus Andronicus, V 1 line 2269; Titus Andronicus, V 3 line 2582; Titus Andronicus, V 3 line 2629; Titus Andronicus, V 3 lines 2640, 2646; Titus Andronicus, V 3 line 2695; Titus Andronicus, V 3 line 2719.

Troilus and Cressida, I 2 line 320; Troilus and Cressida, I 2 line 434; Troilus and Cressida, II 2 line 1097; Troilus and Cressida, II 2 line 1103; Troilus and Cressida, IV 4 line 2478; Troilus and Cressida, IV 4 line 2483; Troilus and Cressida, V 3 line 3339.

Twelfth Night, I 5 line 545; Twelfth Night, III 1 line 1401; Twelfth Night, V 1 line 2441.

Two Gentlemen of Verona, II 2 line 580; Two Gentlemen of Verona, II 3 line 625; Two Gentlemen of Verona, II 3 line 646; Two Gentlemen of Verona, II 4 line 789; Two Gentlemen of Verona, II 7 line 1044; Two Gentlemen of Verona, II 7 line 1053; Two Gentlemen of Verona, III 1 lines 1298, 1304; Two Gentlemen of Verona, III 2 lines 1526, 1527; Two Gentlemen of Verona, IV 4 line 2009.

Venus and Adonis, lines 69, 102, 212, 380, 445, 512, 971, 983, 984r, 988, 1001, 1076, 1093, 1114, 1198.

Winter's Tale, II 1 line 732; Winter's Tale, II 1 line 741; Winter's Tale, III 2 line 1480; Winter's Tale, V 1 line 3016; Winter's Tale, V 2 line 3155; Winter's Tale, V 2 line 3197; Winter's Tale, V 2 line 3253.

Teeth: plural of tooth. Application to tooth-like parts of other objects (saws, combs, etc.) first recorded 1520s. Teeth can symbolise attack and defence, for they are the primary weapon for most animals. Baring one's teeth, as in a snarl, is commonly seen as a defensive action. Teeth can also be linked to age. The most rudimentary way to tell the age of an animal is to look at their teeth, the amount of wear on them will be a decent indicator. Old English *toth* (plural *teth*), of Germanic origin; related to Dutch *tand* and German *Zahn*, from an Indo-European root shared by Latin *dent-*, Greek *odont-*.

All's Well That Ends Well, III 2 line 1405.

Antony and Cleopatra, I 5 line 602; Antony and Cleopatra, III 4 line 1761; Antony and Cleopatra, III 13 line 2470; Antony and Cleopatra, V 2 line 3766.

As You Like It, I 1 line 69; As You Like It, II 7 line 1064.

Comedy of Errors, II 2 line 415; Comedy of Errors, V 1 line 1687.

Coriolanus, I 3 line 430; Coriolanus, II 3 line 1492; Coriolanus, III 1 line 1772.

Hamlet, III 3 line 2345; Hamlet, IV 7 line 3191.

Henry IV, Part I, III 1 line 1677; Henry IV, Part I, V 2 line 2816.

Henry IV, Part II, IV 5 line 3101; Henry IV, Part II, V 3 line 3501.

Henry V, II 1 line 552; Henry V, III 1 line 1106.

Henry VI, Part I, I 2 line 232; Henry VI, Part I, III 1 line 1318.

Henry VI, Part II, III 2 line 2007; Henry VI, Part II, IV 7 line 2637.

Henry VI, Part III, I 4 line 495; Henry VI, Part III, V 6 line 3048; Henry VI, Part III, V 6 line 3073.

Henry VIII, I 2 line 359.

Julius Caesar, II 3 line 1133; Julius Caesar, IV 3 line 2086; Julius Caesar, V 1 line 2392; Julius Caesar, V 1 line 2416.
King John, I 2 line 198; King John, II 1 line 663; King John, IV 3 line 2176.
King Lear, IV 3 line 2865.
Love's Labour's Lost, V 2 line 2250.
Macbeth, III 4 line 1308.
Measure for Measure, III 2 line 1645.
Merchant of Venice, I 1 line 58.
Merry Wives of Windsor, V 5 line 2700.
Much Ado About Nothing, V 1 line 2195.
Othello, III 4 line 2386.
Pericles, I 4 line 461.
Rape of Lucrece, line 1838.
Richard II, I 1 line 197; Richard II, I 3 line 464.
Richard III, IV 4 line 2845.
Romeo and Juliet, I 3 lines 396, 397.
Sonnet XIX line 3.
Taming of the Shrew, IV 1 line 1627.
Tempest, III 2 line 1442.
Titus Andronicus, III 1 line 1402; Titus Andronicus, III 1 line 1421; Titus Andronicus, III 2 line 1461.
Two Gentlemen of Verona, III 1 line 1407; Two Gentlemen of Verona, III 1 line 1410.
Venus and Adonis, lines 289, 1135.
Winter's Tale, IV 4 line 2731.

Tempest: violent storm, mid-13c., from Old French: *tempeste*(11c.). Figurative sense of violent commotion is recorded from early 14c.
Antony and Cleopatra, I 2 line 244.
Hamlet, III 2 line 1887.
Henry IV, Part I, V 1 line 2627.
Henry IV, Part II, II 1 line 807; Henry IV, Part II, II 4 line 1673.
Henry V, II 4 line 1002.
Henry VI, Part II, III 1 line 1638; Henry VI, Part II, III 2 line 1783; Henry VI, Part II, III 2 line 1860; Henry VI, Part II, IV 9 line 2867; Henry VI, Part II, V 1 line 3187.
Henry VI, Part III, II 5 line 1191; Henry VI, Part III, V 6 line 3041.
Henry VIII, I 1 line 141; Henry VIII, IV 1 line 2500.
Julius Caesar, I 3 lines 426, 431.
King John, III 4 line 1384; King John, IV 3 line 2185; King John, V 1 line 2210; King John, V 2 line 2328.
King Lear, II 4 line 1588; King Lear, III 2 line 1740; King Lear, III 4 line 1814; King Lear, III 4 line 1826.
Macbeth, I 3 line 123.
Merry Wives of Windsor, II 1 line 625; Merry Wives of Windsor, V 5 line 2581.
Midsummer Night's Dream, I 1 line 137.

Othello, II 1 line 786; Othello, II 1 line 800; Othello, II 1 line 844; Othello, II 1 line 976.
Pericles, I 2 line 344; Pericles, III 0 line 1173; Pericles, IV 1 line 1566; Pericles, IV 4 line 1909; Pericles, V 3 line 2558.
Rape of Lucrece, line 1839.
Richard II, I 3 line 484; Richard II, II 1 line 954; Richard II, III 3 line 1683.
Richard III, I 4 line 877; Richard III, IV 4 line 3354.
Romeo and Juliet, III 5 line 2244.
Sonnet CXVI line 6.
Tempest, I 2 line 313; Tempest, V 1 line 2122; Tempest, V 1 line 2197.
Titus Andronicus, I 1 line 509; Titus Andronicus, IV 2 line 1852.
Troilus and Cressida, I 3 line 476.
Twelfth Night, III 4 line 1939.
Venus and Adonis, lines 258, 475, 822.

Temple: side of the forehead, early 14c., from Old French: *temple*: side of the forehead, probably originally the thin stretch of skin at the side of the forehead. Possibly associated with *tempus span: timely space* (for a mortal blow with a sword), or from the notion of stretched, thinnest part.
Henry VI, Part I, V 4 line 2809.
Henry VI, Part III, I 4 line 543.
Henry VIII, III 2 line 1981.
King John, II 1 line 402.
Merchant of Venice, I 1 line 176.
Midsummer Night's Dream, IV 1 line 1599.
Othello, IV 1 line 2472.
Richard II, III 2 line 1570.
Richard III, IV 4 line 3195; Richard III, V 5 line 3897.

Tench: freshwater fish. Middle English: from Old French: *tenche*, from late Latin: *tinca*.
Henry IV, Part I, II 1 line 657; Henry IV, Part I, II 1 line 658.

Tercel: a male goshawk; male falcon, late 14c., from Old French *tercel* (c. 1200), from Medieval Latin *tertiolus*, from Latin *tertius* third, a third, from root of *tres*. Various theories as to why it is called this; one says it's because the males are a third smaller than the females, another because a third egg in the nest (smaller than the other two) is believed always to produce a male bird.
Troilus and Cressida, III 2 line 1704.

Terra: Latin: literally, earth.
Henry V, I 2 line 183.
Henry VI, Part II, IV 7 line 2677.
Love's Labour's Lost, IV 2 line 1147.
Titus Andronicus, IV 3 line 1885.

Terrene: of, or like earth. Middle English: from Anglo-Norman French, from Latin: *terrenus*, from *terra*: *earth*.

Antony and Cleopatra, III 13 line 2438.

Thigh: thigh is literally, the thick or fat part of the leg. Old English: *þeoh, þeh*.
As You Like It, I 3 line 525.
Coriolanus, II 1 line 1069.
Cymbeline, IV 2 line 2712.
Henry IV, Part I, IV 1 line 2330; Henry IV, Part I, V 4 line 3097; Henry IV, Part I, V 4 line 3124.
Henry IV, Part II, IV 5 line 2969.
Henry VI, Part II, III 1 line 1649.
Julius Caesar, II 1 line 929.
Midsummer Night's Dream, III 1 line 994.
Othello, III 3 line 2107; Othello, V 2 line 3618.
Passionate Pilgrim, lines 128, 129.
Romeo and Juliet, II 1 line 818.
Twelfth Night, I 3 line 243.
Venus and Adonis, line 895.

Thill-horse: a shaft horse, to pull the thill or fill of a wagon.
Merchant of Venice, II 2 line 660.

Thistle: prickly herbaceous plant, Old English: *thistel*. Emblem of Scotland since 15c.
Henry V, V 2 line 3033.
Midsummer Night's Dream, IV 1 line 1556.
Much Ado About Nothing, III 4 line 1556; Much Ado About Nothing, III 4 line 1560.

Thorn: Old English: *þorn*: sharp point on a stem or branch, earlier thorny tree or plant. Figurative sense of, anything which causes pain, is recorded from early 13c. Also an Anglo-Saxon and Icelandic runic letter (þ), named for the word of which it was the initial. Little is mentioned by Shakespeare with regard to thorns, save that they are generally used by him as the emblems of desolation and trouble. Denoting sin, sorrow and hardship, the thorn is one of the most ancient symbols in the world; together with the rose it represents pain and pleasure, and the thorn is an emblem of Christ's passion, as with the crown of thorns.
All's Well That Ends Well, I 3 line 446; All's Well That Ends Well, IV 2 line 2027; All's Well That Ends Well, IV 4 line 2458.
As You Like It, II 7 line 991.
Hamlet, I 3 line 532; Hamlet, I 5 line 825.
Henry IV, Part I, I 3 line 506.
Henry VI, Part I, II 4 line 955; Henry VI, Part I, II 4 line 997.
Henry VI, Part II, III 1 line 1345.
Henry VI, Part III, III 2 lines 1662, 1663r; Henry VI, Part III, V 4 line 2874; Henry VI, Part III, V 5 line 2908.
Henry VIII, II 4 line 1597.
King John, IV 3 line 2171.
Love's Labour's Lost, IV 3 line 1441.

Midsummer Night's Dream, I 1 line 82; Midsummer Night's Dream, II 2 line 660; Midsummer Night's Dream, III 1 line 871; Midsummer Night's Dream, III 2 line 1059; Midsummer Night's Dream, V 1 line 1978; Midsummer Night's Dream, V 1 line 2098r.
Passionate Pilgrim, lines 238, 384.
Pericles, IV 6 line 2087.
Rape of Lucrece, lines 543, 1186.
Richard II, IV 1 line 2320.
Romeo and Juliet, I 4 line 522.
Sonnet XXXV line 2; Sonnet LIV line 7; Sonnet XCVIX line 8.
Taming of the Shrew, Prologue 2 line 202.
Tempest, IV 1 line 1916.
Venus and Adonis, line 650.
Winter's Tale, I 2 line 488; Winter's Tale, IV 4 line 2543.

Throat: Old English *throte, throtu*, of Germanic origin; related to German *Drossel*.
Antony and Cleopatra, II 5 line 1092; Antony and Cleopatra, II 6 line 1368; Antony and Cleopatra, II 7 line 1461; Antony and Cleopatra, III 5 line 1811.
As You Like It, I 1 line 51; As You Like It, II 5 line 823.
Coriolanus, III 2 line 2300; Coriolanus, IV 5 line 2862; Coriolanus, IV 5 line 2892; Coriolanus, V 4 line 3736; Coriolanus, V 4 line 3793; Coriolanus, V 6 line 3854; Coriolanus, V 6 line 3881.
Cymbeline, III 4 line 1754; Cymbeline, IV 2 line 2514.
Hamlet, I 1 line 174; Hamlet, II 2 line 1647; Hamlet, IV 7 line 3271; Hamlet, V 1 line 3601.
Henry IV, Part I, II 2 line 823.
Henry IV, Part II, I 2 line 379; Henry IV, Part II, I 2 line 385.
Henry V, II 1 line 529; Henry V, II 1 line 553; Henry V, II 1 line 574; Henry V, II 1 line 595; Henry V, III 2 line 1241; Henry V, IV 1 line 2041; Henry V, IV 4 line 2387; Henry V, IV 4 line 2403; Henry V, IV 7 line 2528; Henry V, IV 7 line 2581; Henry V, IV 8 line 2723.
Henry VI, Part I, I 1 line 104; Henry VI, Part I, II 4 line 1010.
Henry VI, Part II, IV 1 line 2171; Henry VI, Part II, IV 2 line 2332.
Henry VI, Part III, V 6 line 3004.
Julius Caesar, I 2 line 359.
King Lear, I 1 line 176.
Love's Labour's Lost, III 1 line 776; Love's Labour's Lost, IV 3 line 1330; Love's Labour's Lost, V 2 line 2798.
Macbeth, II 2 line 691; Macbeth, II 3 line 799; Macbeth, III 4 line 1291; Macbeth, III 4 line 1292.
Measure for Measure, II 4 line 1183; Measure for Measure, IV 3 line 2141.
Merchant of Venice, I 3 line 488.
Othello, III 3 line 2032; Othello, III 4 line 2184; Othello, V 2 line 3722.
Pericles, II 5 line 1074.
Richard II, I 1 line 47; Richard II, I 1 line 60; Richard II, I 1 line 128.

Richard III, I 2 line 270; Richard III, I 3 line 653; Richard III, V 4 line 3878.
Romeo and Juliet, I 4 line 583.
Taming of the Shrew, IV 3 line 2094.
Tempest, I 1 line 50; Tempest, III 3 line 1617.
Timon of Athens, I 2 line 392; Timon of Athens, III 5 line 1353; Timon of Athens, IV 1 line 1574; Timon of Athens, IV 3 line 1801; Timon of Athens, IV 3 line 2158; Timon of Athens, V 1 lines 2463, 2466.
Titus Andronicus, II 1 line 607; Titus Andronicus, III 1 line 1415; Titus Andronicus, V 2 lines 2498, 2513, 2514.
Troilus and Cressida, IV 4 line 2568.
Twelfth Night, I 3 line 151; Twelfth Night, III 4 line 1699.

Throstle: thrush, Old English: *throstle*.
Merchant of Venice, I 2 line 253.
Midsummer Night's Dream, III 1 line 958.

Thrush: type of songbird, Old English: *thyrsce*.
Winter's Tale, IV 3 line 1733.

Thunder: Old English: *thunor*. The verb is Old English: *thunrian*; figurative sense of, to speak loudly, threateningly, bombastically, is recorded from mid-14c. According to an erroneous fancy the destruction occasioned by lightning was effected by some solid body known as the thunder-stone or thunder-bolt. The thunder stone is the imaginary product of the thunder, which the ancients called *Brontia*, mentioned by Pliny as a species of gem, and as that which, falling with the lightning, does the mischief. It is the fossil commonly called the Belemnite, or Finger Stone, and now known to be a shell. Thunder, it was muted, had the effect of rousing eels from their mud, and so rendered them more easy to be taken in stormy weather.
Antony and Cleopatra, III 13 line 2354; Antony and Cleopatra, V 2 line 3494.
Coriolanus, I 4 line 562; Coriolanus, I 6 line 642; Coriolanus, II 1 line 1216; Coriolanus, III 1 line 2057; Coriolanus, V 3 line 3662.
Cymbeline, IV 2 line 2670; Cymbeline, V 4 line 3177; Cymbeline, V 4 line 3240; Cymbeline, V 4 line 3245; Cymbeline, V 4 line 3265.
Hamlet, I 2 line 331; Hamlet, II 2 line 1559; Hamlet, III 4 line 2444.
Henry V, II 4 line 1003.
Henry VI, Part I, I 4 line 558; Henry VI, Part I, III 1 line 1259; Henry VI, Part I, III 2 line 1512; Henry VI, Part I, V 3 line 2451.
Henry VI, Part II, I 4 line 651; Henry VI, Part II, I 4 line 674; Henry VI, Part II, IV 1 line 2260.
Henry VI, Part III, II 1 line 754.
Henry VIII, V 4 line 3331.
Julius Caesar, I 3 line 420; Julius Caesar, I 3 line 475; Julius Caesar, I 3 line 500; Julius Caesar, I 3 line 527; Julius Caesar, II 2 line 971.
King John, I 1 line 28; King John, II 1 line 722; King John, III 1 line 1045; King John, III 4 line 1423; King John, V 2 line 2457.

King Lear, II 1 line 979; King Lear, II 4 line 1522; King Lear, III 2 line 1683; King Lear, III 2 line 1691; King Lear, III 2 line 1722; King Lear, III 4 line 1947; King Lear, IV 6 line 2710; King Lear, IV 7 line 2949.
Love's Labour's Lost, IV 2 line 1263.
Lover's Complaint, line 327.
Macbeth, I 1 line 1; Macbeth, I 1 line 3; Macbeth, I 3 line 97; Macbeth, III 5 line 1450; Macbeth, IV 1 line 1547; Macbeth, IV 1 line 1626; Macbeth, IV 1 line 1638; Macbeth, IV 1 lines 1649, 1650.
Measure for Measure, II 2 lines 875, 878, 879.
Merry Wives of Windsor, V 5 line 2579.
Midsummer Night's Dream, IV 1 line 1673.
Othello, V 2 line 3583.
Passionate Pilgrim, line 68.
Pericles, II 1 line 567; Pericles, II 1 line 581; Pericles, III 1 line 1195; Pericles, IV 2 line 1805; Pericles, V 1 line 2415.
Richard II, I 3 line 376; Richard II, III 3 line 1693.
Richard III, I 4 line 994.
Sonnet XIV line 6.
Taming of the Shrew, I 2 line 644; Taming of the Shrew, I 2 line 754.
Tempest, I 1 line 1; Tempest, I 2 line 320; Tempest, II 1 line 923; Tempest, II 2 line 1081; Tempest, II 2 lines 1106, 1124; Tempest, II 2 line 1196; Tempest, III 3 line 1626; Tempest, III 3 line 1661; Tempest, III 3 line 1680; Tempest, V 1 line 2065.
Titus Andronicus, II 1 line 550; Titus Andronicus, II 1 line 610.
Troilus and Cressida, II 3 line 1224; Troilus and Cressida, II 3 line 1421; Troilus and Cressida, IV 5 line 2756.
Twelfth Night, I 5 line 546.
Venus and Adonis, line 288.
Winter's Tale, III 1 line 1193.

Thunderbolt: from mid 15c.
Antony and Cleopatra, II 5 line 1151.
As You Like It, I 2 line 323.
Cymbeline, V 4 line 3231.
Henry IV, Part I, IV 1 line 2346.
Julius Caesar, IV 3 line 2066.
King Lear, III 2 line 1682.
Tempest, II 2 line 1123.

Thyme: plant of the mint family, late 14c., from Old French: *thym, tym* (13c.), from Latin: *thymum*, from Greek: *thymon*, possibly from *thyein: burn as a sacrifice*, which would indicate the plant was used as incense.
Midsummer Night's Dream, II 1 line 628.
Othello, I 3 line 681.

Tide: Old English: *tid: point or portion of time, due time.* Meaning, rise and fall of the sea (mid-14c.) is probably via notion of fixed time, specifically, *time of high water*. Old English seems to have had no specific word for this, using *flod* and *ebba* to refer to the rise and fall.

Antony and Cleopatra, I 4 line 474; Antony and Cleopatra, III 2 line 1652.
Comedy of Errors, IV 1 line 999.
Coriolanus, V 4 line 3781.
Henry IV, Part I, IV 1 line 2288.
Henry IV, Part II, II 3 line 1219; Henry IV, Part II, V 2 line 3377; Henry IV, Part II, V 3 line 3434.
Henry V, I 2 line 294; Henry V, II 3 line 844; Henry V, IV 1 line 1946; Henry V, IV 1 line 2110; Henry V, V 2 line 3293.
Henry VI, Part I, I 1 line 88; Henry VI, Part I, II 5 line 1171; Henry VI, Part I, V 5 line 2859.
Henry VI, Part II, I 4 line 705.
Henry VI, Part III, I 4 line 454; Henry VI, Part III, I 4 line 472; Henry VI, Part III, II 5 line 1107; Henry VI, Part III, III 3 line 1741; Henry VI, Part III, IV 3 line 2234; Henry VI, Part III, IV 6 line 2405; Henry VI, Part III, V 1 line 2649; Henry VI, Part III, V 4 line 2836.
Henry VIII, V 4 line 3286.
Julius Caesar, III 1 line 1486; Julius Caesar, IV 3 line 2229.
King John, II 1 line 314; King John, II 1 line 364; King John, III 1 line 1006; King John, IV 2 line 1873; King John, V 6 line 2621.
Midsummer Night's Dream, III 2 line 1088; Midsummer Night's Dream, V 1 line 2047r.
Rape of Lucrece, lines 696, 832, 1718, 1840.
Richard II, II 2 line 1096; Richard II, III 2 line 1501.
Richard III, I 2 line 190; Richard III, I 2 line 291; Richard III, I 3 line 465; Richard III, I 4 lines 911, 912, 916; Richard III, II 4 line 1561; Richard III, IV 4 line 3155.
Romeo and Juliet, I 3 line 399; Romeo and Juliet, III 5 line 2289.
Tempest, I 1 line 68; Tempest, V 1 lines 2063, 2108.
Timon of Athens, I 2 line 395; Timon of Athens, III 4 line 1304.
Titus Andronicus, III 1 line 1225; Titus Andronicus, IV 2 line 1744.
Troilus and Cressida, II 3 line 1351; Troilus and Cressida, III 3 line 2035; Troilus and Cressida, V 1 line 3023.
Two Gentlemen of Verona, I 1 line 61; Two Gentlemen of Verona, II 2 lines 579r, 580; Two Gentlemen of Verona, II 3 line 630; Two Gentlemen of Verona, II 3 line 633; Two Gentlemen of Verona, II 3 line 644; Two Gentlemen of Verona, IV 3 line 1823.
Venus and Adonis, lines 999, 1001.

Tiger: Old English *tigras* (plural), also in part from Old French *tigre* (mid-12c.), both from Latin *tigris; tiger*, from Greek *tigris*, possibly from an Iranian source.
Comedy of Errors, III 1 line 729.
Coriolanus, III 1 line 2129; Coriolanus, V 4 line 3758.
Henry V, III 1 line 1097.
Henry VI, Part III, I 4 line 567; Henry VI, Part III, I 4 line 596; Henry VI, Part III, III 1 line 1405.
King John, III 1 line 1185.
King Lear, IV 2 line 2384.

Macbeth, I 3 line 105; Macbeth, III 4 line 1397; Macbeth, IV 1 line 1580.
Midsummer Night's Dream, II 1 line 608.
Rape of Lucrece, lines 1006, 1030.
Richard III, II 4 line 1538.
Romeo and Juliet, V 3 line 2976.
Sonnet XIX line 3.
Timon of Athens, IV 3 line 1876.
Titus Andronicus, II 3 line 880; Titus Andronicus, III 1 lines 1182, 1183; Titus Andronicus, V 3 line 2530; Titus Andronicus, V 3 line 2740.
Troilus and Cressida, I 3 line 499; Troilus and Cressida, III 2 line 1729.
Twelfth Night, V 1 line 2250.
Two Gentlemen of Verona, III 2 line 1532.
Venus and Adonis, line 1118.

Tilth: Old English: *tilþ*, from *tilian*: to till, as in turn, the soil.
    Measure for Measure, I 4 line 396.
    Tempest, II 1 line 861.

Tithe: Old English: *teogoþa* (Anglian), *teoþa* (W.Saxon) *tenth*, Retained in ecclesiastical sense while the form was replaced in ordinal use by *tenth*. Usually refers to a division of agricultural land, or those associated with it: tithe-woman, tithe-pig etc.,
    All's Well That Ends Well, I 3 line 401.
    Hamlet, III 4 line 2493.
    Henry IV, Part I, III 3 line 2066.
    King John, III 1 line 1076.
    Measure for Measure, IV 1 line 1883.
    Romeo and Juliet, I 4 line 580.
    Timon of Athens, V 4 line 2593.
    Troilus and Cressida, II 2 line 1008.

Timber: Old English: *timber: building, structure,* later, *building material, trees suitable for building*.
    As You Like It, III 3 line 1575.
    Hamlet, IV 7 line 3154.
    Henry VI, Part III, II 1 line 682.
    Henry VIII, I 2 line 426.
    Love's Labour's Lost, V 2 line 2579.
    Othello, II 1 line 817.
    Troilus and Cressida, I 3 line 493.

Toad: Old English: *tadige, tadie*. Among the vulgar errors of Shakespeare's day was the belief that the head of the toad contained a stone possessing great medicinal virtues. It was also generally believed that the toad was highly venomous; a notion to which there are constant allusions in Shakespeare's Plays. Also known as a *paddock*.
    As You Like It, II 1 line 560.

Cymbeline, IV 2 line 2438.
Henry VI, Part III, II 2 line 983.
King Lear, III 4 line 1923; King Lear, V 3 line 3285.
Macbeth, IV 1 line 1553.
Othello, III 3 line 1931; Othello, IV 2 line 2809.
Rape of Lucrece, line 901.
Richard II, III 2 line 1423.
Richard III, I 2 line 192; Richard III, I 2 line 332; Richard III, I 3 line 713; Richard III, IV 4 line 2876; Richard III, IV 4 line 2942r.
Romeo and Juliet, II 4 line 1356r; Romeo and Juliet, III 5 line 2128.
Tempest, I 2 line 490.
Timon of Athens, IV 3 line 1868; Timon of Athens, IV 3 line 2077.
Titus Andronicus, II 3 line 837; Titus Andronicus, IV 2 line 1756.
Troilus and Cressida, II 3 line 1379; Troilus and Cressida, V 1 line 2992.
Winter's Tale, IV 4 line 2150.

Toadstool: late 14c., apparently just what it looks like: a fanciful name from Middle English *tadde:* toad + stole (stool). Toads themselves were regarded as highly poisonous, and this word is popularly restricted to inedible or poisonous fungi, as opposed to mushrooms (e.g. toad-cheese, a poisonous fungi).
Troilus and Cressida, II 1 line 877.

Tokened: plagued with spots.
Antony and Cleopatra, III 10 line 2074.

Tongue: *tunge: organ of speech, speech, language*. The spelling of the ending of the word apparently is a 14c. attempt to indicate proper pronunciation. Meaning, foreign language, is from 1530s. As a verb it meant, *drive out by order or reproach* (late 14c.).
All's Well That Ends Well, I 2 line 282; All's Well That Ends Well, I 3 line 501; All's Well That Ends Well, II 4 line 1227; All's Well That Ends Well, IV 1 lines 1931, 1933; All's Well That Ends Well, IV 1 line 1934; All's Well That Ends Well, IV 1 line 1943; All's Well That Ends Well, IV 1 line 1976; All's Well That Ends Well, V 3 line 2727.
Antony and Cleopatra, I 1 line 39; Antony and Cleopatra, I 2 line 190; Antony and Cleopatra, II 2 line 786; Antony and Cleopatra, II 3 line 996; Antony and Cleopatra, II 5 line 1165; Antony and Cleopatra, II 7 line 1467; Antony and Cleopatra, II 7 line 1525; Antony and Cleopatra, III 2 line 1609; Antony and Cleopatra, III 2 lines 1649, 1650; Antony and Cleopatra, III 3 line 1702; Antony and Cleopatra, III 3 line 1706; Antony and Cleopatra, III 7 line 1955.
As You Like It, I 1 line 52; As You Like It, I 2 line 372; As You Like It, II 1 line 563; As You Like It, II 5 line 844; As You Like It, II 7 line 978; As You Like It, III 2 line 1239; As You Like It, III 2 line 1343; As You Like It, III 5 line 1771; As You Like It, IV 1 line 1942; As You Like It, IV 1 line 1951; As You Like It, IV 3 line 2085; As You Like It, V 4 line 2442.

Comedy of Errors, II 1 line 345; Comedy of Errors, III 2 line 772; Comedy of Errors, IV 2 line 1091; Comedy of Errors, IV 2 line 1101; Comedy of Errors, IV 4 line 1270; Comedy of Errors, V 1 line 1747.
Coriolanus, I 1 line 110; Coriolanus, I 6 line 643; Coriolanus, II 1 line 1143; Coriolanus, II 2 line 1254; Coriolanus, II 3 line 1430; Coriolanus, II 3 line 1469; Coriolanus, II 3 line 1477; Coriolanus, II 3 line 1653; Coriolanus, II 3 line 1658; Coriolanus, III 1 line 1753; Coriolanus, III 1 line 1770; Coriolanus, III 1 line 1917; Coriolanus, III 1 line 2035; Coriolanus, III 1 line 2058; Coriolanus, III 2 line 2235; Coriolanus, III 2 line 2286; Coriolanus, III 2 line 2305; Coriolanus, III 2 line 2326; Coriolanus, III 3 line 2435; Coriolanus, IV 3 line 2672; Coriolanus, V 1 line 3318.
Cymbeline, I 4 line 453; Cymbeline, I 6 line 741; Cymbeline, II 3 line 991; Cymbeline, III 1 line 1413; Cymbeline, III 2 line 1511; Cymbeline, III 4 line 1734; Cymbeline, III 4 line 1756; Cymbeline, III 4 line 1844; Cymbeline, V 3 line 3031; Cymbeline, V 4 line 3299; Cymbeline, V 5 line 3580; Cymbeline, V 5 line 3731.
Hamlet, I 2 line 363; Hamlet, I 2 line 469; Hamlet, I 3 line 545; Hamlet, I 3 line 604; Hamlet, II 2 line 1584; Hamlet, II 2 line 1668; Hamlet, III 1 line 1842; Hamlet, III 2 line 1884; Hamlet, III 2 line 1939; Hamlet, III 2 line 2273; Hamlet, III 4 line 2395; Hamlet, III 4 line 2396; Hamlet, III 4 line 2429; Hamlet, IV 5 line 2970; Hamlet, IV 7 line 3266; Hamlet, V 1 line 3418; Hamlet, V 2 line 3775; Hamlet, V 2 line 3822.
Henry IV, Part I, I 1 line 82; Henry IV, Part I, I 2 line 119; Henry IV, Part I, I 3 line 416; Henry IV, Part I, I 3 line 421; Henry IV, Part I, I 3 line 555; Henry IV, Part I, I 3 line 573; Henry IV, Part I, II 4 line 1056; Henry IV, Part I, II 4 line 1230; Henry IV, Part I, III 1 line 1669; Henry IV, Part I, III 1 line 1756; Henry IV, Part I, IV 1 line 2226; Henry IV, Part I, V 2 line 2830; Henry IV, Part I, V 2 line 2850; Henry IV, Part I, V 4 line 3048.
Henry IV, Part II, Prologue 1 line 1; Henry IV, Part II, Prologue 1 lines 7, 38; Henry IV, Part II, I 1 lines 126, 131; Henry IV, Part II, I 1 line 142; Henry IV, Part II, I 1 lines 155, 159; Henry IV, Part II, II 2 line 1135; Henry IV, Part II, IV 1 lines 2254, 2256; Henry IV, Part II, IV 3 lines 2599, 2600; Henry IV, Part II, IV 4 line 2817; Henry IV, Part II, V 5 lines 3731, 3747.
Henry V, I 2 line 379; Henry V, III 2 line 1161; Henry V, III 7 line 1674; Henry V, V 2 line 3089; Henry V, V 2 line 3099; Henry V, V 2 line 3101; Henry V, V 2 line 3138; Henry V, V 2 line 3162; Henry V, V 2 line 3174; Henry V, V 2 line 3263; Henry V, V 2 line 3272.
Henry VI, Part I, I 2 line 322; Henry VI, Part I, II 4 line 994; Henry VI, Part I, II 5 lines 1125, 1127; Henry VI, Part I, III 1 line 1285; Henry VI, Part I, III 4 line 1741; Henry VI, Part I, IV 1 line 1855; Henry VI, Part I, V 3 line 2498; Henry VI, Part I, V 3 lines 2528, 2531.
Henry VI, Part II, I 1 line 241; Henry VI, Part II, II 3 line 1139; Henry VI, Part II, III 1 line 1438; Henry VI, Part II, III 1 line 1553; Henry VI, Part II, III 2 line 1749; Henry VI, Part II, III 2 line 1795; Henry VI, Part II, III 2 line 1843; Henry VI, Part II, III 2 line 1949; Henry VI, Part II, III 2 line 2010; Henry VI, Part II, IV 1 line 2217; Henry VI, Part II, IV 1 line

2277; Henry VI, Part II, IV 2 line 2477; Henry VI, Part II, IV 7 line 2724; Henry VI, Part II, IV 7 line 2741; Henry VI, Part II, V 1 line 3072.
Henry VI, Part III, I 4 line 485; Henry VI, Part III, I 4 line 552; Henry VI, Part III, II 1 line 671; Henry VI, Part III, II 1 line 708; Henry VI, Part III, II 2 line 947; Henry VI, Part III, II 2 line 964; Henry VI, Part III, II 2 line 970; Henry VI, Part III, II 2 line 979; Henry VI, Part III, II 2 line 988; Henry VI, Part III, II 6 line 1312; Henry VI, Part III, III 3 line 1754; Henry VI, Part III, V 5 line 2926.
Henry VIII, I 1 line 71; Henry VIII, I 1 line 83; Henry VIII, I 2 line 389; Henry VIII, I 2 line 402; Henry VIII, I 4 line 739; Henry VIII, II 1 line 994; Henry VIII, II 2 line 1059; Henry VIII, II 2 line 1139; Henry VIII, II 3 line 1203; Henry VIII, III 1 line 1663; Henry VIII, III 1 line 1673; Henry VIII, III 1 line 1685; Henry VIII, III 2 line 1849; Henry VIII, III 2 line 2145; Henry VIII, III 2 line 2359; Henry VIII, V 1 line 2822; Henry VIII, V 1 line 2918; Henry VIII, V 3 line 3205; Henry VIII, V 3 line 3230.
Julius Caesar, I 2 line 101; Julius Caesar, I 2 line 216; Julius Caesar, II 1 line 946; Julius Caesar, II 4 line 1145; Julius Caesar, III 1 line 1490; Julius Caesar, III 2 line 1772; Julius Caesar, V 1 line 2397; Julius Caesar, V 5 line 2717.
King John, I 1 line 92; King John, II 1 line 775; King John, III 1 line 1106; King John, III 1 line 1113; King John, III 1 line 1183; King John, III 1 line 1190r; King John, III 1 line 1233; King John, III 3 lines 1339, 1351; King John, III 4 line 1423; King John, III 4 line 1556; King John, IV 1 line 1653; King John, IV 1 line 1685; King John, IV 1 lines 1686, 1688, 1689; King John, IV 2 line 1774; King John, IV 2 line 1855; King John, IV 2 line 1875; King John, IV 2 line 1985; King John, IV 3 line 2115; King John, V 1 line 2213; King John, V 2 line 2405; King John, V 2 line 2448; King John, V 6 line 2587; King John, V 6 line 2594.
King Lear, I 1 line 80; King Lear, I 1 line 251; King Lear, I 4 line 717; King Lear, II 4 line 1444; King Lear, III 2 line 1768; King Lear, V 3 line 3292; King Lear, V 3 line 3435.
Love's Labour's Lost, I 1 line 128; Love's Labour's Lost, I 1 line 171; Love's Labour's Lost, I 2 line 395; Love's Labour's Lost, II 1 line 500; Love's Labour's Lost, II 1 line 558; Love's Labour's Lost, II 1 line 738; Love's Labour's Lost, II 1 line 753; Love's Labour's Lost, III 1 line 774; Love's Labour's Lost, III 1 line 928; Love's Labour's Lost, IV 2 lines 1261, 1267; Love's Labour's Lost, IV 3 line 1361; Love's Labour's Lost, IV 3 line 1582; Love's Labour's Lost, IV 3 line 1685; Love's Labour's Lost, V 1 line 1743; Love's Labour's Lost, V 2 line 2149; Love's Labour's Lost, V 2 line 2152; Love's Labour's Lost, V 2 line 2166; Love's Labour's Lost, V 2 line 2252; Love's Labour's Lost, V 2 line 2253; Love's Labour's Lost, V 2 line 2303; Love's Labour's Lost, V 2 line 2324; Love's Labour's Lost, V 2 line 2599; Love's Labour's Lost, V 2 line 2659; Love's Labour's Lost, V 2 line 2678; Love's Labour's Lost, V 2 line 2785; Love's Labour's Lost, V 2 line 2805.
Lover's Complaint, lines 100, 121.
Macbeth, I 5 line 370; Macbeth, I 5 line 420; Macbeth, I 7 line 491; Macbeth, II 3 line 835; Macbeth, II 3 line 909; Macbeth, III 2 line 1204; Macbeth, IV 1 line 1562; Macbeth, IV 3 line 1855; Macbeth, IV 3 line

2078; Macbeth, IV 3 line 2115; Macbeth, V 5 line 2386; Macbeth, V 8 line 2495.
Measure for Measure, I 1 line 51; Measure for Measure, I 4 line 385; Measure for Measure, II 2 line 800; Measure for Measure, II 2 line 907; Measure for Measure, II 4 line 1019; Measure for Measure, II 4 line 1168; Measure for Measure, II 4 line 1205; Measure for Measure, III 2 line 1696; Measure for Measure, IV 3 line 2231; Measure for Measure, IV 4 line 2333; Measure for Measure, V 1 line 2834.
Merchant of Venice, I 1 line 115; Merchant of Venice, I 1 line 118; Merchant of Venice, II 2 line 719; Merchant of Venice, II 3 line 785; Merchant of Venice, II 6 line 938; Merchant of Venice, III 2 line 1371; Merchant of Venice, IV 1 line 2183.
Merry Wives of Windsor, I 4 line 482; Merry Wives of Windsor, II 3 line 1153.
Midsummer Night's Dream, I 1 lines 191, 197r; Midsummer Night's Dream, II 2 line 659; Midsummer Night's Dream, III 1 line 1025; Midsummer Night's Dream, III 2 line 1105; Midsummer Night's Dream, III 2 line 1336; Midsummer Night's Dream, III 2 line 1417; Midsummer Night's Dream, IV 1 line 1774; Midsummer Night's Dream, V 1 line 1941; Midsummer Night's Dream, V 1 line 2148; Midsummer Night's Dream, V 1 line 2187; Midsummer Night's Dream, V 1 line 2210; Midsummer Night's Dream, V 1 line 2285.
Much Ado About Nothing, I 1 line 126; Much Ado About Nothing, I 1 line 127; Much Ado About Nothing, II 1 line 408; Much Ado About Nothing, II 1 line 415; Much Ado About Nothing, II 1 line 561; Much Ado About Nothing, II 1 line 655; Much Ado About Nothing, III 2 lines 1211, 1212; Much Ado About Nothing, III 4 line 1572; Much Ado About Nothing, IV 1 line 1895; Much Ado About Nothing, IV 1 line 1968; Much Ado About Nothing, V 1 line 2165; Much Ado About Nothing, V 1 lines 2241, 2244r; Much Ado About Nothing, V 3 line 2510.
Othello, I 2 line 223; Othello, II 1 line 887; Othello, II 1 line 893; Othello, II 3 line 1370; Othello, III 3 line 2134; Othello, V 1 line 3274; Othello, V 2 line 3520; Othello, V 2 line 3521.
Passionate Pilgrim, lines 7, 11, 64, 71, 307, 351, 372.
Pericles, I 1 line 82; Pericles, I 1 line 158; Pericles, I 2 line 274; Pericles, I 2 line 293; Pericles, I 4 lines 429, 411; Pericles, II 1 line 655; Pericles, II 5 line 1087.
Rape of Lucrece, lines 129, 212, 278, 521, 821, 944, 1127, 1265, 1271, 1514, 1516, 1588, 1668, 1699, 1769, 1831.
Richard II, I 1 line 49; Richard II, I 1 line 52; Richard II, I 1 line 108; Richard II, I 1 line 195; Richard II, I 3 lines 458, 463, 470; Richard II, I 3 line 534; Richard II, I 3 line 545; Richard II, I 3 line 557; Richard II, I 4 line 625; Richard II, II 1 line 687; Richard II, II 1 line 806; Richard II, II 1 line 836; Richard II, II 1 line 920; Richard II, II 3 line 1228; Richard II, III 2 line 1429; Richard II, III 2 line 1474; Richard II, III 2 line 1502; Richard II, III 2 line 1607; Richard II, III 2 line 1629; Richard II, III 3 line 1725; Richard II, III 4 line 1941; Richard II, IV 1 line 1989; Richard II, IV 1 line 2197; Richard II, V 1 line 2381; Richard II, V 2 line 2451;

Richard II, V 2 line 2470; Richard II, V 3 line 2607; Richard II, V 3 line 2696; Richard II, V 3 line 2708; Richard II, V 5 line 2849.

Richard III, I 1 line 99; Richard III, I 2 line 256; Richard III, I 2 line 274; Richard III, I 2 lines 353, 355; Richard III, I 2 line 382; Richard III, I 3 line 827; Richard III, II 1 line 1228; Richard III, III 7 line 2405; Richard III, IV 4 line 2810; Richard III, IV 4 line 3034; Richard III, V 3 lines 3695, 3696.

Romeo and Juliet, II 2 line 908; Romeo and Juliet, II 2 line 1023; Romeo and Juliet, II 2 line 1026; Romeo and Juliet, II 3 line 1092; Romeo and Juliet, II 6 line 1486; Romeo and Juliet, III 1 line 1683; Romeo and Juliet, III 2 line 1750; Romeo and Juliet, III 2 line 1814; Romeo and Juliet, III 2 line 1822; Romeo and Juliet, III 5 line 2279; Romeo and Juliet, III 5 line 2356; Romeo and Juliet, IV 5 line 2690.

Sonnet XXIII line 12; Sonnet LXIX line 3; Sonnet LXIX line 6; Sonnet LXXXI line 11; Sonnet LXXXIX line 9; Sonnet XCV line 5; Sonnet CII line 4; Sonnet CII line 13; Sonnet CVI line 14; Sonnet CXII line 6; Sonnet CXXVII line 14; Sonnet CXXXVIII line 7; Sonnet CXLI line 5; Sonnet CXLV line 6.

Taming of the Shrew, Prologue 1 line 122; Taming of the Shrew, I 1 line 386; Taming of the Shrew, I 1 line 503; Taming of the Shrew, I 2 line 648; Taming of the Shrew, I 2 line 757; Taming of the Shrew, I 2 line 807; Taming of the Shrew, II 1 line 1064; Taming of the Shrew, II 1 line 1065; Taming of the Shrew, II 1 line 1067; Taming of the Shrew, IV 1 line 1627; Taming of the Shrew, IV 2 line 1886; Taming of the Shrew, IV 3 line 2041.

Tempest, II 1 line 729; Tempest, II 2 line 1094; Tempest, II 2 line 1140; Tempest, III 1 line 1328; Tempest, III 2 line 1407; Tempest, III 2 line 1428; Tempest, III 2 line 1508; Tempest, III 3 line 1607; Tempest, IV 1 line 1767.

Timon of Athens, I 1 line 215; Timon of Athens, IV 3 line 1956; Timon of Athens, IV 3 line 2066; Timon of Athens, IV 3 line 2094; Timon of Athens, V 1 line 2411.

Titus Andronicus, II 1 line 610; Titus Andronicus, II 1 line 684; Titus Andronicus, II 3 line 776; Titus Andronicus, II 3 line 914; Titus Andronicus, II 4 line 1062; Titus Andronicus, II 4 lines 1063, 1064; Titus Andronicus, II 4 line 1069; Titus Andronicus, II 4 lines 1091, 1102, 1112; Titus Andronicus, III 1 line 1174; Titus Andronicus, III 1 line 1237; Titus Andronicus, III 1 lines 1261, 1263; Titus Andronicus, III 1 line 1274; Titus Andronicus, III 1 line 1372; Titus Andronicus, IV 2 line 1842; Titus Andronicus, IV 4 line 2113; Titus Andronicus, V 1 line 2227; Titus Andronicus, V 1 line 2285; Titus Andronicus, V 2 lines 2492, 2493; Titus Andronicus, V 3 line 2537; Titus Andronicus, V 3 line 2591; Titus Andronicus, V 3 line 2620.

Troilus and Cressida, I 2 line 257; Troilus and Cressida, I 3 line 520; Troilus and Cressida, I 3 line 613; Troilus and Cressida, II 1 line 967; Troilus and Cressida, III 2 line 1779; Troilus and Cressida, III 3 line 2153; Troilus and Cressida, IV 5 line 2664; Troilus and Cressida, IV 5 line 2713.

Twelfth Night, I 2 line 112; Twelfth Night, I 3 line 201; Twelfth Night, I 5 line 586; Twelfth Night, II 2 line 677; Twelfth Night, II 5 line 1173; Twelfth Night, III 4 lines 1615, 1618; Twelfth Night, III 4 line 1751; Twelfth Night, V 1 line 2246.
Two Gentlemen of Verona, II 3 line 640; Two Gentlemen of Verona, II 3 line 641; Two Gentlemen of Verona, II 6 line 944; Two Gentlemen of Verona, III 1 lines 1174, 1175; Two Gentlemen of Verona, III 1 line 1415; Two Gentlemen of Verona, IV 1 line 1586.
Venus and Adonis, lines 237, 351, 447, 797, 798, 871, 1025, 1029, 1091, 1099.
Winter's Tale, I 2 line 75; Winter's Tale, I 2 line 164; Winter's Tale, I 2 line 448; Winter's Tale, II 2 line 885; Winter's Tale, II 2 line 906; Winter's Tale, II 3 line 1043; Winter's Tale, II 3 line 1064; Winter's Tale, II 3 line 1138; Winter's Tale, III 2 line 1454; Winter's Tale, IV 4 line 2135; Winter's Tale, V 1 line 2841; Winter's Tale, V 1 line 2953.

Tongue-tied: from about 1530c.
    Henry VI, Part I, II 4 line 947.
    Sonnet LXXXV line 1; Sonnet CXL line 2.
    Henry VI, Part III, III 3 line 1713.
    Julius Caesar, I 1 line 63.
    Midsummer Night's Dream, V 1 line 1943.
    Richard III, III 7 line 2356; Richard III, IV 4 line 2928.
    Troilus and Cressida, III 2 line 1861.
    Winter's Tale, I 2 line 83.

Tooth: see Teeth.
    All's Well That Ends Well, I 1 line 159; All's Well That Ends Well, II 3 line 936.
    As You Like It, II 7 line 1078.
    Comedy of Errors, V 1 line 1501.
    Coriolanus, V 3 line 3604.
    Cymbeline, V 4 line 3329.
    Henry IV, Part I, II 2 line 765.
    Henry IV, Part II, IV 5 line 3027.
    Henry VI, Part III, I 4 line 552.
    Henry VIII, I 3 line 627.
    King John, I 1 lines 197, 220; King John, III 1 line 1185.
    King Lear, I 4 line 814; King Lear, II 4 line 1414; King Lear, III 6 line 2068; King Lear, V 3 line 3268.
    Love's Labour's Lost, V 2 line 2560.
    Macbeth, III 2 line 1186; Macbeth, IV 1 line 1569.
    Measure for Measure, V 1 line 2399.
    Much Ado About Nothing, II 1 line 647; Much Ado About Nothing, III 2 line 1219; Much Ado About Nothing, III 2 line 1223; Much Ado About Nothing, III 2 line 1260; Much Ado About Nothing, V 1 line 2104.
    Othello, III 3 line 2096.
    Richard II, I 3 line 603.
    Richard III, I 3 line 759; Richard III, II 4 line 1513.

Taming of the Shrew, I 2 line 628.
Tempest, IV 1 line 1916.
Troilus and Cressida, IV 5 line 2927.
Venus and Adonis, line 1139.
Winter's Tale, IV 3 line 1730; Winter's Tale, IV 4 line 2263.

Tortoise: 1550s, altered (perhaps by influence of *porpoise*) from Middle English *tortuse* (late 15c.), *tortuce* (mid-15c.), *tortuge* (late 14c.). Others propose a connection with Latin: *tortus*: *twisted*, based on the shape of the feet. The classical Latin word was *testudo*, from *testa*: *shell*.
    Romeo and Juliet, V 1 line 2851.
    Tempest, I 2 line 462.

Tree: Importance of the oak in mythology is reflected in the recurring use of words for, oak, to mean, tree. In Old English and Middle English, also, thing made of wood, especially the cross of the Crucifixion and a gallows, 12c. Old English: *treo, treow*: *tree* (also wood).
    Antony and Cleopatra, I 4 line 495; Antony and Cleopatra, III 6 line 1873; Antony and Cleopatra, IV 14 line 2983.
    As You Like It, II 1 line 563; As You Like It, II 3 line 707; As You Like It, II 5 line 820; As You Like It, II 5 line 845; As You Like It, III 2 lines 1126, 1130; As You Like It, III 2 line 1226; As You Like It, III 2 line 1227; As You Like It, III 2 line 1239; As You Like It, III 2 line 1284; As You Like It, III 2 line 1334; As You Like It, III 2 line 1336; As You Like It, III 2 line 1359; As You Like It, III 2 line 1471; As You Like It, III 3 line 1564; As You Like It, IV 3 line 2079.
    Coriolanus, II 1 line 1119.
    Cymbeline, III 3 line 1666; Cymbeline, V 5 line 3687.
    Hamlet, II 2 line 1302; Hamlet, III 2 line 2082.
    Henry IV, Part I, II 4 lines 1410, 1411; Henry VI, Part I, III 1 line 1676.
    Henry VI, Part I, II 4 line 963.
    Henry VI, Part II, II 1 line 839; Henry VI, Part II, II 1 line 840; Henry VI, Part II, II 1 line 843; Henry VI, Part II, III 2 line 1900; Henry VI, Part II, III 2 line 2017.
    Henry VI, Part III, II 5 line 1151; Henry VI, Part III, V 2 line 2736; Henry VI, Part III, V 6 line 3041; Henry VI, Part III, V 7 line 3126.
    Henry VIII, I 2 line 427; Henry VIII, III 1 line 1623; Henry VIII, V 4 line 3275.
    Julius Caesar, II 1 line 828.
    King John, V 6 line 2620.
    King Lear, II 3 line 1253; King Lear, V 2 line 3107.
    Love's Labour's Lost, IV 3 line 1684; Love's Labour's Lost, V 2 line 2198; Love's Labour's Lost, V 2 lines 2846, 2854.
    Macbeth, III 4 line 1426; Macbeth, IV 1 line 1607; Macbeth, IV 1 line 1650; Macbeth, IV 1 line 1663; Macbeth, V 5 line 2400.
    Measure for Measure, IV 1 lines 2316.
    Merchant of Venice, III 5 line 1893; Merchant of Venice, V 1 line 2445; Merchant of Venice, V 1 line 2536.

Merry Wives of Windsor, II 3 line 1121; Merry Wives of Windsor, II 3 line 1133; Merry Wives of Windsor, IV 4 line 2227; Merry Wives of Windsor, V 5 line 2643.
Much Ado About Nothing, II 1 line 600.
Othello, IV 3 line 3062; Othello, V 2 line 3316; Othello, V 2 line 3716.
Passionate Pilgrim, lines 136, 380, 395.
Pericles, I 1 line 67; Pericles, I 1 line 165; Pericles, I 2 line 266.
Phoenix and the Turtle, line 2.
Richard II, II 3 line 1207; Richard II, II 4 line 1338; Richard II, III 4 line 1888; Richard II, III 4 line 1909; Richard II, III 4 line 1924.
Richard III, I 2 line 347; Richard III, III 7 line 2377.
Romeo and Juliet, II 1 line 829; Romeo and Juliet, II 2 line 833; Romeo and Juliet, II 2 line 957; Romeo and Juliet, III 5 line 2101; Romeo and Juliet, V 3 line 2936; Romeo and Juliet, V 3 line 3092.
Sonnet XII line 5.
Tempest, II 2 line 1211; Tempest, III 2 line 1429; Tempest, III 3 line 1587.
Timon of Athens, IV 3 line 1911; Timon of Athens, V 1 lines 2494, 2500.
Titus Andronicus, II 3 line 733; Titus Andronicus, II 3 line 830; Titus Andronicus, II 3 lines 1024, 1029; Titus Andronicus, V 1 line 2180; Titus Andronicus, V 1 line 2273.
Troilus and Cressida, I 3 line 518.
Twelfth Night, II 5 line 1042.
Venus and Adonis, lines 172, 283, 411.

Tributary: late 14c., paying tribute. The noun sense of one who pays tribute is recorded from early 15c. Meaning, stream that flows into a larger body, which is recorded from 1610s in this sense.
Cymbeline, IV 2 line 2359.
Hamlet, V 2 line 3691.
Romeo and Juliet, III 2 line 1827.
Titus Andronicus, I 1 line 181; Titus Andronicus, III 1 line 1410.
Venus and Adonis, lines 683, 1067.

Tripe: c.1300, from Old French: *tripe: entrails used as food* (13c.), of unknown origin. Applied contemptuously to persons (1590s).
Henry IV, Part II, V 4 line 3565.
Taming of the Shrew, IV 3 line 1976.

Trout: Old English: *truht: trout*, in part from Old French: *truite*. In late 17c. slang, trusty trout was used in a sense of confidential friend.
Measure for Measure, I 2 lines 181.
Twelfth Night, II 5 line 1049.

Trundle-tail: a curly tailed dog. 1540s, possibly from Middle English *trendle* wheel, suspended hoop (early 14c.), from Old English *trendel* ring, disk. Also probably in part from Old French *trondeler* to roll, which is of Germanic origin.

King Lear, III 6 line 2071.

Trunk: mid-15c., originally, box, case, from Old French: *tronc*: alms box in a church (12c.), also trunk of a tree, trunk of the human body, from Latin: *truncus*, originally, mutilated, cut off. The meaning *box, case* is likely to be from the notion of the body as the *case* of the organs. English acquired the other two senses of the Old French in late 15c., main stem of a tree and torso of a human body.
    Henry IV, Part I, II 4 line 1432.
    Henry IV, Part II, IV 5 line 3126.
    Henry V, III 6 line 1621.
    Henry VI, Part II, III 2 line 1827; Henry VI, Part II, IV 10 line 2973.
    Henry VI, Part III, III 2 line 1656.
    King John, V 2 line 2423.
    King Lear, I 1 line 189.
    Measure for Measure, III 1 line 1300.
    Merchant of Venice, IV 1 line 2068.
    Romeo and Juliet, V 1 line 2874.
    Timon of Athens, IV 3 line 1918.
    Twelfth Night, III 4 line 1924.

Tuft: late 14c., perhaps from Old French: *touffe: tuft of hair*.
    As You Like It, III 5 line 1728.
    Love's Labour's Lost, IV 2 line 1235.
    Merry Wives of Windsor, V 5 line 2635.
    Richard II, II 3 line 1207.
    Winter's Tale, II 1 line 642.

Turf: *turf, tyrf: slab of soil and grass, also surface of grassland*.
    As You Like It, III 4 line 1637.
    Cymbeline, V 3 line 3038.
    Hamlet, IV 5 line 2891.
    Henry V, IV 1 line 1858.
    Midsummer Night's Dream, II 2 line 695.
    Tempest, IV 1 line 1772.

Turkey: 1540s, guinea fowl (*Numida meleagris*), imported from Madagascar via Turkey, by Near East traders known as turkey merchants. The larger North American bird (*Meleagris gallopavo*) was domesticated by the Aztecs, introduced to Spain by conquistadors (1523) and thence to wider Europe, by way of North Africa (then under Ottoman rule) and Turkey (Indian corn was originally turkey corn or turkey wheat in English for the same reason). The word turkey was first applied to it in English 1550s because it was identified with or treated as a species of the guinea fowl. The Turkish name for it is *hindi*, literally, Indian, (c.1600, contracted from *poulet d'inde*) literally, chicken from India, based on the common misconception that the New World was eastern Asia. The New World bird itself reputedly reached England by 1524 at the earliest estimate, though a date in the 1530s seems more likely. By 1575, turkey was becoming the usual main course at an English Christmas.

Henry IV, Part I, II 1 line 667.
Taming of the Shrew, II 1 line 1206.

Turkey-cock: see Turkey.
Henry V, V 1 line 2901; Henry V, V 1 line 2903.
Twelfth Night, II 5 line 1059.

Turtle: reptile, c.1600, marine tortoise, from *tortue: turtle, tortoise*, of unknown origin. The English word is perhaps a sailors' mauling of the French one.
Love's Labour's Lost, IV 3 line 1553; Love's Labour's Lost, V 2 line 2853.
Merry Wives of Windsor, II 1 line 644; Merry Wives of Windsor, III 3 line 1442.
Phoenix and the Turtle, lines 23, 31, 34, 58.
Taming of the Shrew, II 1 line 1056; Taming of the Shrew, II 1 line 1057.
Troilus and Cressida, III 2 line 1828.
Winter's Tale, IV 4 line 2037; Winter's Tale, V 3 line 3449.

Turtle-doves: Originally applied to all pigeons, now mostly restricted to the turtle dove. A symbol of gentleness from early Christian times, also of the Holy Spirit, and of peace and deliverance from anxiety.
Henry VI, Part I, II 2 line 790.

Tusk: Old English: *tux, tusc.*
Venus and Adonis, line 1138.

Twig: Old English: *twigge.*
All's Well That Ends Well, III 5 line 1630; All's Well That Ends Well, III 6 line 1831.
Henry V, V 2 line 3025.
Henry VI, Part II, III 3 line 2130.
Measure for Measure, I 3 line 314.
Richard II, III 4 line 1896.
Taming of the Shrew, II 1 line 1103.

Udder: milk gland. Old English *uder*, of West Germanic origin; related to Dutch *uier* and German *Euter*.
As You Like It, IV 3 line 2118.

Union: a pearl.
Hamlet, V 2 line 3915.

Universe: 1580s, the whole world, cosmos, from Old French: *univers* (12c.).
Henry V, IV 0 line 1790.
Sonnet CIX line 13.

Urchin: Still used for, hedgehog, in non-standard speech in Cumbria, Yorkshire, Shropshire. Applied throughout 16c. to people whose appearance or behaviour suggested hedgehogs, from hunchbacks (1520s) to goblins (1580s) to bad girls (c.1530); meaning, poorly or raggedly clothed youngster, emerged 1550s, but was not in frequent use until after c.1780. Sea urchin is recorded from 1590s (a 19c. Newfoundland name for them was whore's eggs). Late 13c., *yrichon*: hedgehog.
    Merry Wives of Windsor, IV 1 line 2245.
    Tempest, I 2 line 476; Tempest, II 2 line 1086.
    Titus Andronicus, II 3 line 836.
    Venus and Adonis, line 1127.

Urine: early 14c., from Old French: *urine* (12c).
    Macbeth, II 3 line 789.
    Measure for Measure, III 2 line 1620.
    Merchant of Venice, IV 1 line 1982.

Vale: river-land between two ranges of hills, c.1300.
    Antony and Cleopatra, IV 11 line 2895.
    Comedy of Errors, V 1 line 1552.
    Cymbeline, IV 2 line 2547.
    Henry VI, Part II, II 1 line 810.
    Henry VIII, I 1 line 43.
    Lover's Complaint, line 2.
    Othello, III 3 line 1927.
    Titus Andronicus, II 3 line 829; Titus Andronicus, V 2 line 2342.
    Troilus and Cressida, I 2 line 157.

Valley: late 13c., from Anglo-Norman *valey*, Old French: *valee*: *a valley*.
    Cymbeline, III 3 line 1685.
    Henry V, III 5 line 1441.
    Midsummer Night's Dream, IV 1 line 1661.
    Passionate Pilgrim, line 356.
    Sonnet CLIII line 4.
    Titus Andronicus, II 3 line 819.
    Winter's Tale, II 3 line 1053; Winter's Tale, V 1 line 3071.

Vegetive: late 14c., endowed with the power of growth, Middle English transferred sense was, characterised by growth.
    Pericles, III 2 line 1327.

Vein: c.1300, from Old French: *veine*, from Latin: *vena: a blood vessel*, also *a water course, a vein of metal, a person's natural ability or interest*, of unknown origin. The mining sense is attested in English from late 14c. Figurative sense *of strain or intermixture* (of some quality) is recorded from 1560s; that of a humour or mood, natural tendency is first recorded 1570s.
    Antony and Cleopatra, II 5 line 1085.
    As You Like It, II 7 line 991.
    Comedy of Errors, II 2 line 413; Comedy of Errors, IV 4 line 1331.

Coriolanus, I 1 line 134; Coriolanus, V 1 line 3338.
Cymbeline, IV 2 line 2610.
Henry IV, Part I, I 3 line 452; Henry IV, Part I, II 4 line 1370.
Henry IV, Part II, IV 1 line 2271.
Henry V, I 2 line 264; Henry V, II 3 line 835; Henry V, IV 2 line 2184.
Henry VI, Part I, IV 7 line 2352.
Henry VI, Part III, I 1 line 104.
King John, II 1 line 743; King John, III 1 line 1203; King John, III 3 line 1345; King John, III 4 line 1520; King John, V 2 line 2316.
Love's Labour's Lost, IV 3 line 1397; Love's Labour's Lost, V 2 line 2478.
Measure for Measure, II 2 line 830.
Merchant of Venice, III 2 line 1546; Merchant of Venice, III 2 line 1631.
Midsummer Night's Dream, I 2 line 300r; Midsummer Night's Dream, III 2 line 1116.
Pericles, I 4 line 512; Pericles, II 1 line 653.
Rape of Lucrece, lines 470, 478, 491, 1505.
Richard III, I 2 line 233; Richard III, IV 2 line 2716; Richard III, IV 2 line 2719.
Romeo and Juliet, I 1 line 105; Romeo and Juliet, IV 1 line 2461; Romeo and Juliet, IV 3 line 2566; Romeo and Juliet, V 1 line 2872.
Sonnet LXVII line 10; Sonnet XCVIX line 5.
Tempest, I 2 line 388.
Timon of Athens, I 2 line 394.
Troilus and Cressida, I 3 line 456; Troilus and Cressida, II 3 line 1423; Troilus and Cressida, IV 1 line 2273; Troilus and Cressida, V 3 line 3313.
Venus and Adonis, line 145.
Winter's Tale, V 3 line 3363.

Venison: late 13c., from Old French: *venesoun*: *meat of large game, especially deer or boar*, also *a hunt*, from Latin: *venationem*.
   As You Like It, II 1 line 569.
   Cymbeline, III 3 line 1682; Cymbeline, IV 4 line 2927.
   Merry Wives of Windsor, I 1 line 73; Merry Wives of Windsor, I 1 line 75; Merry Wives of Windsor, I 1 line 179.

Venom: early 13c., from Anglo-French and Old French: *venim*, from Latin: *venenum*: *poison*, earlier (pre-classical) *drug, potion*, probably originally *love potion*. The meaning, bitter, virulent feeling or language, is first recorded c. 1300.
   Antony and Cleopatra, V 2 line 3767.
   As You Like It, II 1 line 560; As You Like It, II 3 line 678.
   Comedy of Errors, V 1 line 1500.
   Coriolanus, IV 3 line 2546.
   Cymbeline, III 4 line 1756.
   Hamlet, II 2 line 1584; Hamlet, IV 7 line 3245; Hamlet, IV 7 line 3308; Hamlet, V 2 line 3974; Hamlet, V 2 lines 3978, 3979.

Henry IV, Part II, IV 4 line 2793.
Henry V, V 2 line 2999.
Henry VI, Part II, III 2 line 1960.
Henry VI, Part III, II 2 line 983.
Henry VIII, I 1 line 182.
Julius Caesar, IV 3 line 2029; Julius Caesar, V 3 line 2586.
King John, III 1 line 978.
King Lear, IV 3 line 2505.
Macbeth, III 4 line 1307; Macbeth, IV 1 line 1555.
Pericles, III 1 line 1197.
Rape of Lucrece, lines 583, 901.
Richard II, I 1 line 175; Richard II, II 1 line 701; Richard II, Ii 1 line 844r; Richard II, III 2 line 1422.
Richard III, I 2 line 192; Richard III, I 3 line 758; Richard III, IV 1 line 2532.
Timon of Athens, IV 3 line 1869.
Titus Andronicus, V 3 line 2538.
Troilus and Cressida, IV 2 line 2301; Troilus and Cressida, V 3 line 3330.
Twelfth Night, III 2 line 1407.
Venus and Adonis, line 938.
Winter's Tale, II 1 line 650.

Venus: from Latin, in ancient Roman mythology, the goddess of beauty and love, especially sensual love, from *Venus: love, sexual desire, loveliness, beauty, charm.* Applied by the Romans to Greek *Aphrodite*, Egyptian *Hathor*, etc. Meaning, second planet from the sun, is attested from late 13c.
  Antony and Cleopatra, I 5 line 542; Antony and Cleopatra, II 2 line 924.
  As You Like It, IV 1 line 1973.
  Cymbeline, V 5 line 3568.
  Henry IV, Part II, II 4 line 1553.
  Henry VI, Part I, I 2 line 343.
  Love's Labour's Lost, II 1 line 757.
  Merchant of Venice, II 6 line 914.
  Midsummer Night's Dream, I 1 line 178; Midsummer Night's Dream, III 2 line 1094; Midsummer Night's Dream, III 2 line 1143.
  Much Ado About Nothing, IV 1 line 1701.
  Passionate Pilgrim, line 144.
  Rape of Lucrece, line 109.
  Romeo and Juliet, II 1 line 810; Romeo and Juliet, IV 1 line 2371.
  Tempest, IV 1 line 1799.
  Titus Andronicus, II 3 line 763.
  Troilus and Cressida, III 1 line 1524; Troilus and Cressida, IV 1 line 2222; Troilus and Cressida, IV 5 line 2653; Troilus and Cressida, IV 5 line 2803; Troilus and Cressida, V 2 line 3239.
  Venus and Adonis, lines 25, 200, 207, 838, 881, 1079.

Verdure: c.1300, fresh green colour, from Old French: *verdure*: *greenness*, from *verd*, variant of *vert*: *green*, from Latin: *viridis*, of unknown origin. Perhaps ultimately from a root meaning, growing plant. Meaning, green plants, vegetation, is attested from c.1400.
    Tempest, I 2 line 187.
    Two Gentlemen of Verona, I 1 line 51.
    Venus and Adonis, line 528.

Vesper: referring to Venus; late Middle English: from Latin: *vesper*: evening (star).
    Antony and Cleopatra, IV 14 line 2986.

Vine: c.1300, from Old French: *vigne*, from Latin: *vinea*: *vine*.
    Antony and Cleopatra, II 7 line 1515.
    Comedy of Errors, II 2 line 563.
    Cymbeline, IV 2 line 2395.
    Henry V, V 2 line 3022.
    Henry VI, Part I, II 5 line 1086.
    Henry VIII, V 5 lines 3418, 3433.
    King Lear, I 1 line 86.
    Rape of Lucrece, line 266.
    Richard III, V 2 line 3436.
    Tempest, IV 1 line 1828.
    Timon of Athens, IV 3 line 1880.

Vineyard: from the Latin: *vinum*.
    Henry V, III 5 line 1394; Henry V, V 2 line 3035.
    Measure for Measure, IV 1 lines 1826, 1827, 1830.
    Tempest, II 1 line 861; Tempest, IV 1 line 1778.

Violet: early 14c., small plant with purplish-blue flowers, from Old French: *violette*, from *viole*: *violet*, from Latin: *viola*. The colour sense (late 14c.) developed from the flower. An old superstition is alluded to by Shakespeare, when he makes Laertes wish that violets may spring from the grave of Ophelia. The violet has generally been associated with early death.
    Cymbeline, I 5 line 593; Cymbeline, IV 2 line 2543.
    Hamlet, I 3 line 489; Hamlet, IV 5 line 3060; Hamlet, V 1 line 3574.
    Henry V, IV 1 line 1950.
    King John, IV 2 line 1739.
    Love's Labour's Lost, V 2 line 2843.
    Measure for Measure, II 2 line 940.
    Midsummer Night's Dream, II 1 line 629.
    Pericles, IV 1 line 1563.
    Richard II, V 2 line 2489.
    Sonnet XII line 3; Sonnet XCVIX line 1.
    Twelfth Night, I 1 line 7.
    Two Gentlemen of Verona, II 5 line 456.
    Venus and Adonis, lines 145, 958.
    Winter's Tale, IV 4 line 1999.

Viper: 1520s, from Middle French: *vipere*, from Latin: *vipera: viper, snake, serpent*, from *vivus: alive*, living. It formerly was believed (mistakenly) that the viper does not lay eggs. Applied to persons of spiteful character since at least 1590s. The only venomous snake found in Great Britain. Replaced native adder. The flesh of the viper was formerly regarded as possessing great nutritive or restorative properties, and was frequently used medicinally; hence viper wine, wine medicated with some kind of extract from vipers, used 17c.
    Coriolanus, III 1 line 2067.
    Henry V, II 1 line 551.
    Othello, V 2 line 3644.
    Pericles, I 1 line 112.
    Richard II, III 2 line 1539.
    Troilus and Cressida, III 1 lines 1618, 1619.

Viperous: snake-like (see viper).
    Coriolanus, III 1 line 2099.
    Cymbeline, III 4 line 1760.
    Henry VI, Part I, III 1 line 1296.

Vixen: Old English: *fyxen* (implied in adjective *fyxan*), feminine of *fox*. The figurative sense, *ill-tempered woman*, is attested from 1570s.
    Midsummer Night's Dream, III 2 line 1374.

Vomit: late 14c., act of expelling contents of the stomach through the mouth, from Latin: *vomitare:* to vomit often, frequentative of *vomere: spew forth, discharge*. Concerning the matter so ejected, it is attested from late 14c. The verb is recorded from early 15c.
    Cymbeline, I 6 line 612.
    Henry IV, Part II, I 3 line 705.
    Othello, II 3 line 1216.
    Rape of Lucrece, line 754.
    Richard III, V 3 line 3833.
    Titus Andronicus, III 1 line 1370.

Vulture: late 14c., from Anglo-French *vultur*, Old French *voultour*, from Latin *vultur*, earlier *voltur*, perhaps related to *vellere* to pluck, to tear. Figurative sense is recorded from 1580s.
    Henry IV, Part II, V 3 line 3554.
    Henry VI, Part I, IV 3 line 2076.
    King Lear, II 4 line 1414.
    Macbeth, IV 3 line 1928.
    Merry Wives of Windsor, I 3 line 384.
    Rape of Lucrece, line 607.
    Titus Andronicus, V 2 line 2337.
    Venus and Adonis, line 572.

Wagtail: used, in an opprobrious sense, to signify an officious person.
    King Lear, II 2 line 1134.

Waist: middle part of the body, also part of a garment fitted for the waist, late 14c., probably from Old English: *wæst*: *growth*, hence, where the body grows.
>**Hamlet**, II 2 line 1334.
>**Henry IV, Part I**, II 4 line 1316.
>**Henry IV, Part II**, I 2 line 458.
>**Henry VI, Part I**, IV 3 line 2048.
>**King John**, II 1 line 517.
>**King Lear**, IV 6 line 2732.
>**Love's Labour's Lost**, IV 1 lines 1020, 1021; Love's Labour's Lost, IV 3 line 1517.
>**Measure for Measure**, III 2 line 1551.
>**Merry Wives of Windsor**, I 3 line 341.
>**Much Ado About Nothing**, III 2 line 1232.
>**Rape of Lucrece**, line 57.
>**Tempest**, I 2 line 316.
>**Troilus and Cressida**, II 2 line 1020.

Walnut: Old English: *walhnutu: nut of the walnut tree*, literally, foreign nut, from *wealh*: *foreign*. So called because it was introduced from Gaul and Italy, distinguishing it from the native hazel nut. The Late Latin name for it was, *nux Gallica*, literally, *Gaulish nut*. Applied to the tree itself from 1600 (earlier walnut tree, c.1400).
>**Merry Wives of Windsor**, IV 2 line 2120.
>**Taming of the Shrew**, IV 3 line 2029.

Wart: Old English: *wearte*.
>**Comedy of Errors**, III 2 line 900.
>**Hamlet**, V 1 line 3627.
>**Merry Wives of Windsor**, I 4 line 545; Merry Wives of Windsor, I 4 line 550; Merry Wives of Windsor, I 4 line 558.
>**Troilus and Cressida**, I 2 line 290.

Wasp: Old English: *wæps, wæsp*
>**Henry IV, Part I**, I 3 line 571.
>**Henry VIII**, III 2 line 1900.
>**Rape of Lucrece**, line 890.
>**Taming of the Shrew**, II 1 line 1058; Taming of the Shrew, II 1 line 1062.
>**Titus Andronicus**, II 3 line 870.
>**Two Gentlemen of Verona**, I 2 line 265.
>**Winter's Tale**, I 2 line 488; Winter's Tale, IV 4 line 2763.

Waspish: irascible, quick to take offence; spiteful, 1560s.
>**As You Like It**, IV 3 line 2010.
>**Julius Caesar**, IV 3 line 2032.
>**Taming of the Shrew**, II 1 line 1059.
>**Tempest**, IV 1 line 1812.

Wat: term for hare.

Venus and Adonis, line 720.

Water: Old English: *wæter*; believed to be a living force. Also, measure of quality of a diamond, c.1600. Meaning, to dilute, is attested from late 14c. To make water *urinate* is recorded from early 15c.
  All's Well That Ends Well, I 3 line 529; All's Well That Ends Well, III 6 line 1811.
  Antony and Cleopatra, I 2 line 243; Antony and Cleopatra, I 2 line 265; Antony and Cleopatra, I 3 line 371; Antony and Cleopatra, II 2 lines 916, 920; Antony and Cleopatra, II 6 line 1324; Antony and Cleopatra, II 6 line 1328; Antony and Cleopatra, IV 14 line 2990; Antony and Cleopatra, V 2 line 3455.
  As You Like It, II 7 line 1088.
  Comedy of Errors, I 2 line 199; Comedy of Errors, II 1 line 293; Comedy of Errors, II 2 line 515; Comedy of Errors, III 2 line 867.
  Coriolanus, II 3 line 1695; Coriolanus, III 1 line 2046; Coriolanus, V 2 line 3446; Coriolanus, V 6 line 3845.
  Cymbeline, II 3 line 999; Cymbeline, III 1 line 1433; Cymbeline, III 1 line 1498; Cymbeline, V 5 line 3696.
  Hamlet, IV 7 line 3335; Hamlet, V 1 lines 3359, 3360, 3361; Hamlet, V 1 line 3506.
  Henry IV, Part I, II 1 line 727; Henry IV, Part I, II 4 line 1001; Henry IV, Part I, III 1 line 1637; Henry IV, Part I, V 1 line 2703.
  Henry IV, Part II, I 2 line 275; Henry IV, Part II, I 2 line 276r; Henry IV, Part II, II 1 line 887.
  Henry V, II 4 line 906; Henry V, III 5 line 1408; Henry V, III 7 line 1662; Henry V, IV 6 line 2505; Henry V, IV 7 line 2628.
  Henry VI, Part I, I 2 line 322; Henry VI, Part I, II 4 line 994; Henry VI, Part I, II 5 lines 1125, 1127; Henry VI, Part I, III 1 line 1285; Henry VI, Part I, III 4 line 1741; Henry VI, Part I, IV 1 line 1855; Henry VI, Part I, V 3 line 2498; Henry VI, Part I, V 3 lines 2528, 2531.
  Henry VI, Part II, I 4 line 666; Henry VI, Part II, I 4 line 704; Henry VI, Part II, III 1 line 1330; Henry VI, Part II, IV 1 line 2188.
  Henry VI, Part III, I 4 line 521; Henry VI, Part III, IV 8 line 2565; Henry VI, Part III, V 4 line 2812; Henry VI, Part III, V 4 line 2882; Henry VI, Part III, V 6 line 3035.
  Henry VIII, II 1 line 930; Henry VIII, II 1 line 967; Henry VIII, IV 2 line 2607.
  Julius Caesar, III 1 line 1516.
  King John, II 1 line 317; King John, II 1 line 422; King John, II 1 line 649; King John, IV 3 line 2133; King John, IV 3 line 2160; King John, V 2 line 2333.
  King Lear, I 4 line 832; King Lear, II 4 line 1578; King Lear, III 1 line 1623; King Lear, III 2 lines 1687, 1688; King Lear, III 2 line 1763; King Lear, III 4 line 1924; King Lear, IV 3 line 2485; King Lear, IV 6 line 2803.
  Love's Labour's Lost, I 1 line 293; Love's Labour's Lost, I 2 line 384; Love's Labour's Lost, V 2 line 2098; Love's Labour's Lost, V 2 line 2100.

Lover's Complaint, lines 283, 289, 293, 306.
Macbeth, I 3 line 181; Macbeth, II 2 line 706; Macbeth, II 2 line 734; Macbeth, III 1 line 1109; Macbeth, V 3 line 2307.
Measure for Measure, III 2 line 1620; Measure for Measure, IV 3 line 2274; Measure for Measure, IV 3 line 2282.
Merchant of Venice, I 1 line 35; Merchant of Venice, I 3 lines 345, 346; Merchant of Venice, II 2 line 614; Merchant of Venice, II 7 line 1030; Merchant of Venice, III 2 line 1502; Merchant of Venice, V 1 line 2554.
Merry Wives of Windsor, II 3 line 1177; Merry Wives of Windsor, III 3 line 1441; Merry Wives of Windsor, III 3 line 1573; Merry Wives of Windsor, III 3 line 1583; Merry Wives of Windsor, III 4 line 1736; Merry Wives of Windsor, III 5 line 1761; Merry Wives of Windsor, III 5 line 1766; Merry Wives of Windsor, IV 1 line 1895.
Midsummer Night's Dream, I 1 line 218; Midsummer Night's Dream, II 1 line 534; Midsummer Night's Dream, III 1 line 1023; Midsummer Night's Dream, V 1 line 1906.
Much Ado About Nothing, V 1 line 2073.
Othello, II 1 line 777; Othello, III 3 line 1642; Othello, IV 2 line 2863; Othello, V 2 line 3465.
Pericles, II 1 line 589; Pericles, II 1 line 631; Pericles, II 1 line 728; Pericles, III 1 line 1229; Pericles, III 1 line 1260; Pericles, III 2 line 1406; Pericles, IV 2 line 1765; Pericles, IV 2 line 1809.
Rape of Lucrece, lines 643, 805, 1009, 1603, 1611, 1662, 1796, 1799.
Richard II, II 1 line 745; Richard II, III 2 line 1462; Richard II, III 3 lines 1693, 1695, 1697; Richard II, IV 1 line 2175; Richard II, IV 1 line 2231; Richard II, IV 1 line 2234; Richard II, IV 1 line 2251.
Richard III, I 4 line 854; Richard III, II 2 line 1341; Richard III, II 3 line 1477; Richard III, IV 4 line 3341.
Romeo and Juliet, I 4 line 562; Romeo and Juliet, II 3 line 1131; Romeo and Juliet, V 3 line 2948.
Sonnet XLIV line 11; Sonnet LXIV line 7; Sonnet CIX line 8; Sonnet CXXXV line 9; Sonnet CLIV line 14r.
Taming of the Shrew, Prologue 1 lines 49, 57; Taming of the Shrew, Prologue 1 line 136; Taming of the Shrew, IV 1 line 1637; Taming of the Shrew, IV 1 line 1751, 1752, 1757.
Tempest, I 1 line 70; Tempest, I 2 line 86; Tempest, I 2 line 272; Tempest, I 2 line 463; Tempest, I 2 line 485; Tempest, I 2 line 554; Tempest, I 2 line 644; Tempest, II 1 line 767; Tempest, III 2 line 1397; Tempest, III 3 line 1641; Tempest, IV 1 line 1781.
Timon of Athens, I 1 line 27; Timon of Athens, I 2 line 398; Timon of Athens, I 2 line 444; Timon of Athens, II 2 line 752; Timon of Athens, III 6 line 1523; Timon of Athens, III 6 lines 1527, 1532; Timon of Athens, IV 3 line 2135; Timon of Athens, V 1 line 2337.
Titus Andronicus, I 1 line 363; Titus Andronicus, II 1 line 639; Titus Andronicus, II 4 line 1068; Titus Andronicus, III 1 line 1198; Titus Andronicus, III 1 line 1392; Titus Andronicus, III 1 line 1409; Titus Andronicus, IV 2 line 1791.

Troilus and Cressida, I 3 line 563; Troilus and Cressida, III 2 line 1670; Troilus and Cressida, III 2 line 1720; Troilus and Cressida, III 2 lines 1837, 1843; Troilus and Cressida, III 3 line 2193.
Twelfth Night, I 1 line 33; Twelfth Night, I 3 line 235; Twelfth Night, I 5 line 451; Twelfth Night, II 1 line 639; Twelfth Night, III 4 line 1649; Twelfth Night, IV 2 line 2079; Twelfth Night, V 1 line 2257; Twelfth Night, V 1 line 2434.
Two Gentlemen of Verona, II 1 line 437; Two Gentlemen of Verona, II 4 line 831; Two Gentlemen of Verona, III 2 line 1459; Two Gentlemen of Verona, IV 4 line 1872.
Venus and Adonis, lines 114, 513, 675.
Winter's Tale, I 2 line 50; Winter's Tale, I 2 line 211; Winter's Tale, III 2 line 1428; Winter's Tale, III 3 line 1600; Winter's Tale, IV 4 line 2062; Winter's Tale, IV 4 line 2162; Winter's Tale, IV 4 line 2518; Winter's Tale, V 1 line 2997; Winter's Tale, V 2 line 3191.

Water-fly: This little insect which, on a sunny day, may be seen on the surface of ponds, is used as a term of reproach by Shakespeare.
Hamlet, V 2 line 3739.
Troilus and Cressida, V 1 line 2964.

Water-gall: A watery appearance in the sky, accompanying the rainbow; a secondary or broken rainbow.
Rape of Lucrece, line 1639.

Water-rat: semiaquatic rodent, also known as a water-vole.
Merchant of Venice, I 3 line 345.

Water-spaniel: A large spaniel of a breed characterised by a curly water-resistant coat, often used in hunting to retrieve waterfowl.
Two Gentlemen of Verona, III 1 line 1345.

Wave: moving billow of water, 1520s, from wave, replacing Middle English: *waw*, which is from Old English: *wagian: to move to and fro.*
Comedy of Errors, III 2 line 810.
Henry VI, Part III, I 4 line 455; Henry VI, Part III, II 6 line 1289; Henry VI, Part III, V 4 lines 2828, 2840.
Julius Caesar, I 2 line 203.
Love's Labour's Lost, V 1 line 1790.
Macbeth, IV 1 line 1605.
Pericles, II 4 line 571; Pericles, IV 1 line 1614.
Rape of Lucrece, lines 1282, 1489.
Sonnet LX line 1.
Tempest, I 2 line 324; Tempest, I 2 line 540; Tempest, II 1 lines 819, 811.
Titus Andronicus, III 1 line 1225r.
Twelfth Night, I 2 line 63; Twelfth Night, III 4 line 1939; Twelfth Night, V 1 line 2429.
Venus and Adonis, lines 106, 841.

Winter's Tale, IV 4 line 2022.

Wax: substance made by bees. Old English: *weax*. Also, grow bigger or greater. Old English: *weaxan: to increase, grow.*
    All's Well That Ends Well, I 2 line 307.
    Hamlet, III 4 line 2476.
    Henry IV, Part II, I 2 line 477; Henry IV, Part II, IV 5 line 2969.
    Henry V, I 2 line 380.
    Henry VI, Part II, III 2 line 1757; Henry VI, Part II, IV 2 line 2384.
    Henry VI, Part III, II 1 line 799; Henry VI, Part III, III 2 line 1532.
    King John, V 4 line 2512.
    King Lear, IV 6 line 2881.
    Love's Labour's Lost, IV 1 line 1032.
    Merry Wives of Windsor, IV 4 line 2246.
    Midsummer Night's Dream, I 1 line 53; Midsummer Night's Dream, III 1 line 994.
    Passionate Pilgrim, line 89.
    Rape of Lucrece, lines 229, 1291, 1714.
    Richard II, I 3 line 370.
    Romeo and Juliet, I 3 line 461; Romeo and Juliet, III 3 line 2007.
    Timon of Athens, I 1 line 62; Timon of Athens, V 3 line 2549; Timon of Athens, V 4 line 2638.
    Titus Andronicus, III 1 line 1172.
    Troilus and Cressida, V 1 line 2984.
    Twelfth Night, II 5 line 1116.
    Two Gentlemen of Verona, II 4 line 863.
    Venus and Adonis, lines 537, 586.

Weasel: Old English: *weosule, wesle: weasel*, with a base sense of stinking animal, because the animal has a foul, musky smell. To meet a weasel was formerly considered a bad omen.
    As You Like It, II 5 line 831.
    Cymbeline, III 4 line 1902.
    Hamlet, III 2 line 2255; Hamlet, III 2 line 2256.
    Henry IV, Part I, II 3 line 941.
    Henry V, I 2 line 315.
    Rape of Lucrece, line 358.

Weather: Old English: *weder;* pronunciation changed 15c.
    As You Like It, II 5 line 827; As You Like It, II 5 line 855; As You Like It, V 4 line 2529.
    Cymbeline, III 3 line 1670.
    Henry IV, Part I, III 1 line 1610; Henry IV, Part I, III 1 line 1611.
    Henry IV, Part II, III 2 line 1938.
    Henry V, III 2 line 1235.
    Henry VI, Part II, IV 10 line 2896; Henry VI, Part II, V 1 line 3007.
    Henry VIII, I 4 line 684.
    King John, IV 2 line 1840; King John, V 1 line 2214.
    King Lear, III 1 line 1618; King Lear, III 1 line 1619.

Love's Labour's Lost, I 2 line 440; Love's Labour's Lost, IV 1 line 1070; Love's Labour's Lost, IV 2 line 1176.
Merchant of Venice, II 6 line 926; Merchant of Venice, II 9 line 1158.
Merry Wives of Windsor, III 2 line 1326.
Much Ado About Nothing, I 3 line 351.
Passionate Pilgrim, line 160.
Rape of Lucrece, line 166.
Richard II, III 3 line 1803.
Taming of the Shrew, IV 1 line 1632.
Tempest, I 1 line 46; Tempest, II 1 line 847; Tempest, II 1 line 849; Tempest, II 2 line 1102; Tempest, V 1 line 2027.
Troilus and Cressida, V 3 line 3305.
Twelfth Night, I 5 line 526.
Two Gentlemen of Verona, II 1 line 526.
Venus and Adonis, lines 422, 994.
Winter's Tale, III 3 line 1498; Winter's Tale, III 3 line 1559; Winter's Tale, III 3 line 1597; Winter's Tale, V 1 line 3056; Winter's Tale, V 2 line 3164; Winter's Tale, V 2 line 3229.

Web: Old English: *webb*: *woven fabric*. Meaning, spider's web, is first recorded early 13c. Applied to the membranes between the toes of ducks and other aquatic birds from 1570s.
   All's Well That Ends Well, IV 3 line 2158.
   Henry V, V 1 line 2906.
   Henry VIII, I 1 line 106.
   King Lear, III 4 line 1911.
   Lover's Complaint, line 95.
   Othello, II 1 line 956; Othello, III 4 line 2253.
   Richard III, I 3 line 710.
   Romeo and Juliet, I 4 line 561.
   Troilus and Cressida, II 3 line 1232.
   Venus and Adonis, line 1013.
   Winter's Tale, I 2 line 394.

Weed: plant not valued for use or beauty. Old English: *weod, uueod: grass, herb, weed*. Meaning *tobacco* is from c.1600. The verb meaning, to clear the ground of weeds, is late Old English: *weodian*.
   Antony and Cleopatra, I 2 line 194.
   As You Like It, II 7 line 940.
   Coriolanus, II 2 line 1342; Coriolanus, II 3 line 1594; Coriolanus, II 3 line 1672; Coriolanus, IV 5 line 2869.
   Cymbeline, IV 2 line 2808; Cymbeline, V 1 line 2974.
   Hamlet, I 2 line 339; Hamlet, I 5 line 769; Hamlet, III 2 line 2149; Hamlet, III 4 line 2553; Hamlet, IV 7 line 3220; Hamlet, IV 7 lines 3321, 3323.
   Henry IV, Part II, IV 1 line 2411; Henry IV, Part II, IV 4 line 2802.
   Henry V, IV 1 line 1853.
   Henry VI, Part II, I 3 line 490; Henry VI, Part II, III 1 line 1308.

Henry VI, Part III, II 6 line 1271; Henry VI, Part III, III 3 line 1931; Henry VI, Part III, IV 1 line 2080.
Henry VIII, V 1 line 2836.
King Lear, IV 4 lines 2518, 2520; King Lear, IV 6 line 2690; King Lear, IV 7 line 2917.
Love's Labour's Lost, I 1 line 98r; Love's Labour's Lost, V 2 line 2743; Love's Labour's Lost, V 2 line 2790.
Macbeth, V 2 line 2242.
Measure for Measure, I 3 line 310; Measure for Measure, III 2 line 1779.
Midsummer Night's Dream, II 1 line 635; Midsummer Night's Dream, II 2 line 727.
Much Ado About Nothing, V 3 line 2538.
Othello, I 3 line 680; Othello, IV 2 line 2815.
Pericles, IV 1 line 1561.
Rape of Lucrece, lines 246, 332, 921.
Richard II, II 3 line 1325; Richard II, III 4 line 1902; Richard II, III 4 line 1908; Richard II, III 4 line 1915.
Richard III, I 3 line 586; Richard III, II 4 lines 1497, 1499; Richard III, III 1 line 1675.
Romeo and Juliet, II 3 line 1065; Romeo and Juliet, V 1 line 2848.
Sonnet II line 4; Sonnet LXIX line 12; Sonnet LXXVI line 7; Sonnet XCIV line 12; Sonnet XCIV line 14; Sonnet CXXIV line 4r.
Tempest, IV 1 line 1720.
Titus Andronicus, I 1 line 86; Titus Andronicus, II 1 line 565; Titus Andronicus, III 1 line 1170; Titus Andronicus, V 3 line 2741.
Troilus and Cressida, III 3 line 2122.
Twelfth Night, V 1 line 2476; Twelfth Night, V 1 line 2476.
Two Gentlemen of Verona, II 7 line 1017; Two Gentlemen of Verona, III 2 1501.
Venus and Adonis, lines 968, 1077.
Winter's Tale, IV 4 line 1856.

Welkin: the sky or heaven. Old English: *wolcen: cloud, sky*, of West Germanic origin; related to Dutch *wolk* and German *Wolke*.
Twelfth Night, II 3 line 758; Twelfth Night, III 1 line 1292.

Wezand: alternative spelling for *weasand*: *windpipe*; called also, formerly, *wesil*.
Tempest, III 2 line 1486.

Whale: large *sea fish*, Old English: *hwæl*.
All's Well That Ends Well, IV 3 line 2303.
Hamlet, III 2 line 2257; Hamlet, III 2 line 2258.
Henry IV, Part II, IV 4 line 2786.
Love's Labour's Lost, V 2 line 2250.
Merry Wives of Windsor, II 1 line 627.
Pericles, II 1 lines 610, 612; Pericles, III 1 line 1259.
Troilus and Cressida, V 5 line 3478.

Wheat: Old English: *hwæte*.
    Antony and Cleopatra, II 6 line 1256.
    Hamlet, V 2 line 3693.
    Henry IV, Part II, V 1 line 3155; Henry IV, Part II, V 1 line 3156.
    King Lear, III 4 line 1913.
    Merchant of Venice, I 1 line 123.
    Midsummer Night's Dream, I 1 line 193.
    Tempest, IV 1 line 1771.
    Troilus and Cressida, I 1 line 47.

Whelk: large marine snail, Old English *weoloc, wioloc*, from Proto-Germanic *weluka* (cf. Middle Dutch *willoc*, Dutch *wulk*). The spelling with *wh-* dates from 15c., respelling of Old English *hw-* attested from 11c., but not the common form until after c.1400; also added to some borrowed words, such as *whelk*, and some native words formerly spelled with simple *w-* or *h-*, for example: *whore*. Proper pronunciation has been much in dispute in educated speech.
    Henry V, III 6 line 1568.
    King Lear, IV 6 line 2680.

Whelp: Old English: *hwelp: whelp, young of the dog*. Also applied to wild animals. Sense of *scamp* first recorded early 14c.
    Antony and Cleopatra, III 13 line 2368.
    Cymbeline, V 4 line 3291; Cymbeline, V 5 lines 3905, 3913.
    Henry IV, Part I, III 3 line 2157.
    Henry V, I 2 line 253.
    Henry VI, Part I, I 5 line 609; Henry VI, Part I, IV 7 line 2290.
    Henry VI, Part III, III 2 line 1649.
    Julius Caesar, II 1 line 992.
    Tempest, I 2 line 419.
    Timon of Athens, II 2 line 769.
    Titus Andronicus, II 3 line 1033; Titus Andronicus, IV 1 line 1640.

Whetstone: a stone used for sharpening tools. Old English *hwetstan*.
    As You Like It, I 2 lines 191, 193.
    Macbeth, IV 3 line 2112.
    Troilus and Cressida, V 2 line 3137.

Whirlwind: 14c, probably from Old Norse: *hvirfilvindr*.
    Hamlet, III 2 line 1888.
    King Lear, III 4 line 1859.
    Rape of Lucrece, line 637.
    Taming of the Shrew, V 2 line 2648.
    Timon of Athens, IV 3 line 1989.
    Two Gentlemen of Verona, I 2 line 279.

Wildcat: early 15c. Meaning, *savage woman*, is recorded from 1570s.
    Merchant of Venice, II 5 line 896.
    Taming of the Shrew, I 2 line 745.

Wilderness: Old English: *wildeornes*: land inhabited only by wild animals.
    Henry IV, Part II, IV 5 line 3032.
    Henry VI, Part II, III 2 line 2054.
    Measure for Measure, III 1 line 1379.
    Merchant of Venice, III 1 line 1354.
    Rape of Lucrece, line 595.
    Richard II, IV 1 line 2057.
    Titus Andronicus, III 1 line 1182; Titus Andronicus, III 1 line 1224.
    Two Gentlemen of Verona, IV 1 line 1615.

Willow: Old English: *welig*. From time immemorial the willow has been regarded as the symbol of sadness. Hence it was customary for those who were forsaken in love, to wear willow garlands; a practice to which Shakespeare gives several allusions.
    Hamlet, IV 7 line 3315.
    Henry VI, Part III, III 3 line 1930; Henry VI, Part III, IV 1 line 2076.
    Merchant of Venice, V 1 line 2455.
    Much Ado About Nothing, II 1 line 572; Much Ado About Nothing, II 1 line 600.
    Othello, IV 3 line 3049; Othello, IV 3 lines 3063, 3065rr, 3067rr, 3071rr, 3074; Othello, IV 3 line 3080rr; Othello, V 2 line 3602rr.
    Twelfth Night, I 5 line 559.

Wind: Figurative phrase *which way the wind blows* for *the current state of affairs* is suggested from c.1400. Normal pronunciation evolution made this word rhyme with kind and rind (Donne rhymes it with mind), but it shifted to a short vowel 18c., probably from influence of windy, where the short vowel is natural. A sad loss for poets, who now must rhyme it only with sinned and a handful of weak words. Symbolic of emptiness and vanity since late 13c. to perceive by scent, get wind of, early 15c., from *wind*. Of horns, etc., make sound by blowing through, from 1580s.
    All's Well That Ends Well, I 1 line 107; All's Well That Ends Well, III 6 line 1840; All's Well That Ends Well, V 2 line 2622.
    Antony and Cleopatra, I 2 line 243; Antony and Cleopatra, II 2 lines 918, 926; Antony and Cleopatra, II 7 line 1374; Antony and Cleopatra, III 6 line 1893; Antony and Cleopatra, III 10 line 2108.
    As You Like It, II 1 line 554; As You Like It, II 7 line 943; As You Like It, II 7 line 1075; As You Like It, III 2 line 1201; As You Like It, III 3 line 1587; As You Like It, III 5 line 1704.
    Comedy of Errors, I 1 line 66; Comedy of Errors, I 1 line 111; Comedy of Errors, I 2 line 218; Comedy of Errors, III 1 line 701; Comedy of Errors, III 1 line 708; Comedy of Errors, III 2 line 907; Comedy of Errors, IV 1 line 999; Comedy of Errors, IV 1 line 1044.
    Coriolanus, I 4 line 527; Coriolanus, I 9 line 868; Coriolanus, III 2 line 2290; Coriolanus, V 2 line 3487; Coriolanus, V 3 line 3559.
    Cymbeline, II 4 line 1203; Cymbeline, III 3 line 1641; Cymbeline, III 4 line 1757; Cymbeline, IV 2 line 2389; Cymbeline, IV 2 line 2545; Cymbeline, IV 2 line 2751.

Hamlet, I 2 line 345; Hamlet, I 3 line 483; Hamlet, I 3 line 542; Hamlet, I 3 line 595; Hamlet, II 2 line 1460; Hamlet, II 2 lines 1547, 1559; Hamlet, III 2 line 2228; Hamlet, IV 1 line 2633; Hamlet, IV 3 line 2755; Hamlet, IV 7 line 3153; Hamlet, IV 7 line 3203; Hamlet, V 1 line 3542; Hamlet, V 2 line 3750.
Henry IV, Part I, I 1 line 4; Henry IV, Part I, I 3 line 369; Henry IV, Part I, II 2 line 754; Henry IV, Part I, III 1 line 1572; Henry IV, Part I, III 1 line 1647; Henry IV, Part I, III 3 line 2099; Henry IV, Part I, IV 1 lines 2324, 2335; Henry IV, Part I, V 1 line 2624; Henry IV, Part I, V 1 line 2674.
Henry IV, Part II, Prologue 1 line 5; Henry IV, Part II, I 2 line 509; Henry IV, Part II, III 1 line 1725; Henry IV, Part II, IV 1 line 2401; Henry IV, Part II, IV 5 line 2995; Henry IV, Part II, V 3 line 3495; Henry IV, Part II, V 3 line 3496.
Henry V, II 2 line 647; Henry V, III 0 line 1063; Henry V, III 3 line 1312.
Henry VI, Part I, II 3 line 892.
Henry VI, Part II, II 1 line 729; Henry VI, Part II, II 1 line 791; Henry VI, Part II, III 1 line 1588; Henry VI, Part II, III 2 lines 1764, 1766; Henry VI, Part II, IV 1 line 2233.
Henry VI, Part III, I 4 line 439; Henry VI, Part III, I 4 line 584; Henry VI, Part III, II 1 line 709; Henry VI, Part III, II 5 lines 1108, 1110, 1111; Henry VI, Part III, II 5 line 1159; Henry VI, Part III, III 1 line 1454; Henry VI, Part III, III 2 line 1485; Henry VI, Part III, III 3 line 1745; Henry VI, Part III, IV 3 line 2334; Henry VI, Part III, V 1 lines 2649, 2653; Henry VI, Part III, V 2 line 2737; Henry VI, Part III, V 4 line 2826.
Julius Caesar, I 3 line 426; Julius Caesar, II 4 line 1159; Julius Caesar, IV 1 line 1895; Julius Caesar, IV 3 line 2053; Julius Caesar, V 1 line 2420.
King John, II 1 line 348; King John, III 4 line 1543; King John, IV 2 line 1750; King John, V 2 line 2353; King John, V 2 line 2367; King John, V 7 line 2673.
King Lear, I 2 line 424; King Lear, I 4 line 631; King Lear, II 3 line 1263; King Lear, II 4 line 1606; King Lear, III 1 lines 1622, 1628; King Lear, III 2 line 1678; King Lear, III 2 line 1691; King Lear, III 2 line 1723; King Lear, III 2 line 1755; King Lear, III 4 line 1849; King Lear, III 4 line 1893; King Lear, IV 2 line 2374; King Lear, IV 6 line 2710; King Lear, IV 7 line 2927; King Lear, IV 7 line 2948.
Love's Labour's Lost, IV 2 line 1177; Love's Labour's Lost, IV 3 line 1434; Love's Labour's Lost, V 2 line 2171; Love's Labour's Lost, V 2 line 2866.
Lover's Complaint, lines 7, 86, 103.
Macbeth, I 3 line 109; Macbeth, I 3 line 184; Macbeth, I 7 line 497; Macbeth, IV 1 line 1604; Macbeth, V 5 line 2412.
Measure for Measure, III 1 line 1359.
Merchant of Venice, I 1 line 19; Merchant of Venice, I 1 lines 24, 26; Merchant of Venice, I 1 line 161; Merchant of Venice, I 1 line 175; Merchant of Venice, I 3 line 347; Merchant of Venice, II 6 lines 925, 928; Merchant of Venice, II 6 line 980; Merchant of Venice, III 2 line 1460; Merchant of Venice, V 1 line 2445.

Merry Wives of Windsor, III 2 line 1345; Merry Wives of Windsor, IV 5 line 2395.
Midsummer Night's Dream, II 1 lines 455, 457; Midsummer Night's Dream, II 1 line 499; Midsummer Night's Dream, III 2 line 1129; Midsummer Night's Dream, III 2 line 1180; Midsummer Night's Dream, IV 1 line 1584; Midsummer Night's Dream, IV 1 line 1655.
Much Ado About Nothing, II 3 line 917; Much Ado About Nothing, III 1 line 1143; Much Ado About Nothing, V 2 line 2456r.
Othello, II 1 line 768; Othello, II 1 line 776; Othello, II 1 line 844; Othello, II 1 line 977; Othello, II 3 line 1195; Othello, III 1 line 1553; Othello, III 1 line 1557; Othello, III 3 line 1923; Othello, IV 2 line 2827; Othello, IV 3 line 3077; Othello, V 2 line 3637.
Passionate Pilgrim, lines 137, 232, 411.
Pericles, I 1 line 145; Pericles, II 1 line 570; Pericles, II 1 line 581; Pericles, II 1 line 640; Pericles, III 1 line 1193; Pericles, III 1 line 1245; Pericles, III 1 line 1274; Pericles, III 3 line 1465; Pericles, IV 1 line 1603; Pericles, IV 1 line 1605; Pericles, IV 1 line 1614; Pericles, IV 2 line 1683; Pericles, IV 4 line 1891; Pericles, V 0 line 2157.
Rape of Lucrece, lines 362, 366, 376, 386, 699, 1382, 1841.
Richard II, I 4 line 619; Richard II, II 1 line 955; Richard II, II 2 line 1123.
Richard III, I 3 line 732; Richard III, IV 1 line 2523.
Romeo and Juliet, I 1 line 132; Romeo and Juliet, I 4 line 602; Romeo and Juliet, I 4 line 606; Romeo and Juliet, II 5 line 1382; Romeo and Juliet, III 5 lines 2238, 2241.
Sonnet XIV line 6; Sonnet XVIII line 3; Sonnet LI line 7; Sonnet CXVII line 7.
Taming of the Shrew, Prologue 1 line 15; Taming of the Shrew, Prologue 2 line 198; Taming of the Shrew, I 2 line 599; Taming of the Shrew, I 2 line 751; Taming of the Shrew, II 1 line 977; Taming of the Shrew, II 1 line 983.
Tempest, I 1 line 11; Tempest, I 2 line 259; Tempest, I 2 line 387; Tempest, I 2 line 699; Tempest, II 2 line 1103; Tempest, III 3 line 1640; Tempest, III 3 line 1680; Tempest, V 1 line 2063.
Timon of Athens, V 4 line 2569.
Titus Andronicus, II 2 line 707; Titus Andronicus, II 3 line 747; Titus Andronicus, II 4 line 1087; Titus Andronicus, III 1 line 1361; Titus Andronicus, IV 1 lines 1641, 1648; Titus Andronicus, IV 2 line 1823; Titus Andronicus, IV 3 line 1939; Titus Andronicus, V 3 line 2607.
Troilus and Cressida, I 3 line 476; Troilus and Cressida, I 3 line 498; Troilus and Cressida, I 3 line 551; Troilus and Cressida, I 3 line 712; Troilus and Cressida, II 2 line 1067; Troilus and Cressida, III 2 line 1682; Troilus and Cressida, III 2 line 1843; Troilus and Cressida, IV 4 line 2483; Troilus and Cressida, V 3 line 3322; Troilus and Cressida, V 3 line 3405r.
Twelfth Night, I 5 line 526; Twelfth Night, II 5 line 1087; Twelfth Night, V 1 line 2605.
Two Gentlemen of Verona, I 2 line 277; Two Gentlemen of Verona, II 3 line 647.

Venus and Adonis, lines 209, 323, 325, 358, 479, 703, 987, 1068, 1104, 1106, 1111.
Winter's Tale, I 1 line 31; Winter's Tale, I 2 line 64; Winter's Tale, I 2 line 211; Winter's Tale, II 3 line 1117; Winter's Tale, IV 4 line 1999; Winter's Tale, IV 4 line 2487; Winter's Tale, V 1 line 3017.

Windgalls: swellings in the legs of a horse.
Taming of the Shrew, III 2 line 1412.

Windpipe: trachea, 1520s, from wind in the breath sense + pipe.
Henry V, III 6 line 1505.
Timon of Athens, I 2 line 391.

Windy: Old English: *wendig*.
Hamlet, I 2 line 283.
Henry VI, Part III, II 5 line 1191.
King John, II 1 line 789.
Much Ado About Nothing, II 1 line 692.
Rape of Lucrece, line 1839.
Richard III, IV 4 line 2923.
Sonnet XC line 7.
Twelfth Night, III 4 line 1705.
Venus and Adonis, line 71.

Wing: late 12c., *wenge*, from Old Norse: *vængr: wing of a bird, aisle*.
All's Well That Ends Well, I 1 line 206; All's Well That Ends Well, II 1 line 699; All's Well That Ends Well, III 2 line 1477.
Antony and Cleopatra, III 10 line 2086; Antony and Cleopatra, III 12 line 2201; Antony and Cleopatra, V 2 line 3580.
Coriolanus, V 4 line 3743.
Cymbeline, I 6 line 818; Cymbeline, III 2 line 1558; Cymbeline, III 5 line 2134; Cymbeline, V 3 line 3028; Cymbeline, V 4 line 3269; Cymbeline, V 5 line 3944.
Hamlet, I 5 line 765; Hamlet, II 2 line 1230; Hamlet, III 4 line 2501.
Henry IV, Part I, III 2 line 1853; Henry IV, Part I, V 1 line 2687.
Henry IV, Part II, IV 4 line 2813; Henry IV, Part II, IV 5 line 3125.
Henry V, I 2 line 458; Henry V, III 0 line 1053; Henry V, IV 1 line 1956; Henry V, IV 1 line 2016.
Henry VI, Part I, I 1 line 15; Henry VI, Part I, I 1 line 80; Henry VI, Part I, IV 2 line 2011; Henry VI, Part I, V 3 line 2516.
Henry VI, Part II, I 3 line 427; Henry VI, Part II, II 4 line 1215; Henry VI, Part II, IV 1 line 2156; Henry VI, Part II, IV 7 line 2694.
Henry VI, Part III, I 1 line 51; Henry VI, Part III, II 2 line 871; Henry VI, Part III, II 3 line 1039; Henry VI, Part III, V 6 line 3009; Henry VI, Part III, V 6 line 3015; Henry VI, Part III, V 6 line 3018.
Henry VIII, I 4 line 668; Henry VIII, V 1 line 2976.
Julius Caesar, I 1 line 73; Julius Caesar, V 2 line 2492.
King John, II 1 line 304.
King Lear, IV 6 line 2613.

Love's Labour's Lost, V 2 line 2170.
Macbeth, I 4 line 296; Macbeth, III 2 line 1226; Macbeth, IV 1 line 1564.
Merchant of Venice, I 1 line 15; Merchant of Venice, III 1 line 1264.
Merry Wives of Windsor, II 2 line 993.
Midsummer Night's Dream, I 1 line 248; Midsummer Night's Dream, II 2 line 653; Midsummer Night's Dream, III 1 line 997; Midsummer Night's Dream, III 2 line 1421.
Much Ado About Nothing, II 1 line 533.
Phoenix and the Turtle, lines 4, 10.
Rape of Lucrece, lines 53, 558, 1000, 1060.
Richard II, II 1 line 983.
Richard III, IV 3 line 2786; Richard III, IV 4 line 2805; Richard III, V 2 line 3451; Richard III, V 3 line 3578.
Romeo and Juliet, I 4 line 513; Romeo and Juliet, I 4 line 560; Romeo and Juliet, II 2 line 915; Romeo and Juliet, II 5 line 1382; Romeo and Juliet, III 2 line 1736.
Sonnet LXXVIII line 7.
Tempest, III 3 line 1627; Tempest, IV 1 line 1789.
Timon of Athens, II 1 line 658.
Titus Andronicus, III 2 line 1507; Titus Andronicus, IV 4 line 2099.
Troilus and Cressida, II 2 line 1035; Troilus and Cressida, II 2 line 1130; Troilus and Cressida, III 2 line 1663; Troilus and Cressida, III 3 line 1950; Troilus and Cressida, IV 2 line 2303; Troilus and Cressida, V 8 line 3609.
Twelfth Night, II 5 line 1138.
Two Gentlemen of Verona, II 6 line 973; Two Gentlemen of Verona, II 7 line 986.
Venus and Adonis, lines 77, 326.
Winter's Tale, IV 1 line 1636; Winter's Tale, V 3 line 3450.

Winged: having wings.
    Antony and Cleopatra, IV 15 line 3207.
    As You Like It, IV 1 line 1915.
    Comedy of Errors, II 1 line 290.
    Cymbeline, III 3 line 1623; Cymbeline, III 3 line 1631; Cymbeline, III 5 line 2023; Cymbeline, IV 2 line 2758.
    Henry IV, Part I, III 1 line 1697; Henry IV, Part I, IV 4 line 2578.
    Henry V, II 0 line 470; Henry V, V 0 line 2846.
    Henry VI, Part I, II 5 line 1091; Henry VI, Part I, IV 7 line 2273.
    Henry VI, Part II, III 3 line 2130.
    Henry VI, Part III, I 1 line 285.
    King Lear, III 7 line 2195.
    Midsummer Night's Dream, I 1 line 245.
    Othello, I 3 line 620.
    Pericles, IV 0 line 1540.
    Rape of Lucrece, lines 1267, 1779.
    Richard II, I 3 line 426.

Richard III, II 1 line 1213; Richard III, II 2 line 1316; Richard III, V 3 line 3813.
Romeo and Juliet, II 2 line 875.
Sonnet LI line 8.
Taming of the Shrew, II 1 line 1056.
Troilus and Cressida, II 3 line 1332.

Winter: The Anglo-Saxons counted years in winters. Old English: *ænetre: one-year-old*. As a verb, to pass the winter (in some place), late 14c.
Antony and Cleopatra, V 2 line 3496.
As You Like It, II 1 line 554; As You Like It, II 3 line 695; As You Like It, II 5 line 827; As You Like It, II 7 line 861; As You Like It, II 7 line 1075; As You Like It, III 2 line 1216; As You Like It, III 4 line 1608; As You Like It, V 4 line 2528.
Comedy of Errors, III 2 line 861; Comedy of Errors, V 1 line 1751.
Coriolanus, I 4 line 527; Coriolanus, I 9 line 868; Coriolanus, III 2 line 2290; Coriolanus, V 2 line 3487; Coriolanus, V 3 line 3559.
Cymbeline, II 4 line 1176; Cymbeline, III 4 line 1732; Cymbeline, IV 2 line 2617; Cymbeline, IV 2 line 2658; Cymbeline, IV 4 line 2918.
Hamlet, V 1 line 3545.
Henry IV, Part II, I 3 line 667; Henry IV, Part II, IV 4 line 2782; Henry IV, Part II, IV 4 line 2842.
Henry V, III 3 line 1327.
Henry VI, Part II, I 1 line 88; Henry VI, Part II, II 4 line 1159; Henry VI, Part II, III 2 line 2029; Henry VI, Part II, V 3 line 3320.
Henry VI, Part III, II 3 line 1075; Henry VI, Part III, IV 8 line 2586; Henry VI, Part III, V 2 line 2737; Henry VI, Part III, V 5 line 2920; Henry VI, Part III, V 7 line 3112.
Henry VIII, III 2 line 2057
Julius Caesar, I 2 line 189.
King John, V 7 line 2689.
King Lear, II 4 line 1324; King Lear, II 4 line 1346.
Love's Labour's Lost, IV 3 line 1586; Love's Labour's Lost, V 2 lines 2838, 2859.
Macbeth, III 4 line 1352.
Measure for Measure, II 1 line 582; Measure for Measure, III 1 line 1305.
Merchant of Venice, III 1 line 1296.
Merry Wives of Windsor, IV 4 line 2225.
Midsummer Night's Dream, II 1 lines 470, 481.
Othello, III 3 line 1824.
Passionate Pilgrim, lines 160, 161.
Pericles, IV 3 line 1871.
Rape of Lucrece, lines 1269, 1306.
Richard II, I 3 line 511; Richard II, I 3 line 514; Richard II, I 3 line 561; Richard II, IV 1 line 2247; Richard II, V 1 line 2374.
Richard III, I 1 line 2; Richard III, II 3 line 1466.
Romeo and Juliet, I 2 line 298.

Sonnet II line 1; Sonnet V line 6; Sonnet V line 13; Sonnet VI line 1; Sonnet XIII line 11; Sonnet LVI line 13; Sonnet XCVII line 1; Sonnet XCVII line 14; Sonnet XCVIII line 13; Sonnet CIV line 3.
Taming of the Shrew, IV 1 line 1640; Taming of the Shrew, IV 3 line 2073.
Tempest, I 2 line 434; Tempest, V 1 line 2033.
Timon of Athens, II 2 line 863; Timon of Athens, III 4 line 1178; Timon of Athens, III 6 line 1466; Timon of Athens, IV 3 line 1959.
Titus Andronicus, III 1 line 1145; Titus Andronicus, V 2 line 2488.
Troilus and Cressida, IV 5 line 2623.
Two Gentlemen of Verona, II 4 line 822.
Venus and Adonis, line 824.
Winter's Tale, II 1 line 629; Winter's Tale, III 2 line 1449; Winter's Tale, IV 3 line 1727; Winter's Tale, IV 4 line 1944; Winter's Tale, IV 4 line 1949; Winter's Tale, IV 4 line1952; Winter's Tale, V 3 line 3345.

Wither: 1530s, alteration of Middle English: *wydderen: dry up, shrivel* (c. 1300), apparently a differentiated and special use of *wederen: to expose to weather*.

All's Well That Ends Well, I 1 lines 163, 164, 165.
Antony and Cleopatra, II 2 line 963; Antony and Cleopatra, IV 15 line 3242.
Cymbeline, IV 2 line 2686; Cymbeline, V 4 line 3248.
Hamlet, IV 5 line 3060.
Henry IV, Part I, III 3 line 2011.
Henry IV, Part II, II 4 line 1232; Henry IV, Part II, II 4 line 1547; Henry IV, Part II, IV 5 line 3126.
Henry V, IV 1 line 2149; Henry V, V 2 line 3144.
Henry VI, Part I, II 4 line 1044; Henry VI, Part I, II 5 line 1086; Henry VI, Part I, IV 2 line 2004.
Henry VI, Part II, III 2 line 2062; Henry VI, Part II, IV 10 line 2951.
Henry VI, Part III, II 5 lines 1206, 1207; Henry VI, Part III, III 2 line 1644.
King Lear, IV 2 line 2379.
Love's Labour's Lost, II 1 line 540; Love's Labour's Lost, IV 3 line 1586.
Macbeth, I 3 line 140; Macbeth, II 1 line 629.
Merry Wives of Windsor, I 3 line 321; Merry Wives of Windsor, V 5 line 2726.
Midsummer Night's Dream, II 1 line 418.
Othello, V 2 line 3316.
Passionate Pilgrim, line 178.
Pericles, II 2 line 800; Pericles, IV 4 line 1916.
Rape of Lucrece, lines 716, 1219, 1305.
Richard II, II 1 line 818; Richard II, II 4 line 1338; Richard II, V 1 line 2342.
Richard III, I 3 line 679; Richard III, II 2 lines 1313, 1314; Richard III, III 4 line 2026; Richard III, IV 4 line 3208.
Romeo and Juliet, I 2 line 280.

Taming of the Shrew, II 1 line 1087; Taming of the Shrew, II 1 line 1258; Taming of the Shrew, IV 5 line 2310.
Tempest, I 2 line 645.
Timon of Athens, IV 3 line 2248.
Titus Andronicus, III 1 line 1243; Titus Andronicus, III 1 line 1309.
Troilus and Cressida, I 3 line 758; Troilus and Cressida, V 2 line 3100.
Venus and Adonis, lines 438, 1204.
Winter's Tale, V 3 line 3450.

Withers: 1570s, probably from a dialectal survival of Old English: *wider: against, contrary, opposite*. Possibly so called because the withers are the parts of the animal that oppose the load.
Hamlet, III 2 line 2135.
Henry IV, Part I, II 1 line 648.

Withering: to wither.
Midsummer Night's Dream, I 1 line 7; Midsummer Night's Dream, I 1 line 82.
Sonnet CXXVI line 4.

Wolf: Old English: *wulf*. Wolves as a symbol of lust are ancient, e.g. Roman slang *lupa*: whore, literally, she-wolf. The equation of *wolf* and *prostitute*, sexually voracious female, persisted into 12c., but by Elizabethan times wolves had become primarily symbolic of male lust. The image of a wolf in sheep's skin is attested from c.1400
Comedy of Errors, IV 2 line 1111.
Coriolanus, II 1 line 923; Coriolanus, IV 6 line 3153.
Cymbeline, III 3 line 1645.
Henry IV, Part II, I 2 line 472; Henry IV, Part II, I 2 line 473.
Henry VI, Part I, I 3 line 410; Henry VI, Part I, I 5 line 615; Henry VI, Part I, V 4 line 2701.
Henry VI, Part II, III 1 line 1356.
Henry VI, Part III, I 4 line 551; Henry VI, Part III, II 4 line 1100; Henry VI, Part III, V 4 line 2887; Henry VI, Part III, V 6 line 3002.
Henry VIII, I 1 line 228.
Julius Caesar, I 3 line 532.
King John, II 4 line 56.
King Lear, II 4 line 1505; King Lear, III 1 line 1630; King Lear, III 4 line 1889; King Lear, III 6 line 2023.
Macbeth, II 1 line 632; Macbeth, IV 1 line 1569.
Merchant of Venice, IV 1 line 2005; Merchant of Venice, IV 1 line 2069.
Midsummer Night's Dream, II 1 line 554; Midsummer Night's Dream, V 1 line 2221.
Rape of Lucrece, lines 728, 929.
Richard III, IV 4 line 2815.
Romeo and Juliet, II 4 line 1200.
Sonnet XCVI line 9.

Timon of Athens, IV 3 line 2035r.
Troilus and Cressida, I 3 line 574; Troilus and Cressida, II 1 line 866; Troilus and Cressida, III 2 line 1843.
Twelfth Night, III 1 line 1366.
Venus and Adonis, lines 480, 1119.
Winter's Tale, III 3 line 1560.

Wolves: see Wolf.
As You Like It, V 2 line 2347.
Henry IV, Part II, IV 5 line 3032.
Henry V, III 7 line 1779.
Henry VI, Part I, I 1 line 88.
Henry VI, Part II, III 1 line 1473; Henry VI, Part II, IV 1 line 2154.
Henry VI, Part III, I 1 line 259; Henry VI, Part III, I 4 line 440; Henry VI, Part III, I 4 line 551.
King Lear, III 7 line 2192.
Macbeth, III 1 line 1109.
Much Ado About Nothing, V 3 line 2533.
Othello, III 3 line 2086.
Rape of Lucrece, line 216.
Tempest, I 2 line 425.
Timon of Athens, III 6 line 1535; Timon of Athens, IV 1 line 1566; Timon of Athens, IV 3 line 1876.
Winter's Tale, II 3 line 1153.

Wolvish: see Wolf.
King Lear, I 4 line 837.
Merchant of Venice, IV 1 line 2073.
Romeo and Juliet, III 2 line 1798.

Womb: Old English: *wamb, womb: belly, uterus*.
All's Well That Ends Well, I 3 line 463.
Antony and Cleopatra, I 2 line 116; Antony and Cleopatra, III 13 line 2451.
As You Like It, II 1 line 554; As You Like It, II 7 line 943; As You Like It, II 7 line 1075; As You Like It, III 2 line 1201; As You Like It, III 3 line 1587; As You Like It, III 5 line 1704.
Coriolanus, I 3 line 368; Coriolanus, III 3 line 2484; Coriolanus, V 3 line 3631.
Cymbeline, V 4 line 3184.
Hamlet, I 1 line 156.
Henry IV, Part I, I 1 line 24; Henry IV, Part I, III 1 line 1573.
Henry IV, Part II, IV 3 line 2602rr; Henry IV, Part II, V 4 line 3569.
Henry V, II 4 line 1028; Henry V, IV 0 line 1791.
Henry VI, Part I, IV 5 line 2169; Henry VI, Part I, V 4 line 2734.
Henry VI, Part III, III 2 line 1641; Henry VI, Part III, IV 1 line 2260.
Henry VIII, II 4 line 1559.
King John, II 1 line 479; King John, III 1 line 959; King John, IV 3 line 2157; King John, V 2 line 2434.

King Lear, I 1 line 13; King Lear, I 4 line 805.
Love's Labour's Lost, IV 2 line 1217.
Lover's Complaint, line 1.
Macbeth, V 8 line 2493.
Measure for Measure, I 4 line 395.
Midsummer Night's Dream, II 1 line 501.
Othello, I 3 line 729.
Pericles, I 1 line 156; Pericles, III 1 line 1230.
Rape of Lucrece, lines 600, 709.
Richard II, I 2 line 235; Richard II, II 1 line 732; Richard II, II 1 line 767; Richard II, II 2 line 1003.
Richard III, I 3 line 695; Richard III, IV 1 line 2524; Richard III, IV 4 lines 2842, 2848; Richard III, IV 4 line 2935; Richard III, IV 4 line 3103; Richard III, IV 4 line 3237.
Romeo and Juliet, II 3 lines 1068, 1069; Romeo and Juliet, V 1 line 2876; Romeo and Juliet, V 3 line 2983.
Sonnet III line 5; Sonnet LXXXVI line 4; Sonnet XCVII line 8.
Tempest, I 2 line 224.
Timon of Athens, IV 3 line 1666; Timon of Athens, IV 3 lines 1865, 1874.
Titus Andronicus, II 3 line 986; Titus Andronicus, IV 2 line 1814.
Twelfth Night, V 1 line 2439.
Venus and Adonis, line 288.
Winter's Tale, II 2 line 916; Winter's Tale, IV 4 line 2425.

Wood: Old English: *wudu*, earlier *widu*: tree, trees collectively, the substance of which trees are made.
    As You Like It, II 1 line 560; As You Like It, II 1 line 581; As You Like It, III 3 line 1544; As You Like It, V 4 line 2554.
    Cymbeline, IV 2 line 2808.
    Hamlet, IV 7 line 3151.
    Henry IV, Part I, I 2 line 280.
    Henry VI, Part I, V 3 line 2250.
    Henry VI, Part II, IV 10 line 2889.
    Henry VI, Part III, III 2 line 1662; Henry VI, Part III, V 4 line 2874.
    Julius Caesar, III 2 line 1687.
    Love's Labour's Lost, IV 3 lines 1593, 1594.
    Macbeth, III 2 line 1226; Macbeth, IV 1 line 1659; Macbeth, IV 1 line 1665; Macbeth, V 2 line 2212; Macbeth, V 3 line 2247; Macbeth, V 4 line 2327; Macbeth, V 4 line 2328; Macbeth, V 5 line 2394; Macbeth, V 5 lines 2405, 2406; Macbeth, V 8 line 2509.
    Merry Wives of Windsor, V 5 line 2653.
    Midsummer Night's Dream, I 1 line 171; Midsummer Night's Dream, I 1 line 222; Midsummer Night's Dream, I 1 line 258; Midsummer Night's Dream, I 2 line 356; Midsummer Night's Dream, II 1 line 508; Midsummer Night's Dream, II 1 lines 566, 567; Midsummer Night's Dream, II 1 line 598; Midsummer Night's Dream, II 1 line 612; Midsummer Night's Dream, II 1 line 617; Midsummer Night's Dream, II 2 line 689; Midsummer Night's Dream, III 1 line 971; Midsummer

Night's Dream, III 1 line 972; Midsummer Night's Dream, III 2 line 1129; Midsummer Night's Dream, III 2 line 1359; Midsummer Night's Dream, IV 1 line 1596; Midsummer Night's Dream, IV 1 line 1668; Midsummer Night's Dream, IV 1 line 1697.
Richard II, III 1 line 1382; Richard II, III 3 line 1792.
Sonnet CXXVIII line 2; Sonnet CXXVIII line 8; Sonnet CXXVIII line 12.
Taming of the Shrew, Prologue 1 line 50; Taming of the Shrew, Prologue 2 line 202.
Tempest, I 2 line 457; Tempest, I 2 line 460; Tempest, II 2 line 1080; Tempest, II 2 line 1098; Tempest, II 2 line 1162; Tempest, II 2 line 1247.
Timon of Athens, IV 1 line 1599; Timon of Athens, IV 3 line 1896; Timon of Athens, IV 3 line 2249.
Titus Andronicus, I 1 line 145; Titus Andronicus, II 1 line 685; Titus Andronicus, II 2 line 698; Titus Andronicus, IV 1 line 1593.
Two Gentlemen of Verona, II 3 line 620; Two Gentlemen of Verona, V 3 line 2140; Two Gentlemen of Verona, V 4 line 2150.
Venus and Adonis, lines 108, 762, 848.

Woodbine: *wudubinde*, a climbing plant, from *wudu*.
Midsummer Night's Dream, II 1 line 630; Midsummer Night's Dream, IV 1 line 1587.
Much Ado About Nothing, III 1 line 1105.

Woodcock: Old English: *wuducoc*, from *wudu*. The woodcock has generally been proverbial as a foolish bird, perhaps because it is easily caught.
All's Well That Ends Well, IV 1 line 1995.
Hamlet, I 3 line 602; Hamlet, V 2 line 3962.
Henry VI, Part III, I 4 line 500.
Love's Labour's Lost, IV 3 line 1407.
Much Ado About Nothing, V 1 line 2232.
Taming of the Shrew, I 2 line 708.
Twelfth Night, II 5 line 1108; Twelfth Night, IV 2 line 2075.

World: Originally, life on earth, this world (as opposed to the afterlife), sense extended to the known world, then to the physical world in the broadest sense, the universe (c.1200). Old English: *woruld, worold: human existence, the affairs of life*, also *the human race, humanity*.
All's Well That Ends Well, I 1 line 174; All's Well That Ends Well, I 3 line 339; All's Well That Ends Well, I 3 line 354; All's Well That Ends Well, I 3 line 400; All's Well That Ends Well, I 3 line 514; All's Well That Ends Well, II 3 line 912; All's Well That Ends Well, II 4 line 1208; All's Well That Ends Well, II 4 line 1239; All's Well That Ends Well, III 2 line 1422; All's Well That Ends Well, III 6 line 1822; All's Well That Ends Well, IV 2 line 2055; All's Well That Ends Well, IV 2 line 2060; All's Well That Ends Well, IV 3 line 2386; All's Well That Ends Well, IV 4 line 2424; All's Well That Ends Well, IV 5 line 2506; All's Well That Ends Well, V 3 line 2913.

Antony and Cleopatra, I 1 line 16; Antony and Cleopatra, I 1 line 47; Antony and Cleopatra, I 2 line 287; Antony and Cleopatra, I 3 line 342; Antony and Cleopatra, II 2 line 729; Antony and Cleopatra, II 2 line 763; Antony and Cleopatra, II 2 line 824; Antony and Cleopatra, II 3 line 979; Antony and Cleopatra, II 3 line 985; Antony and Cleopatra, II 6 line 1222; Antony and Cleopatra, II 7 line 1373; Antony and Cleopatra, II 7 line 1446; Antony and Cleopatra, II 7 line 1448; Antony and Cleopatra, II 7 line 1452; Antony and Cleopatra, II 7 line 1483; Antony and Cleopatra, II 7 lines 1519, 1520; Antony and Cleopatra, III 4 line 1785; Antony and Cleopatra, III 5 line 1806; Antony and Cleopatra, III 10 line 2070; Antony and Cleopatra, III 11 line 2113; Antony and Cleopatra, III 11 line 2183; Antony and Cleopatra, III 13 line 2253; Antony and Cleopatra, III 13 line 2270; Antony and Cleopatra, IV 6 line 2710; Antony and Cleopatra, IV 8 line 2799; Antony and Cleopatra, IV 8 line 2805; Antony and Cleopatra, IV 9 line 2858; Antony and Cleopatra, IV 14 line 2983; Antony and Cleopatra, IV 14 line 3052; Antony and Cleopatra, IV 14 line 3083; Antony and Cleopatra, IV 15 line 3179; Antony and Cleopatra, IV 15 line 3230; Antony and Cleopatra, IV 15 line 3238; Antony and Cleopatra, IV 15 line 3259; Antony and Cleopatra, V 1 lines 3297, 3301; Antony and Cleopatra, V 1 line 3328; Antony and Cleopatra, V 2 line 3438; Antony and Cleopatra, V 2 line 3491; Antony and Cleopatra, V 2 line 3540; Antony and Cleopatra, V 2 line 3555; Antony and Cleopatra, V 2 line 3755; Antony and Cleopatra, V 2 line 3781.
As You Like It, I 1 line 104; As You Like It, I 1 line 140; As You Like It, I 2 line 180; As You Like It, I 2 lines 302, 303; As You Like It, I 2 line 334; As You Like It, I 2 line 346; As You Like It, I 2 line 390; As You Like It, I 3 line 417; As You Like It, I 3 line 540; As You Like It, II 3 line 657; As You Like It, II 3 line 701; As You Like It, II 7 lines 907, 916; As You Like It, II 7 line 953; As You Like It, II 7 line 964; As You Like It, II 7 lines 1037, 1057; As You Like It, III 2 line 1202; As You Like It, III 2 line 1376; As You Like It, III 2 line 1377; As You Like It, III 2 line 1494; As You Like It, III 5 line 1705; As You Like It, III 5 line 1731; As You Like It, IV 1 line 1876; As You Like It, IV 1 line 1968; As You Like It, V 1 line 2196; As You Like It, V 3 line 2364; As You Like It, V 4 line 2557.
Comedy of Errors, I 1 line 35; Comedy of Errors, I 2 line 199; Comedy of Errors, II 1 line 293; Comedy of Errors, II 2 line 495; Comedy of Errors, II 2 line 541; Comedy of Errors, III 2 line 862; Comedy of Errors, V 1 line 1872.
Coriolanus, I 1 line 247; Coriolanus, I 4 line 563; Coriolanus, I 9 line 833; Coriolanus, I 10 line 912; Coriolanus, II 1 line 1197; Coriolanus, II 2 line 1333; Coriolanus, II 2 line 1375; Coriolanus, III 1 line 2055; Coriolanus, III 1 line 2117; Coriolanus, III 3 line 2507; Coriolanus, IV 3 line 2548; Coriolanus, IV 3 line 2567; Coriolanus, IV 4 line 2733; Coriolanus, IV 5 line 2846; Coriolanus, IV 5 line 2930; Coriolanus, IV 5 line 2988; Coriolanus, IV 6 line 3010; Coriolanus, IV 6 line 3065; Coriolanus, V 2 line 3477; Coriolanus, V 3 line 3545; Coriolanus, V 3 line 3633; Coriolanus, V 3 line 3669.

Cymbeline, I 1 line 108; Cymbeline, I 4 line 396; Cymbeline, I 4 line 428; Cymbeline, II 1 line 903; Cymbeline, II 4 line 1198; Cymbeline, III 1 line 1425; Cymbeline, III 1 line 1463; Cymbeline, III 3 line 1662; Cymbeline, III 3 line 1677; Cymbeline, III 4 line 1758; Cymbeline, III 4 line 1877; Cymbeline, IV 2 line 2457; Cymbeline, IV 2 line 2641; Cymbeline, IV 2 line 2659; Cymbeline, IV 2 lines 2699, 2722; Cymbeline, V 1 line 2983; Cymbeline, V 4 line 3197; Cymbeline, V 4 line 3287; Cymbeline, V 5 line 3406; Cymbeline, V 5 line 3645; Cymbeline, V 5 line 3767; Cymbeline, V 5 line 3799; Cymbeline, V 5 line 3829.
Hamlet, I 1 line 102; Hamlet, I 2 line 311; Hamlet, I 2 line 338; Hamlet, II 2 line 1283; Hamlet, II 2 line 1339; Hamlet, II 2 line 1346; Hamlet, II 2 line 1402; Hamlet, II 2 line 1477; Hamlet, III 2 line 2049; Hamlet, III 2 line 2066; Hamlet, III 2 line 2092; Hamlet, III 2 line 2129; Hamlet, III 2 line 2162; Hamlet, III 2 line 2266; Hamlet, III 3 line 2339; Hamlet, III 4 line 2454; Hamlet, IV 1 line 2670; Hamlet, IV 5 line 2862; Hamlet, IV 5 line 2967; Hamlet, IV 5 line 3006; Hamlet, IV 5 line 3010; Hamlet, IV 6 line 3104; Hamlet, V 1 line 3369; Hamlet, V 1 line 3543; Hamlet, V 2 line 3971; Hamlet, V 2 line 4008; Hamlet, V 2 line 4046.
Henry IV, Part I, I 2 line 302; Henry IV, Part I, I 3 line 482; Henry IV, Part I, I 3 lines 494, 514; Henry IV, Part I, I 3 line 540; Henry IV, Part I, II 3 line 954; Henry IV, Part I, II 4 line 1122; Henry IV, Part I, II 4 line 1221; Henry IV, Part I, II 4 line 1351; Henry IV, Part I, II 4 line 1466; Henry IV, Part I, III 1 line 1637; Henry IV, Part I, III 2 line 1917; Henry IV, Part I, III 3 line 2216; Henry IV, Part I, V 1 line 2709; Henry IV, Part I, V 1 line 2741; Henry IV, Part I, V 2 line 2838; Henry IV, Part I, V 4 line 3011; Henry IV, Part I, V 4 line 3045; Henry IV, Part I, V 4 line 3117.
Henry IV, Part II, Prologue 1 line 11; Henry IV, Part II, I 1 line 213; Henry IV, Part II, II 1 line 746; Henry IV, Part II, II 2 line 971; Henry IV, Part II, II 2 line 1012; Henry IV, Part II, II 4 line 1614; Henry IV, Part II, III 2 line 2182; Henry IV, Part II, IV 5 line 2932; Henry IV, Part II, IV 5 line 3048; Henry IV, Part II, IV 5 line 3120; Henry IV, Part II, IV 5 line 3127; Henry IV, Part II, V 2 line 3373; Henry IV, Part II, V 3 line 3508; Henry IV, Part II, V 5 line 3649; Henry IV, Part II, V 5 line 3672; Henry IV, Part II, V 5 line 3701.
Henry V, II 1 line 758; Henry V, III 2 line 1200; Henry V, III 2 line 1211; Henry V, III 6 lines 1470, 1475; Henry V, III 6 line 1556; Henry V, III 7 line 1644; Henry V, III 7 line 1650; Henry V, III 7 line 1677; Henry V, IV 1 line 1914; Henry V, IV 1 line 2109; Henry V, IV 3 line 2293; Henry V, IV 8 line 2717; Henry V, IV 8 line 2753; Henry V, V 1 line 2892; Henry V, V 2 line 3016; Henry V, V 2 line 3366.
Henry VI, Part I, I 4 line 545; Henry VI, Part I, II 2 line 804; Henry VI, Part I, II 2 line 809; Henry VI, Part I, III 2 line 1567; Henry VI, Part I, III 3 line 1618; Henry VI, Part I, IV 4 line 2111; Henry VI, Part I, IV 4 line 2132; Henry VI, Part I, IV 5 line 2150; Henry VI, Part I, V 2 line 2443; Henry VI, Part I, V 4 line 2706.
Henry VI, Part II, I 1 line 26; Henry VI, Part II, I 2 lines 277, 281; Henry VI, Part II, I 2 line 294; Henry VI, Part II, I 2 line 318; Henry VI, Part II,

II 3 line 1122; Henry VI, Part II, II 4 line 1198; Henry VI, Part II, II 4 line 1244; Henry VI, Part II, II 4 line 1253; Henry VI, Part II, III 1 line 1517; Henry VI, Part II, III 2 line 1731; Henry VI, Part II, III 2 line 1746; Henry VI, Part II, III 2 line 1836; Henry VI, Part II, III 2 line 1990; Henry VI, Part II, III 2 lines 2056, 2057; Henry VI, Part II, III 2 line 2076; Henry VI, Part II, III 2 line 2102; Henry VI, Part II, IV 1 line 2196; Henry VI, Part II, IV 2 line 2316; Henry VI, Part II, IV 10 line 2962; Henry VI, Part II, V 2 line 3257.
Henry VI, Part III, I 4 line 608; Henry VI, Part III, II 1 line 664; Henry VI, Part III, II 3 line 1033; Henry VI, Part III, II 5 line 1122; Henry VI, Part III, II 6 line 1330; Henry VI, Part III, III 2 lines 1636, 1658; Henry VI, Part III, V 2 line 2740; Henry VI, Part III, V 5 line 2901; Henry VI, Part III, V 5 line 2943; Henry VI, Part III, V 6 line 3048; Henry VI, Part III, V 6 line 3069; Henry VI, Part III, V 7 line 3117.
Henry VIII, II 1 line 903; Henry VIII, II 1 line 953; Henry VIII, II 3 line 1256; Henry VIII, II 4 line 1503; Henry VIII, II 4 lines 1564, 1566; Henry VIII, II 4 lines 1597, 1604; Henry VIII, III 2 line 2073; Henry VIII, III 2 line 2096; Henry VIII, III 2 line 2270; Henry VIII, IV 2 line 2589; Henry VIII, IV 2 line 2754; Henry VIII, IV 2 lines 2763, 2769; Henry VIII, V 1 line 2936r; Henry VIII, V 3 line 3233; Henry VIII, V 5 line 3447.
Julius Caesar, I 2 lines 213, 220; Julius Caesar, I 2 line 226; Julius Caesar, I 2 line 402; Julius Caesar, I 3 line 433; Julius Caesar, I 3 lines 522, 524; Julius Caesar, II 2 line 1005; Julius Caesar, III 1 line 1271; Julius Caesar, III 1 line 1377; Julius Caesar, III 1 lines 1429, 1430; Julius Caesar, III 2 line 1664; Julius Caesar, IV 1 line 1875; Julius Caesar, IV 3 line 2001; Julius Caesar, IV 3 line 2082; Julius Caesar, V 5 line 2677; Julius Caesar, V 5 line 2698; Julius Caesar, V 5 line 2761.
King John, I 1 line 36; King John, I 1 line 118; King John, I 1 line 129; King John, II 1 line 417; King John, II 1 line 573; King John, II 1 line 806; King John, II 1 lines 876, 889, 890; King John, III 3 1335; King John, III 4 line 1424; King John, III 4 line 1490; King John, III 4 line 1495; King John, III 4 line 1533; King John, IV 1 line 1721; King John, IV 2 line 1829; King John, IV 2 line 1867; King John, IV 3 line 2088; King John, IV 3 line 2143; King John, IV 3 line 2171; King John, V 1 line 2241; King John, V 2 line 2335; King John, V 2 line 2362; King John, V 2 line 2394; King John, V 2 line 2400; King John, V 4 line 2514; King John, V 7 line 2704; King John, V 7 line 2753.
King Lear, I 1 line 20; King Lear, I 1 line 186; King Lear, I 2 line 380; King Lear, I 2 line 442; King Lear, I 4 line 579; King Lear, II 1 line 1008; King Lear, II 2 line 1229; King Lear, II 4 line 1581; King Lear, III 1 line 1626; King Lear, III 2 line 1684; King Lear, IV 1 line 2258rr; King Lear, IV 6 line 2639; King Lear, IV 6 line 2743; King Lear, IV 6 line 2755; King Lear, IV 6 line 2757; King Lear, V 1 line 3077; King Lear, V 3 line 3210; King Lear, V 3 line 3236; King Lear, V 3 line 3505.
Love's Labour's Lost, I 1 lines 12, 14; Love's Labour's Lost, I 1 lines 31, 32; Love's Labour's Lost, I 1 lines 169, 178; Love's Labour's Lost, I 2 line 409; Love's Labour's Lost, II 1 lines 488, 495; Love's Labour's Lost, II 1 line 588; Love's Labour's Lost, IV 3 lines 1329, 1335; Love's Labour's Lost, IV 3 line 1384; Love's Labour's Lost, IV 3 lines 1656,

1687; Love's Labour's Lost, V 1 line 1799; Love's Labour's Lost, V 1 lines 1829, 1833, 1836; Love's Labour's Lost, V 2 line 2273; Love's Labour's Lost, V 2 line 2363; Love's Labour's Lost, V 2 line 2373; Love's Labour's Lost, V 2 line 2477; Love's Labour's Lost, V 2 line 2501r; Love's Labour's Lost, V 2 line 2509r; Love's Labour's Lost, V 2 lines 2731, 2738; Love's Labour's Lost, V 2 line 2785.
Lover's Complaint, line 7.
Macbeth, II 1 line 628; Macbeth, II 4 line 972; Macbeth, III 1 lines 1125, 1127; Macbeth, III 2 line 1188; Macbeth, IV 2 line 1821; Macbeth, V 5 line 2411.
Measure for Measure, I 2 line 206; Measure for Measure, II 1 line 510; Measure for Measure, II 2 line 809; Measure for Measure, II 4 line 1183; Measure for Measure, III 1 line 1296; Measure for Measure, III 1 lines 1361, 1364; Measure for Measure, III 1 line 1474; Measure for Measure, III 2 line 1516; Measure for Measure, III 2 line 1518; Measure for Measure, III 2 line 1562; Measure for Measure, III 2 line 1730; Measure for Measure, III 2 line 1738; Measure for Measure, IV 3 line 2241; Measure for Measure, IV 3 line 2249; Measure for Measure, V 1 line 2441; Measure for Measure, V 1 line 2926.
Merchant of Venice, I 1 line 79; Merchant of Venice, I 1 line 82r; Merchant of Venice, I 1 line 174; Merchant of Venice, I 2 line 196; Merchant of Venice, II 7 line 1024; Merchant of Venice, II 8 line 1122; Merchant of Venice, III 2 line 1441; Merchant of Venice, III 2 line 1620; Merchant of Venice, III 5 line 1918; Merchant of Venice, IV 1 line 1949; Merchant of Venice, IV 1 line 2229; Merchant of Venice, V 1 line 2548; Merchant of Venice, V 1 line 2614; Merchant of Venice, V 1 line 2639.
Merry Wives of Windsor, II 1 line 588; Merry Wives of Windsor, II 2 line 797; Merry Wives of Windsor, II 2 line 921; Merry Wives of Windsor, III 4 line 1666; Merry Wives of Windsor, IV 1 line 1904; Merry Wives of Windsor, IV 5 line 2386.
Midsummer Night's Dream, I 1 line 198; Midsummer Night's Dream, II 1 line 483; Midsummer Night's Dream, II 1 lines 598, 599, 511; Midsummer Night's Dream, IV 1 line 1701; Midsummer Night's Dream, V 1 line1916.
Much Ado About Nothing, I 1 line 86; Much Ado About Nothing, I 1 line 162; Much Ado About Nothing, I 1 line 177; Much Ado About Nothing, II 1 line 413; Much Ado About Nothing, II 1 line 645; Much Ado About Nothing, II 1 line 696; Much Ado About Nothing, II 3 line 1048; Much Ado About Nothing, III 5 line 1612; Much Ado About Nothing, IV 1 line 1919; Much Ado About Nothing, IV 1 line 1941; Much Ado About Nothing, V 4 line 2660.
Othello, I 2 lines 292, 298; Othello, I 3 line 425; Othello, I 3 line 504; Othello, I 3 line 602; Othello, I 3 line 657; Othello, I 3 line 669; Othello, I 3 line 761; Othello, II 3 line 1338; Othello, III 3 line 2007; Othello, III 3 line 2056r; Othello, III 3 line 2063; Othello, III 4 line 2186; Othello, III 4 line 2254; Othello, IV 1 line 2615; Othello, IV 2 line 2910; Othello, IV 2 line 2933; Othello, IV 2 line 2987; Othello, IV 3 line 3090; Othello, IV 3 line 3095; Othello, IV 3 line 3096; Othello, IV 3 line 3103; Othello, IV 3

line 3107; Othello, IV 3 lines 3108, 3109, 3110; Othello, IV 3 line 3113; Othello, V 1 line 3265; Othello, V 2 line 3476.
Passionate Pilgrim, lines 4, 30, 82, 371.
Pericles, I 1 line 94; Pericles, I 1 line 200; Pericles, II 1 line 689; Pericles, II 3 line 909; Pericles, II 4 line 981; Pericles, III 0 line 1146; Pericles, III 1 line 1227; Pericles, III 2 line 1407; Pericles, III 2 line 1412; Pericles, IV 1 line 1549; Pericles, IV 1 line 1640; Pericles, IV 3 line 1820; Pericles, V 1 line 2235; Pericles, V 1 line 2347.
Rape of Lucrece, lines 79, 118, 169, 436, 459, 462, 598, 1373.
Richard II, I 3 line 504; Richard II, I 3 line 570; Richard II, II 1 line 706; Richard II, II 1 lines 727, 738, 740; Richard II, II 1 lines 793, 795; Richard II, III 1 line 1385; Richard II, III 2 lines 1446, 1463; Richard II, III 2 line 1504; Richard II, III 2 line 1518; Richard II, III 4 line 1864; Richard II, IV 1 line 2061; Richard II, V 1 line 2358; Richard II, V 3 line 2728; Richard II, V 5 lines 2750, 2751, 2757, 2758, 2768, 2814.
Richard III, I 1 line 22; Richard III, I 1 line 159; Richard III, I 2 line 303; Richard III, I 2 line 309; Richard III, I 2 lines 431, 439; Richard III, I 3 line 531; Richard III, I 3 line 605; Richard III, I 3 line 606; Richard III I 3 line 685; Richard III, I 4 line 839; Richard III, I 4 line 915; Richard III, I 4 line 1008; Richard III, I 4 line 1077; Richard III, II 1 line 1207; Richard III, II 2 line 1342; Richard III, II 2 line 1363; Richard III, II 3 line 1436; Richard III, II 3 line 1442; Richard III, III 1 line 1574; Richard III, III 2 line 1819; Richard III, III 2 line 1883; Richard III, III 5 line 2138; Richard III, III 6 lines 2195, 2198; Richard III, III 7 line 2435; Richard III, IV 1 line 2526; Richard III, IV 3 line 2769; Richard III, IV 4 line 2819; Richard III, IV 4 line 3182.
Romeo and Juliet, I 2 line 278; Romeo and Juliet, I 2 line 370; Romeo and Juliet, I 3 line 461; Romeo and Juliet, II 2 line 923; Romeo and Juliet, II 2 line 946; Romeo and Juliet, II 2 line 1002; Romeo and Juliet, II 4 line 1359; Romeo and Juliet, III 1 line 1604; Romeo and Juliet, II 5 line 1428; Romeo and Juliet, III 2line 1779; Romeo and Juliet, III 2 line 1741; Romeo and Juliet, III 3 line 1887; Romeo and Juliet, III 3 lines 1888, 1890, 1891; Romeo and Juliet, III 5 line 2330; Romeo and Juliet, V 1 lines 2883r, 2884; Romeo and Juliet, V 1 line 2892; Romeo and Juliet, V 3 line 3068.
Sonnet I lines 9, 13, 14; Sonnet III line 4; Sonnet IX lines 4, 5, 9, 10, 11; Sonnet XI line 8; Sonnet XIX line 7; Sonnet XXXIII line 7; Sonnet LV line 12; Sonnet LVII line 5; Sonnet LIX line 9; Sonnet LXIX line 1; Sonnet LXXI lines 3, 4, 13; Sonnet LXXII line 1; Sonnet LXXV line 8; Sonnet LXXXI lines 6, 11; Sonnet XC line 2; Sonnet CVII line 2; Sonnet CXII lines 5, 14; Sonnet CXXIX line 13; Sonnet CXXXVII line 10; Sonnet CXXXVIII line 4; Sonnet CXL line 13; Sonnet CXLVIII line 6.
Taming of the Shrew, Prologue 1 line 7; Taming of the Shrew, Prologue 1 line 108; Taming of the Shrew, Prologue 2 line 211; Taming of the Shrew, Prologue 2 line 290; Taming of the Shrew, I 1 line 315; Taming of the Shrew, I 1 line 422; Taming of the Shrew, I 2 lines 599, 607; Taming of the Shrew, II 1 line 1004; Taming of the Shrew, II 1 lines 1102, 1103; Taming of the Shrew, II 1 line 1141; Taming of the

Shrew, II 1 line 1161; Taming of the Shrew, II 1 line 1237; Taming of the Shrew, III 2 line 1381; Taming of the Shrew, III 2 line 1423; Taming of the Shrew, III 2 lines 1502, 1503; Taming of the Shrew, IV 1 line 1648; Taming of the Shrew, IV 1 line 1649; Taming of the Shrew, IV 2 line 1839; Taming of the Shrew, IV 2 line 1861; Taming of the Shrew, V 2 line 2508; Taming of the Shrew, V 2 line 2515; Taming of the Shrew, V 2 line 2674.

Tempest, I 2 line 168; Tempest, I 2 line 190; Tempest, III 1 line 1326; Tempest, III 1 line 1342; Tempest, III 1 line 1362; Tempest, III 3 line 1630; Tempest, V 1 line 2220; Tempest, V 1 line 2335.

Timon of Athens, I 1 line 5; Timon of Athens, I 1 line 59; Timon of Athens, I 1 line 172; Timon of Athens, II 2 line 716; Timon of Athens, II 2 line 841; Timon of Athens, III 1 line 991; Timon of Athens, III 2 line 1079; Timon of Athens, III 5 line 1336; Timon of Athens, IV 3 line 1754; Timon of Athens, IV 3 line 2019; Timon of Athens, IV 3 line 2022; Timon of Athens, IV 3 lines 2079, 2098.

Titus Andronicus, I 1 line 173; Titus Andronicus, I 1 line 222; Titus Andronicus, I 1 line 274; Titus Andronicus, I 1 line 316; Titus Andronicus, II 1 lines 623, 624; Titus Andronicus, IV 2 lines 1799, 1800; Titus Andronicus, V 2 line 2339; Titus Andronicus, V 2 line 2371.

Troilus and Cressida, I 2 line 195; Troilus and Cressida, I 3 line 761; Troilus and Cressida, II 2 line 1127; Troilus and Cressida, II 2 line 1159; Troilus and Cressida, II 2 line 1204; Troilus and Cressida, II 3 line 1408; Troilus and Cressida, II 3 line 1454; Troilus and Cressida, III 2 line 1823; Troilus and Cressida, III 2 line 1852; Troilus and Cressida, III 3 line 1877; Troilus and Cressida, III 3 line 2051; Troilus and Cressida, IV 1 line 2261; Troilus and Cressida, V 1 line 2963; Troilus and Cressida, V 10 lines 3672, 3673r.

Twelfth Night, I 1 line 90; Twelfth Night, I 3 line 219; Twelfth Night, I 3 line 236; Twelfth Night, I 5 line 300; Twelfth Night, I 5 line 531; Twelfth Night, II 4 line 979; Twelfth Night, III 1 line 1333; Twelfth Night, III 1 line 1364; Twelfth Night, III 2 line 1439; Twelfth Night, IV 1 line 1964; Twelfth Night, V 1 line 2507; Twelfth Night, V 1 line 2620.

Two Gentlemen of Verona, I 1 line 7; Two Gentlemen of Verona, I 1 line 71; Two Gentlemen of Verona, I 3 line 324; Two Gentlemen of Verona, II 4 line 828; Two Gentlemen of Verona, II 7 line 1034; Two Gentlemen of Verona, III 1 line 1077; Two Gentlemen of Verona, III 1 line 1226; Two Gentlemen of Verona, III 1 line 1386; Two Gentlemen of Verona, V 4 line 2223.

Venus and Adonis, lines 8, 18, 32, 550, 655, 778, 783, 879, 947, 1097, 1211.

Winter's Tale, I 1 line 32; Winter's Tale, I 2 line 75; Winter's Tale, I 2 line 354; Winter's Tale, I 2 line 396; Winter's Tale, II 1 line 695; Winter's Tale, II 1 line 761; Winter's Tale, II 3 line 1017; Winter's Tale, II 3 line 1079; Winter's Tale, V 1 line 2834; Winter's Tale, V 2 line 3121; Winter's Tale, V 2 line 3199; Winter's Tale, IV 4 line 2258; Winter's Tale, IV 4 line 2346; Winter's Tale, V 3 line 3374.

Worldling: a sophisticated person of experience.

As You Like It, II 1 line 598.
Henry IV, Part II, V 3 line 3508.

Worm: to move like a worm, c.1600. In figurative senses attested from 1620s, suggesting patient, sinuous progress. The ancient category of these was much more extensive than the modern, scientific, one and included serpents, scorpions, maggots, and the supposed causes of certain diseases. As an insult meaning, abject, miserable person, it dates from Old English: *wurm*, variant of *wyrm: serpent, dragon*.

Antony and Cleopatra, V 2 line 3698; Antony and Cleopatra, V 2 lines 3710, 3713r; Antony and Cleopatra, V 2 line 3715; Antony and Cleopatra, V 2 line 3718; Antony and Cleopatra, V 2 lines 3721, 3723; Antony and Cleopatra, V 2 line 3735.
As You Like It, III 2 line 1179; As You Like It, III 4 line 1616; As You Like It, IV 1 line 1886.
Cymbeline, III 4 line 1756; Cymbeline, IV 2 line 2605.
Hamlet, I 5 line 827; Hamlet, IV 3 line 2732r; Hamlet, IV 3 lines 2738, 2739.
Henry IV, Part I, II 1 line 717; Henry IV, Part I, V 4 line 3051.
Henry IV, Part II, Prologue 1 line 35; Henry IV, Part II, II 4 line 1635; Henry IV, Part II, IV 5 line 3010.
Henry V, II 4 line 988.
Henry VI, Part I, III 1 line 1296.
Henry VI, Part II, III 2 line 1953.
Henry VI, Part III, II 3 line 859.
Henry VIII, IV 2 line 2722.
King John, III 4 line 1414.
King Lear, III 4 line 1898; King Lear, IV 1 line 2286.
Love's Labour's Lost, IV 3 line 1485.
Macbeth, III 4 line 1306; Macbeth, IV 1 line 1563; Macbeth, IV 2 line 1777.
Measure for Measure, III 1 line 1239.
Merchant of Venice, II 7 line 1057.
Merry Wives of Windsor, V 5 line 2642; Merry Wives of Windsor, V 5 line 2647.
Midsummer Night's Dream, II 2 lines 661, 673; Midsummer Night's Dream, III 1 line 995; Midsummer Night's Dream, III 2 line 1104; Midsummer Night's Dream, III 2 line 1441.
Much Ado About Nothing, III 2 line 1224; Much Ado About Nothing, III 3 line 1450.
Othello, III 4 line 2257.
Pericles, I 1 line 150; Pericles, II 3 line 866; Pericles, IV 1 line 1634; Pericles, IV 2 line 1689.
Rape of Lucrece, lines 899, 997, 1299.
Richard II, III 2 line 1555.
Richard III, I 3 line 686; Richard III, IV 4 line 3197.
Romeo and Juliet, I 1 line 171; Romeo and Juliet, I 4 line 564; Romeo and Juliet, III 1 line 1613; Romeo and Juliet, V 3 line 3054.

Sonnet VI line 14; Sonnet LXXI line 4; Sonnet LXXIV line 10; Sonnet CXLVI line 7.
Taming of the Shrew, V 2 line 2666.
Tempest, III 1 line 1315.
Timon of Athens, IV 3 line 1869.
Twelfth Night, II 4 line 1012.
Venus and Adonis, lines 642, 955.

Wormwood: c.1400, folk etymology of Old English: *wermod* related to vermouth, but the ultimate etymology is unknown. Possibly, *wer: man + mod: courage*, from its early use as an aphrodisiac. Figurative use, however, is usually regarding its bitter aftertaste. Perhaps because of the folk etymology, it formerly was used to protect clothes and bedding from moths and fleas. There is, also, some use of this plant in weaning infants.
    Hamlet, III 2 line 2073r.
    Love's Labour's Lost, V 2 line 2790.
    Rape of Lucrece, line 924.
    Romeo and Juliet, I 3 lines 411, 415.

Wren: Old English: *wrenna*. The bird's name in other languages usually denotes royalty, regarding its golden crest.
    Cymbeline, IV 2 line 3010.
    Henry VI, Part II, III 2 line 1723.
    King Lear, IV 6 line 2721.
    Macbeth, IV 2 line 1749.
    Merchant of Venice, V 1 line 2563.
    Midsummer Night's Dream, III 1 line 949.
    Pericles, IV 3 line 1839.
    Richard III, I 3 line 532.
    Twelfth Night, III 2 line 1469.

Wrinkles: fold or crease in the external body, late 14c.; in cloth or clothing from early 15c., implied in wrinkling, probably from stem of Old English *gewrinclod*: wrinkled, crooked, winding.
    All's Well That Ends Well, II 4 line 1223.
    Antony and Cleopatra, I 2 line 99; Antony and Cleopatra, I 5 line 553; Antony and Cleopatra, III 11 line 2151.
    Hamlet, II 2 line 1301.
    Henry VI, Part III, V 2 line 2741.
    King John, II 1 line 818; King John, IV 2 line 1936.
    King Lear, I 4 line 810.
    Measure for Measure, I 3 line 294.
    Merchant of Venice, I 1 line 86; Merchant of Venice, IV 1 line 2215.
    Rape of Lucrece, lines 326, 613, 1503.
    Richard II, I 3 line 530; Richard II, II 1 line 857; Richard II, IV 1 line 2268.
    Richard III, I 1 line 9; Richard III, I 3 line 628.
    Romeo and Juliet, II 4 line 1200.

Sonnet III line 12; Sonnet LXIII line 4; Sonnet LXXVII line 5; Sonnet XCIII line 8; Sonnet C line 10; Sonnet CVIII line 11.
Taming of the Shrew, IV 5 line 2310.
Timon of Athens, IV 1 line 1569; Timon of Athens, IV 3 line 1830.
Titus Andronicus, III 1 line 1132.
Troilus and Cressida, I 1 line 69; Troilus and Cressida, II 2 line 1070; Troilus and Cressida, II 2 line 1099.
Venus and Adonis, lines 153, 159.
Winter's Tale, V 3 line 3320.

Yew: Old English: *iw, eow*. It symbolises both death and immortality, being poisonous as well as long-lived. Although various reasons have been assigned for planting the yew tree in churchyards, it seems probable that the practice had a superstitious origin. As witches were supposed to exercise a powerful influence over the winds, they were believed occasionally to exert their formidable power against religious edifices. To counteract, therefore, this imaginary danger, some may have planted the yew tree in their churchyards; not only because of its vitality as an evergreen, but as connected, in some way in heathen times, with the influence of evil powers. From ancient medical authorities, it would seem that the juice of the yew is a rapidly fatal poison; next, that the symptoms attendant upon yew poisoning correspond, in a very remarkable manner, with those which follow the bites of poisonous snakes; and lastly, that no other poison but the yew produces the *lazar-like* ulcerations on the body, upon which Shakespeare, in this passage, lays so much stress. It appears that every Englishman, while archery was practised, was obliged to keep in his house either a bow of yew or some other wood.
Macbeth, IV 1 line 1574.
Richard II, III 2 line 1527.
Romeo and Juliet, V 3 line 2936; Romeo and Juliet, V 3 line 3092.
Titus Andronicus, II 3 line 843.
Twelfth Night, II 4 line 951.

Zephyr: mid-14c., from Old English: *Zefferus*, from Latin: *Zephyrus*, from Greek: *Zephyros: the West wind* (sometimes personified as a god), probably related to *zophos: the West, the dark region, darkness, gloom*. Sense of, mild breeze, is c.1600.
Cymbeline, IV 2 line 2543.

www.ingramcontent.com/pod-product-compliance
Lightning Source LLC
Chambersburg PA
CBHW072117290426
44111CB00012B/1689